W9-CNL-273

A HISTORY OF

GEORGETOWN UNIVERSITY

VOLUME I

Georgetown should be a school first in character & merit in America.

JOHN CARROLL to ROBERT MOLYNEUX,
February 3, 1807

A HISTORY OF

GEORGETOWN UNIVERSITY

FROM ACADEMY TO UNIVERSITY
1789–1889

VOLUME I

ROBERT EMMETT CURRAN
Foreword by John J. DeGioia

Georgetown University Press | *Washington, D.C.*

This text of this book is set using the Meridien typeface family with Myriad as the supporting sans serif typeface and Sloop for the script elements that appear in the front matter.

The ornamental images used in the chapter opening pages are details of the stained glass window in Healy Hall (photographed by James Schaefer).

The book is printed on 70# Somerset matte paper by R.R. Donnelly and Sons, Willard, Ohio.

Cover and interior design and composition by Naylor Design, Inc., Washington, DC.

Library of Congress Cataloging-in-Publication Data

Curran, Robert Emmett.
    A History of Georgetown University / Robert Emmett Curran ; foreword by John J. DeGioia.
        v. cm.
    Includes bibliographical references and index.
    Contents: v. 1. From academy to university, 1789–1889 — v. 2. The quest for excellence, 1889–1964 — v. 3. The rise to prominence, 1964–1989.
    ISBN 978-1-58901-688-0 (v. 1 : cloth : alk. paper) — ISBN 978-1-58901-689-7 (v. 2 : cloth : alk. paper) — ISBN 978-1-58901-690-3 (v. 3 : cloth : alk. paper) — ISBN 978-1-58901-691-0 (set : alk. paper)
    1. Georgetown University—History. I. Title.
    LD1961.G52C88 2010
    378.753—dc22

                                                                    2009030489

15 14 13 12 11 10   9 8 7 6 5 4 3 2
First printing

Printed in the United States of America

FSC
Mixed Sources
Product group from well-managed forests, controlled sources and recycled wood or fiber
Cert no. SCS-COC-000648
www.fsc.org
© 1996 Forest Stewardship Council

Lord, teach me to number my days aright that I may gain wisdom of heart.

PSALM 90

In memory of Michael Foley and all his heart-wise companions through Georgetown's two centuries.

TITLES IN THIS SERIES

A History of Georgetown University: From Academy to University, 1789–1889, Volume 1
A History of Georgetown University: The Quest for Excellence, 1889–1964, Volume 2
A History of Georgetown University: The Rise to Prominence, 1964–1989, Volume 3

CONTENTS

Appendices

FOREWORD

From the Jesuit tradition of education and the American spirit of independence, Georgetown has grown from the Catholic academy founded by Archbishop John Carroll that first educated six students, into a global research university with more than 1,300 faculty members that today welcomes 15,000 students from more than 130 countries to our campuses each year. *A History of Georgetown University,* volumes 1–3, captures the compelling narrative of the people and the traditions that have made this remarkable transformation possible.

Georgetown's first hundred years saw great change in Archbishop Carroll's academy. From the very start, we had assets of incalculable value: the extraordinary vision of our founder, and a commitment to pluralism, inclusiveness, and support for the highest ambitions of this country. In the decades leading to the Civil War, Georgetown transformed itself from something not much more than a high school—our first student, William Gaston, was only thirteen years old when he entered—to a full college. In 1851, Georgetown established the nation's first Catholic medical school. And at the close of Georgetown's first century, the leadership and extraordinary vision of Patrick Healy, SJ, laid the foundation for our emergence as a university. Perhaps the most symbolically significant step was Father Healy's decision to construct the building that would bear his name, and to reorient the college to have it positioned away from the river and directly facing the city of Washington, DC, thereby permanently linking our campus and community. Over the next hundred years, Georgetown expanded in enriching ways by becoming a more diverse community committed to educational excellence in each of our nine schools. In the early twentieth century, as a direct response to the tragedy of World War I, Georgetown opened the nation's first school dedicated to the study of international affairs and to the preparation of a new type of public servant. After World War II, in response to the nation's new, international economy, we founded a school of business.

Georgetown has seen immense growth and change in the size and diversity of our community, in the breadth of scholarship, and in the physical expansion of our campus. We have seen the university grow from an outstanding regional university that is recognized for superior undergraduate teaching and highly regarded for our schools of medicine and law, to an exceptional national research university, and now as an aspiring global university. Yet we know that the Georgetown University of today is only possible because we move forward in the traditions espoused by John Carroll and animated by our identity as a Catholic and Jesuit university. The commitment to education, service, and academic freedom that brought the first Georgetown community together in 1789 continues to inspire and motivate our faculty, students, and alumni today.

In over two centuries, our university has become something that John Carroll and our other early leaders could never have imagined. Sometimes, when I see the Gilbert Stuart portrait of John Carroll that hangs on the wall in my office, I wonder what he would think of his little "Academy." I suspect that he would marvel at how far we have come, how much we have accomplished, and how much we have contributed to the educational and social landscape of our city and our nation. I also think that he would remind us of our continuing responsibility to fulfill our promise and potential and to strive to become the university we are called to be.

We are deeply grateful to Robert Emmett Curran for creating this wonderful record of our work as a community to fulfill this mission over the past two centuries. In the words of the 28th Superior General of the Society of Jesus, Father Pedro Arrupe, we seek to foster a community of "women and men for others"—individuals who are committed not only to intellectual inquiry, but to advancing human knowledge in service to others and, in turn, advancing the common good.

—John J. DeGioia
President, Georgetown University

PREFACE

When the first volume of this history, titled *The Bicentennial History of Georgetown University: From Academy to University, 1789–1889,* was published in 1993, I noted that it was appearing much later than the bicentenary of the university that had originally occasioned it. Little did I realize that it would not be until the end of the first decade of a new century before the companion volumes would be in print, two decades removed from the event it was supposed to commemorate. Lateness, however, can bring some benefits.

Father Timothy Healy had envisioned a bicentennial history that would carry Georgetown's story up to 1964, with the retirement of Father Edward Bunn, who is commonly considered to be the university's second founder. To go beyond that, Father Healy reckoned, would be to plunge into historical waters that were still making their way to shore and carrying along many persons still very much part of the Georgetown scene. Even in the 1980s that constricted coverage of the university's past made little sense to me. Ending Georgetown's history in the middle of the 1960s was to miss a great, if not the greatest, part of the narrative that was the university's by the end of its second century. My intention early on was to carry the history to 1989. From the prespective of another fifteen years I decided finally to bring it—through an epilogue—as close to the present as I could, knowing that recent history is always quite different from the older kind to which there is paradoxically greater access with less of a tendency to bring presuppositions to the weighing of people and events. Georgetown as a vital institution should have a living history that tries as best as it can to tie past to present. However realized, that has been my aim.

This edition consists of three volumes. Volume 1 is a revision of the 1993 volume that covers Georgetown's initial century. The second volume traces Georgetown's history through its next seventy-five years, from 1889 to 1964. Two very strong presidents bookended its second hundred years: Joseph Havens Richards and Edward Bunn. Richards, in his ten-year tenure

(1888–98), renewed Patrick Healy's aspirations to make Georgetown a full-fledged American Catholic university in the nation's capital. "Situated as we are at the nation's Capital, and enjoying an exceptionally fine reputation," he wrote in September 1894, "we have an admirable field for development into one of the greatest, perhaps the greatest institutions of the country." Richards's efforts to create a broad cadre of academic specialists to direct advanced studies, do research in the arts and sciences, as well as develop the facilities and funding to support them, failed in great part but they set the standard for Georgetown's quest to become an elite research university over the course of its second century.

With Richards's departure, that quest was essentially put on hold for the next twenty years while his successors concentrated their attention on the college, and the professional schools of law and medicine reverted to their separate spheres. In that interim the configuration of the university changed as the professional schools of dentistry, nursing, and foreign service were added piecemeal, and the preparatory school, which had been the heart of Georgetown during its first century, was finally unlinked from the university and relocated in Maryland. In the 1920s "The Greater Georgetown" campaign was a formal attempt by a new president, John Creeden, to create an endowment to enable the university to develop the centralized facilities and faculty that would make it a bona fide comprehensive institution of higher education. That campaign proved to be a crushing disappointment and Creeden's successor had little interest in pursuing his plans. The Depression, however, ironically proved to be a catalyst for the effective resumption of "The Greater Georgetown" as the next president, Coleman Nevils, took advantage of the favorable building conditions to construct a new home for the medical and dental schools, a classroom building, and a student residence.

The second "Great War" of the twentieth century transformed the main campus of Georgetown into a testing center for the Army; most of the medical, dental, and nursing students became members of the training corps of the various services. To compensate for the loss of male students, females were admitted to the graduate school and the school of foreign service for the first time. In the immediate postwar era enrollment nearly doubled as the GI Bill opened the university's doors to many who earlier could not have considered such an education.

Edward Bunn (1952–64) brought the university into the modern world of higher education by centralizing the administration of its schools, introducing planning as a mechanism for shaping the development of the university, by recruiting, particularly in the medical center, a faculty who was more committed to research and publication, and by overseeing an unprecedentedly ambitious building program largely funded by the federal government. By the time he stepped down as president at the end of 1964, "Doc" Bunn had earned the title of "founder of the modern Georgetown."

The third volume, with the exception of the epilogue, covers the shortest part of Georgetown's history, barely a quarter of a century, yet arguably its most important one in terms of its development as a university. Edward Bunn's immediate successor, Gerard Campbell, completed the modernization of the university in the 1960s and brought it into the mainstream of American university life by restructuring the governance of Georgetown and allowing, for the first time, participation of faculty in the process; establishing the first comprehensive capital development campaign; and completing the democratization of student enrollment by admitting African Americans and women into all the schools of the university.

The last three decades of the twentieth century have proved to be the most dynamic in Georgetown's history as the institution acquired national and international stature. Its enrollment at both the undergraduate and professional levels not only doubled but the diversity and quality of the student body increased dramatically as well. The caliber of the faculty improved impressively across the three campuses. Strong administrative leadership in those decades developed the institution's academic and financial strengths. No one was more responsible for Georgetown's rise to prominence as a university than Timothy Stafford Healy, who as president from 1976 to 1989, gave the university an unprecedentedly national voice as he became one of the most influential leaders in higher education by articulating its ideals and challenges, as well as defining the unique Catholic and Jesuit traditions that inform Georgetown. Healy personally led the university in becoming more diverse in both the student body and faculty, and he was highly instrumental in sextupling the institution's endowment during his tenure. By the time he stepped down from office at the end of Georgetown's second century, he had brought the university to the brink of becoming a truly great institution.

The organization of the three volumes is partly chronological, partly thematic. Volume 1 follows a broadly chronological pattern, with the exception of chapters 7 and 8, which deal with student culture and education, respectively, during the antebellum era. In volume 2 the chronological approach prevails, aside from chapter 4, which covers the development of intercollegiate sports at Georgetown from the 1890s through the 1920s. Volume 3 employs a topical approach within the larger timelines of the period we have come to know as "The Sixties," as well as that of the fifteen years following the "Sixties" that has yet to receive a distinguishing label. In organizing the volumes in this way, I have tried to minimize the repetition inherent in such a treatment.

ACKNOWLEDGMENTS

In the course of nearly a quarter century of work on this history, I have amassed many debts. The board of advisors that Father Healy established to supervise the project was very helpful in the early planning. Several members were especially invaluable: John Rose was an unfailing resource for the history of the medical center; Father Brian McGrath generously shared with me over the course of many hours his extensive knowledge of Georgetown's history from the 1930s to the 1980s; and Dorothy Brown, Paul Mattingly, and James Scanlon read all three manuscripts. The published text has profited immensely from their critiques. When the bicentennial volume was published in 1993, I said that had they themselves been the authors, Georgetown's history would have been the richer. Having benefited from their comments on the second and third volumes, I can repeat that with even more assurance. Georgette Dorn provided great help by translating documents in Italian and Spanish. Hubert Cloke, John Hirsh, John Farina, Christopher Kauffman, Dolores Liptak, Timothy Meagher, and Paul Robichaud, CSP, also generously read and responded to various chapters.

I would like to thank also the following archivists and historians for their assistance: Sister Felicitas Powers, RSM, the Reverend Paul Thomas, and Tricia Pyne of the Archives of the Archdiocese of Baltimore; Francis Edwards, SJ, of the English Province Archives of the Society of Jesus; Edmond Lamalle, SJ, of the Roman Archives of the Society of Jesus; Henry Bertels, SJ, librarian at the Roman Curia of the Society of Jesus; John Bowen, SS, of the Sulpician Archives of Baltimore; Hugh Kennedy, SJ, and John Lamartina, SJ, of the Maryland Province Archives of the Society of Jesus at Roland Park, Baltimore; and Paul Nelligan, SJ, of the Archives of the College of the Holy Cross.

The university has been consistently generous in its support of this project. A university leave from 1985 to 1987 allowed me to begin the research in Europe and in this country. The university also provided research assistants for the project: Keith Allen, Mark Andrews, Anne Christensen, Katherine

Early, Tracy Fitzgerald, Bruce Fort, Patricia Jones, Ellen Kern, James Miller, Mark Sullivan, and Yang Wen put in countless hours, largely in the tedious task of compiling and entering information for the student-faculty databanks. Sally Irvine and Barbara Shuttleworth, my two original assistants, were marvels at organizing the research and setting high standards in coordinating it. Anna Sam, my research associate for several years, was virtually a coauthor of the bicentennial volume. Grants from the graduate school in recent years assisted me significantly in bringing the project to a close.

At the Joseph Mark Lauinger Library, several persons have been especially instrumental in the preparation of these three volumes: Artemis Kirk, university librarian; John Buchtel, head of special collections; Jon Reynolds, university archivist from 1970 to 2000; Lynn Conway, his successor; Lynn's assistant, Ann Galloway; and David Hagen, of the Gelardin New Media Center. Patrick J. McArdle, associate athletic director, was a rich source of information for the history of Georgetown sports. At Georgetown University Press, director Richard Brown has shown a steady, not to mention resourceful, hand in shepherding this edition through its long and twisting path toward publication. Rebecca Viser was invaluable as photo editor in locating and securing permissions for the many illustrations in the three volumes.

It is with added pleasure that I acknowledge the photography of James Schaefer, associate dean for academic affairs and financial aid in the Graduate School of Arts and Sciences. Jim has photographed the campus over many years and we acknowledge with gratitude his permission to use many of his photographs throughout the three volumes.

Finally, to my wife, Eileen, whose patience and support have meant more than she can ever realize, I give heartfelt appreciation.

ABBREVIATIONS

It should be noted that bold, single-letter designations (e.g., **C**, **L**, or **M**) are used throughout the text to identify an alumnus of Georgetown College or one of the university's professional schools (together with appropriate dates) while triple letters (e.g., CAS, CLS, CMD, GMD, LAW, or MED) in regular roman type identify either the College of Arts and Sciences or the Schools whose statistics are summarized in the tables.

AAB	Archives of the Archdiocese of Baltimore
ACHR	American Catholic Historical Researches
APF	Archives of the Sacred Congregation for the Propagation of the Faith
ARSI	*Archives in Rome of the Society of Jesus*
C	College of Arts and Sciences Alumnus
CAS	College of Arts and Sciences
CJ	[Georgetown] *College Journal*
CLS	College and Law School
CMD	College and Medical School
CP	John Carroll Papers
CUAA	Catholic University of America Archives
CW	*Catholic World*
EPA*	English Province Archives
GMD	Graduate and Medical Schools
GP	Gaston Papers, Southern Historical Collection, University of North Carolina
GUA	Georgetown University Archives
GUSC	Georgetown University Special Collections

HRS	*Historical Records and Studies*
HEQ	*History of Education Quarterly*
L	Law School Alumnus
LAW	Law School
M	Medical School Alumnus
MED	Medical School
MHM	*Maryland Historical Magazine*
MPA*	Maryland Province Archives at Georgetown University
MPARP*	Maryland Province Archives at Roland Park
SHC	Southern Historical Collection
WL	*Woodstock Letters*

* *Institutional records, official correspondence, and historic documents in the provincial
depositories of the Society of Jesus.*

PROPOSALS

FOR ESTABLISHING AN

ACADEMY,

AT GEORGE-TOWN, PATOWMACK-RIVER, MARYLAND.

THE Object of the proposed Institution is, to unite the Means of communicating Science with an effectual Provision for guarding and improving the Morals of YOUTH. With this View, the SEMINARY will be superintended by those, who, having had Experience in similar Institutions, know that an undivided Attention may be given to the Cultivation of Virtue, and literary Improvement; and that a System of Discipline may be introduced and preserved, incompatible with Indolence and Inattention in the Professor, or with incorrigible Habits of Immorality in the Student.

The Benefit of this Establishment should be as general as the Attainment of its Object is desirable. It will, therefore, receive Pupils as soon as they have learned the first Elements of Letters, and will conduct them, through the several Branches of classical Learning, to that Stage of Education, from which they may proceed, with Advantage, to the Study of the higher Sciences, in the University of this, or those of the neighbouring States. Thus it will be calculated for every Class of Citizens—as READING, WRITING, ARITHMETIC, the easier Branches of the MATHEMATICS, and the GRAMMAR of our NATIVE TONGUE will be attended to, no less than the LEARNED LANGUAGES.

Agreeably to the liberal Principle of our Constitution, the SEMINARY will be open to Students of EVERY RELIGIOUS PROFESSION.—They, who in this Respect differ from the SUPERINTENDENTS of the ACADEMY, will be at Liberty to frequent the Places of Worship and Instruction appointed by their Parents; but, with Respect to their moral Conduct, all must be subject to general and uniform Discipline.

In the Choice of Situation, Salubrity of Air, Convenience of Communication, and Cheapness of living, have been principally consulted; and GEORGE-TOWN offers these united Advantages.

The Price of Tuition will be moderate; in the Course of a few Years, it will be reduced still lower, if the System, formed for this SEMINARY, be effectually carried into Execution.

Such a Plan of Education solicits, and, it is not Presumption to add, deserves public Encouragement.

The following Gentlemen, and others, that may be appointed hereafter, will receive Subscriptions, and inform the Subscribers, to whom, and in what Proportion, Payments are to be made :—In Maryland—The Hon. CHARLES CARROLL, of CARROLLTON, HENRY ROZER, NOTLEY YOUNG, ROBERT DARNALL, GEORGE DIGGES, EDMUND PLOWDEN, Esqrs, Mr. JOSEPH MILLARD, Capt. JOHN LANCASTER, Mr. BAKER BROOKE, CHANDLER BRENT, Esq; Mr. BERNARD O'NEILL and Mr. MARSHAM WARING, Merchants, JOHN DARNALL, and IGNATIUS WHEELER, Esqrs, on the Western-Shore; and on the Eastern, Rev. Mr. JOSEPH MOSLEY, JOHN BLAKE, FRANCIS HALL, CHARLES BLAKE, WILLIAM MATTHEWS, and JOHN TUITTE, Esqrs.—In Pennsylvania—GEORGE MEAD and THOMAS FITZSIMMONS, Esqrs, Mr. JOSEPH CAUFFMAN, Mr. MARK WILCOX, and Mr. THOMAS LILLY.—In Virginia—Col. FITZGERALD, and GEORGE BRENT, Esq;—and at New-York, DOMINIC LYNCH, Esquire.

SUBSCRIPTIONS will also be received, and every necessary Information given, by the following Gentlemen, Directors of the Undertaking :—The Rev. Messrs. JOHN CARROLL, JAMES PELLENTZ, ROBERT MOLYNEUX, JOHN ASHTON, and LEONARD NEALE.

We the Subscribers promise to pay to the Rev. Messrs. John Carroll, James Pellentz, Robt. Molyneux, John Ashton & Leonard Neale, or to their order, or to the order of any of them, the sums severally annexed to our names; that is, one third, June 1st 1787; one third Decr. 1 1787; and one other third June 1st 1788 —

PART ONE

THE ACADEMY: BEGINNINGS, 1773–1830

To all liberally inclined to promote the Education of YOUTH.

BE it known by these presents, that I, the underwritten, have ~~appointed~~ *humbly requested* *Edwd. Weld Esqr. & Lady* to receive any generous donations for the purposes

set forth in a certain printed paper, entitled,

Proposals for establishing an Academy, at George-Town, Patowmack-River, Maryland;

for which *they* will give receipts to the benefactors, and remit the monies received by *them* to me the aforesaid underwritten, one of the directors of this undertaking.

Conscious also of the merited confidence placed in the aforesaid *Edward Weld Esqr. & Lady* I moreover ~~authorize~~ *desire* *them* to appoint any other person or persons to execute the same liberal office, as *they are humbly requested* ~~is authorized~~ by me to execute.

~~Given at~~ *Maryland,* this *30th* day of *March* 17 *87*—

Signed and sealed

J. Carroll

CHAPTER 1

"Our Main Sheet Anchor for Religion"

I am greatly obliged to you for still remembering our Academy, which is indeed to be our main sheet anchor for Religion. We now hope to get it under way, . . . early next summer.

JOHN CARROLL TO CHARLES PLOWDEN
from Maryland to Lulworth Castle October 23, 1789

The "Rising Church of America"

In 1773 John Mattingly (1745–1807) was trying to remember the Maryland he had last seen as a young schoolboy in 1760, thirteen years before—trying to remember for the Roman officials who were asking. He remembered priests riding out to rural chapels on Sundays and feast days to hear confession, say Mass, preach, and catechize. "The natives," he told the inquiring Roman officials, "do not live in towns or villages, but each family separate and apart, on its own farm." The priests themselves lived on farms, plantations, in fact, that were large enough to support the work of many missionaries. Alas, even a fifteen-year-old could realize that those plantations were not properly run. There were so few priests, he recalled, and they so overworked in meeting the spiritual needs of their people, that "they cannot apply their minds to temporalities." To that schoolboy, the priests were sacred characters living apart from the social and political affairs of profane society, venerated but necessarily aloof. That was the church he knew or had heard about: twenty-three priests, eight native-born and fifteen immigrant, for a

Facsimile of the fund solicitation that in 1787 went to each prospective donor "inclined to promote the Education of YOUTH," along with a copy of the Proposals for establishing an Academy at George-Town. In this notice, Carroll declares himself the official underwriter of the institution whose establishment he had been considering on and off for more than three years. (Georgetown University Archives)

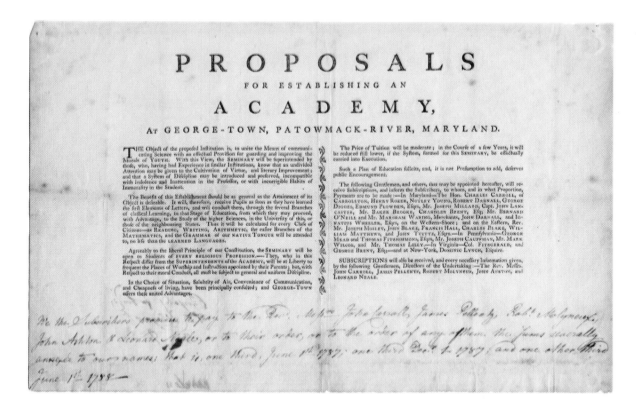

Facsimile of broadside proposing an Institution whose "Plan of Education solicits, and it is not Presumption to add, deserves public Encouragement." (Georgetown University Archives)

Catholic population of somewhat more than twenty thousand souls clustered in rural communities in Maryland and Pennsylvania. "No bishop has ever yet penetrated into those parts," he added.

The chief reason of this is, that the followers of the Puritanical sect prevail there, and wage a continual war with the episcopal order. They have brought it about that no bishop of the Anglican Church has ever dared to establish a see there. In this the Catholics have done the same, for fear of giving heretics an occasion to start a persecution against the Catholic Church.[1]

John Mattingly had left his native Maryland in 1760 to study at the English College at Saint Omer in French Flanders. Since the late seventeenth century the Maryland Catholic gentry had sent their sons to the Jesuit school (known as St. Omers in English) begun in 1593 for English recusants under the auspices of the Spanish Crown. Mattingly, like more than a third of the Maryland students at St. Omers, eventually entered the Society of Jesus in 1766. By 1773 he was the dean and professor of controversial theology at the English College in Rome.[2] As the lone Marylander in Rome, he was a natural choice for the officials of the Congregation for the Propagation of the Faith (Propaganda Fide) to question about the state of the American mission. The Congregation under whose jurisdiction the church in British America fell had particular reason to be interested in the mission. In the previous month, August, Pope Clement XIV had released the Brief ordering the suppression of the Society of Jesus throughout the world, the culminating act of a campaign against the Society that had been building in Europe for a generation. The campaign united an odd combination of opponents—*philosophes*, Jansenists, Eurocentrists—who severally found the Society a unique threat to progress or orthodoxy or uniformity in the church, depending on the opponent's particular vantage point. Since all the priests in British America had been Jesuits, they and their property now came directly under the Congregation.

In what spirit Mattingly compiled this report for the Propaganda we can only guess. We do know that he, unlike most of his fellow ex-Jesuits, received a pension from the Congregation and, having been denied permission to return to Maryland, spent the next thirty-four years as a traveling clerical tutor to English gentry.[3] The world of Catholic America, which he had earlier recalled for Roman officials, was on the verge of a dramatic change, in which the suppression of the Society of Jesus would play a significant role, the American Revolution an even greater one.

Catholics in British America

Although Maryland had been founded in 1632 by an English Catholic nobleman, Sir George Calvert, the first Lord Baltimore, Catholics from the beginning had been a very small minority there, usually numbering less than a twelfth of the population. In the first fifty years of the colony's existence, freedom of religion more or less prevailed so long as the Calverts were in power. With separation of church and state as the official policy of the colony, the Jesuits who accompanied the settlers to the Chesapeake area had to resort to the same means that the gentleman planters did to sustain themselves and their ministry. Through grants of land from the Lord Proprietor under the headright system, bequests, and acquisition of property, the Society of Jesus came to be a major landowner in Maryland by the eighteenth century, possessing seven estates, of which several were more than two thousand acres in size. On one of these estates, at Newtown in St. Mary's County, the Jesuits established a preparatory school in 1677 for students planning to attend St. Omers. And there apparently was a contemporary, possibly even older school run by the Society in St. Mary's City, then the capital of the colony.

Even in those first five decades, the position of the Calverts and their Catholic associates was unstable. Twice in the first fifteen years of the colony's history, the Calvert government was overthrown. In the first revolution in 1645, two English Jesuits, Andrew White and Thomas Copley, were taken back to England in chains; three others sought refuge in Virginia. A decade later these priests were forced again to seek sanctuary across the Potomac.

After the Glorious Revolution reached Maryland in 1689 Catholics found themselves, at least theoretically, subject to the same discrimination they had fled England to avoid. The Anglican Church in British America was thus established by law (i.e., its clergy were supported by taxes). Catholics could not vote, practice certain professions, bear arms, or worship publicly. They were sometimes doubly taxed. To educate their children in a Catholic school was to risk disqualifying a child from any inheritance or worse.

For the most part these penal laws went unenforced, but the status of Catholics (as well as other dissenters) was clear. Periodically, there were threats to invoke the laws, the last coming as late as the 1750s during the French and Indian War, when Catholics in Maryland were accused, or at least suspected, of conspiring with the Catholic enemy. Jesuits were arrested on a few occasions on charges that ranged from saying mass to being French agents, but they were never convicted or imprisoned. Several attempts were made to seize the extensive property of the Jesuits, but such measures were always stopped by the Protestant gentry in the upper house of Maryland, who had many ties by marriage to Catholics. In general, the Catholic gentry managed to flourish economically, despite their political and religious disabilities. The period from 1720 to 1750 was one of great prosperity for the leading Catholic families. Through land speculation, industrial ventures, agriculture, and commerce, Catholics like Charles Carroll, James Digges, and Richard Bennett accumulated considerable fortunes. At his death in 1749, Bennett was reputed to be the richest man in America. A generation later, Charles Carroll of Carrollton enjoyed the same reputation.

The imposition of political penalties for nearly eighty years apparently motivated relatively few, at least among the gentry, to abandon their faith. Indeed, the percentage of Catholics in Maryland seems to have grown slightly in the late colonial period. Indentured Irish servants were one cause for this increase; converts another. Conscientious Anglicans repeatedly complained that Jesuits were taking advantage of the indifferent ministry and of the scandalous private lives of too many clergymen of the Church of England to win converts to Rome. Moreover, a number of prominent Protestant families, such as the Hansons and the Stones, had Catholic branches by the middle of the eighteenth century. In the same period there was a sharp increase in the number of children whom the Catholic gentry were sending abroad for their education in the recusant schools at Saint Omer and Bruges (Brugge)—both in Flanders. Indeed, more Americans went to St. Omers College in the eighteenth century than to Oxford and Cambridge combined.[4] The Boones, Boarmans, Brookes, Carrolls, Digges, Neales, Semmes, and Sewalls, among others, all sent several sons to St. Omers. The result was a harvest of vocations—thirty-six Jesuit novices in the period from 1724 to 1773 alone. And colonial American girls went to convent schools in the Low Countries. Thus the Carmelites, the Poor Clares, and the Benedictines had similar increases in the novitiates because they taught the daughters of the same Maryland families.

The Jesuit schools in Newtown and St. Mary's City were already closed at the beginning of this penal age. Not until the middle of the 1740s did another one open, and that for only a brief period. Father Thomas Poulton started the school at the Jesuit plantation of Bohemia on the upper Eastern Shore of Maryland, but it only lasted about four years. Bohemia was a good site for a Catholic academy in a colony that now outlawed such enterprises since it was located in a peninsular area disputed by Maryland and Delaware, a quarrel not settled until Mason and Dixon plotted the true line of demarcation between the two colonies and Pennsylvania twenty years later. Bohemia began, like Newtown, as a preparatory school for St. Omers and was a distinct success until Poulton's death closed it in 1749.

By the time of the Peace of Paris in 1763, the position of Catholics in America seemed rather unpromising. In Maryland they were a significant minority, whose aristocracy was tenuously clinging to the proprietary family to protect their rights and interests (in 1713 the Calverts had regained legal authority, if not all of their old power, by embracing the Anglican faith). In Quaker Pennsylvania there was greater religious toleration than in Maryland, although the few thousand Catholics in Philadelphia and the southeastern region remained suspect. In virtually all the other colonies their religion was proscribed by law. If Catholics in America were, as John Adams remarked, "as rare as earthquakes," it was no accident. Indeed, the less contact one had with Catholics, the more anti-Catholicism flourished in the colonies. All the antipopery in the cultural baggage of the English Reformation survived the sea passage to the New World. If nothing else, the imperial rivalry between Catholic France and Protestant England kept it alive in the colonies. Bloody Mary, the Spanish Armada, Foxe's *Book of Martyrs,* and Titus Oates all fed the depiction of Catholicism in textbooks, sermons, pamphlets, and songs. The hanging of the papal effigy was a hallowed part of the Guy Fawkes Day ritual in British America. Nor was the *haute culture* outside the prevailing temper. At Harvard College, a lecture in the annual Dudleian lectures was devoted to "detecting, convicting and exposing the idolatry, errors and superstitions of the Romish church."[5]

So unpromising had conditions become for Catholics in America by 1760 that Charles Carroll of Annapolis advised his son to settle in Louisiana once he completed his legal studies in London.[6] Charles Carroll of Carrollton did not take his father's advice. He returned instead to Maryland, and he brought home from Europe a vision shaped by the writings of Montesquieu and other *philosophes.* He was convinced that the party of privilege, which had for so long been the refuge of Catholics, would not be the dominant force shaping the colony's future. Through his leadership in Maryland the Catholic gentry began to place its fortunes on the rising "Country" Party, which was laying the groundwork for revolution. When the revolution came, the Catholic communities in Maryland and Pennsylvania, though divided like nearly every other group in the civil war, provided leaders who played significant roles in the establishment of the new state and federal governments. Most notably, Charles Carroll placed his life, honor, and considerable fortune behind the patriot cause.

Effect of the War and the Jesuit Suppression on Catholics

No American Catholic was more directly affected by the confluence of the American Revolution and the suppression of the Society of Jesus than Carroll's cousin, John Carroll (1735–1815). The son of an Irish immigrant who, through a well-connected marriage and a successful country store, had earned enough to become a prosperous planter-merchant in Prince George's County in Southern Maryland, Carroll had studied first for two years at Bohemia, then, with Charles Carroll, crossed the Atlantic to St. Omers in 1748. Like his cousin, he was deeply influenced by the more moderate currents of the Enlightenment mediated by French Catholic intellectuals in the Low Countries. Unlike Charles, John, as an eighteen-year-old in 1753, entered the novitiate of the Jesuits at Watten in the Netherlands. Ordained in 1761, he subsequently taught in the English colleges at Liège and Bruges.[7] Undoubtedly he, like John Mattingly, would have remained in Europe, had not the suppression occurred, since the English Province of the Society was not in the habit of sending its intellectuals to the colonies. But the suppression changed all that.

Carroll himself had seen its various stages at close hand. He had been at Liège when the faculty and students of St. Omers had been forced to flee secretly to escape the order of the French authorities to close the school and disband. The school relocated to Austrian-controlled Bruges, where Carroll himself was eventually transferred in 1771, only to be asked to accompany the son of a young English Catholic nobleman on a tour of Europe. For the next two years Carroll acted as a peripatetic tutor for Charles-Philippe, the son of Lord Stourton, as they made their way through France, Germany, Austria, and Italy. By October of 1772, they were in Rome, with Carroll concealing his Jesuit identity. "Our catastrophe is near at hand," he wrote an English Jesuit in January of the next year, "if we must trust to present appearances, & talk of Rome."[8] Carroll had so often heard such rumors of impending doom that he felt cause to hope that this was more of the same, but the hardening opposition to the Society that he had found in Rome had so alienated him that he began to think seriously about requesting leave to return to America. Events quickly overtook him. In September 1773, the College of Bruges, where Carroll had returned at the completion of his tour, received the fatal news of suppression. "I am not, and perhaps never shall be, recovered from the shock of this dreadful intelligence," he informed his brother, Daniel, in Maryland. "The greatest blessing which in my estimation I could receive from God, would be immediate death. . . . What will become of our flourishing congregations [in Maryland] . . . and those [in Pennsylvania] cultivated by the German fathers?"[9] A month later, Carroll and his Jesuit confreres were ordered at bayonet point by the Austrian authorities to quit the college. Carroll, who had already decided that with the expiration of the Society he was now his "own master," needed no permission from church or state before sailing for Maryland in the spring of 1774.[10]

In order to be with his widowed mother whom he had not seen in twenty-five years, John Carroll had already reluctantly turned down Lord Arundell's invitation to become the family chaplain at Lulworth Castle in Dorset.[11] Instead, he became, in effect, chaplain for his own extended family, serving two congregations in the Potomac Valley, one on the Maryland side at a chapel adjoining his mother's plantation in Rock Creek, Montgomery County, and another one in Acquia, Virginia, where his sisters, Ann and Eleanor, had married into the Brent family. Now that he was no longer under vows, he felt no obligation to take orders from the former Jesuit superior in America, John Lewis, who remained nominally in charge of the former Jesuits in Maryland and Pennsylvania. But less than two years after his return to Maryland, Carroll found himself caught up in the revolution against English rule that had already turned bloody and was rapidly carrying the colonies to independence. When the Continental Congress commissioned three of its members to attempt to persuade the French Canadians to join the colonists' cause in 1776, Charles Lee suggested to John Hancock that "some Jesuit or Religieuse of any other Order (but he must be a man of liberal sentiments, enlarged mind and a manifest friend to Civil Liberty) . . . would be worth batallions" to such a mission. "Mr. Carroll has a relative who exactly answers the description."[12] John Carroll, despite his conviction that when ministers of religion "take a busy part in political matters, they generally fall into contempt," if not discredit the whole enterprise, nonetheless agreed to join his cousin, Charles Carroll of Carrollton, as well as Benjamin Franklin and Samuel Chase. He knew enough about the political complacency of the Canadians to have little hope that they would join the revolution, especially in light of the virulent anti-Catholicism lately revived among Protestant Americans by the Quebec Act.[13] Carroll's misgivings were all too soon borne out by the cold reception the four commissioners received in Montreal. Two weeks after arriving, the priest headed home with an ailing Franklin. The other two followed shortly afterwards.

That failed mission was the extent of Carroll's involvement in the American Revolution, but he remained its firm supporter and celebrated the civic and religious liberties that the new states established for their citizens, including Catholics. In the middle of the war he could scarcely contain his enthusiasm in informing Charles Plowden, an old friend from the Lowlands, "the fullest & largest system of toleration is adopted in almost all the American states: publick protection & encouragement are extended alike to all denominations & R[oman] C[atholics] are members of Congress, assemblies, & hold civil & military posts as well as others."[14] When the defeated British army marched out of Yorktown, the bands played "The World Turned Upside Down." For Carroll it was a time to realize how much the old order had been shaken and how much improved prospects were now for minorities like Catholics who had suffered discrimination under the colonies of the Crown. "An immense field is opend to the zeal of apostolical men," he reported to Plowden in the fall of 1783. "Universal toleration throughout this immense country, and innumerable R. Cats going & ready to go into the new regions bordering on the Mississippi, perhaps the finest in the world, & impatiently clamorous for Clergymen to attend them. The object nearest my heart is to establish a college on this continent for the education of youth, which might at the same time be a Seminary for future Clergymen. But at present I see no prospect of success."[15]

Carroll's "Lengthened Shadow"

No institution is merely the shadow of a single individual, but Philip Gleason is surely right in claiming that Georgetown in its founding and early years was "almost literally the lengthened shadow of one man."[16] Without Carroll there would have been no initiative, among either clergy or laity, for beginning a school. Nor would there have been any movement to organize the Catholic clergy, once the old ties to Rome through England had been severed by the suppression and the revolution. For Carroll the necessity of a school quickly became an integral part of his plan for organizing a republican church.

Had his brother priests in Maryland taken any action to address the new situation, it is questionable whether Carroll would have stirred himself to do so; but they did little beyond carrying out their established ministries. "The clergymen here continue to live in the old form," Carroll complained to Plowden in 1782. They gave little or no thought to the larger world or the next generation. Some, he thought, were deluding themselves that the Society of Jesus would be quickly restored.[17] It is ironic that Carroll, who had a very divided mind about any restoration of the Society, was the one who took the initiative to ensure the preservation of its property.

Carroll saw the estates as the key to providing an adequate and capable clergy for the rapidly expanding Catholic population (by Carroll's estimate, approximately 25,000 in Maryland, Pennsylvania, and New York alone).[18] The property was considerable, some 12,677 acres of prime land in the seven plantations of Southern Maryland and the upper Eastern Shore.[19]

Following the lead of the ex-Jesuits in England, Carroll in 1782 devised a plan whereby all the ex-Jesuits in America would choose representatives to adopt "some system of administration, settled with the joint concurrence of all, and founded on principles of justice and equality," to provide a foundation for the support of the present clergy, active and retired, and for "the good of Religion" in general.[20] Carroll prodded his former superior, Father Lewis, into giving his consent to a meeting of all the clergy at the White Marsh plantation in Prince Georges County in June 1783 to discuss Carroll's plan. Only six of the twenty-two former Jesuits attended. Nevertheless, out of that meeting and two subsequent ones over the next year and a half came the "Representative [or Select] Body of the Clergy," six elected representatives who were charged with the administration of the property and the distribution of its income. As the constitutions of the group made clear, the property belonged to them alone. Should the Society of Jesus ever be restored, the property would then revert to the Society, but until such time no one, neither pope nor papal congregation nor bishop, would have any power over it.[21]

From the beginning, it is clear, the preservation of the property, the appointment of a bishop, and the establishment of a school were all interconnected. As Carroll remarked later to some ex-Jesuits who were opposing the creation of a bishopric (as well as the school), if the school were to be "a nursery" for the priesthood, "an independent Ecclesiastical Superior is principally if not essentially necessary to render the school competent to all the purposes of its establishment."[22] Carroll left no doubt that his principal interest in wanting the academy was to prepare young men for the priesthood. As he admitted years later when the school was finally on the verge of opening, "Their education was not my principal goal, when I conceived the idea for it. I had the intention of training students for an ecclesiastical seminary . . ." which he hoped to found once the academy or college was established.[23]

At their last meeting, in October 1784, the representatives of the clergy, hoping to prevent Rome from naming a local priest as vicar-apostolic (and thus a direct representative of Propaganda), sent a petition to the Holy See asking that John Lewis be made their formal ecclesiastical superior, since it was no longer appropriate that they come under the Vicar-Apostolic of London.[24] In fact, Rome had already acted, appointing Carroll not vicar-apostolic but superior. After labyrinthian inquiries involving the French Crown, the papal nuncio at Paris, and Benjamin Franklin (the American ambassador to France), the Holy See had been satisfied that the new government wanted no role in the religious affairs of its people, but would prefer spiritual authority over its citizens to be exercised by fellow Americans rather than by subjects of a foreign power (Rome had been considering replacing an English vicar-apostolic with a French one, since France was now the leading Catholic ally of the new republic). With the encouragement of Franklin, the Holy See instead appointed John Carroll the "head of the missions in the provinces of the new Republic of the United States of

America."[25] Carroll received official word of the appointment in November 1784. He was not yet a bishop, with power to ordain, and indeed he did not press Rome on the matter until the Select Body finally committed itself to founding the school.

By the time Carroll did become superior, he had reluctantly dropped his plans for a school. Apparently, his first soundings for financial assistance, both at home and abroad, had found little to give him encouragement. William Strickland, an English ex-Jesuit who was president of the academy at Liège established in the wake of the suppression of the Society, warned Carroll that Liège was still "in its infancy," struggling for funds and direction, even though it was in its second decade and had begun under much better circumstances than those Carroll faced.[26] By the end of 1784 the new superior had concluded that Catholics in America were "too inconsiderable in point of wealth to erect & support a college; & we Clergymen are too few to supply a sufficient number of masters for the entire education of youth, if even such a College existed." Besides, as he reflected to a fellow priest in Philadelphia, "being admitted to equal toleration, must we not concur in public measures, & avoid separating ourselves from the Community?"[27] Public colleges were opening in Pennsylvania and Maryland, with no restrictions against Catholics. Why retreat at this point to form their own educational enclave?

A Catholic College for America

The revolution, like the Great Awakening a generation before it, set off a wave of college foundings, but on a scale that dwarfed the offspring of the earlier religious revival. Six had begun in the three decades before independence; twenty-three were chartered between 1782 and 1800.[28] The post-Revolutionary period also marked the birth of the academy in America. Fifty-two were established in New England alone.[29] The sudden interest in education, especially at the higher level, was very logical. If the United States was to survive as a republic, education was essential for those who would lead. Most of the new colleges had affiliations with religious denominations, with the Presbyterians being the most active promoters—of eleven colleges all told. Hampden-Sydney (1776), Liberty Hall [now Washington and Lee] (1783), Transylvania (1783), Dickinson College (1783), Blount [now Tennessee] (1794), and Union (1795) are the major survivors of the educational network that the Presbyterians created from New York to Tennessee in the postwar period. But if the 1780s and 1790s, as Jurgen Herbst points out, "witnessed the emergence of the American private college," this was largely taking place on the frontier, in the rapidly developing western areas of the new states.[30]

In the older areas the trend seemed to be state-supported, if not state-controlled, schools. In 1779, the Pennsylvania legislature created a University of the State of Pennsylvania, which was essentially a reorganization of the College of Philadelphia, with the Presbyterians replacing the Anglicans as the dominant group. Nonetheless, the new university was charged by law to have an ecumenical governing board, which was to include the senior ministers from the Anglican, Baptist, German Calvinist, Lutheran, Presbyterian, and Roman Catholic churches in the City.[31] William Smith, a Scottish immigrant and Anglican churchman, was in a sense a victim of that reorganization. The president of the College of Philadelphia, he had gained a respected reputation on both sides of the Atlantic for his views on education. But, during the national crisis that led to the revolution, Smith had vacillated between loyalty to the Crown and the emerging nation, and that eventually caused his dismissal from the college. He moved south to Chestertown on the Eastern Shore of Maryland, where he became master of the Kent County School, an Anglican academy. Smith quickly sought not only to raise the academy to the level of a college but to receive funding from the new state as part of a projected state university system. In May 1782 the Maryland assembly incorporated the school as Washington College. By this time even Smith knew how the "winds of war" were blowing. Classes started the following year. Two years later the legislature committed itself to provide an annual fund of £1,250 for the college. The next year, 1785, the state chartered St. John's College on the western shore in Annapolis, granted it an even larger fund of £1,750, and joined the two institutions together as the state university.[32]

Carroll was well aware of these developments. At the invitation of the Maryland legislature, he sat on St. John's first board of trustees and in 1788 served as the president of that body. Washington College, for its part, with William Smith presiding, had already given him an honorary degree at its second commencement in 1785. This represented an interesting turn for Smith, who in the 1750s had written a series of essays in which he raised the shibboleth of the popish menace and concluded that a long-time Catholic conspiracy was at the root of the French-Indian war.[33]

Carroll was now genuinely optimistic about the new climate. As he wrote to Plowden in February 1785:

Two Colleges are now erecting in this State, by private contribution and public endowment. They are established on a liberal plan open to Masters and Scholars of every denomination. Similar foundations exist in other states. Notwithstanding the danger for morals in these mixed Colleges, I still think that much advantage will be derived from them: & I hope that as we R.C. are unable to raise or support one ourselves, providence has ordained these as a resource for the exigencies of Religion. For in these Colleges, I trust there will amongst the Catholic youth trained in them be some from time to time inclined to an Ecclesiastical state. . . .

Apparently Carroll's idea was to establish a house near each of the new colleges in Philadelphia, Chestertown, and Annapolis, where a priest could attend to or even act as housemaster for those youths ("perhaps one or two every year") who were interested in the priesthood. Beyond that, a small seminary would be necessary, with two priests providing the intellectual and moral training for the candidates, once they finished their collegiate preparation.[35] Over the first six months of 1785, Carroll pursued this plan by attempting to attract Catholic professors he had known at Liège and elsewhere to apply for positions on the faculty in the three colleges, noting his influence with the ones in Maryland.[36]

By the end of that year, Carroll had revived his intention of beginning a separate academy. "The object nearest my heart now, & the only one, that can give consistency to our religious views in this country, is the establishment of a school, & afterwards of a Seminary for young clergymen."[37] It is not clear what caused him to revise his plans so sharply in 1785. Developments at Chestertown and Annapolis did not prove disillusioning to him. As late as 1790 he noted the "principles of perfect equality, as to Religion" that prevailed at St. John's.[38] (By that time he could regard the Annapolis college only as a competitor for younger students and a possible place for the graduates of his academy to pursue professional training in law and medicine.) Carroll, it is true, had detected some increase in anti-Catholic feeling in the region, occasioned by the publication of a pamphlet written by Charles H. Wharton, a former Jesuit priest and one of his cousins, who had converted to the Protestant Episcopal Church. Carroll had published a lengthy rebuttal of Wharton's attacks on the dogmas and practices of Roman Catholicism in the fall of 1784.[39] For a time he feared that Catholics would find themselves experiencing the same discrimination that had been their lot for most of the colonial period. Wharton's tract had appeared in the spring of 1784, a few months before Carroll first discussed his plan for forming houses for prospective seminarians near the local colleges. Had that "Wharton" scare, coupled with his discouragement at the prospects of funding and staffing a college, caused him to turn to an alternative that would not isolate Catholics? As he reflected to a friend in December of 1784, would not Catholics, by starting their own school, "be marked, as forming distinct views, & raise a dislike which may terminate in consequences very disagreeable to us?"[40]

When the Wharton controversy died quickly, Carroll perhaps had second thoughts about his own academy. There is evidence too that the more he pondered the need for priests to serve the Catholic population rapidly growing in the former colonies and spilling out into the territories no longer closed to settlement, the more he concluded that a Catholic school was the only way to provide for them. Carroll had apparently considered the possibility of continuing to rely upon the English recusant community in Flanders for the education of the American Catholic elite. He was still very much the Anglo-American. Had he been able to obtain for Americans the financial support that the Liège Academy provided for those considering the ecclesiastical state, it is possible that Carroll would have never developed his plan for Georgetown. But Liège restricted scholarships to English subjects; Americans had to pay £40 per year,[41] a sum that Carroll found "impracticable for many Americans," and they were bound to serve as prefects or assistants in the school after they completed their education.[42] This was clearly unacceptable to Carroll.

His English friend and fellow ex-Jesuit, Plowden, was counseling Carroll to provide his own educational institutions for "the rising church of America."[43] Carroll, in turn, came to believe firmly that establishing their own school(s) was the best investment American Catholics could make. His academy, Carroll wrote Plowden, was to be "our main sheet anchor for Religion."[44] (A sheet anchor was the large, spare anchor carried amidships, to be cast overboard in emergencies. It was, in other words, the rock bottom support of a ship in crisis.) The more Carroll reflected on the church that he now headed and the immigrant priests (all too many of them clerical vagabonds whom he was forced to use because he had no priests of his own), the more he calculated what was at stake in the school he was starting. If it failed, those who would govern the fate of the American Church would likely be such as "the missionary adventurers, as we have lately seen."[45]

Plans for Church and School

In early 1786 Carroll reported to a Roman official that to relieve a shortage of priests, "we plan to build a school where boys will be trained in piety and in the discipline of the *litterae humaniores*."[46] In November 1786 the general chapter of the Select Body of the Clergy, at a meeting at White Marsh, passed three major resolutions: (1) that the appropriate religious authority in the United States be a bishop, chosen by themselves and dependent on the Holy See only in those matters "universally acknowledged as its undoubted prerogative"; (2) that a special committee consider the expediency of incorporating their property in the State of Maryland; and (3) that they erect a school "for the education of youth & the perpetuity of the body of Clergy in this country." The three resolutions were interrelated. And, as the Chapter's circular letter explained, "we formed the plan of a school of general education for youth; but more especially that it may be a nursery of future clergymen. . . . To compleat this scheme a Bishop will certainly be necessary."[47] And to finance the school it was necessary to secure the property as fully as possible.

The Chapter appointed five directors of the school, including Carroll, and authorized a general financial subscription to be carried out throughout the United States, the West Indies, and Europe to support the enterprise. To enable Carroll to begin construction on a building, the sum of £100 sterling was appropriated from the sale of a tract of land.[48]

Immediately there was opposition to all of this from the members in the Southern District, comprising St. Mary's and Charles Counties. This heartland of the old Maryland Mission was also home to the movement for the restoration of the Society of Jesus in America.[49] Leonard Neale (1746–1817), one of five brothers from Charles County who had been members of the Society, was the movement's leader. Neale and his colleagues resented the consequences that the actions of the chapter would have upon the former property of the Society, which they obviously regarded as a sacred trust. Both a bishop and a school represented threats to it. A bishop would very likely lay claim to the property. The school was already spending and dissipating some of it, and probably much more would follow. All this they elaborated upon in a circular letter through which they intended to nullify the decisions made at White Marsh.

Carroll wasted no time in responding to their allegations. As he reminded Neale, he had taken pains before the White Marsh meeting to discuss the necessity of the school with virtually all of them and all had been supportive of the idea. (One delegate to the meeting was spreading the story that the resolutions were the result of a conspiracy on the part of a majority of the delegates, who had kept the business of the bishop or the school from the clergy in general.) In fact, Carroll contended, it was "universal knowledge" that all the issues—the school, incorporation, and the bishopric—would be on the agenda of the chapter. Neale was especially concerned about the "extensiveness" of the school. Carroll pointed out that if they expected the school to be a "nursery" for ecclesiastics, they had to admit youths who were mere children. "The sooner youths are put under virtuous & careful hands," he added, "the less danger there will be of corruption in their morals & principles." In America, unlike Europe, there were unfortunately no elementary religious schools to inculcate the first elements of learning and discipline, hence the need for a comprehensive academy.

Carroll assured them that he would do everything that prudence dictated to prevent the school from becoming a burden upon their estates. "Till the experiment is made," he observed, "it is difficult to tell what the contributions of seculars will amount to . . . ," but all should bear their fair share. As to the obligation they had to hold the property in trust for the restoration of the Society, he pointed out that the property being used to fund the proposed school had been acquired since the suppression of the Society, and suggested that the vital role that education had played in the work of their former society should tell them how much his proposed academy was one that "St. Ignatius would glory in as coming from his most zealous children . . ."[50] "[T]he Society," he reminded one member of the Southern District, "rendered no service more extensibely [sic] than the education of youth."[51]

The schools of the Society in Europe were not calculated merely to supply its order with members, or the Church with ministers, but to diffuse knowledge, promote virtue & serve Religion. This is just the end we propose by our school, & tho' no members should take to the Church, we conceive this end alone well worth our most earnest concurrence. . . .

At any rate, the property, including the school, would be turned over to the Society, as soon as it should be restored. No bishop would ever have any power over it. But if they hoped to produce native priests, a bishop was absolutely essential; as was a school, which would be "the only source for new members," Carroll deftly pointed out, "in case of a reestablishment." Having said all this, Carroll reminded them that in establishing the Select Body of the Clergy they had pledged themselves to abide by the decisions the majority of the districts reached at the general chapter.[52] "My hopes are perhaps too sanguine," he confessed to one priest in Southern Maryland, "but God is my witness, that in recommending a school . . . I think I am rendering to Religion the greatest service, that will ever be in my power."[53]

The "White Marsh" opposition proved to be short-lived. By March 1787 Neale and his associates, convinced of the "reasonableness" of Carroll's plans for school and bishopric, were "as urgent as any to have them carried into execution."[54]

Financing the Institution

The second of the three resolutions, obtaining a bishop, proved to be the easiest. The American clergy, through Carroll, asked the Holy See, in recognition of republican sensibilities about independence, to appoint a bishop elected by his fellow priests and not dependent on any Roman Congregation for his authority. Rome consented to their request and authorized the Americans, "as a special favor and for this first time," to elect as bishop "a person eminent in piety, prudence, and zeal for the faith," from among themselves.[55]

The results of the May 1789 election were predictable, although Carroll declared that he was "stunned with the issue of this business."[56] He had been functioning as a bishop for five years in all but sacramental power. Carroll received twenty-four of the twenty-six votes cast.[57]

The first of the chapter's goals, incorporation of the property within the state of Maryland, took six years to effect, although the reasons for the delay are not clear. At last, in late December 1792, the General Assembly of Maryland passed "An Act for securing certain estates and property for the support and uses of ministers of the Roman Catholic religion." The Catholic clergy was thus legally enabled to establish a civil corporation of three to five trustees to control and manage the property they had acquired in Maryland but had hitherto been able to hold only as individuals. Now, a decade after the Revolution, the state acknowledged that "it is highly reasonable and just to grant unto ministers of the Roman Catholic religion, who are citizens of this

State, that legislative aid, without which they will be destitute of that protection and security to their property, to which they are entitled equally with every other sect or denomination of Christians."[58]

Of the three goals, establishment of the school proved the most difficult. Finances were a major obstacle. Carroll hoped to secure "considerable subscriptions" from the Catholic laity in America, although he had no illusions that they would be sufficient to meet the expenses of the initial construction of buildings and the securing of faculty.[59] In accordance with the directives of the general chapter of 1786, Carroll put together a network of agents from New York to Virginia to receive (and presumably encourage) contributions to the academy.

Certainly there was cause to hope that this initial fund-raising campaign would be successful. In the Chesapeake country a disproportionate number of Catholics were among the wealthiest gentry. Charles Carroll of Carrollton alone was reputedly worth more than £200,000. The agents themselves, with few exceptions, constituted the Catholic landed and mercantile elite in America, from Charles Carroll to Thomas Fitzsimons of Philadelphia. Printed "PROPOSALS FOR ESTABLISHING AN ACADEMY AT GEORGE-TOWN, PATOWMACK-RIVER, MARYLAND" were distributed broadly in America and Europe. The reaction at home was disappointing, to say the least. The agents neither attracted major contributions nor made any themselves.[60] Clearly, the Catholic elite did not consider the prospective academy its own best investment toward a learned and disciplined leadership in the next gen-

The following Gentlemen, and others, that may be appointed hereafter, will receive Subfcriptions, and inform the Subfcribers, to whom, and in what Proportion, Payments are to be made :—In Maryland—The Hon. CHARLES CARROLL, of CARROLLTON, HENRY ROZER, NOTLEY YOUNG, ROBERT DARNALL, GEORGE DIGGES, EDMUND PLOWDEN, Efqrs, Mr. JOSEPH MILLARD, Capt. JOHN LANCASTER, Mr. BAKER BROOKE, CHANDLER BRENT, Efq; Mr. BERNARD O'NEILL and Mr. MARSHAM WARING, Merchants, JOHN DARNALL, and IGNATIUS WHEELER, Efqrs, on the Weftern-Shore ; and on the Eaftern, Rev. Mr. JOSEPH MOSLEY, JOHN BLAKE, FRANCIS HALL, CHARLES BLAKE, WILLIAM MATTHEWS, and JOHN TUITTE, Efqrs.—In Pennfylvania—GEORGE MEAD and THOMAS FITZSIMMONS, Efqrs, Mr. JOSEPH CAUFFMAN, Mr. MARK WILCOX, and Mr. THOMAS LILLY.—In Virginia—Col. FITZGERALD, and GEORGE BRENT, Efq;—and at New-York, DOMINIC LYNCH, Efquire.

SUBSCRIPTIONS will alfo be received, and every necefary Information given, by the following Gentlemen, Directors of the Undertaking :—The Rev. Meffrs. JOHN CARROLL, JAMES PELLENTZ, ROBERT MOLYNEUX, JOHN ASHTON, and LEONARD NEALE.

Detail from the 1787 broadside. It lists the Gentlemen and Directors as the agents authorized to receive monies needed for the proposed Academy at George-Town, Patowmack-River, Maryland. (Georgetown University Archives)

eration.[61] Carroll apparently had failed to persuade them that what he was beginning was more than a preparatory school for clergymen. There was no Phillips family to be found within Catholic America.[62]

The war had left the country financially pressed; the 1780s were hard times in general for schools, particularly those that were trying to establish themselves. There was a rising tide against the public funding of colleges by the mid-1780s. St. John's and Washington Colleges did not escape the consequences of the change in opinion. St. John's was unable to open until 1789 because of defaulting subscribers. An "Old Soldier" summed up the prevailing opinion in Maryland about using state funds for higher education in 1785:

Let anybody show what advantage the poor man receives from colleges, who is scarcely able to feed and clothe his family, pay his public just and necessary demands, and teach his children to read the Bible and write their names; what are colleges to these? Why should they support them? I must confess I don't know, unless it is to serve those who are in affluent circumstances, whose children can be spared from labor, and receive the benefits.[63]

By 1805 the legislature had voided the act that created the University of Maryland.[64]

Independence had cut not only the political ties to England but financial ties as well. The traditional British patronage of American colleges practically stopped. Several of the old colleges, including Yale, Dartmouth, Rhode Island, and New Jersey, sent agents to Europe to raise money. Only Dartmouth had any success, and that only indirectly. President John Wheelock in 1783 persuaded two Englishmen to donate equipment for a scientific laboratory.[65] Carroll had no qualms about seeking funds in England and the Continent. He had no choice but to hope that European benefactors would be able to supply what Americans could or would not. Plowden quickly burst the bubble of Carroll's hope. English Catholics, he informed his friend, were glutted with appeals for their generous support, not only support of the Liège Academy but of other schools, chapels, and other pious enterprises as well. "In these circumstances," he wrote Carroll in June 1787, "I fear that your petition, however interesting it be, will not be much countenanced by the few Caths. in this country, who have the means to support it . . ."[66] Nor did the ex-Jesuits in England hold out any hope for Carroll that some money might become available from the assets of the Society in England which were then being litigated.[67]

Carroll's fund-seeking in England was in fact harmed further by a pamphlet published in Dublin in 1788. The author was an Irish priest, Patrick Smyth, whom Carroll had appointed pastor of the church in Frederick, Maryland, in October 1787 but who had returned to Ireland a few months later after a dispute with the former pastor, an ex-Jesuit, over Smyth's salary. Before Smyth left, Carroll had learned that he was already spreading stories that there was a prejudice against those who had not been Jesuits.[68] Smyth denied the charge at the time but his Dublin pamphlet soon substantiated that and more. It scornfully depicted the former Jesuits as rich country squires and slaveholders who were irreparably harming religion by clinging to their estates rather than meeting the religious needs of the expanding Catholic population. Smyth charged, without foundation, that Carroll had deliberately passed up the public endowments that the Pennsylvania assembly was offering to any denominations who wished to erect colleges. This was but one manifestation of a small-mindedness that was bent on confining the institutional center of the Church to one of the least promising states in the Union. Smyth wrote:

It only betrays the shallowness of vulgar penetration to stand amazed at this ingenious stroke of policy. Maryland hath always been, and at all hazards, it seems, it must continue to be, the seat of our faith in North America. From its limited situation on all sides, no gratuitous territory can be expected. Something, however, may be done by beggarly subscription; and a snug little house, called a College, is now a-building in Georgetown, to shew the world how the *amor patriae* supercedes what foolish devotees style, the Good of Religion. A man owes much gratitude to the place of his nativity.[69]

Carroll dismissed Smyth's work as that of an "imagination, pregnant with suspicion."[70] Nonetheless he prepared a detailed rebuttal which he sent to Ireland to be published, should Smyth's pamphlet get a wide circulation.[71] Friends in Ireland and England counseled silence. ("A silent contempt," Strickland thought, "is the only answer it deserves.")[72] Carroll's reply went unpublished, although Smyth's pamphlet made its way as far as Rome. What damage it did to Carroll's fund-raising efforts in the British Isles is unclear, but it temporarily impeded his attempts to secure financial assistance from the Holy See. Two students whom Carroll had sent to Rome to study at the Propaganda College were summoned by Leonardo Antonelli, the Cardinal Prefect of the Congregation of the Propaganda, to be interrogated about Smyth's charges. A confidant of Carroll's warned him that the cardinal still suspected the Americans of trying to resurrect the Society of Jesus in the United States, despite the Brief of Suppression.[73] Carroll felt constrained to point out to Antonelli in 1790 that of the thirty priests who had come to America and received faculties from him since 1784, only seven were former Jesuits. "I think I should be guilty of a most grievous crime and deserve punishment," he added, "if I should strive to promote the restoration of the Society rather than the spread of the Faith."[74]

Carroll solicited contributions from European prelates and nobility during the next several years. The opportunity to patronize an establishment that would further the progress of religion and offset in America the losses the Church was experiencing

John Carroll's Episcopal seal adopted in 1790. The design incorporates an image of the Blessed Virgin and the keys of Peter, the two he selected as patrons of the nation's first bishopric. The Virgin is surrounded by thirteen stars that represent each of the United States of America. After his consecration, John Carroll published "A Short Account of the Establishment of the New See of Baltimore in Maryland," as well as the discourse delivered on the occasion of his consecration at Lulworth Castle, a translation of the authorizing papal bull, and extracts from the Bill of Rights of some of the States. (From *The Life and Times of Archbishop Carroll* by John Gilmary Shea.) (Georgetown University Archives)

in Europe was the primary theme of Carroll's appeal. Unfortunately, he was no more successful on the Continent than he had been in the British Isles. Cardinal Antonelli made vague promises of future help for the school. Carroll begged that his congregation grant the academy an annual sum of two hundred gold pieces. Eventually in 1792, Propaganda pledged a nominal subsidy of one hundred scudi for three years, about a tenth of what Carroll had sought. Carroll was so desperate for money to sustain the school that he kept pressing Propaganda for the sum, which was finally granted in 1794.[75] At the time of his consecration in England (August 1790) as bishop of Baltimore, Carroll also obtained some benefactions from individuals, which amounted to more than £500, some of which he was able to apply to the school.[76]

For the most part, however, the Americans were left to their own resources. In May 1789, the general chapter authorized a new subscription campaign focused on the clergy, but there is little evidence that this drive attracted any significant aid. The chapter was increasingly dependent on revenues derived from their own lands in order to fund the new institution. At that meeting they authorized that the salary of the still-to-be named president be paid annually from the income of a certain tract of land held by them.[77]

"George-Town, Patowmack-River, Maryland"

In 1787 John Carroll had acquired as a site for his school a one-acre plot on a rise overlooking the Potomac River outside the village of "George-Town."[78] The decision to locate there had been made at the general chapter in 1786. An urban setting for a school was both an American and a Jesuit tradition. This pattern continued throughout the Federal era, but many educational leaders, and especially the Presbyterians, believed that republican education could not take place in the city, and hence located their new colleges in smaller towns, where students presumably would not face the temptations that city life bred.[79]

Georgetown certainly qualified as a small town. In the late 1780s it was a river port of some two-hundred and fifty houses and a number of sheds and shanties and perhaps fifteen hundred persons.[80] Founded in 1751, Georgetown became the leading tobacco port in the region in the last quarter of the century. The town grew rapidly after tobacco commerce revived dramatically following the Treaty of 1783, which officially and successfully ended the War for Independence. Scottish immigrant merchants made fortunes in the flourishing trade as did planter-merchants who increasingly migrated to the area from Southern Maryland. By 1790 it had replaced Annapolis as the commercial and social center of the Maryland tobacco region. A French visitor in that decade found it "a rather pretty, rather crowded, rather commer-

The port of George-Town on the Patowmack-River in 1790. (Engraving courtesy of the Prints and Photographs Division, Library of Congress)

cial little town . . ."[81] For the Maryland gentry of Southern Maryland, it became the urban center of their culture.[82]

Georgetown, however, was not itself the urban center of Maryland. That distinction belonged to the older town, Baltimore, which was the fastest growing urban area in the country. In 1782 its population was 8,000; eight years later Baltimore, with a count of 13,503 inhabitants, was the fifth largest city in the nation. In the next decade the number doubled. The cause of this extraordinary growth was Baltimore's ideal location in the fall zone between the Piedmont and Tidewater areas. As Europe had developed food shortages that became desperate toward the end of the eighteenth century, the importance of grain increased enormously as a "money crop" on the backcountry farms of Maryland, Virginia, and Pennsylvania. Of all the Maryland ports, including Georgetown, Baltimore was by far the closest to this farming region. As one Baltimore merchant advertised in 1767, "The situation of our town to an extensive back country, which is now well cultivated and from which we draw large quantities of wheat, flour and flaxseed, renders it fair for a place of considerable trade."[83] By the 1780s Baltimore had monopolized the grain market and become the flour milling center of the Chesapeake region.[84] Since grain, in contrast to to-bacco, had a year-long production cycle, required a multitude of ships to transport its loose bulk, and generated secondary industries, Baltimore was, no doubt, "a booster's delight."[85]

The American clergy, in electing Carroll as bishop, had unanimously chosen Baltimore as his episcopal see because of its central location in Maryland.[86] But Carroll apparently never gave any thought to locating his academy there. For one thing, six months before the General Chapter approved his plan for the academy, Carroll had chaired a meeting for the purpose of establishing a nonsectarian college in Baltimore. That school, with Carroll's support as well as that of Episcopalian and Presbyterian clergy in the city, eventually opened, but it had a short history.[87] George-town, on the other hand, had no schools. More important, Baltimore had a very small Catholic presence, only about 7 percent of the population. And most of them were working class folk, hardly the group able to sup-port an educational institution, nor the focus of the Jesuit tradition in education.[88]

In the "Proposals for establishing an Academy," Carroll mentioned the "Choice of Situation, Salubrity of Air, Convenience of Communication, and Cheapness of Living" as the principal reasons for the choice of George-town. If the phrase was something of a cliché in college promotional lit-erature, there was, nonetheless, truth to the claims. The town, perhaps in population a third Roman Catholic, was undoubtedly the urban center of the Maryland Catholic gentry. It was well situated enough to afford "con-venience of communication" as well as a country setting for the institu-tion. And as Carroll noted, costs in Georgetown were relatively cheap, certainly in comparison to Baltimore or Philadelphia. In anticipating the narrow margin within which the school would perforce operate, this was no mean consideration. As for its salubrious air, the hilltop setting seemed especially healthy in a wooded area cooled by Potomac breezes. George-town, in fact, was the first of many schools to choose such an elevated setting. Health may have been the primary reason but image was another. The "College on the Hill" became a common nineteenth-century ideal.[89] For Carroll, the school, like Winthrop's colony, was to have a life larger than its own.

The selection for the Potomac area as the permanent site of the federal capital was a triumph of the Potomac gentry over the upstart Chesapeake merchants, but this had no substantial influence upon Carroll's choice of Georgetown.[90] Although Georgetown (as well as Baltimore) was one of the chief players in the bidding contest that had been taking place since 1783, Carroll confessed to Plowden that he had given "little thought of [it] when I recommended that situation for the academy."[91] Still, he in-stantly recognized the potential importance this development would have for his school. "Our academy, from its situation," he allowed, "will prob-

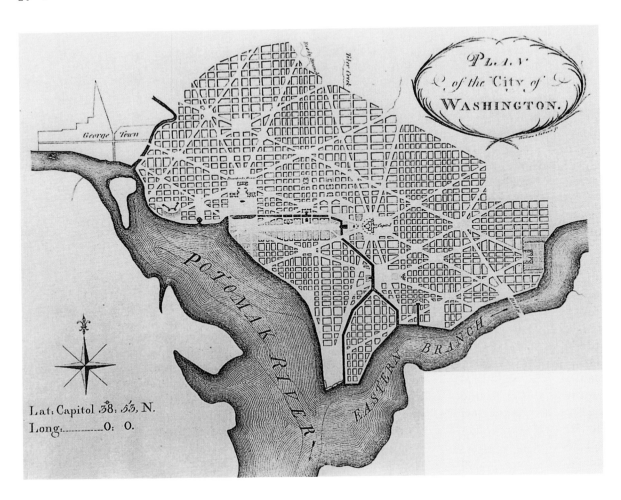

Map of the federal city with George-Town in the upper left quadrant. (Reprinted with permission of the Library of Congress from *The City of Washington: An Illustrated History,* Thomas Froncek, ed.)

ably be conspicuous. Commissioners under the direction of the President are to determine the particular spot, in a district of about 50 miles, lying on that river. The knowledge, I have of the Country, makes me confident, it will be either at George Town, or, what would answer better for our school, within four miles of it."[92] Carroll was fairly sure that President George Washington would choose a site within the tidewater of the Potomac to allow access by water to the federal capital, which eliminated most of the backcountry area under consideration.[93] Of course, his confidence was bolstered by the fact that his brother, Daniel, was one of the commissioners. And, as things turned out, the site they chose matched his wish perfectly.

A Residential College Intended for "Students of Every Religious Profession"

"We shall begin the building of our Academy this summer," Carroll wrote Plowden in March 1788:

In the beginning we shall confine our plan to a house of 63 to 64 feet by 50, on one of the most lovely situations, that imagination can frame. It will be three stories high exclusive of the offices under the whole. Do not forget to give & procure assistance. On this academy is built all my hope of permanency, & success to our H. Religion in the United States.[94]

Construction actually began in mid-April 1788. The contractors, five Georgetown laymen, engaged Henry Carlisle, a "carpenter and joiner," to erect the shell of the three-story, hip-roofed building. They apparently made very clear how little money they had to spend. Carlisle estimated his costs at £493.5 for the materials, "lower By 20 Pr Cent than Ever I Undertook," and £450 for his labor. The contractors thought they could do better than that and supplied their own materials.[95] Carroll was hopeful of having the building "under roof" by the end of that year, but lack of money delayed the finishing of the building for more than three years.[96] Not until January of 1789 did Carroll raise the £75 needed to acquire the deed to the one-acre plot of ground on which the first building was rising.[97]

This first building, which eventually became known as "Old South," had ten or eleven rooms in which students and faculty held classes, studied, and ate. Its attic served as a dormitory for the students.[98] Carroll had initially intended to have the students seek their own lodgings in town, at least until additional buildings could be constructed, but even before formal classes began in 1792, students were living on campus, and as many as possible were soon crammed into the garret of the building.

Carroll was particularly concerned with student discipline. He found American colleges notoriously deficient in this regard. A tendency for students to fend for themselves in town lodgings rather than live in a dormitory under strict rules was a growing feature of college life in the period.[99] Republican educators, like Benjamin Rush, the Presbyterian president of Dickinson College in Pennsylvania, typically regarded dormitories as relics of "monkish ignorance" and totally incompatible with enlightened institutions of learning where individual responsibility, not group herding, was the key to the formation of moral character.[100] Carroll was all for moral formation, but had no prejudice against boarding schools. On the contrary, he seemed to feel that the current laissez-faire attitude toward student living was a large part of the scandal he found in much of the American collegiate scene.

The Academy's first
building, Old South, in 1788.
(Georgetown University Archives)

The Jesuit schools that Carroll had known in the Lowlands—St. Omers, Liège, Bruges—unlike most European colleges of the Society, had been boarding institutions with strict discipline, which included the wearing of uniforms (modified cassocks) by their students. Carroll intended, *mutatis mutandis,* to achieve a similar environment at Georgetown. "The students of the academy are to be distinguished by some peculiar badge in their dress," he wrote in his plan, "without which they are never to appear in publick. . . ." They were to avoid profanity as well as "disorderly [behavior]or publick houses, or gaming tables." Hazardous games and drunkenness were also to be strictly forbidden.[101] Still, he had no intention of imposing a monastic regime upon students who were being educated for life in a republic.

Nor did he intend to secure discipline by requiring a religious test for entrance. Not only was it to be open to all Catholics who qualified but also to "Students of Every Religious Profession." This was again a part of the Jesuit continental tradition, as well as a growing practice in American schools. Virtually all schools in the young republic, both nonsectarian and denominational, were becoming more pluralistic in the religious affiliations of their students. Most actually barred religious qualifications for admission. Carroll's correspondents in England, notably Plowden and Strickland, had reservations about the compatibility of such religious toleration with the effective discipline and piety that were the soil for the seed of vocations. But Carroll never wavered in this regard. His Catholic institution was not going to be a Catholic ghetto. Since Catholic schools in Europe were open to Protestants, it was all the more fitting in America, with its unprecedented provision for religious liberty, that Catholic schools be ecumenical. That religious liberty

THE Object of the proposed Institution is, to unite the Means of communicating Science with an effectual Provision for guarding and improving the Morals of YOUTH. With this View, the SEMINARY will be superintended by those, who, having had Experience in similar Institutions, know that an undivided Attention may be given to the Cultivation of Virtue, and literary Improvement; and that a System of Discipline may be introduced and preserved, incompatible with Indolence and Inattention in the Professor, or with incorrigible Habits of Immorality in the Student.

The Benefit of this Establishment should be as general as the Attainment of its Object is desirable. It will, therefore, receive Pupils as soon as they have learned the first Elements of Letters, and will conduct them, through the several Branches of classical Learning, to that Stage of Education, from which they may proceed, with Advantage, to the Study of the higher Sciences, in the University of this, or those of the neighbouring States. Thus it will be calculated for every Class of Citizens—as READING, WRITING, ARITHMETIC, the easier Branches of the MATHEMATICS, and the GRAMMAR of our NATIVE TONGUE will be attended to, no less than the LEARNED LANGUAGES.

Agreeably to the liberal Principle of our Constitution, the SEMINARY will be open to Students of EVERY RELIGIOUS PROFESSION.—They, who in this Respect differ from the SUPERINTENDENTS of the ACADEMY, will be at Liberty to frequent the Places of Worship and Instruction appointed by their Parents; but, with Respect to their moral Conduct, all must be subject to general and uniform Discipline.

In the Choice of Situation, Salubrity of Air, Convenience of Communication, and Cheapness of living, have been principally consulted; and GEORGE-TOWN offers these united Advantages.

was the prerequisite for both enlightened inquiry and discussion, and those in turn were the best hope for Christian reunification.

Nor was social status to be a criterion. "Thus it will be calculated," the initial prospectus declared, "for every Class of Citizens."[102]

John Carroll's Vision

As 1788 passed into 1789, George Washington was elected first president (in January) and took the oath of office on April 30 in New York City, the nation's first capital. (Twelve of the original thirteen states had ratified the Constitution by November 1789.) Still the building on Georgetown's heights remained unfinished. "I think we shall get enough of [the Academy] completed this summer to make a beginning of teaching," John Carroll wrote Plowden in the late winter of 1790; "but our great difficulty will be to get a proper President or Superintendent."[103] Plowden had already resisted Carroll's repeated invitations to become the first president, as had several other acquaintances in Europe, including John Mattingly. The qualifications

Detail from the 1787 broadside that defines the "Object of the proposed Institution" and declares it to be "open to students of EVERY RELIGIOUS PROFESSION." (Georgetown University Archives)

that Carroll mandated assured the virtual impossibility of finding someone for the position. He had earlier explained these to his English friend:

You see, he must be a person old enough to carry a considerable weight of authority & respect; experienced in the detail of government for such a place of education; & capable of embracing in his mind a general & indeed universal plan of studies, of which the academical institution is only a part. He should have considerable knowledge of the world, as he will be obliged to converse with many different persons: and he should be capable of abstracting his mind from the methods used in the colleges, where he has lived, so as to adopt only as much of them as is suited to the circumstances of this country; and of substituting such others, as are better adapted to the views and inclinations of those with whom he has to deal. You see I require a good deal; but all I mention, is necessary to give reputation & permanency to the plan; for you may be assured, that in the Institutions of other professions, they have procured from Europe some litterary [sic] characters of the first class: and this likewise makes me desirous of not falling behind hand with them . . . [104]

Some of Carroll's English friends found his presidential description absolutely quixotic. There were few priests who approached the ideal president he depicted, and they were already engaged. William Strickland wondered why Carroll thought he needed a man of such "universal knowledge & brilliant talents." This kind of president was fitting for a college offering philosophy and belles-lettres but hardly necessary for a grammar school. If he was concerned about building a reputation, let him make sure he secured "diligent and vertuous Masters . . . with proper Regulations." The school would establish its own character, no matter what the president's credentials. If Carroll wanted to develop the academy into something greater later on, he could easily do so. Far better to start modestly and grow gradually than to reach for the sky with grand plans that could only end in the collapse of the institution. "Permanancy," he counseled, "is an object of higher Consideration than the temporary honor of the day."[105]

Carroll does seem to have been thinking on a grander scale than an academy. John Witherspoon and William Smith, two "litterary characters of the first class" whom Carroll likely had in mind, were hardly presiding over mere academies at Princeton and Chestertown. Indeed, virtually as soon as the school opened "at George-Town, Patowmack-River," all references to the "academy" disappeared.

In Carroll's plan for the school, drawn up apparently in 1788 or 1789, when he was expecting the school to begin, it is clear that he envisioned a very comprehensive course of studies.[106] The curriculum would be both classical and practical. Latin and Greek ("the Learned Languages") would be emphasized no more than reading, writing, arithmetic, English grammar, and geography.[107] If there was a demand for it, French would also be offered. (Given the popularity of France in the mid-1780s, Carroll no doubt expected that there would be such a demand.) At St. Omers, as at most

American colleges, the minimal age, "as a rule," had been fourteen. At Georgetown, it was set at eight, putting it slightly below the average minimal age of admission at other American academies."[108] St. Omers expected boys to have an elementary knowledge of Latin. Georgetown required that entrants have the ability to read their own language. St. Omers set out a five- or six-year curriculum, from "Rudiments" to "Rhetoric," that constituted the core of Jesuit humanistic education. Carroll was proposing a curriculum that would range from preparatory studies for the traditional Jesuit education to the higher level of rhetoric. Having completed the course of studies, such a student might then proceed, "with Advantage, to the Study of the higher Sciences," in one of the universities of the nearby states or in the seminary Carroll intended to open in a few years.[109] In fact, it replicated in intention the course of studies offered at St. Omers College and its preparatory school at Boulogne when Carroll had been a student in Flanders in the 1740s.[110] The education that colonial American Catholics had been able to obtain at Newtown or Bohemia *and* St. Omers, Carroll now wanted to provide at Georgetown. As the English Jesuits had discovered a generation before, there was no local church or community to provide the elementary education necessary as a foundation for the liberal arts of the college curriculum. But it was this combining of grammar school and college that Strickland found unrealistic.

Carroll, of course, could point to other American schools that were as comprehensive. William and Mary had abolished its lower school only a few years before Carroll first proposed his academy. Other institutions, such as Washington College in Virginia and Dickinson in Pennsylvania, were evolving from grammar school/academies into colleges. At any rate, Strickland's criticism did not deter Carroll from his aim—to found a school that in quality and reputation would rank with any that were springing up in the new country.

Foregoing a Charter for the School

If Carroll was so concerned with reputation and public stature, one has to ask why he made no attempt to have his school chartered, at a time when a dozen new or old schools from Maine to Georgia were receiving charters.[111] Despite his family's political connections (his cousin, Charles, was the president of the Maryland Senate until 1789; his brother, Daniel, was a delegate to the Constitutional Convention of 1787), it was no simple matter for him to obtain a charter for Georgetown. To possess a charter, of course, was to be protected from the unlimited liability that owners of institutions risked. On the other hand, charters in the late eighteenth century carried a liability of their own. To receive a charter was to give a public character to an institution and thus make it dependent on the chartering authority.

Americans had inherited the European concept of the college or university as a civil corporation. Education was regarded as a civic value; hence the necessity of government to be able to influence, if not control, the schools it authorized to grant degrees, even those with religious affiliations. (In most colonies, of course, there had been a formal connection between church and state; the colleges had been conducted by the established church.) In a republic without an established church, the awareness of the civic role of colleges was even stronger since an educated citizenry was considered essential to the preservation of a society in which the people were declared sovereign.

Carroll did not need to look far to see how intrusive government could be in attempting to control colleges. In 1779 the Pennsylvania legislature had converted the private College of Philadelphia into the public University of the State of Pennsylvania by virtually forcing upon the institution a new set of trustees. When William Smith and the old trustees attempted to regain their charter rights as founded in 1740, they were told that such "corporations, which are the creatures of society, can, under the bill of rights, plead [no] . . . exemption from legislative regulation."[112] That is, Pennsylvania could not afford to have a college become a kingdom unto itself. Subsequently, the Presbyterians were very circumspect in seeking charters for their other academies or colleges in order to avoid state interference. Even though Benjamin Rush intended Dickinson to be a Presbyterian counterforce to the radical University of the State of Pennsylvania, he was careful to disguise its denominational character.[113] At Liberty Hall in western Virginia, the Presbyterians deliberately sought incorporation as an academy rather than as a college, to minimize the threat of legislative interposition. Even so, a decade later the legislature attempted to change the academy into a college under its control.[114] In Tennessee, the Presbyterian schools were legally not denominational but independent institutions accountable to the legislature.

Jurgen Herbst has suggested that Carroll, shrewdly reading the signs of the times that showed a growing backlash against higher education and all too aware of the atavistic distrust of Catholics in American society, decided to found an academy that would not require a state charter to grant degrees and hence would elude state interference. By this strategy Carroll "kept to himself" his real intention to found a seminary for future priests and kept the control of the institution within the church. When the school finally received a federal charter a generation later, it lost none of its independence because its governing structure remained intact. In this way Georgetown arose as "the most private" of the private colleges that came to characterize American education in the new nation.[115]

How much of this "strategy" Carroll consciously pursued, the record does not resolve. It is true that there is no mention of "Catholic," much less anything hinting of "seminary for future clergymen," in the prospectus. Not until 1814 would the college publicly advertise that "the object of this institution is principally for the education of those who profess the Catholic religion."[116] But it was hardly a secret who was behind the enterprise. For the first time Catholics were beginning a college in America—with no charter, little or no money, no president or faculty. What they had was Carroll's vision, a remark- ably serendipitous location, and a future that was anybody's guess. "The academy will be opened in a few days," Carroll was finally able to report to Plowden in October 1791. But he had to add that it was opening "not so advantagiously, as I hoped. No president *pro dignitate loci.* I can hardly forgive my friends at Liège. Here was an opportunity for infinite services to the cause of God and his church."[117] It was scarcely an auspicious start.

CHAPTER 2

"To Give Perpetuity . . ."

At length I am safe arrived here after a journey of three days. Now you may congratulate me of being at that place where I have so long desired. The College will be opened immediately.

WILLIAM GASTON TO HIS MOTHER
from George Town, 5 November 1791

Georgetown's First Decade

In its first decade Carroll's institution became something more, and something less, than an American St. Omers College. For the American Catholic gentry of the Chesapeake region, it became a natural successor to the recusant school they had patronized before the revolution. Like St. Omers, it was international in both students and faculty, but with an internationalism that transcended the Anglo-American world and brought tensions that were to affect the development of Georgetown by the first decade of the next century.

Its location in the new capital of the country did "give a weight" to its establishment, even in the early years, as a rising elite, consisting partly of Chesapeake Catholics, identified with the new school. Identification, however, did not include financial support, much less control of the college. Just as the District of Columbia suffered from economic depression and political uncertainty about its own future status by the turn of the century, Georgetown experienced its own recession because of internal political turmoil,

Robert Plunkett, first president of Georgetown, from 1791 to 1793. This is a presumed likeness painted in the late nineteenth century from eighteenth-century descriptions. (Georgetown University Archives)

inept leadership, and competition from a rival institution in an even more rapidly growing urban center, Baltimore.

The First President

In Carroll's efforts to attract a distinguished ex-Jesuit from England to head his academy, he had virtually pleaded with Charles Plowden to accept the position or at least find someone "capable of filling this place with credit and advantage."[1] Other overtures to British and continental friends also brought no commitment. "The fate of the school will depend much on the first impression made upon the public," he wrote Plowden in 1790.[2] When construction of the academy was nearing completion in the fall of 1791, Carroll still had not found a president. Robert Molyneux (1738–1808), *faute de mieux* the best qualified of the available ex-Jesuits in America, could not then be prevailed upon to head the school. Nor could Carroll blame him. As he admitted to Plowden, "he has not the activity of body, or the *vivida vis animi* for such an employment."[3]

Carroll finally persuaded a recent immigrant, Robert Plunkett (1752–1815), to become the first president. The thirty-nine-year-old Plunkett, an alumnus of the English College at Douai, had joined the Society of Jesus four years before its suppression.[4] Having been ordained a priest sometime afterwards, Plunkett had received permission from Propaganda Fide in 1789 to go to America as a missionary.[5] He had set sail for the United States in 1790, in the company of Charles Neale and four nuns who had been sent to establish the first Carmel in the new country. He was stationed at the plantation at White Marsh when Carroll turned to him almost by default to head his academy. The bishop had no illusions about Plunkett, who had volunteered for the American mission because of its perceived pastoral, not educational, needs. But, for the moment, he had no one else to turn to in order to open his academy.

The First Faculty and the Sulpicians

Typically in the eighteenth century, one or two individuals constituted the faculty of an academy. Even colleges rarely numbered more than five or six professors, with an equal number of tutors. Yale, the country's largest college with an enrollment of approximately two hundred and fifty students, had a permanent faculty of three: a president, a professor of divinity, and a professor of mathematics and natural philosophy.[6] In a society where the clergy continued to monopolize the teaching profession, Carroll necessarily had to look to the Catholic clergy at home and abroad to staff his academy. His re-peated attempts to lure English ex-Jesuits to Georgetown for this work had produced one uninterested priest, Robert Plunkett, who reluctantly became the first president of the institution and lasted eighteen months in the office. Among the score of ex-Jesuits in America there were few, if any, who could be spared from missions and parishes and who also had the aptitude to teach. Carroll was all too aware that "the provincials of England were not in the habit of sending hither many of their best subjects, . . ." and the Society had now been suppressed, except in Russia, for nearly twenty years.[7]

In the first fifteen years of Georgetown College, three ex-Jesuits served as president—two Englishmen and one American—as well as one Sulpician who was of French descent and from the West Indies. The original faculty itself was composed of two diocesan priests, four Sulpicians, nine seminari-ans or candidates for the Sulpician seminary, at least eight former students fulfilling their "tuition repayment" oaths as tutors or student prefects, and seventeen lay faculty who taught mathematics, English, fencing, and music. As with the students, there was a heavy faculty turnover, more than half staying less than two years.

As one revolution had created the possibility of establishing a Catholic college in post-colonial America, so another was in a large sense responsible for staffing it. At the very time Carroll was vainly searching for a president, the Sulpicians, amid the growing turmoil of the French Revolution, were seeking to relocate themselves and their seminarians. Carroll, thinking it premature, had initially been cool to the Sulpician offer to establish a semi-nary in his diocese at their own expense. The Cardinal Prefect of Propaganda, Leonardo Antonelli, urged Carroll to accept their offer, if only to defuse charges by some disgruntled clerics like Patrick Smyth that the bishop want-ed to keep America as a preserve for ex-Jesuits.[8] When the Sulpicians per-sisted, Carroll finally recognized the providential nature of their availability as "a great & auspicious event for our new Diocese."[9] By July of 1791 Father Francis Charles Nagot, three of his fellow Sulpicians, and five seminarians had arrived in Baltimore and Carroll quickly utilized these seminarians—French, British, and American—to staff his new college.[10]

Jean-Edouard de Mondésir, a seminarian from France, had arrived in Baltimore in July 1791. In late October he was sent to Georgetown and was the first person to reside in the yet uncompleted building. He "wears a cas-sock," one former Jesuit noted.[11] (The Maryland ex-Jesuits, reflecting the outlaw status of priests during the colonial period, ordinarily wore conserva-tive civilian dress.) He became the first professor, teaching French and Latin while learning English from Plunkett.[12] Since the classics were to be the core of the curriculum, de Mondésir also set about learning Greek in order to in-troduce students to that language as well. For the next ten years de Mondésir shuttled between Georgetown and Baltimore, teaching everything from French to Greek to philosophy. During the College's first five years three other seminarians served on the school faculty, plus one candidate for the priesthood from Ireland. In 1795, Benedict Flaget (1763–1851) was the first Sulpician appointed to teach French and geography. That year the faculty numbered eight.

The bishop had realized from the outset that funds for his fledgling institution would be "scanty." One area in which he hoped to economize was that of faculty salaries. Thus, candidates for the priesthood or seminarians were to be preferred for the core subjects of Latin and Greek, since they presumably would need less remuneration, perhaps £30 ($80) plus year-round room and board at the college. Other faculty, such as "the meer English teacher" could be paid £80 annually, far below the average college or academy salary of £150 to £200 which Carroll considered ""enormous."[13] In fact, aside from Plunkett and Francis Neale (1756–1837), all the faculty hired in the first five years (seminarians, candidates, Sulpicians, and laymen) received annual salaries of £75 each, plus room and board. (It should be noted that the Maryland pound was still in use. The dollar [as a silver coin] was issued in America in 1794 but was not yet the "dominant" currency.)

The First Student–Safe Arrived

"At length I am safe arrived here after a journey of three days," William Gaston (**C** 1791–93) wrote his widow mother from "George Town" in early November of 1791. "Now you may congratulate me of being at that place where I have so long desired. The College will be opened immediately."[14] The thirteen-year-old Gaston had set out from his mother's home in New Bern, North Carolina, the previous spring to attend the new Catholic institution only to discover that it was not yet ready. For the past several months he had been studying privately with an Irish Dominican, Francis Fleming, in Philadelphia.[15] Fleming assured Mrs. Gaston after leaving her son with his new teachers, "He is charmed with every circumstance of his new scene, & I hope, will make a most rapid progress."[16]

Unfortunately, the building was still not habitable and William had to spend the next three weeks living above the City Tavern on Falls Street (now M Street) in Georgetown while continuing his private studies with Fleming. Finally, on January 2, 1792, classes began, with but two students in attendance—Gaston and Charles Philemon Wederstrandt (**C** 1791–93), a distant relative of John Carroll from the Eastern Shore of Maryland. Nevertheless, despite a severe winter that froze even the harbor waterways of Georgetown and Baltimore for months, the number of students steadily increased as word spread of the long-awaited opening of the academy.[17] By June there were more than forty students, not only from Maryland but from well beyond. "Our College has got a great reputation," Gaston informed his mother:

From all quarters boys come to it. From the West Indies we have four . . . From Philadelphia we have two, from New York one (three more are daily expected) from Wilmington N° Carolina we have also one, . . . ; from Virginia, three, & several from all parts of Maryland. It increases so much that they have determined to build [the hall] 130 ft. longer & a story higher, for it is only two stories high at present. But the most material thing is the goodness, not the number of the boys. For at the Last Judgement God will not demand of us how numerous we were, but how good we were . . . [18]

President Robert Plunkett, for one, was very impressed by Gaston's piety and intelligence. At the end of the first term he assured Gaston's mother that "he is the best scholar & most exemplary youth in GeoTown."[19] Gaston spent his six-week summer vacation in Baltimore at the newly established Sulpician Seminary at the invitation of his teacher, Jean-Edouard de Mondésir. Gaston had found de Mondésir a magnetic force, whose conversation about God could make the boy's heart "almost burst with crying."[20] The first student seemed destined to become the first fruit of Carroll's plan to seed a future clergy at his academy. Plunkett even confided to his mother that the boy had the makings of a bishop.[21] But a chronic cold and other symptoms of incipient consumption forced him to return to New Bern in April 1793 at his mother's insistence, despite Plunkett's assurances that his health was sound.[22]

William Gaston (1778–1842). He was the first student and is here portrayed in the mid-1830s at the height of his long and distinguished career in public service. (By G. Cooke, engraving by A. B. Durand, courtesy of the Library of Congress.)

Billy Gaston departed with the intention of returning but he never did. When his health improved sufficiently for him to resume his formal education, he decided to enroll at Princeton. Francis Neale, who had taken charge of Gaston's spiritual life at Georgetown and had sent him off to North Carolina with a copy of his devotional manual, *The Pious Guide to Prayer and Devotion*, was crushed by the news.[23] Despite Neale's bitter warning that the Presbyterians "of all heresies" were the most opposed to "the truths of the Gospel,"[24] Gaston persisted in his resolve and eventually graduated from the Presbyterian college. He went on to become a highly accomplished lawyer, politician, and judge in North Carolina, but he remained a staunch Catholic and a good friend of Georgetown. He not only sent his son and grandsons there for schooling but was also responsible for expediting passage in Congress of the Act that chartered the college in 1815.

Student Demographics

Gaston's piety and intelligence may have been exceptional, but in general he was typical of the first generation of Georgetown students: young, Catholic, small-town, and transient.[25] Nearly three-quarters of the two hundred and seventy-five students were between ten and sixteen years old, although they ranged in age overall from six to twenty-nine.[26] More than three quarters (80%) were Catholic. A bare majority were English in ethnic origin, with substantial minorities of French (22%) and Irish (13%), as well as some of Portuguese, Scottish, Dutch, Italian, Hispanic, Scandinavian, Welsh, and German extraction, and combinations of them. The students came largely from urban areas (70.9%), nearly twice as many from towns such as Georgetown and New Bern as from cities like Philadelphia and New York.[27] More than half (55%) were boarders, either on campus or in nearby private homes. Nearly two-thirds of the students attended Georgetown for less than two years.

American colleges at the end of the eighteenth century were usually local or regional schools. In New England an estimated ninety-one percent of the students were natives of that region.[28] In contrast, Carroll's academy from the beginning was a national, indeed international, school (see table 2.1, in appendix F). In the first decade nearly one-fifth of its students came from outside the United States, the French West Indies supplying most of them (forty students). Maryland and the District of Columbia accounted for nearly four-fifths of the Americans, with Pennsylvania, Virginia, and New York the other significant sources. A few months after the opening of classes, Bishop Carroll made a national appeal for the school through his pastoral letter to the American Catholic community in May of 1792. He exhorted "as many of you as are able" to send "your sons to this school of letters and virtue." "I know and lament," he added, "that the expense will be too great for many families." He trusted that they would experience its benefit indirectly through the schools that Georgetown graduates would subsequently establish or be involved in in their own local areas.[29] The tuition and board were formidable, £10 and £30 respectively, or approximately $107, more than a laborer's annual pay, and a fourth of an artisan's. Among both academies and colleges, Georgetown's fees were comparatively high.[30] In the first decade, tuition was paid in a variety of ways. A semi-barter economy allowed more individuals to attend the school than the formal tuition rates indicate. Students paid in everything from brandy to oats, from the use of adjacent properties to supplies of bread flour. A few parents even supplied slaves for the college's use as laborers in lieu of tuition. At least a couple of widows also paid for their sons' educations by working as laundresses or seamstresses for the college.

Other students, who gave promise of religious vocations, had their fees paid by others, usually priests in their home regions.

But if class, as Carroll had promised in his original proposal, did not prove an insurmountable obstacle to a Georgetown education in its early decades, the large majority of students still came from the American Catholic gentry and the rising middle class. As we have seen, Carroll had already begun trying to establish a network of Catholic support for the institution in cities from New York to Alexandria. If American Catholics had been slow to provide money for Georgetown, they quickly sent their sons in large numbers, once the doors opened. By 1796, enrollment had reached nearly one hundred, a size that few colleges of the period surpassed. The old families of Southern Maryland (an increasing number of whom had been moving to Georgetown and the District) formed the core of the large Catholic majority (more than 80%) in the school. Nearly all the students from Maryland were Catholic (97.4%), but probably less than two-thirds (60%) of those from the District were. The Carrolls, Fenwicks, Edelens, Brents, Hills, Neales, Medleys, Pyes, and Youngs all had sons in the first classes. Given the high degree of intermarriage among Maryland Catholic families, it is no surprise to find that approximately half of the Chesapeake Catholic students were related.[31] For instance, Thomas (**C** 1792–95) and William Brent (**C** 1792–96), grandnephews of John Carroll, had at least eight cousins in the school: a Carroll (William), a Brent (Robert), three Sims (Daniel, Joseph, and Patrick), two Hills (Clement and William), and a Young (Ralph), and there were probably more.[32] Even outside the old Maryland Catholic network, kinship was a common characteristic. Indeed, brothers and cousins constituted nearly half (45%) of the student population during the first decade.

Of the Chesapeake Catholic students, about two-thirds came from urban areas—more than two-fifths (43%) from towns; the rest (about 17%) from Baltimore; and somewhat fewer (nearly 40%) came from rural areas, almost all in Southern Maryland. Those from Southern Maryland were mainly sons of the Anglo-American gentry: planters, merchants, and professional men, such as three of the original subscribers from that region, Francis Hall, Edmund Plowden, and Notley Young. Hall was something of a newcomer among the gentry. A fourth generation Marylander, whose grandfather had converted to Catholicism and whose father had studied at St. Omers, Hall owned nearly two thousand acres in Prince George's and Frederick counties. On his plantation, "Pleasant Hill," in Prince George's County he also operated a store. He had represented Prince George's in the Lower House of Maryland and at various conventions during the 1770s and 1780s.[33] He sent two sons to Georgetown, Richard (**C** 1793–96) and Francis (**C** 1799–1802). Edmund Plowden, a great-grandson of Sir Edmund Plowden, who had been given title to a palatinate north of Baltimore's colony in 1634, was a planter in St. Mary's County and a member of the Lower House at various times from 1777 to 1797. By the 1790s Plowden had begun selling land in St.

Mary's to acquire lots in the District of Columbia; although at his death he still owned 2,315 acres in his native county.[34] His sons, Edmund (**C** 1799–1803) and William Hammersly, (**C** 1804–9) attended Georgetown. Notley Young, the brother-in-law of John Carroll, was a Prince George's planter who owned much of the land from which the federal district was formed. He was also a director of the Bank of Columbia and served on the commission that oversaw the construction of the original college building. Records show that he had one child, Notley Jr. (**C** 1799–1802), at the college, and possibly a second.

The Southern Maryland Catholic tended to stay longer than the average student. Almost two-thirds (60%) stayed for more than two years; nearly two-fifths (38%) for more than three; and nearly one-fifth (19%) for four or more years.

The District of Columbia Catholic students were more of a mix ethnically: English (64%), Irish (27%), and French (6%). Their fathers tended to be merchants, professional men, politicians, planters/landowners, or persons who combined these occupations. Most prominent was the convert Thomas Sim Lee (1745–1819), twice governor of Maryland (1779–84, 1792–94). After completing his second term in Annapolis, Lee, a planter, had moved his home from Frederick County to Georgetown and enrolled his two sons, John and Archibald in the college. Colonel John Fitzgerald (**C** 1739–99) of Alexandria was another notable father. Fitzgerald had emigrated from Ireland, settled in Alexandria before the Revolution, married a Digges, and become a prosperous merchant in that town. A friend of George Washington, Fitzgerald acted during the Revolution as secretary and aide-de-camp to him as the Commander of the Continental Army from 1776 until 1778. Following the war, he was mayor and collector of the port of Alexandria. He was among the original agents for the college. Also prominent was John Carroll's nephew, Robert Brent (1763–1819), a prosperous merchant-planter whose family quarry near Acquia Creek in Virginia supplied the stone for many federal buildings. Brent served as the first mayor of Washington City. His wife, Mary, was the daughter of Notley Young. The Brents had their only son, Robert, at the college (**C** 1797–99) in the first decade. Mrs. Brent's brother-in-law, Peter Casanove, a prosperous Georgetown merchant, land speculator, and future mayor of the town, also had a son at the college. Casanove was married to Anne Young, another daughter of Notley Young, and, like Young, Casanove owned land on the site chosen for the federal city, as did James Fenwick, a sea captain and tobacco trader. Fenwick sent two sons to the college.

Alexander Doyle, an Irish American native of Port Tobacco, in Charles County, was a Georgetown merchant and trustee of Holy Trinity Church who sent three sons to the college. Even though Doyle could well afford it, his sons were given free tuition for twelve years by formal contract in exchange for their father's efforts in the construction of Trinity's church.[35] The other local Irish-American students, however, seem to have included some from families of modest means, who either depended on others to pay their tuition or paid in kind.[36]

The Baltimore Catholics were multi-ethnic and mainly unrelated. As noted in the last chapter, the town had about a thousand Catholics in 1790, approximately seven percent of the population. In the 1790s Catholics had tripled their numbers and by 1800 constituted more than a tenth (12%) of the city's inhabitants, but apparently a majority belonged to the working class.[37] The most prominent Baltimorean to send a son to the college in the first decade was David Williamson, a Scottish merchant, who was a convert to Catholicism and related by marriage to Bishop Carroll. Another son of a well-to-do merchant was Robert Walsh (**C** 1797–1800), who became a noted writer, editor, and publisher in Philadelphia and Paris in the first half of the nineteenth century. Most of the Baltimore students were of French extraction, refugees from Sainte-Domingue (the island was then under French control). All but one came to Georgetown between 1796 and 1798, the years in which the Sulpician refugee, William Louis DuBourg, was president.

As noted above, the West Indies were a major source of students during the first decade. Like their Maryland counterparts, the Catholic gentry of St. Croix, Sainte-Domingue, and Barbados had sent their sons to the recusant schools in Flanders during the eighteenth century. Georgetown was the inheritor of that tradition. So the Jordans of St. Croix, who had had two sons at Bruges and Liège in the 1770s, sent another to Georgetown in 1793. Others came from Guadeloupe, Martinique, St. Lucie, and Demerara in British Guiana. Half of the students from the Indies entered in 1792–93, during the height of the revolution in Sainte-Domingue. Indeed eight of the twenty were from that island. At least thirteen other refugees from Sainte-Domingue, not including those who came by way of Baltimore, followed them to Georgetown later in the decade. Like the Marylanders who crossed the Atlantic for their education, the West Indians came to Carroll's academy for the duration, on the average about two and a half years. Two of the West Indians, Pierre and Marc Fontaine of Martinique, remained for a decade.

The Catholic middle class families in both New York and Philadelphia were significant supporters of the school in the early years. The New York merchant, Dominick Lynch, an original agent for the college, sent his five sons down from New York to Georgetown. His Philadelphia counterpart, George Meade, also had a son at the college. Most of the Philadelphia students, however, seem to have been young men of modest or slender means whose tuition and board were paid by clergymen or prominent laymen because it was hoped that they might have a vocation to the priesthood. Leonard Neale (1747–1817), the pastor of St. Mary's Church (Philadelphia), supported several such students at Georgetown, as did one of his trustees at St. Mary's, Thomas Fitzsimons, the renowned Pennsylvania patriot and framer of the Constitution.

Called to the "Service of the Church"

Carroll had built his hopes on Georgetown as "our main sheet anchor for religion" precisely because he saw its potential as a producer of pious and intellectual youth who would constitute the core of an enlightened and zealous American clergy. "We trust in God," Carroll remarked to Plowden in 1787, "that many youths [from the academy] will be called to the service of the Church."[38] To what extent did Georgetown fulfill that hope in its first fifteen years?

Financial aid from outside private sources for individuals contemplating a career in the ministry was commonplace in American colleges and academies, especially in the north. Georgetown was no exception. Between 1791 and 1805, approximately thirty-seven students had their tuition and/or board paid, at least partially, by priests. The Neale brothers, Leonard and Francis, were particularly active in sponsoring potential seminarians, as was William Louis DuBourg (1766–1833).[39]

During DuBourg's short tenure as president (1796–98), sixteen students received such clerical support, five of them from Baltimore, DuBourg's previous place of residence. In 1797, both DuBourg and Francis Neale, in lieu of salary increases as president and vice president, were "allowed to choose and admit a youth of good character & capacity & promising disposition as a student in the college," with the expenses to be borne by the college.[40] Eighteen of the thirty-seven priest-supported students were from Maryland, ten from Baltimore. They tended to stay a relatively long time; nearly half of them remained for more than two years, a quarter of them for more than four. The large majority were Anglo-American (twenty-three students), with the French and Irish significant minorities (seven and five students, respectively). Two students from the West Indies had similar financial support. The students who received aid seem to have been both poorer than the average and outside the extended family networks from which Georgetown drew its students (only six of these thirty-seven were related to other Georgetown students). In exchange for their tuition and board, some of the students taught classes at the college, usually after they completed their own studies. In 1800, those receiving a free education were required to commit themselves under oath to teach at the clerical salary for six years, if the president so desired. For instance, Thomas Poole, from St. Mary's County, was at Georgetown from 1796 to 1804, teaching at the school during his last four years there. He had taken the oath in 1801 to serve as a teacher for six years in return for his education. However, three years later he entered the Baltimore Seminary. Other students given such aid were immigrants, like Michael Cuddy (C 1797–1800) from Ireland, whose expenses were paid by the Sulpician, Benedict Flaget. After three years at Georgetown, Cuddy also entered the Baltimore Seminary in 1800, only to die prematurely in 1804.

Of the two hundred and seventy-seven students at Georgetown between 1791 and 1805, sixteen (6%) entered the seminary or novitiate. In comparison with New England colleges, a quarter of whose graduates chose the ministry, it was a small number.[41] Even within the Anglo-American world, the recusant schools at Saint-Omer and Douai also sent approximately a fourth of their students to the novitiate or seminary.[42] Carroll was obviously disappointed that the college had yielded so few vocations, barely one a year. He had hoped to get that many vocations from the residences for Catholic students that he had considered setting up near the new colleges in Philadelphia and Annapolis.[43]

Of the sixteen Georgetown students who did pursue the priesthood or religious life, six had had financial support at the college. Thirteen became Jesuits, of whom five were ordained priests and one, Joseph Mobberly (**C** 1798–1804), became a brother. The other three entered the Baltimore Seminary, one of them, James Moynihan (**C** 1802–5), at the age of forty-two in 1808 (and the only one eventually ordained). Six of the sixteen were from Southern Maryland, including two Fenwicks, Enoch (**C** 1793–97) and Benedict (**C** 1793–1801), both of whom eventually became presidents of the college. Benedict, the younger, served two terms (ninth and twelfth presidencies) while Enoch, the older, served as Georgetown's eleventh president. Indeed the Chesapeake Catholic community accounted for thirteen of those first sixteen vocations. The most "exotic" seminarian was James Ord (**C** 1800–1806), who entered Georgetown under the care of the ex-Jesuit, Notley Young, and who later came to believe that he was a son of the Prince of Wales.[44] Ord was one of the first novices received into the restored Society of Jesus in 1806 (at the age of seventeen), and he later taught at Georgetown, but he left the Society in 1811 and joined first the U.S. Navy, then the U.S. Army. (His descendants later attended Georgetown.)

In keeping with Carroll's intention that the school be "open to Students of every religious Profession," nearly a fifth of the students during the first ten years were non-Catholic. Most of them were local residents, from Georgetown and adjacent towns within the newly formed District of Columbia, which lacked any other school. At least three of the early non-Catholic students were the sons of artisans. For the most part, however, the students' fathers were merchants and professional men, including Secretary of the Navy Benjamin Stoddert (in President George Washington's administration), Robert Peter, the first mayor of Georgetown, Robert Suter, owner of the jolly Old Scotsman Tavern in Georgetown, and John Gannt, the secretary of the Board of Commissioners of the federal city. Peter, a Scotsman who was the earliest tobacco exporter in the area, had four sons at the college.

Since these "locals" lived in the immediate area and were mainly non-Catholics, they were also largely day students, including the two grandnephews of George Washington, Augustine (**C** 1793–94) and Bushrod (**C** 1794–95). The two sons of Gustavus Scott, an Anglican who was health commissioner

The three Stoddert children portrayed from sometime during 1789. Benjamin Stoddert was serving in President George Washington's cabinet at the time. The oldest child, Benjamin Jr. (right), was enrolled at Georgetown in 1792, the year after William Gaston and Charles Philemon Wederstrandt entered the academy's first classes. This charming oil by Charles Willson Peale has in its background one of the earliest known, albeit somewhat romanticized, views of the Town of George. (The Dumbarton House Collection, copy courtesy of Mrs. Douglas Woods Sprunt.)

of the District and one of the organizers of the Potomac Canal Company, were, as student boarders, exceptions in this regard.[45]

"Ratio Studiorum" at Georgetown

It seemed to me [John Carroll had once confided to Charles Plowden] that at Liege far from encouraging young men to extend the circle of their knowledge, the heads of the College esteemed no merit but that, of the study of their dictates. . . . the Hebrew lesson was a mere mockery; even the cultivation of Latin elegance was thrown aside; and as to our native language, there was scarcely a book of it in the Library worthy of being studied. No modern author of any science or in any language was introduced into it. Thus genius and talent were cramped, & a habit of inapplication was acquired, which few escaped.[46]

While intent upon unfettering "genius and talent," Carroll nonetheless envisioned a curriculum for Georgetown that was essentially the course that he had gone through at St. Omers, the preparatory school for Liège. Based on the *Ratio Studiorum,* the system or plan of education that the Society of Jesus had first formulated at the end of the sixteenth century, the new college's curriculum was a humanistic concentration in which Latin enjoyed primacy, with Greek, English, mathematics, and geography in supporting roles. As the prospectus of 1798 stated, "The study of the dead languages, that foundation of universal knowledge . . . ought to engage a large proportion of the attention of the professors." French was available as an elective.[47]

The Jesuit *Ratio* called for five "schools" or classes which did not strictly and necessarily correspond to the years of one's education. A student could pass from one class to another after he had demonstrated a certain proficiency at the lower level. Nonetheless, Carroll assumed that ordinarily the professor of Latin and Greek would progress with his students from class to class. Students began by studying Latin, Greek, French, and English grammar, and then gradually applied their knowledge of it by reading the literature of each language. The centerpiece was the study of the classics. They read Caesar's *Gallic Wars* as well as Lucian's *Dialogues* and the orations of Cicero. They also translated portions of the New Testament from the Greek. The intensive concentration on the ancient languages brought discernible results. William Louis DuBourg, a Sulpician with high standards, was impressed by the "extraordinary proficiency" that many of the students had acquired in so short a time.[48]

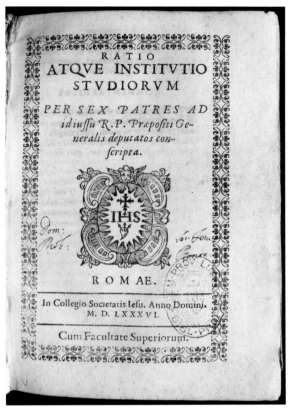

The first printing of the *"Ratio"* (1586) was published by the Society of Jesus and distributed from Rome to the Jesuit provinces throughout the world for classroom trial and comment. This rare, preliminary edition is the only known copy in North America. (Purchased with funds generously provided by Mrs. S. R. Straske, Paul Straske, and Homer Hervey. Georgetown University Special Collections)

In keeping with developments in Jesuit education in the eighteenth century and Carroll's own concerns, there was considerable stress on the vernacular, as well as on the study of mathematics, geography, and history.[49] English was taught not only in its formal structure and as a medium for *eloquentia perfecta*, but also as a second language for the foreign students. As early as 1794, William Scott's primer was being used to instruct students in the mechanics and the art of elocution.[50] There were no *belles-lettres* in the original curriculum, the lack of which was one reason for William Gaston's transfer to Princeton (which did formally offer them).[51] But Georgetown was among the first American schools to include French within its curriculum. American colleges were reacting to the national infatuation with France as a result of the key role that country had played in the War of Independence, but the legacy of the Lowland preparatory schools might have played a role in this decision as well.[52] The arrival of the French Sulpicians no doubt strengthened the place of French in the curriculum, as did the presence of a large number of French-speaking student emigres. Thus, French study at Georgetown survived the backlash against France at the close of the decade, unlike its fate in other colleges. Robert Walsh reported to his father in the fall of 1798 that he was "paying particular attention to French" in his studies.[53]

French remained an integral part of the curriculum throughout the next century.

Despite its liberal thrust, the curriculum gave significant attention to vocational preparation as well. For most of its first decade, the college offered, in effect, two courses of study: classical and English (a common practice in English grammar schools and early American academies, e.g., Phillips Exeter).[54] For all students, mathematics included not only the formal elements of the subject but the practical applications, ranging from bookkeeping to surveying, that were commonplace necessities in a mercantile society. John Gough's *Treatise of Arithmetic in Theory and Practice* was a common text. In Book III Gough dealt with "mercantile arithmetic," including chapters on "Estimating Imports and Exports," "Interest," "Compound Interest," and "Fellowship" (how to determine shares from profits in a partnership).[55] Robert Gibson's *A Treatise of Practical Surveying* was another text widely used in the first decade of Georgetown's schooling.[56] John Hamilton Moore's *The New Practical Navigator* served as a very useful application for geography, geometry, trigonometry, and astronomy.

There was no teaching of Hebrew or natural science as such. Students advancing to the seminary would begin the private study of Hebrew at that point. And as an academy Georgetown offered no natural philosophy, as natural science was then known. But, as associated with Copernicus, Descartes, and Newton, "The New Learning" had made great inroads at all the older American colleges by the middle of the century.[57] The history of the United States was offered to the more advanced students. For religious studies, a history of the Bible and a catechism were the only formal religious textbooks used, but, besides the translating of the Scripture, students were encouraged to use devotional manuals, such as the *Pious Guide, The Daily Christian,* and *The Garden of the Soul.* Examinations and repetitions, on weekly, monthly, and yearly schedules, were integral parts of the pedagogy, which put a premium on students' ability not only to memorize but also to explain and interpret, to demonstrate their talent for original composition in both vernacular and classical languages, to solve mathematical problems, and to answer historical or geographical questions. As early as 1796 the public was invited to judge for itself the worth of a Georgetown education by witnessing the students' performance during their end-of-year oral examinations.[58]

Robert Molyneux, the Second President

Robert Plunkett served as president for less than two years. As he increasingly settled into the plantation society of the Catholic gentry in Maryland, he tired of holding the reins of Carroll's college until some more appropriate president could be found. According to William Gaston, Plunkett resigned in December 1792 but apparently also agreed to stay on until June 1793 so

Carroll could find a successor.[59] When the academy that the English ex-Jesuits had established at Liege in Flanders was closed
by the French Revolution in 1792, Carroll expressed hope
that "the catastrophe" might at last provide a capable president for Georgetown, but that hope also faded to disappointment.[60] Finally, in June 1793, Robert Molyneux
(1738–1808), who had initially resisted the bishop's
pressures on behalf of Georgetown, became its second president. Then Plunkett moved happily off to
rural Maryland as a missionary planter.[61]

The son of a distinguished Lancaster family, Molyneux had been educated in the recusant schools
of St. Omers, Liège, and Bruges. Charles Plowden
and the two Carrolls, John and Charles of Carrollton, were fellow students. In 1771 he had been sent
by Jesuit authorities to British America. During the
revolution Molyneux was pastor of St. Mary's Church
in Philadelphia. His erudition and elegant manner made
him very popular in Philadelphia society with both the
American gentry and the French diplomatic community.

He was always deeply concerned about education. As pastor
of St. Mary's he had begun a school for children. He also was the
first publisher of Catholic books in the United States. On the eve of the Revolution he had brought out A *Manual of Catholic Prayers* (1774). A catechism
and Joseph Reeves' *History of the Old and New Testament* followed. From the
outset Molyneux was a strong supporter of Carroll's efforts to establish
Georgetown College. Carroll deeply respected his judgment and savored his
humor, but found him somewhat too easy-going and indolent for effective
leadership, "never calculating today for tomorrow; . . . of sound judgement,
in things, where he is not to be an actor: but of the greatest timidity & irreso-
lution possible, where he is."[62] Nonetheless, Carroll as bishop of Baltimore
had pressed Molyneux to leave Philadelphia and become president of the
new academy, when his first attempts to secure a president from England
failed. Accordingly the genial Englishman had finally accepted in 1793.

As president, Molyneux underwent no revolution in character. Still the
college grew steadily during his three-year tenure. The number of faculty
and students both increased. Student enrollment jumped from seventy-six
to nearly a hundred in the next three years. One of the faculty, Edouard de
Mondésir, wrote in May of 1794 to Gaston:

On my return hither, I found great alterations in every line. We are now five professors. One more is daily expected, a French man who knew English before he came to
this continent, formerly assistant to the professor of Rhetorick at Rouen, perfectly
versed in the Greek & Latin, as also in most of the modern European languages. An

Robert Molyneux
(1738–1808). As a former
Jesuit and emigré from
England, he served as
the second president of
Georgetown from 1793
to 1796. As a Jesuit in the
restored Society, he again
served as Georgetown's fifth
president from 1806 to 1808.
This presumed likeness was
painted about eighty years
later from descriptions of
the erudite Englishman.
(Shea, *Memorial of the First Century
of Georgetown College*)

immense building will soon afford room for at least a hundred boarders, at which period the number of tutors must be considerably augmented.[63]

The Jesuit European schools had been, for the most part, nonresidential ones. St. Omers, as a boarding school for English recusant children, was an exception. From its inception, Georgetown followed the Flanders tradition. But the limited space for housing in the original college building meant that many students lived in private homes nearby, usually with people who had connections with the college. George Fenwick, for instance, usually housed anywhere from seven to ten boarder students in the 1790s. By the beginning of the second academic year Carroll had already decided to expand the facilities in response to the growing enrollment.[64] First, an infirmary, a two-story frame building, was added. Then, at its November 1792 meeting, the Chapter authorized a structure for classrooms, study hall, and dormitories.[65] A few acres contiguous to the north side of the original lot were purchased from John Threlkeld for the site and construction began in 1794.[66] Leonard Harbaugh, a Baltimore engineer who had already designed and built Trinity chapel for the Georgetown Catholic community and would later build both the Treasury and War Office buildings in Washington, was very probably the architect and builder.[67] The four-story brick building, with its front measuring 154 feet, dwarfed the original edifice which stood directly south (hence the eventual names of Old South and Old North for the two buildings). "[A] noble one it is," Carroll reported to Plowden in 1795.[68] Modeled after Nassau Hall at Princeton, the new tripartite, center-pediment structure housed everything under its roof. It quintupled the dormitory space, added several classrooms, and provided a spacious chapel for the students. Carroll's new college, towering over the Maryland side of the river, now had a very prominent place in the Georgetown landscape. A French visitor in 1797 was struck at how "notably large" this rising building was for the area.[69] Indeed, there was nothing in the town to compete with Old North, and in the rising federal city, only the capital itself promised to be grander. Compared to the small scale of the buildings then represented in Washington's republican architecture, Old North was monumental, a testament to Carroll's ambition for his school.

His financial means still fell far short of his vision. The corporation pledged to fund the construction through income from the Society's Maryland plantations, which were still seen as the chief financial support for Georgetown College. In reality the plantations provided very little income; and other external sources, such as the modest subsidy from Rome, hardly compensated for this shortfall.[70] Within nine months of the college's opening the directors had to raise the fees for room and board and slash President Plunkett's salary from £100 to £40 in order to meet expenses. Unsurprisingly, the revenue from the land fell considerably short of meeting the formidable costs of the new construction, which were in excess of £10,000.[71] The directors and the bishop were forced to utilize any funds they could attract to complete the

Old North, Georgetown's second major academic building, was begun in 1794 and completed in early 1797. It was here, on the front porch, that former President George Washington was formally received and introduced by President DuBourg to the students in August 1797. (Georgetown University Archives)

building: including the Propaganda money, part of an endowed scholarship, a benefaction from former President Plunkett, and a loan from a Baltimore bank.[72] Significantly, unlike their counterparts connected with New York's Columbia College and other emerging urban colleges, the Catholic elite continued to fail to provide financial support for the institution.[73] The only benefaction from a Catholic layman in the 1790s was a grant of $1,600 by Joseph Ecke of Philadelphia to establish a scholarship. The wealthy Maryland Catholics sent their sons to Georgetown, as they had to St. Omers, but they gave little more than tuition. The extensive lands known to be owned by the ex-Jesuits in Maryland and Pennsylvania may have been a factor— giving the false impression that the college needed no outside support to buy whatever was needed. The Catholic gentry, after the English tradition, supplied chapels galore in the Maryland countryside, but nothing of note for education. Whatever the reason, Georgetown College in its first generation was sans endowment.

As a result, the new building was not opened until the spring of 1797. In late 1796, Carroll had already acceded to Molyneux's entreaties to be relieved of the burdens of office because of his poor health, undoubtedly worsened by the pressures of financing Old North.[74] In October 1796, William

Louis DuBourg, an energetic Sulpician, was named the third president. The bishop had finally secured someone who seemed to embody all the qualities he had sought in a president for the college.

From Academy to College

William Louis DuBourg, third president of Georgetown from 1796 to 1798, was one of several erudite Sulpicians who contributed significantly to the growth of that "complete nursery of learning." The courtly emigré also raised that "nursery" from academy to college during his brief but energetic tenure. (Engraving from Shea, *Memorial of the First Century of Georgetown College,* 23)

Without the Sulpicians, it is hard to imagine the college surviving its first fifteen years. The four Sulpicians who taught at Georgetown constituted a remarkable band of talented and zealous men: John Baptist David, Benedict Joseph Flaget, Ambrose Maréchal, and William Louis DuBourg. They were part of an extraordinary group of French emigrés who played a dispropor-tionately large role in molding the institutional matrix and culture of the American Catholic community in the early national period.[75] DuBourg was arguably the most influential of them all. Together with the students from the West Indies, these emigrés gave a cosmopolitan cast to the school, and brought as well a rich pedagogical tradition, within the world of clerical formation.

DuBourg was born in Saint-Domingue (afterwards Santo Domingo), in the West Indies, where his family had made its fortune in coffee. After the death of his mother, he was sent as a young child to Bordeaux for schooling. His classical studies eventually brought him to Saint-Sulpice in Paris, where he quickly fell under the influence of Jacques-Andre Emery, the superior general of the Society (la Compagnie de Saint Sulpice). Ordained in 1790, DuBourg was put in charge of a boarding school at Issy, in southern France, from which he was forced to flee in August 1792, five days before a raiding party of Jacobins murdered four of his seminarian instructors.

Spain was his first refuge, but growing restric-tions, owing to the Spanish suspicion of hetero-doxy among the French clergy, led to his impromptu decision to go to America. Within two years of his arrival at Baltimore in 1794, he was chosen president of Georgetown. In his "Mémoires," de Mondésir described him as ut-terly unique, neither "traditionally" Sulpician nor typically Jesuit but some *tertium quid*

of rare activity and resourcefulness. His fecundity in pro-ducing all kinds of means to carry out his enterprises was astonishing. He could make an arrow of any kind of stick. Whatever his undertaking might be worth and whatever risks he might run, he went ahead.[76]

Impatient "to work all wonders at once," as his biographer has put it, the then thirty-year-old DuBourg immediately set out to make the five-year-old institution the best in the country.[77] In fact, at Georgetown he transformed an academy into a college in more than name.

He significantly expanded the size of the faculty by adding sixteen new teachers over the next two years. Twelve were laymen (there had been only three during the first five years). Not only did he enlarge the faculty but he increased annual salaries, at least for some deserving individuals. When, for instance, de Mondésir returned in 1796, his new salary was set at £120, John Wilson was appointed professor of mathematics at £112, Joseph Brooks, a carpenter, was hired for £100. Others, such as Enoch Fenwick, a recent student, and Charles Boarman, a lay professor, received the standard £75, although Boarman, a former Jesuit, also received tuition credits for his three sons.[78]

The curriculum was also enlarged. "The sphere of education, in this College, was, for a time, unavoidably contracted," the prospectus announced in 1798; "it has expanded itself gradually, and the College now offers the promising prospect of being a complete nursery of learning equal to those in the United States whose institution was earlier. . . ." DuBourg was ready to introduce "the higher sciences" of history, moral and natural philosophy, as well as Spanish. Music, dancing, and drawing were also offered for the first time. He was intent on providing Georgetown with all the marks of an elite college. A seal was adopted, based closely on the Great Seal of the United States. Uniforms were now made standard wear, one of blue coats with red waistcoats for Sundays and special occasions.[79]

DuBourg was very imaginative in promoting the college's public image. He quickly seized the importance of "the Washington Connection." "It is no inconsiderable recommendation to public favour," the prospectus observed, "that the College is an extensive and most convenient edifice, situated on one of the healthiest spots and commanding one of the most delightful prospects in the United States; and that it is so near to the City of Washington, which being the centre of the Federal Government, will offer the best examples of, and incentives to attain literary eminence."

DuBourg, a man of considerable charm and expansive personality, also cultivated the society of the energetic and affluent, such as immigrants Thomas Law and James Barry who as merchant speculators represented the new wealth and the new society in the booming District of Columbia. Law, the son of the Bishop of Carlisle and brother of Lord Ellenborough, Chief Justice of England, had been an East Indian merchant before emigrating to the United States in 1795 to pursue the financial opportunities inherent in transforming plantations into capital city real estate. He acquired large tracts of land on Greenleaf's Point and elsewhere, began a sugar refinery, and married Martha Washington's granddaughter.[80] Law's friend, James Barry, who came from a family of shipping merchants in Cork, Ireland, had arrived in

New York City in 1788. Convinced that the nation's new capital was going to become an international center for trade, Barry moved south to the federal district and joined Law in his land ventures, though on a distinctly smaller scale.[81] The Barrys quickly became close friends of Bishop Carroll. Law enrolled a son at the college, Barry a nephew. Through them DuBourg secured an invitation to meet George Washington at Mount Vernon in July 1797, and a month later the recently retired first President of the United States made a formal visit to the campus.

Nevertheless, for all of DuBourg's large vision and undeniable magnetism, his impulsive temperament made him a poor leader. Within his first year as president he alienated de Mondésir and another French confrere on the faculty. Both left in May of 1797.[82] Moreover, wherever DuBourg went, he left behind a trail of debts, a monument to grand plans half realized. Georgetown was no exception. Debts were soon mounting from faculty expenditures, stagnant enrollment, and what was perceived as DuBourg's lavish style of administration. Indeed, a silver service and a grand piano hardly seemed appropriate for a college struggling to meet the payments on its main building.[83] Wealthy patrons failed to materialize, and the speculative real estate market in the District collapsed in the late 1790s. Law himself lost some $700,000.[84] And the tobacco trade, the traditional center of Georgetown's economy, was suffering—the plantations from soil exhaustion and the merchants from the loss of markets due to the French Revolution.

The reaction from the ex-Jesuits who had to pay the bills for DuBourg's prodigality was predictable. Even before DuBourg had become president, concern about the mounting costs at the college had increased. In June 1796 the trustees of the corporation had authorized the sale of certain land and the use of its proceeds as well as other monies to meet the debts owed by the school.[85] This in turn had offended the Representatives of the Select Body of Clergy, who thought it their business to make such decisions, since they elected those trustees every three years. The six representatives—including John Bolton, who had originally opposed the use of land to fund a college, as well as two of the Neale brothers, Charles and Francis, who continued to regard the land as a sacred trust—were obviously unhappy to see the college swallowing up more and more of the assets of the corporation.[86] The following October, the representatives chose Augustine Jenkins, another former opponent of Carroll's plan, as well as Francis Neale to join John Ashton, Charles Sewall, and James Walton as trustees.[87] Meeting at St. Thomas Manor the next spring (March 1797), the trustees resolved to proceed with the sale of the land; and they arranged a special election among the members of the Select Body of Clergy to choose a committee of three to determine the dispute between the trustees and the representatives, as well as to determine in what manner the directors of the college should be chosen.[88]

When the Select Body subsequently elected two of the trustees, Ashton and Sewall, to the special committee, it was hardly surprising that that committee now decided that the representatives somehow lacked the power they claimed. They also dictated that the trustees should choose the board of directors for Georgetown College, to consist of five members elected every three years from among the "Select Body." Those directors would have power to appoint and remove the president and vice-president and to superintend the economy of the college.[89] The first directors were Francis Neale, Robert Plunkett, John Ashton, Charles Sewall, and Francis Beeston.

The new directors quickly utilized their authority to curtail spending by DuBourg and the Sulpicians. At their first meeting in October 1797 they re-appointed DuBourg, but instead of Flaget, they named Francis Neale vice-president and gave him control over finances. Moreover, they asked that DuBourg submit to them at their next meeting an account of the financial state of the college.[90] "[A]fter a careful examination of the Accounts," the debt was estimated to be only $800 "more or less."[91] Giovanni Grassi, afterwards president of the college from 1812 to 1817, later claimed that DuBourg left the institution $20,000 in debt in 1798. But as DuBourg's biographer notes, "existing records . . . are insufficient to support such a claim."[92] Perhaps the directors were reporting only the debt from the current year's operations, although that seems doubtful. Nonetheless, the college was clearly put on an austerity budget. Board and tuition had remained virtually unchanged during the decade; enrollments were down by eleven, from ninety-eight to eighty-seven. Under Neale's authority the faculty salaries were soon cut. Lay professors now received £75, the old standard salary; ecclesiastical students £40. The mathematics professor, Wilson, his salary reduced from £112 to £75, was the first to leave in the spring of 1798.[93]

In January 1798, by an act of the General Assembly of Maryland, the property of the college had been included within the holdings of the corporation of the Roman Catholic Clergymen.[94] This was the first official recognition of the school by any public lay authority. That act was passed, the Assembly declared, "to give perpetuity" to Georgetown College, by making it part of a legal corporation. The earlier incorporation act of 1792 had affected only the property that had been acquired by the Society of Jesus in Maryland before 1776. Carroll, Molyneux, and John Ashton had continued to be the legal holders of the Georgetown property. In June of 1796 the trustees had initiated the process of consolidation. But the urgency of the change did not seem to impress them until the fall of 1797.

DuBourg survived for another year after the consolidation began, but the animus against him was growing. The trustees of the corporation, if not those of the college, felt that he was audaciously scheming, not only to Frenchify Georgetown but to seize it from their control. The corporation's directors, at their December 1798 meeting, claimed to have received notice "that certain persons, not admitted to the participation of the incorporated property of the Clergy, have not only attempted to be the sole and entire administrators of said College, but also to make that property their own . . ." Francis Neale, who sat on both bodies, was probably the instigator of the charge. They went on record with two formal resolutions:

1. That no person or Society of men, except the present incorporated Body of the R.C. Clergy, ought to be in possession of any part of the College property even for a time. . . .
2. That a letter shall be sent to the Bishop of Baltimore, informing him that the Body Corporate are in possession of strong proofs of a plan being laid by some clergymen of the Seminary to take the College from us, who had been at great expense in building it, and that the Board of Trustees do oppose a scheme so highly unjust.[95]

Within the week, DuBourg resigned.[96] Carroll, who had great respect for DuBourg, felt there had probably been blame on both sides. "[N]ational attachments, that bane of all communities, where they are suffered to exist, have been the original cause of the mischief. He was too fond of introducing his countrymen into every department; and the Directors had too strong prejudices against every thing, which was derived, in any shape, from France . . ."[97] In reality, Carroll found his former Jesuit brethren the chief culprits as he later confided to Plowden. If Georgetown had failed to realize Carroll's hopes after a decade, their narrow and rigid views, epitomized by their Francophobia, were largely responsible, to his mind.[98] Indeed, Carroll had attempted to remove Francis Neale from Georgetown in the spring of 1797 but the protest of the trustees of Trinity Church, all prominent laymen who were important to the college, apparently forced the bishop to reconsider.[99] Of course, ex-Jesuits had no monopoly on Francophobia in the late 1790s. It had been DuBourg's misfortune to have been president at the very height of the tensions between the United States and France (the two countries were engaged in a "quasi-war" at sea during 1798), the culmination of a decade that had increasingly divided Americans over the meaning and implications of the revolution in France. Even refugees from that revolution like DuBourg were highly suspect in the eyes of the Neales and their fellow Maryland priests. In that climate, ambition and brilliance became the stuff of conspiracy.

By 1798 frustration had also probably made ex-Jesuits particularly prone to paranoia. The efforts of the Neales and others to revive the Society of Jesus in America by joining with the Jesuits who had survived in White Russia had led nowhere. Then suddenly, it seemed, the Sulpicians were in their midst, seemingly ubiquitous, "reaping," as Philip Gleason saw it,

the harvest planted by generations of Jesuit laborers in the vineyard, supported by properties that had once belonged solely to the Society of Jesus, intruding themselves into the college erected at such cost and loading it with debts. Small wonder that the directors of Georgetown were 'not . . . on the best of terms' with DuBourg.[100]

The Neales of Maryland

With the departure of DuBourg, the Neales took over the administration of Georgetown. The board (with Carroll's sanction) named Leonard Neale president and his brother Francis vice president. Descended from a family that traced its roots to the first generation of Maryland settlers, including Calverts and Brookes, Leonard Neale was one of seven brothers who had studied at the recusant colleges in the Lowlands. Three of them—William, Charles, and Leonard— had entered the Society of Jesus before the Brief of Suppression (1773). Following the suppression, Leonard had worked in England. In 1780 Propaganda sent him to Demerara (British Guiana), where he found the natives more receptive to Catholicism than the English settlers. However, unable even to construct a church, Neale received permission to leave the mission and return in 1783 to Maryland.[101] For ten years he was stationed at St. Thomas Manor, near his home at Chandler's Hope in Charles County. Neale shared Carroll's conviction that the American church in its temporal jurisdiction should be independent of Propaganda Fide, and fully supported the efforts to establish the property that had belonged to the Society of Jesus on a secure basis. Although he had initially opposed the legal alienation and transfer of titles for some of this property to establish Georgetown, he became a firm supporter of the college.

Rt. Rev. Leonard Neale, D.D. (1746–1817). As fourth president of Georgetown, he served from 1799 to 1806. With his help, Alice Lalor, an Irish emigré, and two companions opened Visitation Academy for the education of young ladies. (Georgetown University Archives)

From 1793 to 1799 Leonard Neale was pastor of St. Mary's Church in Philadelphia. During the 1793 and 1798 yellow fever epidemics he ministered heroically and repeatedly to the sick and dying in that city. He himself contracted the disease during the second epidemic and never fully recovered his health.

A deeply spiritual man, he likely had a significant role in the production in 1792 of the *Pious Guide*, along with his brother, Francis. He had a particular gift for stirring sensitive hearts to religious life. One such was Alice Lalor, an Irish immigrant in Philadelphia. Neale encouraged her and two associates to set up a quasi-religious community in Philadelphia. When he was called to become president of the college in 1799, the three women came to Georgetown, and close by the college, under Neale's guidance, established a formal religious community according to the Visitandine rule and a school for girls as well. In 1800 he was named Bishop Carroll's coadjutor.

If spiritual direction and personal sanctity were hallmarks of Neale's presidency, educational administration was not. With the assistance of his equally severe brother Francis, Leonard tended to run the college as an ecclesiastical seminary. The office of prefect of morals was established and the regulations for students were tightened and more strictly enforced. Candidates for the seminary were segregated from the other students. Non-Catholic students were also segregated in off-campus lodgings. This practice had been instituted even before the Neales by the directors in 1797, apparently out of concern for the numerous non-Catholics being admitted by DuBourg. The number does not seem to have been any greater than it had been under Plunkett and Molyneux, but virtually all the earlier non-Catholics were local or day students. At any rate, DuBourg that same year had to publish in a Georgetown newspaper an advance notice of the section of the prospectus which dealt with separate housing for "students professing other tenets" to assuage "the anxiety of some of the Friends of this Institution." This may have been a compromise that DuBourg had struck with the directors. What is clear is that after DuBourg left, non-Catholics practically disappeared from the college.[102]

Carroll, who himself regarded discipline as an essential instrument of education, soon had cause to complain that the Neale brothers were putting off parents by their "rigorous regulations not calculated for the meridian of America. Their principles are too monastic; and with a laudable view of excluding immorality, they deny that liberty, which all here will lay claim to."[103]

One of the first measures taken by the Neale brothers was the elimination of the lay faculty that DuBourg had added. The directors, noting that "secular masters of worldly dispositions in the College mixing with the scholars are a great obstruction to . . . [the nurturing of vocations] & that a unanimity of sentiments & views will greatly contribute to promote it," sought clergy from Carroll to staff Georgetown in place of laity.[104] Four lay faculty left within the next seven months, including the fencing instructor. Carroll, probably with some satisfaction, sent to Georgetown two Sulpicians, John Baptist David and Ambrose Maréchal. The rest of the faculty during the six years of the Neale administration included a diocesan priest, a seminarian, seven candidates under the "commitment" oath, two probable candidates for the seminary, and two laymen.

The introduction of this oath, according to President Neale, was to ensure continuity in faculty and prefects.[105] Those candidates for the priesthood who were receiving a free education at Georgetown had, in exchange, to commit themselves to serve as professors or prefects for six years.[106] To enable them to continue their education while teaching, the directors also authorized Neale to extend the course of studies to include philosophy. The directors also claimed that pressure from parents made it necessary to implement the course in natural and moral philosophy that the prospectus had promised two years before. The reputation of the college, they contended, was at stake.[107]

The course expansions at that time actually grew out of a mixture of vindictiveness and fear.[108] DuBourg, once back in Baltimore, had started a college at St. Mary's. That the enrollment of the new college was supposed to be limited to students from the West Indies was small comfort to Georgetown, which was still drawing so heavily from that region. Leonard Neale admitted to Carroll that Georgetown had instituted the philosophy course in order to preempt DuBourg, who would certainly attempt to create a complete course of studies to the detriment of the older college.[109] As early as 1793 the Sulpicians had attempted to start an academy in Baltimore for day students, both in lieu of seminarians and in the hope of attracting some individuals to the seminary, but Carroll had suppressed it then because of Georgetown.[110] When Carroll's instinct to suppress DuBourg's new college was voiced in 1800, the Sulpician superior in Baltimore pointed out to the bishop that "in a country where equal liberty is the basis of political government," schools should enjoy as much liberty. Carroll admitted the logic of Nagot's protest and allowed them to take whom they would as students.[111]

With the seminarians bound by oath to remain at Georgetown, the Sulpician Seminary in Baltimore found itself with no students at the beginning of the next school year. Carroll, rather than oppose the Neale brothers outright, decided upon another course of action. If the Georgetown seminarians could not go to the Sulpicians, he would bring the best qualified Sulpician philosopher to them. In the fall of 1801, the Sulpicians agreed to send Ambrose Maréchal to Georgetown to become the second professor of philosophy. (De Mondésir had already returned to Georgetown to become the first.)[112]

In a further attempt to reconcile their differences, the Sulpicians offered in 1802 to close their college and transfer the students plus some faculty to Georgetown. The trustees of the Corporation thought it might well be the salvation of their college. For the foreseeable future the Sulpicians appeared to represent the best source of faculty for any Catholic institution of learning. Without them Georgetown was already suffering. "The College," the trustees observed to the members of the Select Body, "is not supplied sufficiently with capable Masters, to raise its credit & estimation in the eyes of the public: few students are sent to it, & consequently it declines in reputation, & in the means of subsistance & improvement." Hence they considered the proposal so important that they recommended that the Select Body, which alone could approve such a merger, choose two or three representatives to pursue the matter with the Sulpicians.[113] Subsequently, both the middle and northern Maryland districts of the Select Body approved the trustees' recommendation. The northern district found the proposed union "a matter of the utmost importance for Religion in the United States," and urged that it be accomplished "by all means."[114] The middle district, which included the college, was more wary, directing the projected representatives to agree to no terms that would "commit the Interests, or accumulate the debts, either of the Corporation, or of the College."[115] There is no record that the southern district, the group that had traditionally been most hostile to the college, ever even met to consider the proposal. At any rate the proposal went no further.[116]

DuBourg then confirmed the worst suspicions of the Neales by unilaterally announcing in 1803 that the Baltimore college would now be open to all students. DuBourg had learned that Cuban boys would no longer be allowed to study abroad, which provided him a pretext to make enrollment unrestricted. By 1805, he had more than one hundred and twenty-five students and had obtained a charter as a university from the State of Maryland.[117] Georgetown was clearly in its shadow. Robert Walsh, the future editor and writer, whom Carroll called the "equal in extent of literature of any youth I ever knew,"[118] and who had greeted George Washington on behalf of his fellow students in 1797, followed DuBourg to the new university, as did the sons of Dominick Lynch. Two Georgetown faculty also switched to Baltimore.

The number of Georgetown students from Baltimore declined (from six a year under DuBourg to one a year over the next decade) as did the number from the West Indies (only seventeen in the 1800s). Few students actually transferred from Georgetown to St. Mary's (only ten between 1800 and 1810). What hurt Georgetown was not the number of students transferring but the number of those who chose St. Mary's initially instead. St. Mary's replaced Georgetown not only among the emerging Baltimore Catholic community but also among students from the West Indies, Philadelphia, New York, and Charleston, and also tapped strongly into an older Catholic center—the newly acquired Louisiana Territory.[119] Leadership, or lack of it, was one reason for the sharply differing fortunes of the two schools, but Georgetown's decline was also linked to the economic reversals and political uncertainties that the District of Columbia experienced at the turn of the century. Fears about the removal of the capital to Philadelphia or elsewhere continued to grow during the first ten years of the nineteenth century.[120] Meanwhile, Baltimore had become the dynamic economic and cultural center that the District had promised to be when Georgetown had officially opened its doors in 1791.

Georgetown in the first years of the new century became a predominantly local school with more than four-fifths (83%) of the students coming from Maryland and the District of Columbia. And, under the Neales, that student body was overwhelmingly Catholic (only two known Protestants were recorded among the students from 1800 to 1810). The old Catholic families of Southern Maryland and Georgetown were even more prominent on those dwindling student rolls of the 1800s. Indeed, the Boarmans, Brookes, Carrolls, Diggeses, Fenwicks, Hills, Neales, Queens, Semmeses, Sewalls, and Youngs continued to send their sons to the college. Nevertheless, the enrollment plummeted from eighty-seven in 1798 to forty-five in 1806. This in itself was not critical. The size of the student body in the average American college in the early nineteenth century ranged from twenty-five to eighty.[121] But Georgetown's decline in enrollment pointed to the decline of confidence that Carroll had noted and to a new parochialism that was a sharp departure from Carroll's plan and from the norm in the institution's first decade. Far from emerging as an American St. Omers, Georgetown was in danger of becoming a backwater academy.[122]

CHAPTER 3

The Return of the Jesuits

I do not like the late resurrection of the Jesuits. They have a general now in Russia, in correspondence with the Jesuits in the United States, who are more numerous than everybody know. Shall we not have swarms of them here, in as many shapes and disguises as ever a king of the gypsies . . . himself assumed? In the shape of printers, editors, writers, schoolmasters, &c? I have lately read Pascal's letters over again, and four volumes of the History of the Jesuits. If ever any congregation of men could merit eternal perdition on earth and in hell, according to these historians, . . . it is this company of Loyola. Our system, however, of religious liberty must afford them an asylum; but if they do not put the purity of our elections to a severe trial, it will be a wonder.

JOHN ADAMS TO THOMAS JEFFERSON
from Quincy to Monticello, May 6, 1816

Immigration and Revival

Had Georgetown continued to operate as a local academy run by a few diocesan priests and taught by clerical aspirants, it likely would have died a quiet death, long before John Carroll did in 1815. Ironically, the Society of Jesus, whose suppression in 1773 had been the occasion for the "resolve" in 1786 to found Georgetown (to supply for Catholics in the new republic the clergy whom the Society had provided previously), now became, through its restoration in the early years of the nineteenth century, the means of the revival of the school. The "return" of the Jesuits at first seemed merely to undermine further the weak condition of the school when they established a second, and seemingly competing, institution in New York City. But in the long run the Jesuit "intellectual migration" from Europe to America that began in 1806 became the major factor in the preservation and development of Georgetown over its next sixty years. No Jesuit played a more important role than the first president of the college from the Continent, Giovanni Grassi.

The Society of Jesus Restored

Pope Pius VII, freed from his imprisonment at Fontainebleau after Napoleon's defeat at Leipzig, and attempting to revive the church in a postrevolutionary Europe, completely restored the Society of Jesus throughout the world in December 1814. That news was still deeply disturbing to John Adams nearly two years later. Steeped in the Enlightenment's reactionary image of the Jesuits, Adams expected all too soon to have "swarms of them here, in as many shapes and disguises as ever a king of the gypsies . . . himself assumed . . . [as] printers, editors, writers, schoolmasters, etc." putting the young country's republicanism to a severe test.[1] By 1816 Adams' fears were not only hyperbolic but outdated. The Society of Jesus had already been restored in the United States and Jesuits had already been "swarming" to its shores for nearly a decade.

The catalyst for restoration had been Pius VII's recognition in 1801 of the fortuitous survival of the Society in the Byelorussian territories of the late Polish-Lithuanian Commonwealth. (There Catherine the Great had valued the Jesuit schools too much to allow the brief of suppression to be carried out.) Aware of this discreet canonical recognition, a group of six ex-Jesuits in Maryland petitioned John Carroll and Leonard Neale to solicit the Jesuit superior general in Russia on their behalf for permission to rejoin the Society.[2] Most of the six had been actively pressing to link up with the Russian remnant since the 1780s. Indeed, Leonard Neale, along with his brothers, Charles and Francis, had long been among the most active promoters of restoration for the Society.

Nevertheless, Carroll, for several practical and personal reasons, was still much more reserved about the matter than his coadjutor.[3] When Carroll failed to act upon the request of the ex-Jesuits, they presented him with a second petition eight months later, in April 1803, this time signed not only by the six ex-Jesuits, but also by four other priests and five seminarians.[4] The addition to that petition of the signatures of such outstanding priests as William Matthews, John Dubois, and Francis Neale, as well as some of his most promising seminarians, including Enoch and Benedict Fenwick, may have caused Carroll finally to take action. At any rate, he and his coadjutor secured approval from the Jesuit superior general, Gabriel Gruber, for the ex-Jesuits in the United States to renew their vows and to receive novices. Five of the ten ex-Jesuits reentered the Society in 1805. In October 1806 eleven candidates, including the two Fenwicks, Francis Neale, and James Ord, entered the novitiate now established at Georgetown. Eight of these eleven were alumni of the college.[5]

With the Society of Jesus an official presence once more in America, John Carroll began the process of formally entrusting Georgetown College to the order. At his suggestion, the directors of the college unanimously chose Robert Molyneux, who had been appointed superior of the restored Maryland Mission of the Society of Jesus, to succeed Leonard Neale in September 1806 and to thus become the college's president for a second time.[6]

On the Brink of Closing

One of the factors that may have caused Carroll to change his mind and promote the restoration was the renewed hope of securing qualified European Jesuits for his diocese, especially for his struggling college in Georgetown. The ex-Jesuits in England had already preceded their American brethren by reuniting with the Society in 1803. Thus in 1805, Leonard Neale, as president of the college, was counting on English assistance, if not leadership, in reviving the Society in America.[7] Carroll knew, of course, that the English Jesuit community was too weak to assist America. But the Society in Russia was prompt in sending help. Two Jesuits arrived in 1805, three others a year later. Among the latter was a thirty-five-year-old Alsatian priest, Anthony Kohlmann (1771–1836). Originally the French Revolution had driven him to Fribourg in Switzerland for his higher education. There he had decided to become a priest, and once ordained had joined the Congregation of the Fathers of the Sacred Heart, a recently established religious order that hoped to secure recognition as a new Society of Jesus. With that congregation and later with the Society of the Faith of Jesus (with which the former united in 1799), Kohlmann had directed a seminary in Bavaria and colleges in Amsterdam and Berlin. Then in 1805 he was accepted in Russia as a Jesuit novice by Father General Gruber. A year later he was in America assisting another novice-priest, Francis Neale, who had been named novice master at Georgetown.

By the time he came in 1806, Kohlmann found the college very much in decay: a "superb building" but with its walls unplastered, the windows boarded up for lack of glass, and the towers truncated and unfinished, housing twenty-six students in space meant to accommodate two hundred. John McElroy, one of the first novices, remembered that there was frequently no money even for food, much less for finishing the buildings. The president, Leonard Neale, slept on a folding bed in the library. Finally, with $400 from the savings brought by a novice, window glass was installed and the interior of the building completed. A few years later, in 1809, the towers were completed as well.[8]

"The good news," Kohlmann reported to an English Jesuit in early 1807, "is that there is generally a good spirit of piety and of Religion in the house, and I have no doubt that in the new order of things that there is no country in the world at this time more ready to give a foundation to the society than this one. . . ." In particular he was impressed with the large number of applicants for the order, including all the current lay faculty of the college.[9] By 1808 there were eighteen novices, nearly all of whom had studied or taught at the college, a point that Leonard Neale made in justifying "the discipline & principles adopted . . . during my presidency."[10] If the measure of the college was the number of vocations, not students, then Georgetown was flourishing.

Bishop Carroll appreciated the vocations, but he had had no illusions that they could sustain a college whose student population continued to erode. As Carroll pointed out in October of 1805, if the Society were "to rise again," the first object would be to form a generation that would rediscover the Jesuit spirit of piety "and that sound knowledge, sacred & profane, which rendered [the Society] the ornament of the church, and its best defence."[11] There were only sixty-nine students that fall; a year later only sixty-two, most of them day students. Indeed, Carroll urged Molyneux to suspend the college's operations until the new Jesuits could provide the proper faculty that would allow them to begin anew. "[I]n its present state of depression," he wrote Molyneux in December 1806, "it is draining the estates, & all the resources of the Corporation & must finally overwhelm them."[12] Such a ragtag college was sinking any reputation the old Society had for education. "Disagreeable as this truth is, we cannot [in February 1807] shut it out from our minds."[13] Better to consolidate now, Carroll concluded, for the sake of future possibilities. In sum, Carroll was urging a more radical course than the one advocated fifteen years earlier by his English brethren and which he had then firmly rejected—when experience had yet to temper his dreams with prudence.

Despite Carroll's advice, Molyneux and his directors did not close the college. The ailing president struggled to improve the finances and enrollment of the institution. Moreover, he managed for the time being to defer Carroll's transfer of Kohlmann from Georgetown to New York. The bishop was willing to do whatever might be possible to assist his old friend, but the affable Molyneux seemed to be having no better results than the austere Neales had had earlier in reviving the college. "If the love and respect, which you enjoy universally," Carroll confided to the president in May of 1807, "do not restore its credit, it must be certain that there is some radical defect in its constitution, so far as relates to its aptitude to suit the inclinations & genius of my countrymen."[14] When Robert Molyneux died in early December 1808 and Francis Neale was named acting president, there were nearly eighty students in the college, but barely more than twenty were boarders. By that time Carroll had sent Kohlmann to be vicar-general for New York in the Diocese of Baltimore. Since Kohlmann had been teaching philosophy to the Jesuit scholastics or seminarians at Georgetown, four of them accompanied the Alsatian Jesuit to New York, along with the recently ordained Benedict Fenwick.[15] In effect, the college lost most of its faculty.

The New York Literary Institution

Within weeks of his arrival in New York in 1808, Kohlmann, with Carroll's blessing, established a school for boys, the New York Literary Institution, with Fenwick and the scholastics as the faculty. Anthony Kohlmann was a man of vision, even if that vision tended to outrace his means. He quickly grasped the importance of New York City in the young republic. If the church was to have an effective presence there and in the other growing urban centers, education and social service would be the keys to unlock the doors. With the establishment of several new dioceses imminent, it was urgent that the Society in the United States "take possession of Boston, New York & Philadelphia," before other prelates with other priorities were in place. "The establishing of Colleges in the said cities is . . . the only means of increasing & propagating the Society." On November 7, 1808, he was already urging that the superior general send more Jesuits to America for this mission.[16] Barring substantial help from abroad, however, it was highly questionable whether even the schools in New York and Georgetown could both survive.

By the spring of 1809 there were already forty boys in the New York Literary Institution, all day scholars, mostly the sons of merchants and Protestants.[17] A year later the institution moved to a site in the country and began accepting boarders. With the sons of Governor Daniel Thompkins and other leading state officials in the school, Fenwick was understandably optimistic by December 1810 about the future.[18] Kohlmann had been even more enthusiastic three months earlier: "Everyone thinks that if the reputation of the house be kept up," he reported to Strickland, "it will in a short time rivalize any College in this country. . . . The reputation of Geo: College is rather diminishing for want of teachers, & proper persons to govern it," he added, "and I doubt very much whether it will ever succeed, as long as the college of Baltimore subsists."[19]

Part of Kohlmann's original rationale for beginning the Literary Institution had been that it could serve as a preparatory school for Georgetown, attracting the New Yorkers that Georgetown had been losing to St. Mary's during the past decade.[20] This was an argument that Carroll also had used four months earlier than Kohlmann when he appealed to Molyneux to spare at least one of the Fenwicks to help establish a Jesuit presence in New

York.[21] Actually, New York had never been a major source of students for Georgetown either before or after DuBourg opened St. Mary's to Americans. From 1791 to 1802 only eleven New Yorkers, all from the city itself, had attended Georgetown. In the next five plus years there were to be five more. All were Catholics. Most of the students at the Literary Institution, even after it became primarily a country boarding school, were Protestants, and its lack of housing seems to have confined its enrollment to about sixty or seventy students.[22]

Nonetheless, Francis Neale, as president of a school desperate for both faculty and students, saw in the New York institution a plot to undermine Georgetown. To begin, he considered that Kohlmann had abandoned the college, more or less on his own initiative, taken four of the prefects with him, and started his own school in New York. Moreover Kohlmann had further alienated the directors of the college by taking with him part of the school's library.[23] Neale and his Maryland confreres might also have heard from their English Jesuit contacts that Kohlmann was saying to them that the Society ought to concentrate its limited resources on New York and Philadelphia, "the most important Cities of America."[24] When Neale reported his suspicions to Fenwick, his fellow Marylander assured him that there was no "*scheme* or *concerted plan.*" Georgetown's problem was a lack of local support, not a preemption of potential students by a competitor in another region. "For I do really believe," Fenwick wrote, "that if the College of Geo. Town had twenty Professors of the most eminent talents in addition to those it is already furnished with, it would not command twenty additional scholars out of the State of Maryland . . . so great is the fondness of Parents for their Children in this country . . ." He cited Harvard and Columbia as proof of his generalization. "If the College of Geo. Town is to flourish, it must flourish from its obtaining students from Maryland."[25] Georgetown's cosmopolitan composition during Fenwick's own student days in the 1790s seems either to have made no impression upon him or was a lost memory by 1811.

Ironically, Georgetown drew thirteen students from New York—as many students during the five years of the Literary Institution's existence as it had had during the entire eighteen years preceding its establishment. Virtually all of them were Catholic, the majority Irish. Eight of the thirteen became Jesuits, an outcome that Bishop Carroll had hoped would be one fruit of the Society's presence in New York City. Indeed, in terms of Georgetown's original purpose of being a nursery for priests, New York during this period (1808–12) was doing more by far to fulfill it than any other region, including Maryland. But as a competitor for all-too-scarce faculty, the Literary Institution was a continuing threat to the college.

The College and the Neales

At Georgetown the Neales, who still controlled the board of directors, had appointed their nephew, William Matthews (1770–1854), to succeed Francis Neale as president in March 1809. Now thirty-eight years old, Matthews had in 1800 been the first native-born priest to be ordained in the United States. He had taught briefly at the college in the late 1790s, and since 1804 had been pastor of St. Patrick's Church in Washington. Although in 1803 Matthews had been among the signers of the petition for the restoration of the Society of Jesus in this country, he had not yet entered the order. Whether he had simply delayed doing so or whether his uncles persuaded him that the president of Georgetown needed to be a Jesuit, he did become a Jesuit novice the day he assumed the presidency. At the same time he continued as pastor of St. Patrick's.

Related to many of the best Maryland families, including the Calverts, and already emerging as a civic leader (he later became one of the founders of the public library in the city of Washington, in 1811), Matthews provided both leadership and a public presence for Georgetown during his brief term as president.[26] In less than nine months the resourceful Matthews completed the new building, attempted to improve the finances of the college through investments (he was particularly adept at real estate speculation), and increased the enrollment by attracting more day stu-

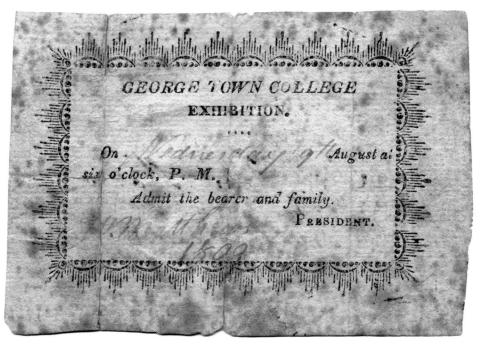

Ticket of admission to the 1809 exhibition (commencement) at Georgetown. (Georgetown University Archives)

Francis Neale, SJ (1754–1837). He served as acting president of Georgetown from December 1808 to March 1809, and as president from 1810 to 1811. (Georgetown University Archives)

William Matthews (1770–1854). A nephew of Francis and Leonard Neale, he was president of Georgetown for about seven months in 1809. (Georgetown University Archives)

dents, many of them children of friends or parishioners. Nonetheless, before the year (1809) was out, he resigned as president, left the novitiate, and returned to St. Patrick's as full-time pastor. Apparently his republican tendency to impose discipline and authority as little as possible upon students and prefects quickly cost him his uncles' confidence and led to his decision to step down.[27]

Francis Neale, once more in the president's office following his nephew's resignation, reinstated the monastic regimen of his brother, a daily order permeated with religious activities. In 1810 Neale also formally instituted a sodality, the traditional spiritual confraternity for students at Jesuit colleges. Members followed a devotional schedule that included daily Mass, regular communion and confession,[28] as well as spiritual reading from the *Pious Guide to Prayer and Devotion* (1792) or *Practical Reflections for Every Day of the Year* (1808), both of which Neale had edited. Little wonder, then, that during the Neale brothers' era, from 1799 to 1812, virtually all the students were Catholic, including the two sons of Elizabeth Seton. One in eight later entered the seminary or novitiate, although relatively few persevered. One who abandoned his studies before ordination was Edward Kavanaugh (**C** 1810–11). The son of an Irish immigrant mill owner and merchant, Kavanaugh left Georgetown after a year to attend St. Mary's in Baltimore and then to study privately for the priesthood in Boston. During the War of 1812 he was forced to drop those plans to work in his father's faltering business. In the 1820s he entered politics, serving in the Maine legislature and the U.S. Congress. In 1843 he became governor of Maine, the first Catholic to hold that office in any New England state.[29]

If Georgetown under the Neales produced a relatively high number of vocations, it was attracting few students in general. By the fall of 1811 total enrollment had dropped from eighty-three to fifty-six students, only nineteen of them boarders. High costs were a factor ($220 for tuition and board), but given the expanding economy of the city, which resulted from rising exports, numerous government building projects, and much ship-building at the Navy Yard, high tuition alone should not have deterred merchants, planters, and government employees from sending their sons to Georgetown.[30] The draconian discipline and general neglect of the school's affairs were probably more decisive elements. Beyond attending to its spiritual and financial aspects, Neale was not really intent on administering the college as an academic institution. When he was elected president in 1809, he had the position redefined to exclude any responsibility for academic affairs. Those duties now fell to the vice-president.[31] Francis Neale continued as master of novices and pastor of Trinity Church, as well as supervisor of finances at the several plantations. He was more or less an absentee president. As one student-teacher at the time recalled, "The Presidents of the College . . . spent much of their time on horseback."[32] In effect, as Carroll had sensed in 1805, operating a college and reviving the Society of Jesus in America were more than the limited resources of the Maryland Mission could afford simultaneously. Adding a second college in New York had only compounded matters. Carroll lamented to Plowden in the beginning of 1812 that the college "has sunk to the lowest degree of discredit."[33] Giovanni Grassi, the new vice-president of Georgetown and one of the recent immigrants, admitted that he felt "compelled . . . to be a sorrowful spectator of the miserable state of this college," with its lost reputation, debts, and "blackguard" students. He had found it a shocking change from Stonyhurst, the Jesuit college he had left in England. He found the novitiate, the hope of the future, in a state of disarray: novices unsupervised, ignorant of the Society they were entering, and departing in large numbers.[34] "I cannot and never will suffer it to be said," he vowed (in October 1811), "that such a College belongs to the Society."[35] To another Jesuit in England,[36] he wrote the following year, "We are in India!!"

Giovanni Grassi

As vice president, Giovanni Antonio Grassi (1775–1849) soon had the opportunity to remedy this situation. Grassi had come to Georgetown by the most convoluted route. A native of Bergamo, he had entered the Society in Italy in 1799. Superiors quickly recognized the extraordinary range of his intellectual and administrative talents. After five years of training he was ordained and made rector of a college in Russian Poland. Within the same year (1805) Grassi and two other Jesuits were ordered to China as part of a Russian mission. But attempts to sail to China from Copenhagen, London, and Lisbon at the height of the Napoleonic Wars proved successively frustrating in the extreme over the next five years. Then, for several years Grassi pursued his research in mathematics and astronomy while studying English at Stonyhurst. At last, in 1810, a new Jesuit superior general, Tadeusz Brzozowski, directed Grassi, not to a new mission in China but to an old one in America.[37]

Less than a year after Grassi's arrival, Brzozowski named him in October 1811 to be both rector (president) of the college and superior general of the Maryland Mission. However, because of the war in Europe, the authorizing letter did not reach Georgetown until the following June. Previously, the presidents had been chosen by either Carroll or the directors since the college still belonged legally to the Corporation of Roman Catholic Clergymen, whose trustees appointed the directors. Yet, according to the Constitutions of the Society, the superior general alone was authorized to name rectors of colleges. But Carroll, who had been informed in June of 1812 of the appointments, told Grassi a month later that the superior general had no authority to name him president.[38] Nonetheless, Carroll urged the directors to respect the general's wish.[39] The directors acted. As the minutes of August 1812 laconically state: [Grassi] "being proposed as president of the College was unanimously elected; and at the same time Rev. Mr. Francis Neale was elected vice-president with control over & management of the temporal concerns of the College."[40] It was DuBourg *redivivus*. But unlike DuBourg, Grassi resisted. With instructions soon obtained from St. Petersburg, he made it clear that this rearrangement of powers was unacceptable. If he was to be president, he would be so according to the norms of the Society, not according to those which had someone else hold the purse strings. The assistant to the superior general had also instructed Grassi that if control of the college remained with the corporation, he should remove the Jesuits from the institution and place them elsewhere. Grassi apparently did not raise this threat to the directors.[41]

In response to Grassi's protest, the trustees of the corporation made him a director of the college, a position DuBourg had not held. But the other directors refused to give him complete control.[42] There was no judgment of Grassi involved in this disposition of duties, as Matthews, the former president, explained in response to Grassi's claims. Such arrangements had been altered several times in the past, in accordance with changing circumstances. Nor was such a separation of authority peculiar to Georgetown. Stonyhurst had a similar structure. And, as Leonard Neale pointed out that September, during his own presidency control over finances had rested with the vice-president (his own brother, Francis, he might have added).[43] The remaining larger question was the authority of Grassi as religious superior over the college, including its finances. Grassi, even before his appointment as president and superior, had approached Charles Neale about ceding the college to the Society. Charles Neale at that time was both the superior of the mission and a trustee of the Corporation. His position was that the religious superior, as superior, had no power over property held by the civil Corporation of Roman Catholic Clergymen.[44] In time, the Neale brothers and Carroll assured Grassi, all the property, including the college, would be turned over to the Society, when it was fully reestablished.[45]

Grassi came to accept this position and to make the best of it. He realized that the trustees had decided to admit into their corporate body only Jesuits in the future, and, if American law required the trustees of a corporation to be citizens, so be it. When Grassi had arrived at Georgetown, among the first things suggested to him was to plan on becoming a United States citizen after five years. He had every intention of doing so, and of having the other immigrant Jesuits join him. Within "a few years" the corporation would then "be composed of Jesuits alone," which would give the superior control over the ancient lands of the Society and the college, all of which he felt had been badly managed."[46]

In reality, Grassi's diplomacy and initiative made the "accountability" division meaningless. Grassi was no DuBourg. He knew how to win people over, partly by keeping a close eye on his budget. When initially he had been named vice-president of the college in the spring of 1811, one of the first things he had done, despite being made responsible for academic affairs only, was to quietly study the financial state of the college. He found that the fees from the few students who paid the full $220 a year could not begin to cover the operating costs of the college, which included free education for students who showed promise of religious vocations. Thus, even with the set-aside income from the two Maryland plantations, St. Inigoes and St. Thomas, the college still had an annual deficit of more than $3,000.[47] Grassi proposed a radical decrease in the tuition and board fees to $125 in order to greatly increase the enrollment by making it possible for the sons of Catholics of more modest means to attend. The idea appealed to everyone from Carroll to Francis Neale.[48] Indeed, on the same day that they elected Grassi president, the directors also approved his tuition reduction plan for

William Leggett (**C** 1815–16).
This Georgetown alumnus
went on to become a noted
journalist in New York City.
(Engraving by A. Seeley from
a painting by R. S. Cummings.
Georgetown University Archives)

the boarder students.[49] A year later, a similar tuition reduction was worked out for the day students. These revised charges made Georgetown relatively inexpensive, compared to colleges in the region. St. John's College in Annapolis charged $150, Mount St. Mary's College in Emmitsburg $400.[50] With these reductions Georgetown's enrollment rose sharply, from fifty-six students and nineteen boarders in the fall of 1811 to seventy-nine and forty-one a year later. By 1815 enrollment at the college totaled one hundred and twenty-nine and ninety-five, respectively. The deficits disappeared. Significantly, in May 1813 the directors moved that Grassi also take over management of St. Inigoes, the most important plantation in the mission.[51]

Physically, St. Inigoes was probably the worst place for Grassi to live since the tidewater area was damp, sultry, and mosquito-ridden. Nevertheless, he went there in the summer of 1813 to make the customary retreat before final vows. There he, like many Jesuits—novices, scholastics, and priests alike—contracted a fever that plagued him all the following year. Eventually he was forced to seek treatments for his health at the sulphur springs in southern Virginia. Despite his now precarious health, he worked steadily at reviving the college, and Georgetown began to regain its status as a national school (see table 3.1 in appendix F). Whereas more than four-fifths (83.7%) of the students during the Neale years (1799–1811) had come from the District of Columbia and Maryland, the proportion dropped to less than two-thirds (61.6%) during Grassi's presidency. New York, Pennsylvania, and Virginia sent unprecedentedly large numbers of students, the two Northern states alone accounting for nearly a quarter of the enrollment.[52] Among the New Yorkers was William Leggett (**C** 1815–16), who left Georgetown to become a midshipman but eventually returned to New York City where he went on to edit several newspapers, including William Cullen Bryant's *Evening Post.*

By 1817, students from Vermont to the Mississippi Territory were on the rolls at Georgetown. Almost overnight, it became an exclusive boarding school, with most of its students (90%) in residence, and most of them living in the rooms which Grassi had had constructed in the new building to replace the original barrack-like dormitories.[53]

These figures certainly indicate that Grassi's tuition reduction achieved its primary purpose of bringing in a broader, more diverse range of Catholic students, as well as many more Protestant students. There was also a decline in kinship ties among the students. Moreover "in kind" payments for tuition were virtually eliminated, but there was also a large increase among those permitted to pay reduced rates based on the new lower tuition.[54] The expanded list of known occupations of fathers, few as they are, is another indicator of increased diversity. Politicians, doctors, military officers, and other professional men now began to outnumber the planters and merchants who had supported the school in earlier years. Even while assorted political events were leading to the War of 1812, it was overall a dynamic decade for the District of Columbia. Its population grew from 24,023 to 33,039, both slave and free; and architects, builders, bankers, editors, lawyers, and other professionals arrived in unprecedented numbers—especially in the boom years after the Treaty of Ghent in 1814 ended the War of 1812. Mayor James Blake of Washington had his son at the college from 1816 to 1818. His Georgetown counterpart, Thomas Corcoran, sent his son William Wilson Corcoran to the college for a year (1813–14). William Corcoran eventually became a financial giant in the city, a co-founder of the Corcoran and Riggs Bank. The architects Benjamin Latrobe and James Hoban also had their sons at Georgetown in 1815. Commodore David Porter sent his seven-year-old son, William David, to Georgetown the following year. Henry Clay of Kentucky, then Speaker of the House of Representatives, enrolled two of his five sons, Theodore Wythe and Thomas Hart, at the college in 1817.

Another sign of the growing diversity among the student body was the increased enrollment of students of Irish and French extraction, and a considerable decrease among those of English extraction. These "newcomers" tended to be urbanites (half of the Irish came from New York City), and were poorer than the traditional Georgetown student. Moreover, a third of the Irish students received outside financial support—proportionately many more than any other single student group receiving aid at the college. And they were also disproportionately represented among the declared candidates for the priesthood. During Grassi's five years as president these Irish-American students accounted for half the vocations, while constituting less than a fifth (16.2%) of the student total.

Meeting Carroll's Initial Purpose

The period from 1805 to 1817 was the golden age of vocations to the priesthood at Georgetown. The school turned out more seminarians during these years than the other two Maryland Catholic colleges combined—St. Mary's in Baltimore and Mount St. Mary's in Emmitsburg.[55] In the year 1815 alone, it contributed the four to the Society of Jesus—George Fenwick, Thomas Mulledy, William McSherry, and James Ryder—who would guide the school during the two decades of its greatest development in the antebellum era. During the Neale years (1799–1811) twenty-four students had gone on to study for the priesthood. Most of them came from either

Maryland or the District and were the sons of Anglo-American merchants or planters, some like George Fenwick (**C** 1807–15), Aloysius Young (**C** 1809–15), and William Queen (**C** 1800–1806) from the old Catholic families. Under Grassi the numbers were even more impressive: twenty-six to the seminary in five years. Partly this reflected the increase in enrollment (245 during Grassi's term as compared to 233 during the much longer Neale presidency), especially in boarders (not one day student entered the seminary or novitiate). But a major factor was the rising presence of the Irish students.

For Catholics at Georgetown, like Protestants at Williams and other denominational colleges of the early nineteenth century, the ministry was the one profession that promised both social mobility and financial support while preparing for it.[56] The Irish in general were prime candidates for both. Six of the thirteen Irish who entered the Society during these years had some kind of financial aid as students at Georgetown. Some, like Thomas Finegan (**C** 1812–15) and Edward Dempsey (**C** 1813–15) of New York, were poor boys and apparently orphans. Both were supported by Catholic laymen who expected them to return as priests to serve the church in New York. However, they entered the Jesuit novitiate in 1815 after a few years at the college. Finegan taught on the faculty both before and after his ordination in 1827. Dempsey taught for a short time but was dismissed from the Society in 1819. Others, such as James Murphy (**C** 1813–14) and James Ryder (**C** 1813–15), were immigrants. Murphy came from the Literary Institution in New York to enroll as a nonpaying boarder in 1813, with the understanding that he could enter the novitiate when Grassi found him ready to do so. The following year he was admitted as a novice. Ryder, having been brought to this country by his widowed mother, entered Georgetown as a thirteen-year-old and became a novice two years later.

Thomas Mulledy (**C** 1813–15) was a Southern variant of the new breed of student—older, self-supporting, and upwardly mobile—who constituted a growing minority in the New England colleges of the early nineteenth century.[57] The son of a ne'er-do-well immigrant farmer in western Virginia, Mulledy had taught at the local academy in Romney before entering Georgetown at the relatively old age of nineteen.[58] He left a depressed area of decreasing economic opportunities for young men and, like so many of the older students in New England from similar backgrounds, eventually chose the ministry.

George Carrell (**C** 1817–20) and William McSherry (**C** 1813–15) were both, in a sense, atypical. Carrell was the son of a wealthy Irish-American family of Philadelphia whose home was the mansion formerly owned by William Penn, and McSherry, the son of a prosperous Irish immigrant who was a planter in western Virginia. Carrell entered the Society in 1820, then left after two years to study for the priesthood at St. Mary's in

Baltimore. Ordained for the diocese of Philadelphia in 1829, he rejoined the Jesuits in 1835, became president of St. Louis University, and finally was appointed Bishop of Covington, Kentucky, in 1853. McSherry, who entered the Society in 1815, eventually served as the seventeenth president of Georgetown.

This rich harvest of vocations under Grassi matured while Georgetown was recovering its inclusive admission tradition. Before Grassi only a tenth of the students were Protestants and virtually all were day students. Now, in 1814 one-quarter of the student body, both boarders and day students, were non-Catholic.[59] At first there was an attempt to reinstitute the segregation of Protestant boarders in a house next to the campus, but this practice was discontinued by 1816.[60] But boarders, no matter what their religious affiliation, were apparently required to attend all the religious exercises then, which practice led to some complaints that the Jesuits were proselytizing.[61] The students were still very young, the median entrance age was twelve, only a slight increase over the past decade. Children as young as six continued to be accepted until 1870. With such young students, Grassi stressed composition by the imitation of the classics: "I have found that our scholars derived great advantage from writing all the translations of the Classical works and by little attention of the Masters to their writing in school they form a pretty good hand, which in this country is the mean object of the education of young men."[62] Most students failed to advance beyond the lower half of the seven-year course of studies.

Making Georgetown's Future

Very much like DuBourg, Grassi quickly became part of the local intellectual and social elites. His scientific interests made him a frequent visitor to the Patent Office and the Navy Yard to consult and be consulted about experiments and to allow the students to watch demonstrations. An enthusiastic mathematician and astronomer, he had calculated the eclipse of the sun in 1811. He frequently paid visits to Congress and received distinguished visitors in return. As rector, Grassi immediately set out to improve the image of the college as a place of culture and learning. Unlike DuBourg, he had a way of making the best of what he had at hand. So he decorated the reception room in Old North with engravings of Piranesi (some of them still adorn the walls of White-Gravenor), which someone had discarded in an obscure corner. He also used the mathematical and astronomical instruments he had brought with him to form the core of a museum there for both students and the general public.[63] For many years people regularly came to the campus to observe the heavens through his telescope. In 1816 he and a mathematics professor launched a balloon on the college grounds as a scientific demonstration in the interests of natural philosophy. Three years earlier, Grassi had revived public exhibitions at the college in connection with the distribution of prizes, a Jesuit educational tradition in Europe, at which the students displayed their learning.[64] Since there were no senior students in the college (ordinarily in European schools they were the major exhibitors of the cumulated knowledge gained in the course of studies), Grassi devised a means for the younger ones to impress an audience. He had constructed a model of the solar system which the students could use to explain the Copernican system during the public "dialogue" he had prepared for them. The large crowd of visitors, including senators and congressmen, were duly impressed. In President James Madison's Washington, the cosmopolitan Grassi provided an ideal link between town and gown.

The faculty in 1813 consisted of five Jesuits: Peter Lavadière (a French priest who had lately arrived in America to join the Society), three scholastics, and Grassi himself. Lavadière quickly proved himself virtually useless, so biased was he against things English. He made little or no effort to learn the language and returned to France in 1814.[65] The subjects taught now were confined to Latin, Greek, mathematics, algebra, writing, and French. Obviously, if the college was to be a college, offering everything from the classics to philosophy, more professors were a *sine qua non.* Strickland had suggested to Grassi in 1812, even before Grassi had been appointed president, that the only way to secure an adequate faculty was to unite the colleges in Georgetown and New York.[66] When Grassi approached Carroll about such a consolidation, the archbishop made clear what shape he now thought it should take. "If either the College of George Town is to be discontinued," he replied to Grassi in November 1812, "or the litterary [sic] institution near New York, undoubtedly it must be the latter . . ."[67]

Grassi, as superior of the mission, thus began the consolidation process by recalling Adam Marshall and James Wallace, two of the Jesuit faculty in New York. Benedict Fenwick, president of the Institution, was happy enough to lose Marshall, who, as he told Kohlmann, had exasperated him by "his total inertia and want of everything."[68] Wallace, a gifted astronomer and mathematician, was another matter. Fenwick asked that Wallace be allowed to stay until November. More important, both Fenwick and Kohlmann strenuously opposed the closing of the school. The Society, Fenwick argued, would dishonor itself by abandoning the commitment it had originally made to the Catholic community in New York by establishing a college there. Grassi pointed out that the mission's superior, Molyneux, had not had the authority to establish a college in the first place. But his chief reason for closing the place, he insisted, was not its apparent "illegitimate" origin but the obvious lack of people to staff it. To let it struggle on for several more years, Grassi explained to Fenwick, would only increase the loss of face over its inevitable collapse.[69] Kohlmann in turn argued not for hon-

or but for demographics. In abandoning New York, his questions emphasized what they were choosing

G: town? to be vexed by the corporation? to starve and to go ragged in St. Mary's
[County] cong[rega]tions, the grave yards for Europeans? and what then will become of the Society? . . .

Stay in New York, he continued, and "in less than 10 years the Society would
be independent in America, and have 60,000 dollars in the banks for it is a
fact, that if any other part of the union will furnish 10 students, N.Y. by its
happy situation will furnish [a] hundred."[70] In other words, the most important city in the country would make the Society prosper by furnishing the
students who would provide the members for its future work. New York,
with more than ninety-six thousand inhabitants by 1810, was the nation's
most populous city. In contrast, the federal city, including the "Town of
George," had about fifteen thousand inhabitants that same year. In ten years,
Kohlmann argued, the Society would have the financial support for its ministries that the plantations had never been able to provide, either for Georgetown or for any of its undertakings.[71] As Kohlmann later put it, "there is no
man acquainted with the . . . State of N.Y. and Maryland that will not pro-
nounce without hesitation that it would be fifty times more for the advantage of the Society to have a college at N.Y. than in any other part of the
union. . . ."[72]

Kohlmann took his case to the superior general in St. Petersburg as well
as to Grassi. Father Brzozowski was impressed enough to advise his regional superior to keep the Literary Institution open, if at all possible, but
Grassi was steadfast in his decision to remove his men from the New York
school.[73] The decline in enrollment in the New York Literary Institution (by
September 1813 there were only forty students there) and the small number of Catholics in the school may have helped shape his thinking, as well
as the fact that the school was owned not by the Society but by laymen of
the parish. But given Carroll's change of heart (since 1808 when he had
encouraged Kohlmann), the decision was probably inevitable. Kohlmann,
after searching for alternatives in staffing it, reluctantly closed the place in
April of 1814.[74] Georgetown gained an unusually gifted faculty member in
Wallace, as well as an elegant set of maps, six students, and a new monopoly on Jesuit higher education in America.[75]

The College during the War of 1812

Although the economies of both New York and Georgetown suffered from
the War of 1812, the war itself played no part in the decision to preserve
Georgetown at the expense of the Literary Institution. If anything, the

British fleet was more of a menace to the maritime traffic on the Chesapeake than that on the Hudson, since the British controlled the lower Potomac and the Patuxent rivers. Raids there among the coastal settlements in the late winter and spring of 1813 forced Grassi to move the novitiate from riverside St. Inigoes, where it had been located the previous fall, to Frederick in the Monocacy Valley of Maryland. Cattle and tobacco were sent to Georgetown for safekeeping, with the tobacco stored in the new building's basement.

Washington itself, as the federal city, seemed very vulnerable. In September 1813, Grassi reassured the parents and public that the college had already started classes "and will continue as usual; the existing state of affairs leaving no apprehension of any further disturbances."[76] The next Tuesday, the college took part in the day of prayer and humiliation that President James Madison had ordered.[77] The area remained free of the rumors of war until the following July, when the British transports were again reported sailing up the Potomac and Patuxent rivers. By late August their fleet was clearly advancing toward Washington. "The people are mobilized for war," Grassi reported in his diary on August 22, 1814. Two days later veteran British troops had landed. They quickly broke the defenses of the raw American militia at the northeast edge of the District. As the British marched through the streets of Washington, the only shot fired at them came from the home of Robert Sewall at Maryland Avenue and Second Street. (His two sons had

British troops burn Washington City in the summer of 1814. (From "History of the Star Spangled Banner," by George I. Svejda, U.S. Department of the Interior, 1969. Reproduction courtesy of "Old News," N. & R. Bromer, Marietta, Pa., 1992)

attended the college in Georgetown a decade earlier.) The day that began as the "Bladensburg races" ended with the British troops burning the Capitol and the president's house, and with the Americans destroying their own ships and stores at the Navy Yard on the Anacostia River.[78] Only the coincidence of a violent thunderstorm prevented the fire from spreading throughout the city.[79]

In Georgetown that evening the flames from the burning buildings were great enough to read by, as Grassi and others watched from the top story of the new building at the college. The townspeople, in panic over the thought of being the next target of the British, were fleeing to the countryside. Many also sent their silverware and other valuables to the college for safekeeping.[80] No one left the college grounds but, as a precaution, the sacred Mass vessels and "other articles of plate" were concealed.[81] The British, however, after putting the War and Treasury buildings to the torch, had returned to their ships the next day. On the 26th, Grassi learned that they had left, sailing for Baltimore harbor and the night-long battle afterwards immortalized in the "Star Spangled Banner."[82] Five days later another school year began without delay.

With many government buildings in ruins, Grassi realized that federal officials might approach him about using the college as its temporary seat of government. In its new building, after all, the college possessed the largest undamaged structure in the area. From Baltimore, Archbishop Carroll advised Grassi to resist any government attempt to take over the college, but if that proved impossible, he should for safety's sake dismiss the students.[83] In late September the Georgetown council authorized the mayor, John Peter, to make Georgetown available to the federal government as an interim capital, "it being ascertained that the Colleges of Georgetown will be cheerfully given up by the Board of Trustees; and that their spaciousness will admit of every comfort and convenience, both to Halls and committee Rooms etc. etc. . . . ."[84] Peter, an alumnus of the college (**C** 1792–93) evidently had persuaded Grassi to allow the town to offer the use of the college facilities. But the federal authorities did not take up this offer.

The Jesuit Restoration Complete

In early December 1814, Giovanni [John] Grassi recorded in his diary: "Received the Brief Sollicitudo omnium Ecclesiarum [restoring the Society of Jesus throughout the world] . . . we all went to the Domestic Chapel where the *Te Deum and the Veni Creator* were recited."[85] Anthony Kohlmann's reaction was characteristically more exuberant: "Novus rerum nascitur ordo:[86] miracles upon miracles and all to the ruin of impiety and to the full triumph of Jesus Christ and his holy Religion over all his enemies."[87] Even the normally reserved Benedict Fenwick could not suppress a *"Te Deum laudamus, te Dominum confitemur.*[88] The Society of Jesus is then completely reestablished!"[89] Pope Pius VII had finally reconstituted the Jesuits throughout the world, giving them the canonical legitimacy for which Carroll and others had been waiting. Fenwick saw the papal action as "tidings peculiarly grateful" to the college since it would enable it to organize completely according to the educational norms and regulations of the Society, with authority in the hands of the rector, together with his consultors. Grassi had already petitioned the directors more than a year earlier to this effect, but not until the following November did the Directors agree to it.[90]

Even before the news of the formal restoration of the Society was received, Grassi had begun the process of applying for a federal charter for the college. It will be recalled that twenty-five years earlier, Carroll had declined to have Georgetown chartered, evidently because he was wary of the intrusive tendencies of state governments in the early national period. But by 1814 there had been a significant shift in the relationship between college and state. A college was no longer regarded as an arm of the state for the training of a provincial elite and the safeguarding of public character but as a form of private enterprise, as independent as any commercial corporation. This new characterization of the college was given classical legal definition in *The Trustees of Dartmouth College versus Woodward* (1819). In that important case, Chief Justice Marshall declared for the whole Court that the college was a private foundation protected by the Constitution as private property, and that the state legislature could not therefore revoke or alter its charter at will.[91]

Actually, the new legal status of colleges and universities had already been defined fifteen years earlier in North Carolina. When the state legislature there attempted to withdraw the land grant to the University of North Carolina on the grounds that it had become sectarian (Presbyterian) and was no longer serving the common good, the state supreme court ruled that the charter of the school was an inviolate contract between its board and the legislature. As the private property of its board, the school could not be destroyed by the legislature. When Chief Justice Marshall ruled in Dartmouth's favor in 1819, he was simply providing the highest judicial sanction for the legal protection already developed at the state level.[92] And with the recognition that chartering an educational institution, even a religious one, created a fundamentally private corporation, there were then no grounds for fearing a violation of the separation of church and state, even with the federal government as the chartering authority.[93]

If Grassi was unaware of these specific judicial developments, he did realize that a charter had become, not a threat to a university's independence, but a safeguard for its integrity. Taking advantage of the fact that

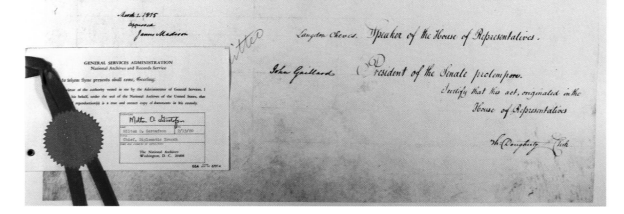

THIRTEENTH CONGRESS OF THE UNITED STATES;

AT THE THIRD SESSION,

Begun and held in the city of Washington, in the Territory of Columbia, on Monday the nineteenth day of September, one thousand eight hundred and fourteen.

AN ACT *concerning the College of George Town in the District of Columbia.*

Be it enacted by the Senate and House of Representatives of the United States of America in Congress assembled, That it shall and may be lawful for such persons, as now are, or from time to time may be, the president and Directors of the College of George Town, within the District of Columbia, to admit any of the Students belonging to said College or other persons meriting academical honors, to any degree in the faculties, arts, sciences, and liberal professions, to which persons are usually admitted in other Colleges or Universities of the United States; and to issue in an appropriate form, the diplomas or Certificates, which may be requisite to testify the admission to such degrees.

several congressmen had had sons in the college, he next sought the legal means for the school to confer academic degrees as well as to prevent the possibility that the government might someday force it to become part of some non-Catholic university, "as has happened elsewhere."[94] Moreover, James Madison was in the President's House, and he was a vigorous promoter of the civil rights of religious minorities, particularly Catholics. Twenty years before, in Congress, Madison had reminded his colleagues that in the Roman Catholic "religion there was nothing inconsistent with the purest republicanism," as many Catholics had proven during the revolution.[95] And there was the special circumstance of having in the Congress a Catholic who was an alumnus of the school, and indeed its first student.[96] He, William Gaston, who had been elected to the House of

The Act was presented to the U.S. Congress for consideration by Congressman William Gaston, loyal alumnus. Facsimile of Georgetown's federal charter, signed by President James Madison on March 1, 1815. (Georgetown University Archives)

Representatives from North Carolina in 1813, was a frequent guest at Grassi's table. In late January 1815, Gaston presented to the Congress a petition of the president and board of directors of the college that they be granted the authority to confer the customary degrees. A week later the bill was reported out of committee and passed by the House of Representatives.[97] The Senate approved it without amendment on February 27 and President Madison signed it into law on March 1, 1815.[98] Georgetown College could now "admit any of the Students . . . to any degree in the faculties, arts, sciences, and liberal professions, to which persons are usually admitted in other Colleges or Universities of the United States . . ."[99] Two years later, Charles and George Dinnies, brothers from New York, were the first recipients of the degree of bachelor of arts.

The Death of John Carroll

"Your friend Mr. Grassi," Carroll wrote to Plowden in October 1815, " . . . continually adds celebrity and reputation to the character of his college. . . ." But, the archbishop added, Georgetown "still wants professors of more eminence and a greater number of them."[100] It was a note Carroll had been sounding ever since the college had opened a quarter of a century before and it is his last known word on the institution he had founded. He died six weeks later on December 3, 1815. Though he was helpless to endow his college with an eminent faculty, he did the next best thing. In his will he bequeathed four hundred pounds sterling in five percent stock to serve as a perpetual fund for the library. And through Grassi and Enoch Fenwick he left a personal library which he had recently inherited from Louvain.[101]

Carroll's college, under Grassi, was becoming at his death the major domestic producer of clergy for his church. It was also rapidly becoming the national college that Carroll had envisioned a generation earlier—open to students of every religion and class. Had Carroll lived another two years he would no doubt have been heartened by the intellectual strengths and diversity of the faculty that Grassi was at last able to assemble, the most promising faculty Georgetown College had ever known, and the kind of

Catholic intellectuals Carroll had in vain attempted to draw to his school at its founding. Only a dozen years after the return of the Jesuits, the college seemed by 1817 on the verge of redeeming Carroll's dream of a Catholic and republican institution of higher learning, blending the best of European tradition and American culture, that was the match of any college in the land.

Rector et Professores Collegii Georgiopolitani

Omnibus praesentes visuris,

Salutem in Domino.

Quandoquidem aequm est, et à Majoribus institutu

ut, qui caeteris ingenio et doctrinâ praestant, meritâ, quâ secernantu

ab illiteratis, decorentur Laureâ, Nos, ad id munus summ

Reipublicae delegati auctoritate, certiores facimus omnes ad quo

praesentes pervenerint, dilectum nobis *Theodorum Jenkins*,

solemni nostræ Artium Facultatis Sessione ad Artium Baccala

reatum unanimâ voce fuisse provectum, singulisque juribus & privilege

ad istum Gradum pertinentibus à nobis fuisse donatum.

Quod, ut omnibus innotescat, has ... Chirographo nostro & Facultatis sigill

munitas dedimus, in Aulâ Collegii no... die vigesimâ septimâ Mensis Julii Ann

Wilhelmus Feiner Rector

... Drewnowski, I.D.

... Kingan Prof. Rhet. & ... Prof. Stud.

... Beuten Prof. Math. & Nat. Phil.

CHAPTER 4

"Instead of a Constellation . . . a Few Unfledged Bodys . . ."

The college has not ten boarders, the ablest & best professors they have had among them have abandoned them year after year and they have not at this time a single member distinguished for literary or scientific attainments—there must be fault somewhere.

RICHARD McSHERRY to WILLIAM McSHERRY
to George Town from Martinsburg, November 27, 1828

Natives versus Continentals

If the decades of an institution's history were reckoned like the seasons of an athletic team, the 1820s would be counted a lost one for Georgetown. In 1817, everything—rising enrollment, growing reputation, brilliant faculty, a federal charter, financial stability—seemed to point clearly to a coming of age for the college. Yet, before the end of the next decade the institution was barely surviving. "The college has not ten boarders," an alumnus wrote in a pessimistic summary in 1828, "the ablest & best professors they have had among them have abandoned them year after year and they have not at this time a single member distinguished for literary or scientific attainments— there must be fault somewhere."[1]

Precisely where the fault lay was a matter of sharply divided opinion. The economic depression that followed the War of 1812 was one obvious factor.

The collapse of the export-oriented economy and the management scandals of the National Bank in the so-called Panic of 1819 deeply affected the commercial classes of all the Atlantic coast cities, from Boston to the District of Columbia. James Neil, a Jesuit scholastic recently returned to New York from Rome, wrote Grassi in February 1820 that he had found "Our country . . . in the greatest misery. Many persons whom I left here with 70 or 80,000 dollars capital are now beggars & lodged in the poor house . . ."[2] Although the continuing operations of the federal government bureaus preserved Washington City from the full impact of the depression, banks failed and real estate sales stagnated. For the District's port towns, the Panic was particularly devastating since their merchants were overwhelmed by shrinking markets and expanding debt that severely curtailed trade with post-Napoleonic Europe.[3] One such merchant, John Walsh of Baltimore, had a son Thomas who badly wanted to return to Georgetown in the fall of 1823. As Walsh explained in an August letter to President Enoch Fenwick, "I calculate to send him again if possible, altho . . . the times are such I cannot afford the expense . . ."[4] Nevertheless Walsh somehow did find the means to send his son for three more years, but many did not. Tuition and board at the college had risen again to $250 by the time Grassi left in 1817. Cut back in 1824 to $175, it was still a steep sum in the hard times of that decade. The overall financial condition of the college, like that of the Jesuit mission, was extremely poor. "Our affairs wear an alarming appearance;" the procurator, Adam Marshall, had already warned Enoch Fenwick in the summer of 1820, "a heavy and empty treasury: immense tracts of land, resembling rather an Indian hunting ground than lands inhabited by men acquainted with the arts of civilized life. All our plantations in a wretched condition. . . ."[5]

In a larger sense, the college was the victim of an intra-Jesuit struggle. The former colonial or "native" Jesuits and their immigrant allies from Britain were aligned on one side; and the Jesuit emigrés from the Continent on the other. These Anglo-American-Irish Jesuits stood consciously for a certain republicanism that stressed reason, openness to American values and culture, and a minimization of traditional religious discipline. The "Continentals" just as consciously stressed metaphysics, institutional authority, and personal asceticism. The former were committed to training virtuous leaders for state as well as church—to preparing young men for life in a republic. The latter were committed to an almost contrary view of the purposes and objectives of the university.

In a sense the "native" Americans were now the ones out of tune with the higher education community, representing as they did the Catholic sector of the republican front that had dominated the mission and identity of all American Colleges in the last quarter of the previous century. But that unique eighteenth-century commonality was rapidly breaking up in the 1820s under numerous parochial, denominational, and conservative pressures.[6] The Continental Jesuits and a few others of like mind within the Maryland Mission, such as John McElroy, tended to regard the Anglo- and Irish-American Jesuits as too much the children of their culture, too enamored of the values of liberty and independence, too lax in nurturing the moral character of their students through the strict enforcement of rules and proper order. For virtually all these Jesuits, there was, at least initially, a deep suspicion of the republican institutions and principles that America epitomized. A good number of them never shook that bias—and never wanted to. "I [do] not wish to see a Society constituted only by Americans," one German even explained in a letter to a fellow Jesuit, a Pole, in 1823:

for I observe they have curious principles: they wish for revolutions, adopt the condemned proposition: "that the Sovereignty resides essentially in the people." They approuve murder, blood shed, just as the Jacobins did in France. . . . Americans wish generally the Institute [the Society] to make room for American manners & opinions, for American Education, with the hatred of Sovereigns and Monarchies.[7]

Understandably, to Europeans who had been uprooted by revolutions in the name of republicanism, the United States seemed in some respects an alien place. Even as well-disposed a European as Giovanni Grassi originally thought it likely that the new United States, under the weight of republican government, would eventually suffer the same fatal collapse that earlier European republics had.[8] However, some, like Grassi, quickly shed their distrust. Others tended to remain strangers to and in their new country.

Most of the issues dividing the two Jesuit "camps" had little to do with Georgetown, but an important one did involve serious questions about the character of Georgetown. Was the university to be an institution open to all? And indeed, was it in its university curriculum and discipline to promote the republican culture of American society? Or did such concerns constitute a betrayal by the university of the Jesuit educational tradition? In the 1820s the new ideas, the new ways were abandoned; the traditionalists prevailed. There was a purging of the Anglo-American Jesuits that would leave the college more dead than alive.

The Making and Unmaking of a Faculty

As Georgetown began its second twenty-five years in 1817, the nation's fifth president, James Monroe, began the first of his two terms as the head of an expanding republic. The year seemed auspicious for the institution. Grassi had finally assembled a faculty that would enable the school to become a college worthy of the name. From New York came Benedict Fenwick and James Wallace; and from England, Roger Baxter. The English Jesuits in 1816 had finally sent, not an accomplished academic, but Baxter, a bright young scholastic. And then there was Grassi himself to teach and lead.

Fenwick, a native of Maryland, was at thirty-five the oldest of the Jesuit newcomers. Anthony Kohlmann, a good judge of learning, found Fenwick's knowledge of Greek and Latin the equal of that of "any scholar" in the country, his French fluent, his grasp of theology "competent," his judgment "quick and penetrating." Fenwick, in his opinion, grasped "the genius of this country better than any other" Jesuit he knew.[9]

Wallace, an Irish immigrant, had taught school in New York City before joining the Georgetown faculty at the age of eighteen in 1805 as a mathematics teacher. Two years later he had entered the Jesuits. Sent in 1809 to the New York Literary Institution, he wrote for his students *A New Treatise on the Use of the Globes and Practical Astronomy or a Comprehensive View of the System of the World* (New York, 1812). One of the first textbooks on astronomy in the United States, the 512-page volume was soon adopted for use at other colleges, including Columbia and Georgetown. (A companion volume on mathematics and general science planned by Wallace was never completed.)

Baxter, an intellectual product of the English Catholic Enlightenment, brought a considerable familiarity with both vernacular literature and *belles-lettres*. His eloquence quickly earned him renown in the pulpit and the press, and within his first year in America he engaged in a widely followed polemical exchange of letters with a Protestant minister in Alexandria on "The Tenets of Catholicity."[10] In 1820 he published an apologetic work developed from that exchange. Titled *The most important tenets of the Roman Catholic Church fairly explained*, it was remarkably ecumenical in its thrust. As a faculty colleague later remarked, Roger Baxter was "the sole preacher, the sole distinguished writer" among them, giving the institution a public voice it had never had previously.[11] At Georgetown he taught rhetoric to the senior students.

If, as Howard Miller has suggested, the natural scientist was the ideal republican educator in a society where scientific knowledge was regarded as a community commodity and as a "particular form of useful knowledge that was the key to the growth of a prosperous and democratic society," Grassi and Wallace met this ideal at Georgetown very well indeed.[12] They also helped to expand the museum at the college, and frequently collaborated on various scientific experiments. In the summer of 1816, on the feast of St. Ignatius, they sent a gas-filled balloon aloft from the college grounds to demonstrate the principles of aerodynamics.[13] By the year 1818 Wallace's reputation as a mathematician had prompted officials in the Department of State to consult him on the calculation of the exact boundary between the United States and Canada as determined by the Treaty of Ghent.[14] Three years earlier when Congress had authorized the recalculation of the longitude of the city of Washington, Grassi and Wallace were asked to undertake the necessary astronomical observations. (This was to be the first stage in the creation at Georgetown of a national observatory in the federal capital.) The two Jesuit astronomers were forced to decline the invitation until such time as they

Title page of Wallace's textbook on astronomy, which he wrote initially for his students at the New York Literary Institution. It was used at Georgetown long after he left the College in 1818. (Georgetown University Special Collections)

A NEW TREATISE

ON THE

USE OF THE GLOBES,

AND

Practical Astronomy ;

OR

A COMPREHENSIVE VIEW

OF

THE SYSTEM OF THE WORLD.

IN FOUR PARTS.

I. An extensive collection of Astronomical and other Definitions.

II. Problems performed by the TERRESTRIAL GLOBE, including those relative to Geography, Navigation, Dialling, &c. with many new and important problems and investigations, particularly useful to the Navigator and Practical Astronomer.

III. Problems performed by the CELESTIAL GLOBE, including those of finding the longitude at sea, new methods of finding the latitude, with only one altitude of the sun, or a star, at any given time, with the method of representing the spherical triangles on the globe, &c.

IV. A comprehensive account of the SOLAR SYSTEM, with the elementary principles, and most valuable modern discoveries in Astronomy to the present time. The nature and motion of COMETS, OF THE FIXED STARS, ECLIPSES, THE THEORY OF THE TIDES, LAWS OF MOTION, GRAVITY, &c. with DIAGRAMS elucidating the demonstrations.

The whole serving as an introduction to the higher Astronomy and Natural Philosophy, is illustrated with a variety of important notes, useful remarks, &c. and each problem with several examples. The necessary astronomical instruments are pointed out, and the most useful tables are inserted in the work.

DESIGNED FOR THE INSTRUCTION OF YOUTH,

AND PARTICULARLY ADAPTED TO THE UNITED STATES.

BY J. WALLACE,

Member of the New-York Literary Institution, &c.

Quid munus Reipublicæ majus aut melius afferre possimus, quam si Juventutem bene erudiamus ?
CICERO.

NEW-YORK :

Printed and published by SMITH & FORMAN,

AT THE FRANKLIN JUVENILE BOOKSTORES,

195 and 213 Greenwich-Street.

1812.

could obtain more precise instruments for the work and in order to carefully compare their observations with those already made in Europe.[15] Before they could do this, however, Grassi was sent to Rome in the early summer of 1817 and, as it turned out, never returned.

He departed reluctantly, going as an emissary for Leonard Neale, now John Carroll's successor as archbishop of Baltimore. Grassi was sent to plead the archbishop's case with Propaganda Fide against dissident priests and lay trustees in his archdiocese. Grassi also hoped to use the trip to press home the need of the Society in the United States for more well-qualified men. To that end he intended to seek permission to recruit volunteers for the mission and to secure approval for sending American Jesuits to Rome for their education in philosophy and theology. Then, too, there was the lure of raising funds for America while in Europe. He had received reports, in fact, of two potential major benefactors in France.[16] So, despite some doubts about the exigencies of such a voyage, Grassi sailed for Europe.[17]

Grassi's mission proved a confirmation of his misgivings. Propaganda had already moved to override the archbishop's opposition in Charleston and Norfolk. Jesuit officials in Rome were very sympathetic to the needs of their confreres in America. Grassi, given permission, found that he could "empty the Novitiates" in Italy and France, so eager were young Jesuits to volunteer for the United States. But the Society was opening colleges in Europe so rapidly that they were absorbing the relatively few men available for such work.[18] He did, however, work out plans to send the first scholastics from Georgetown to Rome for their advanced studies. All he could send to Georgetown two years later, as it turned out, were paintings for a proposed gallery and books for the faculty.[19] Worst of all, he himself was unable to return to America because doctors feared that his inoperable hernia would make a transatlantic crossing dangerous, prone as he was to becoming violently seasick.[20]

By the time Grassi learned of this medical verdict—in the spring of 1819— he had already been dismayed by the earlier news that the new superior, Anthony Kohlmann, had broken up the scholarly "core" of the Georgetown faculty. Roger Baxter was now in Richmond, Benedict Fenwick and James Wallace in Charleston, Francis Neale in Charles County. "What I had procured with so much labour and patience," Grassi complained to Plowden from Rome in November of 1818, "now I see . . . destroyed; I do not know how the College will prosper!"[21] Grassi, all too aware of Kohlmann's volatility and his chronic difficulties with the Anglo-Americans, had deliberately named Charles Neale acting superior of the Maryland Mission and had had Benedict Fenwick appointed president of the college when he left for Rome in 1817. But the superior general, intent on keeping Grassi in Rome, had subsequently appointed Kohlmann superior of that mission. Kohlmann, in turn, took over as rector of the college as well.

Anthony Kohlmann, Tenth President

Anthony Kohlmann's attitude toward Georgetown, of course, was all too well known. Having already lost out in his efforts to suppress the college in favor of the Literary Institution, he had now become convinced that the only prudent thing for the Maryland Mission to do, as John Carroll had also advocated a few years earlier, was to close Georgetown, at least for the near future, in order to concentrate its meager resources on the training of the novices and scholastics. "Anything else," he had previously warned Grassi in December 1816, "will not satisfy either the scholastics or novices, anything else will not save the Society." To neglect their training in order to employ them in keeping the college open would all too certainly drive them out and with them the future of the mission.[22]

Although Anthony Kohlmann did not in fact shut down Georgetown (a step the directors would hardly have endorsed), he seemed well on the way, in the eyes of many, to emptying the place by his own means within three years of his presidency.[23] As with most things concerning Kohlmann, this judgment was somewhat hyperbolic. Nevertheless, in 1820 alone thirty-six students left the college, thirty-four of them boarders. Moreover, enrollment had fallen in three years from a peak of one hundred forty-three to ninety-seven, and the fifty-four boarders among them amounted to slightly more than half of the total students (101) who had been at the college when Grassi sailed for Rome. Undoubtedly, some of that decline was certainly due to the Panic of 1819; some, however, could certainly be laid at Kohlmann's door.

By any measure, Kohlmann's administration was a disaster. Like the Neales, he brooked no violations of discipline in the students. During his three-year term he dismissed ten students, three times the number that had been expelled in the previous history of the college. Many more withdrew. Henry Stuart Foote, later governor of Mississippi, transferred after three months in 1818 to attend Washington College in Virginia. Thomas Jefferson's grandson, Francis Eppes, was another dropout. Eppes, whose father was a member of the House of Representatives from Virginia, had entered Georgetown in the autumn of 1817 but by December was ready to leave. "There are a great many objections to this Georgetown College," he wrote his grandfather. "In the first place they are bigoted Catholics extremely rigid and they require the boys to observe all the regulations of their Church which makes a great interuption in the course of our studies. . . . [T]hey are very strict and punish for the most trivial offence."[24] Despite the self-serving character of the letter (was he perhaps preparing his family for a poor academic report by pleading religious harassment?), Eppes spoke for many students who wanted little or no supervision. The culmination was their revolt in 1818. Their target was a prefect, Stephen Dubuisson, whom they rightly regarded as Kohlmann's chief instrument of repression. Dubuisson, a French emigré, felt it his duty to heavily enforce the rules which the American prefects had until then tended to lightly enforce, if at all. The students organized to kill him (at least Dubuisson and others were so convinced) but the plot was discovered and the six instigators were expelled.[25]

This was the first revolt at Georgetown but by that time rebellious uprisings were commonplace at campuses across the country, from Harvard to North Carolina. Already in 1799, students at Chapel Hill, reacting to disciplinary attempts, had horsewhipped the college president and attacked their professors. And in 1825, students at Virginia, angry over the denial of a lengthened summer vacation, protested and inflicted violence on several of the faculty to the cry of "Down with the European Professors!" The protesters, Steven Novak has argued, were the upperclass heirs of the freedom-loving revolutionary founders of the republic, and they were upset over the conservative turn that American education had taken.[26] Predictably, the result overall was expulsions, harsher disciplinary codes, and a further decline of republican education, in both governance and curriculum. As we noted earlier, Georgetown's student body seemingly became less aristocratic during the dozen or so years after 1810. However, of the eleven students expelled during the Kohlmann years (1817–20), at least four were sons of Maryland's old Catholic families—Fenwick, King, Hall, and Carroll. Two others were from old St. Louis families (one, Francis Jarrott, later became mayor of that city). Of the eleven expelled, ten were Catholics, and all were boarders. All but one were paying full tuition and board. They had been at the college longer than the average student and were further advanced in their studies. These eleven rebels seem mainly to have been sons of the gentry, and they were resisting changes in the hitherto relaxed, traditional discipline at Georgetown. Like administrators at Princeton and other denominational colleges, Kohlmann was intent on establishing a more orthodox educational environment in place of the republican one.

The period was also one in which American higher education in general was searching for a curriculum that would define its purpose and rationalize its worth within society. The Yale report of 1828 was the culmination of the effort to legitimize the preservation of the classical course of studies. Other institutions attempted to find alternatives more in keeping with the realities of American culture, ranging from Harvard's addition of elective courses to its prescribed curriculum through Union College's offering of a parallel scientific course to the University of Virginia's establishment of eight separate schools in the arts, sciences, and professions.[27] Georgetown, of course, experienced its own struggle over the curriculum, in the unhappy intellectual tug-of-war between the Continental Jesuits and their Anglo-American brethren, the "native" Jesuits. Kohlmann wanted a curriculum dominated by Latin and Greek grammar for the sake of the formation of seminary candidates. The "new generation" faculty preferred, instead, a mix of the classics, with a heavy stress on Latin and Greek literature, and a substantial component of mathematics and science. The result: two competing plans of studies—Kohlmann's and the one drawn up by Fenwick, Grassi, and Wallace. As president of the college, Kohlmann quite naturally put his own plan in place. Wallace later protested:[28]

He conceived that Latin alone was sufficient for a Clergyman, and as he valued pretious little the acquaintance of such gentry as Cicero, Virgil or Horace he concluded very wisely that the catechisms of the Council of Trent [were] . . . more sublime & also more useful . . . [for] classical erudition. . . . No profane author was allowed to shew his face within the walls of the Coll. according to his plan, unless in a certain concealed part of the library called Hell or Limbo . . . Many of the poor modern classics, with other similar gentry, who were not in every point strictly orthodox, were on those memorable occasions condemned to the flames, even poor Eustace could not stand the ordeal.

To Wallace and other "Anglo-Americans," Kohlmann was "a Continental" intent on confining education to clerical preparation in a highly traditional society. Little wonder, then, that, despite Kohlmann's orders, Baxter, Fenwick, and Wallace continued to follow their own preferences in the use of texts in the classroom. Their plan of studies was organized around a curriculum that blended tradition (the classics and mathematics) and the new, burgeoning knowledge of the physical sciences with a modest recognition of utilitarian needs. Those in the preparatory classes at the college studied English and Latin grammar, English composition, Latin literature (Caesar's Gallic Wars), French, and arithmetic. In the higher school, the students began in First Grammar with Greek grammar and literature (St. Luke's Gospel), then read several Latin authors, including Sallust and Ovid, while continuing to learn French and arithmetic ("commission brokerage, Buying & Selling of Stocks, Discount, Comp. Interest," etc.). Next, in Humanities (Poetry) they began to study mythology, Greek (Xenophon and Homer), Latin (Livy, Cicero, Virgil), French, algebra and geometry, and history. In Rhetoric they continued with Latin (Cicero, Virgil, and Horace) and Greek (Homer), French composition, geometry, and trigonometry. Thus, *Eloquentia perfecta* was to continue to be the conscious goal that many of the rhetorical texts and methods were designed to achieve. And music, dancing, and drawing were to continue to be offered as electives for interested students.

In the final year, known as Philosophy, the students were expected to concentrate on ethics, ontology, natural theology, and natural philosophy—as science was then called. That last included physics and astronomy. For the small minority that completed the entire course of studies, Philosophy served implicitly as a synthesis and integration to the process of intellectual formation, offering an intellectual cosmos in which the mature student could orient his thinking and behavior.

That curriculum as proposed and implemented by Baxter and his colleagues was still essentially a classical one, but with greater emphasis on literature, both classical and modern, and natural science. It retained

Georgetown's modern language, French, as an integral part of the curriculum (most colleges, including Yale, continued to offer it, at best, as an elective). Significantly, science, not moral philosophy as at so many schools before the Civil War, was regarded as the capstone, the highest form of intellectual integration, and the greatest of "human acquirements." Science, as James Wallace put it in 1812 in the Introduction to his *New Treatise*), was the one in which God "chiefly manifested his greatness and majesty."[29] At graduation an award was given to the senior student who was outstanding in natural science. There was no award for moral philosophy. Despite science's high place in the curriculum, however, Georgetown students had less exposure to it than at many traditional colleges, such as Yale, where students began its study before the senior year.

The Fruits of Factionalism

Another area of division between the Anglo-American Jesuits and those from the Continent was related to the pluralistic nature of religious affiliations within Georgetown's student body. Both Anthony Kohlmann and John McElroy, the treasurer of the college, tended toward a religious enthusiasm that the Anglo-Americans found alien and offensive. One manifestation of this was perceived by some as the proselytization of non-Catholic students. Benjamin Latrobe's son, John, later recalled that he and his brother were virtually the only Protestant students untouched by the efforts to convert.[30] The most publicized incident involved McElroy's conversion in 1817 of a young student, John Swartout, the son of a prominent New York Republican, Samuel Swartout. The father, outraged over what he regarded as the manipulation of the boy's affections,[31] withdrew him from Georgetown. Unfortunately, McElroy subsequently financed the boy's secret return to the college, with Kohlmann's permission. Benedict Fenwick, who was then still rector, sent young Swartout back to his father in tears, as soon as he, Fenwick, discovered what had happened. In the next dozen years there would be only one student from New York enrolled at Georgetown. This abrupt diminution of the New York presence was probably a consequence of the economic depression in that city rather than an overt reaction to heavy-handed evangelization, but to the Anglo-American Jesuits it only confirmed, fairly or unfairly, that Kohlmann's leadership was a menace to both the college and the mission.[32]

In great part, this dissension was over the finances and goals of the North American Mission. Both McElroy and Kohlmann had for some time favored selling the plantations and investing the funds to build up capital so the Mission could concentrate its resources on additional colleges in the major cities. The "native" Jesuits, on the other hand, tended to regard the old estates as the soul of their mission; moreover, they distrusted banks. "[N]ever apply to them," Charles Neale advised the mission procurator in 1822, "without the greatest necessity such as the want of bread. . . ."[33] Kohlmann, they all remembered, had left the mission saddled with a debt of $10,000 in New York and a reputation for financial extravagance and indiscretion.[34] He seemed to be threatening to repeat the New York experience at Georgetown, where the "native" Jesuits perceived that "Continentals" like Kohlmann and his treasurer, John McElroy, were using funds erratically and excessively for such dubious purposes as the support of future novices. Many of these were recently arrived Irishmen, such as John Carney. McElroy had met Carney on a steamer in 1816 and then and there persuaded him to come to Georgetown to enroll as a free student "rather than to be a peddler."[35]

Charles Neale, whom Grassi had left as superior, wrote in frustration to the superior general in the early summer of 1818. He considered that Kohlmann's schemes and behavior were threatening the mission itself:[36]

[He] has thrown out on his own authority Father [Benedict] Fenwick and the mathematics Professor Wallace, most learned men. He has built a novitiate in Washington City and admitted at least 100 students besides the teachers and scholastics. He is so changable by nature that what he builds today tomorrow he will tear down: he alienates by his German customs Americans, so that there is a great danger . . . that the whole Society will perish here.

McElroy's later refusal in 1820 to open the financial books of the college to the directors only fed the worst suspicions of those in the Anglo-American "camp."[37] And when Kohlmann virtually forced the corporation directors to make him the financial agent, their fears grew all the more.

Presumably with Kohlmann's acquiescence, the archbishop of Baltimore, Ambrose Maréchal, had by this time assigned Baxter, Fenwick, and Wallace to parishes in Richmond and Charleston. Dismayed at the direction of affairs in the college, they had not resisted. But, early in 1819, even the archbishop began to be alarmed at the factionalism that was stripping the college of the core of its faculty. Charles Plowden reported these concerns of the archbishop to Grassi in Rome, "The evil, he says, is past remedy in America, and the Soc^ty, he thinks, must absolutely sink and fail in the United States, unless I immediately come to its relief."[38]

Peter Kenney, Special Visitor

The superior general in Russia, increasingly disturbed at the reports coming from America about the factional ethnic discord, sent an Irish Jesuit, Peter Kenney, as Special Visitor of the Society to Georgetown College and the Maryland Mission in 1819. Among his charges as Visitor, Kenney was to identify, if possible, those promising young men in the novitiate who could be sent for their pre-ordination studies to Italy where they could receive the proper spiritual and intellectual grounding necessary for future leadership.[39]

Peter Kenney (1779–1841) had entered the Society in Ireland in 1804 at the age of twenty-five but had had most of his formation in Italy. Back in Ireland after his ordination, he had served consecutively as rector of Maynooth and Clongowes Colleges, as well as superior of the Irish Mission. A man who appreciated both Continental and British cultures, Kenney was a wise choice for the delicate mission that Brzozowski entrusted to him as visitor. He arrived at Georgetown from New York by way of Annapolis in late September 1819, since he was forced to bypass Baltimore where yellow fever was raging, as it was in most of the coastal cities. Kenney quickly won the trust of both factions in the United States through his fairness, openness, and prudence. He saw quickly that both were to blame: the Anglo-American Jesuits for their undisciplined lifestyle and illegal desire to control their own finances through the Corporation, and the Continental Jesuits for their rigidity and imprudence.[40] Kohlmann, he concluded, pious and zealous as he was, was too incurably volatile to continue as superior or rector. "In small matters & in great," Kenney reported to Grassi, "he is of one opinion today & another tomorrow . . ."[41] The Visitor could not identify one Jesuit who had any confidence in him as a leader. And that lack of regard extended to the larger society. Kohlmann utterly lacked Grassi's talent for cultivating and promoting the public image of the institution. Moreover, his heart condition seemed to be worsening; he was not a well man. But there was no available alternate short of Kenney himself, or Grassi, whom Kenney urged the Superior General to send back, if at all possible. He had not found Giovanni Grassi's equal among the Jesuits in the States, nor did any other European Jesuit know the culture and language of the country as Grassi did.[42]

Kenney's experiences at Georgetown also soon confirmed in his mind the wisdom of the superior general's other charge: to select and send some promising young Americans to Italy for their higher studies. If the college was to have a proper faculty, Kenney quickly concluded, it could not count on additional foreign faculty for assistance, but rather had to get the best training for the most promising scholastics in the American mission.[43] Grassi, it will be recalled, had begun to advocate this policy even before he left for Rome; and he had taken with him one scholastic, James Neil, when he left in 1817. Aloysius Young followed a year later, also at Grassi's insistence.

In early June of 1820 Kenney sent six young men to Rome for further studies. These six—William McSherry, Thomas Mulledy, John Smith, Charles Constantine Pise, George Fenwick, and James Ryder—were, like Neil and Young, all alumni of the college who had entered the Society during Grassi's administration. They also had all made their novitiates under Kohlmann at White Marsh and Georgetown. In fact, Kohlmann, along with a group of faculty and students, had joyously accompanied them on June 6 by steamboat to Alexandria where, serenaded by the recently formed student band, the six boarded the schooner *America* and sailed for Cadiz.[44] Three months later they were at the Roman College, just in time for the election of the new superior general, Luigi Fortis, who, since the Society had been recently expelled from Russia, was the first general since the restoration to make his headquarters in the Eternal City.

For Georgetown's immediate future, Kenney had already attempted to reassemble Grassi's faculty. He had proposed the previous October (1819) to make Benedict Fenwick the rector-president with Baxter, Wallace, and Fenwick's brother, Enoch (then pastor of St. Peter's in Baltimore), as his principal faculty. Archbishop Maréchal was reluctant to allow any of them to be withdrawn from their ministries in Baltimore, Charleston, and Richmond, but Kenney tried to persuade him that the college needed all four. He assured Maréchal that their return to Georgetown could ensure that it would continue its crucial educational role of promoting "the good of Religion in this vastly extensive but deeply afflicted Mission."[45] "[I]f the College be not better supported," he wrote again bluntly to the archbishop, "it will sink and Y. Grace will consider, who it is that withholds the only devisable remedy."[46]

The Visitor thus managed in 1820 to get Baxter back from Richmond, but he was not successful in persuading Benedict Fenwick and James Wallace to return. So long as Anthony Kohlmann was superior, Fenwick continued to plead Charleston's pastoral needs as his excuse for not returning to the District. Kenney then recommended that Enoch Fenwick, Benedict's brother, be appointed rector in the summer of 1820. Shortly thereafter he had completed his visitation and returned to Europe to participate in the election of the new general.

A year later, Charles Neale replaced Anthony Kohlmann as superior. Neale then transferred McElroy to a parish in Southern Maryland. Benedict Fenwick thereupon returned to the college to become procurator in 1822. James Wallace never did return, despite Kenney's and Grassi's combined efforts.[47] Without permission from superiors, he had accepted an appointment in 1820 at Columbia College (later South Carolina College) to teach mathematics and natural philosophy, a post he held until 1834 when most of the faculty was let go because of plummeting enrollment. While at the Carolina college, he also occasionally contributed scientific articles to *The Southern Review*.[48] Dismissed from the Society in 1822, James Wallace remained in the ministry, serving steadfastly as a diocesan priest in John England's new bishopric of Charleston, South Carolina, until his death in 1851.

In addition to the return of Baxter and Fenwick to Georgetown, two outstanding Jesuit scholars also joined the faculty there in the 1821–22 academic year—Francis Dzierozynski (1779–1850), originally from Poland, and Thomas Levins (1789–1843), originally from Ireland. Dzierozynski had taught French, physics, music, philosophy, and mathematics at Jesuit colleges in St. Petersburg (Russia) and Mogilev (Belarus). After the Napoleonic Wars ended, he became a professor of theology at the college in Polock (Polish Russia).

Expelled with his brethren in 1820, Dzierozynski went on to Rome where within the year he was given a special assignment by the new superior general, Luigi Fortis. He was sent to the United States to help provide the spiritual and administrative leadership that seemed much needed there. To do that, Fortis appointed Dzierozynski the assistant to the mission superior, Charles Neale. In effect, he was the superior general's permanent representative in the United States.[49] That charge was substantially reinforced in 1823, when Fortis named Dzierozynski mission superior upon the death of Charles Neale. At Georgetown, besides serving as an administrator, he taught philosophy during his first years. A very gentle, prudent, and affable man, Dzierozynski quickly won favor with the students, who shortened his name to "Father Zero."[50] Because of his delicate official position, favor among his own came more slowly.

Thomas Levins was sent by Fortis to Georgetown about six months after Dzierozynski set out for the United States. "His talents are for mathematics, Natural Philosophy & English literature & every opportunity has been given him to cultivate them," Kenney wrote to John McElroy from Ireland in 1822. An alumnus of Jesuit colleges at Clongowes, Dublin, and Stonyhurst, Levins while still a Jesuit scholastic had gone on to the University of Edinburgh to study philosophy. "I am sure," Kenney added in his June letter, "that he will be docile & industrious & that he will sufficiently supply Mr. Wallace's place, tho he cannot arrive to his great name. It was with this view I imagine that he was sent to America."[51] At Georgetown Levins taught natural philosophy and mathematics, and also rapidly acquired a reputation in Washington as a scientist and mathematician. John Calhoun, then Secretary of War, came to regard him as the best mathematician in the country and said so to former President James Madison, who was by then rector of the University of Virginia.[52] Calhoun liked to go from his home in Georgetown to visit the campus in order to discuss philosophy with Dzierozynski and science with Levins.[53] In 1824 Levins was invited to serve as one of the examiners in mathematics at the United States Military Academy, then perhaps the premier school for mathematics and the sciences in the country.

While at Georgetown, Peter Kenney had begun a reform of the curriculum. The seven-year course of studies was retained, from Rudiments through Philosophy, and a formal distinction was introduced between the lower and higher schools. At least one of the faculty suggested that the names of the last four terms should be changed to freshman, sophomore, junior, and senior class, respectively, in accordance with American collegiate practice. However, the traditional Jesuit names endured for another seventy years at Georgetown.[54] Kenney proposed that Carroll's original concept be observed of having a teacher accompany a class through its entire course; but if it ever was adopted, this strategy was quickly abandoned. By 1823, Baxter had put in place the curriculum that he and his colleagues had championed against Kohlmann. And a new language, Spanish, was introduced as an elective at the end of the decade.

Columbian College and the Washington Seminary

Enoch Fenwick (1780–1827) was the first of several extremely reluctant rectors in the 1820s. "I am not much [of anything]," he replied apologetically to Kohlmann in August of 1820 when informed of his appointment.[55] Actually, he deeply resented his removal from Baltimore, where he was involved heart and soul in the construction of the cathedral, "and all this," he wrote the following month to Francis Neale when he was at last at Georgetown, "to take the direction of this College which has one foot in the grave of disgrace and the other beginning to sink."[56] A descendant of one of the original Catholic settlers of Maryland, he had come to Georgetown in 1793 with his brother Benedict from his father's estate in St. Mary's County. William DuBourg regarded him as the best scholar in the college in 1797, when he appointed him to teach Rudiments to the younger students in the lower school. In 1805 he had entered St. Mary's Seminary in Baltimore and a year later joined the first group to enter the Jesuit novitiate in Georgetown.

Enoch Fenwick officially served as president for a little more than four years (1820–25).[57] He became increasingly dejected at the declining enrollment and mounting debt. In the hard times that coincided with his presidency, he found it particularly distasteful to press parents to pay their sons' overdue board and tuition. Usually he exercised little leadership, allowing Roger Baxter, the prefect of studies (1819–24), to run the place as he pleased. Baxter had sometimes troubled superiors on both sides of the Atlantic. Enormously talented, the corpulent, free-spirited, satirical Baxter seemed little interested in intellectual or moral discipline. "Little order and a great deal of liberty," was one recently arrived Jesuit's judgment about his administration.[58] In fact, both Baxter and Fenwick frolicked as equals with the boys. And Baxter declared college holidays when the mood struck him. He scandalized many of his foreign brethren by his prodigious thirst for wine, by his frequent unaccompanied trips to the city, supposedly to visit a woman, and by his general republicanism.[59]

Diploma of Theodore Jenkins, who graduated in 1826 with an AB. (Georgetown University Archives)

By the spring of 1823 there were scarcely thirty boarders at the college, fewer than fifty students in all. Under Fenwick, the reputation of the college was clearly slipping, as even Francis Neale admitted. Lack of leadership coupled with too little discipline was probably one reason, although barely five years before "too much" had provoked loud complaints about discipline.[60] The continuing economic depression was certainly another, probably greater one. There was a third reason for the decline of enrollments from the District and elsewhere. Georgetown had to face the competition of two new schools in the area, Columbian College and the Washington Seminary. In 1821 the General Convention of the Baptists had moved its recently established Institution from Philadelphia to an area of the District just north of what were then the city's boundaries. This institution was granted a federal charter under the title of The Columbian College. By 1823 there were fifty-four students in attendance there, by 1826 nearly eighty.[61] Most of the students were indigent boys preparing for the ministry and were supported by their home congregations.[62]

Meanwhile in Washington City itself Anthony Kohlmann had begun a second school for the Society to operate. In 1815 ground had been broken by Grassi in the federal city for a novitiate building. However, by the time this F Street structure was completed Grassi had returned to Rome, so there was no use for it until George Ironside offered to take it over. A former Episcopal priest, Ironside had been converted to Catholicism by Benedict Fenwick while conducting a school in New York City.[63] Then he moved to Washington in 1817 and leased the empty building so he could open another school. However, when Kohlmann became superior a few months later, he reclaimed the building on F Street between Ninth and Tenth for the Society. This property sat unused until 1820. In October of that year, in accordance with Peter Kenney's plans, it opened under the name of the Washington Seminary as a house of studies for Jesuit scholastics, with Kohlmann as rector. A year later Kohlmann also began a secondary day school in it with the scholastics serving as teachers for the boys. By now he was convinced that boarding schools did not promote religion. Day schools would be cheaper, need fewer persons to staff them, and "religious discipline could be better preserved" with the students directly under the supervision of their parents. The Society, he suggested to the superior general, should concentrate on the lower levels of education in the United States.[64] But when the secondary school actually opened in September 1821, he explained to its Jesuit scholastics that such a concentration on the more elementary courses at the school was a temporary measure "till the return of the Roman Doctors enable us to have it erected into a Metropolitan university."[65]

As Georgetown's enrollment declined, the Seminary's increased. Seventy students were enrolled in classes at the Washington Seminary by the end of the first year; by 1825 there were one hundred and fifty of "all denominations."[66] To support the school Kohlmann sought a dispensation from the Society's prohibition of tuition charges. Ironside, who remained a staunch Jesuit friend, tried to explain why to Father General Fortis in 1825: "we are a proud and independent people, and by no means willing to admit the sincerity of those who neglect their own immediate interest. It is . . . a generally established principle here that he who charges nothing for education either has some sinister design, or is too incapable to bear public inspection."[67] In fact, Georgetown itself had continued to charge tuition, for boarders and day students alike, even after the school had been officially put in the charge of the reestablished Society. Kohlmann's subsequent formal request in 1827 raised the matter again with the superior general, who refused to grant a dispensation. The seminary subsequently closed that year, but the superior general's ruling also forced Georgetown to cease charging tuition. Fees for boarders (lodging only) were accordingly reduced from $175 to $150 annually; and those for day students were dropped even more—from $50 to $5 (and that only as an allowance for "fuel"). Dzierozynski, who as superior was responsible for the actual closing, announced in the local newspapers that any Washington Seminary student could transfer to Georgetown, and as a day student would not be charged any fees.[68] The result was an influx of twenty-five day students in 1828, more day students than had attended Georgetown College in the seven years since Kohlmann had opened his school, but most left within the academic year. This, needless to say, did not ease the financial strain for the college.

Georgetown Students in the 1820s

What few students there were in Georgetown from 1820 to 1828 (only 175 entered as new students), tended to be locals. Nearly three-quarters of these were from the District and Maryland; other southern states accounted for a fifth of the students; the northeastern states sent but six students until 1829 (see table 4.1, in appendix F). Only a twentieth (5%) of the student enrollment was foreign, including Joseph de Mareuil (**C** 1824–25). The son of the French Minister to the United States, he was forced to leave because of the abusive treatment he got from some of his fellow collegians, Louisianans whose "Jacobinical Principles" (according to Dubuisson) could not tolerate the presence of a royalist. More than half (55%) of the students were urbanites, many the sons of merchants and businessmen, such as Alexander (**C** 1820–28, AB) and Nicholas Dimitry (**C** 1828–33). They were the sons of a prosperous Greek merchant in New Orleans (the father had Americanized the name Demetrios). Alexander was the valedictorian of his class. His younger brother was later expelled in the riot of 1833. Over a third (35%) were related to or had family ties within the college. They included the two grandnephews of John

Charles James Faulkner (**C** 1815–22). He had a long and distinguished career in public service, first in the Old Dominion's House of Delegates, then in the U.S. House of Representatives, and finally in the diplomatic corps of the United States. (Photo by J.E.M. Glees. Georgetown University Archives)

Carroll, Thomas William Brent (**C** 1819–21) and Henry Johnson Brent (**C** 1821–22). Many students, including the Carroll kinsmen, went on from Georgetown to complete their studies for the bachelor's degree at other institutions. Even more of them simply left the college after a few years to begin their careers. For instance, Thomas George Pratt (**C** 1822), as an eighteen-year-old, left Georgetown after several months to take up the study of law. Pratt later became governor of Maryland (1844–47) and then served in the United States Senate (1849–57).

Nonetheless, a relatively high proportion of these students (14%) earned degrees. Indeed most who entered at the age of seventeen or older were graduated (the average age at graduation was nineteen). Those who finished at Georgetown were a more balanced group demographically than the entering student body in general. More than a third (40%) were local residents (Maryland and the District), approximately another third from the South (Virginia and Louisiana), and nearly a third from the Middle Atlantic area (New York and Pennsylvania). Of thirteen whose careers can be traced among the twenty-six graduates who entered between 1820 and 1828, five became doctors, four lawyers (with three active in politics and one in law), and two clergymen. Among the politicians were two Baltimoreans, Lewis William Jenkins (**C** 1815–22) and Solomon Hillen Jr. (**C** 1820–28). Both went into public service, Hillen becoming mayor of Baltimore in 1842. Charles James Faulkner (**C** 1815–22) of Virginia was another alumnus who became a highly regarded political figure. He served in the Old Dominion's House of Delegates where he unsuccessfully argued for the gradual abolition of slavery during the crucial debate over that "peculiar institution" in the 1831–32 session. He, unfortunately, is better known for his later role in the Virginia legislation that became the basis of that stringent amendment to the federal statute of 1793 that we know as the infamous Fugitive Slave Law of 1850. In the 1850s he himself was elected four times to the House of Representatives where he served until President Buchanan appointed him U.S. Minister to France.

Alexander Dimitry of New Orleans had a Renaissance-like career as editor, writer, educator, bureaucrat, and diplomat. Among the many positions he held was that of superintendent of education in Louisiana as well as U.S. Minister to Costa Rica and to Nicaragua. In the 1830s his short stories appeared in New York and Philadelphia journals; and by the 1850s he was acclaimed nationally as a distinguished scholar, linguist, and lecturer.

Meanwhile, as enrollments continued to decline at Georgetown, so too did the proportion of Catholics (down to 68% for the decade). A handful of them (4%) went on to study for the priesthood: Samuel Mulledy (**C** 1829–31), the younger brother of Thomas; Thomas Lilly (**C** 1819–27); George Fenwick (**C** 1822–32, AB), the nephew of Benedict, Enoch, and George); James A. Ward (**C** 1829–32); and Samuel Barber (**C** 1822–30, AB). Barber was the son of Jerushe Booth and Virgil Horace Barber, New Englanders and converts who had both entered religious life in 1822, she as a Visitandine, he as a Jesuit. They brought their children with them, including eight-year-old Samuel, into the convent and monastery (Jesuit novitiate), respectively. He, Samuel, followed his father into the Society eight years later.

Still No "Constellation" Supporting the College

By 1825 the two Fenwicks, as well as Baxter, Levins, and Marshall, were all gone from the college. "Instead of a Constellation of Fathers, supporting a College, which might lead millions to Catholicity," George Ironside complained to the father general, "we have a few unfledged bodys, capable only of taking charge of the lowest classes, and about 30 scholars, the greater part of whom are under 12 years of age."[69] The catalyst for the spectacular downturn had been the reports of a miraculous cure in 1824 in which Kohlmann and Dubuisson had played leading roles. Kohlmann, while rector of the Washington Seminary, had befriended a widow, Ann Carbery Mattingly, the sister of the mayor of Washington, who had long suffered from what had been diagnosed as breast cancer and related ailments. When Mrs. Mattingly's condition worsened alarmingly in the late winter of 1824, Kohlmann and Dubuisson invoked the healing powers of a popular priest in Germany. He, Prince Alexander Leopold Hohenlohe, had acquired a considerable reputation and a wide following in Europe for his apparent ability to cure persons who united with him in prayer. On the appointed day, March 10, 1824, Dubuisson, then an assistant pastor in Mattingly's parish, St. Patrick's, brought communion to the gravely ill widow who was living in her brother's home at the time. Within minutes of receiving the host, she stood up and claimed she felt completely well. All symptoms of her illness, including the breast tumor, had vanished.

The cure became a sensation in the city and beyond, the news even reaching Europe. Thousands flocked to Mayor Carberry's home to see the reports confirmed by Mrs. Mattingly herself. Kohlmann, Dubuisson, and their clerical associates, largely Jesuit and Sulpician emigrés, promoted the cure as a powerful proof of the superior claim of Catholicism to the mantle of Christianity. Not for nothing, they remarked, had this cure occurred to such a well-known person "in the capital of America, and in sight of our national councils."[70]

Rev.ᵈ Thos. C. Levins.

Pastor of St. Patrick's Cathedral New York.

The Anglo-American Jesuits were skeptical about the miracle and repelled as well by the way that Kohlmann and others were aggressively using it to prosyletize. All the tensions between the two groups tended to find expression in their opposing views of the Mattingly cure. A month after the event a letter appeared in the *National Intelligencer* that satirized Kohlmann for his overwrought reports about the miracle and stressed that he was in no way associated with Georgetown College. It implied, moreover, that Kohlmann had been responsible at Georgetown for replacing "men of varied and solid learning" with pious incompetents.[71]

Suspicion immediately focused on Levins as the author of the anonymous April letter. Dzierozynski, the regional superior, for some time already had been contemplating sending Levins and Baxter back to Europe for their scandalous behavior and nonconformist views. Indeed he had temporarily transferred Baxter south to St. Inigoes, the Jesuit plantation in the remotest part of Maryland. When Dzierozynski confronted Levins and Enoch Fenwick (Levins's superior) about the letter, both refused to respond to his questions. Then in October of 1824, a series of unsigned but scathing articles about the miracle and about the "ignorant and shallow men, petulant & snarling old women" promoting it appeared in another Washington newspaper.[72] When Dzierozynski got the same silent response from Levins about these articles, he accelerated his efforts to deport both Levins and Baxter. Baxter left in October of 1824; Levins departed from Georgetown for New York. Three months later he was dismissed from the Society by Father General Fortis.[73]

Enoch Fenwick, following his April encounter with Dzierozynski, took himself off to St. Thomas Manor and refused to return even though he was still president and rector of Georgetown. Eight months later Dzierozynski, in desperation, appointed Enoch's brother, Benedict, to serve as vice-rector and president.[74] Dzierozynski regarded Benedict Fenwick as "a man of great wisdom, of good heart, and outstanding prudence."[75] But Fenwick's second term as president was hardly any longer than his first. That same summer he was named Bishop of Boston and went immediately to his new duties. Dzierozynski, left with virtually no alternatives, next appointed Stephen Dubuisson to serve as vice-rector in September of 1825. (Kohlmann himself had been called to Rome by Pope Leo XII a month after the Mattingly cure to teach dogma at the Roman College.)

Stephen Dubuisson (1786–1864) was a double emigré, having been born in Saint-Domingue in the West Indies and reared there and in France. During the Napoleonic Wars he served first in the receiver general's office in Germany, then in Paris as comptroller for the Crown in 1814. In Paris he felt an overwhelming call to the religious life but family needs forced him to defer his vocation. "My first idea," he later recalled, "was to bury myself in a Trappist Monastery," but his confessor had convinced him that in such a revolutionary age the Church could not afford pure contemplatives.[76] Napoleon's

Thomas Levins (1789–1843). Irish emigré and professor of science and mathematics at the College. Despite his dismissal from the Society in 1825, the scholarly Levins eventually bequeathed his library to Georgetown. (Lithograph from a print made by R. Bowen when Levins was rector of St. Patrick's Cathedral in New York City. Georgetown University Archives)

first abdication and exile to Elba in 1814 gave Dubuisson the opportunity to act on his resolve to join the Society of Jesus in America where, so a visiting American bishop told him, there were great needs and even greater opportunities for religion. Finally, he was able to set out from Paris for Georgetown, and, like the Xavier of legend, he did so without taking leave of his family. And, as he later explained to the Father General, "without anyone even having the least idea of my plan."[77]

Highly sensitive and somewhat neurotic, Dubuisson struggled unceasingly to fit into religious life in America. The monastic urge remained strong in him. But much about America, from its republicanism to its egalitarianism, repelled him. Of all his fears, the prospect of having to assume a position of authority was the very worst. Twice within his first three years at Georgetown, while still a scholastic, he was made prefect of studies, which meant that he was responsible for student discipline. On the first occasion he nearly had a breakdown; the second time around, the students nearly broke him since they made plans to assault him. Nevertheless, once ordained, the pious and zealous Dubuisson had found his metier in the pastoral life of Washington and Georgetown. The thought of becoming president of Georgetown petrified him. He felt that he lacked the necessary education, and, as he confided earlier to Father Fortis, he felt too that his monarchical views toward authority, both secular and sacred, made him *"spiritually hors de moi"* as a college president in the United States.[78]

In any case, Dubuisson was president for barely seven months. Practically as soon as he was appointed, he began pleading with the superior to allow him to go to Rome to appeal personally to the general to send home an American to be president of Georgetown. This reaction was not merely the confirmation of his worst fears. His reputation as prefect of studies haunted him with both students and parents. Eventually some began to say openly that he ought to resign.[79] "[I]n the morning," Dzierozynski wrote Fortis in April 1826, "I am not certain that by evening I will still have a Rector."[80] Finally, the superior sent him down to St. Thomas Manor to reconsider his request for a transfer, but in early May Dubuisson informed the superior that he had considered and that he still had to go back to Rome. With Dzierozynski's wary blessing, he departed in June. On the way he preached an eight-day retreat in a Baltimore church and drew huge, appreciative crowds who responded to his words in a way that would have confounded his fault-finding students and impatient colleagues at Georgetown.[81] All too obviously, he was a saintly man who was simply out of his element as a professor, and even more as a college president.

In his place Dzierozynski next appointed William Feiner, a German Jesuit who had been sent to the States in 1822. The thirty-three-year-old Feiner was a virtuous religious and an experienced professor, but he had tuberculosis. As Peter Kenney had remarked when he heard of Feiner's transfer to America, "He is very good & very amiable and may be a great professor of Logic, but . . . he will not long profess any thing in this world!"[82] Moreover, after four years in the Maryland Mission neither his health nor his English had improved substantially. To the Americans that appointment was the ultimate confirmation of European prejudice—to prefer a dying foreigner who could barely write English as president of the college. Whom Dzierozynski could have chosen besides Feiner they did not say, since Feiner was the only Jesuit priest then connected with the college.[83] As he wrote (in Latin) to the Superior General, "I am . . . simultaneously Rector, Minister, Procurator and spiritual Father. I fill these offices as much as I am able."[84] In reality, Feiner was mainly occupied as pastor president, concentrating on the parish of Holy Trinity and the religious discipline of the Jesuit scholastics and students within the college. When his wasting sickness made it impossible for him to continue in the late winter of 1829 (he was dead by June), Dzierozynski turned to yet another Jesuit emigré, William Beschter, pastor of a German church in Baltimore, and the author of the anti-American sentiments expressed in a letter to the Father General three years earlier.

The Acquisition of a Campus

In one respect the dozen years that ended in 1829 marked a period of unique growth for Georgetown College. Most of its campus land was acquired during that time. Since the initial few acres had been obtained for the original buildings, Francis Neale had systematically purchased contiguous lots for the institution from 1798 through 1825. The largest acquisition was made in 1818 when Joseph West, a Montgomery County farmer who had entered the Society as a lay brother, used the proceeds from the sale of his own property to purchase land for a farm directly north and west of the original college grounds. Then, while he was digging irrigation ditches for the farm, West also laid out graceful, connecting paths which in time he terraced and landscaped with trees. Thus were born the famed "College Walks," which virtually encircled the campus for more than forty years. Indeed, some sections of them were to survive well into the next century.[85] In 1828 Francis Dzierozynski purchased seventy-six acres of land on Hickory Hill, adjacent to the northern rim of the campus (the present Reservoir Road). That acreage was intended to augment crop production at the farm.[86]

Another change during the period concerned the legal control of the school. In the course of a protracted dispute between the Maryland Jesuits and Archbishop Maréchal over the Jesuit property in Southern Maryland and the Eastern Shore (the archbishop laid claim to these lands, asserting that legal title devolved to him as the local head of the Roman Catholic Church), the provincial superior, Francis Dzierozynski, under orders from

Wintertime approach to the College Walks designed by Brother West. They graced the campus for more than a century, until the land had to be used for buildings. (Georgetown University Archives)

the general, used the occasion to end the autonomy of the corporation that had been created in 1794 to preserve the property.[87] In 1825 three trustees (Francis Neale, Benedict Fenwick, and Peter Epinette) signed a statement declaring that they held the property solely as a trust for the Society of Jesus and would administer it only with the approval of the superior general. Thereafter the corporation, to which Georgetown legally belonged, was for all intents and purposes controlled by the Jesuit provincial superior.

A New Beginning

Enrollment continued to plummet in the late 1820s. By the fall of 1827 there were barely a score of boarders, about sixty students overall. Opinions varied about the cause of the decline. The Europeans blamed it on the reputation of lax discipline and loose morals that was the legacy of the Anglo-Americans. "It was plain," Dubuisson had written from Rome in the spring of 1827, "that the want of piety among the boys, the love of dressing, the rage of going out, the ruinous habit of visiting confectioners' shops, and too great liberty in reading, have had a large share in producing the evil [at the College] . . . ."[88] The Anglo-Americans laid it squarely at the doorstep of the Continentals who had neither the health nor vision nor language skills to head an American college. Many laymen, they found, refused to entrust their sons to a man who could not write English. The naming of Beschter, one subsequently reported in 1829, had "amazed everyone. Beschter can speak in no language [and] knows very little about a college. . . ."[89] Of the twenty-five students who left the college in 1827, twenty-two were Catholics, mostly from Maryland and Louisiana, traditional centers of Catholic support for the college. This was the immediate occasion for Richard McSherry's letter of complaint to his Jesuit brother about the rapidly deteriorating state of the college. McSherry explained to his brother in November of 1828:

I have deferred sending James [his son] away to school . . . till your return hoping that G. Town college would revive, but believe I will have to send him to Emmitsburg. It appears to me that the Jesuits have managed their affairs very badly in this country, what it is owing to I cannot tell, but think it very bad policy to place foreigners as superiors who know nothing of the country or its institutions.[90]

McSherry's nativistic judgment about the leadership of foreign Jesuits in America was too sweeping. In his five years in America, Giovanni Grassi, very much an Italian, had provided unprecedentedly effective leadership both of the Maryland Province in general and Georgetown College in particular. Francis Dzierozynski, a Pole, in the long run, also had proved a wise leader. Admittedly, the foreign presidents of Georgetown in that decade— Kohlmann, Dubuisson, Feiner, Beschter—left a rather sorry administrative record. But the record of the one American Jesuit president, Enoch Fenwick (discounting his brother's fleeting second term as president), was no better. In truth, ethnically generated fratricidal strife took a deep toll on the college, leaving it virtually moribund by the end of the decade.

William McSherry and four other American Jesuits had completed their studies and been ordained by 1825, but they were detained in Italy, partly because the North American Mission lacked the money for their return passage and partly because the superior general was reluctant to send them

Washington City seen from Georgetown in the 1830s. (Drawing by J. Smith, engraving by J. B. Neagle, 1832. Georgetown University Archives)

back until he was satisfied that the Society in the United States had been sufficiently reformed.[91] Finally in October 1827 Dzierozynski managed to forward $1,200 to cover their traveling expensess. So the first three—William McSherry, Thomas Mulledy, and Aloysius Young—were able to return to Georgetown in December 1828. A year later James Ryder and George Fenwick (third of the Fenwick brothers) followed, sent by the recently elected superior general, the forty-three-year-old Dutchman, Jan Root-

haan. The mantle was passing to them, Kohlmann told McSherry, now twenty-eight, as he and his two companions embarked for the States.[92] By the beginning of the 1829–30 academic year Mulledy was installed as the seventeenth president of Georgetown, and McSherry as the vice president, with Fenwick, Ryder, and Young appointed professors. The direction of the college was now completely in the hands of this first generation of Roman-trained American Jesuits. Less than a decade after the institutional promise engendered by one faculty cadre had ended in frustration and acrimony, a new, energetic one promised to be and to do what would finally set the college on a course that would convert Carroll's vision into reality.

"Georgetown in 1830." (Black & white photograph of painting by James Simpson. Georgetown University Art Collection)

PART TWO

FROM ACADEMY
TO COLLEGE, 1830–60

59.

CHAPTER 5

Building a College and More, 1829–49

The College, thanks to heaven, grows beyond our anticipation. . . . There is every probability of an even greater increase. . . . Some say we lack the resources but I believe that with greater trust in God, and with better management of those we have we can build. . . . While it is a university [in law], it is not one in actuality . . . because we lack suitable professors.

JAMES RYDER to JAN ROOTHAAN
to Rome from Georgetown, January 29, 1831

An Irish American Troika

Over the next two decades, Giovanni Grassi's long-range project for developing a cadre of Roman-trained Americans that could make Georgetown College into a thriving institution of higher education within the Jesuit tradition seemed on the way to being realized. Three of the five young priests who returned home from Rome in 1828–29, Thomas Mulledy, William McSherry, and James Ryder, occupied the president's office for all but a few months of the twenty-two years between 1829 and 1851. They had come back with ambitious plans—plans that focused on making the college more than the academy that in large part it still was (see table 5.1 in appendix F). They wanted Georgetown to be an elite establishment with a large enrollment and more than adequate facilities. They wanted the college to be in reality the

Constructed in 1810, this small brick building housed Georgetown's shoe shop, store, and bakery. (Photograph probably taken several decades before it was razed in 1908. Georgetown University Archives)

university it was in law, with the three higher schools devoted to science, medicine, and legal education, respectively. They envisioned an ample endowment to make all this possible. Finally, they wanted Georgetown at the center of a network linking Jesuit colleges throughout the eastern United States. By the end of the 1840s, despite inevitable crises and persistent problems, they had taken important steps towards the fulfillment of most of these goals.

These three, all first- or-second generation Irish Americans, were also all alumni of the college who had entered the Society in 1815 and had received their early formation from Anthony Kohlmann, then the novice master. The oldest, Thomas Mulledy (1794–1860), was one of the sons of a poor immigrant farmer in Hampshire County, western Virginia.[1] Both Thomas and his younger brother, Samuel, appear to have paid their own way through Georgetown, with the records showing that Samuel paid some of his fees in kind—by giving the college two horses. Both had taught at the local academy in Romney near their home (in what is now West Virginia) before going to Georgetown at the relatively old ages of nineteen and eighteen, respectively.[2] Thomas was a handsome man of imposing physique and charming manner. As a scholastic he had been named first prefect of discipline of the college after the student rebellion against the hapless Dubuisson in 1818. Two years later he was among those chosen by Peter Kenney to study in Rome, even though Anthony Kohlmann found him too proud and quick-tempered, a reputation that Mulledy himself reinforced in Rome.[3] Yet, for all his compelling physical presence, he dreaded speaking in public. During his first year in Rome he balked at giving a public recitation by heart, an act of defiance that was etched deeply in the "institutional" memory of the Jesuit hierarchy.[4] He also gained notoriety for his sometimes contentious defense of American institutions and values. Even in a poem written in honor of Luigi Fortis's election as superior general in 1820, Mulledy could not resist contrasting the republican liberty that America offered the Society with the suppression that the Jesuits had experienced under *l'ancien régime:*

She who ne'er felt the tyrant's galling rod,
Or snuff'd the poison of a Regal Breath;
Joyful accepts th' anointed of her God;
And twines around his brow the freeman's wreath.[5]

During his stay in Europe, Thomas Mulledy began to feel a call to "consecrate his energies and life" to the Indian missions in the American west. The second time that he attempted to get the superior general to overrule the local superior's denial of his request to be sent to Missouri, Mulledy was told that it was vitally important that he, as well as the other returning Jesuits, be at the center of the Society's work in America, not on its fringes.[6] Soon thereafter he was appointed prefect of studies and teacher of mathematics and philosophy at Georgetown. In September 1829, less than a year later, at the age of thirty-five, he was named president of the college for the first of two terms (1829–37, 1845–48).

William McSherry (1799–1839) was also the son of an Irish emigré, Richard McSherry, who had settled first in the West Indies and then in western Virginia. McSherry and his twin, having accumulated considerable wealth as merchants in Jamaica, left that island in the 1780s for the new republic. Richard was prosperous enough by the time he immigrated to the United States to be wearing powdered hair, lace ruffles, and silver knee buckles. He established himself as a planter at "Retirement," a large estate on the northern tip of the Shenandoah Valley in Berkeley (later Jefferson) County, Virginia. He and his wife, Anastasia, eventually had nine children and more than a score of slaves.[7]

In 1813 William, namesake of their father's twin, followed his older brother, Richard, across the Blue Ridge Mountains to Georgetown College (a third brother, James, born in 1814, entered Georgetown in 1829). In February 1815, six months before he turned sixteen, William entered the Jesuit novitiate (as would James in 1833 for a short period before returning to Virginia to practice law in Martinsburg). Over six feet tall, the lanky William McSherry was an amiable and retiring youth who easily caught the eye of superiors, despite modest intellectual gifts and an undistinguished academic record. After his ordination at Rome, he served for two years (1826–28) in the Jesuit College at Turin under Jan Roothaan, soon-to-be superior general of the Society. When he returned to Georgetown in 1828 he was appointed to teach the students in First and Second Humanities. He served as president for one academic year only (1838–39). Nevertheless, William McSherry was a major figure in shaping the college all throughout the 1830s.

The third of the trio, James Ryder (1800–1860), had been brought to the United States as a young boy by his widowed mother. He entered the Society after two years at Georgetown. The most brilliant of the band that was sent to Rome in 1820, Ryder was appointed to teach theology and sacred scripture at the University of Spoleto after his ordination in 1824. There he became a close friend of Archbishop Giovanni Ferretti, later Pope Pius IX. In 1829 Ryder was allowed to return to America, along with Stephen Dubuisson and George Fenwick. At Georgetown he became professor of philosophy and theology for the Jesuit scholastics and, like Thomas Mulledy, James Ryder eventually served two terms as president (1840–45, 1848–51).

Thomas Mulledy, President

During a tour of South Atlantic cities and towns in 1833, Henry Barnard, a New Englander and a recent Yale graduate, visited Georgetown College where he was met by "a jolly faced, big bellied man dressed in a cassock . . . who proved to be the President." Indeed, President Thomas Mulledy was eager to

Thomas Mulledy, SJ
(1794–1860). Trained in
Rome and twice president
of Georgetown, he always
cherished the wearing of
the "freeman's wreath" in
America. (Photograph from
an 1840s daguerreotype.
Georgetown University Archives)

show Barnard his institution—library, chapel, museum, campus—and the visitor was duly impressed. "'[W]ere it not for its Catholicism," he later wrote, "[it] would be a very eligible situation for a youth from 12 to 17. The situation of the college is delightful, I can't imagine any thing finer."[8] Mulledy was, needless to say, a very enthusiastic and effective promoter of the college. As James Ryder had explained three years earlier to Jan Roothaan, the newly elected superior general, in America the president of a Jesuit college needed to have "the virtue of a monk, the shrewdness of a man of affairs and the graciousness of a gentleman." And, above all he needed to be a salesman and Mulledy was "a marvelous salesman."[9]

Within a few months of becoming president in September 1829, Mulledy had tripled the number of boarders in the college—from twenty to sixty. "It is an almost unique occurrence," Stephen Dubuisson, as a former president, observed at the end of 1830. "In less than 6 months, we have grown from 30 to more than 100."[10] Dubuisson, who had suggested that Mulledy replace him in 1826, was amazed as early as April 1830 to see how quickly Mulledy had been able to restore Georgetown's reputation. At that time, in a letter to the father general, Dubuisson remarked on Mulledy's peculiar charm, which, he concluded, worked with both students and the general public.[11]

Under Mulledy the college became a magnet for everyone from presidents to Indian chiefs. Congressmen and senators were regular visitors. Andrew Jackson, then in his first year in the White House, enrolled his ward in 1829; his secretary of state, Martin Van Buren, sent his son. For President Jackson's second inauguration in 1833 the students began the practice of marching in their blue uniforms to the Capitol for the ceremonies. During Mulledy's first year in office the college began the tradition of grand celebrations of the two high feastdays of the republic, Washington's Birthday and Independence Day. Fireworks, cannon salutes, speeches, music, and a banquet were the staples of each celebration. These "patriot" days at Georgetown were usually attended by numerous congressmen, administration officials, generals, and eminent citizens, such as George Washington Custis (the founding father's adopted son) and Daniel Carroll, a framer of the Constitution and the archbishop's brother.

In his first year, President Mulledy was energy personified, not only expanding the enrollment by unprecedented gains but creating a new library, a new museum, and a new chapel. "Nothing escapes his hands," Francis Dzierozynski reported in the spring of 1831 to Rome. "The college is flourishing."[12] By the fall of 1830 there were 161 students in the college, of whom

102 were boarders. The number of non-Catholics would have certainly sur-prised Barnard (60, more than half of them boarders). Indeed, of all the students enrolled in 1830, non-Catholics accounted for nearly half (47.8%); five years before they had been scarcely more than a quarter (26%) of the total. This considerable increase in non-Catholic enrollments was largely due to the great influx of day students consequent on the closing of the Washing-ton Seminary and the elimination of tuition in 1827. During 1830 alone, approximately 110 day students were enrolled at the college, about 70 of them non-Catholics. That was a slightly larger proportion (64%) than the estimated 4,500 non-Catholics residing in the town of Georgetown itself.[13]

Because they were predominantly Protestant and of "slender means," Mulledy was determined to drop day students. "I know well," he wrote Roothaan before he was named president, "that according to the [Jesuit] institute we ought to teach for free, but in this country we are not endowed as in Europe and we can not live without a decent salary."[14] If they were not to be allowed to charge tuition, Mulledy felt, they should at least be able to exclude day students who neither studied religion nor felt its influence through the Mass and other exercises in which the boarders, both Catholic and Protestant, were required to take part. But the day students' greatest defect, Mulledy implied, was not one of creed but of class. So long as the day students remained, he warned, the potential for increasing the number of boarders would be very limited, since "many parents do not wish to send their sons to a college where they are forced to mix with the lowest rabble." He saw the day students simply as a bad influence on the boarders and a constant source of disorder.[15]

Actually the day students were, for the most part, segregated from the boarders in the classrooms. Day students studied virtually no Latin (an hour and a half a week); most of their class time was spent on grammar and math-ematics.[16] They were certainly a more transient group than boarders as well. Nearly three-quarters of these day students stayed less than a year, and vir-tually none went on to study for the priesthood. But fewer day students than boarders were in fact expelled during this period.[17] Nonetheless, the issue quickly became a point of contention between the newly returned American Jesuits and the "Continental" Jesuits at the college. Ryder, McSherry, and Fenwick all supported Mulledy, although the well-connected George Fen-wick did not think the presence of the less affluent day students kept many well-heeled boarders away. Moreover, Beschter and Dzierozynski pointed out that some of the day students were sons of prominent Washingtonians, including the mayor of the city, a bank president, an editor, and the widow of the Emperor of Mexico![18] Admitting day students, most of them Protes-tants, was, according to the defenders of the policy, also an effective way of lessening prejudice against Catholics and promoting conversions.[19] And the open admissions had obviously not deterred President Andrew Jackson and Secretary of State Martin Van Buren from enrolling their sons as boarders in the college. Dzierozynski added that the president of the United States had said publicly "more than once . . . that he *did not know a more honest and disciplined College in America than Georgetown.*"[20] Indeed, the former superior pleaded that the Society must preserve its tradition of educating both rich and poor alike according to their promise and not according to their ability to pay.[21]

Superior General Roothaan assured Dzierozynski that he would not allow Mulledy to make Georgetown exclusively a boarding college.[22] In any case, this goal was only a minor part of the American vision for the province. For the sake of the college they wanted to charge the boarders tuition, partly to provide badly needed facilities—an infirmary and a student center. None had been added for thirty-five years. They also wanted to fully utilize the charter they had from the Congress so as to make the institution a real university. "I am persuaded," Ryder told Roothaan, "that the honor of the Society and the good of religion in this area would be more efficaciously provided for if we made Georgetown College an integral part of a comprehensive university with chairs of Chemistry, Medicine, and Law" so that the students would no longer leave to complete their studies elsewhere, as was then the common practice.[23] They were eager to approve a petition from a prominent doctor to begin a medical school in the city under the auspices of the college. "The school of medicine," Mulledy explained to Roothaan in January of 1830, "would be on a site nearby but apart from the College. Four other professors would unite with this individual [the doctor] to form a competent faculty. I believe this would much aid the college—we would gain many friends."[24] In addition Mulledy was petitioning Rome to grant Georgetown a pontifical charter so that it could award appropriate degrees to Jesuit scholastics or other clerics completing courses of study in theology or canon law, a power that St. Mary's College in Baltimore already possessed.[25]

Beyond expanding the college into a university, Mulledy, Ryder, and McSherry were committed to fundamental changes that would enable the Society in the eastern United States to become a major force in higher education. In their opinion, the key to this development was the abandonment of the Society's plantations that were scattered throughout Southern Maryland and the Eastern Shore. The financial support of the Jesuit ministries in America had been based on those properties since the seventeenth century. But influenced by Anthony Kohlmann's views, the trio was convinced that a slave-based economy could not support anything, whether it be churches or colleges. Instead they saw any income devoured by the costly upkeep and care required for the nearly four hundred slaves. They also contended that until the Society was able to liberate itself from responsibility for the farms and the mission churches attached to the plantations, it would never be able to thoroughly develop colleges and shift its resources to the cities where the future obviously lay. "We cannot have both flourishing colleges and flourishing missions," Mulledy warned.[26] He and his fellow Jesuits aimed to sell both the land and the slaves so the Society could invest the money gained in banks. That in turn would provide capital for the development of Georgetown and other colleges, an idea that Kohlmann had elaborated on nearly a decade before.[27]

The "Continental" Jesuits in Maryland, as well as the older American Jesuits, were in general scandalized by the trio's "grand plans." The plantations, Dzierozynski continued to argue, constituted "a perpetual good" which could not simply be abandoned like an old shirt. The black folk residing on them were not an economic investment, but "children whose care and well-being has been given to us by God."[28] Other Europeans criticized the young president's impulsive and brusque manner, his intolerance of opposition, and the perceived neglect of religious discipline in the college. Thus, within two years of the Americans' return, Rome felt the conflict serious enough to order Peter Kenney back to America as an official visitor once more in 1830.

The Second Kenney Mission

In appointing Kenney the superior of the Maryland Mission and Special Visitor, Roothaan charged him with ascertaining to what extent, if any, the day students were undermining the success of the boarding enrollments at Georgetown. Did "the better families" in America really have an invincible prejudice about free schools? He also wanted him to make a complete examination of the living conditions and financial viability of the plantations. Was it true that the slaves lived virtually as animals because the estates could not support them adequately? If this was the case, the Visitor was to determine whether or not there was both a moral and a financial necessity to sell off the plantations along with their slaves, "and use the revenue for other things."[29]

James Ryder had been importuning Roothaan to send Kenney to America as superior from the time he had returned to Georgetown in 1829. The Americans, of course, expected that Kenney would be very supportive of their position. About their superior general, however, they were less certain. Indeed, in his choice of the consultors assigned to Kenney, the Americans could take little encouragement.[30] Mulledy was the only American among them. The other three were continental Europeans, including Dzierozynski, Dubuisson, and Fidèle de Grivel who was sent by Roothaan to the United States from Stonyhurst with Kenney. And, in fact, Roothaan was now highly suspicious of the Americans' independence, especially Mulledy's. "Keep an eye on this new rector," he warned Dzierozynski in May of 1830, "let him not do everything as he pleases. . . ."[31]

Kenney himself, now fifty-two, was reluctant to undertake such a mission. "I hoped the good news which has reached me of the mending prospects of Georgetown & the increase of number might have caused him [the General] to believe that was not necessary," he wrote John McElroy as he prepared to sail from Liverpool in September of 1830.[32] What he found at the college two months later convinced him that it was in good hands. Mulledy was a dynamic rector who was attracting a rapidly growing number of well-disciplined students. Under his management the college debts had "been nearly wiped out." "I know his defects," he wrote Roothaan, but he reckoned them to be the average ones of human weakness. If anything, Peter Kenney judged that being president seemed to have tempered the "impetuous ardor and excessive love of country" that had made Thomas Mulledy conspicuous in Rome.[33]

Despite the superior general's earlier injunction against the exclusion of day students, Mulledy was able to get the support of Kenney as well as all his consultors, except Dzierozynski, in restricting enrollment to boarders and half-boarders (those who took their meals at the college while living at home), beginning with the 1831–32 school year. A "veritably diabolical book" which circulated among the boarding students but traced to some day students helped to carry the argument for exclusion as did "a virtual general battle" of stonethrowing between boarders and day students in early 1831. Mulledy pressed these points along with a lack of teachers (two lay teachers had to be hired that year for the middle and lower classes), the swelling number of boarders, and parental opposition to day students in justifying the change to Roothaan.[34] Dzierozynski complained bitterly to the superior general that the decision had been made "on grounds which a child could refute," but the decision held.[35] For the next decade day students were restricted to half-boarders, of whom more than half were Catholic (56.4%).

The impact of the decision upon the non-Catholic presence in the student body was dramatic. A year later the number of Protestants in the college had been halved, from sixty to thirty.[36] By the middle of the 1830s, non-Catholics represented scarcely a third of the students, a trend that continued through the 1840s. By 1850 non-Catholics were less than a quarter (24%) of those enrolled, the lowest figure since the 1820s.[37]

Kenney also supported the resumption of the practice of charging tuition (on the grounds that this had long been a privilege extended to the schools conducted by the English Jesuits and only recently withdrawn from them by the former superior general). John McElroy had by that time begun a day college in Frederick (Maryland) and the potential was there for additional colleges in other cities. Already in 1830 Roothaan had permitted the American Jesuits to accept stipends for their religious services to meet their financial needs.[38] A formal request for dispensation from the ban on tuition went to Rome in 1832, and the petition was granted the following year. Even though the exemption permitting tuition charges was ostensibly limited to day students (St. Louis College in Missouri had made the same request at this time), Mulledy quickly utilized it to increase the fees for all Georgetown students. Those for boarders increased sharply from $150 to $200 in 1833; those for half-boarders went from $65 to $90.[39] When day students were readmitted in 1839 (with Mulledy no longer president), their tuition was set at $50, effectively excluding poorer local students who had previously not paid anything.

In 1833 Georgetown College was also granted a pontifical charter authorizing it to award theological degrees—the result of Mulledy's persistent lobbying of Rome. Since the official revival of the Society in America in 1806, Georgetown had been providing a special curriculum in philosophy and theology for the Jesuit scholastics, in effect, conducting a school of divinity. Consequently, as early as 1830 Mulledy had argued that a pontifical degree was absolutely necessary for the intellectual formation of the Jesuit scholastics as well as secular priests.[40] Not by chance, one of Mulledy's old Roman associates, Charles Constantine Pise, then a diocesan priest in Baltimore, petitioned Rome in 1831 for just such a degree from Georgetown in recognition of his theological studies there as a Jesuit scholastic.[41] However, even after it was granted, Kenney apparently had some doubts that Georgetown really needed this charter. He admonished Mulledy to use great prudence in awarding degrees under it. Too many institutions, the Visitor found, even Jesuit ones, made a mockery of their authority by giving degrees to unqualified persons, such as those students at the Jesuit college at St. Louis who could earn bachelor's and even master's degrees without any knowledge of Latin or Greek. The American Jesuits, he feared, would be seen as contributing more than their share to "a superficial system of education. . . ."[42] But Kenney's fears for Georgetown were pointless since the college awarded few, if any, pontifical degrees over the next thirty years.

Kenney was also charged by Roothaan with the task of judging whether Georgetown should sponsor a medical faculty.[43] There is no surviving report of the Visitor's views on the subject, but nothing more was heard about a medical school for the next two decades. Such professional education was foreign to the Society's history, and Jan Roothaan, for one, was skeptical about the prospects of changing this tradition. The medical schools he knew in Europe, he told Mulledy in the spring of 1830, were very "materialistic."[44]

On the matter of the plantations, Rome opted for the status quo. Before Kenney had even completed his investigation of the estates, the superior general, heeding the warnings of Dzierozynski and Dubuisson, decided in 1831 that any radical change regarding them would be imprudent.[45]

A year later Kenney concluded his mission and returned to Ireland. At the beginning of 1833, Father General Roothaan, citing the progress made by Jesuits in America, particularly in developing Georgetown College, formally raised the Maryland Mission to the level of a province of the Society of Jesus and appointed William McSherry the first provincial (regional superior).[46]

Expansion of Facilities

As the student enrollment at the college rapidly climbed toward two hundred, Mulledy began a building campaign to provide much-needed facilities. The first of his projects was a four-story brick infirmary, which was built in 1831. Perpendicular to the original college building but some twenty yards to the west, it was constructed on the site of the first infirmary. That old two-story wooden structure had been an increasingly inadequate infirmary for a long time, but lack of funds had prevented the college from replacing it. By 1831 the college's debt had been reduced to the $2,000 it owed to a bank.[47] Mulledy and his fellows felt that with some resourcefulness, strict management, and trust in God, money could be found not only for the new infirmary but for other buildings as well. An opportunity had arisen in 1831 when a widow who had decided to enter the Visitation Convent asked Mulledy to take her son as his ward. In return she entrusted to him promissory notes worth several thousand dollars. The college president was convinced that the money realized from the widow's debtors would be more than enough to finance the infirmary, which was subsequently built by Nathaniel Marden for $5,775.[48] Francis Dzierozynski, the province treasurer, was impressed that Mulledy had been able to do it without incurring new debt but worried that his ambition for building would lead him into debts far beyond the college's income. Should that happen, "where will [the money] come from[?]," he warned Father General Roothaan. He expected a new outcry for the sale of the farms and slaves.[49]

In the next year Mulledy and his consultors decided to build an even larger multi-purpose structure between the "Old College" and the new infirmary.[50] From Boston, Benedict Fenwick wrote to tell his brother that he could not understand why the Georgetown Jesuits had not chosen to construct "a splendid building four stories high with a colonnade in front and a cupola rising in the centre of the main building twenty feet higher than the roof" which would face toward the city and have the old and new colleges as wings. "That," he estimated, would present such an imposing image as "to leave all other Cath. Institutions in the country completely in the shade."[51] But the focus of the campus was still upon the river, not upon the city, and the $12,000 (the amount authorized by Mulledy for the new building) would barely cover the essentials, much less colonnades and cupolas. Even so, the college had great difficulty raising the money for the project. Mulledy, having vainly attempted to find donors in the hard times of the early 1830s, next tried to finance the building with the $5,000 the college had on deposit in the bank plus a proposed transfer to the builders of some lots it owned in Washington. But the builders, Nathaniel Marden and Matthias Duffey, had no interest in acquiring real estate in the depressed Washington market.[52] However, just when the project seemed dead, a Jesuit pastor in Southern Maryland, James

Neil, offered Mulledy a loan of $12,000 at 6 percent annual interest. The money was his patrimony, which Neill could still possess, since he had not taken final vows. The loan was offered with the understanding that the capital would eventually be given to the Society. Neil meanwhile was to use the interest. With this loan arranged, the builders lowered their price to $11,000 and broke ground in early July 1832.[53] By the following July the new facility was completed. It was ninety-five feet long, fifty feet wide, and four stories high, with a cellar, dining hall, chapel, and auditorium/study hall capable of accommodating more than a thousand persons.

Hard Times at the College

Thomas Mulledy, entering his fifth year as president in 1833, was more than ready to step down. His health had been poor since the cholera summer of 1832. One of his fellow Jesuits at the college found him "worn out."[54] Moreover, in November of 1833 there had been a nerve-wracking student riot that had lasted for nearly three weeks and had resulted in the expulsion of twenty-one students. Some of his confreres later attributed the riot to Mulledy's "receiving every scoundrel" in order to increase enrollment.[55] Most of those expelled had indeed been admitted after the fall of 1832; and the enrollment had increased considerably in 1833 from 130 to 183 (up 40% with 172 of them as boarders). Although Mulledy had sought his release as president before the riot, that unhappy event seemed to make him further intensify his efforts. The superior general was ready to grant his wish for several reasons: Mulledy's seemingly cavalier attitude toward finances, his autocratic style of government, and his failure to set a climate of discipline for either students or Jesuits (the riot of 1833 seemed to confirm the worst of Roothaan's earlier suspicions about Mulledy's laxity towards moral formation).

The problem was to find a suitable replacement. James Ryder, George Fenwick, and Aloysius Young (the other 1828–29 returnees from Europe) were the obvious alternatives but each of the three had serious administrative weaknesses. Ryder cared even less than Mulledy about finances and seemed forever on the road giving retreats and talks. Fenwick had a phobia about exercising any authority, and Young tended to be even more autocratic than Mulledy. John McElroy was the only other possibility, but his limited education and working class background (particularly his social status as a former lay brother in the order) eliminated him as a serious candidate.[56] Moreover, even if someone else could be found, Mulledy was too valuable as a teacher to send elsewhere, which would put his successor in an intolerable position.[57] So the upshot was that Mulledy had to reluctantly remain in office.

By the middle of the decade the finances of the college were, according to one discerning Jesuit observer, *"in a most miserable condition."*[58] Mulledy's loan and payback arrangement for the construction of the new buildings had already been undermined by the depressed economy of the 1830s as well as the sudden dismissal from the Society of his benefactor, James Neil. "The state of our country is very dreadful," a group of young Jesuits reported in early 1834 to a fellow Jesuit studying in Rome. "We are on the very brink of a revolution, owing to the hostility of our President [Andrew Jackson] to the United States Bank. Bankruptcies are very common. Daily we hear of immense mercantile houses breaking and nothing is more universally looked for, if the present state of things continue, than our general ruin."[59] The promissory notes for the outstanding loans that Mulledy had been given by the widow-postulant apparently had proved uncollectable. Even worse, Neil had reclaimed his $12,000 loan when he was dismissed from the Society in 1833.[60] The financial records for the 1830s show that one of the building contractors, Nathaniel Marden, was paid only $5,214 of the $16,275 due him.[61] Then too, Mulledy, like Enoch Fenwick a decade before, was very reluctant to press parents for unpaid fees. Ryder complained as early as 1832 of how "timid" Mulledy was in pressing parents to pay their sons' room and board.[62] And regrettably, the dramatic increase in enrollment was accompanied by a much higher number of defaulting students. Mulledy admitted the problem but considered it a consequence of the depressed economy.[63]

The college in October 1833 had secured from the federal government a land grant of building lots in the city that, theoretically, were worth $25,000. But in the midst of the "War" that Andrew Jackson was waging against the Bank of the United States, there was little likelihood of finding speculators willing to invest in real estate on the southwestern outskirts of Washington.[64] The following year, Susan Decatur, the widow of Admiral Stephen Decatur, agreed to donate $7,000 to Georgetown. She was not able to actually deliver the money until 1837, when she was finally awarded the federal pension she had been seeking since 1820 (the year Decatur died in a duel). Despite substantial annuity payments to Mrs. Decatur for the next twenty-three years ($644 each year), earnings from the gift provided welcome relief to the college, which was on the verge of financial collapse by 1837.[65] William McSherry wrote to Father General Roothaan in Rome in November of that same year:

Yesterday I received a letter from the College written by the Procurator [treasurer], urging me to make some arrangements to procure some aid for them; that it is impossible to continue unless something is done—that at least twenty thousand dollars would be required in order to sustain the college. I have often spoken to Fr. Mulledy of the condition of the college, that the greatest economy should be used, & such advice as I thought ought to be sufficient, but if he has ever regarded my admonitions, it was only for a short time.[66]

Mulledy, in fact, tended to ignore the finances of the place. In late 1837 he had little idea of the extent of the college debts. In fact, when McSherry suc-

Susan Wheeler Decatur, widowed in 1820 by her husband's death in a duel, became one of Georgetown's great benefactors. The portrait, attributed to Gilbert Stuart, is in the collection of Mr. and Mrs. William Machold. (Georgetown University Archives)

ceeded Mulledy as president in January 1838, he inherited a debt of $47,654.54 that Mulledy thought amounted to about $25,000.[67] Thanks both to the Decatur gift and to an increase in student income McSherry was soon able to reduce it to $23,857.36, which was still a crippling amount.[68] The proposed sale of the slaves continued to be the major hope for rescuing the college and the province from their accumulated financial troubles.

"A Tragic and Disgraceful Affair"

Rome's reluctance to disturb the province's slave economy notwithstanding, Mulledy and McSherry persisted in their efforts to end it. In 1835, at the first congregation of the province, a majority of the ten delegates had requested the general's permission to sell the slaves as well as some of the plantations. With the revenue to be thus gained, they asserted that the province could, among other things, strengthen its existing colleges in Georgetown and Frederick and establish new ones in other cities like Baltimore, Philadelphia, and Richmond.[69]

Although the selling of individual slaves was a long-established practice among the Jesuits in Maryland, it was usually done only in order to keep families together or to punish troublesome slaves. Deferred emancipation (the contractual renting out of slaves for a specified number of years, which ended with their legal freedom) had been the chief means previously considered an acceptable way to end slaveholding on the Society's plantations.[70] Mulledy had proposed such a scheme as late as 1830. By 1835, however, new state legislation had made it much more difficult to pursue such a policy. Moreover, persistent financial pressures, particularly at Georgetown, were making a mass sale more expedient, especially since the plantations continued to contribute little or nothing to the needs of the province. Moreover, there was a growing conviction among the Maryland Jesuits that a bilateral division of the Union was inevitable, that the Potomac would likely be the dividing line between the resulting two new federations of states, and that Maryland, as the only slave state within the northern federation, would be forced to emancipate its slaves or perhaps even suffer a slave revolt, such as the one that Nat Turner had led in neighboring Virginia in 1831.[71] Better then to sell the slaves outright, they reasoned. But the possibilities were extremely limited for a mass sale of nearly three hundred slaves to Maryland planters without an undesirable breaking up of families because of Maryland's relatively small plantations. (By that time, most Maryland slaveholders [90%] owned fewer than fifteen slaves.)[72] So, if these slaves were to be sold, they would have to be sold to planters in the Deep South, a decidedly uncommon practice in the state.[73]

Most of the continental Jesuits in Maryland vehemently opposed the sale, as did many of the native American Jesuits, including Joseph Carberry (**C** 1811–15). Carberry had already begun a successful experiment in free enterprise for slaves by dividing most of the St. Inigoes plantation into small farms, which individual slave families were then able to work for themselves in exchange for a modest annual rent. To Jesuits like Carberry, the financial exigencies and the fear of civil war were no justification for breaking the bond that existed between the Society and its black families by selling them, especially to slaveholders in the Deep South.[74] Despite their protests, Superior General Roothaan approved a general sale of the slaves in December of 1836, with the stipulation that their religious needs be met, that the families not be separated, and that the money from the sale be invested to support the education of Jesuits.[75]

The Panic of 1837 delayed the proposed sellout by severely deflating the market value of slaves. Then in January of 1838 Mulledy was appointed to replace the ailing McSherry as provincial. The change seemed to reenergize the new provincial. He wasted no time in completing the project he had been foremost in advocating for the past decade. In June of 1838 Mulledy arranged to sell all the slaves for $115,000 to a pair of Louisiana planters. One of them, Henry Johnson, a former governor of the state, had a nephew at Georgetown.[76] Johnson and his partner paid $25,000 up front for the 272 black people. Mulledy in turn loaned $24,000 of that sum to the college.[77] Mulledy, accompanied by Johnson and local sheriffs, then swept unannounced through the province's four plantations in southern Maryland and gathered the slaves for transport to the port of Alexandria. From there they were shipped to the Deep South. "They were dragged off by force to the ship," a Jesuit manager of one of the plantations reported to the general.[78] "No one does this sort of thing," a continental Jesuit stationed on one of the plantations explained to Roothaan,

except evil persons, such as slave traders who care about nothing but money, or those who by necessity are so pressed by debts that they are forced into such a sale. . . . I tell you this will be a tragic and disgraceful affair. . . . [79]

In that letter to the superior general, Peter Havermans also observed that Catholics and Protestants alike were scandalized. But not only Jesuits complained to Rome about the sale. Archbishop Samuel Eccleston, of Baltimore, also wrote to Roothaan about the scandal that Mulledy had given. Although the full correspondence between the archbishop and the superior general has not survived, it appears that the tragic separation of the black families was among the charges that Eccleston brought.[80] The superior general had also been disturbed to learn earlier that Mulledy had used part of the sales money to reduce the building debts of Georgetown.[81] In June 1839, Archbishop Eccleston and William McSherry, now president of Georgetown, together persuaded Thomas Mulledy to resign as provincial and take his case personally to Roothaan.[82] Mulledy, in shock over what he saw as inexplicable developments, hastily booked passage for Europe. As it turned out, the archbishop and the president had given him prudent advice since, in August while Mulledy was en route, the general sent orders to Mulledy (through McSherry) to resign as provincial until he could clear himself of the charges.[83] By that time Mulledy was already in Italy. When he finally saw the superior general in the early fall, the latter, according to Mulledy, had little to say beyond the observation that "all was now settled." Roothaan, however, had become convinced that Mulledy could not return to America at that time because of the scandal he had given, intentionally or not, in the sale.[84] So he assigned him to work in Nice with the English-speaking community there.

Before the end of the year the province had lost the services of McSherry as well as of Mulledy. For at least five years McSherry had been courageously battling stomach cancer. Suffering acutely from tumorous growths, he had obtained temporary relief in 1835 from medical treatment but gradually he weakened and lost all energy. Then, in response to his pleas, Roothaan had relieved McSherry in October 1837 as provincial. Subsequently, Mulledy named McSherry acting president (vice-rector) of the college as his replacement. But by the time Roothaan, in the wake of Mulledy's resignation, reappointed McSherry provincial—while retaining him as president of Georgetown—the latter was in no condition to lead either province or college. By the fall of 1839 he was in constant pain and terminally ill. At November's close he was in bed, unable to retain any solid food and resigned to his fate ("you had appointed yr place in the grave yard," he told an elderly Brother; "I will take it.").[85] A novena for a cure was begun in union with Prince Hohenlohe on December 12. But William McSherry died two days before its conclusion on December 18, 1839, four months beyond his fortieth birthday. Joseph Lopez, who had been named acting president of the college that month, continued in that position until a permanent successor was installed in the spring of 1840.

James Ryder

With McSherry dead and Mulledy in Europe, James Ryder was the logical choice to succeed McSherry as president. In April 1840 he was installed as the twentieth president of the college, a position he held for most of the decade during two terms (1840–45, 1848–51). Ryder was both a respected and a popular figure with his fellow Jesuits, with the students, and with the outside community, particularly political Washington. As Fidèle de Grivel noted in October 1840, "he succeeds very well with the community & the boys, & strangers: thanks be to God."[86] Dzierozysnki thought him "our great saviour. Never have we had a Rector . . . more honored."[87] As president, Ryder remained as peripatetic as he had been as a professor. Already a well-known lecturer and preacher and influential far beyond the local community, Ryder was perhaps the most renowned preacher in antebellum Catholic America.

He was increasingly in demand as a retreat director and on the lecture circuit in Baltimore, Philadelphia, Cincinnati, and in other Catholic centers.
In Washington and Georgetown his talks attracted
hundreds of persons, including members of the
administration and Congress. In 1844, during the
nativist crisis, he gave a series of three lectures a
week for several weeks in Washington to explain
the nature of Catholicism and "the Church *establishment.*"[88] As pastor of the parish attached to the
college, he was keenly interested in replacing the
dilapidated 1794 chapel with a church fit for a
Catholic university community in the nation's
capital. After being deterred by financial stress
and other obstacles during his initial term in office
(1840–45), Ryder's first act in his second term was
to commit the college to building a new church,
"to be called Trinity," on college property on Thir-

James Ryder, SJ (1800–
1860). Twice president of
Georgetown, he was also an
elected Resident Member of
the Smithsonian Institution
and one of the most
renowned Catholic preachers
in antebellum America.
(Shea, *Memorial of the First Century
of Georgetown College*)

ty-Sixth Street.[89] The church, reflecting Ryder's republican vision, was designed in neoclassical style and completed in 1852. It is still in use in that
same Georgetown parish, as is the now restored eighteenth-century chapel.

However concerned and involved Ryder was overall, he was little interested in the daily operations of the college and left such matters to the vice-
rector, the procurator, and the faculty. (During his first term in office he also
served as provincial superior in 1843 and 1844.) If James Ryder had little
interest in internal government, he was nevertheless very adept at promoting the college. One forum that he frequently used for that purpose was the
lecture and retreat circuit. Just as ministers and agents of Protestant denominations recruited students in many states for their colleges through itinerant
preaching and other publicity, so Ryder attracted students to Georgetown
while filling speaking engagements in many cities and towns of Pennsylvania, Maryland, and Virginia.[90] He also effectively cultivated relations with the
local Washington community, and especially with members of the federal
government. In 1842 he was elected a Resident Member of the new Smithsonian Institution; and he continued to sponsor participation in the semiannual "boosterism" on February 22 and July 4, as well as the quadrennial
marches to the Capitol. In 1841 he had the college students march two by
two in formal dress to William Henry Harrison's preinaugural reception in
Georgetown as well as in the unprecedentedly large inaugural parade three
weeks later (a fitting climax for the election of 1840). When some Democratic students had balked at marching in honor of a Whig, Ryder ordered
them to put aside political partisanship and join the parade in honor of their
country's president.[91] Even before Harrison's inauguration, Ryder had already paid his respects to the weary president-elect. Then, a month after

The College seal, thought to be derived from DuBourg's design, was formally adopted for legal use when Georgetown was formally incorporated by an Act of Congress in 1844. (Georgetown University Archives)

Harrison's inauguration, James Ryder and George Fenwick took part in the funeral that followed his brief fight with pneumonia. With Harrison's successor, John Tyler, a Virginian, Ryder also developed a warm relationship. (The president's sister became a Catholic that spring.) Tyler himself became a regular participant in the commencement ceremonies and recommended students to the college, including his son, Tazewell, who boarded there for nearly two years, from 1843 to 1845. Even after President Tyler left office, Ryder remained his close supporter. In 1859, long retired from Georgetown, Ryder was a key agent in an abortive attempt to revive the "party-less" Tyler's fortunes as the Democratic Party's presidential candidate.[92] (When Tyler had become a "man without a party" in 1844, his successor, James K. Polk, continued Tyler's practice of presiding at the Georgetown College commencement; and he enrolled his nephew there in 1845.)

During President Tyler's term, Ryder was pleased that the Congress approved a bill which in 1844 formally incorporated "Georgetown College" so that its trustees could be recognized as legal agents able to accept and manage property and funds without limit, powers that the original charter of 1815 had not conveyed. It is likely that the manager of the bill in the Senate was William D. Merrick of Maryland (the brother-in-law of Father William Matthews), who was a member of the Standing Committee on the District of Columbia, under whose jurisdiction such matters fell. Under the terms of the incorporation a seal, first devised by William DuBourg in the late 1790s, was now formally adopted for the legal transactions of the institution. That seal incorporates the heraldic eagle used on the Great Seal of the United States, substituting in its talons the earth's globe and the cross for the nation's arrows and olive branch.

The financial condition of the college improved dramatically during Ryder's first term. The institution's debt, approximately $20,000 when he became president in 1840, had virtually been liquidated by 1842.[93] The financial records for the period are incomplete. Some of the debt amortization appears to have resulted from a change in bookkeeping methods rather than from financial improvements, since the province decided to take over the debts of both Georgetown College and St. John's Literary Institute in 1841.[94] It is highly possible, however, that some of this reduction also stemmed from the monies Ryder earned through his lectures. He may also have used his wide-ranging travels and contacts to raise money. In 1852, after he was transferred to Philadelphia, he secured permission to go to California to raise money for a new Jesuit college in Philadelphia and came back with $5,000.[95] It is hardly likely that that was Ryder's first fund-raising trip.

Ryder had inherited a school with a student enrollment that was slightly lower than the peak enrollment under Mulledy. In the spring of 1840 when Ryder became president there were perhaps two hundred students

(170 boarders and about 30 half-boarders).[96] Five years later the total enrollment was as high as it had ever been (211) but there were somewhat fewer boarders (164); by 1850 the total enrollment was lower (183), but there were more half-boarders (51). For the decade there was a significant decline (9.1%) in the general enrollment and a sharp drop (32%) in the number of non-Catholics in the school. Part of the decline may be attributed to Thomas Mulledy's unsuccessful second administration (1845–48), but there were probably larger factors at work, two of which were nationwide anti-Catholic nativism and the competition of the new Catholic colleges.

Nativism and the Mexican American War

In 1845, Ryder, like Mulledy six years before, was forced to take a hurried transatlantic trip to Rome. For Ryder the occasion was persistent rumors accusing him of an affair with a woman.[97] In his place as president, Father General Roothaan named Samuel Mulledy rector and president of Georgetown, an appointment he quickly regretted when the younger Mulledy's alcoholism became all too apparent. Six years after the slave-sale scandal, Thomas Mulledy, his brother, returned as president in September 1845. No longer vigorous, he seemed a shadow of his former self. He enlarged the infirmary building during his second term but did little else as president other than alienate the faculty and drive students away by his despotic manner. The sharpest decline in enrollment during the decade came during his three-year term from 1845 to 1848. Then at the end of Mulledy's second term, Ryder was brought back to Georgetown.[98] He had been serving as president of Holy Cross College since 1843 after satisfying the superior general that his friendship with the woman was an innocent one. As seems likely, the decline in enrollment transcended any difficulties exacerbated by Thomas Mulledy's personality. An alarming anti-Catholic nativism had been heating up for a decade. The sharp rise of Irish immigration, the conversion of prominent Protestants, the attempts of Catholic prelates such as Bishop John Hughes in New York to secure public funds for parochial schools—all had combined to raise the specter of a growing Catholic menace to republican America. And the Society of Jesus was seen by many to be at the heart of the conspiracy, casting its shadow from the Mississippi Valley to the halls of Congress. The painter-inventor, Samuel F. B. Morse, for instance, warned his fellow Americans in 1835 of a plot that European monarchs had concocted to subvert American liberties by funding missionary societies whose chief agents were Jesuits.[99]

"Nearly all the political papers are teeming with articles against the Catholics," James Ward, a young Jesuit at Georgetown, wrote to Samuel Barber in that same year,

& it is the opinion of some that a persecution of some kind or other will soon be ex-
cited against them . . . the parsons & ministers . . . are exerting their utmost efforts to
prove to the American People, that Catholicity is hostile to civil liberty. . . . In the
[Southern Maryland] counties, the Ministers have forbidden their congregations to
have any communication at all with Catholics whom they regard as the most faithless
& treacherous beings in the world.[100]

Subsequently Stephen Dubuisson, who had been successful in securing
funds from the Society for the Propagation of the Faith and was then (in
1836) preparing to publish his memoirs, decided in light of the "ridiculous"
rumors about the missionary societies to remove all material that could give
any appearance of confirming Morse's charges.[101]

By the 1840s the Catholic menace had become a prime topic within the
debating societies of most American colleges. At Yale the Brothers in Unity
Society decided in 1844 that "the Roman Catholic religion [is] inconsistent
with free government." A similar literary society at the University of Pennsylvania that same year judged that self-styled "native" Americans were justified in burning the homes of their Catholic neighbors.[102] At the University
of Georgia, both debating societies in the 1850s decided in favor of the Know-
Nothings; in fact, one supported the proposition that Catholicism "should
not be tolerated in the United States."[103]

Most of the attacks against Catholics were verbal, but there was occasional
physical violence, as the Pennsylvania debate implied. Most notable were
the burning of the Ursuline Convent in Charlestown outside Boston in 1834
and the riots in Philadelphia a decade later when two churches and thirty
homes were burned, fifty persons wounded, and fourteen killed. "'[I]f this
example spreads," a Jesuit reported to Roothaan from Frederick in June of
1844 on the turbulence in Philadelphia, "we could be among the first towns
affected. Things are in such a state that it will not take a conflagration, a spark
will be enough."[104]

Washington itself, given the long-established Catholic community in the
federal city, was something of a haven from nativism. (A short-lived nativist
organization, with initial Catholic involvement, in the late 1830s had foun-
dered over the religious issue.)[105] Ryder continued to give his talks on
Catholicism in Washington during the Philadelphia riots. But he was not
optimistic about the national temper. "No popery is the species of active Protestantism now adays [sic]," he wrote John McElroy, "& where the fear of
chastisement does not prevent, its hostility to every thing Catholic, is rampant." Ryder thought the unpleasant remedy lay in Catholics arming themselves in self-defense in large cities. Baltimore alone seemed safe, he judged,
but only because Catholic hooliganism in that city was "well known & equally dreaded" by even the violence-prone nativists.[106]

In spite of his pessimism, Ryder had organized a "Pilgrim's Day" two years
before the Philadelphia riots. It celebrated the landings in 1634 of the *Ark* and

the *Dove* on St. Clement's Island in the broad reaches of the Potomac River. The idea had originated with George Fenwick, who regretted the heavy overshadowing in the nation's history of his Maryland ancestors by those who concentrated on their New England counterparts. It was, of course, also a way of reminding Americans that Catholics had been in this country long before the potato famine had driven the Irish to America. And with Ryder's generous oversight the celebration became an irenic event, with Catholics and Protestants alike joining in the festivities on the morning of May 9, 1842. The Georgetown College Band and the Philodemic Society led most of the students through the streets of Georgetown to the steamboat *Columbia* hired by Ryder for the trip south on the Potomac. Altogether approximately seven hundred persons, including the mayor of Washington and several members of Congress, went by boat from Washington and Baltimore to St. Inigoes that day. There on the eastern shore of the St. Mary's River at the site of the old colonial capital, Archbishop Eccleston celebrated Mass and Bishop Fenwick preached. Then they all sailed farther up the river to St. Mary's City to be greeted by an ecumenical crowd of about four thousand who joined them in a procession to the ruins of the old capital. For the keynote address of the day Ryder had first sought out William Gaston, but Georgetown's first student, now nearly sixty-four, had declined on the grounds both of age and of not being a Marylander. Instead, William George Read, a distinguished Baltimore lawyer and a convert, and Ryder himself gave talks eulogizing the first planters of Catholicism in the original colonies, "and all without giving the least offence to the Protestants who were present."[107] The celebrations closed with an ode written by George Washington Parke Custis (President Washington's adopted son). Set to the music of the "Star Spangled Banner" it was sung by Charles Carroll's granddaughter, George Fenwick, and the composer. One recently arrived Jesuit from Switzerland, Anthony Rey, thought one result of the event was to move "many parents to entrust the education of their sons to us."[108] And indeed, the number of new students at Georgetown College jumped sharply over the next four years, but few were Protestant.

Two years after the nativist crisis of 1844 the United States was at war with the Republic of Mexico, whose citizens were mainly Catholics. Our federal government, sensitive to the concerns of its Catholic citizens, especially those among the expeditionary force (at least a third of the total), quickly made efforts to secure Catholic chaplains. Anthony Rey and John McElroy, two Jesuits formerly with Georgetown, were among those chosen. The new provincial superior, Peter Verhaegen, thought it providential:

It will serve to destroy those calumnies of the enemies of our Religion who for so long have been charging that Catholics and especially the Catholic clergy of the United States, are opposed to our form of government, that they are not faithful subjects, that they always take the part of the enemy.[109]

He was particularly pleased that President Polk had wanted to meet with the chaplains before they left in May of 1846 for the front.

Besides Rey and McElroy, at least twenty-four Georgetown alumni served in the American army. Two former students and future Confederate generals saw action there, Henry Heth (**C** 1837–38), a recent graduate of the U.S. Military Academy, and William Loring (**C** 1839–40). As was true of the army in general, most of these alumni soldiers (all but two) were Southerners. William Walker (**C** 1838–41) of Mississippi was a lieutenant under General Joseph Johnson. In the climactic assault at the Battle of Chapultepec outside Mexico City in 1847, he was reportedly the first to scale the walls of the massive fortifications. On the battlefield Rey encountered two Georgetown alumni from Mississippi, one of whom he received into the Church on his deathbed. Of the twenty-four alumni known to have participated in the war, three died, including Benjamin Stoddert's grandson, Levi Gantt (**C** 1834–35). Among the other casualties that brought the war close to Georgetowners was the death of Archibald Yell, whose son was in his third year at the college. (The father, a veteran of the War of 1812, had been governor of Arkansas and a congressman from that state before enlisting for the war.) After the father's death in northern Mexico in the Battle of Buena Vista in February 1847, De Witt Clinton Yell (**C** 1845–47) was made a ward of President Polk.

Anthony Rey won praise for his heroic ministry to the troops during the battle of Monterey. Then in January of 1847 the priest disappeared while on his way to visit McElroy. Months later his body was finally discovered, the victim of a bandit raid. McElroy, who because of his age had been confined to hospital work well behind the lines, was recalled in May when the war appeared over, but it dragged on for more than a year. "What a great calamity for each Republic!" Verhaegen wrote to Rome.[110] The war had long since transcended any perceived need or occasion for proving Catholic loyalty.

The Shaping of a Catholic Educational Empire

This antebellum period was one of rapid, exuberant expansion in the number of colleges in the United States. Between 1830 and 1861 hundreds were founded, of which nearly three hundred became permanent or long-lived institutions of higher learning.[111] In the sixty years before the Civil War the rate of increase of attendance at colleges was four times that of the general population.[112] No wonder that one observer could confidently assert that "Our country is to be a land of colleges."[113] By far most of these new colleges were denominational or related to religious denominations. The Catholic Church—or, more precisely, the Catholic dioceses and the societies of teaching religious—were among the leaders in this development in education. Between 1829 and 1849 thirty-one Catholic colleges or literary institutes were founded, including Xavier (1831), Fordham (1841), Notre Dame (1842),

Villanova (1842), Clarke College (1843), Holy Cross (1843), Mount St. Vincent (1847), and Loyola/New Orleans (1849).[114] As many of these names suggest, those Catholic institutions that survived the Civil War (17 of 31) were almost all started by or taken over by religious orders and societies such as the Augustinians, Holy Cross Fathers, Vincentians, and Jesuits, as well as the several congregations of nuns founded especially for teaching. But most of the schools initially were local diocesan enterprises, begun by bishops to supply a clergy as well as to provide educational opportunity and a buffer against barbarism for Catholics and non-Catholics alike in a rapidly changing (and moving) society. Their relationship with the local community was weaker than that of so many new Baptist and other denominational colleges which were financed and at least partly controlled by local persons and local governments. But, given the popular demand for education and the essentially private character of higher education in America through the first half of the nineteenth century, these Catholic colleges, like their Protestant counterparts, were usually considered distinct assets for the local community. They were highly prized institutions in which each community felt the presence of a real investment.[115] Whether in cities or countryside, they fulfilled the ambitions created by the rising aspirations of an emerging middle class.[116]

Protestants made up a substantial part of the student body in Catholic colleges during the second quarter of the nineteenth century, perhaps, as Philip Gleason estimates, as many as a third to a half.[117] For instance, half of the boarders at Santa Clara College in California in 1852 were Protestants, to the amazement of the Italian Jesuits who had begun the school in the previous year.[118] By the 1830s St. Mary's in Baltimore (originally begun in 1791 as a seminary) had a majority of Protestant students.[119] Nevertheless, with Catholic immigration escalating and nativism surging, the exclusive Catholic college, restricted to Catholic students, began to appear—first in Wilmington, Delaware, with the establishment of St. Mary's College in 1839. Others followed in the 1840s. Thus the "ghetto" school evolved. It was to be the dominant type of Catholic college by the late nineteenth century, a clear deviation from the ecumenical course that John Carroll had charted for Georgetown and which Catholic schools in general had followed until the 1840s. At first, Georgetown itself reflected this trend to the extent that its proportion of non-Catholic students continued to decline in the 1840s. Then in the 1850s another change of course occurred; increasingly Georgetown became a college for Southerners.

As Catholic collegiate education became more decentralized and localized, Georgetown began to feel the effects. The decline of the enrollment by nearly a fifth was the most visible one. The sharpest drop in numbers came in the students from the northeast. In the 1840s, they accounted for less than a tenth (9%) of the enrollment.

Of course, Ryder and his fellow Jesuit leaders at Georgetown had long favored a policy of proliferating Jesuit colleges in the eastern United States.

Through their influence the first provincial congregation in 1835 had urged the founding of colleges in Baltimore, Philadelphia, Richmond, and elsewhere. Yet at the end of the decade Georgetown and St. John's Literary Institute in Frederick were still the only Jesuit institutions in the region. In 1837 the Archbishop of Baltimore had wanted the Society to take over St. Mary's College. Thomas Mulledy was in favor of pursuing that opportunity to merge Georgetown with its long-time rival. "With Baltimore now only three hours away by railroad," he observed to the superior general, "one professor of higher studies could teach at both places, as well as one professor of Rhetoric." He envisioned students in the higher classes of Rhetoric and Philosophy alternating between Baltimore and Georgetown.[120] But Roothaan refused to let Mulledy accept it because of the province's financial obligation, especially because of the $47,000 debt that Mulledy had accumulated while president at Georgetown.[121]

In Boston, Bishop Benedict Fenwick had built a school in a rural colony he had established in Maine for Irish immigrants. He offered it to the Maryland Jesuits in 1842, but Francis Dzierozynski, now provincial, and his consultors much preferred an urban college to one in New England's "wilderness." They also favored a day school rather than a boarding college in order to attract poorer youths, as John McElroy had done in Frederick. Fenwick acknowledged the weight of their arguments regarding urban colleges but insisted that it was also necessary to have a rural boarding college to which "the *elite*" in the urban day colleges could be sent when they showed promise of a vocation. Left long enough as students in the cities, he countered, "they will seldom have a vocation . . . to the ecclesiastical state." His proposed college would be restricted to Catholics only, a decision he had made as early as 1838 in response to the nativism he had encountered in Boston.[122]

A "geographic" compromise was subsequently worked out when Fenwick acquired the property of an academy in Worcester and turned it over to the Society. The first president was Thomas Mulledy, who had been allowed to return to the United States to head the new school at Fenwick's insistence.[123] Thus, in the fall of 1843 the College of the Holy Cross opened for classes in central Massachusetts. Owing to its exclusive Catholic enrollment, it was unable to secure a charter from the state for more than twenty years, and during that time its degrees were conferred by Georgetown University.

Within the next ten years the Society had either opened or taken over four more schools on the East Coast, and were making long-range plans for a fifth—in Boston. In 1846 the French Jesuits who had been operating a small college in Kentucky agreed to close it and take over instead the school that Bishop John Hughes had begun in 1841 in the Fordham section of New York City. Then in 1848 the Jesuits reopened in the District the Washington College which they had closed in 1827. That new day school quickly attracted students from the top ranks of the city's establishment, both Catholic and Protestant.[124] By 1851, enrollment in its preparatory and collegiate classes had reached nearly 350. Six years later it was incorporated by Congress as Gonzaga College. In 1851 and 1852 the Maryland Province of the Society established similar colleges in Philadelphia and Baltimore, St. Joseph's and Loyola. St. Joseph's began in Philadelphia in 1851 with preparatory classes only, but a college charter was granted the following year. The new Loyola in Baltimore, as the successor to St. Mary's College, which had closed in 1851, continued its tradition of providing a liberal arts education for the middle class of Baltimore. Within its first year Loyola registered ninety-five students, a third of them from St. Mary's.[125] Few of the sons of the immigrant poor were among Loyola's students in its first half century. Finally, in Boston, Benedict Fenwick's successor, Bishop Joseph Fitzpatrick, agreed to begin raising money for a Jesuit college in his episcopal city, in exchange for the Jesuits' commitment to rebuild Holy Cross, whose main building had been destroyed by fire in 1852.

Of the four new colleges, Holy Cross and Fordham were boarding schools, while St. Joseph's and Loyola were day schools only. The latter required smaller investments of both manpower and money; and some even argued that they also promoted more vocations than boarding schools did.

The network of urban colleges that the repatriated American Jesuits had envisioned in 1830, but had initially been unable to realize for lack of money and men, was now finally a reality—made possible in great part, as we shall see, by the influx of Jesuit refugees from Europe. The Jesuit collegiate network in the East was the fortuitous culmination of religious, social, and economic factors—long-range Jesuit evangelical aspirations through education, episcopal ambitions for Catholic colleges in the growing dioceses, and the social needs of the now more affluent, established urban Catholic population. The student bodies of the new schools were predominantly middle class. Where a tradition of pluralistic Catholic education existed, as in Washington and Baltimore, the student bodies of the new schools continued to be a mix of social groups and religions. Where it did not, as in Boston and Philadelphia, the schools tended to be for the rising Catholic middle class only—a much larger group in Philadelphia than in Boston.[126] Unlike the centrifugal, local character of American higher education in the antebellum period, Jesuit education in the East could now be characterized as a highly centripetal intellectual endeavor. Colleges from Boston to Washington shared the same basic educational tradition, curriculum, and faculty (Jesuits were regularly reassigned from one college to another as needs and priorities developed). With Georgetown, as the oldest and most prestigious, at the center, the Jesuit network linked these colleges as more than local enterprises, even as higher education evolved throughout America.

CHAPTER 6

The 1850s: Refugees, Science, and the Founding of the Medical School

The Jesuits, driven from Rome last spring, and who since May have experienced so friendly an asylum at Ugbrook, from the Clifford family, quitted last Thursday, with their learned superior, the Rev. Marquis Sopranis. The majority, we understand, proceed to the United States, where every encouragement will be afforded them. Their university at Georgetown, near Washington, will shortly be able to rival the best University of Europe.

WESTERN TIMES
London, November 25, 1848

Georgetown in 1850

By mid-century, Georgetown College, as the oldest, was at the center of a rapidly expanding network of Catholic institutions of higher education in the United States, many of them Jesuit schools. While contributing to this overall expansion, Georgetown had also completed two successful decades of growth and consolidation. Its student enrollment was stable, its finances sound, and its intellectual reputation revitalized. This in large part was owed to a new generation of refugees, from Switzerland and Germany and Italy, who continued to have a deep impact on collegiate life in the 1850s. George-town had also established, in the last year of the previous decade, its first professional school, the department of medicine.

A New Wave of Emigrés

Refugees and missionaries from Europe had been an integral part of the college since its beginnings. In the 1790s, the first wave of clerical emigrés, the Sulpicians, had provided Georgetown with its initial faculty. After the restoration of the Society of Jesus in 1805, Jesuit faculty had come from Byelorussia, France, Italy, and from Belgium especially. Between 1819 and 1846 Belgium sent nine Jesuits to Georgetown, including James Van de Velde (1795–1855), who came to the United States in 1817 with the intention of being a missionary in the West. But he taught at Georgetown intermittently until 1831, when he was reassigned to Saint Louis University. He subsequently served as president of that university and also as bishop of Chicago, Illinois, and then Natchez, Mississippi.

While James Ryder was in Italy in 1845, he also had recruited eight priests and scholastics, several of whom became permanent faculty at the college. But it was the intellectual migration generated by the Revolutions of 1848 that had the greatest impact on the intellectual life and reputation of Georgetown in the 1850s.

Those numerous revolutions that erupted throughout Europe produced thousands of refugees, many of them members of religious congregations rightly or wrongly identified with the old political order. In March of that year the Jesuits' superior general, Jan Roothaan, had to flee from Rome in disguise to avoid capture by the anti-papacy republicans. Giovanni Grassi wrote from the Eternal City in June that the cruel eviction of Jesuits throughout Italy, with the exception of Sicily, was worse than that of the suppression in 1773.[1] Nor was it any better for the Society in Germany or Switzerland. Burchard Villiger was a Jesuit scholastic studying theology at Fribourg in 1847 when the Swiss Diet expelled the Society from the republic. With a companion he escaped from Fribourg, which was under siege by a Swiss army sent to execute the order of expulsion. Then, after short stays in the Savoy and in France, where revolutionary forces were also targeting Jesuits as enemies to be displaced, Villiger had to go to Geneva. There he received orders from his superiors to proceed to the United States in the late spring of 1848, along with forty companions from the Upper German Province.[2]

Once the news of the upheavals had reached America (in April 1848), the provincial superior, Ignatius Brocard, wasted no time in extending an offer of asylum to as many refugee Jesuits as the Maryland province could accommodate. He saw this turmoil as the opportunity to provide, for the first time, an excellent theological and philosophical faculty for the divinity school at

Georgetown, as well as a chance to strengthen the collegiate curriculum there, especially in mathematics and the natural sciences, including astronomy. "Perhaps also with their arrival," he suggested to the general, "new houses can be formed in Pennsylvania, Virginia and other states where we have been unable to fulfil our hopes of having schools. . . ."[3] German and Swiss Jesuits were sent in response to his request. Besides Villiger, they included John Bapst, Joseph Duverney, Francis Knackstedt, and Bernard Wiget.

That same year James Ryder, who was beginning his second term as president of Georgetown, offered shelter in America to certain Italian Jesuits who earlier had found refuge in England. Accordingly, Ryder was advised in October 1848 that the exiled director of the observatory at the Roman College, Francisco De Vico, was preparing to lead "a glorious assemblage of Fathers & scholastics" to Georgetown.[4] Ryder had been especially interested in bringing De Vico to Georgetown ever since he had met him in Rome in 1845. In fact, De Vico, who had earned an international reputation for his moon crater discoveries and other important planetary and cometary observations, had already agreed to take on the direction of the Georgetown observatory after a brief earlier trip to the United States. Unfortunately, by the time the twenty-one Italians sailed for the United States, De Vico was too ill to join them. He died in London in November, a few days before the twenty-one landed in New York.[5] All told, twenty-seven Italian Jesuits reached the Maryland Province in the 1848–49 academic year. Even without De Vico, it was an extraordinary band of emigré scholars for it included Benedict Sestini, Angelo Secchi, Hugo Molza, Michael Tomei, Giovanni Battista Pianciani, Joseph Finotti, and Armillini Torquatus. The English newspaper *Western Times* (London) predicted that this remarkable "infusion" of scholars would allow Georgetown University "to rival the best University of Europe."[6] In all, forty-one Germans and twenty-seven Italians arrived in 1848.[7]

By 1851, of the more than two hundred Jesuits working in the Maryland Province nearly a fourth (49 of 213) had come from European provinces.[8] This European influx enabled Brocard to pursue plans for opening new colleges in both the South and East. For years, Jesuit provincials had had to decline the requests of bishops to establish schools in their dioceses. Now, within months of taking office Brocard was able to seriously consider possibilities for Charleston in South Carolina, Erie in Pennsylvania, and Richmond in Virginia. None of these plans came to fruition, but the Jesuit colleges in Washington, Philadelphia, Baltimore, and Boston were direct and indirect beneficiaries of the 1848–49 migrations.

Georgetown reaped the greatest benefits from the European exodus. When Brocard arrived at Washington in January 1848, the college was floundering. In the last year of Mulledy's second term as president there were fewer than ninety full-time students registered. In truth, college enrollments were down sharply all across the country in the late 1840s. Ignatius Combs, the assistant provincial, mistakenly blamed the lagging enrollments, at a time when "other Catholic colleges in the United States are well filled," on the failure of the foreign Jesuits to accommodate their teaching philosophy and discipline to American students.[9] Actually there were only three foreigners, including James Curley, among the fifteen faculty in 1848. Two years later, twelve of the seventeen Jesuit faculty were German or Italian; nevertheless the enrollment had doubled (to 183, including 132 boarders). In the decade after Combs complained to Roothaan, enrollments across the country rose dramatically again (67%). But Georgetown experienced an even more dramatic increase in the 1850s.[10] The great surge in enrollment at Georgetown, to nearly three hundred students by 1859, had many causes, but the presence of the foreign faculty was a major factor in the revival of the college, rather than the reverse. With an expanded corps of teachers the college was able not only to strengthen its core subjects but to add new ones as well. German and Hebrew appeared in the curriculum for the first time and chemistry and physics were regularly offered in science. Moreover, a number of the newcomers immediately began teaching their specialties in philosophy and theology to the Jesuit scholastics, both native and foreign. Francis Xavier Knackstedt offered courses in ethics and natural law; Giovanni Battista Pianciani taught dogmatic theology; Joseph Duverney scripture; Michael Tomei moral theology. In these subjects, language was no barrier since the classes were traditionally taught in Latin. But Italians and Germans also taught mathematics, the classics, French, German, Spanish, physics, chemistry, and music. Benedict Sestini, for instance, offered courses in astronomy and physics, and Angelo Secchi in physics.

Language was a problem both in and out of the classroom for most Italian and German Jesuits. The American scholastics taught English to non-English-speaking scholastics in half-hour classes three times a week.[11] However, the inevitable cultural differences between Europe and America compounded both teaching and living adjustments for these emigrés, particularly the Germans, who tended to disdain American ways and isolate themselves.[12] Then, too, the European Jesuits had no experience whatsoever of life in a boarding school serving lay students and Jesuit students alike—and one situated halfway between country and city at that. As an earlier emigré remarked when he wrote to Rome, "it is not an urban college for vineyards and a farm adjoin it, and it is situated outside a city; nor is it a rural one for our library, museum, and the gardens . . . are almost daily visited by the learned and unlearned, men and women and children alike. . . . [I]t is not a cloister since it is surrounded by no walls; . . . nor is it a secular boarding school for priests and scholastics also live there."[13] Besides, the presence of women on the grounds and guests in the dining room scandalized them. And the American familiarity between generations was something alien to their sensibilities. One Italian Jesuit who came upon George Fenwick and Thomas Mulledy in a field on the campus with their arms around students had to assure himself that the two were doing no wrong; still he reported to Roothaan that he found it extremely inappropriate behavior for a religious.[14] In addition, the hot, humid climate of Washington still worked a fearsome "malarial" seasoning on newcomers. In fact, John Bapst, the young Swiss, had to be sent north to the Maine mission to regain his health before the end of 1848. Two others were moved to Pennsylvania to recuperate,[15] and four died within their first three years in Maryland.[16]

"Strangers by Our Own Firesides"

A further complication for the emigrés was the resurgence of nativism after the Mexican War. A flood tide of mostly Catholic immigrants (2,598,214 in the 1850s, five times the 1840s total), some further ill-advised attempts by some Catholics to secure public funds for parochial schools, a growing temperance movement, and restiveness over the growing sectional crisis nurtured a xenophobia which found convenient targets in Catholics, especially Jesuits. Moreover, in 1853 a papal diplomat, Archbishop Gaetano Bedini, had arrived in the United States as an emissary of the Papal States. One of his official instructions was to explore the possibility of establishing full diplomatic relations between the Holy See and the United States. Bedini, who had been the papal governor of Bologna when the revolution was put down bloodily in the Papal States by the Austrian army, was at once labeled the "Butcher of Bologna" by radical expatriates living in the United States. He was forced to abandon his diplomatic mission in January of 1854 after crowds threatened him in Pittsburgh, Wheeling, and Cincinnati. Shortly after he returned to Washington that same month, a Washington mob seized the stone sent by the Holy See for the Washington Monument, vandalized it, and dumped it into the Potomac. Despite the condemnation of the attacks by U.S. government officials, Bedini left the city hastily after a formal reception at the college (he had previously attended Georgetown's July 1853 commencement).[17]

A year after Bedini's departure, a crowd in Ellsworth, Maine, attacked Father John Bapst, the Swiss refugee who had been sent north from Georgetown because of his health. Earlier, his concern for the Passamaquoddy Indians and the Irish immigrants and his work and teaching in the town of Ellsworth had quickly led to Protestant conversions as well as to some confrontations. He also had become a most outspoken critic of the local public school policy of obliging Catholic children to read the King James Version of the Bible in the classroom. Tensions grew there and elsewhere throughout New England in the early months of 1854. That same summer Catholic churches in Manchester and Bath, Maine, were destroyed. The bishop thereupon moved Bapst to Bangor (on the Penobscot River) for his own protection. However, when he returned to Ellsworth in October a crowd dragged him from the home of a parishioner, stripped off his clothes, tarred and feathered his bare body, and then paraded him about the town for hours on a plank. Afterwards, Bapst assured his superiors that he was hurt "neither in body nor mind." Indeed he felt that the intended shaming had instead won him sympathy from many non-Catholics in Maine. Nonetheless, he saw himself as only the temporary center of "a rising storm."[18]

Eventually Georgetown College found itself near the eye of that storm of nativist unrest. Maryland, and especially Baltimore, was the scene of an on-going confrontation between a rising tide of Catholicism on whose crest Georgetown College rode conspicuously and an ebbtide of antithetical back-flowing nativism. Twenty percent of Baltimore's population was foreign born by 1850. During that decade, job-hunting German and Irish immigrants, many of them Catholics, disembarked and streamed into the city in increasing numbers. In 1852 a somewhat naive Catholic delegate introduced in the legislature a bill to secure funding for sectarian schools. That same year the First Plenary Council of the American Catholic hierarchy convened in Baltimore. The scores of robed prelates and priests who marched to the cathedral provided a spectacle of pomp, a New York journalist noted, "such as Republicans are not wont to look upon."[19] And earlier in 1851, when Archbishop Eccleston died at Visitation Monastery in Georgetown, Church and State had seemed to join in the funeral comfortably. The Marine Band led the parade, then came the Georgetown students in their college uniforms, next a cross-bearer and the clergy, and the hearse, followed by carriages in which President Millard Fillmore, members of the Cabinet, and the mayors of Georgetown and Washington rode in procession. Various Catholic societies marched on foot to complete the solemnities.[20] To many disgruntled and perhaps "unrecognized" non-Catholic Marylanders the growing power of the Catholic Church seemed all too evident and undesirable. In a community disrupted by demographic and socioeconomic changes that were hastening the decline of slavery and its plantation economy, both immigrants and Catholics "served, like lightning rods, to attract the apprehensive attentions of citizens whose old ways of life were disappearing. . . ."[21] Nowhere was the American Party, the political organ of the nativists, stronger than in Maryland. In fact, the American Party elected its candidate mayor of Baltimore in 1854. The following year it captured the state legislature. In 1856 Maryland became the only state to cast its electoral votes for the American "Know-Nothing" presidential candidate, Millard Fillmore. (The former President of the United States came in a distant third in that race.)

Although there were far fewer immigrants in the District than in Baltimore in the 1850 census records (some 4,918 of 51,687), the anti-Catholic animus expressed itself there as well. The recently reopened Washington Seminary, which had attracted a large number of non-Catholic students, suffered a sharp drop in enrollment in 1851. "Considerable opposition had been got up against it," Thomas Lilly reported that September in his diary; "several other schools were put on foot."[22] The Know-Nothing Party itself became a dominant force in Washington the same year that it triumphed in Baltimore. In June 1854, the party gained control of the mayor's office and a majority of the seats on the city council of the city of Washington—positions the Know-Nothings held until a hastily organized Anti-Know-Nothing Party elected a Georgetown alumnus, William Magruder (**C** 1808–9), mayor in 1856 and a majority of the city councilmen a year later. By 1858 Washington's Know-Nothing Party was extinct.

Georgetown itself still had a large Catholic population. Nevertheless, when President James Ryder and his fellow directors had petitioned the Thirty-First Congress in 1850 to change the western boundary of the town so that none of the college grounds would any longer be legally included within the corporate limits and thus subject to local, municipal taxation, they complained to the Congress at the same time of the contemptuous treatment that the college had received from the town over the past four decades. This, they wrote, was despite the considerable revenue they brought to it ($30,000 a year by their claim), the hundreds of local youth they had educated for free, and the poor families they had sustained.[23] The town responded to the college petition by saying that "There is no greater reason why any gentleman's garden within the limits of our town . . . should not be excluded . . . than these lots. . . . Our town is very sensitive on this subject." Five years earlier the grounds of the Visitation monastery and school had been removed from the town's jurisdiction and tax base, the commissioners informed the Congress, "against the wish of the mass of our people." Once again, said they, the petition for redress was "from one of the richest institutions in the land. . . . With what feeble voice we have, we do insist that our town should not be impaired in the integrity of its limits, and our people almost unanimously say the same."[24] The petition (for what would have been *de facto* tax exemption) died in committee at that time.

In February 1855, Charles Stonestreet, then provincial superior, wrote a letter to local newspapers to respond to the hoary charge that Jesuits took an oath to the pope to overthrow non-Catholic rulers. "I am humiliated as a Marylander," he wrote,

to . . . repel the charge of more than latent treason! The Western shore of Maryland, the home of my childhood, has ever been a classic place, cherished in my heart with patriotic pride. There are the remains of my grandfather, a revolutionary soldier, and there, in an adjoining county, is the landing place of 'The Pilgrims of St. Mary's,' whose brightest scenes and best memories are imperishably connected with the Jesuits' name.

. . . I can not help seeing in this, an effort to render me and my brethren in religion, aliens at home and strangers by our own firesides.[25]

Unfortunately, many other Jesuits in the District and Maryland *were* legally aliens. And the less than attractive persistence of Germans and Italians in clinging exclusively to their native speech while openly decrying American ways was providing welcome ammunition for the nativist attacks. As one Marylander warned the superior general in 1854, national and ethnic differences that had previously "unsettled only our houses and colleges" now had much larger repercussions.[26] After the nativist political triumphs in Maryland, Stonestreet wrote in the spring of 1856 to Rome: "we are in a crisis." Indeed, Stonestreet worried that nativism might poison the presidential election that year. "In such a situation prudence seems very much in order for us. . . ."[27] Such prudence apparently dictated strategic name changing. It is interesting to note the anglicization of names, mostly Irish, that appeared in the Maryland Province catalogues during this period. Thus "O'Hagan" became "Hegan," "O'Donoghue" "Donoghue," "O'Callaghan" "Calligan," and "Bauermeister" "Barrister." Where there had been seven priests and scholastics indexed under O' in 1854, there were none by 1858.

In reality, the most serious threat to the emigrés remaining in America came not from nativists but from the Society of Jesus itself. When the counterrevolutionary armies quickly restored the *status quo ante revolutionem* in Europe, the Jesuit superiors in Germany and Italy wanted to recall their members from America. Despite the difficulties of acculturation and acclimatization that the Europeans were certainly experiencing, Ignatius Brocard realized what a disaster it would be to lose these refugees. He pleaded with the superior general not to withdraw the Europeans, who were making indispensable contributions to the education of lay and Jesuit students alike, particularly at Georgetown.[28] Brocard's pleas to Roothaan were successful. Eleven German and Swiss Jesuits remained in the United States, including John Bapst, Joseph Duverney, Francis Knackstedt, Burchard Villiger, and Bernard Wiget. An equal number of Italians, most at their own request, stayed on to work in the colleges and missions, including Angelo Paresce, Joseph Ardia, Anthony Ciampi, and Benedict Sestini. Of fifty-eight European Jesuits who taught at the college between 1845 and 1860, the majority were Italians (55.4%), with Germans and Swiss constituting a strong minority (28.5%). Although their median length of stay was slightly under two years (compared to five and a half years for faculty in the 1830s), twelve remained five or more years at Georgetown.

The Faculty in the 1850s

By 1850 Georgetown, with eight professors and instructors, had a slightly larger than average American college faculty. (Most institutions of higher education in the South only had between four and six faculty each.) In fact, Georgetown's faculty-student ratio was also slightly better than the one in twenty that many major colleges averaged during that period.[29] As a group the Georgetown faculty was very young, with a median age of twenty-five and a half for all faculty who began to teach in the 1840s and 1850s. The oldest member of the college faculty during the 1850s was Father George Fenwick (1801–57), who had been teaching English and the classics at the college since his return from Rome in 1829. Another notable American among the Jesuit faculty of the period was James Clark (1809–85). The son of a Pennsylvania farmer, Clark had received an appointment to the United States Military Academy at West Point, from which he was graduated in 1829. Subsequently, he distinguished himself as an engineer and a mathematician. A convert to Catholicism, Clark enrolled at Mount St. Mary's College to study for the priesthood before entering the Society of Jesus in 1844. For the next thirty-five years, between terms as president of Holy Cross and Gonzaga Colleges, Clark filled many positions at Georgetown, from mathematics and chemistry professor to prefect of discipline to vice president to treasurer.

In the 1850s Georgetown also had a significant increase in lay faculty. They had virtually disappeared since the return of the Jesuits in 1806. For instance, of forty-six faculty who began teaching in the 1830s, all but two were Jesuits. In the next decade only the dancing and drawing instructors were not members of the Society. But in the 1850s, sixteen of forty-seven were laymen who taught not only fencing, music, and dancing but also Latin, French literature, Greek, Spanish, and mathematics. Rising enrollments (more than three hundred students by 1857), and the opening of four additional Jesuit colleges in the East were threatening to swamp faculty resources. "I wish you could come to our relief," President Bernard Maguire wrote during the Panic of 1857 to Stonestreet, then provincial, "or we will have to close doors and break up like all the Banks & merchants of the Country—Not for the want of money but of men— . . ."[30] Lay faculty became the only alternative. Among those teaching music was the German refugee, Charles Bergmann, who was the conductor of the Handel and Hayden Society in Boston (1853–54) and of the New York Philharmonic in New York City (1858–76). Between these appointments he offered courses at Georgetown in the 1854–55 academic year. John Caulfield of the District taught music and was the college organist from 1855 to 1866. An alumnus, James Alexander Simpson (**C** 1815–16), a local landscape and portrait artist who had taught the fine arts periodically at the college in the 1820s and 1830s, rejoined the faculty in the late 1850s. Two other laymen were alumni—Manuel Garcia De Zuniga from Uruguay (1855, AB, 1856, MA) was an instructor in Spanish from 1855 to 1857 and William Wills (1851, AB, 1859, MA) taught Latin, French, Greek, and mathematics. Wills also served as the first athletic director, from 1858 to 1861. Most laymen stayed only a year or two. Although financial records for the period have not survived, it is highly likely that annual salaries for the lay faculty were quite low, probably less than a thousand dollars (Jesuits received none). The average faculty salary at Harvard for the same period was $2,550.[31] In addition, the number of positions open to laypersons depended on the number of available Jesuits. A heavy turnover in lay faculty was inevitable.

The Astronomical Observatory

A chief magnet for some of the Jesuit refugees was Georgetown's newly established astronomical observatory. It was the first of the two-stage improvement that James Ryder had first articulated in 1832. In both his terms as president (1840–45, 1848–51) Ryder seized the opportunity to create the conditions to achieve his goal—to make Georgetown a university in which advanced training in science and the professions would be an integral part of the curriculum. The building of the observatory (1843–44) finally realized in stone what Grassi and Wallace had hoped to do in 1815. By the end of the 1840s three other colleges—North Carolina, Williams, and Western Reserve—had erected similar small observatories. During those years public enthusiasm for these "lighthouses of the skies" was clearly growing, but public funding did not necessarily follow. Neither federal nor state support of science was then considered an appropriate function of a republican government.[32] The development of the observatory at Georgetown was typical of the private character of the astronomy "movement" in antebellum America. Although Ryder gave strong official backing to the project, it was another Irish immigrant Jesuit who was responsible for its physical conception and realization. James Curley (1796–1889) had come to the United States from County Roscommon in 1817, and had taught English at the Washington Seminary before entering the Society in 1827. In 1831 he began to teach natural philosophy and mathematics at Georgetown, subjects he had essentially taught himself from the age of thirteen in his native Ireland.[33]

The idea of an observatory had apparently been long in Curley's mind. Finding the money to build and equip it was another matter for a debt-ridden college. Once again the key source was the legacies of two Jesuit scholastics. Thomas Meredith Jenkins was an aspiring astronomer who in 1841 offered $8,000 he had inherited from his mother, so Curley could begin construction. Jenkins also persuaded some relatives to donate astronomical instruments. And Charles Stonestreet promised another $2,000 from a similar inheritance for instruments.[34] With these pledges and with nearly unanimous support at George-

Architect's rendering of the Astronomical Observatory's south elevation, as seen when facing the ridge on which Georgetown's "lighthouse of the skies" was sited in 1843. (Georgetown University Archives)

PLATE I.

GEORGETOWN COLLEGE OBSERVATORY.

SOUTH ELEVATION.

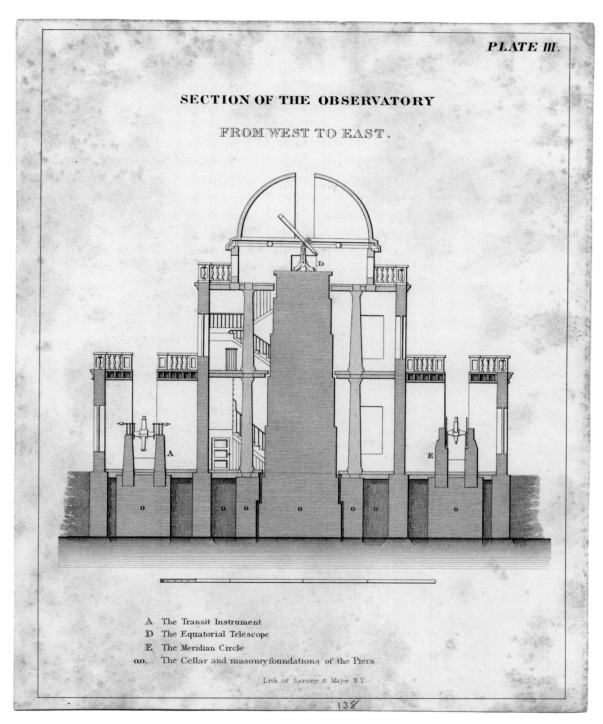

PLATE III.

SECTION OF THE OBSERVATORY

FROM WEST TO EAST.

A   The Transit Instrument
D   The Equatorial Telescope
E   The Meridian Circle
o,o. .... The Cellar and masonry foundations of the Piers

Lith of Sarony & Major N.Y.

Cross section of Georgetown's observatory showing the transit instrument, the equatorial telescope, the meridian circle, and the granite piers sunk in the three-foot-thick masonry foundation embedded in the ridge at the Hilltop. (Georgetown University Archives)

town, Curley secured permission in 1843 (the procurator thought it "a true folly" but felt it "worse than useless" to attempt to preach fiscal sanity amidst such enthusiasm).[35] Curley chose the site, a ridge between the vineyard and the pasture, designed the building with granite piers and three-foot-thick foundations, and ordered the best instruments available in Europe (an equatorial telescope, a large transit instrument, and a meridian circle for measuring the declination of stars). The meridian circle or clock was made in London for approximately £400, and the telescope was made in Germany by Merz and Mahler, the prestigious optical company whose only previous American contracts had been for the City of Philadelphia observatory and for the one at the United States Military Academy in West Point, New York.[36] Construction of the building began in the spring of 1843.

It turned out later that Father Curley had misinterpreted Father General Roothaan's letter as a reply that conveyed permission for the observatory. (Like McElroy, Curley barely read Latin, and Roothaan's sophisticated, elegant Latin was especially complex.) In his 1843 reply the superior general had approved the idea of an observatory in principle and the further planning for it, not its immediate construction. When he subsequently discovered that the United States Navy had just constructed an observatory less than two miles from Georgetown, Roothaan was even more displeased. But if James Curley's Latin was poor, his diplomacy was of another order entirely. He assured Roothaan in a December letter that the Naval Observatory was mainly intended as a depository for instruments, implying that it would complement, not compete with, Georgetown's; and furthermore, that the Georgetown observatory, even before its completion, was building public esteem for the college's commitment to science and thus attracting additional contributions. He ended his explanations by asking if the father general would not himself like to contribute a comet-searcher to their new facility.[37]

Curley's depiction of the naval facility as a depository was technically correct but somewhat misleading—thanks to the Congress. True, it had been created in 1830 as a Depot of Charts and Instruments, but by 1840 it had a full-time staff involved at least indirectly in observations. In 1842 several naval officers, in the hope of creating a national observatory, persuaded the Congress to allocate $25,000 to make the depot a working observatory. But Congress, not wishing to acknowledge that it was funding such a facility, insisted that the facility continue to be called a depository. Whatever its name, by 1844 the Depot had a permanent staff and excellent instruments for astronomical observation.[38]

The superior general, although unfamiliar with the political intricacies of Washington, nevertheless was unmoved by Curley's explanations. If anything, he expected the observatory would be seen not as a monument to science but as a sheer extravagance in hard times. Curley was next instructed to stop the project and take no more contributions.[39] Fortunately for Georgetown's subsequent scholarly history, letters from Rome could and usually did

James Curley, SJ (1796–1889). The first director of the Astronomical Observatory, and, for nearly sixty years, a member of the college faculty, is seated in the chair presented to him by President Abraham Lincoln. Photograph taken about 1865 by Mathew Brady. (Georgetown University Archives)

take several months to reach America in the 1840s. By the time Roothaan's February 1844 letter was in hand, the observatory was virtually completed and its instruments had already been received from Munich and elsewhere.[40] The building had cost approximately $9,000; the instruments perhaps twice that amount.[41]

Francisco De Vico was one of the first Jesuits that Ignatius Brocard sought to bring to America from Italy. De Vico was the renowned director of the Roman observatory, and Brocard was well aware of the impact that such a distinguished scientist could have in Washington, "under the eyes of the government, the Senate, the Representatives from all the States of the Union, . . ." Appropriately alerted, the press was anticipating De Vico's arrival as a coup for the whole country by 1848. De Vico, Brocard observed to Roothaan, could train a generation of astronomers to perpetuate his work in the heart of the republican colossus "so that scientific studies will flourish among us."[42] Unfortunately, as we know, De Vico died before coming to America; but his assistant, Benedict Sestini, was able to carry on his work at Georgetown. The thirty-two-year-old Sestini, a native of Florence, had studied mathematics and physics with the renowned Andrea Carraffa at the Roman College before working under De Vico. He pleaded with Roothaan that with the proper lenses and books he could do in Georgetown "for many years" the work he had been doing in Rome. Obviously undergoing a change of heart, the superior general obliged him by sending both.[43] Within a year of his arrival, Sestini had secured contracts with the federal government for projects involving the study of sunspots. That research was published by the Naval Observatory in 1853.[44] Sestini remained active at Georgetown for twenty years altogether. During that time he published several textbooks on mathematics, ranging from *Analytical Geometry* (1852) to the *Manual of Geometrical and Infinitesimal Analysis* (1871).[45]

Another Jesuit astronomer, Angelo Secchi (1818–78), whose spectroscopic research on luminous stars would later earn him recognition as the "father of astrophysics," did little on-site work at the observatory during his brief stay. Nevertheless one of the highlights of the Georgetown commencement in 1849 was the exhibition of an electrical battery which Secchi had constructed and used to magnetize a hundred-pound bar to hold up a sixteen-hundred-pound weight.[46] However, his research on electrical rheometry for Joseph Henry of the Smithsonian Institution was published by that Institution in 1852 as part of its *Contributions to Knowledge* series.[47] By that time Secchi had been appointed director of the Roman College observatory and was no longer in America.

In 1846 James Curley, in collaboration with astronomers at the Royal Observatory in England and at Washington's Naval Observatory, used the 4.5-inch Ertel transit instrument in the west wing of the observatory to successfully compare a series of observations he had made of transits of the moon. He then calculated the longitude and latitude of the observatory, and by triangulation that of key sites in the District of Columbia, including the Smithsonian Institution, the Capitol, the White House, and the Washington monument.[48] This was the first scientific determination that verified the longitude of the nation's capital, the very calculation that Grassi and Wallace had been asked to make thirty years before. Curley's findings were published in the first (and only) volume of the *Annals of the Astronomical Observatory of Georgetown, D.C.* in 1852. That same year the college also published a mathematics textbook by Sestini.[49]

By 1852 Curley had acquired an astronomical library of some five hundred volumes through both donations and purchases. Among the donors

Map of the main campus in 1853. It should be noted that the Observatory is not sited in this area. Plotted and drawn by Father Curley. (Georgetown University Archives)

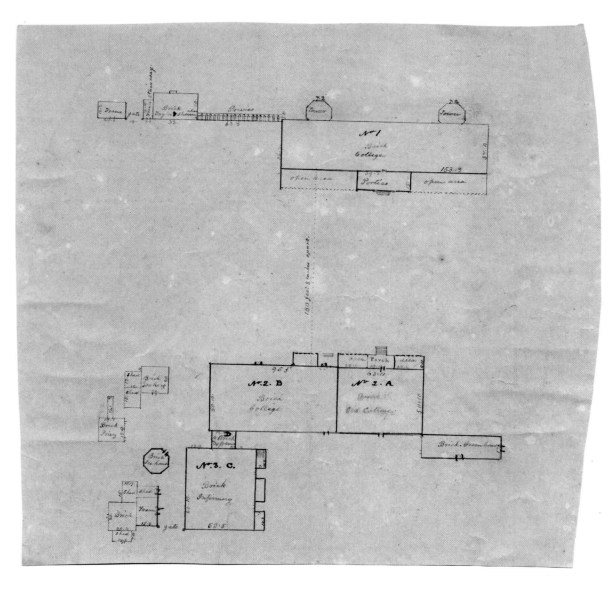

were the Royal Astronomical Society of London, the University of Cambridge Observatory, the East India Company Observatory at Madras, the University of Oxford, the Smithsonian, and Matthew Maury, Superintendent of the Naval Observatory. But after this initial activity, Curley and Sestini made little use of the observatory for scientific research. Curley was immersed in many other duties at the college and tended to regard the observatory as a teaching rather than a research facility. Sestini, unlike Curley, was specially trained in modern astronomy but soon his interests turned to mathematics and away from astronomy. Neither he nor Curley trained any astronomers. The hilltop did not yet provide the congenial environment for scientific enlightenment that Brocard had originally envisioned when he fought to keep the European Jesuits in America.[50]

The Medical Department

First conceived in 1830, the second of Ryder's two-stage efforts toward the making of a university from the college was the establishment of a Georgetown medical department in 1849. Medical schools in the United States had numbered thirteen by 1820; there were to be forty-seven by 1860, one of which was Georgetown's. This proliferation of medical educational institutions derived in part from the need and the desire practitioners had to improve their low status in prescientific medicine in American society. Challenged by the rise of homeopathy and by the anti-elitist bias of the Jacksonians, which were both, among other things, diminishing the licensing power of the medical societies, American doctors sought to bolster their position through professional reform.[51] Both need and desire were addressed by changing the mode of training from apprenticeships to more prestigious teaching programs affiliated with universities. Since dispensaries or infirmaries were usually attached to such institutions, the professional and financial privileges that medical faculty thereby enjoyed were other reasons for establishing medical departments or schools.[52] Thus competition for professional advantage and privilege within communities led to more and more schools.

The Georgetown Medical Department was in part created by such societal pressures. There was already one medical school in the city, the Medical Department of Columbian College, and it controlled access to the city's lone hospital as well as to membership in the newly established national regulatory agency, the American Medical Association.[53] Such an institutional monopoly was intolerable to ambitious medical professionals not connected to the Columbian Medical School, especially in a period when educational institutions that awarded medical degrees were replacing medical societies as the effective licensers in the profession.[54] At the suggestion of John Carroll Brent (**C** 1830–33, AB), a Georgetown graduate and close friend of Ryder, several local doctors approached the president in the fall of 1849 about beginning a medical department under the auspices of Georgetown College.[55] Within two weeks President Ryder and his consulters had approved the arrangement, "so long as no condition or burden be imposed upon the College."[56] In their application to Ryder these doctors made clear their intention to start a "Medical College" in the District of Columbia in the next year, affiliated either with Georgetown or with some other university.[57] Whether as an expedient (fear that the doctors might go elsewhere) or because of his memory of the last, failed attempt to sponsor a medical faculty, Ryder sought no permission from Rome. By this time another Jesuit institution, Saint Louis University, had already established a medical school (1836), without formal Roman approval, when Peter Verhaegen had been president. In any event, the four doctors (Noble Young, Flodoardo Howard, Charles H. Liebermann, and Johnson Eliot) received the initial faculty appointments from Ryder.[58]

Three of these four—Young, Howard, and Eliot—were graduates of the medical department at Columbian, which they were challenging, at least indirectly. Noble Young (1808–83), a native of Baltimore, had grown up in Washington and attended the Jesuits' Washington Seminary. After graduating in medicine from Columbian in 1828, he had built a very successful practice in the District and had been for several years house physician for the United States penitentiary.[59] Johnson Eliot (1815–83), whose family had deep roots in both colonial Massachusetts and Maryland, had gone to work as a druggist's assistant at the age of thirteen. He remained in the pharmaceutical business for eleven years, before studying medicine privately and then at Columbian, where he earned his degree in 1842. Upon graduation Eliot had joined the Columbian faculty as a demonstrator of anatomy.[60] Flodoardo Howard (1814–88), a native Virginian, had also operated a pharmacy in the District before beginning medical studies, first as an apprentice and later as a student in the Columbian department.[61]

The fourth founder of Georgetown's medical department, Charles H. Liebermann (1812–86), was a Latvian who had studied medicine at the University of Dorpat (now Tartu) in Russia. But, while still a student, Liebermann had been imprisoned by the Russian government for his involvement in the Polish independence movement in the 1830s. He and several others managed to escape from their Siberian prison and flee to Germany. There he completed his medical training at the University of Berlin. His subsequent return to Czarist Russia led to a second imprisonment and banishment. After short stays in Holland and England, Liebermann arrived in Washington in 1840, convinced that the nation's capital was the ideal place to practice medicine, despite his lack of English. He quickly developed a highly successful practice but he also quickly concluded that the medical training in the District was far inferior to what he had known in Europe. Thus for Liebermann, at least, the opportunity to improve medical education was a pressing motive along with the professional considerations that prompted all in the group to want to establish a new school.[62]

Constructed in 1850–51 and used until 1869, the medical department's first building was at the corner of F and 12th Streets NW, in Washington, DC. Photograph taken ca. 1885. (Georgetown University Archives)

In the initial organization of the school, Liebermann played the principal role, serving as chief planner and treasurer. Eliot became the first dean. Young, the oldest and professionally the most well established of the group, was chosen president. Young was also the only Catholic. The other three founders, Eliot, Howard, and Liebermann, were Episcopalian, Methodist, and Jewish, respectively, although Eliot later converted to Catholicism. Their approach to Georgetown College had been entirely a practical matter of seeking an affiliation with the only institution in the District, besides Columbian, that was empowered to grant degrees. Indeed, the four had initially favored a relationship with the University of Virginia, but had been persuaded by John Carroll Brent, a relative of Johnson Eliot, that affiliation with the Jesuit college would be desirable but would not entail Jesuit control.[63]

Throughout America in the first half of the nineteenth century, medical education continued to be a proprietary enterprise in which groups of doctors shared control, as well as costs and profits.[64] Thus, because Georgetown was such a proprietary school, its medical faculty was to be responsible not only for its own government but for its finances and facilities as well. A constitution, adopted in April 1850, established rules specifying that each faculty member would share equally in the proceeds from student tuition revenues as well as in the costs of the rental, construction, and maintenance of facilities.[65] The members first leased a building in the fall of 1849 on the southeast corner of F and 12th Streets in northwest Washington. It was to house both lecture halls and an infirmary, and they intended to begin course lectures in May of 1850.[66] But a few months after they acquired the two-story building the members concluded that it was inadequate for their needs and decided to build an additional facility, if it were within their means.[67] They therefore purchased an adjacent lot that same spring and started construction of a modest three-story building containing two lecture rooms and a dissecting lab. So limited were their finances that gas lighting was not added until 1852—more than a year after the building was completed.[68] By then they had also been forced to rent out the first floor to a butcher and some merchants in order to secure additional revenue.[69] Nonetheless, they continued leasing the original building and converted it into an infirmary with twelve beds for "nonresident paupers." An attempt to secure $2,000 in government funding to support the infirmary had already failed in 1850 so the members themselves bore the costs of renovation and conversion, which were approximately $3,000.[70] By the fall of 1850 a six-bed dispensary was functioning in this F Street building, which was also used for surgical operations and clinical lectures.[71] In May of 1851 the first four-month session of classes began. Father Ryder gave the opening address to a large audience.[72]

Fears of Jesuit attempts to take over the school proved premature. Apart from Ryder's inaugural address, the only association that the president of Georgetown College was to have with the medical department would be in the conferring of degrees at commencement, and in ratifying the formal appointments of those professors who would be recruited and selected by the founders (but not in their dismissal). The medical faculty, for its part, seems to have been disappointed in the minimal support they received from these same college authorities, whose control they feared. One source of such frustration was the failure of the college to supply a much-needed chemistry professor to the Medical Department, despite Ryder's initial promise of such assistance and even after repeated pleas for over a year from the founding doctors that they needed such help so that the department might open. Finally the doctors were forced to find their own professor in the spring of 1851.[73]

Another source of frustration was the perception in the new medical department that the college had undermined the doctors' attempt to secure federal funding for their infirmary. Although President Ryder himself had sent a letter to the congressional committee, attesting to his "lively interest in the success of their enterprise," another Jesuit official at the college, probably

MEDICAL DEPARTMENT OF GEORGETOWN COLLEGE,

Corner of F and 12th streets, Washington, D. C.

SUMMER COURSE—FACULTY.

NOBLE YOUNG, M. D., Professor of Principles and Practice of Medicine.

CHARLES H. LIEBERMAN, M. D., Professor of Institutes and Practice of Surgery.

FLODOARDO HOWARD, M. D., Professor of Obstetrics and Diseases of Women and Children.

JOHNSON ELLIOT, M. D., Professor of Anatomy.

JOSHUA RITCHIE, M. D., Professor of Institutes of Medicine.

JAMES M. AUSTIN, M. D., Professor of Materia Medica and Therapeutics.

J. W. H. LOVEJOY, M. D., Professor of Chemistry.

SAMUEL W. EVERETT, M. D., Adjunct Professor and Demonstrator of Anatomy.

The Lectures will commence on the second Monday in May, and continue four months.

Clinical Lectures will be delivered and operations performed on patients from the Infirmary and Public Dispensary attached to the College, commencing in May, and continuing during the year.

The College building has been recently erected at great expense, provided with large and convenient Lecture Halls and Anatomical rooms, and is admirably adapted for Medical instruction.

The supply of material is at all times ample, and every facility is afforded for the successful prosecution of Anatomy.

Fee for the full course	$70
Matriculation, (paid only once,)	5
Graduation	25
Demonstrator's ticket	10
Perpetual ticket	150
Fee for those who have attended two full courses in other Colleges	50

For further information address

FLODOARDO HOWARD, M. D. *Registrar,*

Corner of F and Tenth streets.

☞ The Winter course of Lectures will commence on Monday, November 3, 1851.

The fee for this course is $90—all other charges the same as in the summer course.

The expenses of living in Washington are as moderate as in any other city in the Union.

WASHINGTON, *April 2, 1851.*

Patrick Duddy, the treasurer, had privately disavowed to the same committee any connection of Georgetown College with the new school, convincing at least one medical faculty member that the Jesuits had been responsible for scuttling the attempt to get funding. The medical department's feelings about Jesuit attitudes only worsened at the first commencement in 1852, a joint one held in July with the College, when no mention was made of the first four medical department graduates. Their degrees, it turned out, had already been put in the mail.[74] After that, the medical department held its own separate commencements, usually at the Smithsonian, but the president of Georgetown College did distribute the diplomas. In December 1853, in an effort to improve relations, the medical faculty offered a free course of lectures to as many as six Georgetown College students and invited those "in the class of physiology" to attend any lecture at the medical department that they should choose.[75] Nevertheless, contact between the college and department remained minimal for the next two decades. Thus Georgetown's Medical School continued to be a virtually independent enterprise.

First announcement sent out by Georgetown's new medical department in April 1851. (Georgetown University Archives)

Georgetown Medical Student Demographics

In the fall of 1850 the faculty had recruited students by placing advertisements about the opening of the medical department in newspapers in Alexandria, Baltimore, Georgetown, and Washington. During those first years (1851–60), more than half (52%) of the fifty-seven graduates were from Maryland and the District of Columbia. The South and the Northeast together accounted for about a third more (20% and 14%), and the Northcentral for less than a fifth (14%). The rest of the students (10.7%) were from Europe or Central America. This wide-ranging regional distribution is somewhat misleading since many of the numerous nonlocal students were temporary District residents and were either employed in government departments or in private businesses. The narrow area targeted by the advertising seems a truer reflection of the school's coincidental demographics than of an intended diversity in students' place of origin. Moreover, as a "sundown college" whose classes ran from five in the afternoon until nine o'clock in the evening, the medical department was an ideal place for young men who had other jobs but who aspired to a career in medicine (see table 6.1 in appendix F).

There were virtually no formal requirements for admission to the course of lectures, other than an annual payment of $105 in lecture, matriculation, and clinical fees. This was a fairly modest expenditure for even a low-level government clerk (average annual salary, $1,200). Others, such as school-teachers (average annual salary, $500), would have been much less likely to be able to afford it.[76] For a typical day laborer or unskilled worker, earning $200 or less annually, that Georgetown tuition was a fortune, of course.

To qualify for a medical degree, the candidate had to be twenty-one years of age, "of good moral character, have applied himself for three years to the study of Medicine, have attended two full courses of Lectures" (one of which had to be at the department), pass an oral examination, and submit an original thesis.[77] Except for the thesis, these were standard requirements among most American medical schools of the period. A college degree, or indeed a college education itself, was considered of little value as a prerequisite to medical schooling. Since medicine had relatively low career appeal to college graduates at the time, few college graduates were likely to be candidates for admission (it was at that time a crowded field, with low social status and little monetary promise).[78] However, a one-year apprenticeship was still considered an integral part of medical training; each student was responsible for arranging to work privately for and with a reputable physician. Moreover, the lectures, whose subject matter was basically unchanged from year to year, complemented that medical apprenticeship, as it still did to some degree in Europe. The conventional wisdom of the American academic medical community prevailed—that repetition of the lectures was the best way for students to complement their practical experience as apprentices. Practically speaking, this was functional as well as customary since medical textbooks were virtually unknown.[79]

The median age at graduation for Georgetown medical students was slightly less than twenty-four, with students ranging from twenty-one to thirty-six years in age.[80] Enrollment records indicate that most of the first students had little previous formal education beyond the secondary level. Joseph Eastman (**M** 1863–65) was exceptional even for those times. His formal education consisted of a few months of "winter school" before, at age eighteen, he began working as a blacksmith in New York in 1860.[81] Nevertheless, Eastman earned a creditable medical degree in three years. Only seven medical graduates of the first decade are known to have previously attended college, including three from Georgetown; none took undergraduate degrees.[82] Nearly two-thirds (64.3%) of these same fifty-seven graduates were Anglo-Americans, with those of Irish (16.1%) and French (10.7%) extraction the significant minorities. More than half of them were Catholic

(56.1%). Many, if not most, were already employed when they began their medical education. Charles Allen of Virginia, for instance, had worked at the federal arsenal since 1852. While continuing to work there, he enrolled in the Medical Department in 1859 and received his MD in 1861. Daniel Boone Clarke (**M** 1855–57, MD) had been a pharmacist in the District of Columbia for a decade before beginning classes at Georgetown at the age of thirty. He continued to operate his pharmacy until his retirement from medicine in 1874, after which he served as president of a bank and insurance company, as well as a member of the City Council of Washington. Silas Lawrence Loomis (**M** 1855–57, MD) from Connecticut had attended Wesleyan College there and then taught school in Massachusetts and Rhode Island before moving to Washington in 1854 to open a school at 17th and I Streets, Northwest. He later was appointed professor of chemistry and toxicology at Georgetown and taught for several years (1861–67) before becoming dean of the medical faculty at Howard University. Samuel Jacobs Radcliff (**M** 1851–52) of Washington, a member of the first graduation class, had begun an apprenticeship with Flodoardo Howard at the age of twenty in 1849.

One of the most renowned early graduates of the medical department was Charles Frederic Girard (**M** 1854–56, MD). Girard, a native of France (1822–95), had studied science at the University of Neuchâtel in Switzerland where he became an assistant to the noted biologist Louis Agassiz. In 1848 he followed Agassiz to America and joined the staff of the Smithsonian Institution. Six years later he enrolled in Georgetown's medical department. Following his graduation at the age of thirty-four, he concentrated his energies on zoological studies and eventually gained international recognition for his extensive research publications. In 1861 he was awarded the Cuvier Prize by the Institute of France and returned to his own country in 1865 at the end of America's Civil War. There he finally practiced medicine for thirty years until his death at seventy-three years of age.

The Medical Department Faculty

The traditional five-month program of classes at Georgetown's Medical School was scheduled to run regularly from October through February, six days a week; and the curriculum repeated each year, remaining basically unchanged, until 1876. Students were expected to attend these lectures repeated by the faculty on their specialties for two consecutive years. As early as 1855 the American Medical Association had urged that medical schools adopt a sequential two-year curriculum instead. The Georgetown medical faculty replied by recognizing the force of the AMA argument for a broader, yet less superficial grounding. But they also contended that they did not currently have the means to forego the traditional program, which covered every branch of medical science in outline each session. As a compromise they

did resolve to concentrate on some special aspects of each subject differently in each of the two years.[83] In practice, this concentration seems only to have amounted to scheduling a special lecture that one designated member of the faculty gave at the beginning of each academic year, a custom that seems to have lasted until the Civil War.

The original faculty consisted of the four founders and four of their colleagues. Noble Young, Charles Liebermann, Flodoardo Howard, and Johnson Eliot held appointments in medicine, surgery, obstetrics, and anatomy respectively. Joshua Ritchie (**C** 1827–35, AB), one of only three Georgetown day students who survived the purge of 1831 to graduate, was professor of physiology and materia medica; James Lovejoy, professor of chemistry; Samuel Everett, associate professor of anatomy; and Alexander Young, demonstrator of anatomy. It was a slightly larger than average medical faculty for the period and soon proved a transient one. By 1853 four of these eight original faculty had left; their average length of stay was less than four years. In the first decade alone twenty-six persons received appointments. A majority of them, like the founders, were not Catholics. Four were European immigrants, but most were locals. Twelve or nearly half had medical degrees—six each from Columbian and from Georgetown itself. Typically, few had medical training beyond the basic degree work,

The faculty of the medical department pose for a group photograph in the spring of 1868. Front row (*from left to right*): Silas Loomis, James Morgan, Johnson Eliot, Noble Young, Flodoardo Howard, Thomas Antisell, and Montgomery Johns. Back row: Daniel Hagner, Robert Reyburn, John Harry Thompson, and Warwick Evans. Photograph taken by Alexander Gardner. (Georgetown University Archives)

although most had considerable experience as apprentices in the practice of medicine. The median age at the time of these appointments was thirty years old.

Thomas Antisell (1817–93), a notable addition to the faculty in 1858, was atypical. An Anglo-Irishman, Antisell had been educated at Trinity College and the Dublin School of Medicine before graduating from the Royal College of Surgeons in London in 1839 at twenty-two. After further studies in chemistry in Paris and London he returned to Dublin to teach that subject. As Liebermann had, Antisell involved himself in revolutionary nationalism while a student—in his case the "Young Ireland" movement. For his subversive political activities he was exiled by the ruling English in 1848 and subsequently made his way to New York. The next decade saw him practicing and teaching medicine in New York and New England, as well as working as a geologist on a team surveying the route for a southern railway to the Pacific. In 1858 he accepted an appointment to the Georgetown medical department as professor of chemistry, toxicology, and physiology. He became one of Georgetown's most popular teachers and eventually taught nearly every medical subject—from hygiene, military surgery, and physics, to pathology and urinary therapeutics. In addition, he was the author of several works on hygiene, including a practical study titled *On the Value of the Sewerage of the City of Washington* (1869).

The quality of instruction at the school seems to have been very good for its time. One of the most distinguished graduates of the early period, Daniel Roberts Brower (**M** 1863–64), who subsequently became a professor of neurology and psychiatry at Rush Medical College and Women's Medical College in Chicago, gave high marks in general to his teachers at Georgetown. "Our Alma Mater," he told a later graduating class, "was as well equipped in those days with an able and sufficient teaching force as any in the land." He appreciated Noble Young's personal direction as his preceptor and the sound grounding in the surgery of the day that Johnson Eliot had given him. But the three best teachers, to his mind, had been Thomas Antisell, professor of physiology; Silas Loomis, professor of chemistry; and Montgomery Johns, professor of anatomy. Antisell he found "the most learned man I have ever met . . . ;" Loomis was "masterful in his demonstrations" in the laboratory; and Johns, "a very brilliant man" who knew his subject better than any one Brower had met since. In fact, in 1900, he could still remember working into the early hours of the morning with Johns over a cadaver, until he, Brower the student, could at last head home and Professor Johns could retire to a cot beside the cadaver.[84] Another student of the period echoed these judgments in general, although his opinion of Montgomery Johns was distinctly less enthusiastic than Brower's, probably because he saw less of him. Johns was a good speaker, he conceded, "but digressed very much. . . . I did not get much anatomy from him."[85] Young was one of the few who prepared notes and read his lectures; many worked without notes of any kind. But most, including Young, were apparently effective lecturers, which, given the repetitive nature of the curriculum, was no small blessing. With no textbooks and a small library (mostly medical journals) whose use was limited to the faculty, the formal lectures and informal supervision were the marrow of medical education at Georgetown, a reality that the students recognized all too well. In 1860 they demanded the removal of one of their professors, J. M. Snyder, evidently for missing classes and failing to cover some of his material. Although the faculty gave Snyder, a seven-year veteran of the department, a vote of "full confidence," they also informed him officially that in the future he would be expected to deliver all his lectures and to devote "a full share of attention to diseases of women and children."[86]

Clinical Training and Facilities

Clinical training was minimal at Georgetown, a characteristic common to most mid-nineteenth century medical schools. The only required clinical work was the dissection connected with the study of anatomy, a practice that sometimes had about it the smell of the criminal, since it was widely rumored that professors came by their bodies through graveyard raids.[87] When a mutilated cadaver was left on the front steps of the medical department in 1859, the faculty thought its reputation endangered enough by the prank to bring the matter to the attention of the mayor of Washington and a sitting grand jury.[88] Attempts to provide clinical experience for students in the 1850s were limited by the lack of available hospital facilities. The department's own dispensary, with its six beds, had already proved to be inefficient and too small and was seldom open more than a few months a year. In the spring of 1853 the Georgetown faculty explored the possibility of giving students access to the Washington Asylum.[89] Later in 1853 an attempt was made to build a full-scale infirmary on the site of the original building. Contracts were negotiated and the Sisters of Charity were invited to take charge of the projected facility. (These nursing sisters were already operating the infirmary connected with the Columbian Medical Department.) But a majority of the faculty apparently decided against the contract because they could not afford to undertake the additional expense. One suspects that the resignations of Liebermann and Ritchie from the faculty at this time reflected their frustration over that 1853 decision to abandon plans for the new infirmary.[90] By the end of the decade the faculty was directing its collective efforts at persuading the Congress to establish a general hospital for the entire city that would also provide facilities for clinical instruction by staff physicians, including the professors at the District's two medical colleges, Columbian and Georgetown.[91] But the secession of South Carolina and the rest of the Cotton South in 1860 and the conspicuous drift toward war sidetracked this movement.

Examinations and Degrees

In any case the students had already taken the "clinical" initiative in 1858 by organizing a pathological society whose membership was large enough to meet in the amphitheater of the school. How active it was or how long it lasted is unknown but it is further evidence of student interest in cumulative, self-help learning that extended beyond the lecture hall.[92] It was also reflected in Noble Young's understanding of the progressive nature of medical learning in his 1857 valedictory address to the graduates. "You are not to rest content with what you have [learned]," he urged them. "[Y]ou are to acquire more and more, to become laborers in the field of progress— a progress to continue to the end of time." There would be found "at every step some new and wondrous truth to be investigated and learned."[93] Thomas Antisell struck the note even more eloquently in his commencement address in 1859. Theirs was an age of remarkable progress in both research and practice, he noted in precise detail. In this endless discovery, medical men had been more than mere explorers. If much had been done, Antisell concluded,

still more remains to be done, and to the new generations we look for further and more wonderful improvements in physic than it has been our lot to witness. We hope that you will take part in this race; that you will specially cultivate a taste for some department of the science of your profession, and do not be led into the belief that the men who pursue science become unfit for the daily duties of the profession.

. . . [T]he education you have received is but a portion of the whole education it is hoped you will attain through life. It is but "learning how to learn," but laying the foundation for yourselves to raise a superstructure upon which may attain for you both emolument and reputation. Your duty toward the public is involved in this—to render yourself as capable of serving them usefully as your faculties and opportunities will permit.[94]

At the conclusion of their courses and apprenticeship, candidates for the medical degree had to submit a thesis on an appropriate topic as well as pass an oral examination given by the faculty. The thesis topics were extremely broad and sometimes redundant: "Aneurism," "Medical Education," "Fractures," "Pneumonia," "Peritonitis," and "Inflammation" were typical and recurring titles. To pass the oral examination a candidate needed to be approved by at least five, or a majority, of the examiners, but examinations could be repeated, if necessary. In general, it seems that few candidates failed. The lack of records of student registration for the first decade makes it difficult to exactly determine what percentage of those who matriculated were graduated. By the 1860s, however, Georgetown was apparently granting degrees to a much higher proportion of its students than other medical schools of note. Whereas Pennsylvania and Harvard, for instance, awarded medical degrees to fewer than 40 percent of those who enrolled, Georgetown seems to have been granting them routinely to at least 60 percent of its candidates.

The proprietary nature of the school may have made it more vulnerable, if not to being a "diploma mill," at least to having faculty who tended to give every benefit of the doubt to "revenue-producing" candidates for degrees. A glimpse of such a tendency is provided by the reaction to a degree petition in 1859 from a Welshman who claimed to possess a diploma from the College of Surgeons of England and was seeking a Georgetown degree for its prestige. ("I don't want to practice much in the profession," he assured the faculty in his letter.) The faculty advised him that if he could present a letter from the secretary of the English college attesting to his having earned the degree, Georgetown would award him its degree for £30.[95] Several months later Father John Early, then president, received a letter from an irate Georgetown medical alumnus who lived and practiced in England. He reported that the individual in question had no medical training other than from a course of lectures he had taken at the local English hospital, but that he "has realized some amount of money by quackery of the lowest type, mixed with astrology. . . . As a graduate in Medicine of your College, having attended the full curriculum and paid fees to the amount of $240 besides passing an exam, I must respectfully but firmly beg to enter my protest against the sale of your diplomas in England . . ."[96] However, the Welshman received an honorary degree at the following commencement in 1861.[97]

Finances and the American Medical Association

Throughout the first decade the medical department was barely able to meet expenses. At the end of the 1854–55 academic year, for instance, there was a balance of $142.05 on hand. Plans for expansion, including the proposed full-scale infirmary or new departments of dentistry and pharmacy, became impossible without a willingness on the faculty's part to bear new financial burdens. And the new faculty were increasingly reluctant to become shareholders in an operation that promised more debt than profit. (When a member resigned, his successor was obliged to buy his share in order to join the faculty.) In recognition of this abiding problem, a two-tiered system of sharing was introduced in 1857 so that those faculty members not interested in sharing profits and expenses were allowed instead to pay rent ($50 annually) for using the facilities.[98]

Despite this new arrangement, friction apparently developed between the older members of the faculty and the newer ones over the administration of the common funds. Unfortunately, Charles Liebermann, who had rejoined the faculty, became the victim of the pressures resulting from such proprietary economics. By the late 1850s there was a growing conviction among many of the shareholders (Liebermann's colleagues) that the financial condition of the school had become a scandal. In 1860 they appointed a committee to examine all the "books, papers, vouchers, etc." in Liebermann's possession as treasurer, and to receive from him all the money he held for the department. These auditors found that Liebermann had failed to collect $420 in overdue fees from delinquent students during the last two sessions. A few days later the dean was ordered to take over the treasurer's books permanently as well as the money already collected by Liebermann. Some $137 was taken from him and distributed among the faculty shareholders. Liebermann, a proud and rigorously honest man, resigned in protest from the faculty that same day.[99] A new committee proceeded to collect most of the money owed the school and to distribute that to the shareholders as well. Liebermann "retired" to his private practice, was elected president of the Medical Society of the District of Columbia in 1865, and eventually became connected with the Children's Hospital in the 1870s. Still his abrupt resignation was a sad termination to the service that this highly gifted and farsighted man had given in the establishment of Georgetown's Medical School.

The establishment of the school also gave access to and membership in the American Medical Association. Georgetown therefore had the right to send two representatives to the association's annual meeting, a right it exercised as early as 1855. When the association met in Washington in 1858, Liebermann and Antisell were chosen as delegates. Inherent in the *raison d'être* of the association, of course, was the goal of setting standards for the profession, including the training of doctors at medical schools. The Georgetown faculty were ready enough to follow the AMA's guidelines, as far as it was practical to do so, but they were not prepared to have the association pass judgment on their program and candidates. When the AMA approached the medical departments of both Georgetown and Columbian in 1860 about such an examination, the Georgetown faculty declared that they did "not recognize any right in the [AMA] committee to propose questions affecting the organization of Institutions receiving no endowment directly or indirectly from the Assoc. or Congress."[100] With or without the faculty's cooperation, the AMA went ahead with its investigation and issued a report which evaluated and criticized both schools for tailoring their class hours for the convenience of working students.[101] (Columbian, perhaps under the pressure of the new competition from Georgetown, had switched to a "sundown" schedule in the mid-1850s.) Predictably Georgetown did not alter its hours of instruction. It continued as a "sundown college" for another thirty-five years.

The Presidents during the 1850s

Besides Ryder, three other Jesuits, all alumni, served as president of George-town College during the decade. Ryder completed his second term in 1851. His successor, Charles Stonestreet (1813–85), was a native of Charles County in Southern Maryland. Upon his graduation from Georgetown in 1833, Stonestreet had entered the Society. As a Jesuit scholastic he taught French, mathematics, and grammar at Georgetown while studying philosophy. Be-fore he was named president-rector of Georgetown, he headed St. John's College in Frederick, Maryland, for three years. The low-key, genial, and seemingly omnipresent Stonestreet was a sharp contrast to Ryder, but he quickly won the favor of students, faculty, and superiors. By the end of his first year in office the provincial reported to the superior general (June 1852) that "in every respect Georgetown College is flourishing," and he attributed it primarily to the thirty-nine-year-old Stonestreet.[102] But Charles Stonestreet was president for a little more than a year.

In the summer of 1852 he had to resign as president because he had been named provincial superior of the Maryland Province in place of Ignatius Bro-card who had died suddenly.[103] The board of directors in December elected Bernard Maguire (1818–86) to succeed Stonestreet. Maguire, a native of County Longford, Ireland, had immigrated as a young boy with his family to Frederick, Maryland, where his father worked as one of the contractors building the new Chesapeake and Ohio Canal. Bernard graduated from St. John's College and entered the Jesuit novitiate at Frederick in 1837. As a scholastic he had taught at Georgetown in the 1840s before being ordained in 1850. Like Stonestreet, he had been president of St. John's before being summoned to the District to head Georgetown.[104]

The tall, slender, black-haired Maguire proved a popular, resourceful, and effective president for Georgetown during his two terms (1852–58, 1866–70). Like Ryder, he was a remarkable public speaker, later becoming one of the most renowned preachers on the Catholic mission circuit. One young Jesuit scholastic found himself being drawn back Sunday after Sunday to hear Maguire's catechetical instructions for the students. "He far surpasses anything I heard of him," he wrote. "His arguments are most clear and con-vincing & his language most beautiful."[105] Unlike Ryder, Maguire immersed himself in the daily life of the college. As president he was hard-working, prudent, and strict, yet popular with both students and faculty.[106] Nor did his dedication to detail keep him from pursuing larger goals for the institution.

One of the first steps Maguire took as president was to segregate the pre-paratory department from the college. Since at least the 1830s, a distinction had been introduced between the "preparatory schools" (Rudiments, Third Humanities, Second Humanities) and the "senior classes" (First Humanities, Poetry, Rhetoric, Philosophy) of the seven-year course of studies. By 1851 there was a decision to separate the younger and older students for moral and financial reasons. In particular there was concern about the bad influence the older students had or might have on the younger. The rector and consultors also realized that the indiscriminate mixing of students ranging from eight to twenty-eight years of age was serving to deter older students from choosing Georgetown for their college education.[107] By the 1852–53 academic year, the preadolescents were housed separately from the older students. In 1856 the "lower school" began to follow its own calendar, with classes beginning on September 1, two weeks earlier than the traditional start of the academic year for the college.[108] The reorganization did seem to attract more college-age men. Yet, for a while most students continued to enroll in the preparatory school. But the percentage of older students did increase steadily in the 1850s. By 1858 nearly half (45.2%) were in the senior or college-level classes, up from a third only six years before.

Two years earlier, in June of 1854, construction had begun on a building for the exclusive use of the "juniors." For several years college and provincial officials had been considering plans for a major new edifice that would connect the existing double row of buildings on either the east or west.[109] What they built was a much more modest structure. The building, five stories in height, flanked the "South" or original building on the east, paralleling but somewhat smaller than the contiguous building that had been built under Mulledy to connect to the western side of "South" two decades earlier. The new building contained a playroom, public hall, classrooms, study hall, and dormitory at a cost of $20,000. Gas lighting fixtures were installed, rather than the older oil lamps. (In 1850 the college had already erected its own gas manufacturing unit to provide lighting for buildings and grounds.)[110] By commencement of 1855, the building, long known as the Preparatory Building (today called Maguire Hall), was completed and duly insured by the Potomac Company of Washington.[111]

Even with this addition, the school's facilities were still inadequate to meet the needs resulting from the great increase of students during the decade. With a student enrollment approaching three hundred by the late 1850s, Georgetown was one of the larger colleges in the country. Indeed by 1857 President Maguire began planning another building to provide classrooms and dormitories for the senior students and a library and exhibition hall as well. However, the financial panic of that year and the coming of war three years later combined to put on hold all these plans for expansion. (The nation's fourteenth president, Franklin Pierce, was drifting weakly to the end of his term. And in March of 1857, he was duly succeeded by James Buchanan.) In the very next year, Georgetown also had a new president, John Early (1858–65).

Bernard Maguire, SJ (1818–86). Twice president of Georgetown. Photograph by Mathew Brady.
(Library of Congress)

PRESIDENTS HOUSE.

Published by Thompson & Homans, Washington D.C.

CHAPTER 7

"Alma Mater of the South"
Student Culture in the Antebellum Years

When American children reach a certain age they grow restless and impatient
with being subjugated unless they are disciplined with a strong hand. From the
arrogation of liberties they frequently pass on to insubordination, and at times
they even rebel violently against their superiors. This is not uncommon in
the American colleges. . . .

GIOVANNI GRASSI
letter from Italy, 1819

Growth and Changing Demographics

As historians have noted, college enrollments were up sharply across the
country in the 1850s. Georgetown's growth by far surpassed the national
average. By the 1855–56 academic year, with three hundred and eight students, Georgetown College was one of the largest colleges in the nation; in its
demographics and student culture, it also had become distinctly Southern.

In the 1820s nearly four-fifths (<80%) of Georgetown's students had
come from the local area (District of Columbia and Maryland), and nearly
two-thirds of these were town and city dwellers. They tended to be the sons
of merchants, businessmen, government officials, and planters. From the

Engraving of the antebellum
White House, probably made
after 1850. (Library of Congress)

1830s onward, it could be more truly called a regional school with a preponderate number of its students coming from below the Mason-Dixon line and increasingly from the Deep South—that is, from the cotton-growing states (table 7.1 in appendix F). In that decade, as the college became almost entirely a boarding school, the proportion of local students declined (to 45.8%) while those from the South increased (from 17.4% to 40.2%) and those from the Northeast also increased (from 3.7% to 13%). In the next two decades the South continued to increase its overall representation within the student body, while the North, with the burgeoning number of other Catholic colleges available, decreased its representation considerably (table 7.2 in appendix F). Between 1850 and 1859 there were more students from the Southern states (44.5%) than from any others (table 7.3 in appendix F). Of the four hundred eighty-eight students, Louisiana had the largest proportion (15.1%). But Virginia (9.9%), Georgia (4.3%), South Carolina (3.6%), Mississippi (3.5%), and Alabama (2.6%) also had, for those times, large numbers of young men at Georgetown. And Maryland, a border state, accounted for nearly a fifth (18.7%) of the domestic students in the 1850s. Students from the Northeast had declined to less than a tenth of the enrollment (8.7%). Significantly, unlike most urban schools in the nation, Georgetown, because of the influx of Southerners, became less rather than more urban in its student demographics during the three decades before the Civil War. Less than half the students were from urban areas during those years. Their fathers tended to be military officers, planters, or small-town doctors and lawyers.

Georgetown seems to have benefited from several factors: relatively low living costs; location in the nation's capital; a growing, prosperous federal bureaucracy; a rising middle class in the South seeking education as a form of advancement for its children; and the scarcity of Catholic colleges in the South.[1]

The cost of attending college rose generally in this period, faster than the incomes of most Americans. The average college's tuition and fees were three times in the 1850s what they had been in 1800.[2] Georgetown, by contrast, kept its costs relatively low. Fees for room, board, and tuition actually decreased from $225 in 1825 to $150 by 1830. In 1833, when formal permission was granted to charge tuition, then President Thomas Mulledy had raised the total fees to $200, where they remained for thirty years.[3] Thus, in 1840, those fees put Georgetown approximately in the middle range of colleges, as compared to Yale's $295, Harvard's $263, North Carolina's $160, Brown's $147, and Bowdoin's $130.[4] Moreover, parents still occasionally paid by providing goods or services, including domestic work done by slaves sent along with the students.

Georgetown's location in the District of Columbia was a more important growth factor than its moderate charges. Despite the antigovernment ideology of the Jacksonians, the federal bureaucracy grew significantly in this period, from 20,000 federal employees in 1830 to 50,000 in 1860, exclusive of the military.[5] The size of the government cadre in Washington expanded with the creation of new departments and agencies, such as Interior, and the establishment of specialized bureaus within the old ones. In addition, new government institutions, such as the Smithsonian and the Naval Observatory, created a formal scientific community and helped enlarge a vigorous government building program which in turn created many jobs. In the 1840s the city's population increased by more than two-thirds (70%). Between 1840 and 1860 it nearly trebled, to 61,122 residents.[6] Thus when the Panic of 1857 devastated the economy of many cities across the country, Washington, with its government-based economy, proved an exception, for it experienced the effects of the depression very briefly.

Georgetown College was a direct beneficiary of this dynamic local economy and growing federal bureaucracy. The political elite of Washington continued to have a significant presence at Georgetown during the antebellum period. Whether natural or adopted, the sons of Presidents Andrew Jackson, Martin Van Buren, John Tyler, and Andrew Johnson were all students at the college, as were James Polk's ward and Senator Stephen Douglas's two sons. Cabinet officers, congressmen, government clerks, and local politicians were also prominent among the parents of local students. In 1834 alone, there were at least four students named "Andrew Jackson" at the college. They were the president's own son and the sons of the postmaster general, the president's secretary, and a congressman from Alabama. Four Washington newspaper executives also had sons studying at the college during the 1830s: Francis Blair, editor of the *Congressional Globe;* Duff Green, editor of the *United States Telegraph* (Jackson's official paper until the *Globe* replaced it in 1833); Hezekiah Niles, publisher of *Niles' Register;* and William Winston Seaton, editor of the *National Intelligencer* and five-time mayor of Washington.

Most of the students from Washington during this period, however, were the sons of mid-level military and civil service managers. Of the one hundred and forty-five fathers whose occupations are known, fifty-five were career military. One was Lieutenant James Ord, the reputed morganatic son of George IV of England, who became an officer in the United States Army after leaving the Society of Jesus as a scholastic. His two sons, James Lycurgus Ord (**C** 1835–37) and Placidus Ord (**C** 1835–37), were half-boarders at Georgetown. Another such Washingtonian was Commodore John Rodgers, of the Navy Board of Commissioners, whose son Henry was a full boarder at the college (1835–38). Matthew Fountain Maury, the superintendent of the Naval Observatory, who worked on joint meteorological projects with both Angelo Secchi and Benedict Sestini, sent his nephew to Georgetown in the late 1840s. Another twenty-four student fathers were either government clerks or minor officials during that same period.

While the federal city enjoyed nearly thirty years of prosperity, its satellite, Georgetown, went into a serious economic decline. The Chesapeake and Ohio Canal had proven a disappointing link to the West in competing for trade since the more successful Baltimore and Ohio railroad virtually by-passed Georgetown. The flour mills and cotton factory built along the canal in the 1840s in an attempt to industrialize the community were near bankruptcy a decade later. In the 1850s the town undertook to build a railroad link to the Baltimore and Ohio mainline at Point of Rocks, Maryland, but the town fathers quickly abandoned the project when taxpayers revolted against proposed property assessments to finance construction. In 1856 the town tried unsuccessfully to imitate its Virginia rival, Alexandria, by seeking retrocession to Maryland from the District of Columbia as a means of economic and social revival. (Alexandria had been retroceded to Virginia by the Congress a decade earlier.)[7] The population of Georgetown (as distinguished from Washington City) was smaller in 1850 than it had been in 1830. Even in 1860 there were only 8,733 persons in the community, barely more than the population of thirty years before. An even more telling effect of the depression was the decline in the number of men between the ages of twenty and forty. In 1830 the census count was 1,145; two decades later it was down to 918.[8]

Georgetown, unlike the federal city proper, felt the full brunt of the Panic of 1857. Benedict Joseph Semmes, an alumnus of the college who operated a wholesale grocery business in Georgetown, wrote to his wife in October: "The oldest and strongest merchants are tumbling to the ground. . . . I have lost almost all confidence in individuals, as well as banks. . . . Numbers of businesses failed. . . . Georgetown is a heavy sufferer by these failures, and the whole town is seriously affected." Two weeks later Semmes, burdened with rising debts and depreciating currency, was desperate: "Business has positively come to an end, and our chief difficulty is about money. I . . . am in a constant state of nervous anxiety or depression. . . ."[9] Six months later he decided to move to Memphis.

Semmes was one of five brothers who had attended Georgetown College between 1835 and 1850.[10] Their father, Raphael Semmes, from whom Benedict had inherited the family's grocery business, was a descendant of an old Maryland Catholic family. In fact, during the 1830–50 period one-quarter of the Catholic students from Georgetown were from the old families. These Brents, Brookes, Clarkes, Fenwicks, Kings, and Youngs were, in effect, a roll call of colonial Maryland. By the 1850s, however, few such Georgetown families could afford to send their children to the college. The number of Georgetown students at the college continued to increase in the 1850s (an average of 8.6 students a year) but those who came were poorer, had to have more financial aid, stayed a shorter time, graduated less frequently, and rarely entered the professions or middle-class businesses. There was a decline in the proportion of boarders among them, from half (50%) in the 1830s to less than a quarter (24.4%) in the 1850s. Day students, who had been readmitted in the 1840s, accounted for more than a tenth (11%) of the students by the 1850s. More of them tended to be the sons of working class or lower-middle-class parents than did their boarder classmates. The fathers of the latter were still more likely to be businessmen or professionals rather than artisans or government clerks. In the 1830s, one in seven students (14.4%) graduated; two decades later it was about one in twenty (5.8%).[11] The typical local student could stay barely a year by the 1850s. Moreover, nearly a fifth of all students received financial aid toward the $50 tuition.

The other significant source of local students during this period was the block of southern Maryland counties (St. Mary's, Charles, Prince George's) which continued to have an important if dwindling supply of students. In the 1850s, five of the ten valedictorians were the sons of southern Maryland families: Brent, Neale, Lancaster, Hill, and Semmes. And two-thirds of all Maryland students at Georgetown still came from rural areas, the vast majority of them from the tidewater counties between the Patuxent and the Potomac rivers. They were largely the sons of planters (20%) or professionals—especially doctors (40%), lawyer/politicians (22%), and military men (8%). Predominantly of English stock (85%) and Catholic (72.5%), they had the most kinship ties to the school. Better than one in two (53.6%) either had currently or had had a relative as a student there. Records show that about one in five (18.8%) received substantial financial support, and stayed longer than any other group (nearly two years on the average). Members of the old Catholic families who had remained in southern Maryland continued to patronize the school in relatively large numbers, constituting about two-fifths (42%) of the Catholic families in the area who sent their sons to study at Georgetown. However, the fact that many of them needed financial assistance to keep a son or sons at Georgetown reflected the stagnant state of the regional tobacco economy.[12]

The Stonestreets were a somewhat wealthier-than-average southern Maryland family with sons at Georgetown. Nicholas Stonestreet was a lawyer-planter in Port Tobacco, the county seat of Charles County. He had thirty-eight slaves altogether—at his town house and on his plantation—in 1830.[13] His oldest son, Charles Henry (**C** 1830–33, AB), after early schooling at local academies, was found qualified to be placed in Poetry Class as a seventeen-year-old. (When the father died while Charles was at Georgetown, he remained as a free boarder, presumably because the family could no longer afford the tuition.) His brother Nicholas (**C** 1831–36, AB) was the same age when he entered First Humanities at the college a year later. A third brother, Joseph (**C** 1839–42), was only twelve when he began Humanities in the lower school at Georgetown, but he went on to Princeton later for his AB

Students from below the Potomac

If, overall, there was a decline in the number of long-staying local students in the period, despite college efforts to assist them, the increase from the South more than offset it. In part Georgetown benefited from its location in a suburb of what was perceived as a city of the South. As Colin Burke has noted, Southerners began remaining within their own region for their education long before the culmination of the sectional crisis in the late 1850s.[14] Georgetown (at the "top" of the South) was thus a major beneficiary since it became a college of choice for many Southerners increasingly alienated from Princeton, Yale, and other colleges in the North that had been traditionally popular until sectional differences became more pronounced. Burke has calculated that the Missouri Crisis and its repercussions in the 1820s produced a severe decline in the percentage of Southerners going north for their higher education (dropping from 20% to 11% in one decade).[15] Interestingly, the percentage of Southerners at Georgetown began to climb rapidly in the same period. By the 1850s, the proportion of Southern students, including those from Maryland, at Georgetown was nearly two-thirds of its total collegiate population. Princeton, by contrast, had seen the number of Southerners decline to one-third of its student population.[16] A Georgetown alumnus, Henry Thompson from Alabama, wrote Stonestreet in 1856: "Great credit is due to old G.T. College for in my intercourse with her sons in this state, Ga. & Mis. I find them universally opposed to the 'isms' of the day. They are constitutional gentlemen & lovers of law & order. . . . [W]henever you see them on the battle field (& they are always there) encountering that monster of Iniquity (K. Nothingism) you find them with swords & without scabbards dealing blows, thick & fast. . . . But ah! sir there is Prinston [*sic*] Dartmouth Yale vitiating the minds of their sons giving them Sharps rifles to resist the constitutional authorities of their country & imbrue [sic] their hands in the blood of their Southern bretheren [sic]. The contrast is great and sickening."[17] Many, no doubt, shared Thompson's opinions. Students from the states below the Potomac represented the greatest increase in enrollment at the institution in the 1850s, as well as the largest portion of the student body.

The Southern student attending Georgetown during this antebellum period (1850–59) was most likely (1) to be the son of a lawyer/politician (29.7%), doctor (20.9%), military officer (20.3%), or planter (16.2%); (2) to come from a rural area (37.6%) rather than from a city (32%) or town (30.3%); (3) to be Catholic (67.1%), English (54.0%), French (10.2%), or Irish (15.7%); (4) to have enrolled in the 1850s (nearly 40% entered during the seven years before the Civil War); (5) to be in Rudiments Class as a fourteen-year-old paying full tuition (94.2%); and (6) to stay just over a year.[18]

Among those students from below the Potomac distinct patterns emerge among the three largest ethnic groups: the English, the French, and the Irish. The largest group of students, those of English extraction, were most frequently the sons of those connected with the federal government, through either the military (28.5%) or civil service (25.8%). Planters (11%) and small-town professionals (doctors, 16%; lawyers, 9%) were much less likely to have their sons at Georgetown. English American Southerners were the least urban among Georgetown's students (24.9%). The largest number came from the Tidewater or the Piedmont plantation country. They were the youngest (median age of twelve at entrance), fewer of them were Catholics (44.3%), they were in residence the shortest time (less than a year), and were the least likely to graduate (6.6%). They also had the fewest family connections with the institution (33.5%).

Lewis Addison Armistead (**C** 1830–31) and Walker Keith Armistead (**C** 1846–48) were the sons of General Walker Keith Armistead and Elizabeth Stanley Armistead. Like most of the children of career officers at Georgetown, the Armisteads had a rural upbringing. Lewis was thirteen when he entered George-town's lower school. General Armistead, a veteran of the War of 1812, was afterwards stationed in Boston. But census records show that he owned a plantation with twenty-three slaves managed by a free black overseer in Fauquier County, Virginia.[19]

William Edgeworth Bird (**C** 1838–44, AB), was the son of Colonel Wilson Bird and Frances Casey Bird, of Hancock County in the Piedmont area of Georgia. The Birds lived in Sparta, the county seat of Hancock, but, with more than sixty slaves, they farmed several plantations in the county.[20] Colonel Wilson Bird had originally moved south from Pennsylvania to Alexandria, Virginia, after the Revolution. Then in the 1790s he had relocated to frontier Georgia where he established an ironworks. His wife's father, John Casey, was a doctor in Prince Georges County, Maryland, who also sought new opportunity in Georgia around the turn of the century. And Frances Casey Bird's brother, John Aloysius, may have been the "John Casey" of Maryland, who is listed as one of the early students at Georgetown (**C** 1792–95). This Bird family was related by marriage to the Semmeses.[21] Known simply as Edgeworth, the Birds' son was thirteen when he entered Georgetown's lower school. (Later, during the Civil War he and Sallie, his young wife, exchanged the heartwarming correspondence known to posterity as *The Granite Farm Letters.*)

The second largest ethnic group, the French American, came mainly from the Creole world of New Orleans and southern Louisiana. They tended also to have family connections with Georgetown (46.5% had student or alumni relatives), to be older at entrance (fifteen years on average), to stay longer (nearly two years on average), to have least need of financial assistance (3.7%), and to be twice as likely as the Anglo-Americans to graduate (12%). They were mostly the sons of planters (56%), such as Henri Octave Colomb (**C** 1834–36), from Pointe Coupée Parish, northwest of Baton Rouge. There his father, Louis Colomb, had a sugar plantation.

The third prominent ethnic group from the South, the Irish American (11%), came mainly from the cities (Richmond, New Orleans, Savannah, Charleston) and small towns. As a group they were slightly younger than the French, and stayed longer than their English counterparts, but not as long as

Lewis A. Armistead (**C** 1830–31) was a precollege student at Georgetown who later studied at the U.S. Military Academy at West Point. He served in the U.S. Army before resigning at the outbreak of war in 1861. In the Army of Northern Virginia (CSA), he rose to the rank of brigadier general. (Library of Congress)

the French. A high proportion graduated (15%), and relatively few of them needed financial assistance (7%). They tended to be the sons of young professionals—lawyers (34%) and doctors (28%)—rather than businessmen (8%). Unlike the Dooley brothers, James (**C** 1856–60, AB) and John Jr. (**C** 1856–61), very few could claim to be the sons of immigrants. John Dooley, Sr., and his wife had immigrated to the United States from County Limerick in 1832 and eventually settled in Richmond. There Dooley senior developed a very successful business in hats and furs. James was fourteen when he entered Third Humanities at Georgetown; his brother, John, a year younger when he was placed in Rudiments.

Typical students from the Northeast, by contrast, were either the sons of lawyer/politicians (49.3%) or businessmen (22.5%); from Pennsylvania (48.4%) or New York (39.8%); were mainly city dwellers (64.6%); and Catholics (74%). Ethnically, most were English (46.6%), Irish (32%) or German (7.9%); most, too, entered before 1850, usually as fourteen-year-olds in Rudiments, paid full tuition (90.4%), and stayed less than a year.

Georgetown students, then, were mainly the sons of traditional professionals, whether from the North or South. The fact that so many Georgetown College students were the sons of persons connected with the federal government through politics or the military probably explains the short average stay at the college, an average that lessened throughout the early nineteenth century. Washington as the nation's capital city was inherently a city of transients and the college reflected that. As Georgetown's student population in the antebellum period came increasingly from the South, it actually represented at least four major groups who were drawn to Georgetown for somewhat different reasons. Besides the Chesapeake Catholic elite, there were three other constituencies from below the Potomac. If the prominent Catholic families of Maryland and the District, the mainstay of the school since the eighteenth century, were no longer supporting the school in the same large numbers of previous generations, still they continued to patronize it, along with many Catholic families of more modest means. (In southern Maryland that Catholic elite was increasingly indistinguishable from the less affluent.) Below the Potomac there were three culturally distinct groups: (1) the Anglo-Americans, largely Protestant, for whom Georgetown's location in the nation's capital and at the northern rim of the South meant a convenient and/or proper education; (2) the wealthy French from the Deep South, for whom the college in the 1830s became a religiously and culturally appropriate place to send their sons; and (3) the Irish, for whom, as a rising middle class, Georgetown represented opportunity and status.

Daily Life in the College

The entrance requirements continued to be those set down by Archbishop Carroll: a minimum age of eight, an ability to read, and, for older students, some evidence of good character. The median age of students, at Georgetown and elsewhere, crept upward during the antebellum period; nevertheless, extremely young students could still be found in the preparatory department or lower school. From the 1830s to the 1850s the median age of students entering First Rudiments rose from eleven years and nine months to thirteen years and seven months; the median age of all entering students rose from just under thirteen to just over fourteen. The minimum (and maximum) age continued to be interpreted liberally. In a society where males ordinarily reached puberty at sixteen and continued to grow well into their twenties, the term "youth" had a very broad and elastic application.[22] By the 1830s the students in First Rudiments ranged in age from eight to twenty-five. Yet a six-year-old from Peru was admitted as late as 1858. Although a maximum age had never been set for the lower school, there were periodic efforts to set an admissions ceiling. After Georgetown's "Great Riot" of 1833 the superior general in Rome ordered one, as did an official Visitor in 1860 (who wanted no one older than twelve admitted). But neither policy change was implemented.[23] For instance, William Loring of St. Augustine, Florida, was twenty-one and had already earned his major's stripes in the Seminole War (1836–38) when he entered Rudiments in 1839, and adults as old as twenty-seven were admitted at various times. But the number of older students was small in contrast to northern schools in the North; never more than 4 percent of those entering Georgetown were twenty-one or older; by the 1850s it was barely 2 percent. Patrick Walsh entered First Rudiments in 1860 as a twenty-year-old, having worked until then as a printer's apprentice; but such cases were more and more rare. The narrowing age range for preparatory and college students at Georgetown was one sign of a maturing culture that acknowledged the transition from childhood to adolescence and equated it with the latter stages of education. A more immediate cause was the improved socioeconomic condition of the vast majority of parents who could now afford to send their subteen or teenage sons to Georgetown for their higher education. The decision in 1832 to eliminate day students, albeit temporary, had helped guarantee that Georgetown would not suffer the fate of many early-nineteenth-century colleges. In many such, an increasingly poorer, older student body made the old institutions unworkable as surrogates for or extensions of parental governance.[24]

The majority of its students being sixteen years of age or younger, the governance of Georgetown College continued to be familial. A rigid schedule defined the day for students from rising to retiring (with the exception of the small percentage of nonboarding students). Unlike many other colleges of the period, whose students had already won the right to reside off campus and where faculty supervision was being reduced to a *pro forma* ritual, Georgetown remained a relatively self-enclosed place in which faculty and students interacted closely.[25] The virtually constant presence of faculty and prefects in student lives in and out of the classroom served to underscore the in loco parentis mode of governance by providing rules with a human face that largely offset the severity of the formal, stated regulations. In practice, the Jesuits were hardly considered rigorous disciplinarians. One Chilean student of the 1850s noted: "It would be hard to find a more indulgent people than the Jesuits who run Georgetown. One could state without exaggeration that if something is forbidden it is also nevertheless permissible to break the rule."[26] For the senior students, moreover, there was a certain amount of self-governance, particularly in the realm of extracurricular activities.

James Ryder Randall (**C** 1848–56). Pictured here in 1861, when he was a journalist in New Orleans. In April of that year he penned "Maryland, My Maryland," in reaction to the bloody clash in his native Baltimore between Union soldiers and Confederate supporters. (Georgetown University Archives)

Whenever a young boy was brought to the college by his parent or guardian the president would interview him and decide whether he should be admitted or not (students tended to be admitted throughout the year, although the great majority entered in September). Once admitted and assigned to a class, the new student would be handed over to an older student who was his guide for a three-day orientation to college life. At the end of that period he was officially measured for height and assigned to a place in the ranks. Neither family status, as at Harvard, nor age, nor academic standing, but stature was employed in assigning each student's position in his class. Twice yearly the first prefect, a Jesuit scholastic, had to again measure the height of each student next to a marked tree, in order to confirm or reassign their places in the ranks. (Disciplinary effectiveness seems to have been the basis underlying this ranking by size.) James Ryder Randall remembered that when he entered Georgetown as a nine-year-old in 1848, Francis Neale, "a giant from Charles County, Md., led the ranks . . . to dinner and elsewhere, and I was at the rear end. He was called 'Big Buster' and I 'Little Buster.'"[27]

A college uniform continued to be prescribed and worn for Sunday and holiday dress. By the 1830s it was, in winter, a blue cloth coat and matching pantaloons with a black velvet waistcoat; in summer, white pantaloons with a black silk waistcoat.[28] Students were required to wear these uniforms on official outings into the federal city, such as to observe congressional debates or to participate in inaugural parades. In 1841 they marched three times for President William Henry Harrison: in February when the town gave him an official welcome, in March for his inauguration, and in April at his funeral.

Living conditions were increasingly spartan. In the 1830s the apartments in the [Old] North Building that Giovanni Grassi had constructed were disassembled and rearranged so as to accommodate more students. Most interior room walls were taken down and curtains were installed between beds. These space-saving "partitions" were the only token of privacy that remained in the large halls. Looking back, James Ryder Randall recalled: "We slept in a cold dormitory, in winter, and had to rise at 5:15 in the morning. If we did not get down [in time] to the subterranean wash-room where often the ice had to be broken to get water . . . we were barred out and were obliged to wash at the pump [in the yard which had been the regular washplace until 1823]. . . . Often I . . . in sleet and snow, with wet shoes and shivering frame, performed that task while bitter tears streamed down and froze upon my cheeks, and I thought of my mother and my home, wondering why such affectionate parents as mine were had condemned their little boy to such torture."[29]

The daily schedule followed a quasi-monastic order, as it did in English and European schools. In the 1830s it was:

5:30	Rise	1:15	Study
5:45	Morning prayers	2:15	Classes
6:00	Mass	4:45	Recreation
6:30	Study	5:15	Rosary and study
7:45	Breakfast	7:00	Supper & recreation
8:15	Classes	8:00	Night prayers
11:15	Recreation	8:15	In rooms
11:30	Dinner & recreation		

The student cuisine also seems to have gone from good to bad during that same period. In the 1820s the fare seems to have been simple but essentially the same good victuals for faculty and students: bread and coffee with milk at breakfast; veal or mutton with potatoes and seasonal vegetables at dinner (but rockfish, perch, and mackerel on Fridays and Saturdays); and bread and tea for supper.[30] By the 1840s there was chronic complaining about the food. Ten lines of doggerel summed up student opinion of the then standard dinner dessert: slabs of dried-apple pie:

Of all mean things beneath the skies,
The meanest is dried-apple pies.
The farmer takes his poorest fruit.
Gnarled and wormy and rotten to boot,
And on a dirty string they're strung
And in the garret window hung.
And there they serve as a roost for flies
Until they're made into apple pies.
Tread on my corns, or tell me lies,
But don't pass me dried-apple pies.[31]

In 1846 President Mulledy instructed the Jesuit responsible for the college food to make sure that the boys' table "should be as good as that of the community. . . ."[32] Despite this admonition, the situation seems not to have improved for long, if at all. College presidents and Jesuit provincials alike continued to wrestle with the problem of food. In the last year of the Civil War the provincial superior was forced to replace the father minister, the procurator, *and* the cooks in order to meet the persistent complaints of both Jesuits and students.[33]

College meals were eaten at long wooden tables in silence, except when there were guests in the refectory. As in monasteries, noon and evening meals included public reading aloud from a book selected by one of the faculty. In addition, those students who had been assigned lines of Latin and Greek poetry to memorize as a punishment for disciplinary infractions also had to recite them to the silent diners. By the 1850s, however, a student was appointed at supper to read aloud the day's news from a local newspaper.

"The Religion Uniformly Practiced"

"As the members of the College profess the Catholic religion, the exercises of religious worship are Catholic, but members of every other religious denomination are received, of whom it is only required, that they assist at the public duties of religion with their companions." This statement in the Prospectus of 1833, ambiguous as it may have been, made clear the Catholic but ecumenical character of the college. An earlier prospectus, penned by Giovanni Grassi in 1814, had put it more succinctly: "The object of this institution is principally for the education of those who profess the Catholic religion, which is the religion uniformly practiced by the boarders." Thus, it was intended that a majority of the students of the institution were to be Catholics but, in keeping with the founder's intent, there was never a religious test for entrance. Despite the "Southernization" of the student body from 1830 to 1860, a strong majority of them, about two-thirds, continued to be Catholic, although for a year or two in the middle 1850s a majority of students were apparently non-Catholic. During this period Georgetown also counted the first Jewish and Indian students on its rolls. Marx Edgeworth Lazarus (**C** 1834–35) was descended from a distinguished Southern Jewish family, the Mordecais.[34] His father was a slave-holding merchant in Wilmington, North Carolina. Lazarus was twelve when he entered. Attinoho Shott (John Brandt) (**C** 1831–38) from South Carolina was the first American Indian

The "uniform religious practice" of the students meant daily Mass, morning and night prayers, and common recitation of the rosary. In addition there were seasonal observances, such as the Marian devotions in May and the nine-day recitation of prayers, or novena, to the Sacred Heart in June. Even the Easter Vigil, beginning at 5 a.m. on Holy Saturday and lasting nearly three hours, was a required liturgy for all students, although by the 1840s the long readings from the Old Testament in the service were abbreviated in deference to the students' presence.

Catholic students were required to go to confession and communion at least once a month. College presidents enforced this norm with varying rigor, but they were particularly concerned about those who failed to partake of the sacraments during the annual retreat or at Easter time. In 1831, Thomas Mulledy characteristically gave two Catholic students (one a Brent) who had failed to go to confession twenty-four hours to decide whether they would do their duty or be expelled. The delinquents chose to confess.[35] By the 1850s prefects were making sure that all Catholic students confessed twice monthly. Isidorio Errázuriz, a Chilean, wrote in his diary: "I fear a rupture between the Jesuits and the Chilean students as they want us to go to confession every two weeks. The prefects follow us everywhere.[36] The Chileans finally met with President Charles Stonestreet, and won a dispensation from frequent confession.[37]

Three-day religious retreats were given annually to all the students, usually in the fall term, as early as the 1820s. For over forty years, from 1825 to 1866, Father John McElroy was the usual director of these retreats, which included three meditations a day, public spiritual reading from Thomas à Kempis, and devotions such as the litany of the Blessed Virgin, besides the regular religious exercises. However, by the 1830s the non-Catholic students were allowed to study privately instead during these triduums.

A French priest who taught in a Jesuit college in Kentucky that enrolled even more Protestant students than Georgetown was struck by the few conversions among the students at his school (he could recall but two in nine years) or in other Southern Catholic colleges with large Protestant enrollments.[38] Conversions at Georgetown were a much more common experience, especially in the 1830s and 1840s. Of an estimated 893 non-Catholic students at Georgetown during the period, at least 46 converted (5%). Two-thirds of these converts were from the South (twelve from Virginia alone); and virtually all were of English or Scotch Irish extraction. Only a few were from urban areas (18.6%).

George Fenwick seems to have been responsible for most of these student conversions in the 1830s. He epitomized the tradition of *cura personalis* within Jesuit education; and his room was ever filled with students seeking academic help or food or talk. Lewis Armistead, the son of General Armistead, was thirteen years old when Fenwick baptized him in 1831. Winfield Scott Gibson of Vicksburg, Mississippi, was a Methodist and "filled with prejudice" when he came to the college in 1838; two years later he was baptized while in the infirmary seriously ill. "I have made up my mind & will show you that a protestant's boast 'of following his convictions' is no idle 'bugbear,'" he wrote George Fenwick. And later, "Mr. Mulledy . . . has been in my room . . . several times. . . . We have completely smothered Protestantism—annihilated all their theories . . . overturned their churches & spread Catholicisity [*sic*] throughout the Union &c: &c."[39] Gibson survived to fight in both the Mexican and Civil Wars.

William McSherry found many of the students open to Catholicism but relatively few made the efforts to profess it. "I see in the College," he wrote in 1835, "many Protestants who daily attend Mass, who hear the exhortations, and the applications of Christian doctrine in class as well as on Sundays, the spiritual reading, who discuss privately with us about things Catholic, and who, however, having come here Protestants, become better disposed to Catholics than before, but remain however Protestants or rather nothing or indifferent." He could offer only parental pressure or bad example as explanations for this inertia.[40] Fleming Gardner, a Protestant student from Virginia, wrote a friend about how impressive he found the Holy Week services in 1836: "The Protestants may talk about Idol worship as they please but it [is] impossible to imagine the difference of effect which the appearance of the cross with the naked and bleeding body of the saviour upon it produces."[41] But young Gardner related none of this to his evangelical family, especially that the Sunday observance at Georgetown included sports, fiddle music, and dancing, since he thought "it would only make prejudices stronger."[42]

The Jesuits always required and obtained the permission of parents before they baptized a student or received him into the Catholic Church. However, when he was president, Bernard Maguire tried to gauge the parents' openness to the possibility of conversion when they presented their sons. He once asked a congressman whether he would have any objection to his son becoming a Catholic. The representative from Louisiana confessed that he did not, but added that there was one conversion that he would not tolerate: "if my son leaves this College anything but a good Democrat let him not come home to me." Maguire assured him that they never interfered with a student's political faith.[43] Nor does it seem that they proselytized the non-Catholic students in general, although individual Jesuits, like John McElroy, were known occasionally to become somewhat aggressive in their zeal to save souls. And one unusually zealous Italian Jesuit gradually changed the names of two Protestant brothers in his class, Luther and Calvin Walker. He first addressed and reported them as Martin Luther and John Calvin, then as Martin L. and John C., and finally as Martin and John.

When Robert Ray (**C** 1848–54) mentioned in his valedictory address in 1854 that he had converted to Catholicism during his time in the college, a Baltimore newspaper immediately accused the faculty of proselytizing its Protestant students. The twenty-four-year-old valedictorian replied that his decision had been a mature one and had been made under no pressure.[44] (Orphaned at seventeen, Robert Ray was a native of Missouri and had lived for about a year in Louisiana before entering Georgetown in 1848.)

A somewhat similar case was that of John Aiken (**C** 1834–36) of Jonesboro, Tennessee. He had entered Georgetown as a twenty-year-old, planning

to become a Presbyterian minister. After "a long inquiry" he asked to be baptized as a Catholic the following year. For the next two years he was hounded
by parents and friends for succumbing to the idolatry
of papism. Whether owing to this pressure or not, his
health so deteriorated that he was unable to return
to Georgetown in the spring semester of 1837 to
complete his studies. But Aiken entered the novitiate
of the Society in Frederick later that summer. He was
subsequently ordained in 1846 and returned to
Georgetown as a member of the faculty in 1854.[45]

Sport at Antebellum Georgetown

Organized sport was not part of antebellum student
life, although by the 1850s sport was clearly asserting
itself in student culture. In the eighteenth century
there had been little or no thought given to physical
recreation. The original campus totaling one-and-a-
half acres was hardly conducive to sports promotion
in any case. In Carroll's original plans for the school he
had merely prohibited any "playing" on Sundays. But
within the first two decades of the school's history,
outdoor sports began to be part of the social scene,

Robert Ray, valedictorian
of the class of 1854.
(Georgetown University Archives)

engaging faculty and students alike. Handball was the first popular athletic
activity. In 1821 a Jesuit scholastic wrote a colleague in Rome that Joseph
Mobberly, a former student and now a Jesuit brother, was playing "ball with
all his former dexterity-throws his heels equally as high, and blows at the same
rate."[46] The game was played the year round, between two teams of three
players, on outdoor courts or "ball alleys" that by mid-century dotted the campus—now enlarged to more than a hundred acres.[47] One student remembered
a match between two Jesuits and two congressmen, one being John Breckin-
ridge. Students were ice-skating on a pond on campus as early as the 1830s.
By that time swimming had become a customary summer recreation in the
Potomac. In the fall, at least as early as 1830, students occasionally played
English soccer or rugby. John Carroll Brent wrote his sister in that year that he
had often had his "feet skinned and bruised" in playing the game they called
football. "I am lame with [a blow] I have received today," he told her.[48] Injuries
were a common byproduct of the sport. Charles Stonestreet noted in his diary
in 1840 that "Justin McCarthy broke his arm whilst playing foot-ball."[49] In the
1850s a primitive form of baseball was introduced to campus.

    With popular enthusiasm for sports growing (the first collegiate teams, in
rowing, were then being organized at Harvard and Yale), in 1853 the board of

directors authorized the increase of facilities for exercise, including the construction of additional outdoor handball courts and a wooden gymnasium for the use of senior students.[50] The gym featured parallel bars, rings, and other apparatus for workouts. By 1856 gymnastic lessons were being offered.[51] With a special facility available, students organized a "Gymnastic Association" in 1855, which apparently lasted only a year or so.[52] Unlike their more urbane and more urban Northern classmates, Southern youths had little interest in team sports or organized athletics. Sports continued to be an informal, individual activity in most antebellum colleges.

Holidays in a Twelve-Month College

Although the ten-and-a-half-month school year was long, holidays were frequent. The liturgical calendar was the chief source for observances of holy days of obligation and celebration of the feasts of certain saints. In 1840 there were no fewer than sixteen such holidays, ranging from All Saints Day at the beginning of November to the Feast of St. Ignatius at the end of July. Christmas, Mardi Gras, Easter, and Pentecost all also included minor vacations of three or more school days. Moreover, there were the nation's civic "holy days." The college, as noted earlier, always faithfully observed Washington's Birthday and Independence Day. By the 1850s Thanksgiving, or "Yankee Christmas," as some in the college called it, had become part of the republican cycle of high feast days at Georgetown. A High Mass would begin the day and be followed later by a turkey dinner, with all trimmings, including pumpkin pie. The cadets, sometimes joined by the United States Marine Band, would march to the college villa for exercises and a separate feast. Election Day was no holiday, but by 1856 the students were openly holding a mock canvass. In that election, the Democratic candidate, James Buchanan, was the overwhelming campus winner, receiving ninety-three votes, whereas John C. Fremont, the Republican, received only three—from particularly intrepid souls willing to state publicly their presidential preference. (The secret or Australian ballot was not then in use.) The surprise was the twenty-two student votes for Millard Fillmore, the American Party candidate.[53] (Buchanan, it will be remembered, was the winner of the national election.)

On holidays there were occasional trips, by steamboat on the Potomac down to Mount Vernon, or by canal barge up to Great Falls on the Potomac. In the evenings entertainments were sometimes provided by magic lantern or minstrel shows. By the mid-1840s a trip by collegians to the circus— accompanied by prefects—became an annual event on the student calendar. During the Christmas vacation of 1840 the U.S. Marine Band came to play in the refectory while the students performed dances. (Harking back to a not too distant military and colonial life, stag dancing was then a regular holiday activity.) By the 1850s, the older students were also hosting dances at the college that included young ladies from their own families and from Visitation Convent. The most elaborate outing was the biennial trip to St. Mary's City for Catholic Pilgrims' Day. With the Georgetown band leading, the students used to march through the streets of Georgetown and Washington to the Navy Yard, where they boarded a boat for a 24-hour sightseeing trip to southern Maryland. By 1852 this excursion was primarily a social event also since the students had decided to invite girls from Visitation Convent and elsewhere to join them onboard the river steamer. "No one slept last night aboard ship because of the noise and heat," Isidorio Errázuriz noted in his diary about the trip that year. After more marching, Mass, and speeches in St. Mary's County, quadrille dancing completed Pilgrims' Day and all returned to the boat just before midnight for the long trip home.[54]

For more than a hundred years after Georgetown College opened, students were ordinarily not allowed off campus by themselves. Even boarders from the city or town were seldom permitted home visits. In 1847 the college acquired a villa two miles from campus in the Tenleytown area. The large house and its surrounding eighty acres became a vacation site for student holidays, especially for the cadets, debaters, and other select groups, who held dinners and entertainments there, and for all the students who celebrated Christmas and Easter vacations. (Not until 1851 did students get permission to return to their own homes for these holidays.)

In the first several decades of the college it was assumed and expected that most students would remain at the institution during summer vacation. If one came, for instance, from Georgia or New York, it made little sense to spend two or more weeks traveling to and from home for a six-week vacation.[55] Even after the transportation revolution of the 1820s and 1830s made distant travel much more practical, many students continued as year-round boarders. By the 1820s students were going regularly to one of the Jesuit farms in Maryland or Pennsylvania for their vacation. Students and prefects made the journey on foot to the nearest plantation, White Marsh in Prince George's County, about fifteen miles to the east. Those going to Conewago in southeastern Pennsylvania, some ninety miles north, went by carriage and train. For those traveling to one of the plantations in St. Mary's County, it could be an adventure getting there by ship, and surviving a further adventure once they did arrive. Jerome Mudd, a Jesuit scholastic, took one group of students down the Potomac in the summer of 1820 to the Jesuit plantation at Newtown: "[W]ith a very slight breeze [we] wound around Masons [Roosevelt] Island, when it blew a young hurricane— . . . and by the ignorance or inattention of the captain [the schooner] got aground, and were near upsetting in the bargain." They managed to sail to Newtown, some sixty miles away, three days later. Two weeks later the vacation of the students had to be cut short for fear that they would starve. No preparations, it turned out, had been made for their coming.[56] That turned out to be a blessing in disguise since the area's mosquito-ridden, undrained wetlands were not precisely a health resort. Shortly afterwards several Jesuit scholastics who were moved from Newtown to the other St. Mary's plantation, St. Inigoes, came down with yellow fever; one of them died. "God bless the place," Mudd wrote, "I shall never go there again if I can help it."[57] But Mudd did, and so did many Georgetown students. Into the 1850s they continued to be sent to spend their vacations there and on the other Tidewater farms, despite periodic complaints of Jesuit managers or superiors about the students' heavy-handed fun and destructive behavior. More and more, however, were able to return to their homes during August and September. By 1850 only about thirty students spent the whole summer at Newtown under the care of the college, after the Jesuits at White Marsh had pleaded eloquently to be spared "the hosting."[58] Later that decade the younger and older students who remained for the summer at the college were separated by age and sent to different farms. But not until 1871 did the institution abandon the notion of a year-round college by officially informing parents that they should be prepared to bring their sons home for the long vacation. Those who remained, it was decided, would be charged an additional $60 fee.[59]

Cholera and Death at the College

The threat of disease and sudden death was undoubtedly the worst certainty in the uncertain and precarious world of the early nineteenth century in which the young were particularly vulnerable. In the South the seasonal sicknesses, especially yellow and typhoid fevers, were a yearly danger that abruptly claimed many victims, among them a large number of Jesuit novices and scholastics. Between 1808 and 1860 no fewer than thirty-five Jesuits died from these seasonal fevers in Maryland and the District, seventeen of them at Georgetown.

In the 1830s cholera was the worst summer scourge for much of the country, including Washington and Georgetown. When it was first carried across the Atlantic in the early summer of 1832, it spread with a terrifying relentlessness from Montreal through New York State to the Middle Atlantic area. In Baltimore alone there were nearly nine hundred victims, mostly among the poor.[60] By late August, cholera was also raging through Washington, especially in the crowded quarters of the working class neighborhoods. As one Washingtonian reported to Anthony Kohlmann, "Three out of four die. The attack is sudden—the progress rapid . . . sometimes death comes in two hours after the first stroke."[61] By September a score of persons was dying daily in Georgetown.[62] In all there were about four hundred deaths in the town.[63] When school opened at the college in mid-September, many parents hesitated to send their children into the area. A large number of the Jesuits also fell ill, including the president, Thomas Mulledy. But only one died. A novice, he lived only a few hours after he was unexpectedly stricken on a Sunday in early October. He was buried immediately "as privately as possible in order to prevent alarm among the students."[64] But by December of that year the Jesuits were offering their Masses in Thanksgiving "for the safe deliverance of this Institution from the desolating scourge, which has been felt so generally throughout the country. . . ."[65]

Epidemics of cholera or cholera-like gastrointestinal diseases returned in 1833–34 and in 1844, and again from 1848 to 1854 but never with the overwhelming sense of terror that marked the first summer of acute seizures and agonizing deaths. By the late 1840s the college doctor was imposing special restrictions on greens, fruits, and drinking water during the crises. "We have resumed vegetables thanks to the absence of the cholera terror," a Jesuit at Georgetown wrote in mid-September 1849. "I imagined that I was in reality *a hermit,* when I sat down every day to beef & corn bread, & corn bread & beef."[66] Although at least one student became critically ill in the last extensive cholera outbreak in 1854, none died.

There were relatively few student deaths at the college from any cause: twelve altogether between 1830 and 1860. Much was made of Eugene Picot's death in October 1843 as the first student fatality in the history of the college. The students appointed a committee to express their official sentiments of mourning and resolved to wear crepe for the next month.[67] Institutional memory seems to have failed in this instance since Ignatius Fenwick, a local student, had been buried on the college grounds in 1810. Fenwick, however, may have been sent home to actually die, a common practice, especially for local students like Fenwick. As the proportion of students from beyond the immediate coastal region increased sharply, so did their death rate. All in all, the number of student mortalities was remarkably low for those times; a testament, perhaps, to Carroll's choice of a high and dry hilltop site. Some of those who died, like Picot, were already sick when they returned from their homes to campus. Indeed, three-quarters of them, like Picot, were Southerners. And sadly, one student, the son of the Argentine ambassador, drowned while swimming in the Potomac. Several died from "consumption," or tuberculosis, two of pneumonia. Most of those who died had been at the college less than a year, and their average age was fourteen and a half.

"Ungovernable, and Immensely Imperious"

When Giovanni Grassi reflected on his days in the United States, he noted that American children at boarding schools like Georgetown were honest and mature, but that "[w]hen American children reach a certain age they grow restless and impatient with being subjugated unless they are disciplined with a strong hand. From the arrogation of liberties they frequently pass on to insubordination, and at times they even rebel violently against their superiors." Those raised in a slaveholding culture, he implied, were especially prone to such behavior.[68]

Charles Stonestreet, himself a student in the 1830s, remembered that for many students "no idea of self-restraint seemed ever to have come into their minds. They had run wild among the slaves upon their fathers' farms [prior] to their college term. They were . . . ungovernable, and immensely imperious."[69] Raised in a society where primal honor still set the prevailing standards for child-rearing, especially of males, Southern youths were accustomed to being indulged in their precocious manifestations of sexuality and of manliness, and to regard obedience as a virtue of slaves and lesser folk, but not free men.[70] Placed in an academic community that, in theory at least, imposed monastic-like structures of discipline in order to form character, they resisted when they thought that these structures impeded their freedom or sense of honor. Errázuriz was not alone in thinking that he had personal rights that had not been surrendered by his act of becoming a student. When President Stonestreet admonished him for going off campus without permission, the Chilean answered that he considered himself a free person who was not under anyone's control. When Stonestreet threatened suspension for such resistance, Errázuriz replied that he would happily leave "this funereal establishment."[71] Stonestreet chose to ignore the insult and Errázuriz was subsequently graduated.

Parents often sent their sons to Georgetown precisely to attain for them the discipline that they could not or would not maintain at home. William Burke, himself a schoolmaster in Monroe County, Virginia, admitted to George Fenwick that "My son . . . being his mother's only son, was very much petted, and brought up without those wholesome restraints calculated to curb a disposition naturally impetuous. It was to correct this perverseness by precept, example and persevering moral discipline, that I selected Georgetown College."[72] President Andrew Jackson sent his ward, Andrew Jackson Hutchings, to Georgetown for similar purposes of reform. As one of Jackson's biographers noted: "Always a discipline problem, Hutchings quarreled repeatedly with overseers, abused the slaves, got himself expelled from school . . . and generally behaved in a thoroughly nasty and reprehensible manner."[73] Georgetown proved no better than the president or prior schools in the civilizing of Hutchings. At the faculty's request, President Jackson withdrew his ward after the close of the 1829–30 school year. A guardian of another Virginia student confided to a Georgetown president in the 1840s that he had never seen "in any human being so great an aversion to books or to confinement—or to any thing like regular discipline. . . . He is as unconscious of any moral obligation as a Comanche. . . . He is determined to force you to drive him off."[74]

The college had a hierarchy of sanctions to impose on delinquents. For unpreparedness in class or stealing a pie from the kitchen, for instance, there was "jug" or detention hall where the culprits had to memorize lines of Latin poetry. For more serious offenses, such as insolence or drunkenness, there were whippings or confinement for several days on a regimen of bread and water in a tower room of the North Building (known to culprits as "the sky parlour"). The ultimate sanction, of course, was expulsion. Students were expelled for a wide variety of offenses—from reading novels at Mass to assaulting others with a deadly weapon.

By the 1850s the use of alcohol had become a capital offense as well. In the early nineteenth century the national consumption of alcohol reached an all-time peak, with an annual rate of nearly four gallons per capita by 1830.[75] The college was very much a part of "the Alcoholic Republic" well into the 1830s. At a time when water was still suspect and alcohol considered uncompromisingly beneficial to health, students regularly were served wine and stronger beverages at their meals and for special occasions. In 1827 when twenty-six students went for a June outing across the Potomac into Virginia, they were issued six jugs of wine and four of whiskey as well as food. They brought back two jugs of unused wine.[76] In the winter of 1836, when fire destroyed the laundry house despite the firefighting efforts of students and faculty who had been called out for firefighting at 2 a.m., "Brandy and gin [were given] to them afterwards," a Jesuit official wrote in his diary, "& nearly all got drunk. One attacked a prefect."[77] Periodic curtailments of the dispensing of spirits notwithstanding, alcohol remained an integral part of campus life until two-term President James Ryder was put in charge.

Ryder (1840–45, 1848–51), an ardent temperance advocate, banned the consumption of alcohol by students both on and off campus beginning with the school year of 1840–41.[78] Although the formal announcement did not come until January of 1841, the students' intelligence network had a distant early warning of the impending threat to their drinking habits. In fact, during the preceding August of 1840, a Virginia student wrote to George Fenwick that he dreaded returning to campus with the prospect of living under such "unnecessarily rigid rules—a decrease of old and common privileges [including] a privation from mint Julips [sic]."[79] By 1845 Ryder had extended the ban to the Jesuits as well.[80] When alcohol reappeared in the 1850s, it was in the form of highly diluted wine. By that time it was the foreign Jesuits who were complaining about the draconian prohibition of all alcohol from the college. But Jesuit superiors, out of considerations that ranged from setting a good example for students through conserving money to depriving the nativists of an opportunity to cry scandal, continued the custom of limiting its use as table wine on feast days and special occasions. For the students the drinking of alcohol in any form remained an offense which warranted expulsion.[81]

Smoking also came to be a forbidden practice under Ryder. Nine months after his decree on alcohol, the president began the next academic year by urging the students "that *every one of you abstain totally from the use of tobacco in every shape*!!" Father Ryder is reported to have explained his reasons but,

During the postbellum years, unlike during the Ryder years, senior students were permitted to smoke but only in certain areas of the Georgetown campus. Cartoon from 1880. (Courtesy of *Scribner's Magazine*)

" BE TO MY FAULTS A LITTLE BLIND."

unfortunately, the details have not survived.[82] Presumably, they concerned the incongruity of young gentlemen untidily smoking cigars or chewing and spitting tobacco (since cigarettes were virtually unknown then). By 1852 the abstinence from tobacco was no longer a counsel but a rule; however, failure to observe it carried a less-than-capital-crime punishment: three hundred lines of Latin to be memorized.[83]

Scholastics, who frequently were scarcely older than their charges at the college, were particularly at risk when they attempted to discipline students, either inside or out of the classroom. Here is Mr. Stonestreet's own diary of one fortnight when he, as a twenty-seven-year-old Jesuit scholastic, had the prefect's duties which illustrate those "combat" dangers:[84]

---

18 Mar 1389
 "Mr. [William] Clarke & Lewis Donnell had a scuffle—Lewis was expelled—. . . some disturbance among the boys after studies."

23 Mar 1839
 "Mr. Clarke & Octave Rintrop had a pitched battle after evening schools—Rintrop was taken out of bed and 'expelled'—The French boys & Clifford had a quarrel."

24 Mar 1839
 "After dinner they had a great flare up—Several of the boys from Louisiana attacked John Clifford. Mr. [James] Power came to separate them & got severely beaten with

sticks & stones. They were expelled during vespers – they were Jos & Lewis LeBour-
geois[,] A. Guidry & G. Duffell—The Execrable French 'faction' is now dissolved
and may it never arise. I was made prefect in Mr. Power's place."

25 Mar 1839

". . . Grass & Mr. [Peter O'] Flanagan had a scuffle. . ."

30 Mar 1839

"Mr. [William] Logan & Johnson had a rumpus. Mr. Logan prevented him from
going out—he went out & Mr. Logan gave it to him accordingly[.] After Breakfast
Johnson went to the woodpile and got a stick and Mr. Logan used it on his back
—put him in prison —let out again—. . ."

A school rule forbade students from possessing any sort of weapon, including
"pistols, Guns, swords, daggers, &c."[85] This seems to have been generally
observed, although students easily came by knives and occasionally used
them against prefects and each other. Mr. William Clarke, a rather slightly
built scholastic, eventually began to carry an iron poker under his habit to
discourage further attacks. Stonestreet himself was compelled to maintain
authority in his classroom with his fists. Once after besting a defiant student
at the cost of a black eye and ruined habit, Stonestreet protested to President
Ryder that he had not entered the Society of Jesus to become a prizefighter.
"Why, man," replied Ryder, "you got the better of him—what more do you
want?"[86]

Southerners particularly resented the "shaming" punishments that were
imposed for their infractions. Regarding shame not as the prod of conscience
but as a stigma that no honorable man should endure, students refused, for
instance, to kneel in the refectory in public or to recite Latin "punishment"
passages during meals. And for them to be beaten (a punishment in vogue at
Georgetown during this period) was to be treated like a slave. When struck,
Southerners tended to strike back, sometimes with fists, sometimes with
even more dangerous weapons. Those from Louisiana seemed to be the most
recalcitrant. To protect the young prefects from retaliation, the administrators encouraged them not to strike students themselves but to refer them to
their Jesuit superiors for punishment, corporal or other.[87] But the students
regarded this sort of informing upon them by virtual peers as an even worse
offense than physical blows.

The Riots of 1833 and 1850

A double breach of such "honor" was the proximate cause of the Riot of
1833. Charles Lancaster, a twenty-two-year-old Jesuit scholastic, had taken
a group of students to the Capitol to observe a session of Congress in early
November. On the way back, one of the students, a Virginian, began making

saloon stops, despite Mr. Lancaster's persistent orders to the contrary. The prefect subsequently reported the student, Virginius Newton, to his superiors who promptly expelled Newton for drunkenness and insolence. Newton's fellow collegians then made plans to avenge him that same evening by attacking Lancaster in the dining hall during supper. But another student warned the college authorities, and Mulledy dispatched a group of burly Jesuit brothers who surrounded the Jesuit scholastic at his prefecting post when the students rushed him after the lamps had been extinguished according to a prearranged signal. The frustrated students proceeded to go on a rampage of rock-throwing, fire-setting, yelling, and general resistance. About thirteen students, mostly sixteen-year-olds, were dismissed for their roles in the plot. Protests went on for several more weeks, but the administration refused to take back the expelled students.[88] Instead, it expelled even more, a total of more than thirty. Others left in sympathy. By late January Georgetown College had eighty fewer students.[89]

The Riot of 1833, the worst in Georgetown's history, was tame in comparison with student outbreaks at other American colleges, in both the North and the South, during that period. At the University of Virginia the militia twice had to be called out, in 1836 and 1845, to restore order at Mr. Jefferson's University.[90] No one died at Georgetown; no buildings were burned down. Still, 1833 represented a high-water mark in the expulsion rate at Georgetown. Between 1830 and 1860 some eighty-five students were expelled; nevertheless, a relatively low figure for a Southern college.[91] Most were Southerners (62.6%), and most were relatively young (16 was the median age). There were, despite their unflattering reputation, surprisingly few French expelled (9, opposed to 50 English and 13 Irish). And relatively few day students were expelled, despite a curious double standard that expelled them more readily than boarders for low grades. Protestants were somewhat more prone to expulsion than Catholics. But the most striking figure is the number expelled (55 in 12 years) during President Thomas Mulledy's two terms (1829–38, 1845–48). Mulledy could be an indulgent president, but when challenged in any way, he gave no quarter, as he had likely never given any back at home in Romney, Virginia, and certainly never gave as First Prefect.[92]

Aside from the surge of expulsions during Mulledy's two terms, there were few others in the 1840s and 1850s. In part this was a result of greater selectivity in admitting more mature students. But it was also due to a subsidence of aggressiveness not only among students but within the college administration as well. As the average age of students at Georgetown increased, the number of expulsions decreased. Among the administrators there was a growing reluctance to react by applying this capital sanction, and if and when it was applied, a growing inclination to rescind it by taking back the offender(s) upon appeal and/or apology. Expulsion, for the student and for the family, often became the ultimate shame, and often led parents to disown their sons. Even Mulledy professed to intend to inflict it for only the gravest reasons because of these social consequences.[93] William Morris of Florida pleaded that his expulsion in 1850 for insulting a prefect be lifted so that he could "become an honor to my parents. . . ." He dreaded the thought of returning home. "What am I to say? What am I to do? All my bright prospects for future life will be nipped in the bud and forever blasted."[94] This emotional plea by Morris did not gain his readmission, perhaps because he had already been given a "certificate of honorary dismissal" (his father was an army major), but similar cries by many others proved more successful.

The contrast between the riot of 1833 and the one of 1850 is a study in changing conditions and attitudes. Whereas the earlier one had been instigated by adolescents outraged by the tattling of a prefect and fellow student, and resulted in massive expulsions and walkouts, the later rebellion grew out of a conflict between the administration and senior members of the most elite student organization on campus. The results were an administrative shake-up and, if not a triumph of student rights, at least a recognition, as one historian of youth has put it, "that studentship was a limited status."[95] The parent-child model of governance had been subtly modified.

This later, so-called Ki Yi Yi revolt had its beginnings in early January of 1850 when First Prefect Burchard Villiger refused permission for the Philodemic Society to hold an extraordinary meeting after studies on a Sunday evening. The members met anyway. When Villiger found out about the "after hours" event, he suspended their meetings for a month and deprived them of late study privileges. A formal petition from the student body was delivered to the vice-rector, James Ward, asking that he lift or soften the penalty. It was rejected. After stewing in their anger for several days, the debaters and their sympathizers began a mass protest by refusing to read in the dining room, serve Mass, read prayers, or be silent in the study hall. That night in the older students' dormitory, stones were hurled, firecrackers exploded, and, as the house diarist recorded, "for three hours and a quarter there was chaos." The protests and violence continued throughout the next day. Finally, Ward expelled three students—two Louisianans and a Marylander—whom he considered to be the leaders. The two Creoles left campus; but the third, William Xavier Wills, a twenty-year-old Philosopher, remained behind to plot further strategy. Accordingly, towards the end of dinner the students invited him to come forward and make a speech. But as soon as Wills began, the prefect dismissed the students, who took themselves in a body to Ward's office. When they complained of the unfairness of the dismissals, that there were people more guilty than the three he had sent home, Ward demanded to know who they were. All of us, they responded, we acted in concert. Then, said Ward, you may leave in concert. With earshattering "Hurrahs" and "Ki Yi Yis" they stormed out, smashing a few doors and windows in the process, but generally under the control of their leaders.[96]

About sixty students, in uniform, then marched off through the midafternoon snow to the city, where most of them took refuge in the Globe Hotel, "a third class house," as one of the students later remembered.[97] From there they issued an ultimatum to the administration that they would not return until all were taken back and the first prefect, Villiger, had been removed.[98] Ward refused to negotiate. The students' revolt was soon a much publicized story in the newspapers of Washington and Georgetown. As the Washington *Republic* reported, "A very serious difficulty has occurred in the Georgetown College. It appears that a foreign professor has been tyrannizing over the students for some time and enforcing most humiliating and demoralizing practices."[99] Several congressmen, including a senator from Louisiana, agreed to intercede on the students' behalf.

By January 19 there were only about fifty out of an original one hundred and eighty students left in the college. In the continuing absence of President Ryder, who had been away for several weeks on a preaching tour, Ignatius Brocard, the provincial superior, called Ryder's consultors together to deal with the crisis. Brocard thereupon announced that he intended, "for the honor of the College and the improvement of discipline," to take back all the students. In effect, the honor at issue was the survival of the college and discipline was now to serve for the correction of overreaction. Ward, who, like Villiger, had been very much influenced by two particularly rigorous Central European Jesuits, Joseph Duverney and Francis Xavier Knackstedt, told his superior, "If you want things done that way, name another Vice-President."[100] Brocard did just that, making another faculty member, Father Angelo Paresce, the acting vice president.

Meanwhile another prefect, Bernard Maguire, had on his own been attempting to work out a settlement with the students. Now, with Paresce's support, he quickly worked out an agreement by which all the students were taken back in exchange for a formal apology for any scandal or offense they had given. Robert Ray, years later, after participating in a second and even more lethal rebellion, recalled that he had come out "worse for the weare in both of them."[101] Perhaps so, but the "Ki Yi Yi" revolt brought about changes at Georgetown that ultimately served both the students and the college. Villiger resigned as first prefect and Maguire was named in his place.[102] The next year Brocard assigned Duverney and Knackstedt to Philadelphia and St. Inigoes, respectively. And Charles Stonestreet replaced Ryder briefly as president. He in turn was succeeded within the year (1852) by Maguire himself. William Wills, one of the three originally expelled, not only had been graduated from Georgetown in the summer of 1851 but went on to earn a law degree at Harvard. Moreover, he returned to his alma mater in 1858 to teach languages and mathematics.

Bernard Maguire's handling of another riot within his first semester as president was an indication of the changing nature of governance on the campus. Maguire allowed that student disorder to continue for several days, then addressed the student body at dinner, not as erring children but as "gentlemen" who were acting in a very dishonorable fashion. Surely, he reminded them, they realized that order was a requirement of every educational institution. He treated them as gentlemen and expected them to behave as such. He informed them that he was prepared to dismiss six leaders of the recent disturbance, but he did not name the culprits. Instead he summoned their parents who discreetly took them home.[103] By defining them as "gentlemen," Maguire was implicitly owning that they had a standing that had to be respected. By calling in the parents to enforce his order, he was admitting that *in loco parentis* was no longer an absolute ground upon which to govern. Thus, in societal terms, Georgetown was in transition from the traditional to a more contemporary form of governance in the 1850s.

The Influence of College Life on Careers

Throughout the antebellum era, college life for most students at Georgetown was a self-enclosed culture whose steady influence reached well beyond the classroom. And the center of that culture was the combination of curriculum and extracurriculum, the twin energizers of liberal education at the Hilltop in this period before the Civil War. The next chapter examines the shape of the Georgetown curriculum, formal and informal, and what was "extra" but allied to it, as well as the outcome of such a liberal education as measured in careers.

The waterfront of the port of Georgetown changed little in physical aspect from about 1840 to 1865, although some cultural changes gradually became evident in the city and on the Hilltop. Photograph taken by William Smith. (Georgetown University Archives)

THE MINOR LITERARY EXHIBITION

OF THE

College of Georgetown, D.C.

Will take place on the 27th of February, at 10 o'clock, A.M.

WHEN the following Exercises will be performed by the young Gentlemen, whose names are affixed to them:—

(THE WHOLE ORIGINAL.)

Prologue, ... Mr. James Faulkner, *r.* *

A Discussion, whether Julius Cæsar was slain justly or unjustly.

JUSTLY.	UNJUSTLY.
Mr. P. K. Mooney, *r.*	Mr. J. Faulkner, *r.*
Mr. Lewis Jenkins, *r.*	Mr. Dom. Young, *h.*
	Mr. James Leckie. 1 *g.*

Soliloquy of Andromache over the dead body of Hector, ... Mr. P. Mooney, *r.*

On Melancholy, ... Mr. L. Jenkins, *r.*

The Thunder-storm, ... Mr. J. Faulkner, *r.*

EXPLANATIONS.

Rhetoric.	Four Orations of Cicero, ...	Mr. P. Mooney.
	All Horace's Odes, ...	Mr. L. Jenkins.
	Second Book of Homer, ...	Mr. J. Faulkner.
Humanities.	2d. Book of Xenophon, ...	Mr. D. Young.
	2d. Book of Virgil, ...	Mr. A. Jones.
	1st. Book of Ovid's Elegies, ...	Mr. W. Burk.
	1st. Book of Fontaine's Fables, ...	Mr. J. Jones.
1st Class Gram.	Sallust's gurthine War, and Lucian's Dialogues, ...	Mr. E. Mason,
	Cicero de Senectute, ...	Mr. G. Gardiner.

Εις την παιριδα και τους φιλους. Ωδη. . . . . . . Mr. J. Faulkner, *r.*

"Tara's Hall," translated into Latin Sapphic, ... Mr. P. Mooney, *r.*

"The Meeting of the Waters," translated into Elegiac, . . . Mr. A. Jones, *h.*

Translation of the 7th of Ovid's Elegies, ... Mr. D. Young, *h.*

Latin Translation of an Extract from Franklin's Life, . . . Mr. G. Gardiner, 1 *g.*

Translation of an Extract from Orpheus, "On the Supreme God," . . Mr. J. Leckie, 1 *g.*

Soliloque de Manasses, ... Mr. V. Jarrot, 1 *g.*

Soliloquy of a School Boy at the College-gate, on the point of eloping. paraphrased from Hamlet's, ... } Mr. A. Chardon, 3 *g.*

Dialogue on the Study of History, ... { Mr. J. Patterson, *ru.* Mr. T. Davis, *ru.* Mr. G. Gardiner, 1 *g.* Mr. A. Chardon, 3 *g.*

On Bad Speaking. . . . . Mr. P. Mooney, *r.*

Epilogue, ... Mr. C. Jenkins, 1 *g.*

* There are six classes in the College, each occupying a year, viz. Rhetoric, Humanities, first, second, and third classes of Grammar and Rudiments. The scholars of these classes are designated as above, thus:—*r.* Rhetorician: *h.* Humanist: 1 *g.* 2 *g.* 3 *g.* are scholars of the 1st, 2d, or 3d Classes of Grammar; *ru.* of Rudiments. (Vide Prospectus.)

Georgetown College, February 27, 1821.

CHAPTER 8

"The Great Object of Education"
Curriculum, Student Societies, and Careers

We are told that [liberal studies] contribute nothing toward what are vaguely called the practical purposes of life. . . . Education is looked upon as an end rather than as a means, and courses of study are laid out very much after the fashion of our railroads—the shortest possible routes are adopted, all of which have for their grand terminus the busy marts of the money-making world. The temple of learning . . . seems to have been taken possession of by the money-changers. . . . But what is man, and for what is he intended?

JOHN C. C. HAMILTON, GEORGETOWN ALUMNUS
July 1862, Address to the Philodemics

"To Develop All These Noble Faculties"

During the Civil War, an alumnus attempted to define for the Philodemic Society the uniqueness of Georgetown's educational philosophy:

We are told that [liberal studies] contribute nothing toward what are vaguely called the practical purposes of life. . . . Education is looked upon as an end rather than as a means, and courses of study are laid out very much after the fashion of our railroads—the shortest possible routes are adopted, all of which have for their grand

This 1821 program "exhibits" the liberal studies that dominated the curriculum. It provided a coherent plan and system "by which truth may be sought and acquired." (*Glimpses of Old Georgetown*. Friant et al., Class of 1941, *The Hoya*, 1939)

terminus the busy marts of the money-making world. The temple of learning . . . seems to have been taken possession of by the money-changers. . . . But what is man, and for what is he intended? . . . Has he not a mind endowed with various and wonderful powers and capacities? Is he not a moral being, with the pure precepts of natural law written in his heart? Is he not a social being, owing the ties of a common brotherhood which knit him with mankind? Has he no relation with the Divine Intelligence . . . ? Behold here, then the great object of education! It is to develop all these noble faculties in their full perfection. . . . [1]

Such an academic jeremiad could have been issued at any one of a hundred religious colleges during the mid-nineteenth century. In essence, John C. C. Hamilton (**C** 1845–51, AB), a Washington lawyer, was arguing that an authentic liberal education was not a process for transmitting information or "ready-made truths" but rather a dynamic for catalyzing "thought by which truth may be sought and acquired." Such an education made no claim to prepare a man for any particular occupation but for "his journey in life that in whatever direction his tastes may lead him, he will soon outstrip those who, with less preparation, have started before him." To do this, it was not enough to cultivate the mind but the imagination as well. "The intellectual man," he concluded, "may reason out and understand the wants and sufferings of others, but the man of imagination sees them at a glance, adopts them as his own, and hastens to relieve them." And the necessary means to imparting such a liberal education, as Hamilton realized, was the retention of the classics at the center of the curriculum.[2]

Most of Hamilton's definition of liberal education was commonplace enough, but the emphasis on the imagination ("the great wellspring of sentiment and of human sympathy") reflected an essential dimension of the Jesuit tradition that distinguished its philosophy of learning even while the curriculum that embodied it mirrored those of other antebellum liberal arts colleges, in the main.[3] For Ignatius of Loyola, the imagination is the key to the emotions, which are the source of behavior. In his *Spiritual Exercises*, the manual of self-reformation that Ignatius put together from his personal experiences, he aims at habituating the imagination to radically perceive the roots of reality in the Christian dispensation. The Jesuit educational philosophy adapted this so as to engage the whole person in the act of learning, to make the student his own teacher as a self-initiating learner who brings his own imagination to bear creatively on "the matter" under consideration, to make him an active player in the integrated process, to "place" himself there, whether translating Ovid or reflecting on the Fall of Rome.

The Georgetown curriculum was faithful to the *Ratio* Studiorum's principles of successively arranged objectives and an overall coherent plan of studies into which all parts fit.[4] The basic academic structure changed little between the 1790s and the 1850s. The full course of ordinary studies still extended over seven years. The classics at Georgetown, as at most liberal arts colleges of the era (including the Presbyterian, Methodist, and Baptist networks), remained at the heart of the curriculum. When a student applied for admission he was cursorily examined for his proficiency in English and mathematics and subsequently placed in an appropriate class.

In the lowest class (Rudiments, or First Class in the Preparatory School after 1852) new students began the study of English grammar and syntax as well as mathematics. In the next class (Third Humanities, or Second Class) the "small boys" began the study of Latin and French while continuing mathematics and English, including composition. For Second Humanities (Third Class) they intensified their study of Latin syntax while beginning Latin composition and the study of Latin literature (Caesar's *Gallic Wars*). In mathematics they concentrated on fractions, simple interest, compound proportions, and the like. French grammar and syntax were pursued and geography begun.[5]

With First Humanities, students moved up to the college or the "higher schools" within the course of studies. A second classical language, Greek, was introduced at this point. Besides being expected to learn the whole of Greek syntax and grammar, those in First Humanities read various Greek texts, ranging from the First Book of Xenophon to chapters of Luke's gospel. In Latin they concentrated on works of Sallust, Livy, and Ovid. In French they spent the year on Bossuet's *Universal History*. In the languages, the methodologies employed included recitation, translation, and composition, with the emphasis on the latter two. Students were expected to read, write, and speak the various languages fluently. Father George Fenwick, popular as he was with his classes through his dramatic recreation of Pericles' funeral oration or Livy's history of Rome, was thoroughly demanding in his nightly assignments (twenty to thirty pages of a text being a typical reading).

The second "school" in the college or upper division was Poetry, so named because of the prominence of Latin and Greek poets in the curriculum. The students routinely translated selections from Virgil's *Aeneid,* Homer's *Iliad,* and Horace's *Art of Poetry* as well as his odes. Other Latin and Greek authors they read included Cicero, Catullus, Xenophon, and Thucydides. Side by side with ex-servicemen and aspiring clerks, the sons of lawyers and planters studied the history of Rome and the geography of the ancient world, as well as ancient mythology. In mathematics they all had to focus on algebra and geometry. French offered the *Fables* of La Fontaine as well as advanced composition.

In requiring the study of French, Georgetown was then somewhat exceptional among American colleges. As noted earlier, this had been a regular part of the Georgetown curriculum since the 1790s. In most colleges in the antebellum era, it was offered as an elective, as at Harvard and Yale, or not at all. Nevertheless, complaints persisted about the failure of students to learn French well, the one modern language that was required, despite many years of studying the language four hours a week. "It has always been my desire," Thomas Jenkins of Baltimore wrote to President Enoch Fenwick in 1824,

Arithmetic Premium awarded for mathematics to one of two top students at the exhibition (commencement) for the Class of 1832. (Georgetown University Archives)

"that my boys should be taught to *speak* French. I am much disappointed that they cannot yet *speak* that language." Mark Jenkins had been a student at Georgetown for most of the previous eight years, his younger brother Theodore for two.[6] Eventually one faculty member suggested in the late 1850s that French be made an elective in order to intensify student attention to the core of the curriculum: the classics. As it was, he observed, too many students had no proficiency in French anyhow, no matter how long they had been subjected to its study. Boredom and inept teachers were singled out as the main causes. If Harvard's experience was any guide, however, making French an elective was no quick fix for boredom and a lack of proficiency.[7] Other faculty colleagues thought more demanding standards were the answer to the problem.[8] In any event, French at Georgetown became neither an elective nor a more demanding element of the core curriculum.

Giovanni Grassi, reflecting on American education after he had returned to Italy, had observed as early as 1819 that "Only gold is idolized more than an eloquent speaker. But of all the parts that the great masters agree make up the art of speaking well, it is elocution that the Americans study the most."[9] Thus, Georgetown's pursuit of the *Ratio* Studiorum's goal of *eloquentia perfecta* fitted well with this cultural predilection; and the curriculum's stress on cultivating the powers of eloquent communication climaxed with Rhetoric, the next to highest "school" of the college. The Rhetoricians read the masters of eloquence: Cicero, Demosthenes, and Sophocles. And French further reinforced rhetoric by concentrating study on certain French preachers, such as Massellon. For these it utilized the traditional pedagogy of classical rhetoric.[10] Throughout the year, students analyzed this literature according to the precepts of rhetoric, including the traditional *Institutions* (*Institutio oratoria*) of Quintilian. But there was much other classical literature, including Ovid, Homer, Virgil, Livy, Juvenal, and Tacitus. The study of English literature was also gradually introduced, informally at first in the 1830s and formally by the next decade.[11] The Rhetoricians also made periodic trips to the Capitol when master orators—Calhoun, Webster, or some other member of the House or Senate of similar renown—were scheduled to speak in congressional debate or at a Supreme Court presentation. Besides the languages, the curriculum in this penultimate year involved advanced geometry and trigonometry, as well as Anglo-American history. In addition, faculty members delivered weekly lectures to the two most senior classes on the philosophy of history.

The college had been offering all the branches of mathematics since Grassi's presidency (1812–17). Into the 1830s the books of Euclid provided the basis for instruction in algebra and related subjects. By the 1840s the texts of Charles Davies, the most successful American adapter of the pioneering analytical French works in the discipline of numbers, were commonly used at Georgetown in teaching everything from simple mathematics to trigonometry. As the analytical content of the various branches of mathematics increased, many students, like their peers elsewhere, no doubt tuned out—as their mournful mentors noted.[12] For all the attention to mathematics, it was still an ancillary part of the Georgetown curriculum.

Few students survived this six-year program so as to become Philosophers. Those who did survive, one Jesuit claimed in the 1840s, "not only write Latin fluently and correctly but even speak and debate with ease [in that language]." Such eloquence in a classical language as well as their own invariably impressed outsiders, he reported, and had greatly increased the reputation of the college.[13]

The last or seventh year of college, Philosophy, focused on and embraced its two divisions: moral philosophy (logic, metaphysics, natural theology, psychology, and ethics), and natural philosophy (mechanics, physics, calculus, chemistry, and astronomy). All but the natural sciences were taught in Latin, a Jesuit tradition honored at Georgetown since the beginning of the century, and an advantage for the immigrant faculty. Moral philosophy apparently had a high standing among the older students. James Ryder Randall, the future writer, found Joseph Ardia's logic lectures "decidedly rich."[14] Alexander Dimitry wrote a friend in 1825:

My mother wishes me to remain another year at college. If I do I shall devote those twelve months to the acquisition of philosophical knowledge. Certainly Metaphysics are by far more abstruse than a great many of the transcendent branches of mathematics; still I cannot bear the latter, while I feel a kind of predilection for the former science.[15]

Dimitry did the additional year of philosophy and took his degree.

Besides being the capstone of the curriculum, philosophy carried the burden of providing an objective foundation for religious belief. As several mid-century students affirmed in their theses: Cosmology and natural theology purported to marshal the "metaphysical, physical, and moral arguments" to prove the existence of God, God's characteristics, creation of the world, providential rule, and the necessary relationship between this supreme, unchangeable, and eternal Being and an inherently dependent yet free humanity capable of good and evil. The cosmological argument or design found in nature, for instance, along with other arguments, was used to give what one thesis writer claimed to be "a perfect and absolute demonstration of God's existence."[16] Nature's very existence was proof of God, as the professor of cosmology taught in 1853, inasmuch as "Every thing bears the relation of effect to some thing Else which is its Cause until we come to a first Cause—the necessary being," or uncaused Cause.[17] Nature, together with nature's law, was still seen, at Georgetown as at most denominational colleges of the era, as the scientific revelation of God.[18]

Religious studies as such were not a formal and separate part of the curriculum. Weekly half-hour catechetical instructions were given on Saturdays to separate classes in all the lower and upper schools. There was a common instruction in Christian Doctrine for all Catholic collegians on

Sunday mornings as well, following the college High Mass.[19] Religious studies at Georgetown in the nineteenth century, one scholar has noted, had much more to do with moral training than with intellectual formation.[20] Theology had no place in the curriculum for either junior or senior students. By the 1850s the Catholic preparatory students began their morning classes by reciting portions of the catechism. Non-Catholics were required to memorize lines of Latin poetry as an alternative. Most students considered both forms of recitation the very worst of exercises in education by rote.[21] For the intellectual dimension of the religious experience, philosophy functioned as the queen of the sciences.

Science in the Curriculum at Georgetown

The other focal point of senior year was natural philosophy or science. By the 1830s the college curriculum was responding, somewhat tardily, to the differentiation and specialization that was occurring throughout the scientific world. By mid-century, astronomy, botany, chemistry, mechanics, optics, and physics had all emerged from the umbrella of natural philosophy as distinct disciplines, with their own courses and textbooks. Georgetown's increasingly sophisticated science curriculum clearly reflected these developments. As we mentioned earlier (in chapter 6, this volume), the influx of European refugees, especially after 1848, enabled the college to expand its science offerings, although they were still limited to those courses in philosophy or senior year. One of the stated reasons for the building of the astronomical observatory was to augment the institution's facilities for science.

Thomas Meredith Jenkins, whose inheritance largely underwrote the cost of the construction, wrote to the superior general in 1841 to explain that, while Georgetown had an outstanding reputation in the humanities, it was rightly criticized for giving so little attention to the sciences. An astronomy observatory, he felt, would be the best way to change that reputation in a society that equated quality education with the prominence of science in the curriculum.[22] And during its first decades, the observatory functioned more as a teaching than research facility. James Wallace's *Use of the Globes and Practical Astronomy* (New York, 1813) continued to be the basic textbook through the early 1840s. Written while he was a scholastic teaching at the New York Literary Institution, Wallace's text, unlike most of those available in the late eighteenth and early nineteenth centuries, detailed the mathematical calculations needed to determine patterns of celestial bodies, rather than sheer memorization of formulae. It was designed for students at three levels, and presupposed for the more advanced ones a knowledge of the geometry, algebra, and trigonometry needed to solve the proposed problems.

By 1844 John Herschel's *A Treatise on Astronomy* (Philadelphia, 1836), which was based on more recent developments in the science, had finally replaced Wallace. James Curley and Benedict Sestini together and separately both taught the subject in classroom lectures and demonstrations in the observatory. Nevertheless, for the nonscientific student, their complex matter could be stultifying. "For all that I care," James Ryder Randall wrote, "Tycho, Brahe, Copernicus, Kepler et *'id genus omni'* might never have been. The stars are not dead, therefore they ought not to be dissected and rent piecemeal by these muddy dabblers." That the future journalist had made two astronomers out of one Danish luminary is clue enough to Randall's interest and/or aptitude. In fact, within a week he recorded in his diary that he was reading and enjoying Byron during astronomy class.[23]

In 1836 three students in Rhetoric class petitioned Father Mulledy that a course in chemistry be substituted for the Latin poetry that was part of the required curriculum for that year.[24] Their request was not granted that year; but chemistry, a science in which Americans were more in tune with European advances than physics or mathematics, did appear two years later for the first time in the Philosophers' schedule of courses. That senior class used Edward Turner's *Elements of Chemistry* (London, 1827), a widely used text in American colleges. Botany, one of the derivatives from chemistry, had emerged as a separate branch as the sciences proliferated during the antebellum period. It was taught at Georgetown with its own special text as early as 1838. That was well before most colleges gave any more than a lecture or two on botany.[25] Separate textbooks were also used for instruction in physics and mechanics by the early 1840s.

Chemistry and physics classes often involved both field and laboratory experiments by faculty from the earliest years. And by the 1840s the college had a formal laboratory for the students as well. In 1844, demonstrations of several chemical experiments were featured as part of the year-end public exhibition. Seven students were chosen to give one hundred and fifty demonstrations of such experiments, including some on "atmospheric air," "combustion," "compounds of Carbon and Hydrogen," and "Hydrogen." All but one worked. The one failure led the student chemist, Francis Dykers of New York, to turn to the audience and explain: "Gentlemen and Ladies, it seems to me no go—but what I have said is a fact anyhow!"[26] Sometimes, however, failure could mean more than embarrassment. That same year a student was seriously hurt when an explosion occurred during a physics lab session.[27] The Philosophers also went regularly to observe scientific experiments at the Navy Yard, the Smithsonian, and other research centers. They had been at the Capitol too when Samuel Morse demonstrated his new telegraphic message code in May of 1844.[28] By the 1850s, the Georgetown seniors received an increasingly wide exposure to the range of modern sciences, but no science was taught below that level.

Other Electives in the Curriculum

There were some other electives in the antebellum curriculum: modern languages other than French (Spanish in 1798, German and Italian by the early 1830s), and for the Southern gentry the fine arts (music, dancing, drawing, fencing). These electives consistently drew large numbers of students, despite being offered only during the two holidays of the week (Thursdays and Sundays). James Alexander Simpson, a local artist, taught drawing and painting from 1830 to 1865. John P. Caulfield offered classes in music during the 1850s and 1860s. In 1833, the college announced "a class of Book-keeping for the convenience of those who wish to learn it,"[29] a recognition of the need to accommodate, to some degree at least, parental (if not student) concerns for a "practical" education. Virginian Henry Aylmer, a Petersburg merchant, was delighted to learn that his son, Robert, was taking advantage of the new offering. "No person," he told his son, "can ever attempt to do business in a proper manner without a knowledge of that Important branch so essential to Merchants."[30] One of Thomas Mulledy's first innovations as prefect of studies was to introduce a series of lectures in 1829 about stenography to interested students.[31]

Despite such nods to business training, Georgetown could lay no claim to providing a comprehensive commercial education. General Gustave Beauregard (of later Civil War fame) withdrew his son in the fall of 1859 after one month of study, apparently quite disappointed that the college did not offer the business-oriented training he sought for his offspring.[32] The very next year, on the eve of the Civil War, a Jesuit superior raised the question of inaugurating separate business courses for those wishing to prepare directly for mercantile careers.[33] Other Jesuit institutions, such as Loyola and St. Joseph's, soon afterwards established commercial courses, partly in response to persistent complaints that the classical curriculum was "useless to youth who had to make their living in America."[34] Anticipating the same parental demand, Holy Cross instituted a commercial course parallel to the classical one in its initial academic year (1843).[35] But Georgetown continued to resist implementing such a special business program for many decades. Even those whose parents made clear their desire to have their sons trained for business took the basic course of liberal studies.[36]

The Library

By the 1830s Georgetown possessed one of the largest libraries in the country. The third president, William DuBourg, as part of his grand vision for the college, had been responsible for its beginnings, bringing with him from Baltimore in 1796 more than one hundred volumes, many of them his own.

He set out to build a useful "working" library, including the development of a call number system displayed on bookplates—a system that he most likely devised himself.[37] Later, Giovanni Grassi greatly expanded DuBourg's collection. Using the Carroll legacy of four hundred pounds sterling (invested in 5 percent stock), he built up the holdings in theology, the classics, ancient and modern history, foreign languages, and the sciences, including the purchase of an edition of Diderot's *Encyclopédie* in forty-five volumes. The Jesuits from Belgium were especially active in adding to the collection, particularly in the areas of scripture and history (e.g., the works of the Bollandists). By the 1820s more than five thousand volumes were shelved in the library and its first official librarian was Thomas Levins.

Rapid growth continued in library acquisitions throughout the decade. James Van de Velde, later Bishop of Natchez, who made the first catalog of the library around 1830, listed 11,150 volumes. The contents ranged from Greek and Latin orations to such "modern novelists" as Washington Irving, Daniel Defoe, and Walter Scott.[38] By that time the collection had outgrown its old location in the original building, so in 1831 a new library room was opened in [Old] North. Its door was painted in *trompe l'oeil* style by a local artist, James Simpson, and it showed shelves of nonexistent books supposedly authored by Georgetown faculty. By 1851 the actual collection of real books had nearly doubled. Partly this reflected the vigilance of James Curley (who served as college librarian in addition to all his other duties) and other Jesuits who acquired new and used books at sales. In the early 1850s Charles Stonestreet had nearly nine hundred such bargain books shipped from Rome. But the increase came largely from gifts of individuals and institutions. For example, Burwel S. Randolph gave a great many books, including some from the library of his ancestor Thomas Jefferson. And the French minister gave a Chinese-French-Latin dictionary on behalf of his government.

When Thomas Levins, former faculty member and librarian, was on his deathbed in New York City in 1843, he expressed the wish to make a bequest of his library, together with his collection of precious stones, to Georgetown College in return for a perpetual scholarship for persons to be named annually by his family.[39] Despite Bishop Benedict Fenwick's attempts to get that library for his new school in Worcester, Georgetown did receive both the book and mineral collections. The former numbered nearly two thousand volumes, including a series of first editions of Erasmus, and an extraordinary collection of other great works on mathematics, theology, history, and science.[40]

Use of the college library was originally restricted to faculty, Jesuit scholastics, and senior students. Students in the several debating and historical societies had their own libraries, several of which had substantial holdings by the 1850s (the Philodemic, for one, had more than five hundred volumes). But unlike those in many other colleges, the Georgetown student libraries were minuscule compared to the main one, although they perhaps offered a broader range and probably served student needs better than the college library itself, particularly in the areas of history and modern literature. (The exception was for those students who as Jesuit scholastics were studying philosophy and theology.)

By 1850 Georgetown's library holdings, including those owned by the student societies, ranked fourth behind Harvard, Yale, and Brown.[41] Ten years later the total collection probably comprised more than thirty thousand volumes, more than three times the size of the better-than-average college library of those times.[42] There was no complete, updated catalogue, however; and complaints persisted about the lack of any system for arranging the books or keeping track of those in circulation.[43] A major problem was sheer space. As early as 1852 President Charles Stonestreet was lamenting to superiors in Rome: "Here there is no longer room for books, so that everywhere we begin to turn into a library. . . . [I]f we must build anywhere, Georgetown should get first consideration.[44]

A Pedagogy of Emulation

Throughout the antebellum period, the principle of emulation continued to be a prominent factor pedagogically at the college. There were regular contests within and between classes. For instance, Latin classes were often divided into "Romans" and "Carthaginians" or Second Humanities was pitted against First Humanities in translating Caesar. Then each month at an assembly the prefect read aloud the students' names ranked according to their class standings. (Private reports of "objective" grading by letter or number were as yet unknown.) Each teacher was assumed to thoroughly comprehend the undefined but real standard of excellence against which all students were to be measured. One of the duties of the prefect of studies was to explain how close to or far from that standard the students were in the various subjects. The tone of the prefect's report usually invited an emotional response. Leading students were applauded and those bringing up the rear were jeered by their fellows. Then, the top student in each class was awarded a ribbon (blue with the seal of the college impressed in gilt). "During my first month," one preparatory student of the 1860s later recalled, "I had felt pretty well satisfied with my progress, as I had studied more diligently than I had ever done before, and I rather expected that I would be called upon to wear the ribbon, and was much disappointed when my name appeared about the middle of the list of my class. I then determined that I would have that ribbon the next month. I almost succeeded and the following month got it. During the rest of my time in Georgetown I was awarded the ribbon about half the time."[45] Not everyone appreciated the pedagogical philosophy of such competition. After his first two months at Georgetown, a not pleased and then ribbonless Isidorio Errázuriz noted in his diary that American "colleges are a grand parody forming merchants and adventurers instead of intellectuals."[46]

Semiannual examinations, both oral and written, took nearly a month altogether and were held in January and in June to determine whether students were qualified to pass on to the next class or needed to remain in their present one. In the written examinations, typically the students would be required to compose and to translate Latin, Greek, and English prose and poetry, in degrees of difficulty according to their class year. Progress reports were sent each quarter to parents. After the twice-yearly examinations, the prefect of studies read aloud the formal reports to the assembled students. Both classes and individuals were thus rated in detail for their success or failure in memorizing of texts, their demonstrated knowledge of grammar, and their rendering of translations from Latin, Greek, and French, as well as their application to mathematics. At Lent's beginning in 1842, George Fenwick's assessment (as acting prefect) of the academic state of some aspiring scholars in the school was appropriately unjoyful:

The class of Rhetoric is decidedly the most deficient of all the divisions of the house. We found in it an indifference—an apathy—an evidence of inattention which we never remember to have observed in any other class before. . . . They seem to have lost every thing like emulation. . . . These gentlemen are far from appreciating the jewels they have in their hands. There [sic] very manner of translating their authors was as if they were lulling themselves & their examiners asleep. Poor Cicero! Poor Demosthenes! . . . never would they have recognized their own compositions in the mouths of these Rhetoricians. . . . They have however a long second term in which they may have an opportunity to redeem their character. Should they neglect it we have no difficulty in telling them that the next years [sic] philosophy will be in the regions of nonentity or if it does exist it will not be composed of any of the present members of Rhetoric.[47]

That same term, Fenwick's judgment on the disappointing performance of one Edgeworth Bird in Poetry year was nearly as harsh. The Prefect's Report continued that in his examinations Bird "scarcely answered any thing in his *Ars Rhetorices*— . . . he answerd badly in Virgil both as to translation & prosody[;] that he was below mediocrity in Horace & scarcely made out to reach it in his Homer. . . ." The students in Poetry, like their counterparts in Rhetoric, needed "much more energy" than they had shown.

But Judgment Day at the college was not all faultfinding. A year later that same prefect found much general improvement in the various classes he had examined. One individual in Poetry had so distinguished himself in such a short time that Fenwick gave him the rare power of deciding for himself whether or not to advance to Rhetoric year.[48] Bernard Maguire, more than a decade later, concluded from his examinations that the younger students had shown "a considerable amount of diligence & proficiency" in their classical studies, but warned the higher classes of Poetry and Rhetoric that "no solid scholarship can be expected . . . as long as they persist in the abuse of translations." In the mathematics classes President Bernard Maguire bemoaned the "many who trifle away their time and neglect the opportunities they have of strengthening their reason—of learning to think—which those studies afford them."[49]

Students at the end of each semiannual examination were either promoted or kept in the same class according to their performance in the various subjects. Theoretically a student could remain in a particular class indefinitely, until he demonstrated sufficient mastery of the subject matter to move on. Flunking out was virtually impossible, although on rare occasions the president or prefect of studies asked a parent to remove an academically hopeless child.

In Philosophy year the students held daily discussions among themselves, in Latin, as recapitulations of the lectures they had just heard in logic, metaphysics, or ethics. Once a year public disputations were also held. And finally, the Philosophers had to pass "a rigorous examination" in moral and natural philosophy in order to qualify for the bachelor of arts degree. Their examination consisted of a "proving" by the student who defended one or more theses selected by the examiners from a list of approximately one hundred and twenty-two "theses" proposed in the various subfields of philosophy. Typically this defense might concern "The common sense of nature, having its origin in rational nature, rests upon such a principle, that it cannot be subject to error"; or "The first cause of the world must have been a supreme cause, out of the series of contingent and mutable things"; or "Natural law is necessary, immutable, universal, objectively eternal, and the foundation of all other laws"; or "Duelling, by which two persons, having fixed a time and place, meet in single combat, undertaken by private authority, must be held as repugnant to the laws of nature."[50] The final degree requirement for each Philosopher was the composition of a short Latin thesis, on an assigned topic, which had to be written without aid and within a few hours. "After lunch," Isidorio Errázuriz wrote in his diary in July 1852, "we went with [President] Stonestreet to the Observatory to write our thesis." (By mid-July the Observatory on the hilltop with its overarching trees was the coolest place on campus.) "Stonestreet gave us as topic 'The Characteristics of the Soul.'"[51] Within a few years English was the language used for this thesis, a change brought on, the 1854–55 catalogue suggested, by student pressure "to prepare them for their future professional career."

The Debating Societies

Extracurricular societies, which had come to be such a vital part of education early in the nineteenth century, began to really flourish in the years just before the Civil War, although at Georgetown they did not, as elsewhere, represent the cutting edge of curricular development or an alternative educational opportunity but were rather a complement to the formal educational ideals of Jesuits as teachers. In all their schools an important part of realizing the

Jesuit ideal of *eloquentia perfecta* had traditionally involved the extracurricular realm where music, debating, and dramatics could translate theory into reality. The Sodality, as we saw earlier, was the most important collegiate organization for developing the character and spiritual life of the Christian scholar in a Jesuit school. At Georgetown the Sodality was the oldest of the students' societies, dating at least to 1810. In the 1830s it was vigorous and popular under the leadership of George Fenwick, James Ryder, Felix Barbelin, and others. By 1840 the sodality membership had so increased that the chapel in the original (South) building could no longer hold them all for the public recitation of the weekly office of the Blessed Virgin. By the 1850s, however, with the rising tide of Southerners, many of them non-Catholic, the Jesuits were becoming concerned about both the declining numbers and diminishing prestige of the Sodality. When his fellow Sodalists elected James Ryder Randall their prefect in 1855, he declined the office, not wishing to play "the mealy mouthed hypocrite" that he presumed others would take him to be.[52] A surprisingly large number (a third) of the Sodalists in the 1850s were French, and nearly half were the sons of planter/merchants; the Irish were decidedly underrepresented. A fifth of the Sodalists earned degrees, but only four of them (3%) went on to study for the priesthood. Most became planters, like Henri Octave Colomb, or doctors.

The debating societies occupied the top rungs of the ladder in student society at Georgetown during the antebellum period, understandable in a republican culture that prized rhetoric as the key to public discourse and enlightened citizenship. Literary societies flourished both inside and out of academia. In the fall of 1830 a group of thirty-three students met to organize a debating society which they subsequently named "The Philodemic Society of Georgetown College." James Ryder, then vice president of the College and professor of theology and also the most noted speaker among the Jesuit faculty, was chosen president. Four students were elected to the other Philodemic offices.[53]

In February of 1831 the society was formally approved, as the house diarist put it, so that outstanding students "might get public experience for conducting the business of the republic."[54] (Much later, in 1839, other debating societies were begun: the Philonomosian Society and the Philistorian Society, the latter for younger students.) The constitution and the official badge underscored the republican character of the Philodemic Society. "This Association," its constitution noted, "commenced in the year of our Lord 1830 and the fifty-fourth of the Independence of the United States, . . . and professes to hold as the primary objects of its cultivation Eloquence and Liberty."[55] The society's badge depicted Mercury, the god of eloquence, clasping hands with the goddess of liberty and contained the inscription in Latin: "The Philodemic Society of Georgetown College cultivates eloquence devoted to Liberty."[56] Each year the members elected new members from the upper classes, an honor few, if any, rejected.[57] There were also honorary members (faculty, or distinguished alumni, such as William Gaston, or noted Americans, like Duff Green). Although the president, according to the constitution, could be elected from among either its faculty or student members, in practice he was always a Jesuit who held office at the pleasure of the members. In 1841 they informed Father Samuel Barber that since he had failed to respond to their notification that he had been elected president they had been forced to replace him.[58]

Given the status of oral communication in Southern society, it is to be expected that Southerners dominated the debating societies. The Philodemic's first officers illustrate that regional dominance: Samuel Mulledy of Romney, Virginia, the nineteen-year-old brother of the school's president, was elected vice-president, John Hunter of Maryland was named secretary, John Digges of Maryland was made treasurer, and Eugene Lynch of Virginia was made amanuensis.

From 1830 to 1861 the largest number of debaters came from Maryland, followed by Louisiana, Virginia, the District of Columbia, and Georgia. In all, these four states and the federal enclave accounted for more than three-quarters of the members (87%), and more than half from below the Potomac. They tended to be largely Catholic (76.2%), from rural areas or small towns (62.7%); and the sons of lawyer/politicians, doctors, and military officers. More than a third of the Philodemics (34.6%) graduated. Indeed, four-fifths of the graduates of the period belonged to one or the other of the debating societies. Of those members (188 of 525) whose later occupations are known, nearly half (84) became lawyers or politicians; and about a ninth (21) went on to study for the priesthood or ministry. Most of Georgetown's prominent alumni from the period, including a governor, a lieutenant governor, fifteen members of state legislatures, two U.S. senators, and two congressmen, were members of the Philodemic Society as undergraduates.

Debates were held weekly. Topics ranged from the ancient and classical to the current and local. The topic chosen for the first debate was a standard in debating circles: "Who was the greater man: Napoleon Bonaparte or George Washington?" Unsurprisingly, Washington gained the decision (but Napoleon was judged the greater in a debate on the same topic later that academic year).[59] The shifting sentiment on the issue of slavery was a reflection of hardening sectional attitudes after 1830. The first time the abolition of slavery was debated in March of 1832 (two months after the Virginia legislature had concluded its debate over the abolition of slavery in the state), a bare majority or eleven of the Philodemic members decided that it would be beneficial to the Union if all African Americans, both slave and free, were sent out of the country. Yet, not quite two years later, in October 1833, the members cast their votes against abolition. Nevertheless, as late as 1848 a majority of the Philodemics found that slavery was inconsistent with republican government.[60] That was the last time the issue of slavery was explicitly and publicly debated. But, like their counterparts in other Southern colleges, the members increasingly favored Southern positions by the early 1850s, including the acquisition of Cuba and firm opposition to tariffs.[61]

When Edgeworth Bird, a Philodemic member, was selected as a graduation speaker in 1844, he chose Daniel O'Connell, the Irish emancipator, as his subject. In a March letter he wrote to his mother in Georgia, "I will have to defend the position he has taken with regard to American slavery which," he advised her, "I expect would not prove very agreeable to some of our Georgia slaveholders were they present." Since the college president had suggested the topic, his mother replied her son had no option but to follow his advice. "But . . . you should have it clearly understood," she insisted, "that you do not advocate his ANTI-SLAVERY PRINCIPLES. How can you as the son of a *Southern Slave Holding Planter* defend his proposition in that respect? . . . Unless you have become an *abolitionist* and intend to free them you cannot consistantly [*sic*] defend him."[62]

On other issues a liberal republicanism prevailed, such as support in 1841 for universal suffrage (for males) and opposition to the veto power of the president. In 1847 the members decided that senators should obey the instructions of the legislatures of their respective states, and that colonies were not beneficial to a nation—this during the Mexican War. The emerging nativist tensions were reflected in the society's 1857 decision that the "modification of our present naturalization laws [would] be a judicious measure."[63]

Having initiated the grand celebrations of Washington's birthday and the Fourth of July of the college, the Philodemic Society was responsible for scheduling the program and speakers for the yearly events. The society also inaugurated "Catholic Pilgrims' Day" in May, an observance that continued, with periodic trips to St. Mary's City, until the eve of the Civil War. Then the new college administration, which had no memory of Georgetown's once being a part of the state of Maryland, judged that "the event does not pertain to us."[64]

Georgetown College Cadets

Six years after the establishment of the Philodemic, students took the initiative again with what was to be the second most popular extracurricular activity during the antebellum period by organizing the Cadets. As citizen military rather than professional military, such militia had long been a favorite social forum for young men in America's towns and villages. And it was an institution that continued to flourish, particularly in the South. Indeed in some Southern states, such as Georgia, all males eighteen or over were required to enroll in the militia. Apparently the Southerners took the lead in the formation of a military company at Georgetown in 1836. Robert Aylmer of Petersburg, Virginia, wrote home in November that "the boys are . . . organizing a company which is to be called the College Cadets. . . . Our captain is one of the boys who was here the year before last and has just returned from fight-

Like their counterparts in other American colleges, these staff officers of the Georgetown Cadet Corps were mature, responsible collegians who wore their uniforms proudly. Photograph taken in 1867. (Georgetown University Archives)

ing the Indians in Florida."[65] Possibly this was William Wing Loring, of Florida, who had been fighting the Indians in the everglades since 1832 as a fourteen-year-old. Ironically, at the very time the company was forming at Georgetown, the volunteer military companies at Franklin College, later the University of Georgia, were being abolished by the university authorities for fear of the dangers that students, unruly enough as they were, could pose for both town and gown if they were armed.[66]

At Georgetown the cadets at first drilled with pikes instead of guns. Apparently that first organization was short-lived. In 1852, a second student initiative bore better results with the formation of the Georgetown College Cadets. At least one hundred and seventy-five students served in its two companies over the next eight years. (A separate unit for younger students from the lower school was operational by 1855.) Southerners accounted for about three-quarters of the cadet membership, with the largest representations from Louisiana, Maryland, and Virginia. The records show that the sons of military officers and doctors were the most likely to be cadets, and those of French and German extraction particularly. Only a few tended to join in the debating or other activities. Bayonet and other military drills, target practice at the villa, and marching were all part of the cadet exercises for many years.[67] At the three civic celebrations (Washington's birthday, Independence

Day, and Thanksgiving) the cadets played increasingly prominent roles. They also served more and more as the college's official delegation to state celebrations and other public events, such as inaugurations or the escorting of distinguished visitors to and from the city. One member of the cadets in the late 1850s remembered: "We were proud of our uniform and looked forward to our parades with youthful eagerness. I can recall the warm welcome given us by President Pierce on the occasion of our visit to the White House in 1856 and the part we took in the inauguration of President Buchanan in 1857."[68]

The Drama Clubs

Drama had been always a vital element in Jesuit pedagogy, as a way of reaching beyond the classroom to the larger community, since the establishment of the Society's first college in Messina. Jesuit dramatic productions in the seventeenth and eighteenth centuries in Europe had been elaborate affairs with magnificent stage sets and enormous casts that entertained and instructed audiences that included prelates and kings, as well as the poor and unlettered.[69] Indeed mention of dramatic performances at Georgetown can be found as early as the 1790s, when William DuBourg was president, and intermittently thereafter. However, the first organized drama club did not arise until 1850 when the curtain went up on the Shakespearian Club. In April of that year, under the direction of Father Charles King, the club performed scenes from *King John* as well as some farces.[70] Three years later the Dramatic Association of Georgetown College replaced it and a constitution was written.[71] King was elected president. The members chose the productions and cast the parts.[72] Shakespeare dominated these productions, especially the historical plays (*Hamlet, Richard II, Richard III, Julius Caesar, Macbeth, Henry IV Part I,* and *King John*), but other playwrights like Sheridan (*Pizzaro*) and Bamin (*Damon and Pythias*) were also popular. Usually a Shakespearean play and a farce formed the bill. Initially the audiences consisted of students, faculty, and a few invited guests. In 1859 the administration temporarily forbade performances, apparently because of some scandalous material in particular plays. But the ban was soon lifted. The Dramatic Association was flourishing and popular at Georgetown as the 1860s began, with John Dooley, Harvey Bawtree, and Henry McCullough counted among those starring in the productions. Irish-American students were particularly prominent in the organization, making up nearly a quarter of the membership, roughly twice their numbers proportionately in the college.

In general, Georgetown students had broad latitude in organizing and conducting extracurricular activities. There was one type of society, however, that the Jesuits would not tolerate—the fraternity or secret society widespread in the South by this time. In 1845 three Louisiana students, transfers from Jefferson College in that state, were expelled for, among other things,

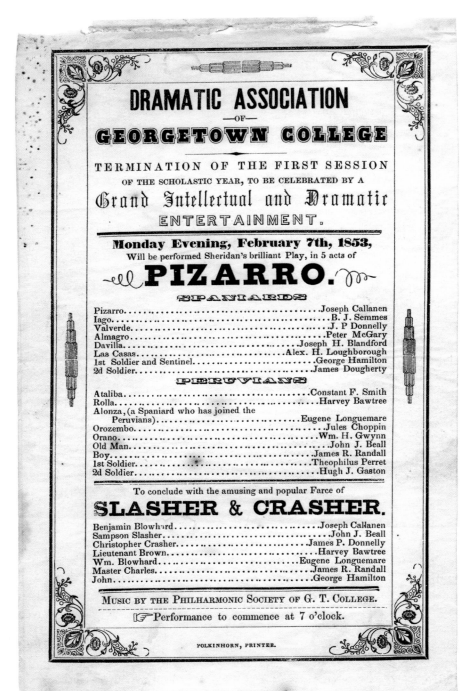

Handbill for an early performance (1853) of Sheridan's "Pizarro," produced by the Georgetown College Dramatic Association, with music by the Philharmonic Society of "G.T. College." B. J. Semmes was cast as Iago, with James R(yder) Randall, George Hamilton, and Hugh J. Gaston among the other luminaries. (Georgetown University Archives)

attempting to start such a society at Georgetown.[73] Social division and caba-
lism had no place in the Jesuit vision of an American college or in the Igna-
tian idea of a university. A Protestant student caught something of the spirit
when he wrote a fellow Virginian at Hampden Sydney College that he dis-
liked the classism he detected in that school but not at Georgetown; "[H]ere
where there are some not only from almost every state but from almost every country we live like a family of brothers— . . ."[74] Moreover, secret societies were seen as antithetical to republicanism. More than a quarter of a
century later an editor in the *College Journal* could honestly boast: "We have
more reasons than one, for congratulating ourselves that from the days of
our patriotic and truly American founder, John Carroll, to the present, no
one here has ever dreamed of adopting the senseless and brutal practices
[hazing] common at English colleges; nor of introducing secret societies,
those other institutions cherished in some American colleges."[75]

The Commencement Exercises

The annual exhibition at the commencement exercises was the grand
showcase in which the college displayed its students' achievements. As at
eighteenth-century American colleges in general, Georgetown's exhibition
originally had been a final oral examination of the students in the various
subjects, to which the public was invited. By 1817, when the first degrees
were awarded, the exhibition was both a graduation exercise and a demonstration of the students' command of *eloquentia perfecta*—their ability to
communicate effectively. Held in late July, it was a community affair that attracted both distinguished and ordinary guests from the city and from the
region—as far away as Frederick (Maryland) and Philadelphia. One English
visitor in 1820 was impressed at the "large and splendid assemblage of bishops, doctors, priests, pupils and spectators of all ranks and religions."[76]
Hundreds of invited guests used to pack the assembly room in Old North
or, after 1833, in the South (Mulledy) Building. Beginning with John
Quincy Adams, presidents of the United States regularly attended and distributed the prizes and diplomas. Cabinet officers, ambassadors, generals,
and other dignitaries were in the audience as well. The Marine Band provided music. Besides the musical selections, there were speeches, demonstrations, plays, and recitations by the students. Unfortunately, the event
commonly lasted at least four hours or more at midday of the hottest and
most humid part of the summer. As the school grew and more events were
added, the length of commencement increased as well. "The length of the
speeches was very wearisome," the college diarist recorded in 1832 after a
six-hour commencement. He admitted that "There was no one who did
not complain. . . ."[77] But the exercises only got longer. By 1852 the uninter-
rupted exercises were beginning at 9 o'clock in the morning and conclud-

Order of the Exercises.

≪⌒⌒⌒⌒⌒⌒⌒⌒⌒⌒⌒⌒⌒⌒⌒⌒⌒⌒⌒⌒⌒⌒⌒⌒≫

Prologue by Master Charles Dinnies, from New-York.

MUSIC.

DEBATE OF CONGRESS ON THE COMPENSATION BILL.

Speech of Mr. Johnson of Ky.	Francis Trubat, of Philadelphia.
Mr. Randolph, of Va.	Edwin Bergh, of New-York.
Mr. Stanford	John B. Blake, city of Washington
Mr. Randolph	Wm. J. Gantt, S. Carolina.
Mr. Webster	Richard A. Wright, Geo. Town,
Mr. Johnson	Daniel O'Brien, Geo. Town.
Mr. Randolph	Lewis Jenkins, Baltimore.
Mr. Johnson	Stephen Durkee, Baltimore.
Mr. Randolph	Joseph Doyne, Maryland.
Mr. Grosvenor	Dominick Young, Maryland.
Mr. Huger	Charles Dinnies, New-York.
Mr. Randolph	Mark Jenkins, Baltimore.
Mr. Wright,	George Dinnies, New-York.
Mr. Clay,	William Waite, New-York.
Mr. Johnson	James Faulkner, Virginia.
Mr. Robinson	Charles Lacoste, New-York.
Mr. Barbour	James Dixon, Baltimore.
Mr. Jackson	James Almeida, Baltimore.
Mr. Pickering	Richard M'Pherson, Maryland.
Mr. Randolph	Joseph Doyne, Maryland.
Mr. Stanford,	Alex. Johncherez, Geo. Town.
Mr. Root	William Jenkins, Baltimore.
Mr. Huger	Charles Dinnies, New-York.
Mr. Grosvenor	John Cremer, Washington.
Mr. Randolph	Henry Gough, Maryland.
Mr. Calhoun	William Carroll, New-York.
Mr. King,	John Dooley, New-York.
Mr. Ross	Elcon Jones, Georgetown.
Mr. Randolph	Thomas Gough, Maryland.
Mr. Hopkinson	William Guinn, Maryland.
Mr Tucker	Robert Neale, Maryland.
Mr. Gaston	Alexander Gaston, N. Carolina.
Mr. Yancey	Perl Durkee, Baltimore.
Mr. Culpepper	Henry Smith, Maryland.
Mr. Sharp	William Lee, Washington.
Mr. Mason	Thomas Jameson, Maryland.
Mr. Chace	James Homans, Washington.
Mr. Dana	James Callaghan, Baltimore.
Mr. Mason	Robert Smith, Maryland.
Mr. Chace	Edward Hoban, Washington.
Mr. Roberts	Robert Mead, Washington.
Mr. Johnson	Henry Riley, New-York.
The Speaker	Peter Menard, Kaskaskia, Illinois Territory.

[handwritten, right margin: I Faulkner entered College July 18 – 1815 left aug' 1822]

MUSIC.

A Latin Ode, by - - -	Francis Trubart, Philadelphia.
A Greek Fragment, by - -	Edwin Bergh, New-York.
Verses addressed by a Father to his Son (in french) by - - -	Paul Mooney, New-York.
A Piece from Lafontaine, by -	Charles Lacoste, New-York.
The Monkey who had seen the World, by	Benjamin Ewel, Geo. Town.
American Sages, a poetic piece, by -	William Jenkins, Baltimore.
Douglas to Lord Randolph, by - -	William Mauro, Washington.
A Piece on Duelling, by - -	John Kellenburgher, Geo. Town.

MUSIC.

A Parliamentary Debate, in the fourteenth year of George II. 1740, on a Bill for preventing Merchants from raising the wages of Seamen in time of war, and thereby inducing them to avoid his Majesty's service.

Sir Charles Wager -	William Wells, Baltimore.
Mr. Fox -	Paul Mooney, New-York.
Sir Robt. Walpole -	Dominick Young, Maryland.
Sir John Barnard -	Jarvis Roebuck, New-York.
Sir Robt. Walpole -	James Patten, Alexandria.
Sir John Barnard -	Jarvis Roebuck, New-York.
Mr. Pitt -	James Dixon, Baltimore.
Sir Robt. Walpole -	James Lynch, Conewago, Penn.
Sir John Barnard -	Jarvis Roebuck, New-York.
Mr. H. Walpole -	Adolphus W. Godwin, New-York.
Mr. Pitt -	John Gray, Georgetown, Col.
Mr. Winnington -	John Warring, Maryland.
Mr. Pitt -	John Gray, Geo. Town,
Mr. Winnington -	John Warring, Maryland,
Mr. Lyttleton -	Richard M'Pherson, Maryland.

MUSIC.

Patriotism, an Ode, by Charles Dinnies, New-York.
The Soldier returning from War, a Poetic Piece, by Henry Gough, Maryland.
A Discourse in praise of Literature, by Thomas Lee, Maryland.
A French Ode in imitation of the 18th Psalm, by N. Preudhomme, Natchitoches.

MUSIC.

The Degree of BACHELOR OF ARTS, *conferred on Charles Dinnies and George Dinnies, from New-York.*

DISTRIBUTION OF PREMIUMS.

MUSIC.

A Discourse on Education, by Charles Dinnies, New-York.
Epilogue, by George Dinnies, New York.

W. DUFFY, PRINTER, GEORGETOWN, D. C.

This somewhat battered and annotated commencement program details the order of exercise for the first conferring of degrees in July of 1817. Charles Dinnies is listed as the salutatorian and his brother George as the valedictorian. Frederick Barber, their classmate, was absent because of the death of his father and did not receive his degree then. The exercises were held in Old North. (Georgetown University Archives)

ing at 4:30 in the afternoon. Before the temperance movement overtook Georgetown in the 1830s, the students were given a "weak mint sling" as they formed ranks in dress uniforms—perhaps to bolster the courage of those who performed and the benevolence of those who merely watched. Then typically, the two hundred or more students would march two by two behind the faculty and the Marine Band to the freshly whitewashed study hall packed with well over a thousand spectators.

The oration topics tended to be timely as much as classical. Thus in 1848, at the end of the Mexican-American War, topics included the "Romance of America" and the "Star Spangled Banner." Two years later, during the sectional crisis over the territorial settlement of that war, the talks were on "The Mission of America," "California," and "The Union." Most of the poems composed for the occasion had classical or historical themes, e.g., "The Passage of the Alps by Napoleon" and "The Death of Caesar" (the latter by William Walker in 1840). But some had moral themes ("Triumph of Temperance," 1841; "War," 1844); some intellectual ("Triumph of Science," 1842).

At the 1842 commencement, with President John Tyler presiding, the original orations included "Byron," "The Pilgrims of Maryland," "Popular Enthusiasm," and the "Destiny of America." Musical interludes were provided by the Philharmonic Society of the college. Pemberton Morris, an alumnus of the college (AB, 1836), gave the annual Philodemic Society address and Thomas Jenkins Semmes spoke the valedictory. The awarding of degrees and prizes completed the ceremony. Besides the bachelor of arts degrees, the master of arts degrees were awarded to those graduates who had distinguished themselves since graduation, usually through the private study of law, and who had petitioned for this recognition. Honorary doctoral degrees (either the Ph.D. or S.T.D.) were also awarded as early as the 1820s. In 1828, judge John Luke Taylor of the Supreme Court of North Carolina was awarded an LL.D. at the request of Bishop John England.

Careers of Graduates and Alumni

Records for the 1830s, 1840s, and 1850s show that fewer than a tenth (<9%) of all the lower and upper school antebellum students graduated (237 of 2,690). But when we restrict our survey to those who entered Georgetown at the college level, the proportion of graduates rises substantially, to more than a third (34.4% or 94 of 275).[78] The vast majority of these graduates were Catholic (82.1%). One-fifth were of Irish extraction, far larger than their proportion of the student population (13.7%). For those in the rising middle class from urban areas, such as the Irish, a college degree had higher value in status and opportunity for advancement than it did for those from more traditional communities, particularly those in the South. The difference in graduation rates between Northern and Southern students at Georgetown only slightly favors the former, but with the Irish factor set aside (20% of all Southern graduates), the difference becomes much greater (from 11% North to 6% South). The median age of graduates continued to increase during the period, from eighteen and a half years in the 1830s to twenty years in the 1860s (tables 8.1, 8.2, and 8.3 in appendix F).

Like their collegiate counterparts elsewhere in that period, most of them went on to enter one of the professions. What distinguished Georgetown was the extraordinary proportion of graduates who chose a mixture of law and public service as a career, as well as the exceptional number who became professional writers and editors. Conversely, a relatively small number entered business or the ministry. A substantial but declining number of graduates chose the field of medicine. Among nongraduates a remarkably large proportion went on to choose a military career.

Of one hundred and forty graduates with known occupations, no fewer than seventy-one (51%) became lawyers, many of whom went into politics or public administration. By contrast, approximately a third (30%) of the graduates from Harvard and Yale in that same period were pursuing careers in law.[79] At colleges in the South, the proportion entering public service was even smaller. Georgetown's physical location and its classical curriculum were undoubtedly both major factors in this career pattern among graduates and other alumni.

A representative yet historically special career may be seen in the case of Charles James Faulkner from Virginia (**C** 1815–22). After graduating from Georgetown, Faulkner served in the Virginia House of Delegates where he argued unsuccessfully for the gradual abolition of slavery during the crucial debate over abolition in the 1831–32 session. But, ironically, he is better known for his work on a Virginia law that became the basis of the infamous Fugitive Slave Law of 1850. In the 1850s Faulkner was elected to the U. S. House of Representatives where he served with distinction for four terms until President Buchanan appointed him U.S. Minister to France.

Walter S. Cox (**C** 1838–43), another well-known Georgetowner, became a prominent lawyer and judge in the District of Columbia, serving as a justice of the Supreme Court of the District for twenty years in the late nineteenth century. John Thomas Doyle (**C** 1832–38), the son of a New York printer and bookseller, became an attorney—first in New York and later in California. Between his legal careers he served as Cornelius Vanderbilt's general agent in Nicaragua for the American Atlantic and Pacific Canal Company. Eventually, in California he went on to serve as a member of the state legislature and write several works on history as well. Richard H. Clarke (**C** 1842–49) of the District, a descendant of one of the original members of Leonard Calvert's council in Maryland, was admitted to the bar in the District of Columbia in 1848, then moved to New York City in 1855 where he became an associate of Charles O'Conor and the author of many books on the history of the United States and the Catholic Church. Robert Ray (**C** 1848–54), who had

Richard Thomas Merrick
(**C** 1837–40) (Georgetown
University Archives)

entered Georgetown as a barely literate 18-year-old orphan and left six years later as class valedictorian, returned to Louisiana where he read law privately and eventually became a judge.

Of course, many alumni who became lawyers left college before earning their AB degrees. Of the five hundred and five alumni (including graduates) from this period (1830–60) whose occupations are known, at least one hundred and forty-three (28.3%) became lawyers.[80] A few of them earned degrees at law schools. Thomas Jenkins Semmes (**C** 1838–42), one of the Georgetown Semmeses, went on for his LL.B. at Harvard, then practiced law in the city of Washington for awhile. In 1850 he moved to New Orleans where he became attorney general of Louisiana. Many more did traditional apprenticeships in law firms, as did the Merrick brothers of Maryland, who subsequently practiced law in the District. Richard Thomas Merrick (**C** 1837–40) was elected to the Maryland legislature in 1849, then went west to Chicago in the middle 1850s to form a law partnership with Stephen A. Douglas. During the Civil War he resumed his practice in Washington. President Franklin Pierce appointed Richard's older brother, William Matthews Merrick (**C** 1827–30), a judge of the District's circuit court. William later served in the House of Representatives for Maryland in the 1870s.

Seventeen of those graduates, mainly of the decade before the Civil War and most of them also lawyers, went into politics or public service. Patrick Walsh (**C** 1860–61), the former printer's apprentice, left school, and like so many of his classmates in 1861, joined the South Carolina Rifle Militia. The war over, Walsh become editor of the Augusta *Chronicle* and then successively a U.S. senator and the mayor of Augusta. John O'Neill (**C** 1839–41, AB), from Frederick, Maryland, moved west to practice law and sit as a judge in Ohio, Missouri, Iowa, and Illinois. In Ohio he held several offices, including that of attorney general. Edward Douglass White (**C** 1857–60) went into law practice in Louisiana, where he was elected to the state senate in 1874. He later served in the United States Senate (1891–94). President Grover Cleveland appointed him an associate justice of the Supreme Court in 1894, and in 1910 he was named chief justice.

There were also five diplomats among these alumni, including Errázuriz and Herran. Isidorio Errázuriz (**C** 1851–52), after receiving his diploma from Georgetown, studied law at the University of Göttingen and then returned to his home in Santiago, Chile. There he became an editor, a politician (serving in the Chamber of Deputies), and a diplomat (minister to Brazil). Tomás M.

Herran (**C** 1857–63), the son of a former president of Colombia and ambassador to the United States, served his country in various capacities, including as chargé d'affaires in Washington. In 1902 he and U.S. Secretary of State John Hay collaborated on the Hay-Herran Convention, which proposed terms for payment and "perpetual control" by the United States of the strip of land in Colombia where the canal was later built. Herran's government afterwards repudiated the subsequent treaties, which led eventually to revolt on the isthmus and finally the establishment of the Republic of Panama.

Tomás Herran (**C** 1857–63)
(Georgetown University
Archives)

Twelve antebellum students (11%) became doctors and one a dentist. Most of the Georgetown alumni who became doctors left well before senior year to begin medical training. Alexander Jenkins Semmes (**C** 1837–46) from Louisiana left Georgetown at the end of Poetry (sophomore) year to pursue the study of medicine at the neighboring Columbian College Medical School. He returned to Louisiana, where he was the resident physician at Charity Hospital in New Orleans, published widely in his field, and in 1858 was elected secretary of the American Medical Association. Another notable alumnus, Samuel Mudd (**C** 1851–52), was also a sophomore when he was expelled by President Bernard Maguire as one of the six instigators of the 1852 college riot. Mudd attended the University of Maryland Medical School, and practiced medicine in Bryantown in Charles County until his ill-fated role in Lincoln's assassination. In all, eighty alumni (15%) whose occupations are known went on to practice medicine. This number is close to the estimated average number of students in Southern colleges who chose medicine during this same period.[81] Moreover, in line with the national trend, there was a sharp decline from the 1840s to the 1850s in the number of Georgetown students entering the field of medicine, from more than a fifth (23%) in the former decade to slightly more than a tenth (13%) in the latter. Medicine had become a very crowded and, financially, a rather unrewarding profession in antebellum America.

Seventeen of the graduates (12.4%) became editors or journalists, a figure matched by no other American college during the period. James Ryder Randall (**C** 1848–56), who became the best-known editor of the antebellum students, was forced to leave the college at the end of his next-to-last year because of a near-fatal case of pneumonia. After his recovery he moved to New Orleans in 1859 and eventually became a journalist and editor. After the Civil War he served as the editor-in-chief of the *Atlanta Constitutionalist.* James Fairfax McLaughlin (**C** 1851–60, AB) became a lawyer and editor of many papers, including the *Catholic Mirror* and *Boston Pilot.* Marx Lazarus, who left Georgetown in 1835, became widely known as a polymath radical reformer, committed at one time or other to Fourierism, Socialism, phrenology, spiritualism, homeopathy, and the anti-slavery movement. He was also a regular contributor to Moncure D. Conway's transcendentalist journal in Cincinnati, *The Dial*.[82]

Nineteen of the first graduates (13.8%) became teachers, ten of them Jesuits. Most of the rest were lawyers and doctors who taught part-time in professional schools. Few made education their profession. Augustine Neale (**C** 1853–60) was superintendent of schools in Charles County as well as a farmer. Tomás Herran's brother, Pedro (**C** 1857–63), became a professor of chemistry in Antioquia College in Colombia.

Sixteen other graduates (11.6%) returned home to carry on as planters or farmers, which was a somewhat higher proportion than the career profile shows for the graduates of Northern colleges (8%) who made their livings in agriculture. But it is at the same time much lower than that of their counterparts in Southern colleges (25%).[83] The proportion of Georgetown alumni in general who made a career of farming was even lower (7%). Those low figures reflect the relatively small percentage of antebellum students who were sons of planters or farmers. Most who did become planters inherited plantations or large farms, such as Nicholas Stonestreet (**C** 1831–36) in Charles County, Maryland, and Edgeworth Bird (**C** 1838–44) in Georgia. Yet many of these planters, like Stonestreet and Bird, also became lawyers.

Given the college's refusal to offer a commercial program or significant commercial courses in its curriculum, it should not be surprising that of these graduates only fourteen (10%) went into business. That was well below the proportion of Southern college graduates (15%) who chose business and far below that of Northern college graduates (20 to 30%) who made this career choice.[84] The proportion of alumni of the college in general from this period (1830–60) who went into business was even smaller (9.1%). There was a steady rise, however, in the proportion of graduates going into business (from 6.1% in the 1830s to 13.3% in the 1850s). Many of the Georgetown graduates who did become businessmen did other work initially. James Dooley (**C** 1856–60) was a lawyer and served in the Virginia legislature before becoming a major developer of Southern railroads and real estate in Richmond—and a multimillionaire. Robert Emmet Doyle (**C** 1842–46) of New York went to the West to seek his fortune in the Gold Rush as a miner but became instead a journalist in San Francisco. Then in the 1850s he became involved in Nicaragua with one of the companies attempting to build a canal across the isthmus. Finally, he returned in 1857 to California where he operated a highly successful stagecoach service from San Antonio to San Diego until the Civil War drove him out of business.

From 1830 to 1860 only sixteen graduates (6%) went on to study for the priesthood or ministry. A total of fifty-three students (2%) of those enrolled at Georgetown in this period eventually entered seminaries. Its origins notwithstanding, Georgetown was not prolific of candidates for the ministry. Even in the halcyon period of Giovanni Grassi's presidency (1812–17), the proportion of students who went on to study for the priesthood was relatively low (<11%), and far below the averages (from 20% to 40%) at New England and Middle Atlantic colleges, but only slightly below the average in Southern colleges in general.[85] Georgetown, like colleges across the nation, experienced a decline in the number of students going into the ministry during this period. From 1840 to 1858 there were never more than two Georgetown students in any given year who entered the ministry. Almost half of those at Georgetown who chose to study for the priesthood entered before 1840. Whereas some few (3.3%) went on to study for the priesthood or ministry in the 1830s, even that small percentage had fallen by half in the 1850s.

The decline of religious vocations was one of the effects of the "Southernization" of the college and the substantial increase of non-Catholics. The profile of the Georgetown student most likely at that time to choose religious ministry for his career is in sharp contrast with that of his counterpart at a denominational college, whether North or South, who was likely to have rural roots. The then typical Georgetown clerical candidate was either town- or city-born, the son of a businessman, and of Irish extraction. About two-thirds of those electing the ministry then came from the Chesapeake (the District, Maryland, and Virginia) and over half of those were from its urban areas. Of the fathers whose occupations are known, less than half (>40%) were businessmen. And at that same time the Irish made up virtually the same proportion (>40%) of these vocations, including John Early (**C** 1834), Martin Morris (**C** 1847–48), James Doonan (**C** 1854–57), and Henry Pinckney Northrop (**C** 1853–56). Early spent only four months at the college before moving to the Jesuit novitiate in Frederick in 1834. (Morris, who entered the Society in 1850 but had to leave to care for his mother, afterwards became a lawyer and eventually the partner of Richard Merrick.) Doonan, from Georgia, entered the Society of Jesus at fifteen in 1857 and in 1882 became the twenty-ninth president of Georgetown. Northrop, a native of New Jersey, went on to Mount St. Mary's to prepare for the priesthood and was consecrated Bishop of Charleston in 1883. When the numbers of those urban-born, Irish American sons of businessmen declined in the college, so did the vocations. Significantly, Holy Cross to the north in Massachusetts, with its dominant urban Irish American population, had replaced Georgetown by the 1850s as the chief supplier of novices for the Society of Jesus in the East.

Still fewer graduates (3) made the military their career. Many, however, who did not graduate went on to the service academies and did become career officers. Indeed, of the Georgetown students whose occupations are known for this period, the third most popular, after law and medicine, was the military. Fifty-seven (11.2%) made careers in the regular army or navy. No other nonmilitary college, North or South, approached this figure in the antebellum period. Over half (55%) were following their fathers in their career choice. More than two-thirds (70%) were of Anglo-American stock.

The vast majority of these students, it should be noted, left Georgetown from the preparatory school. Less than a fifth of them reached the three se-

nior classes. Among even those who entered Georgetown at the college level, however, a relatively high proportion (6.6%) entered the regular military.
William F. Gaston (**C** 1848–52), the grandson of the first student, left Georgetown after Rhetoric (junior) year to attend West Point. After he was commissioned, he served on the frontier until 1858, when he was killed in one of the
Indian campaigns. Julius Garesché (**C** 1833–37) also left as a junior and was
graduated from the U.S. Military Academy in 1841.

Most of Georgetown's notable alumni in the military had only attended
the preparatory department before going on to the service academies. Lewis
Armistead (**C** 1830–31) was dismissed from West Point for poor academic
performance, but eventually he managed to follow his father into the Army.
In 1839 he obtained an appointment as lieutenant, and for his service in the
Mexican War was promoted to major. He too then went to the West, to the
frontier. Henry Heth (**C** 1837–38) received an appointment to West Point

The Hilltop in the 1850s.
Engraving by C. Bohn.
(Georgetown University
Archives)

some years after Georgetown and was graduated next to last in his class in
1847. He spent the next decade in the West, serving at military outposts from
Kansas to Utah. William Wing Loring (**C** 1839–40) left Georgetown to study
law privately and was admitted to the bar in the state of Florida. He also
served as a legislator in the Florida House before joining the United States
Army during the Mexican War. During that campaign (1846–48), in which
he lost an arm, he was promoted to the rank of colonel. He also spent most
of the 1850s on the frontier. Levi Gantt (**C** 1834–35), the grandson of Benjamin Stoddert, who received his bachelor of science degree from West Point
in 1841, was later killed in the Mexican-American War. James Hoban Sands
(1853–59), the son of Admiral Benjamin Sands, left Georgetown after the
final year of preparatory school with an appointment to the Naval Academy,
from which he was graduated in 1863. He was a rear admiral when he returned to the Naval Academy in 1905 as its superintendent.

PART THREE

FROM COLLEGE TO
UNIVERSITY, 1860–89

CHAPTER 9

Georgetown's Blue and Gray

Thursday, Feb. 19th, 1863. Today has been spent in exclusion at the College . . .
and has been [one] of the happiest of my life—contrasting my present temporary
quiet with the experience of the past eighteen months in the army, where with
some exceptions, everything corrupt, low vulgar and debasing in our corrupt
nature is rampant. Would that I was out of it altogether, but it cannot be yet.
I may still do some good where I am . . . God [grant] that this unhappy war
may soon terminate but from present indications it is only commencing.

JOSEPH B. O'HAGAN, SJ, CHAPLAIN
On leave, back at the Hilltop

"Whether the Union Will Be Dissolved . . ."

On December 11, 1859, the Philodemic Society had debated the topic "Should
the South now secede?" That debate continued over several meetings for
two weeks, culminating in a decisive victory for the affirmative. J. Fairfax
McLaughlin remembered that

Our debate that night [December 18] was particularly stormy. The climax was
finally reached, and a scene followed not unlike some of those then frequently occurring in Congress—a free fight. Bill Hodges, of Mississippi . . . sprang at the Vice-
President of the Society . . . Jack Gardiner, of Maryland, rushed at me, . . . Jim Dooley,
of Virginia, Gus Wilson of Maryland, Jim Hohan and Pres Sands, of Washington, . . .

Federal troops "at ease"
on the Virginia side of the
Potomac, sometime after
the Battle of Gettysburg.
Georgetown's buildings
are visible on the hilltop
(left of the tree) above
the Aqueduct Bridge.
(Library of Congress. Georgetown
University Archives)

Paul and Placide Bossier . . . of Louisiana, . . . and many other Philodemics, were mixed up in the mêlée.

Father James Clark finally had to put out the lights to restore order. The president of the college, John Early, thereupon banned any further meetings for the rest of the year.[1]

Early had succeeded Maguire as president in 1858. And, like Maguire, he was an Irish immigrant, having come as a nineteen-year-old to the United States in 1833 to prepare for the priesthood because there was no place for him in the seminary at Maynooth. After a short stay at Mount St. Mary's in Emmitsburg, Maryland, he left—perhaps influenced by John McElroy in nearby Frederick who was from the same county in Ireland—to study at Georgetown. A few months later John Early entered the Society. Georgetown was the third college which the distinguished, somewhat portly Early was to serve as president. He followed Mulledy and Ryder at Holy Cross (1848–51) and then headed Loyola of Baltimore during its first six years (1852–58).[2] By the time he was appointed president of Georgetown, Early had acquired a reputation as a prudent and strong leader from his successful administration of the other two colleges.

The sectional divisiveness that had touched off the violence at the college had been growing throughout the United States for decades but had never been more apparent than over the previous two months. At the beginning of December 1859, fifty-five miles to the west, John Brown, abolitionist and fanatic, had been hanged in what is now Charlestown, West Virginia, for his bloody October raid on the government arsenal at Harpers Ferry, not far from the McSherry estate on the northern rim of the Shenandoah Valley. The mayor of the town, Fontaine Beckham, had been among Brown's victims. His son, James, was an alumnus of the college. Samuel Chilton, the father of another former student, was one of Brown's court-appointed lawyers at his trial. That savage raid and the bitter trial sent shock waves through the South since Brown's desperate blow against slavery seemed to confirm the worst fears of Southerners about Northern intentions. After Harpers Ferry, war seemed only a matter of time. (The western section of Virginia, including Harpers Ferry and old Charles Town, separated from Virginia in November 1861. In 1863 it was formally admitted to the Union as the state of West Virginia.)

The topics recorded in the minutes of the Philodemic Society for the following year (1860–61) are a barometer of the nation's rapidly deteriorating political climate:[3]

John Early, SJ (1858–65). Twenty-fifth president of Georgetown and its firm, resolute leader during seven tense and often difficult years for students and faculty. Photograph taken ca. 1875. (Georgetown University Archives)

October 13, 1860: "Whether the Union will be dissolved in the case of the election of Lincoln as President of the U.S." [After being warmly debated, decided in the negative.]

November 18, 1860: "Ought the Southern States to oppose the coercion of any States of the Union, should any secede in the event of a Black Republican President." [Question decided in the affirmative 8 to 1.]

January 20, 1861: "Is man justified in obeying a law of his country, which he feels to be morally wrong?" [Negative prevails 8 to 2.1]

January 27, 1861: "Is this government founded upon the integral and perspective theory of well-guaranteed security or upon the psychological principles of abstract political economy." [Former wins 6 to 2.]

"[C]ivil War is at hand . . ."

Alexander Dimitry (**C** 1820–26, AB), then U.S. minister to Nicaragua, wrote to his wife in January 1861:[4]

The papers from the States, I dare not write the United States, bring fearful accounts of excitement, exasperation, fierceness and hate. South Carolina has no doubt consummated the last act of defiance to the Union of the States; . . . [her] conduct . . . [though] fully warranted in right by the insolent aggression of the North, is stained, in point of honor by the blackest ingratitude [to Mr. Buchanan who] . . . has been devoted . . . to the rights and interests of the States of the South.

James Talbot (**C** 1838–40), a career military officer stationed in South Carolina at Fort Sumter in Charleston Harbor, had been sent to Washington earlier in January by his commander, Major Robert Anderson, to seek instructions from President Buchanan. He returned ten days later with nothing. When he had presented Anderson's dispatches to the president, the latter could only ask: "Lieutenant, what shall we do?" "I never felt so [frightened] in my life," Talbot later related to a brother officer. "The President seemed like an old man in his dotage."[5] Three months later, Talbot was the bearer of the answer from Buchanan's duly elected successor. Shortly after his inauguration in March of 1861, President Lincoln sent word to the governor of South Carolina that he intended to resupply the fort.[6]

As early as the 1830s, the Jesuits in Maryland had been anticipating a dissolution of the country over the slavery issue. Burchard Villiger, whose stern presence had allegedly been the occasion of the 1850 student revolt at the college, was now provincial superior. After Lincoln had been elected president and South Carolina had seceded, Villiger informed Rome in December of 1860: "Political affairs here are in the greatest turmoil. The dissolution of the states seems inevitable; the economy is nearly destroyed."[7] Two months later Villiger wrote again to say that he thought contingency plans should be prepared to divide the Society in America into two provinces, along sectional lines, with the District of Columbia and Maryland allocated to the Southern one.[8]

In early January of 1861 the college had participated in the national "day of fasting & humiliation," which outgoing President Buchanan declared, "for averting the imminent evils from the Republic." Classes were canceled and the students gathered in the chapel for the litany of the saints and benediction.[9] Georgetown, located in a border area (indeed, in a Southern town), had so far experienced little of the massive withdrawal of Southern students that Northern colleges endured after Brown's raid. Southerners from below the Potomac accounted for half the students at the college at the beginning of the 1859–60 academic year. A year later there was a sharp drop of students from states in the Deep South, particularly from Louisiana and South Carolina, but the region was still by far the source for the largest proportion of students (46.9%). But, as the crisis worsened in January of 1861, some parents began to call their sons home. Others relied on President Early's judgment. "You are on the border," one guardian in Mississippi wrote to him at Georgetown, "and if civil war is to be one of the disastrous results of existing dissensions, the District of Columbia . . . may be one of its theatres." Should war occur, he hoped that Early would remove his charges from "scenes of danger, turmoil and violence, to some place of safety and retirement. . . ."[10] The professors of the medical department, fearing a riot at the time of Lincoln's inauguration, requested in February that they be empowered to make a copy of the record of the degrees the college had awarded to their students over the past decade.[11]

On April 10, ten of the eleven members of the Philosophy Class wrote to explain to Early why they were leaving school—because of "our inability to apply ourselves to our studies . . . while all we have most dear on earth, our country (the South), our parents and our bretheren call loudly upon our presence. . . ." Moreover, they asked that he suspend classes until September. "[C]ivil War is at hand, and may at any moment fall among us with all its horrors, and when we are least prepared to protect ourselves against its danger. . . ."[12] Classes were not suspended, but it was decided to allow the Philosophers to graduate without further studies. Then a few days later the college authorities decided to reschedule commencement in order to avoid a possible riot when Congress reassembled on the Fourth.

But events were outracing attempts to cope with contingencies. That very morning (April 12) Fort Sumter had been attacked by Confederate forces. Almost immediately, parents began to remove their sons from the college. One father, a colonel in the army, knew all too well the potential danger in which the strategic position of Georgetown could put the college. "If the forces of the Southern Confederacy should march upon the Capital," he wrote Early from Cleveland, where he was stationed, "they may cross the Potomac at or above Georgetown, and are as likely to be met by the United

States Troops in your vicinity as any where else. In this event so bloodless a collision as that at Fort Sumter is hardly to be hoped for, and a stray bomb from either party would not discriminate between an unoffending college boy and a member of the opposing corps. . . ."[13] Four days later he ordered his son to return home to Tennessee. Another Southern father in the military, who was stationed in Washington, simply took his son from the college and wrote the president from Richmond on May 6, "we left Washington very unexpectedly, thinking it was dangerous to remain. . . ."[14]

Armed conflict came quickly enough, and only forty miles to the north in Baltimore, where a mob of Southern sympathizers attacked the Sixth Massachusetts Regiment in the street as it attempted to switch trains on its way to Washington. Four soldiers and twelve civilians, including several innocent bystanders, were killed. Many more were wounded; and one of the Baltimoreans reported dead that day was Francis Xavier Ward (**C** 1854–59, AB). When his former roommate, James Ryder Randall, then in New Orleans, heard of Ward's death (erroneously as it later turned out) and what else had happened in his native city, he wrote in his anger the song that became "the Marseillaise of the Confederate cause" and known to all as "Maryland, My Maryland":

The despot's heel is on thy shore,
Maryland!
His torch is at thy temple door,
Maryland!
Avenge the patriotic gore
That flecked the streets of Baltimore,
And be the battle-queen of yore,
Maryland my Maryland!

I hear the distant thunder-hum
Maryland!
The Old Line bugle, fife and drum,
Maryland!
She is not dead nor deaf nor dumb—Huzza! She spurns the Northern scum:
She breathes! She burns! she'll come!
she'll come!
Maryland my Maryland![15]

Randall was not the only Georgetown-connected person to compose music for the Confederate cause. John P. Caulfield, a faculty member who taught music and was the organist at the college, also contributed two of the earliest musical pieces in support of Southern nationalism. In 1860 he published the "Grand Secession March," dedicated to the Charleston delegation that had withdrawn from the Democratic convention in that city. A year later he wrote the music for "Our Southern Flag: A National Song," that celebrated the creation of the Confederacy:

Up! Up with our flag and forever may it be.
And beneath its bright folds
how proudly we'll fight,
For God and for Justice,
For Truth and for Right![16]

Within the week most of the students had hastily departed from the college, with the rest ready to follow.

Alumni in Blue and Alumni in Gray

Four of the ten college seniors (Philosophers) who left in April of 1861 subsequently enlisted in the Confederate Army, but none, apparently, until the following year. Of the sixteen who had graduated in 1860, eleven served in the War between the States, nine for the South, and two for the North. Among those who fought for the Confederacy were Paul and Placide Bossier, James H. Dooley, Augustine Neale, and Warfield Semmes. Of the one hundred and seventy-eight undergraduates who dropped out in the late winter and early spring of 1861, seventy-one left to enlist. Of the more than one thousand total alumni who fought in the war (table 9.1 in appendix F), most served in the Confederate armies (867 of 1,085 or 86%; see table 9.2 in appendix F).

Nearly a quarter (375 or 23.8%) of those Georgetown alumni who wore the Confederate Gray came from two states: Louisiana (208) and Virginia (167). A considerable number (126 or 15%) came from Maryland, a state that did not secede from the Union. Indeed, more than a quarter (27%) of all Maryland alumni took part in the conflict, and most of them (85%) served in the Confederate forces. Extremely high percentages of alumni came from four of the large Southern states. Of those from Louisiana who entered the college between 1830 and 1865, more than half (208 or 58% of 349 total) were in the war. Virginia sent nearly half (46%) of its total Georgetown alumni (167) from that same period, Georgia and South Carolina each sent nearly two-thirds of their total alumni (74 and 42) from that same time span (60% and 61%, respectively). And if one were to subtract the fairly large number of the 1830–65 alumni who can be assumed to have died before the war of natural causes, the proportion would be even greater. In all, nearly three-quarters of the alumni in Gray (645 of 867) came from the Confederacy's eleven states. (Factoring in the prewar death rates indicates Southern alumni service in the war is consistent with that of Southern white males in general.)[17] The alumni in Gray who came from states that did not secede were a little over a fourth (222 of 867) of those who fought for the Confederacy.

Catholic alumni from Louisiana had a slightly higher representation than the non-Catholic, and many more who were professionals or the sons of professionals enlisted than those from plantations. The Bossier brothers, Paul and Placide, were both 1860 graduates, and both enlisted in 1861 in the Third Regiment of the Louisiana Infantry. Edward Douglass White, who had left Georgetown in 1860, ran away from home in 1862 to enlist. Helped by family connections, he was commissioned a lieutenant and detailed to the staff of General W. N. R. Beal. René Toutant Beauregard (**C** 1858) was commissioned a first lieutenant in the First South Carolina Battalion of Light Artillery. Gabriel Fournet (**C** 1856–60, AB) served as a lieutenant colonel under his father who commanded the Louisiana Yellow Jacket Battalion. Robert Ray enlisted as a private in the Third Louisiana Cavalry. Alexander Dimitry served as the assistant postmaster general in the Confederacy. Three of his sons, Alexander (**C** 1855–61), Charles Patton (**C** 1855–56), and John Bull Smith (1867, M.A.), enlisted in Confederate units at the beginning of the war. So did their cousin, Theodore John Dimitry (**C** 1856–59).

Virginia alumni from rural areas were most highly represented (46% of the total), as were the Catholics among them. The four Matthews brothers of Speedwell, Virginia, at Georgetown between 1857 and 1861, all enlisted between 1861 and 1863, the oldest at twenty, the youngest at thirteen in 1862. James and John Dooley both enlisted in the First Virginia Infantry, which was briefly commanded by their father that year. Former President John Tyler's son, Tazewell, and his nephew, Nathaniel, joined Virginia state regiments.

In Georgia, William Edgeworth Bird left Granite Farm in June of 1861 to enlist as a private in the Fifteenth Georgia Infantry. Hugh Gaston (**C** 1848–55, AB) abandoned his rural law practice to become first lieutenant and adjutant of the Forty-Eighth Regiment of the North Carolina Infantry Volunteers. And, despite his antislavery sentiments,[18] thirty-nine-year-old Marx Lazarus (**C** 1834–35) enlisted as a private in the Confederate Army at the outbreak of war. But it was a young man's war. The median age of the Georgetown alumni in Gray was twenty-three.

Far fewer of the Northerners among the 1830–65 alumni are known to have fought in the war. Of the total (218), more than half (129) came from the District, more than a quarter (61 or 28.5%) from Pennsylvania, and the rest (30 or 14%) from New York (see table 9.3 in appendix F). Catholics tended to be underrepresented (52.7%), as did the Irish (14.8%); while Anglo-Americans were overrepresented (59%) among those who wore the Blue. And twenty-four, the median age of Union alumni, was slightly higher than that of their Confederate counterparts.

Of the total Georgetown alumni (153) from the border state of Maryland who fought in the war, most (126 or 85%) went south to join the Confederate forces. These Confederate Marylanders were overwhelmingly from Southern Maryland (75%), of Anglo-American stock (79%), and Catholic (78%). Francis Xavier Ward, whose erroneously reported death in the rioting in Baltimore had been the inspiration for James Ryder Randall's song

"Maryland, My Maryland," survived his wounds and left his law studies to head south to Richmond, where he enlisted as a second lieutenant in the First Maryland Regiment. John Brooke of Upper Marlborough (**C** 1836–37), a federal judge and former president of the Maryland Senate, crossed the Potomac and accepted a judgeship in the new Confederacy. Joseph Stonestreet (**C** 1839–42), a planter in Charles County, followed the same route to enlist as a sergeant in the First Maryland Light Artillery Battery at Fredericksburg. They thus also became men without a country, defending a new nation that did not yet include their own state. Another such, John Prevust Marshall (**C** 1854–59, AB) of the Maryland Line, understood that when he wrote from Virginia in April 1862: "The only hope I have upon earth is to see this Confederacy permanently established and Maryland annexed to it." Marshall had just reenlisted at a time of great crisis for the South.[19] But some Marylanders became frustrated by this isolation from the Confederate cause. William Mitchell (**C** 1852–56) of Glyndon went to the South in 1861 to show his sympathy, but he returned home after encountering much hostility in Virginia over Maryland's failure to secede from the Union.

The District of Columbia alumni who participated in the war were not numerous. Of these (146), more than half (85) fought for the South and, among them, alumni from the town of Georgetown were extremely well represented (37%). Typical was Christopher Charles Callan (**C** 1853–56), who was a staff journalist for the *Alexandria Sentinel* when he joined the Washington Volunteers, a Confederate unit. However, more than two-fifths (35 of 85) of the Georgetown alumni from the District who fought for the Confederacy had already relocated to Southern states before the war began. The Semmes family of Georgetown, scattered in several Southern cities by 1861, soon became prominent in the affairs of the Confederacy. In New Orleans, Thomas Jenkins Semmes (1838–42, AB) helped draft Louisiana's ordinance of secession and was elected a Confederate senator. His younger brother, Alexander Jenkins Semmes, left his position as resident physician at Charity Hospital in New Orleans to become a surgeon for the Eighth Louisiana Infantry; at Memphis, Benedict Joseph Semmes (**C** 1835–40) enlisted as a sergeant in the 154th Tennessee Regiment, the Maynard Rifles; and another kinsman, Bennett Barton Simmes (**C** 1827–28), originally of Charles County, Maryland, became a general in Louisiana.[20]

Of the sixty-one District of Columbia alumni who fought for the Union, ten were career military. Among them were William Macomb (**C** 1831–34) a naval officer who by 1862 commanded the blockading squadron in the Atlantic; Placidus Ord (**C** 1835–37), a colonel, who served on General William Tecumseh Sherman's staff; his brother, James Ord (**C** 1835–37), who was a surgeon in the Third U.S. Artillery; Alexander Aldebaran Semmes (**C** 1840–41), a U.S. Navy regular, who commanded several Union ships in the South Atlantic during the war; and George Cooper (**C** 1833–35), also a commander in the U.S. Navy.

Most of the other alumni who were career military remained loyal to the Union (32 of 46), including Southerners. John C. McFerran (**C** 1838) of Kentucky, a graduate of West Point, was a brigadier general in the Army. Julius Garesché (**C** 1833–37), an 1841 graduate of West Point, began the war as a lieutenant of artillery and ended as a colonel on General William Rosecrans' staff in the Army of the Cumberland. Edward Everett Stone (**C** 1841–42) from Georgia was a regular in the U.S. Navy who chose to retain his commission. He commanded the frigate *Iron Age* in the Union's South Atlantic Squadron. However, a few alumni followed their states out of the Union, including William Wing Loring (**C** 1839–40), who had opposed secession until Sumter. He resigned from the U.S. Army in May 1861 and accepted a commission as a brigadier general in the division of the Confederate Army charged with the defense of western Virginia. William Henry Chase Whiting (1838–40, AB) of Mississippi quit the U.S. Army to become a chief of engineers for the Confederacy's Army of Northern Virginia. William Gardner (**C** 1839–41) of Augusta, Georgia, resigned from the U.S. Army in January 1861 and was promptly commissioned lieutenant colonel of the Eighth Georgia Infantry, and Lewis Armistead (**C** 1830–31) resigned his commission in the U.S. Army in May 1861 to be made colonel of the Fifty-Seventh Virginia Infantry. Captain Henry Heth (**C** 1837–38), a West Point graduate, had resigned as a captain in the U.S. Army the month before; and by January next he was a brigadier general on duty with the Confederate Army in Kentucky.

Placidus Ord (**C** 1835–37). U.S. Army, Adjutant General's staff. Photograph taken in 1861. (Ord Family Papers. Georgetown University Archives)

Besides those who were career military, few Southern alumni fought for the Union. Duncan Walker (**C** 1857–58), at twenty-three years of age, was brevetted a brigadier general to the Union's XIX Army Corps in 1863. He was the son of a former senator from Mississippi who was then governor of Kansas. Francis Blair Jr. (**C** 1836), of St. Louis, was a member of the House of Representatives when the war began. He organized resistance to his secessionist-minded state government and played a key role in keeping Missouri in the Union. He eventually became an army corps commander in the Western theatre of war.

Nearly half the medical department's first-decade graduates served in the war; the vast majority (24 of 32) were surgeons in federal units. The class of 1861 was typical. Five of the eight graduates were on wartime duty as surgeons, four with the Union armies. The Union medical alumni were largely from the District and the Northeast, especially New York, with a significant number of them immigrants. Notable were Silas Lawrence Loomis (**M** 1855–57, MD) and James Peabody (**M** 1858–60, MD) who were surgeons, the latter a chief surgeon, in various military hospitals. Samuel Jacobs Radcliff (**M** 1851–52, MD) became the medical director of the Twenty-Third Army Corps. Those who served in the hospitals and medical units of the South were mostly alumni from Maryland and Virginia. As Georgetown's medical department became a major training facility for the doctors and surgeons needed in the war, the number of alumni in service grew correspondingly. All in all, the Medical School was a mirror image of the college's representation in the war.[21]

The War and the College

Throughout the war, the Jesuits at the college, as ordered by their superiors, kept scrupulously silent about the fratricidal contest. Since a majority of the Jesuits, like their students and alumni, favored the South, and some, like Father Charles Stonestreet, had relatives fighting for the Confederacy, this was both a prudent and a necessary policy. But there were other, in some ways deeper, concerns. The Jesuit superiors feared that the war would prove to be a new occasion for a revival of nativism and attacks on Catholic institutions. Absolute public silence and neutrality seemed the only security. In the U.S. presidential election of 1860 the superior general of the Jesuits had already forbidden his subjects to even vote in that election (since voting in pre-Australian ballot elections meant publicly declaring one's choice). "There seems to be no imminent danger for religion," Early informed the superior general in Rome in May, "but because things are not as favorable for Catholics as they should be through the constitutions of the United States, God knows where finally this civil upheaval will lead."[22] "We are between Scylla and Charybdis," the regional superior reported in late November 1861. Still he was happy that no Jesuit at Georgetown or elsewhere had imprudently taken a public stand on the war, "although there are among us," he admitted, "those who hold tenaciously to their private opinions."[23]

In fact, the sympathy for the Confederate cause among the majority of the faculty was well known. Moreover, some of the college's most prominent local alumni were considered Southern supporters or sympathizers. William Merrick, a District of Columbia federal judge, was placed under federal house arrest in 1861 when he defied the Lincoln administration by issuing a writ of *habeas corpus* in behalf of a father seeking to gain the release of his underage son from federal service. Richard Clarke, an attorney, was imprisoned in 1863 as a suspected Southern spy. (He had been caught sending goods to his Semmes in-laws in the South.) And alumnus William Corcoran left the country in 1862 and leased his Washington home to the French ambassador in order to prevent its seizure by the federal government.

The college authorities attempted also to publicly maintain political neutrality among the students on campus. Presumably under such direction, the Philodemic Society removed anything political from their debate topics. "Are mental enjoyments greater than physical?" "Does vice increase with Civilization?" and "Has the invention of printing been beneficial to man?" now became the typical subjects of formal debates at Georgetown. But the college administration could go only so far in controlling sentiment. If the Jesuits at Georgetown suppressed expression of their convictions about the war, their students quite obviously had no such intentions. Many, of course, left to enlist. Those who stayed wore their allegiance on their sleeves—and more, even in the presence of Northern troops. In February 1861, the cadets at the college burned the effigy of President-elect Lincoln.[24] By the beginning of May, Washington was rapidly becoming a fortified capital encircled by army camps. Lincoln's volunteer Army of the Potomac was preparing to march on Richmond. Second Lieutenant George Gibson Huntt (**C** 1849) of the U.S. Cavalry was sent out to select additional sites for accommodating the military units converging from various Union camps above the Mason-Dixon line. Huntt, remembering perhaps the commanding views of the area from Georgetown's Hilltop, secured permission from President Early to reconnoiter the countryside from the observatory and the top of the preparatory school building. When Huntt and a fellow officer came out of that building, they found the students lined up along the road to the main gate. As they made their way through the ranks, one older student stepped forward, removed his cap, waved it, and shouted: "Three cheers for Jeff Davis and the Southern Confederacy!" The rest of the students responded with an approving roar. Huntt's companion remarked to the crowd: "Hurra! boys, Hurra! I once was a boy myself."[25]

A day or so later, on Saturday, May 4, Father Early received a message from the commander of the Sixty-Ninth New York Regiment who explained that he had been authorized to occupy and billet his troops in "Georgetown Heights & the College, until further orders."[26] The sixty or so remaining students frantically removed all equipment and belongings to the North building. That evening fourteen hundred troops, known as the "Irish Regiment," arrived and took over the buildings on the southern half of the campus. Father Early warned his faculty and staff not to have so much as a conversation with the soldiers, apparently all Irish Catholics. The next day the chaplain of the regiment celebrated Mass for them in the yard. The following Wednesday President Lincoln and several members of his cabinet visited campus to review the troops. The night after that the campus was awakened to the cry of "To Arms! To Arms! The Enemy! The Enemy!" Within minutes the regiment was aroused and marching in double-quick time, toward Washington. But it was soon discovered that it was a false alarm, due to a nervous sentry's confusion over alarm bells ringing for a house fire in the city and the coincidental sound of musketry in the Virginia hills on the opposite river shore.[27]

Students continued to leave the college throughout the 1860–61 academic year. The Philodemic Society, recognizing "that all but three of its members had left College," voted to adjourn until the next October (1861).[28] The direc-

Union soldiers of the Sixty-Ninth Regiment were billeted briefly in Old South and other college buildings in May of 1861. Called the Irish, these New Yorkers (who were mainly immigrants or the sons of immigrants) soon departed for action in Virginia. They were replaced in June by other Union troops, the Seventy-Ninth Regiment. Also from New York, the "Highland" regiment (largely immigrants from Scotland) followed the Sixty-Ninth westward to Manassas by the end of June. (*Harper's Weekly*, June 1861; provided courtesy of HarpWeek, LLC)

tors of the college decided that, with the military occupation, there should be no formal commencement or public awarding of degrees (virtually all the Philosophers had left anyhow). After three weeks the Sixty-Ninth evacuated the college grounds only to be replaced in early June by another New York regiment, the Seventy-Ninth, called the "Highland Regiment," because of its large number of Scots. As the House Diarist makes clear, the Jesuits found them to be "the worst sort of scoundrels," perpetually fighting among themselves with pistols and knives.[29] Fortunately, by the end of the month most of the Seventy-Ninth had followed the Sixty-Ninth westward toward the rail junction at Manassas.

First Bull Run (Manassas)

Christopher Charles Callan (**C** 1853–56) was encamped with the Southern forces near Manassas Junction. He wrote his wife in mid-July of 1861 that his Washington Volunteers consisted of many old friends, including his former classmate, Julius Gantt. "They are all religiously inclined of late," he added, "for we are expecting a battle. I believe and hope that ere many more Sundays I will have the happiness of attending Mass at old Trinity once again. A turn is about to take place in affairs that will work a mighty change! We will be in Washington very soon!"[30]

The following Sunday the few remaining students at the college watched "a huge procession of vehicles" crossing the Potomac over the Aqueduct Bridge (now the Key Bridge) at the foot of the Hilltop. One of them, Louis Otto Hein, remembered seeing the spectacle of picnic parties, "tourists, members of Congress and civil government officials, on their way to watch the progress of the anticipated Union victory at Bull Run. . . ."[31] For most of that day (July 21, 1861), the cannon of the two armies could be heard in Georgetown; as evening approached, the sounds grew louder as though the battle was getting closer. Men on horseback appeared in greater and greater numbers, racing towards Washington. Georgetown President Early, watching from the porch of the South building, remarked to a student: ". . . . the Union forces evidently have met with a serious reverse. They may be in here before night." He was prepared to make every bed available for the wounded.[32] Louis Hein saw the same Sunday picnickers and sightseers he had watched in the morning now returning "panic stricken . . . followed by the fleeing soldiers of McDowell's army, many of whom were without caps, coats and weapons."[33]

David Ramsey (**C** 1848–50) of the District was one of the many Union dead, and Christopher Charles Callan was slightly wounded in the action. Colonel William Gardner of the Eighth Georgia Infantry had his leg badly shattered and never regained full health, although he returned to limited duty and was made a brigadier general several months later. Both the Sixty-Ninth and the Seventy-Ninth, the New York regiments that had camped at the college, had been sent to make futile, wasting charges up Henry Hill on the Bull Run battlefield at the climax of the battle.[34] Both were in the middle of the Union rout; and the regimental commander of the Irish, Captain Thomas Meagher, had his life saved by an army regular, Joseph S. McCoy (**M** 1866–68, MD). In a skirmish three days earlier at Blackburn's Ford, another New York regiment, the Twelfth Volunteer Infantry, had also been routed by the Army of the Shenandoah, except for one private, Charles F. Rand (**M** 1871–73, MD). Alone, he continued to fire at the charging Confederates until their colonel ordered the troops to cease firing because Rand was too brave to die. Spared by this gallantry, Rand left the battlefield safely (and afterwards entered Georgetown Medical). Thirty-six years later Rand was awarded the Medal of Honor for his heroism on the strength of the testimony of those very Confederates he had faced.

The college, as it turned out, was not needed to house the wounded, since most casualties had been left behind in Virginia. The day after that major disaster for the Union forces, Lieutenant Julius Garesché wrote Father Early from the field: "all our sick and wounded, I suppose, are in the hands of the confederate army—At least one third of them must be Catholics—with no Priests to care for them! There is work for half a dozen—I can procure Passes for any number."[35] That same hot July day three Jesuit priests left the college and set out for Manassas.[36] Others followed in their wake as chaplains, with or without commissions. Father Bernard Wiget, the president of Gonzaga College, was among the first to respond and became a familiar sight astride his horse, Jackson, as he visited the troops camped in and around the city. Two former faculty members, Francis McAtee and Joseph O'Hagan, were assigned by the provincial superior as chaplains to the Army of the Potomac. O'Hagan, who joined the heavily Catholic Seventy-Third Regiment in October, originally described them as "the scum of New York society, reeking with vice and spreading a moral malaria around them." Some had been recruited from prisons. But discipline and removal from their old, debilitating slum environment worked its own transformation. O'Hagan soon had a vibrant military parish, which eventually consisted of the Catholics serving in ten Union regiments. More than fifteen hundred soldiers regularly gathered in the fields for the Mass he celebrated on Sundays.[37]

Impact of the War on the College

At its outbreak there had been some concern that the war would close not only Georgetown but the other Jesuit colleges in Worcester, Philadelphia, and Baltimore as well. The concern was not idle. In Maryland alone, five colleges or seminaries had to close, among them St. John's of Annapolis. The loss of Southern students was, of course, a key factor.[38] Georgetown, which had become increasingly dependent on the Deep South during the past three decades, was especially vulnerable, as the drastic decline in enrollment in the first months of the war quickly showed. By the beginning of 1862 John McElroy again brought up an old idea, that Georgetown be converted into a Jesuit seminary since the college had lost its traditional base of support—probably forever, he thought.[39]

When the new academic year of 1861–62 began in September, only about fifty students enrolled. A year later, during Lee's first invasion of Maryland, even fewer students were on hand for the *Te Deum* and benediction at the school opening. James Clark, now president of Holy Cross, perhaps with faculty recruitment in mind, wrote the provincial superior a few days after the Army of Northern Virginia crossed the Potomac, "Georgetown College, being almost suspended, certainly does not need all the teachers they had. . . ."[40] However, that period proved to be the low point of the war for Georgetown, if not for the North. Enrollment steadily increased thereafter, to peak at one hundred and fifty-five in the fall of 1864, nowhere near the prewar level but respectable enough. As happened more than once before in the school's history, when traditional sources dried up, a sharp increase of local enrollments (particularly day students) allowed Georgetown to survive.

The District of Columbia, whose population had more than doubled since the outbreak of war, now accounted for over half the student body in the college. By 1864 day students made up almost a third (30%) of the enrollment. And many more of the students who entered during the war years were Protestants and Jews than were Catholics. By 1864 the Catholic proportion of the college student body had declined to less than two-thirds (59%). Many of the local non-Catholic students were of German stock. For the first time, German students, both Jew and gentile, became a major group (nearly 16%) within the college, outnumbering both the Irish and the French. (The latter had virtually disappeared with the secession of Louisiana in 1861.) By 1863, one-fifth of the entering students were of German extraction, the sons of businessmen or artisans, who had been drawn to Washington and Georgetown from Baltimore and New York by the war's economic opportunities.[41] One local German American was Julius Soper of Georgetown (**C** 1862–66, AB). Having already worked for two years, he entered the college at seventeen in the fall of 1862 in order to study Latin since he intended to become a pharmacist. However, his study of the required classics opened up to him a new world that led him instead into teaching and later into the Methodist Seminary (at Drew University) and a subsequent career as a highly regarded Methodist missionary in Japan.[42]

Other local students included James Valentine Coleman (**C** 1863–69, AB), who would later become a highly successful mine owner in California; Robert (**C** 1861–67, AB) and Stephen Douglas (**C** 1861–67), the sons of the Illinois senator; and Edwin Rogers (**C** 1863–64), the son of Henry Rogers, an inventor and developer of the telegraph industry. John B. Hamilton (**C** 1864–69) of Port Tobacco and Robert Fenwick Brent (**C** 1864–66) of Baltimore were among the students from Maryland.

Many of the new students (81) whose fathers' occupations are on the records were the sons of military officers (some 26). James Cresap Ord (**C** 1864–67) was a third-generation Ord at Georgetown and, like his father and grandfather, he also became a regular army officer. Charles Whipple (**C** 1861–63) of Portsmouth, New Hampshire, was the son of General A.W. Whipple, one of the Union commanders who died at Chancellorsville. Theodoric Porter (**C** 1862–63) was the son of Rear Admiral David Dixon Porter. Altogether, these newcomers constituted a highly transient group. The average student stayed less than a year, and less than a tenth of them (7%) earned degrees.

Pennsylvania was the one state outside the immediate area to continue sending a large number of students, many of them of German descent. Among these Pennsylvanians were Charles Harper Walsh, the grandson of alumnus Robert Walsh, a Philadelphia publisher, and John Brisben Walker (**C** 1863–65), whose later life as military professional, journalist, publisher, capitalist, and reformer surely ranks among the most remarkable experienced by any alumnus in the late nineteenth century.

Financially, the war meant hard times for the college. Inflation forced the first tuition increase in nearly forty years, from $200 to $325. Even so, the college's debts continued to rise, and its ability to provide financial assistance to students declined sharply. In 1861 more than one in seven (14%) had received either free tuition or some aid. By 1864 fewer than a tenth (7%) could be helped, and those seem mainly to have been Southerners stranded by the war. Already by the spring of 1862 Georgetown's president expressed doubt to the consultors that they could afford to award the gold medal annually given the student with the best academic record.[43] Commencement on July 3 was a subdued affair with only sixty persons in attendance. Pointedly, there was no celebration of the Fourth. The Philodemic Society held a dinner on commencement day at which the noted alumnus-lawyer John C. C. Hamilton delivered the address on liberal education already referred to. In his closing remarks to the Philodemics, Hamilton warned sadly that

We may not with impunity turn our eyes from the past. Greece had her Peloponnesian war, where States were arrayed against States in deadly conflict, and the national glory which their joint efforts had built up was prostrated forever. Rome, too, felt the terrible effects civil war engendered by the rival pretensions of Caesar and Pompey. On the tombs of nations, as on those of men, the living often read grave and solemn lessons; how many woes might be spared a people if these warnings were heeded in time.[44]

This cry for peace, by a layman, was the most explicit comment about the war to be publicly uttered at the college during the entire conflict. But by the summer of 1862 peace seemed less than ever a quick victory away. Shiloh and the Peninsular Campaign in Virginia had already brought a scale of carnage and death that made the casualties of First Bull Run (Manassas) (4,878) seem negligible. And the news was to be worse for the divided nation as summer passed into fall.

From Shiloh to Fredericksburg

Already a thousand miles west of the federal city, near a country meeting house known as Shiloh Church in southwestern Tennessee, the Confederate Army of the Mississippi and the hastily assembled Union Armies had fought savagely for two days in early April 1862 for control of the only rail line linking Richmond and the west. Shiloh, as one historian has noted, "launched the country onto the floodtide of total war."[45] The dead and wounded were five times the casualties at Manassas. Among the dead from Georgetown were Edwin Birdsall (**C** 1857–60) of Texas and John W. Laurans (**C** 1852–53) of Louisiana, as well as one of the first members of the medical department faculty, Samuel W. Everett, a surgeon in the Union Army. Benedict Joseph Semmes of the 154th Tennessee Regiment suffered a leg wound that put him in a Mississippi hospital for the next several months. John Bull Smith Dimitry of the Crescent Guards was also severely wounded.

In that same month civilians were allowed to cross the Potomac into Virginia without a pass for the first time since the action at Manassas. A group of Georgetown students took advantage of the opportunity to explore the battlefield. Edward Reily (1861–64), a sixteen-year-old from Pennsylvania, wrote to his sister: "We saw many strange sights and scenes. Strings of baggage-wagons as long as the good old city of McSherrytown, winding their slow course over the heights of Arlington; now a troop of cavalry, again a squad of infantry; here and there . . . an encampment on some hill-side. . . ."[46] It was all part of what constituted the ambitious two-pronged attack on Richmond that George McClellan had conceived as a decisive way to end the war. On the peninsula the Army of the Potomac inched its way between the York and James rivers with excruciating deliberation toward the Confederate capital. Williamsburg finally fell on May 5 after heavy fighting. Father Joseph O'Hagan, with the New York's Seventy-Third, was in the thick of it, deafened by "the roaring of hundreds of pieces of artillery, and the sharp, crackling sound of musketry. . . . The rain was pouring down in unbroken streams. The mangled remains of soldiers . . . were carried past in quick succession." As the Seventy-Third prepared to attack, O'Hagan ordered all the Catholics to kneel and make an act of contrition. A mass of bluecoats fell on their knees in the mud and received their chaplain's absolution. The non-Catholics removed caps and stood silently. Within minutes the regiment was engaged.[47] On the Confederate side, Captain Reuben Cleary led his company in the Seventh Virginia Infantry as the regiment fought a desperate, costly rearguard action to protect the Confederate Army's retreat toward Richmond.

James Dooley, with the First Virginia, was wounded and taken prisoner at Williamsburg. Ten days later at Drewry's Bluff on the James River below Richmond, Daniel Carroll (**C** 1858–59) of the Maryland Carrolls, who had resigned his U.S. naval commission to serve as a midshipman in the Confederate navy, was killed by a shell fragment while manning one of the riverside naval batteries that successfully repulsed the Union gunboats. In the brutal Seven Days' Battle for Richmond, Thomas M. Blount (**C** 1848–52) of Jackson's Corps was killed at Cold Harbor; Charles Francis (**C** 1848–49) of the Second Delaware Regiment and Charles Hester (**C** 1858–61) of the Eighteenth Mississippi Regiment died on Malvern Hill. Johnson Middleton (**M** 1855, MD), an assistant surgeon for the Union army, received a citation for his "untiring efforts to relieve the wounded" at Gaines's Mill, Turkey Bridge, and Malvern Hill. The total in killed and wounded at the end of the week's fighting on the York Peninsula was thirty thousand. Among the Union forces captured was Father O'Hagan, who was briefly imprisoned at Richmond before being released.

"I contracted a severe cold sometime back," Edgeworth Bird informed his daughter, Sallie (Saida), from Richmond at the end of July. "[W]e are entrenching ourselves pretty close to McClellan. . . . By God's blessing, we'll beat them again. One or two more signal victories will so disgust the North with abolition rule, that a peace party . . . may spring up there and this cruel war have an end."[48] Indeed, McClellan's army had been decimated by the prolonged fighting as well as by the dysentery and typhoid the men had contracted in the mosquito-ridden wetlands of the peninsula. But these same terrible forces had also taken a deadly toll among the Confederate troops. Samuel Raborg (**M** 1857), an assistant surgeon of the First Maryland Regiment (CSA), contracted typhoid during the campaign and was forced to resign that summer. Joseph Stonestreet of the First Maryland Light Artillery (CSA) suffered a serious chest wound at Mechanicsville at the beginning of the Seven Days' Battle but he returned to his unit several weeks later. James Dooley, after being released from a Union prison later in November, was discharged due to his shattered arm. His younger brother, John, a slight, intense, and highly sensitive nineteen-year-old, had already left Georgetown and taken his place in the First Virginia.

Despite the weakened state of his troops, Lee turned north in August of 1862 to confront the other army, General John Pope's Army of Virginia, which intended to squeeze Richmond into submission. Instead, at the end of August the two forces found themselves locked in combat on the same ground around Bull Run that had been contested a year earlier. This Second Bull Run was an even greater Southern victory. John Dooley, barely two months in uniform, was in the thick of the penultimate Confederate assault on the center of Pope's line. "[T]he bullets whistle thro' the leaves and ears . . . we have no time to think; such is the excitement, such the feeling with which I am inspired that I rush on with the rest, completely bewildered and scarcely heeding what takes place around." As comrades fell all around him, Dooley blindly moved on at double-quick pace and finally gained the opposite hill and the Union battery on it. Only then, as he later recalled, did he comprehend the "horrid scenes around us! Brains, fractured skulls, broken arms and legs, and the human form mangled in every conceivable and inconceivable manner."[49] Johnson Eliot, one of the Georgetown medical faculty who had heeded Lincoln's call for surgeons, rushed to Manassas, where he ministered to the wounded of both armies before being captured by "Stonewall" Jackson's troops at Chantilly.[50] Among the twenty-two thousand casualties from that three days' battle was Edgeworth Bird who, severely wounded, was sent home to Granite Farm on sick leave for several months.

With nothing between Lee's triumphant army and the federal capital ex-cept the remnants of Pope's scattered and demoralized troops, hysteria swept Washington. Government officials made hurried preparations to move the seat of government to New York.[51] Lincoln reluctantly asked George McClel-lan to take general command again and defend the city. But Lee had already decided that Washington was too well fortified for a direct assault. So he crossed the upper Potomac into western Maryland, intending to give that slave state another chance to secede and so increase the pressure on the fed-eral government to make peace with the Confederacy.

On that march into Maryland, Lewis Armistead, now a general command-ing the Provost Guard, was charged by Lee with preserving a strict respect of property, since Lee hoped that would help persuade Marylanders to join them. But this was the section of the state least sympathetic toward the Con-federacy. John Dooley found the people there "as sour as vinegar." "They are opposed to us all along this [Monocacy] valley, and are or pretend to be fear-ful of punishment from the Yankees."[52] One haven in Frederick was the Je-suit novitiate where Dooley searched out and found former professors and classmates from Georgetown. He was warmly greeted by Angelo Paresce, now the provincial superior, as well as by James Ward, the rector, and by Bernard Maguire, now president of Loyola College. He was surprised to find John Moore Davis (**C** 1860–62) of the District with Maguire. Davis made no attempt to hide his Northern sentiments.[53]

John E. Dooley (**C** 1856–61). CSA, First Virginia Infantry, ca. 1863. (Georgetown University Archives)

Dooley left Frederick on September 10, 1862, with Longstreet's Corps. (Lee had split his army into three divisions in order to conduct a complex, risky campaign that would, he hoped, carry the war still farther north.) Four days later the First Vir-ginia had to race back from Hagerstown to South Mountain because the Army of the Potomac, hav-ing accidentally discovered Lee's plans, was threat-ening to break through his rear guard there and thus imperil his badly fragmented army. Arriving late in the afternoon, the Virginians helped to stem the Union advance and allow an orderly retreat through Boonsboro to Sharpsburg. There Lee was preparing to engage McClellan, even though the latter's army outnumbered his by more than two to one. The indecisive McClellan finally attacked on September 17, in piecemeal fashion, along the five-mile line astride Antietam Creek. After nearly breaking through the thin Confederate ranks at sev-eral points during the morning and early afternoon, the Federals in late afternoon turned the Confeder-ate right. Dooley found his regiment, reduced to

Joseph O'Hagan, S.J. Chaplain, Army of the Potomac. (Georgetown University Archives)

seventeen men, facing a Union charge of thousands. "Oh, how I ran!" he admitted in his diary, "or tried to run through the high corn . . . I was afraid of being struck in *back,* and I frequently turned half around in running, so as to avoid if possible so disgraceful a wound."[54] But even as he and his companions ran pell-mell toward the town, other Confederates were counterattacking. A. P. Hill's division had arrived from Harpers Ferry to save the day and the Confederate army—for three more terrible years.

The bloodiest day in the war had resulted in a tactical stand-off but a strategic triumph for the North. Lincoln was now able to issue his preliminary Emancipation Proclamation and thus change the nature of the conflict. For Dooley and Bird and Armistead it meant a weary withdrawal farther back into Virginia. For Alexander Dimitry that retreat provided a respite in the Shenandoah Valley where he could wonder how old he was and could begin to court "one of the sweetest girls I ever met in my life."[55] Many others were left behind at Sharpsburg, among them Lieutenant Hugh Gaston of the Forty-Eighth North Carolina regiment, who had been critically wounded and captured. President Lincoln visited him during a trip to the battlefield and was reportedly moved to discover that young Gaston was the grandson of the distinguished congressman and jurist.[56] Gaston died of his wounds less than a month later.

Three months later the Army of the Potomac, under a new commander, General Ambrose E. Burnside, attempted to complete what McClellan had failed to do at Sharpsburg. In camp with the Union Army on the Rappahannock near Fredericksburg, Father Joseph O'Hagan wrote a fellow Jesuit at the end of November: "No attempt has yet been made by Burnside to cross the river, and if he attempts it here, it will be at a terrible sacrifice of life. The enemy's works are all in sight on the opposite side, and though not very strong, yet they are very numerous, and in magnificent positions."[57] Burnside's attack two weeks later proved O'Hagan all too accurate in his prediction. Nearly thirteen thousand Union soldiers were killed or wounded as, wave upon wave, they tried in vain to scale Marye's Heights and its fortifications. John Dooley, with the First Virginia (held in reserve throughout the battle), heard "the most dismal moans and groans and the most piteous cries . . . on all sides of us [from] the Yankees."[58] "I am confident that half a million of men could not have taken [the heights]," O'Hagan wrote after the disastrous battle.

I never imagined that so many dead could be left on one field. They were actually in heaps. . . . I do not know what the next programme will be, nor do I care much, provided our poor men are not led to another butchery. It is horrible, and I am only surprised that the entire nation does not rise up against it unanimously.[59]

The College as an Army Hospital

Even before the guns had stopped firing at Manassas the previous September, virtually every large building in the District, including the Capitol, was earmarked to be appropriated for use as hospitals for battle casualties. The government informed Georgetown President Early that he should make provisions for accommodating five hundred wounded soldiers in the southern buildings of the college as well as at the villa in Tenleytown.[60] Apparently, the northern building was spared because of the intercession of General A. W. Whipple, whose two sons were students in the college. (Only thirty students were on the campus as the school year began in September 1862.) Early again warned his fellow Jesuits about giving any offense to Union soldiers by making remarks about the war or politics in general.[61] The provincial superior ordered the community to recite daily Psalm 46: "God is our refuge and our strength, . . . Therefore we fear not, though the earth be shaken."[62]

Two weeks after the college buildings were requisitioned the government ordered Trinity Church converted into a temporary hospital for those who had been wounded at Antietam. The congregation removed the carpeting from the sanctuary and pews, and carpenters hurriedly put planks over the pews to serve as makeshift beds.[63] The military sick and wounded remained there and on campus for the entire first semester of the 1862–63 academic year. The Jesuits refrained from any political discourse but were active in ministering to the afflicted. At the temporary hospitals set up at Georgetown, in Washington, and at the novitiate in Frederick, hundreds were converted to Catholicism, including all the one hundred and twenty soldiers who eventually died.

Among the many funerals in the city that John Early and the other Jesuits attended was one at St. Aloysius Church in January 1863 for another convert and distinguished alumnus, Colonel Julius Garesché. A combined choir from all the Catholic parishes in the city sang Mozart's *Requiem Mass.* Garesché, chief of staff to General William S. Rosecrans, commander of the XIV Army Corps, had been decapitated by mortar fire in Tennessee at the Battle of Stones River on the last day of the old year, while riding next to the general.[64] He was brought back to Washington and given a military burial at Mount Olivet Cemetery. Less than four months later Father Early preached at another military funeral, this time for General Whipple at Trinity Church, with President Lincoln and his cabinet in attendance.[65]

From Chancellorsville to Gettysburg

Joseph O'Hagan, at Georgetown on a brief furlough in the winter of 1863, contrasted "my temporary quiet with the experience of the past eighteen months in the army, where with some exceptions, everything corrupt, low vulgar and debasing in our corrupt nature is rampant. Would that I was out of it altogether, but it cannot be yet. I may still do some good where I am . . . God [grant] that this unhappy war may soon terminate but from present indications it is only commencing."[66] Benedict Joseph Semmes, now a commissary captain on the staff of General Bragg, could only vent his frustration on the North for the waste and destruction. He wrote that spring to his wife:

Teach my children to hate them, to despise them as not only our worst and meanest enemies but the enemies of God and Mankind . . . Even in despotic Europe some were found to rebel, but in their insane hatred of the South and their thirst for our money and lands they submit to a worse despotism than Europe ever saw, in hope of reducing us to a level with our negroes and subjects of their power. If it is God's will that they succeed, my last wish is that none of my blood may live to see it. No Semmes must ever be a Yankee serf. . . . [67]

In the eastern theater of war the Army of the Potomac made another major effort in May 1863 to break through the Confederate lines at the Rappahannock, but with even worse results than in December. Lee's brilliant pincer movement at Chancellorsville tore up the Union forces even though they outnumbered the Confederates by more than two to one. The Virginians inflicted more than seventeen thousand casualties on the Federals. But the Army of Northern Virginia paid its own heavy price for its greatest victory, more than a fifth of its ranks (12,800) dead and wounded, including Thomas "Stonewall" Jackson, Lee's greatest soldier and most able tactician. Two alumni, Francis A. Lancaster (**C** 1852–57) of Philadelphia and William Hayden (**C** 1837–38) of Harpers Ferry, were among the dead of both armies—one in Blue, one in Gray.

Emboldened by this triumph, Lee in early June invaded the North for the second time in nine months. Morale, he calculated, was the Southern advantage that would enable his army this time to win a decisive victory on Northern soil, which would possibly end the war and surely take pressure off Virginia and the beleagured Confederate forces at Vicksburg. John Dooley, in the rear guard on the northward march into Pennsylvania, thought that "never before has the army been in such fine condition, so well disciplined and under such complete control. Perhaps never before have we had a larger effective force, sixty thousand infantry with some two hundred pieces of cannon."[68] There were then at least one hundred and thirty Georgetown alumni with Lee's forces.[69]

On June 30 Major General Henry Heth sent a brigade to the small town of Gettysburg, apparently to purchase shoes, where they inadvertently encountered what was thought to be a small Union force. The next day Heth's entire division joined the attack on what turned out to be the vanguard of the Army of the Potomac, and the Confederates were committed to a battle they had not chosen and had not planned.[70] When the First Virginia finally arrived at Gettysburg, the battle had been raging for two days. In fact, Lee's forces came tantalizingly close to driving the Federal troops from their high ground on Cemetery Ridge and Little Round Top. At dawn on July 3 the First Virginia passed General Lee as it marched to the front. "I must confess that the Gen'l's face does not look as bright as tho' he were certain of success," John Dooley, now a lieutenant, noted.[71] As they awaited orders, Dooley's men passed the time in an orchard pelting each other with green apples. Finally, in the afternoon the order came for them to attack once the artillery in front of them did its work on the line opposite them. After approximately an hour of the artillery exchange ("Never will I forget those scenes and sounds. The earth seems unsteady beneath this furious cannonading. . . ."), the command was given at three o'clock in the afternoon for Pickett's Division, as well as for Heth's and McLaws's, to advance. The First Virginia was in the center of Kemper's Brigade. They marched, for almost a mile, bands playing, coming increasingly under the withering fire of the Union cannon. Their ranks thinned rapidly from the effects of shelling and musketry as they went into double-quick step for the last hundred yards. "Volley after volley of crashing musket balls sweeps through the line," Dooley remembered, "and mow us down like

Union soldiers ferried supplies from the Georgetown port to their encampment on Anolastan (now Roosevelt) Island. Photograph taken ca. 1865. (Library of Congress. Georgetown University Archives)

wheat before the scythe." Still, every senior officer was out front, "Pickett with his long curls streaming . . . Garnett on the right, Kemper in the center and Armistead on the left. . . ."[72] Wounded, Dooley himself went down thirty yards from the copse of trees they had been heading towards. Lewis Armistead, the only general officer remaining, led the remnants of his brigade in a charge against the salient of the Union line. He managed to penetrate the Federal position but fell, mortally wounded, his hand on a Union cannon.[73]

Armistead died in a Federal hospital two days later. Like several other alumni, Dooley was captured and imprisoned (of one hundred and fifty-five men of the First Virginia in Pickett's charge, only thirty-five escaped death or injury).[74] Many Georgetown alumni were among the Confederate wounded, and two others besides Armistead died. In all, it is estimated that the two armies suffered more than fifty-one thousand casualties in the three-day battle. "Our army has seen pretty rough times," Edgeworth Bird wrote his wife a few days after the Confederates had retreated from Gettysburg. He had become quartermaster in Benning's brigade and during the battle had assisted a surgeon. "The Yankees were impregnably posted and on their own soil they fought undoubtedly well. . . . Our loss of noble men is terrible. . . . Oh, my darling, these are sad, sad times."[75] He thought it prudent to settle the family debts with Confederate money while they could. "A few short weeks ago we were confident and jubilant, but Vicksburg, Port Hudson, and the *unfortunate victory at Gettysburg* have changed greatly the fall of our fortunes."[76]

One former Jesuit faculty member saw heaven's hand in the declining fortunes of the Confederacy. John Barrister (Bauermeister), who had come from Germany in 1848, wrote a fellow Jesuit: "[Lee's invasion] is already the second attempt and failure to make conquests for the Slave power: I trust this will be the last. . . . How the Almighty now punishes American pride by the very thing which once made these people so boastful and haughty, I mean their *'Glorious Union and heavenborn Constitution.'* O tempora! O mores! There was a time when the haughty Virginian looked down upon the poor Irishmen, or the humble mechanic from his sashed window with an air of contempt. Now an Irish soldier or a Massachusetts cobler [*sic*] . . . sits on his lofty porch of Corinthian columns, smoking his pipe, or chewing tobacco."[77]

The Medical Department

For the medical department wartimes made for flush times, not bad times (see table 9.4 in appendix F). The only negative impact was a two-week delay of the start of classes in the fall of 1862 because of Lee's first invasion. Student enrollment soared; from 1862 to 1865 the school graduated seventy students, more than it had in the entire first decade of its existence. Consequently, the medical department, in contrast to the college, had to increase tuition only slightly, from $90 to $105, and that late in the war. As the only medical school in the city by 1863 (the Columbian College medical department had suspended classes that same year),[78] Georgetown became a major training center for surgeons for the Union armies. Of the eighty-five students who entered during the war, at least twenty-three served in the military as medical cadets or surgeons. On average they were older than previous new students—nearly twenty-two years old when they entered—and more than half from the Northeast (some 56%). Although the records show that most were still Anglo-American in origin (62%), the greatest ethnic increase was among the German Americans (from 8% to 18%). Many were already ranked as medical cadets while they attended lectures at Georgetown. Amasa Elliott Paine, who had been a private in the Forty-third Massachusetts Regiment, entered Georgetown in September of 1863, earned his medical degree, and was appointed a medical cadet in the U.S. Army in November of 1864. Joseph Eastman (**M** 1863–65, MD) of New York, who had contracted a fever while serving with the Eleventh New York Regiment on the peninsula, was afterwards assigned to duty in Washington's Mount Pleasant Hospital. There he encountered the Georgetown doctors who worked there. Soon after he began classes at Georgetown and qualified as a surgeon in 1865. He later gained distinction as a specialist in women's diseases. William Steinmetz studied at Georgetown while serving as a hospital steward in Washington hospitals. He graduated in 1865 and later became a career captain-surgeon in the U.S. Army. Maurice Tucker graduated in 1862 and became the surgeon for the Thirtieth U.S. Colored Troops. Daniel Roberts Brower was appointed an assistant surgeon upon his graduation in 1864 and before the war's end was the chief medical officer for the Military District of Norfolk. After the war he went to Richmond as head of the Howard's Grove hospital for freedmen. Ralph Walsh (**M** 1861–63, MD), commissioned an assistant surgeon in the United States Army immediately following his graduation, saw service at Gettysburg that summer. Walsh returned to Georgetown in 1873 to become professor of physiology for nearly two decades. Joseph Tabor Johnson (**M** 1863–65, MD) did postgraduate work in New York (Bellevue), Paris, and Vienna before returning to be professor of obstetrics at Howard University. Then, in 1874 he began his long career with the Georgetown medical faculty.

Daniel Roberts Brower (**M** 1863–64), assistant surgeon, Army of the Potomac. (Georgetown University Archives)

In recognition of the needs of their new constituency and in response to a suggestion of the surgeon general, the faculty in February of 1863 approved the establishment of a Chair of Military Surgery, Physiology & Hygiene. Dr. Thomas Antisell was elected to fill the new position.[79] To meet the demand for surgeons, a second five-month session was introduced in the spring of 1864, so that students might complete their training within one year.[80] Also in 1864, apparently impressed by the practical experience that the medical cadets were receiving at the military hospitals, the department required for the first time that all students were to receive similar clinical instruction, either at Providence Hospital or at a military hospital, in order to graduate.[81]

The Long Summer of 1864

William Cowardin (**C** 1858–61) of Richmond had joined the Third Battalion of the Virginia Local Defense in 1863 as a sixteen-year-old. In March 1864 the battalion repulsed a raid by Union cavalry on Richmond and killed its commander, Colonel Ulrich Dahlgren. Papers found on Dahlgren's body apparently disclosed Union intentions to burn the city and assassinate President Davis and his cabinet. However, Union officials disclaimed any responsibility, and their Confederate counterparts professed at that time to accept the disclaimers.[82] (Dahlgren was the son of John Adelphus Bernard Dahlgren, a distinguished U.S. naval officer and inventor.)

Six weeks later Ulysses S. Grant, now commanding all Federal armies, began his own drive across the Rappahannock to take Richmond. John Longyear (**C** 1864–65) traveled from the college with his father, a congressman from Michigan, to watch Burnside's IX Corps break camp in Annapolis and head for the front. As they passed through the city, young Longyear was able to march with his hometown company, the Twentieth Michigan Infantry, until they reached the Long Bridge (now the 14th Street Bridge) and crossed into Virginia.[83] In the West, William Tecumseh Sherman started his march toward Atlanta. But, despite their heavy losses in the summer and fall of 1863, Confederate morale was still high. B. J. Semmes, with the Army of Tennessee, thought he had "never seen the army in such splendid fighting trim, or in such determined and confident spirits."[84]

At the beginning of May 1864, Grant struck heavy Confederate resistance in the Wilderness, west of Chancellorsville. Beaten back with fearsome losses after two days of savage fighting in the nearly impenetrable underbrush and second growth trees, the Union commander did not withdraw, as his predecessors had; instead he maneuvered the army around the Confederate right and headed toward Richmond.

The two armies met again in fierce combat at Spotsylvania Court House and again at the North Anna River over the next month. Each time the Army of the Potomac was repulsed with great loss, but Grant kept maneuvering toward Richmond. "Grant has before him an impossible task," Edgeworth Bird wrote to his wife. "He cannot take Richmond, and I hope and believe is destined to a more hopeless defeat than fell to the lot of McClelland [sic]."[85] The Union disaster two days later at Cold Harbor made Bird a prophet, of a sort. The First Maryland Artillery, captained by William F. Dement (**C** 1841–45) and counting seventeen other Georgetown alumni, was a key battery in the Confederate artillery defenses that inflicted devastating losses on the Federal assault.[86] Once again Grant slipped his army south before digging in and settling in a line of trenches to the east of Petersburg. In a month the Union forces had more than fifty thousand casualties, the Confederates more than thirty thousand. Wounded at Petersburg, James Madison Cutts (**C** 1849–51) of the First Rhode Island Regiment later was awarded a "Triple Medal of Honor" for his heroic actions in the fighting. John Fitzsimmons (**C** 1835–36) of Virginia, Robert Cowan McRee (**C** 1860–61) of North Carolina, and David P. Matthews of Virginia (one of the Matthews brothers) were among the unprecedentedly high number of fatalities. A Georgetown student remembered the wounded being brought to Washington "on the river steamers by thousands every day," and the "long lines of ambulances carrying the wounded men from the steamboats to the various hospitals."[87] The war had become a seemingly endless repetition of murderous battles, each leaving more casualties than the last. "So many thousands of men wounded! It scarcely can be believed . . ." was all that Bernard Wiget could comment in 1864 after tending the victims for more than three years.[88]

Through the long summer of 1864 Grant lay siege to Petersburg and Sherman to Atlanta. Grant pressed relentlessly closer, trying to isolate the entrenched Army of Northern Virginia so he could break through to Richmond. In July, a spectacular attempt to smash the Confederate defenses by exploding a gigantic mine beneath their lines miscarried and ended in a Union disaster. Then in August, a key railroad line south of Petersburg was captured by Union forces, despite furious counterattacks by Henry Heth, who commanded a division of A. P. Hill's Third Corps on the extreme right flank of the Confederate lines. The losses mounted on both sides as summer became fall and the siege lines continued to lengthen. Thomas Alexander (**C** 1860–62) of Virginia, Dent Burroughs (**M** 1857–59, MD) of Maryland, and Alexander Allemong (**C** 1845–48) of South Carolina were among those in gray who died in the trenches. By winter the Confederate defenses stretched nearly forty miles from Richmond to southwest of Petersburg.

In Atlanta, B. J. Semmes had stores for the Army of Tennessee loaded on freight trains in order to provide more mobility against the shelling from the Union guns. By the latter part of August the bombardment was incessant. "About midnight," he wrote his wife Iorantha on the twenty-first, "the fire was so hot at my quarters that I had to get up and vacate to another point a hundred yards distant, but after a while I returned, the shells being as thick there as my quarters."[89] Ten days later the besieged city fell. Semmes got out with part of his stores just before. In putting the best face on the loss, he told Iorantha: "The fall of Atlanta will . . . prolong war at least another year."[90] Charles Rowan Percy (**C** 1859–61) of Louisiana and George W. Hill (**M** 1858–59, MD) of Ohio were among those killed in action during the campaign. As Sherman penetrated deeper and deeper into Georgia, seemingly laying waste everything in his path, Edgeworth Bird in Virginia could only admit that "Revolution in all its horrors is indeed upon us. . . ."[91] "I have already told my negro men," he informed his father, "that in such case, those of them who wish to go to the Yankees could do so; those who did not must take to the roads and keep out of the way."[92] Semmes was still confident that Sherman would eventually suffer in the Deep South what Napoleon had suffered on the way to and from Moscow. "I trust we will all soon make another strong effort to regain our lost ground."[93] John Bell Hood indeed made a foolhardy attack at Franklin three months later. Two weeks after that a sad Semmes confessed that the remnant of the Army of Tennessee was fifteen thousand "ragged, barefooted [men], without blankets or shelter and broken in spirit." He and most of the army were sent home on furlough. Sherman had already reached the sea and was devastating South Carolina on his way north to join Grant in front of Petersburg.[94]

Peace and Assassination

"[Jubal] Early is careening around Washington and Baltimore and frightening the eternal Yankee nation into fits, but I fear [he] will not be able to capture the former," Edgeworth Bird wrote to his wife in mid-July of 1864.[95] For the third summer in a row a Confederate Army had invaded Maryland, this time in an attempt to lift the siege of Petersburg and tilt the upcoming Federal elections in favor of the Democrats and a peace settlement. Early's army of about seventeen thousand seasoned men penetrated the northern limits of the District by July 11. Jesuit scholastics at the college villa could distinctly hear the firing between the Confederate attackers and the federal defenders, many of them civilian government workers, at Fort Stevens three miles away.[96] As Bird suspected, Early lacked the strength to seize the city and shortly afterwards had to withdraw across the Potomac into Virginia. Among the casualties left behind were two Georgetown alumni, John Chichizola (**C** 1856–58) of Alabama, wounded and captured at Silver Spring, and Alexander G. Dimitry (**C** 1855–61) of Louisiana, the son of Alexander Dimitry, killed in action. Dimitry was later buried in the Jesuit cemetery at Georgetown. Four months later Union forces under Sheridan destroyed Early's army at the Battle of Cedar Creek in the Shenandoah. Charles Pettys (**M** 1870–73, MD) who had enlisted in New York State two years earlier as a fifteen-year-old, earned a medal of honor in that October encounter.

By the winter of 1865 everyone knew the war would soon be over. "Our affairs look rather gloomy," Edgeworth Bird admitted in a letter written to his wife Sallie in early January.[97] The South, Angelo Paresce reported to Rome in February, was running out of arms and men. It could continue the conflict, he thought, only by turning to guerrilla warfare.[98] The college, out of respect for the suffering in so much of the land, held no Washington's birthday celebration or Mardi Gras carnival that year. "Even the old flag," Joseph O'Hagan, now back at Georgetown, wrote on that foreboding twenty-second day of February, "seemed unwilling to move on the old Tower . . . as if mourning over the woes of the land of Washington!"[99] Nevertheless, most of the faculty and students went into the city on March 4 to watch President Lincoln's second inaugural.

O'Hagan, who had left the Union army in 1864, was called back to the Army of the James as a chaplain ten days after the inauguration. He had barely reached the York Peninsula when Grant finally broke through Lee's ever thinning lines on April 2, 1865. Unlike McClellan and Meade, Grant pursued his retreating foe westward for a week to eliminate the Army of Northern Virginia once and for all. Eighty miles west of Petersburg, General Edward Ord (a brother of James and Placidus), commanding the Army of the James, turned back the last Confederate effort to break through the encircling Union armies. Hours later the war, for all practical purposes, ended with the surrender of the remnant of Lee's army at Appomattox Court House. At least thirty Georgetown alumni, including Augustine Neale, Henry Ford (**C** 1855–58), Joseph Stonestreet, Francis Xavier Ward, and Luke Tiernan Brien (**C** 1844–46) of Baltimore, were among those who stacked arms in the triangle of the village green on April 9, 1865. Carl Kleinschmidt (**M** 1860–1862, MD), a surgeon with the Confederate Army, parole in hand, walked the two hundred miles home to Georgetown. Theodore J. Dimitry (**C** 1856–59), of Louisiana, deserted and made his way to Danville where he joined the bodyguard being formed to escort Jefferson Davis, who was making his abortive attempt to escape to Mexico.[100]

John Dooley, who had been paroled from a federal army prison in February, had made his way in uniform from Richmond with a friend in late March, apparently expecting that Lee would abandon his position at Petersburg and march west to start a new campaign in the Lynchburg-Danville region.[101] Dooley and his companion were resting at a friend's home just above Lynchburg when word came that Richmond had fallen and Lee was fleeing westward. So they headed south in the hope of joining up with the Army of Northern Virginia. But by the time they reached Danville, on the North Carolina border, they learned of Lee's surrender. Nevertheless, they continued south toward President Davis, because they felt "in honour bound to follow the fortunes of the Confederacy until its cause is hopeless or its hopes of success revive."[102] At Greensboro they found the skeleton of the Confederate government, a caravan of desperate officials, and the hastily packed treasure that Jefferson Davis had brought out of Richmond, as well as the Army of Tennessee, the last remaining Southern army of any significance. Dooley and his companion accompanied the remnants of the Confederate government as far as Charlotte. There he realized that it was "madness to go farther South," deciding instead that returning to Richmond was his only recourse, even though it might well mean "imprisonment, starvation" or even worse. Dooley headed home, demoralized by the South's lack of dedication to pursuing the war to the very end, whether in triumph or trial, and regretting that he had not heeded his college day urge to enter the Society of Jesus instead of chasing the dreams of Southern nationalism.[103]

When the news of Lee's surrender reached Washington, the batteries in the chain of forts that surrounded the capital fired a series of salutes in rotation for several hours. John Longyear remembered the smoke of victory hanging over the Virginia shore "like a blanket."[104] Five days later, on April 14, 1865, Samuel Read Ward, a U.S. Treasury Department employee and Georgetown medical student, went to attend a performance at Ford's Theatre on F Street (the medical department had already scheduled its July commencement there). He went because he hoped to see General Grant, who was reported to be attending the play that evening, together with his wife and the Lincolns. Ward was disappointed when Grant did not appear, but suddenly he heard a shot, saw a man with a dagger spring from the presidential box, shout "Sic semper tyrannis," and jump to the floor, falling as he landed, but limping quickly off the stage.[105] Hickson Field (**C** 1864–65), a student at the college whose father was assistant secretary of the Treasury, was visiting in the lobby of Willard's Hotel with Senator James Nye of Nevada when word came that the president had been shot. Field and the senator ran down F Street to 10th, where they gained entrance to the Peterson House where the mortally wounded president had been taken. Field provided the pocketknife that the president's doctor used to cut away Lincoln's waistcoat and carried away the bloodsoaked garment in the morning, after the president finally expired. Among the doctors futilely treating Lincoln during his last hours was Charles Liebermann, then president of the Medical Society of the District of Columbia.

By the next morning the bells at Trinity Church in Georgetown were tolling, along with those of all the churches throughout the city and in the nation beyond. Black crepe was draped over the porches of the North and South buildings on the campus and over the front gate; on one of the towers of the North building the flag was displayed at half-mast "as a mark of grief," Joseph O'Hagan noted in the official diary of the college.[106] That same day near the college villa in Tenleytown, a faculty member, Father John Guida, was arrested by soldiers who thought he bore a striking resemblance to the man accused of assassinating the president. He was held in a military camp until he was able to convince the authorities that he was not John Wilkes Booth.[107]

Several alumni, however, were ultimately implicated in the assassination. Chief among them was David Herold (**C** 1855–58), who earlier had

Samuel Bland Arnold (**C** 1844–45).

David Herold (**C** 1855–58).

guided Lewis Paine to Secretary of State William Seward's house where Paine stabbed the secretary nearly to death in his bed. Herold not only knew Washington intimately but the roads of southern Maryland as well. And, along with Samuel Bland Arnold (**C** 1844–45), he had also been one of the conspirators in an earlier plan to kidnap Lincoln and spirit him through southern Maryland to a Potomac crossing and a waiting band of abductors in Virginia. Arnold had served briefly in the Confederate Army in 1861, then worked for the Southern government as a civilian clerk. After the assassination Herold guided the injured Booth from Charles County, Maryland, across the Potomac and to the Northern Neck in Virginia, where Booth was himself shot and killed by federal troops. Samuel Mudd (**C** 1851–52) had apparently been involved in the earlier kidnap plot as well: he had met with Booth several times in the fall of 1864 and introduced Booth to the Surratts.[108] When Booth arrived with Herold at Mudd's house in Charles County after the assassination, seeking to have his ankle set, the doctor implausibly claimed not to have recognized either of them.

Herold was one of the four persons hanged for his part in the assassination, and Arnold and Mudd were sentenced to life imprisonment.[109] Had the net been cast wider, other Georgetown alumni would almost certainly have been pulled in as well. Booth, for instance, had brought a letter of introduction from a Confederate agent in Canada to William Queen (**C** 1800–1806), a doctor in Charles County.[110] John C. Thompson (**C** 1838–42),

Samuel Mudd (**C** 1851–52).

(Georgetown University Archives)

Queen's son-in-law, subsequently (before the assassination) had introduced Booth to Mudd.[111]

As it was, three Georgetown alumni were among the six convicted of involvement in the conspiracy. The sole woman among the six brought to trial was Mary Surratt, a Catholic with close ties to local Jesuits. (Father Bernard Wiget, of Georgetown, for one, was her confessor and a character witness at her trial.) Amidst their fears in 1861 about the war providing an occasion for a renewal of anti-Catholicism, Jesuit superiors could hardly have envisioned a worse provocation than a group of presidential assassins with Catholic and Jesuit connections. But despite the hysteria and fury that swept the city and nation in the wake of Lincoln's death, no one sounded an alarm about either a Catholic or a Jesuit plot to bring down the republic. No one pointed the finger at Georgetown for nurturing those who had committed this ultimate act of disloyalty. The Catholic service record in the war, lagging enlistments and draft riots notwithstanding, had effectively discredited the nativist shibboleths of the previous decades.[112] Georgetown had made its own modest contribution to that good record. Of the two hundred and eighteen Georgetown alumni who had fought for the Union, twenty-one (9.6%) had died in service; another thirty-six had been wounded or captured. The number of Georgetown alumni who had served the Confederacy was far greater, of course. Of the eight hundred and sixty-seven in the Confederate service, more also died proportionately (97 or 11%), either from battle wounds or war-related diseases, and another three hundred and thirty-four (38.5%) were either wounded or captured.[113]

Georgetown after the War

For Georgetown itself, the war had proven to be the most serious threat to its survival as an institution. However, had the college been closed in 1861 or 1862, it is unlikely that it would have reopened, given the many other Jesuit colleges in the region competing for limited resources. In that event, the medical department, despite its wartime success, would probably have been forced to look for another academic sponsor. Fortunately, such pessimistic speculation went unfulfilled.

When classes resumed in the fall of 1865, more than two hundred students enrolled in the college, nearly a third of them from below the Potomac, including six Confederate veterans. And John Dooley was among the Jesuit novices who entered that fall. Stephen Mallory, the seventeen-year-old son of the former secretary of the Confederate navy and one of the six veterans, was struck at the lack "of sectional bitterness." Both Southern and Northern students, he found, had the good sense not to raise "the merits of the Union and the Confederate causes."[114] When Bernard Maguire returned as president in January 1866, he found a school in poor condition, financially and physically, as a result of the war, and a student body still strongly Southern but impoverished. He might well have thought that the college, unlike the nation, had survived the war basically unchanged. During the next decade, the consequences of the war for the institution only gradually manifested themselves in ways few would have predicted.

CHAPTER 10

A Decade of Reconstruction and the Founding of the Law School

If we are out of the race where the purse is millions, must our running cease? If magnificence is not within the lawyer's reach, are there no more rewards? Is there to be no place in America for men[?]

CHARLES P. JAMES, FIRST LAW DEPARTMENT
Georgetown Commencement, June 4, 1872

Recovery for the College and the University

Having survived the Civil War, the university reconstructed itself in the new, post-Appomattox society of America under the leadership of two former presidents serving second terms from 1866 to 1873. The college recovered most of its Southern patronage but lost much of the local support that had sustained it through the dark days of the early 1860s. For the college the nation's period of Reconstruction was its period of consolidation and reform. Beyond the college, the university lost one professional school, in divinity, but added another, in law. For the third professional school, the medical department, the decade proved one of contraction and reorganization after the collapse of its wartime enrollments.

The Postwar City of Washington

The war had transformed Washington from a large Southern town housing a small-scale government to a sprawling bureaucratic center supporting the immense military machine that put down the South's rebellion. In 1860 the population of the federal city had been counted at sixty-one thousand. By 1864 that same city's population was estimated to be more than two hundred thousand. However, with peace and demobilization, some of the air went out of that demographic balloon (an 1867 census counted fewer than one hundred and ten thousand persons). But the nation's capital remained a large city, albeit an underdeveloped one: with streets still mostly unpaved, no overall sewerage system, and more than half of its children unschooled. Georgetown, less affected by the war than Washington City, experienced modest growth in ten years (from 8,733 in 1860 to 11,384). Half of the newcomers (1,336) were black, and nearly as many (1,000) were Irish laborers.

Since the early months of the war there had been a steady influx of African Americans, mostly runaway slaves, who came seeing Washington as the "promised land." Both during and after the war, the Congress used the District as a testing ground for the most explosive measures of proposed social change for blacks. In 1862 the District was the first area south of the Mason-Dixon line in which slavery was abolished by federal law. (Proposed and declared ratified in 1865, the Thirteenth Amendment abolished slavery throughout the entire United States, or any place subject to their jurisdiction.) The Congress also extended suffrage to African American males in the District in 1867. (Proposed in 1866 and declared ratified in 1868, the Fourteenth Amendment recognized American citizenship for all persons born or naturalized in the United States, including blacks.) In 1868 a candidate supported by blacks and promising to complete the social revolution became mayor of Washington. In 1869–70 blacks were accorded equal access by law to any place of public entertainment, and to hotels, bars, and restaurants.

But the recognition of their civil rights and the franchise were in themselves poor providers for the most elementary needs of African Americans, of whom two-thirds had been unschooled, untrained slaves just a few years before. Thousands of them had to live in ramshackle housing located in disease-breeding, unsanitary near-swamps in southwest and eastern Washington. As the city's historian noted, "The once half-empty, sprawling city of 'magnificent distances' had suddenly acquired slums as horrifying as those of New York."[1] By 1870 the black community in the District of Columbia had nearly tripled its numbers to more than forty thousand—or nearly one-third (31%) of the population.

For much of the white community such developments were deeply disturbing and were resisted, insofar as was possible. In 1866, both Georgetown and Washington held referendums in which voters overwhelmingly rejected the proposal to grant the franchise to blacks (in Georgetown it failed to gain even one positive vote). Although presumably no adult at the college voted in the referendum (the prohibition by their superiors on Jesuits exercising their franchise being still in force), most shared local negative sentiments. "We have no more colored men in the District. They all turned white last Friday," one Jesuit at the college bitterly wrote to another when the 1867 "Congressional" suffrage bill became law in the District.[2] Editorials in the college newspaper were still arguing in 1875 against the Fifteenth Amendment and for the retrocession of the Georgetown area to Maryland.[3] (Proposed in 1869, the Fifteenth Amendment on universal suffrage [for men] was declared ratified in 1870.) "Politically," an earlier editorial had argued, "the District is, in relation to the country at large, what the forcing-grounds of the Agricultural Department at Washington are to the farmers and gardeners—a field to start strange growths in, and to experiment upon, generally."[4] Maryland, however, as a Southern state that had not seceded, offered a sanctuary from the social engineering of Reconstruction from which it was legally exempt, as the states of the former Confederacy were not.

The college was still very self-consciously Southern. "We of the South," the Georgetown *College Journal* observed in 1874, "are sometimes reproached for the lack of those qualities which distinguish the thrifty people of the North—energy, perseverance, punctuality, economy, and the rest of the matter-of-fact virtues." The charge, the writer continued, was hardly justified, given the radically different conditions that set the two sections apart. An urban environment and a vigorous climate in the North had made for "healthy competition. . . . Moreover, no inferior race has ever existed to any extent in their midst . . . but every one has had to work for himself."[5]

For some, the devastating consequences of war and the politics of Reconstruction at both the local and national levels meant the end of a cherished antebellum republican society. In 1867 and again in 1868, Reconstruction bills and their supplements imposed a military rule that treated the former Confederates as a conquered enemy. Most white Southerners were outraged. In this spirit John Dooley, now a Jesuit scholastic, addressed the Goddess of Liberty whose statue had been placed atop the Capitol's dome during the latter part of the war:

But do you ask how men unfamed as these
Can manage so the populace to please
That they obtain position and the time
For perpetration of such shameless crime?
The Negro freedmen and the worthless whites
With equal intellects have equal rights
And these combining with designing knaves
Must vote for Generals mute or quondam slaves
(Or if they be not mute or freedmen blacks)
(Still chains and stripes disgraceful mark their backs)
Who when elected don't forget to lend

A helping hand to each abetting friend.
Thus friend aids friend and vice obtains control
Since only vicious men approach the poll:
For those same laws that set the Negro free
Reduced his master to his slavery.
Transferring from the master to the Slave
The power to choose 'twixt honest man & knave. . . . [6]

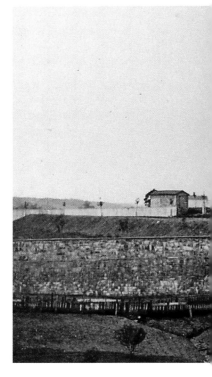

In Georgetown, the most visible human signs of a failing economy and society were not only the misery of emancipated blacks but also the obvious distress of the impoverished Irish who overcrowded many rundown dwellings west of Wisconsin Avenue and near Trinity Church and the college. A student at the college in the late 1860s remembered a staff member distributing food daily at the front gate to poor blacks and poor whites.[7] An 1870 census listed at least a thousand such whites, many of them living in abject circumstances.[8] Violence was also for many years a frequent occurrence among them. "Jerry Donovan, who was beaten on Sunday by Dan McCarthy died today." John Early thus noted in his diary without comment the death in 1871 of an Irishman who had lived close to the gate of the college.[9] Begun in the 1850s when rising vagrancy and thefts had become a concern, the college wall completed the insulation of the campus from its neighbors by the summer of 1866. The town that same year granted the president and directors permission to close First Street (now N Street) from Warren (Thirty-seventh) to College Street and to enclose the college property.[10] Accordingly, a masonry wall with a gate was built around the eastward-facing section of the campus.

The College and the City Government

Compounding the economic downturn, the largely undeveloped infrastructure, and the occasional racial turmoil in the District was the fear that Congress might actually relocate the nation's capital to the Mississippi Valley, where cities like Cincinnati and St. Louis were petitioning for a change in the seat of government. In this unsettled atmosphere, a movement to consolidate the District as one political jurisdiction that could provide an "umbrella" of efficient and progressive government grew increasingly attractive. Thus, in 1871 the District Territorial Act joined together Washington, Georgetown, and the remaining area of the District into one political enclave with an ap-

Detail from a photograph of the completed college wall with shanties below on Warren (Thirty-seventh) Street. Photograph taken ca. 1867. (Georgetown University Archives)

pointed governor and council, as well as its own elected house of representatives and a nonvoting delegate to the Congress. Richard Merrick (**C** 1837–40) was the Democratic candidate for delegate but he lost to his Republican opponent by a margin of more than four thousand votes. Henry Cooke, president of the First National Bank of Washington and younger brother of the New York financier, Jay Cooke, was appointed governor. But real power lay with the head of the board of public works, Alexander "Boss" Shepherd, a former gasfitter's assistant who had well and shrewdly exploited the commercial opportunities in wartime Washington to gain control of local banks. His was a key voice among those calling for a new relationship between the local and federal communities. This Territory of the District of Columbia lasted only three years, but in that time its board of public works largely accomplished the modernization of the area's streets and sanitation, if not of its school buildings. But the board piled up such enormous debts (spending approximately five times more than all previous District governments had in the preceding seventy years) that Congress revoked the territorial arrangement and took back direct control in 1874.[11]

The college continued to be sensitive to its reputation as a pro-Southern institution in a city now dominated by liberal (mainly Northern) Republicans. Thus, although some college officials discussed in 1872 the possibility of applying to the federal government for rental payments for the use made of college buildings by federal troops during the war, they decided not to in order "not to excite remarks and rake up reminiscences about the Southern proclivities of many of ours."[12] Five months later, college officials did file for $7,500 compensation, but only when they were assured that the federal government was routinely granting such requests under the Quartermaster Stores Act of 1864. Eventually the government paid the college approximately $2,400, despite the Quartermaster General's objection that church-related institutions should not qualify since they paid no taxes.[13]

Under the short-lived territorial government the college was taxed for heating and cooking gas, even though it was producing its own. Nonetheless, the college administration was wary of protesting too strenuously, since it feared that might only jeopardize its property exemption.[14] In 1872 the territorial government, while regrading the Georgetown streets in order to lay new water pipes and sewers, cut off the college system from the main lines, apparently in order to conserve water. Pleading by both college officials and friends for several weeks finally secured a special legislative act that ordered resumption of water service from the nearby Georgetown reservoir that had originally been built for the whole federal district by the Army Corps of Engineers.[15]

Both Bernard Maguire and John Early (Early succeeded Maguire as president of Georgetown for a second time in 1870) were accomplished diplomats, adept at reconciling the college to the new society in Washington. Both Presidents Johnson and Grant presided at Georgetown commencement exercises during their terms, as did General William Tecumseh Sherman in 1871, and Governor Cooke in 1872. (Sherman's son, Thomas, had entered the college in 1869.) Jesuits at the college had already begun to serve the new communities of black Catholics that formed in Washington and Tenleytown in the late 1860s. They went out to St. Ann's and St. Augustine's parishes, not only to satisfy pastoral needs but intellectual ones as well. For instance, Father Anthony Cicci gave several lectures on chemistry in 1869 to black Catholics in Washington.[16]

Nonetheless, the college as a whole remained a conservative, pro-Southern Democratic stronghold. In the 1872 mock presidential election on campus, Greeley easily defeated Grant, fifty-three to fifteen.[17] Moreover, in reporting on the dominance of military units and artillery in the inaugural parade the following March, the *College Journal* commented that such a spectacle—of President-elect Grant, "surrounded by a large number of armed men, with bayonets glittering, caused many . . . to think of the time when victorious Caesar, the destroyer of his country's liberties, attended by a consular army, triumphed through the streets of Rome." It was not an auspicious event for the republic, concluded the *Journal* on the first day of April 1873.[18] Students and faculty took encouragement from the brief revolution against the Republican government of Louisiana in the fall of 1874 to hope that Reconstruction was on its last legs. And there was great excitement when the Democrats won back control of the House of Representatives in 1874. Both students and faculty attended closely the impeachment trial of Secretary of the Interior Belknap in 1876, barely disguising also their delight over the other mounting scandals of the Grant administration.[19] Redemption from the excesses of Reconstruction seemed to be imminent in the 1876 Presidential election. The traditional mock election, following the mock conventions, was held on campus. All except the youngest boys were obliged to vote. Several students in blackface, as well as others carrying carpetbags and umbrellas, were escorted to the polls by the college cadets in a somewhat heavy-handed satirical comment on the Republican candidate. Not surprisingly, the campus tally was ten times more for Tilden than for Hayes (101 to 11).[20] For the next several weeks the campus intensely followed the developments over the actual, hotly contested election. (As it turned out, two sets of returns from each of four states were ultimately handled in favor of the Republican candidate.) Georgetown alumnus William Corcoran, a banker and a leading figure in the local Democratic party, confidently but mistakenly assured Patrick Healy that on November 24 "there was no doubt whatever about the election of Mr. Tilden."[21] When the special Electoral Commission finally awarded Hayes the disputed votes on March 2, 1877, there was outrage on the Hilltop among the faculty as well as among the students. Indeed, on March 5 (the day after the inauguration) the official college diarist took note of the "compromise" with unconcealed bitterness: "Inauguration of President? Hayes, who was declared elected by fraud, bribery & corruption."[22]

Patrick Healy

In 1867 Father Joseph O'Callaghan was appointed prefect of studies (dean) at the college in order to take on responsibilities that had formerly been included in the president's duties. Subsequently, while he, the new prefect, was returning home from a meeting in Rome in January of 1868, the schooner on which he had taken passage encountered a severe storm. The huge waves that crashed through the schooner's rigging and decks killed several passengers, including O'Callaghan.[23] Patrick Healy, who had been acting prefect in O'Callaghan's absence, was thereupon named the new prefect of studies.

The thirty-five-year-old Father Healy was, in a sense, an improbable candidate for such an important position at a still Southern college. Born in 1834 in central Georgia, he was the second son of a white immigrant planter, Michael Healy, and his black, common-law wife, Mary Eliza. Mary Eliza's half sister, Ellen Craft, also a slave in Georgia, became a celebrated figure in Abolitionist circles after she and her husband made a successful escape to a free state in the North in 1848. Several years before that, Michael Healy, anxious to provide for his own children—all slaves according to Georgia law—had sent the older five (one daughter and four sons), including Patrick, to schools in New York and Massachusetts for their education. At Holy Cross the four Healy brothers came under the influence of George Fenwick. He helped the young students cope with being marginal—neither white nor black—in a white "Anglo" world, especially after the death of their father in 1850 (their mother had died a short time before). Under Fenwick's tutelage the four Healys were all instructed and baptized as Catholics. Three eventually studied for the priesthood. Patrick's oldest brother, James, became the second bishop of Portland, Maine; a younger brother, Sherwood, was appointed vicar-general of the archdiocese of Boston. Michael, also younger, became a naval commander in the Revenue Cutter Service. In Alaska he was known as "Hell-Roaring Mike" during his lively nautical career in what is now a branch of the U.S. Coast Guard. (Three of the five sisters—Martha, Josephine, and Eliza—also entered religious life; Eliza became superior of her community in Montreal.)[24]

Patrick Healy had first come to Georgetown in the late summer of 1850, having just graduated from Holy Cross. The Jesuit superiors were aware, of course, of his mixed-race background and so-called illegitimate status. "If you think these are no impediment," John Early, then president of Holy Cross, wrote the provincial superior, "I consider him as a young man in every way worthy of being rec[eive]d."[25] Within days, Healy entered the novitiate at Frederick, Maryland. After teaching at Holy Cross in Worcester and at St. Joseph's in Philadelphia, he was sent to Rome in 1858 to complete his philosophical and theological formation. Impending civil war in Italy forced his Jesuit superiors to transfer Patrick and other Jesuit scholastics to Leuven (Louvain) in Belgium, where Patrick earned his licentiate at the Jesuit theologate on Minderbroederstraat.[26] He was assigned to Georgetown in 1866 to teach philosophy to scholastics.

Although Patrick was the lightest complexioned of the Healy brothers and usually passed as white, he was still legally a black man in nineteenth-century American society. This would seem to explain why his previous periods of formation and teaching assignments had all been in the North or abroad. It also probably explains why his superiors initially restricted his teaching at Georgetown to Jesuit scholastics. Nonetheless, at the very time when concerns and rumors about black social and political revolutions were stirring fear and reaction among many whites in Washington, his superiors unhesitatingly appointed a partly African American Jesuit to a key academic position at Georgetown. Stephen Mallory (**C** 1865–69), the son of a former Confederate cabinet officer, who took Healy's philosophy course in his senior year, remembered him as "a finished scholar, a remarkable linguist, and the clearest thinker and expounder of his thoughts that I have ever met."[27] In his new position Patrick Healy also gradually and gracefully took his place in Washington's social life. Cora Semmes, Benedict's sister who had married Joseph Christmas Ives and had two sons at Georgetown, became a fast friend.

So did Julia Gardiner Tyler, the ex-president's widow, whom Healy baptized, along with her daughter and granddaughter, in 1872 at the Visitation Convent.[28]

Curricular Reform

During the twelve eventful years that he was prefect of studies, Patrick Healy accelerated the modernization of the curriculum begun before the war by downplaying the classics somewhat and at the same time increasing the presence of the sciences, which previously had been limited to the final year of the course of studies. Under Healy, students began the study of chemistry and physiology as Poets (or sophomores). Rhetoricians (or juniors) were introduced to organic chemistry and mechanics. Philosophers (or seniors) took physics and botany. This was a clear departure from the *Ratio Studiorum,* which since Renaissance times had paid relatively scant attention to the sciences and mathematics. But as the regional superior, Joseph Keller, explained to Roman authorities, in America as in France and England, it was now necessary to stress these disciplines more than had traditionally been done. If their graduates were to have influence in society, it was vital "to make them very adept in the sciences."[29] Whether the initiative was Keller's (whose authority would have been needed to make such changes, in any case) or Healy's, the sciences at Georgetown soon became an integral and substantial part of the curriculum.

Patrick F. Healy, SJ. Prefect of Studies from 1868 to 1880. Photograph taken ca. 1877. (Georgetown University Archives)

Healy also increased the emphasis on English literature. George F. Holmes, a distinguished scholar who held the chair of history and literature at the University of Virginia, was invited to give a series of monthly lectures on English studies and literature to the senior students in the 1870–71 academic year.

But if science and vernacular literature were given more emphasis in the curriculum, Healy continued to regard the classics as central to liberal education. He attempted to set more rigorous and demanding standards for Greek and Latin studies. In his 1870 Prefect's Report he applauded the senior classes for handling well more subject matter than they had been accustomed to previously or, indeed, had been expected to know. It was his intention, he told them, to bring them to a point where they could read classical languages with facility and write them with elegance.[30] Oral and written examinations continued to be held twice yearly, now not only for the classics but for mathematics and the sciences as well. Philosophers were still expected to write theses in order to graduate. By 1871 the academic calendar had also been modernized, with the two semesters ending in January and June.

Since the 1840s students had been given the option of remaining an additional year to do further work in the various branches of mathematics and philosophy (including natural philosophy) in order to receive the master of arts degree. In 1867 six such degrees were awarded. Then, under Healy the college began to offer its first formal "postgraduate" program, which included courses in the history of philosophy, natural law, and "special branches of science." Master of arts degrees were awarded to some twenty-one graduates of this program between 1869 and 1873. Those traditional master's degrees previously given to alumni on the basis of their postcollegiate achievements were thereafter designated as "honorary" when they were awarded.

Woodstock College

Since 1806 Georgetown had provided higher studies in philosophy and theology for the Jesuit scholastics (many of whom had also served as teachers and prefects of discipline for the lay students). Moreover the College had received its pontifical charter in 1833, which authorized it to award degrees to graduates of these philosophy and theology "schools." However, for two decades at least, pressure had been building to relocate the scholasticate or formation center for scholastics or at least to separate it academically from Georgetown College. Jesuit superiors in both America and Rome worried about the economic costs of formation in an expensive city such as Washington and the dubious economics of Jesuit students taking the time to double as teachers and prefects.[31] In 1855 the superior general, Peter Beckx, suggested that Georgetown College be converted from an undergraduate college into a general training center reserved for all Jesuit scholastics in the United States. Charles Stonestreet, the Maryland provincial superior at the time, protested that it would be folly to close Georgetown College, "the mother of American science and piety; known in Europe and virtually everywhere . . . [and] even by Protestants it was recently called 'The Sebastapol of Religion.'"[32]

Stonestreet's successor as provincial, Burchard Villiger, conceded a few years later that Georgetown, with its apparent exploitation of Jesuit students as part-time teachers, was hardly an apt place for their religious and intellectual formation. He suggested as a permanent scholasticate the Jesuit farm at Conewago, in southeastern Pennsylvania, "where the air is healthy and there are no distractions." For the time being (February 1859), he proposed moving the scholastics to Boston where John McElroy had constructed a college that he had been unable to staff and open.[33] Nearly two years later, Villiger's suggestion became an order when an official visitor from Rome directed that all the Jesuit scholastics be transferred to Boston until adequate facilities could be provided at Conewago as a scholasticate for all Jesuits in the United States. However, the Civil War as well as a lack of money delayed any construction at the farm in Conewago.[34] The scholastics remained at

Boston until 1863, when rising costs so exceeded revenues that the Jesuit authorities were forced to recall the scholastics to their separate provinces and missions.[35] The Maryland scholastics returned to Georgetown.

Meanwhile, opposition to the Conewago decision mounted. At the provincial congregation held in the fall of 1861 in Baltimore, all the delegates, with the exception of Angelo Paresce, the provincial superior, had favored keeping the scholasticate at Georgetown. Nonetheless, the superior general kept pressing Paresce to locate the scholasticate in a rural spot. In 1861 a generous bequest of land in Pennsylvania by the Duchess of Leeds, Charles Carroll's granddaughter, enabled the provincial superior to begin looking at affordable sites closer to Georgetown.[36] In 1864 he found a suitable tract of land (139 acres) some twenty miles west of Baltimore, on the Baltimore and Ohio railroad line. There, at Woodstock, he had a building constructed for the imposing cost of $232,000.[37] From Georgetown came both the nucleus of the library and the faculty. Fathers Benedict Sestini, Anthony Cicci, Camillus Mazzella, and Dominick Pantanella, along with several scholastics, all departed for this new Woodstock College in 1869. The loss of such a significant part of the faculty, especially the scholastics, forced Georgetown to turn to lay professors to fill the vacuum. The college engaged eighteen lay faculty over the next five years. These included recent graduates Stephen Mallory and John Hedrick, who taught part-time while they worked for master's degrees in the new Georgetown graduate program. There were also some students in the new law department who became part-time college teachers. But they were a highly transient group; two-thirds of them remained only a year or less. At the college, except for certain traditional peripheral subjects (such as music), the employment of lay faculty continued to be regarded as a stopgap measure, to be used only until Jesuits were available to replace them.

Student Demographics

Bernard Maguire, whom Rome appointed president of Georgetown for the second time at the close of the Civil War, recalled that "We could not depend on the South now ruined by the reverses of War & the students were from every section of the country perfectly united & marching under the old flag. . . ."[38] That indeed did become the pattern by the late 1870s (table 10.1 in appendix F). But in the decade after Appomattox (1865–75), Southerners—notably from Virginia, Louisiana, and Georgia—returned to the college in surprisingly large numbers and soon comprised almost a third (31.7%) of the students. In 1865 and 1866 alone, more than one hundred young men from below the Potomac entered the college as first-year students. Among the fathers of those postwar Southern students there were a former governor of Virginia (John Floyd), two Confederate generals (Carnot Posey, Bennett Barton Simmes), the Confederate secretary of the navy (Stephen Mallory), a Confederate congressman (Charles Wells Russell), and the notorious guerrilla leader John Singleton Mosby. John Hedrick, the son of Benjamin Sherwood Hedrick, was also an entering student in 1866. The senior Hedrick had been forced to resign from the faculty of the University of North Carolina in 1856 when his antislavery views became public.

The Southern students at Georgetown during the Reconstruction years (from the war's end through 1877) differed somewhat from their antebellum predecessors in several ways. Before the war, nearly two-fifths (39%) of Georgetown's Southerners had been from rural areas; now the largest group or more than a third of them (37%) hailed from cities and the second largest or a third came from small towns (33%). The professions of law and medicine continued to rank highest as the occupations of their fathers, but business had supplanted military and planter occupations for the other fathers. The length of stay of the Southerners as collegians was also briefer (less than a year) than it had been earlier. At fifteen, they were, on average, a year older than their fellow students from other regions. Approximately half were non-Catholic. Every tenth Southerner had no father—understandable since more than a quarter million adult Southern men died during the war.

Those from the Northeast and Northcentral regions together made up a third (33.2%) of the student population, considerably more than their antebellum proportion. Among them were William Garesché (**C** 1869–71, AB), the nephew of Julius Garesché; Ignatius Donnelly (**C** 1867–68), the son and namesake of the Western Grange and Populist reformer; Henry Walters (**C** 1865–69, AB), who afterwards became president of the Atlantic Coast Line and the founder of the prominent Baltimore art gallery; James Francis Tracey (**C** 1869–74, AB) of New York, later an associate justice of the Supreme Court of the Philippines; and Henry Collins Walsh (**C** 1867–68, 1874–80), who went on to edit the *Catholic World* and *The Smart Set*.

In the five years of President Maguire's second administration (1866–70), enrollment in the college declined from a high of 231 in 1866 to a low of 162 in the year 1870. The chief reason for that disturbing drop was the loss not of Southern but of local students. Day students had made up a quarter of the college enrollment in 1865; by 1870 they accounted for only a tenth of the enrollment. The introduction of public schooling throughout the District probably had some minor impact; but demilitarization and the reduction of the government bureaucracy toward prewar levels were even more consequential. A third factor was an upward change in the minimal age requirement in 1870. Since John Carroll had originally set the minimal age for admission at eight years, the college had continued to receive some very young students. In fact, in the immediate postwar years no fewer than fifty boys between the ages of six and eleven were admitted. By the end of the decade, however, a shift in attitude and policy was deemed necessary. Indeed, when the nine-year-old Eugene Francis Arnold ran away in 1869, the official Jesuit diarist had written, "I hope he is the last of the babies."[40] A year later the authorities determined that no one under the age of twelve ("an age at which one is capable of appreciating the advantages of college life") should be accepted in the future.[41] With few exceptions this became the rule in the 1870s and thereafter.

Maguire found his postwar students "more studious, more obedient & they all felt the necessity of hard work—Many of them had spent some years under military discipline & now came to devote themselves to serious work. . . ."[42] Nevertheless, among the five hundred and seventy-two students who entered between 1865 and 1869, there were only eighteen veterans, all but one of them former Confederate soldiers. William Cowardin, who served as sergeant of the Boys' Batallion of Richmond, was still not sixteen years old when, in poor health, he returned to the Hilltop he had left in 1863. Like John Dooley the war had left Cowardin tuberculous, but unlike John Dooley, he survived the disease to serve for many years on the faculty—first at Georgetown and then at Holy Cross. Cowardin was one of five Confederate Army veterans who eventually entered the Society of Jesus. Another, Stephen Mallory of Florida, the son of the Confederacy's secretary of the navy, was at seventeen a veteran of both the Rebel army and navy. And many of those who had been too young for combat duty had nevertheless been caught up in the war and deeply affected by it. John Carroll Payne (**C** 1869–76, AB) remembered his naive thrill as a seven-year-old encountering a Confederate burial party in the midst of their grisly work on the battlefield of Second Manassas in September 1862. Later that summer his grandmother's house was used as a hospital (he was staying there since his mother had died and his father was in the army). One night in the downstairs parlor filled with the wounded, the young Payne had to man a broom to keep the rats away from them. "I could hear the drip, drip of the blood [from a soldier's leg] dripping to the floor and seeing the bright eyes of the rats under his bed, . . . I screamed out loud with horror, so bad were my nerves. . . ." Nonetheless, the end of hostilities three years later and the dispersement of the armies, his "source of constant excitement," left the now ten-year-old Virginian feeling that "my every-day life was flat . . . all my pleasure had been destroyed."[43]

The war had almost totally disrupted education in the South. One alumnus wrote in 1867 to Maguire about the possibility of entering his nephew in the college. The latter was, he owned, "a well grown lad; but owing to the terrible & trying scenes through which the southern country has been passing for some years, we have had no schools, and his education has been greatly neglected."[44] Payne, whose schooling had similarly suffered, found himself much behind his Northern classmates in academic learning ("arithmetic, grammar and geography") although not in "world[ly] knowledge."[45] After two years of hard studying, Payne began to collect "every medal the college could grant . . ."[46]

The Class of 1869—Georgetown's most notable class in the nineteenth century. Those identified include Walter Abell, seated at the right; Stephen Mallory, seated at the center; Henry Walters standing at the right; and James Coleman, standing at the left. (Georgetown University Archives)

Beyond the disruption of education in the South was the unaccustomed poverty that now marked the South's former privileged groups. "Those who before the civil war wore purple," wrote Father Francis McAtee from Southern Maryland, "now lack food and clothing."[47] John Carroll Payne arrived at Georgetown clothed in homespun clothes and, for his first few years, was rather miserable in the presence of well-dressed Northerners. The war had left Payne's lawyer father, like so many Southerners of his class, in financial ruin. He wrote the authorities at Georgetown College and Georgetown Visitation Convent in 1867 to ask if they would take his son and two daughters as students on the strength of his promise to pay for their education when he could. Both schools accepted them on that condition. That same year, another alumnus, General Bennett Barton Simmes of Louisiana (**C** 1827–28), inquired about the possibility of aid for his two sons, one of whom was already at the college. "[T]he result of our terrible conflict has so reduced my means," he stated, "that I fear my inability . . . to have my only two sons educated at George Town College—Sad, indeed, must be the tale, that your Southern children must tell. Their future is full of gloom—the South *must educate and trust to God for his* [sic] *future.*"[48] (The general was also given tuition assistance.) Many other Southerners were given similar help by the college. Indeed, one-third of the Confederate veterans received help. The percentage of Southerners given financial aid during the initial postwar years nearly quadrupled. Nearly a seventh (about 16%) of the students from below the Potomac were given either free tuition and board or reduced fees. Including those from Maryland, Southern students, who constituted just over half (51%) of the student population, received two-thirds (66%) of the financial assistance given by Georgetown. Most of these Southerners were from Maryland and Virginia.

The Religious Ethos

Defeat and poverty also seems to have helped cultivate a more religious sensibility in the postbellum students (at least many of the Southern ones). A sign of the changed temper of the times was the large number of students joining the Sodality, which replaced the debating societies as the most popular organization on campus. Indeed, Sodalists outnumbered debaters by nearly three to one. Southerners were particularly prominent in the Sodality, a marked change from their prewar pattern. For instance, eleven of the seventeen Confederate veterans who enrolled in the postwar years were Sodalists. In all, about a third of the Southern students belonged to the Sodality. Since the Sodality was restricted to Catholics, who were only a little more than half (57%) of the student body in the years immediately following the war, this meant that virtually half the Catholics (48%) in the school and a majority of those from the South (56%) were Sodalists. Ironically, their overall numbers declined in the next decade, despite the great increase of Catholics within the school (to more than 80% by 1880).

In general, the religious ethos intensified during the years following the war. The daily routine of Mass and common prayers continued for all students, as did seasonal devotions such as the Marian observances in May and the novena to the Sacred Heart in June, and new devotions, both daily and seasonal, were added. Stations of the Cross were erected for the first time in the students' chapel, and weekly confession became a requirement. In 1869 there was an elaborate Corpus Christi procession around the walks, with the cadet military companies as honor guard for the reserved Sacrament, and a band provided sacred music.[49] A novena to St. Aloysius was introduced and his feast was elaborately celebrated on June 21. In conformity with the decree of the First Vatican Council (1869–70), St. Joseph's feast in March also became an annual solemn liturgical occasion at Georgetown. In 1872 his statue was placed in the infirmary garden, the first such monument on campus. John McElroy, then ninety years old, gave the address of dedication.

The College Sodality. Robert Douglas, son of Senator Stephen Douglas, is seated third from the left, next to the Jesuit moderator. Photograph taken by Alexander Gardner, ca. 1865. (Georgetown University Archives)

A highlight of the academic year now was the feast of the Immaculate Conception in December, which paralleled and, in terms of intensity, to some degree replaced the earlier secular celebrations of Washington's birthday and the Fourth of July. At a solemn high Mass attended by the entire student body the new Sodalists were received into the organization. Then, in the evening there was a formal address by a Jesuit and a solemn renewal by all of their promise to keep the rules of the Sodality faithfully. Benediction and a grand feast for the sodalists, complete with speeches and readings and toasts, ended the feast day. And gradually the civic "holy days" dropped out of the yearly calendar of events at the college. By 1872 and thereafter, February 22 was simply another class day, and the Fourth of July fell during what had come to be the summer vacation. In the immediate postwar years Thanksgiving Day was the major occasion for the college's revived cadet corps to march to the villa and, accompanied by the U.S. Marine Band, to there display their martial skills. But records after 1869 seem to indicate that the holiday ceased to be observed, and the grand review of the student military company on parade became part of the celebrations included in the religious observances of the month of May during the next decade.

Another important development in the spiritual culture of the students was the establishment on the campus of the Confraternity of the Apostleship of Prayer, a voluntary association for practicing and spreading devotion to the Sacred Heart. The Confraternity was also promoted nationwide by the *Messenger of the Sacred Heart,* a devotional magazine founded by Benedict Sestini at Georgetown in 1866. Through articles in the *Messenger* and the listing of the monthly prayer intentions, the students were kept abreast of the declining temporal power of Pope Pius IX (increasingly identified with the suffering Heart of Jesus), as well as of the need to confirm the supreme moral and spiritual authority of the pope in the face of the impending collapse of his political authority. Those who could not join the Papal Zouaves in defending the pontiff and the Papal States from the armies of Garibaldi and Victor Emmanuel (as John Surratt had done in 1865) were encouraged to at least make reparation through their prayers for the attacks.[50]

When Rome finally fell to the soldiers of the Italian nationalists in 1870, abruptly suspending the Ecumenical Council (Vatican I) and forcing the pontiff to take shelter in the Vatican enclave, the students needed no prompting from the Jesuits to express their feelings. In early November, while President Early was in Baltimore welcoming back Archbishop Spalding from Rome, a spontaneous demonstration took place on campus. "At seven o'clock last evening," George Hamilton wrote to his father, "the boys assembled *en masse* for the purpose of protesting against the occupation of Rome by Victor Emanuel [sic] and of the imprisonment of the Pope. . . . Many fine speeches were made by the boys; And various resolutions were passed, all expressing indignation . . . and sympathy for the Pope . . . It was resolved . . . that since the Pope is now deprived of all his possessions and revenues, a subscription should be raised for his benefit. . . . every boy is subscribing."[51] (The Papal States within Italy, as well as Rome itself, had been taken over and annexed to Italy earlier that year.)

When Archbishop Spalding came to Washington the following Thanksgiving Day, his visit became the occasion for a solemn demonstration of support and sympathy for the "prisoner of the Vatican." The college presented the archbishop with a check for $500, more than half of which had come directly from the students.[52] A second demonstration was held at the college in June of 1871, and another collection went to Pius IX, along with a handsomely written tribute from the faculty and students:

Your children in this distant hemisphere are not willing to believe that peoples nearer than they to that ancient seat of your authority, of which you have been unjustly robbed, can be more faithful, more devoted to you than themselves. . . . We, the professors and students of Georgetown College, wish to reiterate the protest . . . against the indignities to which your Holiness has been subjected . . . and to add the hope . . . that the days of your Holiness' liberation are rapidly approaching, though the period be undiscerned by human wisdom. Bless us, Holy Father, that we may ever be faithful to the teachings of our Infallible Head, and . . . know that no truer or warmer hearts beat in your behalf than those of your American children, the students of Georgetown college.[53]

As the provincial, Joseph Keller, wrote the superior general, "The afflictions of the Holy Father have made ultramontanes of all of us here. . . ."[54] Pius

IX, one of the faculty confessed, was "the only being on earth whom I would gladly, if I could, cross the ocean to see . . . and I know the warmth of sentiment which animates our students in regard to His Holiness and his violated rights." He proudly noted that the November Georgetown rally on behalf of the pope "was the *first* held by Catholic students in the United States, was an *entirely spontaneous* movement, and was managed by themselves alone."[55]

Three years later at another mass meeting Georgetown students voted to send with a group of pilgrims an American flag to be raised at Lourdes (the shrine where Mary was reputed to have identified herself in 1854 under the title of the Immaculate Conception, the first doctrine to be infallibly defined by a pope).[56] The flag was then to be taken to the Vatican for the pope's blessing, and finally back to Lourdes for permanent display. "It was a perfect success," Cora Semmes Ives wrote Patrick Healy about the ovations they had received at both Lourdes and Rome. "They think that Catholicity is antagonistical to liberty, but when they see America standing foremost in her devotion to the Holy See, & that our faith does not trammel our liberty it will have a wonderful moral effect."[57] (Her two sons, Eugene Semmes Ives (**C** 1870–78) and Frank J. Ives (**C** 1871–74) had carried the flag.) The irony of Southern "rebels" presenting an American flag to the pontiff was not lost on them, but the mother at least took it as a sign "that she must give up thinking of the lost hopes of a once prosperous nation, but try & love that flag which has crushed her people into submission."[58] Whatever their mixed feelings, in the pilgrims one could easily imagine a new motto framing the school's mission:"For pope, country, and Georgetown."

Another sign of the heightened religious sensibility at Georgetown was the increase in vocations to the priesthood during the immediate postwar period. In the entire thirty years before the war the total number of vocations is known to have been fifty-two. Of those who entered the college in the six postwar years between 1864 and 1870, twenty-three studied for the priesthood, including five Confederate veterans. Moreover, ten of the twenty-three were from the South, a radical change from the antebellum pattern. Timothy O'Leary had been born in Ireland but had immigrated with his family to the Staunton area of western Virginia in 1853. A member of the Virginia home guard, he made his way to Baltimore through the federal lines in 1863 in the hope of joining the Jesuits. Sent to Georgetown for additional academic preparation, O'Leary entered the novitiate in 1864. Thomas Ewing Sherman (**C** 1869–72, AB), the son of the famous Union general, entered the Society, despite the bitter opposition of his non-Catholic father, after earning his B.S. at the Sheffield Scientific School at Yale. The younger Sherman became a noted Catholic preacher and apologist throughout the country in the 1880s and 1890s. John Dooley, who entered the Society in 1865, returned to Georgetown in 1868 to teach and study theology, but the tuberculosis that he had acquired during his long imprisonment on Johnson's Island steadily worsened and left him an invalid by 1870. He died at Georgetown

Left: Thomas H. Stack (**C** 1866–68). Afterwards, as a Jesuit, he became president of Boston College. Photograph taken ca. 1872. (Georgetown University Archives)

Right: Francis Barnum (**C** 1866–72). Afterwards, as a Jesuit, he became a missionary to Alaska. Photograph taken ca. 1868. (Georgetown University Archives)

in May 1873, remembered "as a choice and beautiful soul that God left us for a while to show us how virtue may be made amiable."[59]

John Patrick Farrelly of Arkansas (**C** 1870–73) studied for the priesthood in the Diocese of Little Rock and eventually became Bishop of Cleveland. John Hedrick of North Carolina (**C** 1866–71, AB) entered the Society in 1879. Thomas Stack of Virginia (**C** 1866–68), who had been an artilleryman during the war, came to Georgetown after hearing Bernard Maguire preach a mission in Virginia. He entered the Society in 1868 and later was president of Boston College. Francis Barnum (**C** 1866–72) of Maryland, the son of a railroad capitalist and Baltimore hotel owner, became a noted Jesuit missionary to Alaska, a prison chaplain, and a retreat master. The next decade, however, would only produce a total of two vocations.

The Postwar Student Societies

With the exception of the Sodality, these proved to be lean years for the traditional student extracurricular activities. The Philodemic debating society sponsored a reunion of its alumni in 1867, in effect the first alumni reunion in the college's history. From that first reunion came a resolution to "regather" every three years. Subsequent "Triennial" celebrations took place in 1871 and 1874 but ceased thereafter. The Dramatic Association had failed to survive the war. In its place a Dramatic Reading Association was formed in 1868 to provide a modest showcase for eloquent literature. Student minstrels were inaugurated in 1865, with no higher object than to provide what would be viewed in the twentieth century as crude escapist entertainment. In those days the minstrels were naively described by one such group as ways "to amuse—to create a tiny oasis in the monotony of our daily life."[60] The college cadets were reorganized in the winter of 1865–66, their commander a lay faculty member and former Confederate army officer, Colonel Edmund Crimmins. For several years the cadet companies of both older and younger students drilled and trained on campus and at the villa. Periodically, the Corps demonstrated their skills by marching through Georgetown or to Washington. In February 1869 they paraded to the city to greet President-elect Ulysses S. Grant. Annual reviews were held on either Thanksgiving Day or May Day for which prizes, donated by friends of the college, were awarded for sharpshooting and precision drills. But, as one student recalled, "drill was not very popular, for there was no great military spirit among the boys."[61] That was typical of the temper of postwar America in general. (The National Rifle Association was also founded in 1871 precisely to rekindle a martial spirit that its sponsors feared the country was losing; for a number of years, the NRA remained a barely viable organization.)[62] Less than a tenth of the students (about 8% altogether) joined either company. By 1871 college authorities had decided that they could no longer enforce obligatory drill[63] and, unsurprisingly, the cadet corps disappeared by the middle 1870s (about the same time as the institutional requirement of a uniform for all lay students was quietly discontinued).

One new organization that flourished was the *College Journal.* It began publishing in 1872 at the initiative of some students with guidance from a Jesuit professor, Edmund Young, who had founded a similar student publication a few years earlier at Santa Clara College.[64] Among the *Journal's* founders were William Caidwell Niblack (**C** 1864–74, AB), the son of an Indiana congressman; Henry Collins Walsh (**C** 1867–89), the grandson of Robert Walsh and later editor of *Lippincott's Magazine* as well as the *Catholic World;* and William Henry Dennis (**C** 1869–74). (Dennis was the grandson of the headmaster of the Quaker school on Long Island that the Healy children had first attended after they left Georgia.) William Dennis brought considerable publishing experience to the paper since, as a thirteen-year-old, he had built his own printing press in Philadelphia and was publishing and printing his own journal by 1869.

For that journal he put together a network of boy writers in several cities. Officers of Georgetown's *College Journal* were elected by the members, including the faculty member who served as its president. To fund the publication, a joint stock company was formed by the twenty-five charter members whose membership shares cost five dollars each.[65] In addition, subscriptions were solicited from students and alumni, as were advertisements. In the first decade of the *Journal,* the students themselves set the type for the four- to eight-page publication, but they hired an outside job printer for the actual printing.[66] The monthly was a combination newspaper, journal of opinion, and literary magazine. In addition to providing campus and alumni news, the *College Journal* published editorials on national and international events, poems, essays on literary subjects, obituaries, and occasional reviews of political events. Short stories also became a standard feature in the late 1880s.

The Rise of Organized Sports

The decline of traditional organizations like the debating and drama societies was offset by and partly caused by the rise of organized sports. Recreation patterns began to change in American colleges in the aftermath of the war. Swimming and skating on the canal, as well as handball, continued to be popular at Georgetown. Cycling became a campus fad as early as the late 1860s. (Invented in 1839 in Scotland, the bicycle was already much used abroad when Americans took to it.) By 1869 professional velocipedists were giving classes to students willing to pay to learn the art.[67] "Every afternoon," one student remembered, "a group of us would wheel around the walks."[68] By the early 1870s billiard tables were being installed in campus buildings. Boxing also became a popular activity in the postwar years.

Such individual recreation could not really compete with the first organized athletic teams at Georgetown, the baseball clubs. Baseball had been informally played on campus since the 1850s, when interest in the sport was growing in the northeast, culminating in the establishment of the National Association of Base Ball Players in 1858. (The Baseball Club of Washington was organized in 1859.) That year also saw the first intercollegiate baseball game, between Amherst and Williams. Although the sport was played in both Northern and Southern cities well before 1861, the Civil War may have inadvertently made baseball truly the national pasttime since it was much played in Northern and Southern military camps alike throughout the conflict. [69] And, after the collapse of the Confederacy, interest in baseball, spurred by newspaper publicity and by teams touring by rail, became a national mania as semiprofessional and amateur clubs multiplied across the reunited land. Among the latter were the many college teams that began to form and to play games against other colleges and municipal teams.[70]

Baseball at Georgetown followed this pattern. As early as the spring of 1866 intramural teams were playing games before spectators on the college grounds at the southeastern corner of the campus.[71] The first two clubs were organized the following autumn, their names, the Quicksteps and the Stonewalls, reflected the lingering impact of the war. The sport then was really a form of softball, played with gloveless fielders and a pitcher who had to throw a large, soft ball underhanded within the borders of a home plate. Consequently, high-scoring games, involving more than forty runs, were common. By 1869 baseball fever had struck the campus, including the faculty (the Jesuit diarist was recording that "Baseball occupies the attention of all").[72] Class teams were formed, as well as the two collegiate nines. At each game many spectators, both students and visitors, crowded the banks surrounding the playing field. President John Early was as much an enthusiast as anyone, even permitting extra holidays so students could go to Washington to watch games between the local semiprofessional club, the Washington Olympics, and teams from other cities, such as the Boston Red Stockings. Not everyone on campus, however, was caught up in the baseball mania. When President Early granted students yet another permission in 1872 to attend a game in Washington, Prefect Patrick Healy was disgusted: "Such things have been done before," he wrote in the official diary, "but it is a sorry practice, at best. The Schools of a University dismissed to see a BB. match!!"[73]

By 1868 the college had already clearly recognized the importance of organized sport as an integral part of student recreation in an educational community and was advertising its athletic facilities and promotion of sports culture as a way of attracting students. The catalogue noted that "organizations for the practice of athletic sports," like the two baseball teams, "are encouraged. The grounds afford every facility for physical exercises, and are provided with ball-alleys and gymnastic apparatus." The competition between the Quicksteps and Stonewalls rapidly built up. For a decade the two clubs were, in effect, the athletic center of Georgetown. In May of 1870 the playoff of a grand championship was begun; when rain halted the game, the students (both players and spectators) were given a partial holiday the next day so that the contest could be completed.[74] By the early 1870s the two teams were vigorously recruiting students from within the college. "These clubs," John Carroll Payne recalled, "would recruit from the boys coming over from the 'small boys' side [who had their own teams] and solicit all newcomers. . . ."[75] Payne himself was captain of the Quicksteps and of the College Nine. Southerners, in fact, seem to have won their fair share of positions on the various teams, a reflection, no doubt, of their increasingly urban background. On the 1872 College Nine, for instance, four of the eight starters were from the South.[76] A series of games between the two clubs each spring determined "the Champion Nine"; then the best players from both teams were chosen to represent Georgetown in games with outside baseball clubs.

Columbian College was the first intercollegiate opponent, playing a home-and-home series of six games (three at each college) with the Georgetown team in the spring and fall of 1870. Georgetown retired the trophy, a gilded baseball, by winning four of the six contests, the last two by the improbable

The Georgetown College Nine of 1875–76. Seated, from left to right: B. Campbell McNeal, Thomas J. Timmins, John Carroll Payne (captain), and Francis W. Dammann. Standing, from left to right: John Giraud Agar, James B. Risque, Edward A. Dolan, Thomas F. Mallan, James P. Dolan. Photograph taken ca. 1875. (Georgetown University Archives)

scores of 73–14 and 69–24. The college team was playing not only other college nines but municipal teams as well, including the Nationals and the
Olympics, the two Washington representatives in the National Association of
Professional Base Ball Players (newly formed that same year).[77] By the summer of 1871 the college team was traveling to play Mount St. Mary's of Emmitsburg, at a "neutral" site in Baltimore. By 1872 the younger boys were
playing contests against outside teams, such as Gonzaga Preparatory.

Postbellum Finances at the College

Despite the rising operating costs due to the hiring of lay faculty, and the decline in revenue resulting from the smaller enrollments of the early 1870s, the
college was able to keep its tuition and other fees at the Civil War level through
the 1870s. In part this was due to income from wartime property investments,
which the college corporation sold at a substantial profit afterwards.[78] Another steady source of income was produce sales from the sixty-three acre
farm north of the campus where Jesuit brothers and the mostly black farm
hands raised oats, potatoes, tobacco, cattle, and sheep. And at Georgetown
itself there was a vineyard behind the North building that produced grapes for
wine making. Then in 1874 stonemasons and carpenters, brought from Pennsylvania, constructed a large barn [later the O'Gara Building] on the hill west
of the college buildings to house draft animals and farm equipment.

   Already by 1867 the college had a capital fund of approximately $10,000,
and expected regular income for that year to amount to at least $12,000. The
college was also the beneficiary of several substantial legacies, totalling over
$25,000 in the late 1860s.[79] This substantial financial improvement revived
plans for a new building at Georgetown. Both Maguire and Early had entertained ideas for a new building early as 1858 but had been forced to post-
pone action because of lack of funding.[80] "The state of the finances of the
college is such to permit the undertaking of a building without danger," the
regional superior wrote to Rome in 1867.[81] The greatest needs were for a library, science laboratories, and a lecture hall. Construction of a new theologate in the late sixties proved a temporary interruption but by the early
1870s John Early was ready to begin consulting architects and discussing
matters of site and design with fellow Jesuit officials.

The Law Department

In 1870, the last year of Bernard Maguire's presidency, the university established its second professional school, the law department. Legal education in
the early nineteenth century, like its medical counterpart, had almost exclusively been developed and acquired through apprenticeships and case read-

ings in private offices. However, there were a few private law schools, like the Litchfield Law School in Connecticut (1784), and some proprietary schools affiliated with universities. Most of these latter were short-lived, but some chairs of law were established in universities. The earliest one was held by George Wyethe at the College of William and Mary in 1779; and James Ryder had proposed one for Georgetown in 1830. But in the egalitarian, anti-intellectual climate of Jacksonian America, formal education for lawyers won little support and bar admissions standards declined. By 1840 there were only nine university-affiliated law schools in the whole nation. By the eve of the Civil War, only nine state jurisdictions (of thirty-nine) even required a definite, minimal period of apprenticeship. Consistent professional standards were virtually nonexistent.[82]

Nonetheless, there were forces at work in the antebellum period that eventually made the formal study of the law and accredited entry to its practice a nationwide necessity. One such compelling force was the general reform of the law that had been going on since the beginning of the century through the Americanization and federalization of the common law. Other evident forces were the move toward codification, the establishment of the principle of judicial review, and other developments that put a premium on learning the principles of law rather than on its practice according to case-by-case interpretations of the fair application of law in a country whose growing complexity and consolidation were making society both interrelated and uniform as well as more and more legalistic. Thus, by 1860 there were twenty-one law schools in the country, and the School of Jurisprudence at Columbia University in the City of New York was preeminent. There Professor Theodore W. Dwight defined the hegemony of institutional legal education when he stated clearly that "principles before practice is the true watchword."[83] As public demand for greater control of fair legal practice was expressed in the bar associations and by a cry for standardized entrance examinations, the need greatly increased for law schools to provide intellectual formation for the profession in an academic setting. By 1870 members of the legal profession had to some degree accepted institutional academic training as an ideal and norm for the profession at least, but not a prerequisite for the practice of law. A vast majority of America's lawyers continued to receive their preparation through private apprenticeships that were more or less modeled on the English system.[84]

In Washington, where there was no law school, the growth of the government bureaucracy during the war provided an additional incentive for establishing one—the large civil service offered a market for students. In response, Columbian College established a law department in 1865 that scheduled all classes after 3 p.m. so as to accommodate federal workers. Georgetown followed with its own, similar "sunset" law school five years later.

Unlike the private initiative that had developed the medical department, the impetus for this new department came from within the university itself.

In fact, the university had been considering such a school for over a decade. In 1859 President John Early had approached William Merrick, then a federal judge, about the desirability of starting a law school. Merrick had in turn approached a fellow judge about joining the enterprise as a faculty member, but when that jurist declined, Early apparently pursued it no further.[85] Four years after the end of the war Early's successor revived the project. By September of 1869 the official diarist of the college recorded that "[T]he establishment of a law department is being seriously discussed by our friends in Washington. The medical faculty press it very warmly."[86] Why the latter should have taken such an active part in promoting a law school at Georgetown is not known. It is possible that in an emerging culture of professionalism in which the American university was seen as a major shaper and controller of the professions, the medical faculty were convinced that the addition of a law department at Georgetown would have a favorable impact upon the reputation and prestige of the entire institution. At any rate, it was a part-time member of the medical faculty, Joseph M. Toner, who convinced three local lawyers of the need to make Georgetown a complete university by establishing a law school.[87] When these three committed to form the core of a faculty, the directors of the university approved the establishment of the school in March 1870.[88]

From the beginning, Maguire and his directors intended the law department to be a closely integrated professional component of the university, not the independent affiliate that the medical department was. To ensure this, they specified that the president of the university was to serve as president of the department. As such, Maguire took on the task of selecting the law faculty and offering financial support for the new school.[89] Three of the first six he recruited were Catholics. By early June, when Maguire made the public announcement of the formation of the school at the college commencement, he had already secured a faculty of six lawyers and jurists for the first term of the school, which began in the fall of 1870. They included the three who had originally met with Toner—Judge Charles P. James, Charles W. Hoffman, and Martin F. Morris. James and Hoffman were appointed vice president and secretary-treasurer, respectively, of the new school.

Charles James, a graduate of Harvard College, had moved his law practice from his native Cincinnati to Washington during the Civil War. There he had been named to serve on the congressional commission appointed to codify the *Statutes of the United States*, an experience that gave him an exceptional comprehension of federal jurisprudence. James was appointed Professor of Law of Real and Personal Property.

Charles Hoffman was no stranger to Georgetown's administration since he had taught various subjects at the college, both before and after the war. The son of a Frederick County farmer, Hoffman had grown up in western Maryland and earned his bachelor's degree at Mount St. Mary's and then taught for three years at Georgetown. Then he served an apprenticeship in a

Martin Morris (**C** 1847–48).
Professor of constitutional
law. Photograph taken ca.
1880. (Georgetown University
Archives)

Frederick law office, and went on to practice law several years there before returning to Washington and Georgetown College for another three-year stint—from 1867 to 1870.[90] During the next twenty years, the "pioneering" years of the Law School, Hoffman taught criminal law and served as dean as well, from 1877 to 1890. Dean Hoffman was also law librarian of the United States Supreme Court from 1873 to 1893.

Martin Morris (1834–1909), the only Georgetown alumnus among the original law faculty (**C** 1847–48), had been brought to this country from Ireland by his parents as a small boy. For ten years he was a scholastic in the Society of Jesus but he felt obliged to leave in 1860 in order to care for his widowed mother. He qualified in law, was admitted to the Maryland Bar in 1863, and practiced in Baltimore for several years before moving to Washington in 1867 to become a law partner of Richard Merrick. For the next thirty-five years he taught the history of the law (later constitutional law) at Georgetown, and continued to teach even after he was named an associate justice of the Court of Appeals of the District of Columbia in 1893.

The other three faculty were justice Samuel Freeman Miller, J. Hubley Ashton, and General Thomas Ewing, Jr. The most distinguished and gifted of the new faculty, Justice Miller (1816–90), had given up a medical practice in Kentucky for the law in the 1840s. His strong antislavery convictions finally led him to move to Iowa in 1850 and eventually to leadership of the Republican party in that state. President Abraham Lincoln named him an associate justice of the Supreme Court in 1862. For four years Miller taught Constitutional Law and Equity at Georgetown. He was the sole member of the original faculty who was paid a salary ($250 in 1870–71).[91] The rest were reimbursed by sharing any profits that the school realized.

J. Hubley Ashton (1836–1907) also brought a distinguished record to the new school, having served as assistant attorney general of the United States from 1865 to 1868 and as acting attorney general in 1865. A Pennsylvanian, Ashton had graduated from the University of Pennsylvania in 1854 and then studied law in a traditional apprenticeship before going into practice in Philadelphia. During the war he was a district attorney in Pennsylvania; and in the late 1860s he represented the U.S. government in several international claims cases, notably the one involving Mexico in 1868. His appointment at Georgetown was as professor of pleading practice and evidence.

Thomas Ewing, Jr. (1829–96), the son of Senator Thomas Ewing, had practiced law in Kansas with his adopted brother, William Tecumseh Sherman, later to be the Union's great Civil War general. Ewing became a member of the Antislavery Party in Kansas and played a key role in forcing the Buchanan administration to abandon the Lecompton Constitution in 1858. In the Civil War as a brigadier general commanding the forces in the Kansas-

Missouri theatre, Ewing had distinguished himself by suppressing the guerrilla activities of the notorious William Quantrill and by successfully deflecting a much larger Confederate force attempting to take St. Louis in the fall of 1864. Coming to Washington to practice law after the surrender at Appomattox, he soon gained prominence as the very able trial lawyer for three of the defendants in the Lincoln assassination case. Later he served successfully in a similar capacity for President Andrew Johnson during his impeachment trial before the Senate. Ewing was, as one biographer noted, "a man of much personal magnetism, of a liberal scholarly mind, and great courage and independence of character."[92] At Georgetown he was appointed lecturer in international law.

All in all, it was an impressive faculty. Ashton, Miller, and James had undoubtedly been sought because of their reputations as well as for their obvious expertise. Indeed, local newspaper announcements about Georgetown's new law school in 1870–71 mentioned only their names. Both Miller and Ashton remained on the faculty for four years, James for three years. The curriculum itself encompassed a good deal more than the technical knowledge of the law. As one of the law school founders and its first dean, Justice James, in his address to the first graduates of the school, explained to them that learning the law meant gaining an appreciation of the culture and history that has produced it, "a study of history, of the forms and political operation of governments, of the condition of nations and their peculiar productions. . . ."[93]

But, as the size of the faculty shrank during the next ten years—a decline coincident with the country's economic decline after the Panic of 1873—so did the curriculum. By 1878 the historical and international courses had disappeared. Property and Contracts, Criminal Law, Law of Evidence, Pleading and Practice, and Equity Jurisprudence now constituted the offerings of the two-year program. Four professors now made up the regular faculty. But courses broad in scope and touching on the philosophy, history, and ethics of the law continued, in one way or another, to be part of the early curriculum. The method of instruction was still chiefly by lecture.

Although the university did emphasize the wide range of advantages that the city of Washington afforded any person considering the study of the law, the actual recruitment was surprisingly narrow. The catalogue reminded a potential newcomer that "Besides opportunities of hearing the arguments and forming the acquaintance of the most distinguished members of the American Bar, he has here the rare privilege of witnessing all the forms of judicial procedure from those of the petty local courts up to those of the Supreme Court of the United States, and of consulting the Law Library of Congress, which contains a collection of Law books unsurpassed in variety and extent." Nevertheless, the targeted student market was in reality a very limited, local one; and, significantly, the advertising for the school was confined to the newspapers in the Baltimore and Washington area. The Georgetown law department, like its medical counterpart, was an evening school for part-time students already working in the area and was taught exclusively by part-time faculty until well into the twentieth century (1921).

The first classes began on the first Wednesday of October in 1870 at a central downtown location, the Colonization Building on the northwest corner of Pennyslvania Avenue and 4-½ Street (the present site of the East Wing of the National Gallery). This building served as a home for the department until classes were moved in 1872 to the old Washington Seminary building on F Street near old St. Patrick's Church and the National Portrait Gallery. The early enrollments were highly encouraging. The first class of twenty-five included six students from Georgetown College, three of them graduates. Among these six was Alexander Porter Morse (**C** 1858–60, **L** 1870–72, LLB), who had spent two years at the college before going on to earn his bachelor's degree at Princeton. A Confederate army veteran, Morse was in Washington working as a correspondent for several Louisiana newspapers in 1870. He later became a specialist in international law. Eugene Brady (**C** 1865–70, AB, **L** 1870–72, LLB) of Richmond, Virginia, was a recent Georgetown graduate who in his final year had held most of the prestigious student offices in the college—president of the Philodemic, prefect of the Sodality, commander of the cadet corps. Another Georgetown College graduate in one of the first law classes was George E. Hamilton (**C** 1865–70, AB, **L** 1870–72, LLB) of Charles County, Maryland. After graduation Hamilton joined the firm of Morris and Merrick and then in 1885 the Georgetown faculty. His long tenure in the Law School included two terms as dean for a total of more than thirty years.

Few of the other first students who entered seem to have had any prelegal college education. At that time there were no academic prerequisites for admission, and the records show that the median age of entering students was nineteen. Students were only required to pay the eighty dollars tuition per year and to pass the examinations given in the several courses. Ten of the first twenty-five students, including Brady and Morse, did so and, having passed, became the first graduates in June 1872. Thus, they were *ipso facto* entitled to admission to the bar of the Supreme Court of the District.[94] Championed by Theodore Dwight in the 1850s, this privilege had subsequently been extended by local jurisdictions to many law schools throughout the country. At Georgetown this *ipso facto* privilege did not survive the decade. An ultimately successful movement afoot in the 1870s eventually required a standard test for admission to the bar.[95]

At the first commencement, Justice James, as dean, warned the graduates that they were entering a profession that was losing its traditional status in American society. Science [technology] was "outstripping" law as a source of learning and power. The capitalists of postwar America were hopelessly outdistancing lawyers in the acquisition of wealth and regarding them as servants to secure their holdings. "If we are out of the race where the purse is

Gonzaga College on F Street NW, Washington, served as the second home for the law department from 1872 to 1882. Photograph taken ca. 1874. (Georgetown University Archives)

millions," James asked, "must our running cease?" Success, he replied, never justified amoral expediency. Besides, he reminded them the "lawyer's work will always be as respectable as it always has been," so long as he has "the learning that befits his duty, the culture that befits his time, and the integrity that befits a man." To be that, in brief, was to ensure that the lawyer would continue to hold the highest rank in America, "the rank of a true gentleman."[96]

Enrollment remained modest for the first decade (table 10.2 in appendix F). After peaking at a total of fifty-six students in the 1872–73 academic year, it plummeted under the general economic impact of the Panic of 1873. By 1877 there were only twenty-four students in the school. For the entire decade the average yearly enrollment was thirty-seven, and the majority of students were Anglo-American and Catholic.

Since it was a proprietary school, the lawyers were responsible for its expenses; they also shared in any profits. As relatively light as expenses were during the first few years ("less than three thousand dollars per annum," according to the first yearly statements),[97] the faculty still had to borrow money from the college during at least the first two years to meet its obligations. Once they moved to a new facility where they were able to rent out excess space to the medical department and others, the financial situation seems to

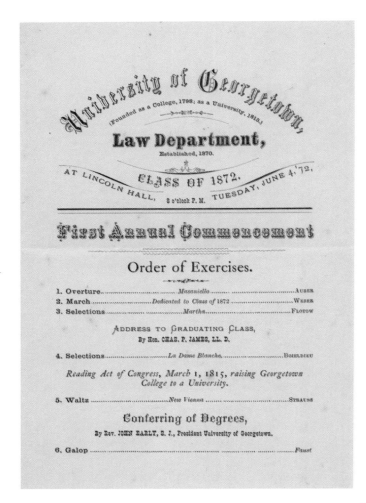

Program for law department's first commencement in 1872. The dean, Justice Charles James, addressed the first ten graduates at Lincoln Hall. The degrees were conferred by President John Early after the reading of the Act of Congress (March 1, 1815), which raised Georgetown College to a university. (Georgetown University Archives)

have stabilized, despite the hard times. By 1876 the faculty of three was sharing $1,664.71 in profits.[98]

The Medical Department

For the medical department, the period marked the beginning of a long depression that lasted well into the middle of the 1880s. In 1867 student fees had produced such abundant revenues that each faculty member was paid a dividend share of $1,267.24.[99] Seven years later the faculty members were required to pay $110.65 each to the department to meet expenses.[100] Enrollment remained high (more than a hundred students) in each of the immediate postwar years (1866–69), then it dropped sharply (table 10.3 in appendix F). In 1868 there were forty-six graduates. By 1876 there were fewer than forty medical students in the whole school and only six graduates. In part this decline was inevitable with the coming of peace and the revival of Columbian University's medical department in 1866. Like Georgetown it too experienced declining enrollments during the 1870s.[101] The raising of academic standards during that period seems also to have been a factor in the enrollment downturn.

Some war veterans were among the one hundred and eighty-five students who enrolled in the medical department between 1866 and 1868. Sixteen had seen service with the Union Army, two with the Army of the Confederacy. Notable among the Union veterans were William Goodman of Annapolis (**M** 1868–70), who had gone on to serve as a hospital steward after losing his left arm in the battle at Fredericksburg; Joseph Nelson Clark (**M** 1865–67), who was a survivor of Andersonville and subsequently a witness against Captain Henry Wirz at his trial; Daniel Smith Lamb (**M** 1865–67), who afterwards was professor of anatomy at Howard University and a pathologist at the Army Medical Museum for over fifty years, as well as one of the District's medical leaders; and Charles Volney Pettys (**M** 1870–73), who had won the Medal of Honor at Cedar Creek. Other students of this period were John Thomas Winter (**M** 1867–70), one of the founders of the short-lived National University (1884–1902) and president of its medical depart-ment; and George Lloyd Magruder (**M** 1868–70), of the District, who was on the medical faculty for twenty-three years (1883–1906), thirteen as dean (1888–1901). In general, the postwar medical students were a mature lot. The median age of those who entered in the ten years after Appomattox was twenty-three. Few apparently had any previous college education; most were non-Catholic (60.6%) and of Anglo-Saxon extraction (62.8%). Almost all came from the Washington metropolitan area or the Northeast; and about six in every ten earned degrees.

The department began some curricular reform in 1867 at the height of the postwar boom, with Thomas Antisell providing the initiative. Henceforth, to graduate, candidates were required to show proof of attendance at a course of clinical instruction at Providence Hospital, where members of the faculty now worked. (This requirement was later extended to Freedmen's and Columbia Hospitals, where Georgetown faculty also lectured.)[102] Oral examinations were also introduced for students completing their first year of courses.[103] The use of textbooks by faculty came to be encouraged, if not required, during these years.[104] By 1869 it was stated policy that each of the faculty submit a syllabus of proposed lectures for review by his superior.[105] An executive committee was also established to oversee "all matters relating to the welfare of the college."[106] There was a sharp rise in student fees. In 1868 the faculties from the George-town Medical Department and the National Medical College each agreed to charge the same flat rate of $135 for a full course of lectures.[107]

But there was substantially little change in the faculty itself during the decade. One distinguished newcomer was a nonphysician, Benjamin Sher-wood Hedrick, who had become chief of the division of chemistry, metal-lurgy, and electricity in the U.S. Patent Office in 1861, then returned to North Carolina briefly to take part in an early reconstruction program in his home state. Dispirited by the corruption and muddle of the Grant administration, he resumed his position at the Patent Office and then joined the Georgetown medical faculty as professor of chemistry in 1872.[108]

When surging enrollments had briefly but severely overtaxed the facilities of the department during the 1866–69 years, the faculty considered expand-ing the building, then decided instead to relocate to larger rented quarters on the corner of Tenth and E Streets in northwest Washington.[109] That move in 1869 also put the school next to an extraordinary medical research facility, the new Army Medical Museum, which occupied Ford's Theatre and con-tained, as the 1874 Georgetown catalogue later boasted, "the most valuable collection of Surgical and Medical Pathological Specimens in the world. . . ." This federal facility not only provided a clinical museum but also housed a medical library of nearly forty thousand volumes.[110]

The move to E Street was also the occasion for a reorganization and staff-ing increase of the faculty. A new chair in clinical medicine was added, bring-ing the total faculty to eight. As of March 1868 the branches taught were:

(1) Principles and Practice of Medicine, General Pathology, and Medical Ethics; (2) Obstetrics and Diseases of Women and Children; (3) Principles and Practice of Surgery, Military Surgery, and Fractures and Dislocations; (4) Materia Medica, Therapeutics, and Medical Jurisprudence; (5) Physiology, Hygiene, Physiological Chemistry, Urinary Pathology, and Therapeutics; (6) Anatomy; (7) Chemistry and Toxicology; (8) Operative Surgery, Histology, Microscopic and Pathological Anatomy; and (9) Clinical Medicine. The title of the school was changed at that time to "the Medical Faculty of Georgetown College."[111]

In 1870 the faculty attempted to expand their programs considerably. That same fall they decided that it was "expedient that Schools of Pharmacy & Dentistry be established in connection with Georgetown College."[112] This was not completely realized, however. The first professor of pharmacy, Oscar Oldberg, was appointed. However, the one-year program produced only three graduates over the next two years and disappeared by 1873. Dentistry as a school was pursued no further. In fact, consolidation, not expansion, prevailed at the school in the next decade.

The Search for Georgetown's Next President

By 1869 Bernard Maguire was no longer vigorous and enthusiastic; his health was clearly failing. When Joseph Keller took office as provincial in the fall of 1869, he wrote to Rome about this and about the fact that he was unhappy with the list of candidates that the province consultors had already sent to Rome to be considered as Maguire's successor in the presidency of Georgetown. Keller regarded the top candidate, Charles Stonestreet, who had briefly been president in the 1850s, as too old (he was fifty-six) and not sufficiently active for the position. At least, Keller added, Stonestreet, if appointed would have "an outstanding man as his assistant, Father Healy, whom I would have much preferred as Rector, except for the problem related to his background."[113] Stonestreet proved to be unacceptable to the superior general. The following March the provincial and province consultors composed a new *terna* or list of three candidates for Georgetown. That new list in 1870 placed Patrick Healy first and Joseph O'Hagan second. "Clearly Healy is the best qualified . . . ," Keller commented, "despite the difficulty that perhaps can be brought up about him."[114] Rome apparently decided that "the difficulty" eliminated Healy. Then, when Rome did act, it named no one on the new *terna*, but instead reappointed the fifty-six-year-old John Early.[115]

When Early's three-year term as president was coming to an end in the winter of 1873, it was clear that his health was too poor (he was suffering from kidney disease) for him to continue in office.[116] This time Keller made no attempt to secure Healy for the position. Instead, he made clear to Rome that

he and his consultors now wanted John Bapst to be named rector of Georgetown. (The climate of Washington had driven Bapst north two decades before
and he was by this time president of Boston College.) Informed by the superior general that Bapst could not be released from Boston, the provincial and
his advisors persisted. Two *ternae* were sent to Rome, one for Georgetown and
one for Boston, listing Bapst and Patrick Healy, respectively, in the top positions. This strongly suggests that the "difficulty" superiors were concerned
about related more to Healy's biracial background and so-called slave status
than to his illegitimate birth. (It will be recalled that nineteenth-century "mis-
cegenation" laws in Georgia forbade a legal marriage between whites and non-
whites.) The local superiors were presuming that mixed race would not have
the potential for problems in New England (where Patrick Healy's two brothers were among the archdiocesan clergy) that it might well pose in Washington for the head of an important institution in a Southern city.

Before Rome could respond, however, John Early died suddenly on May
23, 1873. Keller immediately appointed Healy acting rector and the directors
of Georgetown College took the initiative and elected him president the following day. More than a year later, Rome reluctantly confirmed his appointment as rector.[117] In such fashion did Patrick Healy come to be the twenty-
eighth president of Georgetown. It proved to be as serendipitous for the
institution as John Carroll's original choice of site had been. Under Healy's
leadership, Georgetown made considerable progress in the transition from
college to university that had been begun by the earlier generation of Jesuits,
including Ryder, Maguire, and Early.

CHAPTER 11

Patrick Healy and the Idea of a University

Here we are, then, the great Catholic University, "inchoate."

GEORGETOWN COLLEGE JOURNAL,
Student editorialist, October 1875

"The Oxford of America"

Georgetown College, reported a Washington correspondent for a Philadelphia newspaper in 1876,

is certainly destined to become one of the great Catholic Universities of the United States—probably *the greatest* Catholic University—at no distant day. Its site is magnificent, and it has all the natural qualifications for becoming the Oxford of America. Situated on the Potomac, and . . . lying on the verge of the capital, it has all that the most ambitious university could command. . . . Its President . . . is greatly respected both without and within the college walls. He combines remarkable administrative abilities. . . . I cannot help wondering that some effort towards making Georgetown College a national University is not made under his regime, as he seems to be the right man to lead such a movement.[1]

The writer, Maurice Egan, a graduate student at Georgetown, was perhaps being as disingenuous as he was chauvinistic in his appraisal of Georgetown's future. But two years previously, at a meeting of officials from the college and the Maryland Province, President Patrick Healy had won from his Consultors a provisional commitment to take steps to make Georgetown a university.[2] Over the next eight years Healy pursued that goal on several fronts. He con-

Patrick F. Healy, SJ (1873–82).
Twenty-eighth president of
Georgetown. (Georgetown
University Archives)

structed new facilities for the college, broadened its curriculum, and altered its paternalistic form of governance. He brought the professional departments of medicine and law within the control of the university and raised the academic standards of both. He endeavored to make Georgetown a university that was Catholic, not only by tradition but in the composition of its student body as well.

The Emergence of the American University

When President Healy explained to the superior general, Peter Beckx, his desire in 1875 to change the nature of the institution from college to university, the latter was puzzled. Was not Georgetown already a university, having not only a liberal arts college but also professional schools? Moreover, Healy's proposal for new buildings and new programs seemed to Father General Beckx to be very ambitious, if not downright unrealistic, in its presupposition of available resources, human and monetary, that the institution lacked and had little or no hope of acquiring. "We can neither create individuals," said Beckx, "nor make them in a day, nor rob other colleges. . . ."[3]

Beckx was scarcely alone in his puzzlement over this new vision and meaning of "university." "[N]o university [in the 1870s]," a leading historian of American education has written, "could be certain exactly what was meant by a university."[4] In the United States, since the seventeenth century, a university had been understood to mean an institution of higher education which possessed the power to issue the full array of academic degrees. By the 1870s it had come to indicate a collection of disparate schools in the United States, usually loosely connected in purpose and administration. But during that decade a new understanding of higher education was emerging under the pressure of the proliferation and specialization of knowledge in postbellum America. Financed at least partly through the Morrill Land-Grant Bill (1862), new institutions of higher education, such as Cornell and the Massachusetts Institute of Technology, were established. Others, such as the Universities of Michigan and California, were revitalized.

Daniel Coit Gilman, in his inaugural address at the University of California (in Berkeley), said in 1872 that the word "university" is "the most comprehensive term that can be employed to indicate a foundation for the promotion and diffusion of knowledge—a group of agencies organized to advance the arts and sciences of every sort, and train young men as scholars for all the intellectual callings of life."[5]

At Cornell, Andrew D. White was organizing just such an institution by creating a complex structure that combined vocational training, classical instruction, scientific research, and applied technology. By 1870 this new university, heeding the original desire of Ezra Cornell to "found an institution where any person can find instruction in any study," provided its more than two hundred and fifty first-year students (then the largest entering class in America's educational history) the choice of fourteen departments, ranging from the arts in general through public service to agriculture, in which to pursue their intellectual and professional goals.[6] At Harvard, Charles Eliot, acting on the principle that science and mathematics could no longer be subordinated to the classics or metaphysics ("We would have them all, and at their best"), committed the college to a virtually total elective curriculum as a fundamental element of Harvard's conscious attempt to become a university uniquely American.[7] The academy, the new wisdom insisted, had to train students in the art of making choices for the complex, specialized world they would be entering.[8] Eventually, it also had to adapt so as to respect the growing *laissez-faire* sentiments of students on evolving curricular requirements. ("We want free trade and no protection in College studies," as one student later put it to Gilman in 1884.)[9] Gilman himself had already been involved in an enterprise in Baltimore that was to give new meaning to the word "university." That was what one sociologist has termed "perhaps the single, most decisive event of the history of learning in the Western hemisphere," the establishment of the Johns Hopkins University in 1876 as the first American institution of higher education whose primary purpose was the cultivation of research and the training of scholars, especially in the natural and social sciences.[10] Yet, of all these nineteenth-century "makers" of the university in America, Eliot most shared with Healy in the vision and idea of a university, despite some radical differences between them.

Within the American Catholic community there had already been some call for its own university—for a comprehensive Catholic institution of higher education. When the nation's bishops assembled at the Second Plenary Council of Baltimore in 1866, under the prodding of presiding Archbishop Martin John Spalding, they expressed the desire to have "a great college or university . . . in which . . . all the letters and sciences, both sacred and profane, could be taught!"[11] Isaac Hecker, Orestes Brownson, and other Catholic intellectuals also decried the fact that the Church in the United States, despite its numbers and wealth, lacked what several petty German states and "even impoverished Ireland" had had the imagination and courage to institute, "a concentration of the endowments, the instructors, and the pupils in one grand institution . . . to give a much better and higher kind of education."[12]

A Catholic newspaper in Brooklyn, the *Tablet,* edited by a Georgetown alumnus, strongly suggested that the Catholic community already possessed in its oldest college an institution that had "the elements of success" for becoming a university: the requisite college and professional schools, plus its location in the country's capital.[13] The *College Journal* agreed that Georgetown College, despite serious shortcomings, was "the great Catholic University, *inchoate*."[14] A student columnist in the middle 1870s saw the institution "in a condition that reminds one of a crab that has cast off its shell:—not a crab in going backwards, but one recently emancipated from its cramped integuments, and although in its most rapid growth, at its weakest stage."[15] More extensive facilities for classes, library, and scientific experimentation were a primary need, the *Journal* argued, particularly necessary in order to expand to a college population ranging from eight hundred to a thousand. Also, declared the *Journal*, the preparatory school had to be eliminated and, in keeping with the character of a university, the *in loco parentis* supervision of students should be discontinued. (Many older students, the editorialist presumed, would prefer to seek housing in either Washington or Alexandria.) As a university, Georgetown would need to further adapt its curriculum, as it was already beginning to do, to the needs of applicants "who wish to dispense with the ancient languages," and introduce an appropriate elective system. And further, declared the editorialist, Georgetown needed an endowment. "We can do little in the matter of the university of the future," he concluded, "without millionaires to help us in realizing the design," something the college had previously lacked utterly. But Georgetown had one advantage. "With a tithe of the great income which such colleges as Harvard . . . possess," it could nonetheless compete in attracting a critical mass of outstanding faculty from among the Society's ranks either in the States or in Europe, as had been done before by the talented German and Italian Jesuits who had transformed the faculty in the decade before the war.[16]

Crucial Decisions

Committing Georgetown to the university ideal was certainly the explicit intention of both Healy and the regional superior, Joseph Keller. At the official consultation in the February 1874 meeting, both had urged that substantial changes be formulated so that the institution might accommodate itself to the emerging new order of higher education. Both agreed also that the primary, immediate need was for new physical facilities. The possibility was raised of abandoning the present site in favor of Hickory Hill, the portion of the college property north of the New Cut Road (now Reservoir Road), or even of relocating everything to a completely different site far from the city but close to a railroad line. (For some time there had been rumors in the city that either urban expansion or the building of a long-sought railroad spur into Georgetown, or both, would jeopardize the integrity of the present campus.) In the end, any relocation ideas were dismissed because of the enormous expenses involved in constructing a new campus *ab ovo*. It was decided, instead, to add new buildings to the existing ones, for classrooms and laboratories, a library, a chapel, and so on.

At Healy's urging, the consultors, anticipating the need for additional student housing, also decided to abandon the traditional group dormitory in favor of private rooms for older students, many of whom were already voting with their feet against the present system that perpetually monitored their activities. Such a recognition of individual responsibility, Healy suggested, was one essential step they needed to take to become a Catholic university in more than name.

Finally, alive to the reality that "many in these times . . . flee our schools unless another curriculum is available to them," the officials agreed in 1874 to broaden the course of studies. Although the classical course would still hold "the first place and honor" within the curriculum, students would henceforth have the option of selecting "the so-called commercial and scientific course, so that all may find with us everything that they desire. . . ."[17] These plans would not be realized until 1879, and then not successfully.

The Jesuit superior general's skepticism about the wherewithal that Healy had for doing all that he hoped to do to convert Georgetown into a university proved to be a hidden blessing. With approval delayed until the fiscal feasibility of the project was demonstrable, Healy had time to convert the construction plans for several buildings, similar to existing ones, to one master plan for a single grand edifice boldly different from the city's much used Federal style. We do not know whether Healy aimed to pattern the new building after university structures he had known at Louvain, but we do know that originally he consulted Patrick C. Keily on the basic design for the building. The New York church architect was noted primarily for his Romanesque style. Healy indicated in 1873 that he intended to choose someone closer to home to do the actual execution.[18]

Accordingly, in the fall of 1874 he engaged the services of two emigré architects, the Austrian John L. Smithmeyer (1832–1918) and his Prussian associate, Paul Pelz (1841–1918). (Pelz later submitted the winning design for the Library of Congress building.) The site chosen for the new building was between the North Building and the Preparatory Building. Smithmeyer and Pelz designed a massive five-story structure of heavy stone masonry, rounded arches, turrets, and two soaring spires. The style, while fashionably eclectic, did emphasize Romanesque features primarily. Whatever its inspiration, it embodied and expressed a vision of ancient learning and culture.[19] The imposing structure, 312 feet long and 95 feet wide, with a central clock tower climbing about two hundred feet, was sited to face east toward the Capitol. For the first time in its history the university was constructing a building that fronted not the river but the city, as if to state visually its intention of becoming an enduring Catholic university in the capital city of the United States.

The architectural team had completed the approved design by the spring of 1876, although construction did not begin until late in 1877. In keeping with Georgetown's tradition, it was conceived as a multifunctional, integrated learning facility that could house administrative offices, classrooms, laboratories, assembly hall for twelve hundred persons, a library for one hundred thousand volumes, and student living quarters. The provincial superior remained opposed to such a single large building, in part because of his desire to return the theologate from Woodstock to Georgetown (which would necessitate additional quarters). But he abandoned this notion finally and deferred in May 1876 to Healy's plan.[20] Although the superior general in Rome thought the building too large and ornate, and the estimates of its cost too low, he gave permission in 1877 for Healy to begin construction, with the understanding that he could not spend more than $100,000 on it.[21]

From the days of their very first building campaign ninety years before, Georgetown's leaders had always had great difficulty in raising money for construction, but the fund-raising that Healy was proposing made the former projects puny in comparison. Georgetown had very little capital to finance the work. The institution had lost most of its unencumbered funds during the Panic of 1873, when a Baltimore bank in which it had invested $31,000 failed.[22] The superior general had already forbidden any further sale of land—in the past a favorite device for raising money.[23] After three months of frustrating negotiations with banks in Washington, Baltimore, and Philadelphia, Healy finally persuaded a Baltimore bank to lend $100,000 at 6 percent interest, with the college property serving as collateral.[24]

The college's economic situation was further aggravated by the tax that the commissioners of the District of Columbia voted to impose on the institution's property. Healy protested that the law protected Georgetown as a religious institution from such taxes, but in order to preserve the university's credit, he did pay in the spring of 1878 the $30,909.24 assessed to Georgetown.[25] Although alumni and friends of the university eventually persuaded the Congress to return the money, this 1878 tax bill put even greater pressure on those proposing to finance the new building.[26]

In advising Healy on the prospects for financing the enormous project to which he was committing the university, Father General Beckx had warned him earlier that "you can little rely on the gifts of friends in undertaking a project of this magnitude. The very building convinces people that we are rich."[27] Nonetheless, for the first time since John Carroll's original proposals went out in 1787, Healy undertook a fund-raising campaign for the university. In December 1877 he sent a lithograph of the architects' rendering of the new building to William Corcoran, the oldest living (and presumably richest) alumnus, together with a plea that Corcoran take the lead in contributing to the building and the establishment of chairs and fellowships for faculty and students. Corcoran's reputation for charitable works was well-known, Healy added, and "as Georgetown College has the exclusive right to claim you as one of its many children, I address myself first to you in order that your name and cooperation may be a means of inducing others to aid us in our efforts to make the buildings of the college worthy of its age & reputation, worthy of its many noble-minded alumni, and of the great and sacred cause that inspired its foundation."[28] Corcoran, who had had scarcely any contact with the college after his brief schooling there in 1813, indeed had become the city's leading benefactor, having completed his art gallery five years earlier and assisting many private institutions. Ironically, at this very time, he was leading a major endowment campaign at Columbian University, where he was president of the corporation. He had already donated an estate valued at $150,000 to that institution, toward their fund-raising goal of $250,000.[29]

William Corcoran (**C** 1813). President, the Society of the Alumni of Georgetown College. (Georgetown University Archives)

Corcoran agreed to lend his name to the effort and contributed $2,000, but the subsequent appeal to other alumni produced a pittance of $450 only.[30] However, the Healy campaign did provide the occasion for the establishment of a permanent alumni association. An earlier effort among alumni of the three departments had produced an organization in 1875 that lasted barely a year. In 1880 Healy invited representatives of the alumni to form a new association, and in that year a constitution was drawn up and officers elected for the Society of the Alumni of Georgetown College. Corcoran was chosen as president, Senator Francis Kernan (**C** 1833–36) as vice president, and Healy as treasurer. Thereafter the alumni began to have annual reunions at commencement. At the first one in 1881 a committee was formed from the three schools within the university to work on liquidating the debt on the new building.[31] It produced nothing. Two years later at their gathering, the president of the university persuaded them to undertake the more modest responsibility of meeting the interest payments on the university debt for the new building during the next ten years. A year later they had secured pledges of $2,000 in annual contributions for the next ten years, an amount barely enough to service the debt for a few months each year.[32]

Healy spent most of the eighteen months from December of 1878 to June of 1880 on the road trying to raise money for the new building. His sometimes precarious health had led him to undertake a "curative" transcontinental sea voyage in 1878–79. With Father Joseph O'Hagan, then president of Holy Cross, he set out for San Francisco in early December on a cruise by way of the Isthmus of Panama. Although Father Healy thought his own health "better than it has been in years" (few shared his opinion), he also agreed to accompany O'Hagan, who had been ordered to sea because of his generally poor health, in order to see what he could raise by face-to-face contacts with alumni scattered across the country.[33] Two weeks out of Boston, the fifty-two-year-old O'Hagan suffered a fatal stroke aboard the ship in the Gulf of Mexico. Healy continued alone to northern California. His subsequent return journey took him to San Francisco, Salt Lake

City, Denver, St. Louis, Chicago, Milwaukee, Detroit, Buffalo, New York City, Philadelphia, Boston, Baltimore, and many smaller places. He traveled tirelessly in the hope of securing gifts either for the building or for scholarships. Aside from a few benefactors, such as James V. Coleman (**C** 1863–67, 1869, AB; **L** 1871–73, LLB), a young mining entrepreneur of San Francisco who contributed $10,000 for a museum in the new building, Healy received virtually nothing from the hundreds of persons he managed to see. Father General Beckx's warning had proved all too true. Paupers, people thought, did not erect academic palaces like the one that was rising over Georgetown. For all his strenuous peregrinations, Healy managed to raise less than $60,000. People promised him many things, from oil wells to stock to property. Few delivered. In February 1881, the *College Journal* asked plaintively,

[W]hy is it that not a week goes by in which there is not heralded to the world the good fortune of some one or other of our Protestant universities and colleges in the matter of bequests, endowments or foundations [Yale had received a million dollars the year before, Princeton $1.2 million] while . . . apart from three or four scholarships, averaging $6,000 each, there is not a dollar of endowment on the oldest Catholic university in the country?[34]

In his fund-raising efforts from San Francisco to Bangor, Healy had seemingly approached every Catholic of wealth, old and new, from Carrolls to Grants, many of them with at least some Georgetown connection. At a time when the Harvards and the Hopkinses were forging the ties between academia and big business by attracting massive endowments (Harvard's grew from $2.4 million in 1869 to $12.6 million by 1900),[35] Georgetown failed to find enough benefactors to fund even one building budgeted for less than a quarter of a million dollars. Of course, relatively few Georgetown graduates had gone into business (only 11% between 1830 and 1870); most graduates continued to enter the professions of law and medicine, although the percentage of alumni in general who were making careers in business was on the rise (20% of those entering in the 1870s). Then too, most of Georgetown's alumni were in the South, the most impoverished region of the country. (Significantly, Healy included no southern cities on any of his fundraising tours.) The lingering effects of the economic recession had undoubtedly also reduced the ability of some potential donors to invest in Georgetown. And increasingly wealthy Catholics tended to send their sons to Harvard or Yale or Princeton. By the 1890s Harvard had approximately three hundred Catholics among its students, far more than Georgetown could then count among its collegians.[36] That no doubt affected the willingness of many other targeted donors. Whatever the reasons or extenuating circumstances, the truth is that Patrick Healy found monied American Catholics no more willing to invest in education than John Carroll had nearly a century earlier.

"Oh for the Money to Do It!"

The cornerstone for the building was laid on December 12, 1877, black laborers having in the previous two months razed the handball courts and excavated the ground. Stonemasons began their work on the front and side walls the next day, using rusticated bluestone from a quarry on the Virginia side of the Potomac west of Georgetown.[37] Four months later bricklayers arrived to lay the rear wall to complement the red brick of the contiguous buildings in the newly formed quadrangle. Fireproofing, in the form of liquid silicate of soda, was applied as the building rose. Progress was rapid until the late spring, when incessant rain, a defaulting stone contractor, and a shortage of stonemasons brought the work to a virtual halt.[38] Nonetheless, by early October the iron girders were all in place and the walls were rising rapidly. By December the towers were climbing as well.

So too were the costs of the building. "I have been borrowing right & left since you went away," the vice president, O'Hagan's nephew, Father John Mullaly, wrote Healy as 1879 began.[39] "There is a good deal more to be done yet. Oh for the money to do it!"[40]

Mullaly, unable to pay the stonemasons and carpenters, was forced to suspend work for two months. Nonetheless, by April, the roof was nearly

The New Building in 1880, showing the huge, frontal mound of dirt from the excavation work. Funds for removal of the unsightly mound and the building's completion were not available until shortly before the Centennial Celebration in 1889. (Georgetown University Archives)

complete. The university had already spent more than $150,000 merely on the building shell, far more than the original estimate for the entire project.[41] That month the provincial superior ordered Healy to leave the interior unfinished until he had the money to pay for it.[42]

In November of 1879 the last part of the exterior, the south tower, was finally finished; spectators and photographers poured onto campus to view and record this architectural colossus. This also provided Healy an occasion to order prayers of thanksgiving for the successful completion of the building exterior and to urge supplications "that He who has given us [the means] to begin will vouchsafe to raise up benefactors who will enable us to complete the great work undertaken to His greater glory."[43]

In the following spring (1880), with the approval of his board of directors, Healy decided to resume work, even if it meant borrowing more money.[44] By that time the costs had exceeded $200,000, forcing Healy to secure another loan for $120,000.[45] Many of the debt service payments were made by borrowing money from banks or friends or alumni. Nevertheless, with a few gifts in hand and the promise of some large benefactions, work began on the interior of the building, and most of the facilities were in use by the academic year 1881–82. But the library and assembly hall both remained unfinished for another decade, for lack of funds. By 1882, the building had cost the university $437,373, including the interest on the debt.[46]

Although desperate to reduce the growing six-figure debt, Georgetown had scant means to do so. But the administrators cut expenses sharply by laying off many of its staff on both campus and farm. In 1881 the college leased both the farm and villa in the District in order to realize some immediate revenue from the rents. And, despite the superior general's prohibition, it began to sell some properties: city lots in Washington, a farm in Virginia, a villa in Pennsylvania. The money realized was far too little to dent the mountain of debt the institution had incurred to raise its new building. "The financial condition of the College," the House diarist remarked laconically in the fall of 1881, "continues in an unsatisfactory condition."[47]

The Faculty of the College

In 1874–75 Georgetown College had a faculty of twenty-five, only nine of whom taught at the college level. Even if diversification within the curriculum was desirable, Georgetown's numbers hardly permitted it. Harvard at that same time had more than forty faculty, and Johns Hopkins began in 1876 with a faculty of twenty-four. Even before the worsening financial condition of the college forced the dismissal of all lay faculty in the early 1880s, few laymen were appointed. There was a tacit commitment to maintaining, to the extent possible, an exclusively Jesuit faculty in the college. In 1874 there were only three laymen on the faculty, one a former Jesuit. He,

Daniel Kelly, taught chemistry at the Hilltop and physiology at the Medical School. A native of Kilkenny, Ireland, Kelly had entered the Society of Jesus following his graduation from Stonyhurst College in England. At Stonyhurst, he had been an assistant at the observatory and subsequently professor of physics. After he left the Society, Kelly did an apprenticeship in medicine, then in 1872 came to Washington. On the strength of letters of introduction and recommendations from English Jesuits, Kelly was admitted as a student in the Georgetown medical department and was appointed professor of chemistry and physiology in Georgetown College.[48] At the college he quickly distinguished himself as a teacher by his emphasis on research and experimentation in his chemistry class. Following his graduation from the Medical School in 1875, he was appointed professor of chemistry and toxicology there while retaining his post at the college.

For the most part, however, Healy, like Eliot during his early years at Harvard, sought faculty not for their research potential but for their teaching promise. Certainly that was true of the other two Georgetown laymen. Edward Forney, a former minister who had converted to Catholicism from the German Reformed Church, was appointed in 1874 to head a newly established Department of English Literature and Declamation.[49] The professor of German in the middle 1870s was Louis Schade, a refugee from the 1848 revolution, who had been prominent in Democratic politics before the Civil War. In 1870, with the backing of William Corcoran, he began publishing a weekly newspaper in Washington, the *Sentinel*. Earlier, in 1865, he had also served as the attorney for Captain Henry Wirz, the only Confederate executed after Appomattox.

Edward Holker Welch was a distinguished Jesuit addition to the faculty in 1878 as professor of rational philosophy. Welch, a graduate of Harvard, had done postgraduate studies in philosophy in Europe, where he was attracted to Catholicism. After becoming a Catholic in 1845, Welch returned to Harvard for additional study in law and literature (LL.B. and M.A.). Then in 1851 he entered the Society of Jesus. For twenty years he was professor of biblical literature at Boston College; and he also did pastoral work in that city before he joined the Georgetown faculty.

With the broadening of the curriculum, especially in the sciences, it was imperative that future Jesuit teachers secure the requisite pedagogical specialization. Accordingly, in the late 1870s, the Society began to send its seminarians to outside institutions for advanced training, especially in the sciences. In 1879 the three young Jesuits who taught the sciences at Georgetown went up to Cambridge to take the six-week summer course in quantitative analysis at Harvard; and two of them returned the following summer for additional study. One, Joseph Havens Richards, was reported to President Healy as a person having excellent promise as a scientist,[50] the other, H. T. B. Tarr, was later appointed to teach the summer course in chemistry when it was organized for scholastics at Georgetown in 1882.[51]

Two earlier efforts to make Georgetown a center of professional science had already failed. In 1876 Thomas Antisell approached the administration about establishing a scientific school in Washington affiliated with the university. The college faculty debated the proposal but decided only to seek more information about the planned school. Nothing further came of it.[52] Two years later, when the United States Senate authorized a new site for the naval observatory, President Healy offered to house it on the Hickory Hill portion of the campus. The federal commission which finally selected the site did examine the Georgetown plot but eventually chose higher ground farther up Massachusetts Avenue.[53]

Establishing a graduate school per se was not part of the Healy vision of Georgetown as a university, nor was it a priority for Eliot at Harvard. A few Georgetown graduate students continued studies for the master of arts degree, usually while teaching the preparatory students, but essentially their graduate work was a tutorial program in philosophy. Maurice Francis Egan, a graduate student in the 1870s, recalled that "Regular graduate courses did not then exist." M.A. candidates did have to write a thesis on a suitable topic, similar to the undergraduate requirement in senior year, but the program had few other mandatory tasks. From his memoirs Egan makes it clear that he spent more time in the Washington salons of Mrs. John Vinton Dahlgren and others than he did on campus, aside from his teaching obligations.[54]

College Demographics in the Healy Years

Despite the lofty aims of the administrators, Georgetown College remained primarily a preparatory school. The median entering age was fifteen. Enrollment during the 1875–90 period fluctuated between one hundred and fifty and two hundred and fifty students, but most were in the junior or preparatory classes.[55] (As late as 1890 there were only eighty-three students in the senior classes of the school.) Fewer than one-third of those who entered as preparatory students reached the senior classes in the college; less than a fifth (17%) of the student body entered at that level (although by the 1880s the proportion of new collegians was rising slightly).

In other ways, however, the student demographics were changing (table 11.1 in appendix F). Under Healy, Georgetown became a school for Catholics from the North. In 1875 there were equal numbers of students from the Washington area (D.C. and Maryland), from south of the Potomac, and from north of the Mason-Dixon line. By the 1880s the numbers of those from the South had been halved; more students were now coming from New York and Pennsylvania than all the southern states combined. Those from the Northeast, Northcentral, and West now accounted for slightly more than two-fifths (40.1%) of the enrollment. Nearly three-quarters of the students were city dwellers, and by the 1880s, slightly more than four-fifths (80.3%)

of them were Catholic also, a sharp change from the pluralism of the ante-bellum period—and the highest proportion in the school's history since the quasi-monastic era of the early 1800s under the Neale brothers. It is quite likely that this concentration was in part a natural consequence of the increasingly Catholic ethos of student life as we noted in our earlier review of the postbellum years. In part, too, Healy, a graduate of an exclusively Catholic school (Holy Cross), seems to have promoted the same policy, at least informally, at Georgetown.[56] Even among the Southerners, historically the most non-Catholic in their composition, the overwhelming majority were now Catholic (82%). Besides the declining numbers of Protestant students, only a few Jewish students continued to attend the school, mostly locals, such as the Nordlinger brothers—Napthali (**C** 1880–83) and Isaac (**C** 1880–83, AB), the sons of a Georgetown clothier. At least at the college level, Healy was setting the institution on a course in which student religious homogeneity was seen as the ideal within the scope of its mission. Georgetown was to be not just a Catholic university, but one primarily for Catholics.

The rising proportion of Catholics in the college (80.5%) was also a consequence of the increased presence of Irish Americans. By the end of the 1880s the Irish Americans (30.5%) were beginning to threaten the status of the Anglo-Americans (43.5%) as the largest ethnic group. They were part of a burgeoning Irish middle class who put a high value on a college education in a Catholic institution. As the oldest such college, Georgetown inevitably attracted the sons of many of them, including some of the wealthier and the more socially ambitious. The greatest number (42%) of the Irish were from the Northeast, the sons of businessmen, lawyers, and white-collar workers. They tended to be older than the average non-Irish student, and their median entering age was sixteen. Moreover, nearly a third entered at the college level. Only a tenth (10%) sought financial assistance, while somewhat more of the other students (12%) needed some kind of aid. These Irish Americans also stayed longer (two years, on the average) as compared to a little more than a year for the general student population. More than a fifth graduated (23% compared to 12% of the others). In fact, Irish students constituted nearly half (45%) of those who matriculated in the 1870s and 1880s and then went on to graduate. Among the notable Irish American graduates was Daniel William Lawler (**C** 1877–81), one of five sons of General John Lawler of Wisconsin who attended Georgetown. Daniel later became a prominent Minnesota lawyer and Democratic mayor of St. Paul. By the late 1870s St. Patrick's Day had been added to Georgetown's calendar. In fact, it became a minor holiday under the presidencies of Patrick Healy (1873–82) and James Doonan (1882–88), who both readily identified with the Irish heritage of their fathers.

Besides the tacit discouragement of non-Catholic applicants, other factors probably accounted for the sharp decline in southern students at Georgetown in the 1880s. (Ironically the two Jesuits who headed the institution from 1873 to 1888, Healy and Doonan, were native Georgians, from the heart of the South.) In any case, the southern economy continued to worsen in the last two decades of the century. Unlike the various fee exemptions given in the immediate postwar years, no effort seems to have been made to assist southern families with connections to Georgetown to send their sons to the college in the 1880s. Despite the financial pressures on the college, more than one student in ten (11.4%) received some sort of financial aid. In fact, Healy established Georgetown's first formal scholarship program, which provided free tuition to one day student from each parish in the District of Columbia.[57] The majority of the others given financial assistance were boarders who were granted a reduction in tuition and other fees. But during that decade apparently not one southern student received financial help. One might be tempted to suggest that Healy was striking back, at least subconsciously, at the plantation society that had considered him an outcast, but that hardly explains Doonan's record. Even so, more than a third of these southern students were kin to alumni (36% as compared to 29% of non-Southerners). Nevertheless, there were now far fewer of them. They did stay longer than the typical student (more than two and a half years) but less than a tenth (7%) remained long enough to earn an AB.

Among those Southerners at Georgetown was a transplanted Northerner, Silas Moore Patterson (**C** 1875–76). He was the son of John James Patterson, a Union Army veteran who had moved to South Carolina after the war and was elected by the Republican legislature to the United States Senate in 1873. Another Southern student who distinguished himself in public service was Robert Foligny Broussard (**C** 1880–83) from Louisiana, son of a planter. (He later received his law degree from Tulane.) Elected to Congress in 1897 and then to the United States Senate in 1912, he was known as the "watchdog of the Louisiana sugar industry," the Democrat who successfully advocated protective legislation for beleaguered domestic sugar producers. Charles Wells Russell (**C** 1870–73, **L** 1881–83, LLB) from Wheeling was also one of the more notable students in this period. His father had served in the Confederate Congress, and the younger Wells went on after graduating to serve for many years in the Department of Justice before being named assistant United States attorney general in 1905. He was also the author of a play, *Cuba Libre* (1897), a novel, *Lays of the Season* (1909), and a book of poetry. Another son of a former Confederate leader was Condé Benoit Pallen (**C** 1875–80, AB) of St. Louis. Pallen was militantly antiprogressive. He became the editor of *Church Progress* in his home city and later the distinguished chief editor of the *Catholic Encyclopedia* (1904–20). He was also the author of several well-known studies of literature and philosophy (*The Philosophy of Literature, Epochs of Literature, What Is Liberalism?*). Also notable were Alexander Stephens (CLS 1888–96), the nephew of Alexander Stephens, who had been vice-president of the Confederacy, and Thomas Roberts Ransom (CLS 1883–86; 1885, AB) the son of Senator Matt Whitaker Ransom, of North Carolina.

Of those who graduated from the college in the 1880s, nearly three-quarters were from the Northeast (41.7%) and the local (Washington) area (30.6%). In the main, they were Catholic (91.4%), the sons of professionals (law, medicine, education, and the military) and businessmen. In this period two-thirds were from cities, and nearly half were Irish American. Three-quarters of them had entered Georgetown at the college level. Of those who began as freshmen or higher, almost half (44%) graduated, and nearly as many (40%) had previous connections with the school. Nearly a tenth of these graduates had financial aid, and four-fifths (80%) were boarders. A surprisingly large number went on to professional schools. Of the known occupations of the graduates who had matriculated during the 1880s, more than half (52.7%) became lawyers; more than a fifth (22%) became doctors. Indeed, a third of these graduates earned a second Georgetown degree in either the law or medical departments. However, Ernest Laplace of Louisiana (**C** 1876–80, AB), went on to earn an M.D. at the University of Louisiana Medical School four years later; then he studied surgery at the Faculté de Médecine in Paris. He subsequently worked with Louis Pasteur and Joseph Lister, among others, and later was a distinguished surgeon-teacher at the University of Pennsylvania Medical School. Very few of these graduates entered the business world. Most Georgetown collegians who had such expectations or ambitions tended to leave before the senior year, as President Healy publicly complained at one commencement. Indeed, he blamed parental pressure for the departure of such students before, as he pointed out, they had had the chance to study philosophy, the capstone of liberal education calculated to instill life-guiding principles.[58] During these same years, even fewer went on to study for the priesthood (2%). One who did was Thomas Ewing Sherman (**C** 1869–74, AB), the son of General William Tecumseh Sherman. Subsequently, Thomas Sherman earned a B.S. at Yale (1876) as well before entering the Society of Jesus, where he became a well-known preacher and lecturer.

Curricular Reform

In 1875, a three-year, nonclassical program—first termed the English Course, and then, beginning in 1881, the Scientific Course—was offered to those who were "well grounded in the elementary studies of Geography, History, Grammar and Composition" and wished "to devote themselves to English Literature, Mathematics, Sciences, and the Modern Languages."[59] There had been some pressure from alumni and students to begin a concentration or major in science, if not the outright establishment of a scientific school, as Sheffield and Lowell had done at Yale and Harvard, respectively. "But," pointed out the *College Journal* in 1872, "to establish such a course, buildings and apparatus of a most expensive character and a corps of professors capable of filling the several chairs of science, must be provided." Georgetown, it added, did not possess the endowment that enabled institutions such as Yale and Harvard to found scientific schools. Until benefactors came forward, it concluded, it was idle to "consider the subject."[60]

In fact, the new course was not the basis and foundation for such a scientific concentration; it was simply the same classical course without Latin and Greek. Those who chose to complete the program received a Bachelor of Science degree. In any case, if the "Scientific Course" was meant to attract more older applicants to the college, it failed miserably. Only thirty-three (10%) of all entering students enrolled in the new college program between 1875 and 1885. Nor did it persuade business-minded students to complete their education at Georgetown rather than to drop out. Between 1879, when the college first awarded the B.S. degree, and 1883, only seven students completed the nonclassical program. As a historian has remarked about Harvard's similar failure to attract students to its nonclassical courses during this period, those who then cared enough to attend college and graduate were seeking the "prestige or the educational values attributed to the long-established classical curriculum."[61]

In 1886, four years after Patrick Healy left Georgetown, the "scientific" program was officially dropped at Georgetown. And, in fact, a Bachelor of Philosophy was substituted in the mid-1880s for the Bachelor of Science; then in the late 1880s both degrees were awarded, but apparently only as alternate consolations for those who failed to complete the full requirements for the classical course. Of those who entered in the 1880s and received a B.S., more than three-quarters (80%) went on into either law or medicine. Charles McGahan (**C** 1876–81, BS) was typical. He earned an M.D. at Dartmouth in 1885 and then went into practice as a physician in Chattanooga, where he also served on the faculty of the local medical college. McGahan eventually became director of the National Association for the Study and Prevention of Tuberculosis.

By the late 1880s Georgetown had renounced any and all curricular pluralism. "The plan of studies," the 1888–89 catalogue announced in no uncertain terms, "is based on the idea that a complete liberal education should aim at developing all the powers of the mind, and should cultivate no one faculty to an exaggerated degree at the expense of the others. . . . The same course is obligatory upon all; to render it in any considerable degree elective would be to defeat its very end and aim. . . . only students who intend to enter the classical schools will be admitted." *Pace* Harvard and even many of Georgetown's sister Jesuit schools, such as St. Louis and Fordham, which were beginning, if reluctantly, to diversify and follow the elective principle, Georgetown chose to retain its monolithic classical curriculum, united structurally by Latin and Greek, even if this meant remaining a small undergraduate college.[62]

Although it did reject substantial curricular diversity at the time, the institution had earlier modernized somewhat by giving increased attention to elementary science courses. Thus, in 1873 the study of chemistry was extended over a two-year period (sophomore and junior years) and French was discontinued as a requirement for those classes. Each science class met three hours weekly; and monthly lectures, with appropriate experiments, were given by appointed juniors, typically on such subjects as chlorine, arsenic, and hydrofluoric acid. Laboratory sessions were part of these courses in 1873, but regular laboratory work in which students could perform their own experiments did not begin until 1880. Then a chemistry laboratory was fashioned out of the small boys' playroom in the basement of the preparatory building (Maguire).[63] Moreover, Georgetown was one of the first schools to use Ira Remsen's then avant-garde textbook in its sophomore chemistry course in the late 1880s. Earlier, the course text, adapted from Fresenius, was prepared for the sophomores and juniors by the chemistry professor, T. B. Tarr, SJ, and printed in 1882 by the press in Georgetown.[64] Moreover, a government report on the teaching of chemistry and physics in institutions within the country had already cited Georgetown in 1880 for its strong concentration on chemistry.[65] In class hours and laboratory requirements for all senior students, the college had a stronger science component than most other liberal arts colleges.

In the senior year, students studied physics and mechanics. Hour-long classes were held six days a week, with professors lecturing and performing experiments for five days and students required to review the essential matter and repeat the experiments each Saturday.[66] The study of astronomy continued as the final phase of the physics course, with nightly observations in April and May at the observatory on the Hill.[67] By the 1880s physics students were spending two hours weekly on their own experiments and original investigation.[68] The results of those experiments were at times displayed at exhibitions in the college museum. In the spring of 1882, for instance, William Cahill, a senior, demonstrated his "electric lamp," which employed mercury as an improved source of energy for the Werdermann lamp.[69]

More typical was the practice of student lectures, usually accompanied by experiments relating to the "investigation" being explained. "Specimens" were also given at the close of each semester so that appointed students could present demonstrations of experiments ("Heat, Motion and Force," "Electro-magnetism and Its Uses," etc.). All the students of the class were also quizzed by members of the faculty on topics related to the principles of physics (e.g., general properties of bodies [molecular forces, three states of matter], hydro-statics [law of transmission of pressure, absorption of gases by solids and liquids, velocity of efflux of a liquid], pneumatics [gases, diffusion of gases; water pumps], acoustics [intensity, pitch, and timbre of sound, physical theory of music], heat [expansion, force of liquids in expanding, solidification]).[70]

Despite this recognition of science's new place in the world of knowing, Georgetown attempted to set careful limits to the authority of such knowl-

Detail from a photograph of the chemistry laboratory, probably as it was used from 1880 onward. Photograph taken ca. 1890. (Georgetown University Archives)

edge. As one student observed in the introduction to his "specimen": "If we should succeed in showing you our advancement in science, we hope you will see that it is advancement as taught in a Catholic college, and as protected by the Catholic religion. This is an age of scientific infidelity," in which Catholic scholars had the obligation to refute the "intellectual atheism" inherent in "the pernicious doctrine of the Evolutionists."[71] Charles O'Donovan (1875–78, AB), the author of "The Nightmare of Science," was unabashedly polemical. He accused science, transformer of the modern world, of the epistemological imperialism of trying to subvert everything to itself, including religion. The doctrine of evolution, he conceded, might be true as an explanation of the development of life among the lower animals, but could hardly be the key to the existence of life from "the original all-pervading Cosmic vapor and [of] the most enlightened man. . . ."[72] Already in 1874 the *College Journal* had published an essay by an Irish archbishop who attempted to refute Darwin's theory that the origin of species is derived by descent, with variation, from parent forms through the natural selection of those best adapted to survive in the struggle for existence. "If any portion of oxygen, nitrogen, or carbon," the prelate wrote, "or any particles of earth or water, could, of their own nature, by simple amalgamation, produce an organism, no reason could be assigned why all the atoms in existence should not have been organisms long ago."[73] In 1884 invited by President Healy to address students and faculty, alumnus Condé B. Pallen attacked the teachings of Darwin and Herbert Spencer for their incompatibility with religious orthodoxy.[74]

This sometimes antievolutionary mood notwithstanding, the extracurricular activities at Georgetown reflected the new scientific consciousness and the president's attempts to raise the quality of intellectual life within Georgetown. In 1876, Healy established the Toner Scientific Circle, named for its benefactor, Doctor Joseph Toner. Intended to promote scientific knowledge, the Circle hosted monthly lectures by distinguished scientists. Among the speakers in the 1880–81 academic year were James E. Hilgard, superintendent of the United States Coast and Geodetic Survey, on "Tides and Tidal Action in Harbors"; Dr. Thomas Antisell, distinguished member of the medical department, on "The Solidification of Our Globe"; W. B. Taylor, of the Smithsonian Institution, on "The Limitations of Scientific Thought"; and Simon Newcomb, a director of the U.S. Naval Observatory, on the "Progress of Astronomy."[75] The lectures drew not only students and faculty but, at least occasionally (as for the Newcomb lecture), members of the Washington intellectual community as well.

Each member of the Toner Circle was required to write a paper on some scientific topic, which served as the basis for the competition for the Toner Scientific Medal. The competition was intended to "awaken [the] taste for personal observation and investigation in some one of the many branches of the natural sciences." Competitors were required to give illustrated lectures on their topics. In 1882 the winning topic, the "Archeology of the District [of Columbia]," was delivered with arrowheads, stone axes, and pottery fragments for exhibits. Also-rans were "The House Fly," with microscopic slides illustrating the insect's anatomy, and "Gold and Silver Ores," featuring specimens collected from the Dakota Territory by a student who hailed from there. Judges, recruited from the university faculty, the Smithsonian, and government agencies, questioned the candidates and examined the lecture exhibits before rendering their decision.[76]

Besides the "specimens" in physics, seniors were also required to participate in regular public disputations in which certain students were chosen to defend and others to attack various propositions related to metaphysics, natural psychology, natural theology, cosmology, and ethics. The propositions, culled from scholastic philosophy, were expected to be defended logically and substantively. Varying little from year to year, they ranged from "There is a natural law and it is immutable" through "From the admirable order of the world, it is clearly evident that a certain superior intelligence lies behind it" to "Dueling is illicit." Not all the topics were innocent of contemporary immediacy. In 1874 Thomas Ewing Sherman was one of the defenders of the proposition: "There is a natural right to property." "The question is an important one," the *College Journal* observed, "in view of the Communistic developments of the day."[77] (Ten years before Karl Marx had presided over the First International, and in 1867 he had published the first volume of *Das Kapital*.) Two years later, a year after the passage of the Fifteenth Amendment to the Constitution, the seniors defended the proposition that "The right of suffrage may be granted to every citizen but it is not an innate nor a necessary right of every citizen in a Democratic any more than in a Monarchical community."[78]

General examinations, both written and oral, continued to be an important part of the Georgetown curriculum. They occurred at the conclusion of each semester (except for seniors, who faced examinations only in the spring), and typically they took up a month of the academic calendar. Written exams were limited to the languages, both classical and modern. A numerical grading system had been in use since 1867, antedating efforts at most colleges to introduce a more formal element of academic control. Monthly marks were read aloud by the dean at assembly and certificates of achievement ("tickets") were distributed to students who managed the highest grades in various subjects. At the end of each semester "grand tickets" were awarded to those in each class who scored the highest out of a possible 300-point total. Emulation was still very much a reigning principle, and "The moderately zealous," the *College Journal* opined, "will be quickened by the competition they will encounter in their classes, and the idly-disposed will have been shamed into unexpected industry. . . ."[79] Indeed, under Healy's presidency, for the first time in school history, students were threatened with dismissal for academic failure— that is, for being on the "condemned list" for three straight months.[80] By the middle of the 1870s scholastic achievement was clearly not only the chief objective of a Georgetown education but it was also intended, through the grading system, to serve as a means of ensuring character formation or discipline as well.[81] It was not coincidental that confinement in the jug and much of the rest of the old penal system for disciplining students were discontinued during that same decade.

In an effort to underscore the new focus on science, mathematics, and history, special prizes were endowed in the 1870s. The very first, a gold medal for the best historical essay, was established in 1874 by Martin Morris, an alumnus and professor of the law department. His colleague, Charles Hoffman, established a prize in mathematics the following year. That same year Joseph Toner funded

"Ticket" awarded in 1880 to William Hunter, in Rudiments, for excellence in the First Elements of English (shown actual size, and signed by P. F. Healy, SJ; Georgetown University Archives)

a medal in natural philosophy or physics. In announcing these medals at the 1875 commencement, Patrick Healy pointed out that such endowments were a novelty in the history of the institution. But his expressed hope was that before Georgetown completed its first century, its commitment to the sciences would not only be symbolically recognized through prizes but incarnated in the shape of a building exclusively devoted to science.[82]

These medals, together with other annual prizes, were distributed, along with degrees at the year-end commencement, held (until 1879) in late June in the student assembly hall of the Mulledy Building. Gone were the five-hour ceremonies; now speeches and distribution of awards and degrees were completed in less than two hours. Presidents of the United States and other political or religious dignitaries still presided over the college exercises, including distinguished alumnus John Lee Carroll (**C** 1844–46), then governor of Maryland, who was invited in 1878 to preside at the ceremonies. In the 1870s the practice of conferring honorary degrees was begun; in the initial decade, most went to members of the law or medical departments. And, beginning in 1880, the preparatory school held its own commencement and separate prize giving.

Student Opinion and American Society

During Healy's tenure there was a renewed emphasis on public speaking. In 1874 he secured from Richard Merrick, an alumnus, an endowment of a prize for debating. Beginning in the spring of 1875 the Merrick Prize debate was held annually under the aegis of the Philodemic, with dignitaries from the government and local community serving as judges and with a large audience in attendance. In 1880 Chief Justice Field, Senator Allen Thurman of Ohio, and Representative Randall Gibson of Louisiana sat as judges for the debate on the topic "Would it be to the interests of the United States to assume the political control of any canal constructed across the isthmus that separates the Atlantic and Pacific oceans?" The subjects were consistently topical; for example, in 1879: "Is it right and expedient to prohibit Chinese immigration?"; and in 1886: "Resolved, That greater dangers threaten the Republic of the United States from combination of capital than from combination of labor." When the new building (later named Healy Hall) opened in 1881, the Philodemic Society was the sole student organization allotted its own room there. One barometer of the reviving prestige of debating was the large number of senior students who applied to join the society. More than half the graduates during Healy's tenure were members of the Philodemic.

Another form of elocution promoted as an extracurricular activity during the Healy administration was declamation, or public recitation. Students competed in monthly public readings of poems and speeches before fellow students and invited guests. At the end of the academic year a declamatory champion was chosen by several distinguished judges who selected the best orator from among the year's monthly winners. Reporting on one of these early readings by John Agar, the *College Journal* noted in 1875: "'Murillo's slave' was a difficult piece to render, on account of the variety of emotions expressed in it; but, difficult as it was, the reader did it ample justice. The inflections of his voice were well managed: good judgment and the careful study he had given the poem, did the rest."[83]

The Reading Room Association was founded during Patrick Healy's first year as Prefect of Studies (1868). The organization was intended to keep students abreast of current events and intellectual developments. In aid of that, the association subscribed to a wide variety of newspapers and journals, including the *Baltimore Sun, New York Herald, St. Louis Times, Catholic World, Scribner's Monthly,* and the *Scientific American.* Since the 33,500-volume college library was still generally closed to students, the Reading Room and the libraries of the various student societies, which together housed nearly four thousand volumes, were important and well-used.[84] Indeed, the establishment of the prizes in history, debating, and science had generated efforts by 1874 to increase the holdings in the student libraries in these subject areas.[85] At the same time there was a growing conviction that a union of the libraries would maximize their value and eliminate the duplication inherent in a system that had the same basic collections in several libraries. So in 1876 the two debating societies consolidated their libraries. Four years later all the student libraries were combined, and a student library committee was elected to oversee them and the association's reading room. By 1888 a library for all three societies was under one management in the new building.[86] The university library collection totaled forty-five thousand volumes by that time.

Student opinion, shaped in part by the traditional curriculum and reflecting the various explicit and implicit opinions of the faculty and administration, remained more or less conservative and anti-statist about most social and political issues. Highly antagonistic to the anticlerical, rationalistic, liberal movements stirring throughout Europe, the students were very defensive in opposing liberalism. They declared vigorously that religion offered "no impediment to true progress, no barrier to the development of thought, no obstacle to the fullest activity of genuine freedom."[87] Moreover, this fervent viewpoint envisioned the dark clouds of liberalism and socialism gathering even in the United States.

Bookplates (two shown here of about a dozen) were placed in books provided by the student societies that maintained the Students' Library. (Georgetown University Special Collections)

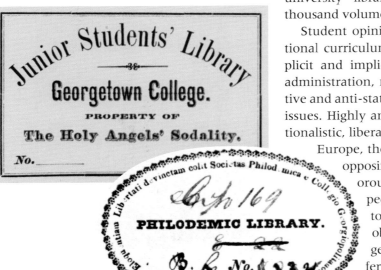

A propos of the policies of Reconstruction, the *Journal* editors observed that "The events which have marked the course of our domestic politics during the past few years, show how slight is the barrier which divides a mighty republic from an unprincipled despotism." Virtue they saw as the key to the preservation of liberty, and religion alone was the guarantor of that virtue.[88] The *Journal* editors repeatedly decried these centralizing tendencies of the federal government, which, as a direct result of the Civil War, were in their opinion a repudiation of the intentions of the founders. "Schemes of national education, with a vast university annexed, and enterprises of a more material, but of no less dangerous and centralizing a character all of which could be safely and successfully conducted by individuals or corporations, begin to call for special laws and legislation, and no one can see where this agressive [sic] movement is to terminate."[89] Compulsory public education was particularly offensive to these articulate students. As early as 1874, it was seen as an invasion of the right of parents to raise and nurture their child as they saw fit. "Legislation of this character," the *Journal* added, "carries us back to the days of State dictation in matters of conscience and religion, from which our Revolution released or ought to have released us."[90] Temperance was another area where the state was seen to be attempting to coerce by law public behavior that could only be achieved through individual virtue. In other words, the students saw an increasingly corrupt society trying to save itself through an all-intrusive state. "This dependence on mere legislation," the student paper concluded, "is already preparing many to accept it as a means of enforcing social equality between classes and races where none exists at present, as a resource for regulating prices and values which the exigencies of trade and commerce can alone control, and for still other purposes."[91] In brief, students were prone to use the language and ideology of liberalism as the means to argue for conservative ends.

Behind much of the stirring for social reform among both southern black and northern white laborers in the 1870s, the student press at Georgetown saw the spectre of communism. (Marx, Engels, and Bakunin were at that very moment turning unquestioned certitudes into shocking uncertainties.) In a long essay in 1875 on "Communism," the writer attacked its philosophical presuppositions that disavowed the right to property. If, in fact, the editor reasoned, "no one could own permanent property, there would arise in a short time the greatest necessity and indigence among the people," since no one would care to endure hardship to acquire it. He was nonetheless puzzled that such a philosophy would "have found so many advocates even in our country, where worth is the only standard by which we measure our citizens, [w]here property is every day changing hands, and every industrious man is becoming at least independent if not rich. . . ."[92]

That summer the violent railroad strike of 1877 that steamed along the tracks of the Baltimore and Ohio and Pennsylvania Railroads from Baltimore to Pittsburgh was especially shocking to the college community. At the following commencement one of the student orators examined "Communism in the United States." The speaker traced the uprising to the false expectations that communism planted in the minds of workers regarding property rights and lawful authority.[93]

Student Government and the Athletic Association

In keeping with his conviction that a system of pervasive, uncompromising discipline was hardly compatible with the civilities appropriate to a university environment, President Healy quickly reformed much of the structure of student living at Georgetown. By 1873 he had not only discontinued the ancient institution of "jug" but he had also had the detention room converted into a billiard parlor. Then, in the dining room he replaced the long wooden, refectory tables with smaller ones, and discontinued the monastic practice of public reading during meals. Attendance at Mass was made optional, and smoking was allowed. He also wanted at least the older students to live in private rooms rather than in dormitories under the constant watch of prefects. But if Patrick Healy felt that the institution had to treat students much more as maturing adults rather than as children *in loco parentis,* he was not prepared to go as far as Charles Eliot at Harvard. Eliminating all discipline and disclaiming any responsibility for training character was not for Jesuit educators.[94] Indeed, Healy was rigorous about enforcing the rules that remained. Between 1874 and 1881 at least twenty-eight students were dismissed, mostly for off-campus intoxication or for insubordination to faculty.

As one of his students recalled after his death, "Father Healy was not what would be called a 'popular' man."[95] He was referring primarily to the resentments that Healy's plans to reform the institution had aroused among the faculty, but his assessment surely extended to many students as well. Healy was rather remote from them. How much of this remoteness was a natural defense against the indignities and injustices that his biracial origins generated is unclear. What is clear is his firm, explicit conviction that students had to be responsible for shaping much, if not most, of their own education—a responsibility that transcended the Georgetown classroom.

The first year of Healy's administration marked the genesis of student government and the democratization of the student extracurriculum at Georgetown. In November of 1874 the leading members of the newer student activities—the *Journal,* the cadets, and the band—sponsored a mass meeting of their fellow students (a good number belonging to all three) to rally support for these organizations. A committee was named to solicit names of potential subscribers for the paper, and another committee was formed to organize a football team.[96] Such mass meetings took place irregularly over the next several years to authorize and regulate student activities that ranged from athletics to political clubs. By 1880 the meetings functioned collectively as an informal student government, known as the "yard."[97]

Athletics became the initial beneficiary of this attempt at the consolidation and self-regulation of student organizations, when the athletic association was formed several months later by the same leaders who had called the November 1874 mass meeting. The athletic association consisted of elected student officials and representatives of each campus sport, including baseball, gymnastics, crew, and billiards. This association was responsible for overseeing and regulating the recreation facilities and for funding of these sports. (Such associations were common on most American college campuses by the 1870s.) One of the first activities that the new organization sponsored was a public benefit, a series of readings, to pay for the gymnasium completed that same year—a wooden building housing a rowing machine, parallel bars, rings, weights, and dressing rooms. Under the association's auspices, track and field began at Georgetown in 1875. Thereafter, each November an "Athletic Sports" intramural competition was held on campus for several weeks. It was a combination of picnic contests (wheelbarrow races, sack races, greased-pig chase) and olympic events (dashes, jumps, hurdles, three-mile walk, mile run, shot put, rifle-firing). In 1879 a kind of marathon was added, a three-hour "go as you please" (run, walk) event in which the winner covered more than nineteen miles in the allotted time.[98] The three-week carnival was the highlight of the fall semester throughout the late 1870s as students, accompanied by band and cannon, converged on the front lawns and walks to both participate in and witness the events. The "Athletic Sports" festival continued to be popular until the late 1880s, when a more organized sport, football, replaced it.

The two independent baseball clubs, the Stonewalls and the Quicksteps, seem to have been the victims of athletic consolidation. They both disappeared after the 1875 spring season, but a college nine survived after a fashion. Baseball lagged much behind other campus sports in student interest during the Healy years. The new rage was crew. A decade earlier, students had petitioned for holidays to watch baseball games; now they sought an early release from classes in order to rush to the Aqueduct Bridge (predecessor of the Key Bridge) to watch a race between local rowing crews.

Ironically, Georgetown discovered crew at the very time it was declining as a national collegiate sport. It had been a popular urban sport since the 1820s, and Harvard and Yale had formed boat clubs as early as the 1840s. By the 1850s several New England colleges were contesting annually for supremacy in intercollegiate regattas. Indeed crew became the first big-time college sport, with collegewide teams, special facilities, paid coaches, and enthusiastic betting on the contests.[99] In 1871 Harvard took the lead in forming the Rowing Association of American Colleges. By

The Georgetown crew training on the Potomac. University buildings appear on the Hilltop to the left of center, and the town's buildings and wharves are shown to the right at the river's edge. Photograph taken ca. 1881. (Georgetown University Archives)

1873 eleven colleges were members, including some of the newer land-grant schools, among them Cornell and the University of Massachusetts. When the latter won championships that apparently embarrassed the elite New England schools, Harvard and Yale withdrew and restricted their future competition to each other. With their secession in 1876, the national association and its national regattas came to an end.[100] That was also the very year that a group of students led by John Agar, T. P. Kernan, and James Dolan formed the Georgetown College Boat Club. Tryouts were held to select the six best oarsmen to man each shell. Very quickly, the Georgetown crews bargained for the use of the Potomac Club's boathouse and several of its shells, as well as a coach.[101] Distinctive colors, a necessity in a sport where the competition took place at a great distance from spectators, were also immediately chosen by a student committee. Then a group of Georgetown Visitation students were invited to make the blue and gray banners for the shells, and, as elsewhere, those crew colors quickly became the official school colors. A "Boat Song" was even written for the crew.[102] The Boat Club collected money through a written appeal to alumni and a series of fund-raisers, including public "musical and liter-

ary entertainments" by student and professional singers, as well as billiard tournaments. Thus, by 1877, the members managed to build their own boathouse, designed by J. L. Smithmeyer, on the Potomac just west of the college, and buy three boats.[103] Four years later, a late winter flood washed away the shells and virtually wrecked the boat house. The sport was moribund for the next decade.[104]

In the early 1880s, with lacrosse already a popular sport in Baltimore, the preparatory students at Georgetown started to play it, but the game failed to interest the collegians. For most of the 1880s baseball, still played in the fall and spring, was the only organized sport at Georgetown. Sporting their own uniforms for the first time in 1885, the "Baseball Nine" played a motley array of opponents, including local semipro clubs, other colleges (Columbian, Gallaudet, the Naval Academy), and high schools. With the modernization of the equipment and the standardization of the game's rules, both scores and enthusiasm plummeted.

In any case, another organized sport was forcing baseball from the fall calendar by 1887. Football, or a crude combination of rugby and soccer, had once been part of a well-established hazing ritual on many college

Like their collegiate "musical ancestors" of the 1870s and 1880s, these members of the Mandolin Club were an established part of Georgetown's social life. Photograph taken ca. 1896. (Georgetown University Archives)

campuses before the Civil War. Although hazing was not part of the Georgetown tradition then, the sport was played informally at the college as early as 1840, when it was recorded that one student broke his arm.[105] However, not until late 1874 or five years after the first intercollegiate game was played between Rutgers and Princeton in 1869 did a Football Association form at Georgetown. Football, rugby style, was growing in popularity in American collegiate circles. A month after the 1874 student meeting gave birth to the Football Association at Georgetown, the *College Journal* remarked on the large number of students playing between the newly erected goalposts in the front yard north of the handball courts. The writer was suitably enthusiastic that "Football has now completely supplanted base-ball. . . ."[106] But this initial football fever proved fleeting. The Football Association quickly died (the general Athletic Association, formed the next year by virtually the same students who had formed the Football Association in 1874, made no mention of football). A decade later, in 1883, a Georgetown team was finally formed. Two games, both losses, were played with Gallaudet.[107] The team did become part of the Athletic Association, however, and a student was elected to manage the team (as in baseball), but four years elapsed before the team played outside competition again. By that time the game, under the influence of Walter Camp of Yale, was evolving rapidly into American football. In November 1887, the Georgetown football team defeated the Emerson Institute on the college field, 46–6, then split a pair of games against local high schools. By the following October the college diarist was reporting that "Foot-ball is all the rage among the boys."[108] The 1888 team won four of six games against local clubs; Alexandria High School defeated Georgetown, as it had the previous year. In 1889 the team improved its record with five victories and one defeat, with Virginia (34–0) and Gallaudet (10–4) among its victims.[109]

Beyond the world of sports student social life was still almost exclusively intramural. Stag dances continued to be a regular feature. Magic lantern shows survived as an occasional entertainment. The major annual event in the social calendar of the students in the 1870s was their Mardi Gras. Capping the weeks-long work of a student planning committee, the Shrove Tuesday carnival began at sundown with the first early supper. Joyously elaborate, it featured everything from oysters to pancakes and was followed by a series of short plays. The highlight of the long evening was a masked ball, in which most of the costumed students staged a grand entrance, two by two, to the strains of a march supplied by a hired orchestra. Costumes ranged from harlequins and princes to knights and ghosts. And they all finished off the evening in formal dancing, four-step gallops and the like, until the grand unmasking during a second midnight supper.[110]

The Medical School

One of Patrick Healy's intermediate goals that was linked to making Georgetown into a university was the transformation of its medical department from an independent proprietary operation to a professional school of the university with rigorous academic standards and a highly trained, specialized faculty. Like Eliot, Healy saw the radical improvement of the professional schools as a prerequisite to the attainment of university status.[111] The field of medicine itself was becoming increasingly specialized. Anatomy, for instance, was now subdividing into physiology, pathology, and bacteriology. More and more American and European doctors were flocking to Berlin or Vienna, both meccas of late-nineteenth-century medicine, for advanced training. Much more emphasis was being put on clinical education, or "bedside teaching," as a complement to classroom lectures and laboratory work in the formation of doctors. The leading schools in the United States were beginning to adopt a graded three-year program in place of the repetitive two-year program, with Harvard the first to do so in 1871.[112]

At the beginning of classes for the 1874–75 academic year of the Medical School, President Healy delivered the opening address, usually given until then by one of the medical faculty. Whether by invitation or on his own initiative, Healy used the occasion to indicate his attitude toward the importance of a comprehensive, contemporary medical education. If, he speculated, one of the professors of the school of medicine at the ancient University of Salerno were to present himself before the examining board of a modern medical school, he would surely fail to earn a diploma. Inevitably, the nature of medicine was progressive. "It cannot therefore be a matter of wonder that in these days more is expected of the candidate for a degree than ever before." He happily noted that the Georgetown faculty had been particularly rigorous in examining last year's candidates for graduation (Healy's first). The criterion was to be quality, not quantity. He had demanded that measure in the college and he expected it in the professional schools as well. If numbers fell because of higher demands, so be it. Ticket-driven commercial considerations were to be no excuse for the failure to advance the standards of the profession.[113]

At the 1876 commencement, Noble Young, then sixty-seven years old and the featured speaker, announced his formal retirement from the faculty. That was the beginning of a sweeping reorganization of the faculty. Begun by Healy, that reorganization was meant to end the school's independent status and bring it abreast of developments in the world of medical education. "After much discussion," as the minutes of the university board of directors put it, the entire faculty of the school submitted their resignations and Healy declared the governing board of the Medical School dissolved. Four members of the faculty, including the three founders—Young, Flodoardo Howard (sixty-two years old), and Johnson Eliot (sixty-one years old)—were then appointed professors emeriti. Young was also given the title of president of the faculty. The resignations of five others were accepted. Healy, now the chief academic officer of the school, had the university board of directors officially put in place a new set of standards for the school regarding the admission and training of students. Then he reappointed six members, including the dean, Robert Reyburn, and five who had joined the faculty the previous year. He also named six other professors and assistants.[114] The school, now clearly under the direction of Georgetown's president, by this restructuring had become an integral department of the university. The nucleus of the new faculty were the six recent appointees: Samuel Busey, Francis Asbury Ashford, Joseph Tabor Johnson, Carl Kleinschmidt, Charles Hagner, and Daniel Kelly.

Busey (1828–1901), a graduate of the University of Pennsylvania Medical School, had been professor of materia medica at the school for five years in the 1850s and a leader in Washington medical circles before failing health forced his retirement in 1858. A decade later, his health restored, he reopened practice in Washington and in 1870 founded the city's Children's Hospital. A pioneer in pediatric medicine, he had been appointed professor of diseases of children at Georgetown in 1875, while he was serving as president of the Medical Association of the District of Columbia. He played a key role in the Georgetown reorganization a year later; and his new position was professor of the theory and practice of medicine.

Ashford (1841–83), a native of Virginia and a Civil War veteran, had come to Washington immediately after the war to study medicine. An 1867 graduate of the Columbian Medical College, Ashford had assisted Busey in the founding of Children's Hospital. Five years later he was appointed to the Georgetown faculty as professor of surgery. In the reorganization he now became treasurer of the college and a year later was named dean, a position he held until his premature death from heart disease in 1883.

Johnson (1845–1921), Kleinschmidt (1839–1905), and Kelly were all Georgetown graduates who had also done clinical work and advanced studies abroad. Johnson, a descendant of John Alden and Priscilla Mullen, had first been a student at Columbia College in New York at the outbreak of the Civil War. He earned his medical degree at Georgetown in 1865, then did postgraduate work at Bellevue Hospital Medical College in New York. In 1868 he had been appointed professor of obstetrics at the new Howard University. After two years he went to Europe to observe obstetrical surgery in hospitals in Dublin, Edinburgh, London, Paris, and Vienna; and then he returned to Georgetown as lecturer of obstetrics. He remained at Georgetown for forty years, serving eventually as president of the medical department. During his long professional career he served also as president of the American Gynecological Society and of the Medical Society of the District of Columbia.

Kleinschmidt, a native of Prussia, had emigrated to America around 1857. Settling in the District, he had earned his M.D. at Georgetown in 1862, then joined the Texas Rangers of the Confederate Army as an assistant surgeon. After making his way on foot to his home in Georgetown from Appomattox after the surrender, he returned to Germany, where he did postgraduate work at the University of Berlin. Back in Georgetown in private practice, he founded a short-lived hospital in 1874, then joined the Medical School a year later as professor of physiology. An ardent reformer in medical education, he published "The Necessity for a Higher Standard of Medical Education" in 1878. He later was the first president of the D.C. Board of Medical Examiners.[115]

In subsequent years other accomplished medical specialists joined the faculty, including Swan Moses Burnett (1847–1906), John Brown Hamilton (1847–1917), and Frank Baker (1841–1918). Moreover, the distinguished and talented Thomas Antisell rejoined the faculty in 1881 as professor of chemistry and toxology.

Burnett, the son of a Tennessee doctor, had studied with his father before completing his medical education in Cincinnati (Miami Medical College) and New York (Bellevue). He had gone to Europe in 1875 to study ophthalmology in London and Paris. Returning to the states, he established the Eye and Ear Clinic at the Central Dispensary in 1878. That same year he was appointed to the chair of ophthalmology at Georgetown's Medical School, a position he held for the next twenty-eight years. At Georgetown he developed a postgraduate course in his specialty in 1881.[116] He was a notable and prolific writer in ophthalmology and otology and a prominent member of the emerging scholarly community within the profession.

Hamilton, a graduate of Rush Medical College in Illinois in 1869, had served as a surgeon in the United States Army before joining the U.S. Marine Hospital Service in 1876. Appointed surgeon general in 1880, Hamilton had already succeeded in reorganizing and reforming that service when he was appointed professor of surgery at Georgetown in 1884. He was noted for his brilliance in clinical instruction. While at Georgetown, he also served as a delegate to the international medical congress held in Berlin in 1890. Later Hamilton was editor-in-chief of the *Journal of the American Medical Association*.[117]

Frank Baker had come late to medicine. The descendant of an old New England family, he had fought in the Civil War with the Thirty-Seventh New York Volunteers, then entered government service. (Walt Whitman and John Burroughs were two colleagues there who became lifelong friends.) Only in 1880 did he take a degree in medicine from Columbian University. Nevertheless, Baker was qualified to join the Georgetown faculty three years later as professor of anatomy. During his thirty-five years at the school, "Daddy" Baker became the institution's institution, known to the students for his kindly Socratic method ("O, yes, Mr. Smith, you must know that; come, now, you have forgotten it!"), as well as for his effective demonstrations of anatomy through the use of lantern slides and dissection.[118] A polymath whose interests extended from anatomy to zoology, Baker contributed many papers to scientific societies and published extensively. He was later the editor of the *American Anthropologist* and coeditor of the *Medical Dictionary* (1890). He was also the founder of the biological and zoological societies of Washington, as well as one of the founders of the National Geographic Society (1888), and was elected president of the Association of American Anatomists.[119]

Curricular reform was implemented two years after the faculty reorganization and was largely the work of Busey and Kleinschmidt. The academic program was increased from a two-year repetition of courses to a three-year cumulative, or graded, program. Students were required to pass a written examination, anonymously graded, at the completion of each annual segment of the program. The academic calendar was lengthened from five to seven (later eight) months. For the first time, a preliminary admission examination was given to all candidates who applied.[120] Clinical training was made an integral part of the program, and the anatomy course included a rigorous training in dissection. Beginning in 1878, students attended fourteen lectures a week, Mondays through Saturdays, and were assigned clinical work at Providence and Children's Hospitals, as well as the college dispensary, on Wednesdays and Sundays. Written final examinations also replaced the traditional oral ones. In effect, Georgetown progressed to the forefront of the reform movement among medical schools in the United States.[121] Charles Eliot, the president of Harvard, wrote in April of 1878 to

Healy: "I was very glad to learn that you took such a stand in behalf of a proper system of medical education . . . [and] to refuse to teach medicine any longer by the old and disgraceful methods. . . ."[122]

For all its academic reforms, the Medical School continued to be a "sundown college," however. Both its faculty and students were still part-time. As a graduate of the period later wrote, trying "to satisfactorily fill a position in the day-time and study medicine at night" was virtually impossible.[123] With this upgrading of standards, a decline in enrollment was inevitable, from fifty-six in 1872–73 to twenty-seven students a decade later. The number of graduates also declined; by the early 1880s, the yearly average was six. Medical students in the 1880s continued to be relatively old when they began their formal training (many nearly twenty-four years old); more tended to be non-Catholics than a decade before (up from 54% to 60%), less urban (down from 75% to 66% with city origins), and more likely to continue in government service after earning the M.D. (more than one-fifth of the total in the 1880s as opposed to one-twentieth in the 1870s). Many went to work as medical examiners in the Pension Bureau. Although most of these students were still of English, German, or Irish origin, the circle of pluralism slowly widened (see table 11.2 in appendix F). In 1883 Louis Kolipinski (a Polish American) graduated and then joined the faculty as curator of the museum. He later studied in Berlin and Vienna before returning as professor of surgery at the National Medical College and resident physician at Children's Hospital. In 1885 the college did admit a Japanese applicant who was employed at the Navy Yard, but for African Americans the racial barrier remained. In 1875, the school refused to recognize tickets, or admission slips, from Howard University, thus effectively barring Howard students from attending Georgetown classes.[124]

Three of the notable graduates of that period were George Martin Kober (**M** 1871–73), Thomas Taylor (**M** 1878–81), and James Dudley Morgan (**C** 1874–81, **M** 1883–85). To avoid being drafted into the Prussian army, the then sixteen-year-old Kober (1850–1931) had emigrated from Germany to New York in 1866. There he worked as a barber's apprentice for a year before joining the United States Army. As a hospital steward he began an apprenticeship in surgery at army posts in Pennsylvania. Transferred to the Surgeon General's office in Washington, he entered Georgetown's medical department as a student in 1871. After Kober completed his studies at Georgetown, he served for nearly two decades as an army surgeon in expeditions against the Indians in Nevada and Idaho as well as at various frontier forts in the West. In 1888 he resigned his commission and began his long career as a teacher and, eventually as dean, of the Georgetown medical faculty.[125]

Taylor, born in Scotland in 1820, already had a distinguished record behind him as an inventor and chemist when, in 1878, he matriculated in medicine at Georgetown. After studying at the University of Glasgow in the 1830s, Taylor had invented several electrical condensers and batteries, and

Georgetown's faculty ca. 1890. Among those in the first row are George Magruder (third from left), and to his left, L. W. Lovejoy (president of the faculty), Joseph Tabor Johnson, and Carl Kleinschmidt. Robert Reyburn is second from the right. Among those in the second row: Francis Asbury Ashford (second from left), and George Kober (third from left). (Georgetown University Archives)

had even demonstrated in 1851 that an electric current could be transmitted without wires. That same year he came to work in the United States. During the Civil War he served on the staff of the Ordnance Department and then of the Department of Agriculture. There he was chief of the microscopy division from 1871 to 1895. He was also one of the founders of the Washington Chemical and Biological Societies.

James Dudley Morgan, a native Washingtonian, had studied law for a year at Columbia University Law School in New York before a brief stint at Bellevue Medical College in 1883. The son of a distinguished physician, Morgan joined the faculty at Georgetown after two years of postgraduate study in Paris. He taught clinical medicine at Georgetown for more than two decades and published in many scientific journals.

To provide more clinical instruction within the school, the faculty opened a medical dispensary in 1879. It was intended to provide clinics in obstetrics, skin diseases, surgery, and children's diseases, among others, and a maternity ward was included. Confident that such a teaching hospital would enjoy public confidence among both rich and poor, the dispensary was set up to serve both paying and charity patients. But its somewhat complicated connections to the Central Dispensary (the city's hospital) in the same block (four Georgetown medical faculty taught there and several Georgetown students had clerkships) forced the new dispensary's closing in 1883.

The Law School

During the first fifteen years of its existence, the law department remained a respected but small program. Then in the middle 1880s enrollments began a dramatic climb that continued into the 1890s. In 1881 there were thirty-eight law students in the department; five years later there were one hundred and sixty. By 1889 there were ninety-six graduates. As the 1890s began, the Law School was the largest school within the university, with an enrollment of more than two hundred and fifty.[126]

In 1879 the Law School's treasurer, William Dennis, had urged President Healy to undertake an aggressive campaign to attract students from outside the region. The school, he informed Healy, already had a good number of such students. With the connections some faculty also had with members of the Hayes administration, he was confident the school could win political patronage appointments for its out-of-town students.[127] Four years later the faculty also began a recruitment campaign. In order to attract more students, they decided at a meeting in May of 1883 to make the curriculum more practice-oriented.[128] The moot court that had been established in 1875 was now expanded and given more emphasis. The Law School also began to advertise much more widely in religious, ethnic, and secular papers—from the *Boston Pilot* to the *Peoria Democrat* to the *Emerald Vindicator* to the *Atlanta Constitution*. But the curriculum seemed to be little changed, nor was it particularly oriented to "outsiders." And, while the proportion of nonlocal students did increase substantially at the school, there is no clear evidence that they were coming to Washington primarily for a Georgetown legal education.

The economic recovery from the depression that had followed the Panic of 1873 was perhaps a factor in Georgetown's growth. Columbian Law School, which had had an enrollment of one hundred and sixty-seven in 1871, experienced a downturn by the mid-1870s. But by 1882 Columbian was back to its 1871 level and continued to increase.[129] Meanwhile, Georgetown had nearly doubled its enrollment from twenty-eight to forty-eight by lowering its tuition in 1879 from $80 to $50, but the numbers declined again in the following three years. Probably the demise of the National University, a local law school founded in 1869, and the return of the Democrats to the White House in 1885 were more pertinent growth factors.

The changing demographics suggest the impact that the Cleveland administrations (1885–89, 1893–97) had upon the Law School (table 11.3 in appendix F). In the 1870s the majority of Georgetown's relatively few law students were Catholic and from cities (both 80%). And nearly three-quarters of the students (70%) were either from the capital area or the Northeast. By the end of the 1880s those figures had changed: only about two-thirds of the students were now from cities (70.1%); fewer than two-thirds (64%) were from the District, Maryland, and the Northeast. By the early 1890s, Catholics constituted slightly more than half of all the students (52.2%). Those from cities accounted for less than two-thirds (57%) and those from rural areas now made up more than a quarter of the enrollment. At the same time, the proportion of Irish students rose in the 1870s to slightly more than a fifth (from 16% to 21%) in the early 1890s. By that time, southern students accounted for a fifth of the students (up to 22% from 13% in the 1870s). Mainly, the changes reflected the patronage patterns of the Cleveland administrations, with Southerners and the Irish as the chief beneficiaries.

Also significant in the school's growth was the increasing number of Georgetown College students who went on to the law department, many of them immediately after graduation. In the 1880s approximately one hundred and fifty students from the college, nearly half of them graduates, enrolled in law, and more than half of them earned law degrees.

The most important reason for the sudden growth of the school, however, was the decision of the local legal bureaucracy, the D.C. Bar Commission, to require three years of formal legal education as a condition for admission to the bar.

On the whole, few law students entering in the 1880s and early 1890s had a college education, much less a degree. James Edwards Clements (**L** 1875–81, LLB), while not typical, does illustrate that point. Clements

The law department's fourth building at Sixth and F Streets, NW, Washington, DC. Photograph taken ca. 1884. (Georgetown University Archives)

went to work as the principal of a public school in Ballston, Virginia, immediately after his graduation from St. John's Academy in Alexandria in 1873. Twenty-two years old when he began in the law program at Georgetown two years later, Clements spent seven years studying for his degree while he continued working as a school principal. The average law student spent much less time than Clements getting a degree (two years) and was younger (nineteen) at entrance, of course. A very high proportion of them completed the program in the 1880s (75%); in the next five years this dropped to about two-thirds (62%).

Among the law students graduated during those years were Matthew John Kane (**L** 1885–86) who later became chief justice of the Oklahoma Supreme Court; Theodore Weld Birney (**L** 1885–87, LLB), grandson of James Gillespie Birney, the abolitionist and Liberty Party presidential candidate, and son of William Birney, a district attorney in Washington, D.C.; and William Rogers Clay (**L** 1885–87, LLB.; 1888, LLM), who became chief justice of the Supreme Court of Kentucky.

In 1878 the school had established a one-year master's program, "devoted especially to proficiency in Practice" and to advanced courses. Like the bachelor's program, this did not become popular until the 1880s. Then, in 1883, with the three-year requirement facing potential applicants for the bar, an LLM was suddenly very useful. So the faculty decided to stress the "usefulness" of this master's program in its advertising.[130] Many Georgetown law students began to fill the additional year requirement by earning a master's degree. By 1887 there were nearly as many persons earning the LLM degree as the LLB. The LLB remained a two-year program.[131]

The school itself moved twice during the early 1880s. In 1882 the razing of the Washington Seminary forced a relocation to the Lenman Building at 1425 New York Avenue, NW. Two years later the school had to move once more, to the southeast corner of Sixth and F Streets, NW.[132] The faculty made several attempts to persuade the university to construct a building for the school, but the financial exigencies of the institution throughout the 1880s were hardly conducive to funding any major construction for the Law School.

Under Healy's direction the university assumed an even greater control of academic affairs in the Law School. Like its medical counterpart, the department was directed to introduce written examinations for both junior and senior years by 1880. In the late 1870s professors and lecturers began to receive salaries (from $200 to $450 by 1883).[133] Healy himself taught a course in legal ethics in the 1875–76 school year. The faculty remained stable through much of this period: Charles Hoffman (dean from 1876), Richard Merrick, and Martin Morris were the nucleus of Georgetown's Law School. And in 1883 William A. Richardson was a distinguished addition as lecturer on statutory and administrative law. A former student of Justice Joseph Story at Harvard Law School, Richardson had served as secretary of the treasury during the Grant administration before being named a judge in the Court of Claims in 1874. In 1885 he became chief judge there.[134] When Richard Merrick died that same year, his replacement in constitutional law was another prestigious addition to the faculty, Chief Justice Stephen Field.

Most of the new law faculty during the 1880s, unlike those of the Medical School, were recent Georgetown graduates. Despite the great increase in enrollment, the teaching faculty increased by only a little. By 1889 there were still only eight professors.

"No President Ever Did More"

It is now thought likely that during much of his presidency Patrick Healy suffered untreated from some undiagnosed form of epilepsy. From at least 1878 he experienced recurrent headaches and occasional weak spells that forced him to keep to his bed for days on end. His trip to the West in 1878–79 had been recommended partly to help him regain his health, and he did

The Healy Building viewed from the Chesapeake & Ohio Canal. (Courtesy of the Class of 1953, *Ye Domesday Booke/Lauinger*). (Lauinger Library)

return from the nine-month journey much improved. This apparently persuaded his Jesuit superiors that they could leave him in office until he completed the new building (his second three-year term expired in 1880).[135] However, by 1881 the old symptoms had returned and Healy spent much of that year living in Maine with his brother, James, trying to recuperate. He finally returned to Georgetown in early February 1882, claiming he had regained his health. Three days later he fell in his room during a "weak" spell and cut himself badly.[136] On February 16, he submitted his resignation as president. The next day the house diarist noted: "Fr. Healy left in the after noon for the North. . . . Fr. Healy held the office of Rector nine years during which time he introduced many and salutary changes. He erected the magnificent new stone building, which will be a monument for all time."[137] "No president ever did more," the editor of the *Journal* declared in March, "to put the College upon a broad and firm basis . . . and prepare the field which it may one day enter into possession of and hold, as a great Catholic University."[138]

Patrick Healy lived for another three decades but he never recovered his health. He was able to do very limited pastoral work in Providence, in New York, and finally again Washington until his death in 1910. By that time it had become customary to refer to him as "The Second Founder of Georgetown." The New Building did indeed become his monument, and eventually was named for him. But if the structure was the symbol of the institution's commitment to becoming a distinctive university, the raw two-story mound of dirt that remained so long in front of it was a reminder of the uncompleted quest, the yawning gap that persisted between reach and grasp.

Instead of an endowment, Georgetown now showed a debt of nearly $300,000. Instead of a large community of mature scholars, the college continued to be a small school of mostly young boys, with a virtually nonexistent graduate program. Nonetheless, the Georgetown that Patrick Healy left in 1882 was a far different place than the one he had come to sixteen years earlier. If the preparatory school still had the largest number of students, the ethos, focus, and standards of the place were now decidedly set by the college. Under Healy's leadership, the college had revitalized both its curriculum and its standards. The two professional schools, medicine and law, had more or less shed their proprietary status and become integral parts of the university. The Medical School had begun to acquire a faculty distinguished for its research and contributions to the field. The Law School, while still relatively new and small, was well-positioned to undertake the dramatic expansion it would realize in the next decade. And, like Carroll, Healy had provided the institution with a definition of the essential link between heritage and mission, had given it a radically new sense of itself, and had provided some of the resources needed to begin the passage from college to university.

CHAPTER 12

Georgetown in 1889
"She Began with Our Fatherland"

She has been the guiding star of Catholic education. For an hundred years has she held her course of usefulness and honor. . . . She began with our fatherland, and as long as that fair fatherland endures so long must she endure. . . .

DANIEL J. GEARY, STUDENT ORATOR
at the Centennial, 1889

The Centennial Celebration

In February 1889, Georgetown celebrated its centennial. For three days, church and state dignitaries, alumni, faculty, and students—more than a thousand in all—gathered on and off campus for academic assemblies, dinners, and reunions to honor Georgetown on the completion of its first century as an educational institution. The United States Marine Band provided the music for the whole three-day celebration, and the student cadet corps served as the honor guard for the distinguished guests. More than eighty thousand visitors passed through the gates of the college. Banners with Latin, Greek, and Russian inscriptions adorned buildings and archways throughout the campus.[1] Sixteen hundred candles illuminated all the college windows facing east to the city and south to the river. On the final evening there was a massive fireworks display on the Hilltop. The official Jesuit diarist was moved to record this centenary triduum as "the greatest event in the history of George-town College."[2]

Whatever its intrinsic importance, the event marked the first time that the university had publicly celebrated its own beginnings. Curiously, in 1839, halfway through the first hundred years, no one had seemed aware that that year was in any way special to Georgetown. Indeed, as noted earlier, "1789" has little claim as an actual founding date. It was the beneficiary of an immigrant Jesuit's simple mistake in calculating the age of the first building. And so, during the centennial festival a banner on the original building identified it in Latin as "The house which here you see, tottering from weight of years, John Carroll, of the Society of Jesus, under happy auspices began, by laying the foundation stone, in the year 1789."[3] But, in fact, that date for the laying of the cornerstone is a year late. Nonetheless, for more than four decades, beginning in the 1840s, the founding of the "Academy at Georgetown" had been equated with the construction start-up of its first building, supposedly in 1789.[4]

James Doonan

The idea of a centennial celebration had originated with Patrick Healy a dozen years earlier. Healy (prefect of studies, 1868–80; president, 1873–82) first conceived it largely as a fundraising measure. His successor and fellow Georgian, James Doonan (1841–1911), promoted it vigorously during the latter years of his generally undistinguished six-year presidency (1882–88). Doonan was the first graduate of Georgetown to become president of the institution. His amiable, easygoing manner made him much more popular with students and alumni than his reserved, scholarly predecessor could ever be. Other than eliminating the bachelor of science program, he was largely content to let the college drift and the professional schools go their own way again. Still, the large debt that Healy had left behind was greatly reduced during Doonan's two terms, so he was popularly perceived as the president who had saved Georgetown from the financial disaster that Healy's grand plans came close to producing.

The enormous debt of the college had indeed been cut back before 1889 by more than half from the nearly $300,000 that had burdened Patrick Healy in the last exhausting years of his administration. However, Doonan had accomplished this not by succeeding where his predecessor had failed—by attracting benefactors—but, first, by being allowed to do precisely what had been ruled absolutely off-limits to Healy. That is, he was permitted to sell two large tracts of Georgetown land—the farm on Hickory Hill and the villa in Tenleytown. Second, Doonan was also the fortuitous recipient, as the community's superior, of a large legacy left to a Jesuit brother at Georgetown. Altogether these three transactions netted the university more than $170,000.[5] In July 1888, the regional superior reported to the superior general in Rome that George-town no longer had any real financial difficulties.[6] The debt was now under fifty thousand dollars, a serious one to be sure, but one that could be serviced with relative ease.[7]

In the late 1880s, Doonan also began to promote the idea of a centennial as an occasion that would allow the university to acquire the financial means to do what it had long desired. At the college commencement in 1888, in language usually not associated with celebratory occasions, Doonan admit-ted that on the eve of Georgetown's centennial it would be pretentious to claim that the university had become "what we would [wish to] see her." The main reason for this, he suggested, was the relative poverty of the Cath-olic community during most of Georgetown's history. But, he went on, if the university, in its "dowerless existence of a hundred years," had been able to achieve what they were now able to celebrate, they should have every con-fidence that during the second century they might finally realize the high aims of their founders.[8]

The message was unmistakable. Georgetown's sons were now in a posi-tion to change their alma mater's financial condition and there was no better occasion than the centenary to begin. Typically, Doonan had done virtually nothing by way of follow-through to prepare for the centennial by the time his presidency ended in the summer of 1888. And, despite an appeal from some alumni to the superior general in Rome that Doonan be kept on as president-rector for an additional three-year term so that he could preside over the centennial celebrations, Joseph Havens Richards was named in his place.[9]

Joseph Havens Richards

Richards was an Anglo-American descendant of one of the first families of the seventeenth-century Plymouth Bay colony. His father, Henry Livingston Rich-ards, was an Episcopalian pastor in Columbus, Ohio, when he became in-volved in the Catholic Movement. He converted to Catholicism two months after his son Joseph's birth in 1851. The senior Richards then went into busi-ness and relocated his family, first to Jersey City, then to Boston, in 1869. There he enrolled his son as a freshman at Boston College.[10] After his junior year, the now twenty-year-old Joseph Havens Richards entered the Society of Jesus. In 1878, during the course of his studies, he was sent to Georgetown for five years to teach physics and mathematics. While there Richards was one of the five scholastics chosen to attend Harvard for special studies in science. By the summer of 1888, at the age of thirty-six, he had completed his training in the Society. But his broad learning transcended his formal education. From his father he had inherited a love of learning that was fostered by his "habit of deep and constant reading" in many fields. In Richards, Georgetown had a

The Society of the Alumni at the centennial on February 21, 1889. In the first row, sixth from the left is James Doonan, seventh from the left is Joseph Havens Richards, eighth is Martin Morris, ninth is George Hamilton. In the third row from the top, Robert Ray is second from the left, with his right arm on the porch post. (Georgetown University Archives)

Joseph Havens Richards, SJ (1888–98). Thirtieth president of Georgetown. (Georgetown University Archives)

second Healy, a president with a broad vision and an intense capacity for work and for getting things done. Nevertheless, he quickly found that the situation he had inherited was more than enough for his enormous energy. As he wrote his mother shortly after taking over: "I am from morning to bedtime in a perfect whirl of business that leaves me no time to even so much as think, and that sends me to bed with the consciousness of a mountain of work still undone."[11]

If Doonan had left Richards a greatly reduced debt, he had also left unreduced the two-story mound of dirt in front of the new college building. It was a painful reminder of the unfinished state of the edifice that Patrick Healy had envisioned as the central symbol of Georgetown University. That fall of 1888 Richards made plans to hastily complete the auditorium and library sections of the building.[12] Yet, by January of the following year, a month before the scheduled centennial celebration, Father Provincial Thomas Campbell had to give Richards permission to borrow "a great sum of money in order that the university might be whole and still ours."[13] The mound of earth disappeared quickly and construction resumed. Then, only days before the celebration in February 1889, Francis Riggs gave $10,000 for the library and promised more, if needed.[14] Riggs Library and Gaston Hall were soon the visible results of this new vitality.

One of the new president's earliest previous actions had concerned the observatory program. Determined to revitalize it, Richards had appointed the Austrian Jesuit astronomer, John Hagen, as the new director in December 1888. The forty-one-year-old scholar-scientist had been doing astronomical research studies in Prairie du Chien, Wisconsin, when a chance visit to Georgetown and Woodstock in 1887 had brought him to the attention of Richards. So, four months after his appointment as president-rector, Richards was able to have Hagen transferred to Georgetown.[15] It was the beginning of the most productive era of the observatory and an indication of the "second Healy's" commitment to making Georgetown the university of Healy's vision.

When Richards took office, the college, with approximately two hundred students, was the largest school of the university, but nearly two thirds of these students (60%) were still in the preparatory department. The medical school faculty, encouraged by Doonan's laissez-faire leadership, had seized the opportunity in 1886 to incorporate themselves as an independent legal body and to build a new, three-story facility. Located on H Street between Ninth and Tenth Streets in northwest Washington, the Romanesque structure housed their lecture rooms and clinical facilities. But the medical department only had eighty-four students. Law, with one hundred and sixty-eight students, was the one Georgetown school experiencing rapid growth.

"All Is Not Yet Done"

If 1789 was weak on historical grounds as a founding date for the university, it was strong on symbolic value, since it made Georgetown's beginnings coincident with that of the federal government and of the Roman Catholic hierarchical church in America. These three themes surfaced repeatedly in the observance of the university's centenary. The Centennial Oration by Martin Morris, dean of the law faculty, explicated Georgetown's special link with the republic:

One hundred years ago . . . when Washington, Franklin, Adams, Hamilton, Jefferson, Madison and Robert Morris, our seven wise men . . . were laying deep and strong the foundations of our Federal Union—in that same year the foundations also were laid of this Republic of the Intellect by one who had participated with the framers of the Federal Constitution in that heroic struggle for human independence—not merely for American independence, but for the independence of mankind . . . John Carroll, of Maryland, was the Romulus of our University.[16]

Undeniably, Carroll was the link not only to the republic, but also, as its first bishop in 1789, to the hierarchical church as well. Carroll had founded Georgetown at the very moment of the creation of the institutional Catholic Church in America so that it might grow in wisdom and truth in a republic that depended for its survival on a free and educated citizenry. Of the three gold medals that were awarded to mark the event, one went to President Grover Cleveland for the United States; one went to Cardinal Archbishop Gibbons for Baltimore, first see of the church in the United States; and one went to John Gilmary Shea for his biography of John Carroll, first of Baltimore and first of Georgetown.

A major theme that all the centennial speakers iterated was John Carroll's frequent appreciations of the unique educational opportunities America afforded. In the centennial sermon at the memorial Mass, former President Doonan emphasized that the repression of American Catholics during the colonial period had initially forced the young Carroll to quit his

The medical department's new building on H Street, NW, Washington, DC, in 1886. Engraving from ca. 1887.

(Georgetown University Archives)

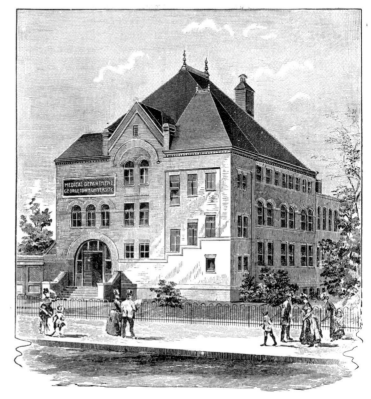

native land for conscience's sake and to go abroad to secure an education. Then the subsequent savage suppression of the Society of Jesus drove him from Flanders back to British America, Doonan noted, and he quickly became an active supporter of the revolution that followed shortly after his return. When the United States became the first of the modern colonies to successfully rebel against a motherland, Carroll was as deeply impressed as any of the makers of that revolution with the heaven-given "mission of proving to the world the possibility of a self-governed and self-governing nation . . . [because] he saw a land under whose impartial, tolerant government the church of his faith . . . would flourish as a goodly tree planted by the water's edge."[17] If it is an axiom that the king should be wise and good, Doonan pointed out, then in a government where every man is king, should he not be intelligent and upright, wise and good? To make every man such was the purpose Carroll had in founding Georgetown.

Not that Georgetown saw itself as a people's university, as an institution of higher learning with a special mission to provide education for the unpolished immigrant and the untutored poor. It was, like most contemporary colleges, avowedly elitist. As Martin Morris contended in the keynote address, "it is too much to hope that, until the millennium is ushered in, a liberal education will be within reach of more than a small minority. . . . It is this small minority that is to leaven the mass. All free government, however democratic in theory, is necessarily aristocratic in fact. The few must always administer it; the few must always guide and control it."[18] Ironically, it was his law department that was probably the most faithful to Carroll's original provision that Georgetown be open to students of "every class." Working people of modest means were still able to afford the part-time education necessary to obtain the LLB. The medical department, on the verge of ending its sundown schedule, would soon be beyond the reach of those economically below the middle class. By the last decade of the nineteenth century Georgetown College was more than ever the preserve of the children of monied Catholics, either from the old immigrations or from Central and South America (nearly a tenth of the students were coming from those regions by 1890).

For most of its first century Georgetown had been predominantly a Southern school. So it was fitting that, for the alumni banquet held at Willard Hotel on the second evening of the celebration, February 21, an alumnus from Tennessee was chosen to respond to the toast to "Our Country." "We revere the memory of our sacred dead," he avowed, "but we are heartily glad that the Union and the Constitution were saved, and that they are our common heritage to-day!"[19] By 1889 it was noticeable that Southerners were an ever-smaller minority at Georgetown, both in the college and the professional schools, as Northerners, particularly those of Irish and German ancestry, became a dominant presence. Four out of every ten students were now Irish Americans.

In this regard the speakers made little note of Georgetown's tradition of religious pluralism among its students. Morris, the centennial orator, did mention the international "household" from which the university drew its students, "even from the nations of Europe and Asia." But no mention was made of Carroll's provision that Georgetown be open to those of "every religious profession." Indeed the proportion of non-Catholics, at least in the college, had also been declining since the Civil War. By 1889 Georgetown College was virtually a ghetto school. Of its two hundred students that year, fewer than fifteen were non-Catholic, a sharp drop from the prewar years when non-Catholic students had occasionally outnumbered the Catholic students.[20]

Much was also made during the centennial triduum of Georgetown's distinction as the oldest Catholic university in the United States. At the entrance to the New Building (later named Healy), a banner heralded "Calverton, 1640; Newtown, 1677; Bohemia, 1740; Georgetown, 1789." These were the schools that Jesuits had conducted in early, Catholic Maryland. And two small ship's cannon, reputedly from the *Ark* and the *Dove,* flanked the main entrance to the New Building as a symbol of Georgetown's connection to the seventeenth-century beginnings of Catholicism in British America. Doonan, in fact, the previous June had been responsible for securing the cannon from the Jesuit farm just below St. Mary's City.[21] Used for seemingly endless salutes to the various guests and events, they played a prominent role in the noisy, joyful celebration. Still the planners of the centennial did not go as far as that university official who, forty-five years later, celebrated a "Founders Day" to honor "the progenitors of Georgetown University" who in 1634 "projected a seat of learning" at St. Mary's City.[22] (That reference to long-ago Jesuit aspirations conveniently made Georgetown at least *in voto* two years older than Harvard, of course.)

Both the 1889 banners and speeches praised Georgetown as "the mother of colleges" but they made no attempt to site its real foundation in Cecil Calvert's Maryland. It sufficed to list the many Jesuit colleges from Worcester to Santa Clara that had followed in Georgetown's wake; and to claim, as a student orator did, that Georgetown "has been the guiding star of Catholic education."[23] Earlier he spoke of Georgetown's progress, "from the modest academy that Carroll placed upon the banks of the Potomac" to "a university whose schools of arts, science, literature, medicine and law give it place among the foremost institutions of the land."[24] It was, in effect, the coda of the themes played during the celebration. Even the dean of the youngest of Georgetown's schools boasted that his school had already "assumed a foremost place among the Law Schools of the country. . . ."[25]

Beneath the commemorative boasting lay the worrisome truth that, as Georgetown entered its second century, it no longer could be considered the premier Catholic institution of higher education. Within the network of Jesuit colleges at least two universities, St. Louis and Fordham, were to

Formal photograph of the revived Georgetown College Company of Cadets at the centennial. (Georgetown University Archives)

some degree challenging Georgetown by their vigorous development as centers of higher learning. The establishment in 1879 of the New York–Maryland Province of the Society had incorporated Jesuits of the New York region into the former Maryland Province. That, in the next several decades proved a major setback for Georgetown's attempts to develop as a national university. After numerous protests by members of the old province about the newly named, larger province, the official name was changed to Maryland–New York. But, despite this nod to historical precedence, the Jesuit center of gravity, at least in the East, had shifted from Washington to New York. Fordham, not Georgetown, soon became the focus of Jesuit plans to establish a premier university in what promised to be the new intellectual capital of the country.[26]

Another new obstacle to Georgetown's development was the Catholic University of America. Georgetown was no longer the only Catholic institution of higher learning in the District of Columbia. Martin Morris, in his Centennial Oration, was moved to recall George Washington's dream of founding a great university in the federal city, which in turn prompted him to ask:

But are we not realizing the dream of Washington? . . . Institutions grow; they are not made. They do not spring up in a night, perhaps to vanish like an exhalation before the morning sun. . . . All human institutions that are destined to last must come up from small beginnings. It has taken a century to develop our country into a mighty nation and a united people. The same century has developed the College founded by John Carroll into a great and prosperous university, fully competent to hold her place among the universities of the world. But all is not yet done.[27]

The mustard-seed metaphor was surely meant to make Georgetown's simple origins contrast favorably with the sophisticated origins of the new Catholic university across town. Morris was aware that the decision had been made to situate in the nation's capital the Catholic University of America that the hierarchy had agreed to establish during the Third Plenary Council of Baltimore. The Jesuits, through their provincial superior Robert Fulton, had at the time of the Council strenuously opposed the idea of such a national university. When it was further proposed to put the future university in Washington, they objected that that was an insult to Georgetown, as well as to Woodstock College, the Jesuit theologate some thirty miles north.[28] Sometime during the course of these deliberations, Bishop John Keane, the newly appointed first president-rector of the Catholic University, approached President-Rector Doonan about the possibility of acquiring Georgetown's buildings and property for the new institution (or so Doonan interpreted it). Doonan made clear that, despite Georgetown's then burdensome debt, there was no intention to sell.[29]

On the last day of the centennial celebration, Father John Murphy, a Georgetown official, read to the assembly a cablegram from Bishop John Keane, then in Rome: "Richards, Georgetown: Congratulations and Best wishes. Keane." Terse cablegrams were the stuff of transatlantic communications in the late nineteenth century. But Murphy's comfortable interpretation was that Keene's four words effectively dispelled any uncomfortable suspicions of any rivalry between the two institutions. Several months later President Richards invited President Keane to address the annual banquet for the alumni. The new rector assured his listeners that the new university represented no threat either to Georgetown or any other Catholic college since its focus would be exclusively on postgraduate studies.[30] That may have pleased and reassured the alumni, but it hardly reassured Georgetown's administrators. Even then, in 1889, they were already intent on reviving the graduate programs in philosophy and in the arts, and they were also looking into ways

Obverse (left) and reverse (right) of the Alumni Medal of the Centennial. Designed by William F. Quicksall (C 1861) and produced for die stamping by Francis A. Cunningham (C 1864). The medals were issued as a memorial of the formal celebration in February 1889. (Shea, *Memorial of the First Century of Georgetown College*)

Distinguished guests and faculty assembled on the porch of Old North during the celebration of the centennial. Photograph taken ca. 1889. (Georgetown University Archives)

to add new graduate programs in other fields, including theology. Moreover, within a very few years the Catholic University administrators did decide it was necessary to offer undergraduate courses. Subsequently they also attempted to take over Georgetown's medical and law schools. So, for the next three decades, despite the brave words of the centenary, this unfortunate rivalry kept a dark cloud over Georgetown.

To the Second Century

In July 1889 Father James Curley died, three months shy of his ninety-third birthday and nearly six decades after his arrival at Georgetown in 1831. His early teaching years at the college were also the years in which Thomas Mulledy, William McSherry, and James Ryder were pressing forward eagerly with their ambitious plans for the institution. With the building of the observatory, now almost a half century old, Curley himself had helped substantially in the realization of those dreams for Georgetown. James Curley had outlived not only his three Irish American contemporaries but also Bernard Maguire and John Early, the dreamers and planners of the next generation.

His time in life had all but spanned the institution's. And for six decades he taught, prayed, and lived the ups and downs of Georgetown's evolution from college to university. It seemed fitting that he should die during the institution's centenary. With James Curley's passing, an era appeared to also pass for Georgetown.

As the institution began its second century, it was now clearly more than "the college on a hill" but much less than the Healy building symbolized. If past was prologue, the future promised no less distinctive a history for Georgetown University than the past ten decades had proven to be for Georgetown College.

Trompe l'oeil painting by James Simpson in 1831 on the library door of Old North. (*CUSC*)

Appendices

Georgetown Student Enrollments, 1791–1889

All enrollment figures for the college and preparatory department together are based on information from the student databank that we established for all students who entered between the 1791–92 and 1870–71 academic years. The figures thereafter (1871–72 through 1888–89) are taken from surviving records, primarily published catalogues and entrance books.

Figures for the medical department (afterwards Medical School) during the first seven years (1851–58) are based on all available information and show only those who graduated from the program, probably half or fewer of those who enrolled.

Data for the law department (afterwards Law School) are compiled from records kept from its beginnings in the 1871–72 academic year through the 1888–89 academic year.

GEORGETOWN ACADEMIC YEAR	ACADEMY & COLLEGE STUDENTS	GEORGETOWN ACADEMIC YEAR	ACADEMY & COLLEGE STUDENTS
1791–92	69	1808–09	53
1792–93	74	1809–10	43
1793–94	86	1810–11	31
1794–95	82	1811–12	53
1795–96	86	1812–13	80
1796–97	71	1813–14	90
1797–98	70	1814–15	106
1798–99	58	1815–16	107
1799–00	68	1816–17	119
1800–01	64	1817–18	108
1801–02	58	1818–19	75
1802–03	45	1819–20	69
1803–04	37	1820–21	61
1804–05	40	1821–22	49
1805–06	33	1822–23	44
1806–07	34	1823–24	43
1807–08	47	1824–25	52

continued

GEORGETOWN ACADEMIC YEAR	ACADEMY & COLLEGE STUDENTS	GEORGETOWN ACADEMIC YEAR	ACADEMY & COLLEGE STUDENTS
1825–26	37	1838–39	187
1826–27	38	1839–40	174
1827–28	65	1840–41	149
1828–29	112	1841–42	156
1829–30	150	1842–43	157
1830–31	138	1843–44	186
1831–32	173	1844–45	185
1832–33	177	1845–46	139
1833–34	150	1846–47	113
1834–35	155	1847–48	111
1835–36	140	1848–49	136
1836–37	131	1849–50	165
1837–38	154		

GEORGETOWN ACADEMIC YEAR	ACADEMY & COLLEGE STUDENTS	MEDICAL DEPARTMENT STUDENTS	LAW DEPARTMENT STUDENTS
1850–51	165	—	
1851–52	176	4	
1852–53	222	3	
1853–54	260	3	
1854–55	283	9	
1855–56	308	5	
1856–57	311	8	
1857–58	333	8	
1858–59	317	34	
1859–60	313	36	
1860–61	286	29	
1861–62	120	22	
1862–63	140	43	
1863–64	204	66	
1864–65	192	127	
1865–66	263	75	
1866–67	290	124	
1867–68	252	108	
1868–69	251	113	
1869–70	206	74	
1870–71	212	81	
1871–72	179	62	25
1872–73	187	56	46
1873–74	170	65	56
1874–75	196	72	37
1875–76	208	80	34
1876–77	194	35	39
1877–78	182	38	31

continued

GEORGETOWN ACADEMIC YEAR	ACADEMY & COLLEGE STUDENTS	MEDICAL DEPARTMENT STUDENTS	LAW DEPARTMENT STUDENTS
1878–79	146	42	24
1879–80	149	51	28
1880–81	170	41	48
1881–82	180	28	38
1882–83	202	26	45
1883–84	195	34	45
1884–85	201	35	66
1885–86	197	40	64
1886–87	175	37	96
1887–88	202	47	145
1888–89	206	84	168

All Degrees Conferred by Georgetown University from 1817 through 1889

YEAR	A.B.	PH.B.	B.S.	A.M.	M.D.	LL.B.	LL.M.	PH.D.	LL.D.	OTHER DEGREES CONFERRED
1817	2									
1818	2									
1819	1									
1820	1									
1821	1									
1822	4									
1823	1									
1824	3			1*						
1825	3									
1826	4									
1827	4									
1828	--									
1829	--									
1830	3									
1831	--			3*						
1832	7									
1833	7									
1834	4			1*						
1835	6									
1836	6									
1837	4									
1838	4									
1839	4									
1840	7									
1841	4									
1842	8									
1843	6									
1844	8			1*						
1845	6									

YEAR	A.B.	PH.B.	B.S.	A.M.	M.D.	LL.B.	LL.M.	PH.D.	LL.D.	OTHER DEGREES CONFERRED
1846	7			2*						
1847	5			4*						
1848	8			2*						
1849	6			4*						4 A.B. for Holy Cross College
1850	3			5*						
1851	7			6*						4 A.B. for Holy Cross College
1852	15			2*	4					6 A.B. for Holy Cross College
1853	15			4*	3				1	
1854	10			1*	3				1	
1855	16			7*	9					4 A.B. for Fordham College
1856	2			9*	5					
1857	10			5*	8					
1858	9			2*	8					
1859	9			4*	9				3	2 A.B. for Holy Cross College
1860	16			14*	10					
1861	11			2*	8					
1862	6			3*	3					5 A.B. for Holy Cross College
1863	9			2*	15					6 A.B. for Holy Cross College
1864	8			4*	1				1*†	5 A.B. for Holy Cross College
1865	6	1		6*	35					
1866	5			7*	18					
1867	6			6	40					5 A.M.*
1868	7			5	48			2		1 A.M.*
1869	7			1	28					7 A.M.*
1870	4			5	29			1†	2*	1 A.M.*
1871	10			12	16					4 Pharm.B.
1872	12			6	20	10			5*	4 Pharm.B.
1873	11			3	24	23			1*	1 Pharm.B. & 1 A.M.*
1874	14			2	11	17				
1875	7			4	6	12		1	2*	
1876	7			2	13	18				
1877	7			3	2	15			2	
1878	14				4	6				
1879	9		1		6	4	3			
1880	10			1	13	16	2		2*	
1881	8		3	1	5	11	5	2	1*	
1882	7		2	3	7	12	5	1†	1*	1 A.M.*
1883	11		1	3	4	16	1		1*	2 A.M.*
1884	4	1	3	3	7	20	9	1†		1 A.M.*
1885	14	1		2	11	20	11		4*	
1886	10			1	10	22	19		1*	
1887	11	2	2	3	5	38	34	1		
1888	11	2	4	8	12	52	22			
1889	12	2		18	14	60	35	8	20*	26 A.M.*

* Honorary Degree   † Doctorate in Music

Members of the Board of Directors from 1797 to 1817 and from 1844 to 1889

The incomplete data in some of the following lists reflect the fact that there are no records in the archives of any action taken by the board of directors between 1815 and 1844 nor is there any indication that any board functioned publicly during that time. It may well be that after the full restoration of the Society in 1814, Giovanni Grassi applied to the college the governing structure required by the Constitutions of the Society of Jesus; that is, to make the four consultors of the rector also directors of the college. That could explain how Anthony Kohlmann, as Superior of the Maryland Mission, was able to make himself rector-president of the college in 1817. In any case, it was still largely an external board in 1815, with three of the five members from outside the college. Moreover, two of them, Leonard Neale and William Matthews, were not Jesuits and therefore not consultors. Kohlmann would likely have experienced opposition from the Fenwicks (Benedict and Enoch), as well as from Francis Neale (a Jesuit) and his nephew William Matthews, the likely directors had the board continued as it had been constituted before the restoration—that is, as an external board.

At any rate, by the 1830s the consultors were clearly operating as the board, dealing with all matters—finances, construction, personnel—normally the purview of boards. When McSherry died in 1839, the consultors chose his successor. When the college was incorporated in 1844, the directors named were apparently the consultors; unfortunately the records of the consultors for this period are somewhat incomplete.

Directors of Georgetown College from 1797 to 1817

John Ashton, 1797–1803
Francis Beeston, 1797–1810
G. B. Bitouzey, 1803–9
Joseph Eden, 1806–8
*Enoch Fenwick, SJ, 1809–15
Giovanni Grassi, SJ, 1812–17
*William Matthews, 1806–15
Jean-Edouard de Mondésir, 1800–1803
Charles Neale, SJ, 1810–12
*Francis Neale, SJ, 1797–1806;
   1808–9; 1812–15
*Leonard Neale, 1809–15
William Pasquet, 1808–12
Robert Plunkett, 1797–1808
Charles Sewall, 1797–1800
Notley Young, 1803–12

*May also have served beyond this date.

Directors of Georgetown College from 1844 to 1889

Charles Bahan, SJ, 1879–81
*Samuel Barber, SJ, 1844
J. B. Becker, SJ, 1882–83
Robert Brady, SJ, 1858–59
Daniel Boone, SJ, 1857–59
Alphonse Charlier, SJ, 1856–63
Anthony Ciampi, SJ, 1850–51;
   1872–73
James Clarke, SJ, 1854–57; 1859–61;
   1867–69; 1875–79
William B. Cleary, SJ, 1875–77
James Collins, SJ, 1887–88
Ignatius Combs, SJ, 1844–45
Edward Connelly, SJ, 1884–86
William R. Cowardin, SJ, 1881–84;
   1885–97
*James Curley, SJ, 1844–80
Edward J. Devitt, SJ, 1883–86
Jerome Daugherty, SJ, 1889–96
James Doonan, SJ, 1879–88
Patrick Duddy, SJ, 1849–54; 1859–64
John Early, SJ, 1858–66; 1870–73

Peter Flanagan, SJ, 1844–45
John G. Fox, SJ, 1888–90
Samuel Frisbee, SJ, 1886–88
Cornelius Gillespie, SJ, 1888–89
Francis B. Goeding, SJ, 1889–90
Benedict Guldner, SJ, 1882–83
Patrick F. Healy, SJ, 1868–82
Charles Jenkins, SJ, 1864–65; 1867–72;
   1873–75
Thomas M. Jenkins, SJ, 1848–49
John F. Lehy, SJ, 1888–89
*Thomas Lilly, SJ, 1844
Daniel Lynch, SJ, 1850–57
Bernard A. Maguire, SJ, 1852–58;
   1866–70
E. McNerhaney, SJ, 1862–63
James Moore, SJ, 1853–54
John A. Morgan, SJ, 1874–75
John Mullaly, SJ, 1869–71; 1875–82
Samuel A. Mulledy, SJ, 1846–48
Thomas F. Mulledy, SJ, 1845–48
Joseph O'Hagan, SJ, 1864–65
M. O'Kane, SJ, 1883–86
John E. Pallhuber, SJ, 1855–56
Angelo Paresce, SJ, 1848–50
Albert Peters, SJ, 1865–69
Anthony Rey, SJ, 1844–46
Joseph Havens Richards, SJ, 1888–98
James Ryder, SJ, 1840–45; 1848–51
Henry J. Shandelle, SJ 1883–84
Thomas Stack, SJ, 1884–85
Charles H. Stonestreet, SJ, 1851–52;
   1861–62; 1863–64
John Sumner, SJ, 1873–74
William H. Sumner, SJ, 1889
James Tehan, SJ, 1863–64
Francis Vespré, SJ, 1845–48
Burchard Villiger, SJ, 1854–55
James Ward, SJ, 1845–50; 1864–68
Edward H. Welch, SJ, 1886–90
William Whiteford, SJ, 1877–79;
   1880–83
Bernard Wiget, SJ, 1851–53
Edmund Young, SJ, 1865–67; 1871–75

*Probably served before this date.

APPENDIX D

Presidents, Prefects, and Deans in Georgetown's First Century

Presidents from 1791 to 1889

Robert Plunkett, 1791–93

Robert Molyneux, 1793–96

William Louis DuBourg, SS, 1796–98

Most Reverend Leonard Neale,
1798–1806

Robert Molyneux, SJ, 1806–8

*Francis Neale, SJ, 1808–9

†William Matthews, 1809

Francis Neale, SJ, 1809–12

Giovanni Grassi, SJ, 1812–17

Benedict Joseph Fenwick, SJ, 1817

Anthony Kohlmann, SJ, 1817–20

Enoch Fenwick, SJ, 1820–25

*Benedict Joseph Fenwick, SJ, 1825

Stephen L. Dubuisson, SJ, 1825–26

William Feiner, SJ, 1826–29

John William Beschter, SJ, 1829

Thomas F. Mulledy, SJ, 1829–38

William McSherry, SJ, 1838–39

*Joseph A. Lopez, SJ, 1839–40

James Ryder, SJ, 1840–45

Samuel A. Mulledy, SJ, 1845

Thomas F. Mulledy, SJ, 1845–48

James Ryder, SJ, 1848–51

Charles H. Stonestreet, SJ, 1851–52

Bernard A. Maguire, SJ, 1852–58

John Early, SJ, 1858–65

Bernard A. Maguire, SJ, 1866–70

John Early, SJ, 1870–73

Patrick F. Healy, SJ, 1873–82

James A. Doonan, SJ, 1882–88

‡Joseph Havens Richards, SJ, 1888–98

**Prefects of Studies from
1811 to 1889**

Giovanni Grassi, SJ, 1811–17

Roger Baxter, SJ, 1819–24

William Feiner, SJ, 1825–26

James Neill, SJ, 1826–27

Peter Walsh, SJ, 1827–28

Thomas F. Mulledy, SJ, 1829–31

William Grace, SJ, 1831–33

Thomas F. Mulledy, SJ, 1833–37

William McSherry, SJ, 1837–39

George Fenwick, SJ, 1840–41

James Ryder, SJ, 1841–43

George Fenwick, SJ, 1843–45

Thomas F. Mulledy, SJ, 1845–48

James Ryder, SJ, 1848–51

Charles H. Stonestreet, SJ, 1851–52

Bernard A. Maguire, SJ, 1852–53

Francis Knackstedt, SJ, 1853–54

Bernard A. Maguire, SJ, 1854–58

John Early, SJ, 1858–65

Bernard A. Maguire, SJ, 1866–67

Joseph O'Callaghan, SJ, 1867–68

Patrick F. Healy, SJ, 1868–80

William Whiteford, SJ, 1880–81

James A. Doonan, SJ, 1881–82

James B. Becker, SJ, 1882–83

Edward Devitt, SJ, 1883–86

James A. Doonan, SJ, 1886–88

Joseph Havens Richards, SJ, 1888–99

Deans of the Medical Department from 1851 to 1889

Johnson Eliot, 1851–76

Robert Reyburn, 1876–77

Francis Asbury Ashford, 1877–83

James William Lovejoy, 1883–88

±C. Lloyd Magruder, 1888–1901

Deans of the Law Department from 1870 to 1889

Charles P. James, 1870–73

George W. Paschal, 1873–75

±Charles W. Hoffman, 1876–90

*Served as Acting President.

†Novice in the Society of Jesus at that time.

‡The celebrator of Georgetown's first one hundred years served well beyond the centennial celebration of 1889.

±These distinguished scholar-administrators both served beyond Georgetown's centennial year.

Original Georgetown College Buildings by Construction Date

Old South, 1788 (razed in 1904)

Old North, 1795

Infirmary, 1792 (razed in 1831)

Gervase Hall, 1831 (enlarged in 1848)

Mulledy Hall, 1833

*****Medical Building,** 1851 (abandoned in 1869)

Maguire Hall, 1854

O'Gara Hall, 1874 (razed in 1985)

Healy Hall, 1877

†**Medical Building,** 1886

Located at 12th & F Streets, in northwest Washington.
†*Located on H Street, between 9th & 10th, in northwest Washington.*

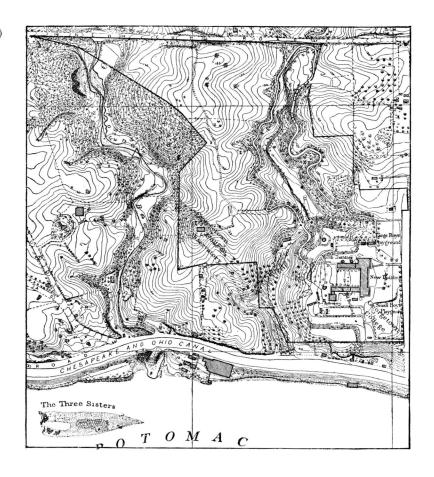

APPENDIX F

Summary Tabulations of Demographics for Students at Georgetown from 1791 to 1889

The U.S. geographic regions noted in these summaries of data for Georgetown students include the following jurisdictions, territories, and states: **Local:** District of Columbia (D.C.) and Maryland; **Northeast:** Connecticut, Delaware, Maine, Massachusetts, New Hampshire, New Jersey, New York, Pennsylvania, Rhode Island, and Vermont; **Northcentral:** Illinois, Indiana, Iowa, Michigan, Minnesota, Ohio, Wisconsin, and Missouri (after 1865); **South:** Alabama, Arkansas, Florida, Georgia, Kentucky, Louisiana (territory after 1803, state after 1812), Mississippi, North Carolina, South Carolina, Tennessee, Virginia, West Virginia (after 1863), Texas (until 1865), and Missouri (until 1865); **West:** Arizona, California, Colorado, Idaho, Kansas, Montana, Nebraska, Nevada, New Mexico, North Dakota, Oklahoma, Oregon, South Dakota, Texas (after 1865), Utah, Washington, and Wyoming.

The eighteenth- and nineteenth-century American, European, and South American communities from which Georgetown students came are classified herein by size in their various urban and rural locales:

Country = fewer than 1,000 inhabitants
Town = 1,000 to 9,999 inhabitants
City = more than 10,000 inhabitants

Throughout these tabulations, surnames have been used in determining likely ethnic groups for those students whose national extraction or family histories are unknown.

Until the 1850s, the religious affiliation of students was not recorded at Georgetown or at most educational institutions in America. Thus, to identify that affiliation we have used information compiled from all available sources. These include account books, membership lists for extracurricular activities, school programs, attendance rolls, etc. Of the students whose religion cannot be established by these means, the conservative assumption has been made that at least half of them were Protestants. The resulting figures are consistent with those from the later 1850s and beyond when religious affiliation begins to be noted in the entrance books of Georgetown and most other academies, colleges, and universities. However, for students in Georgetown's professional schools, the figures are based on known religious affiliations only.

Percentages of religious vocations among Catholics are calculated against the total number of Catholic students known to have attended Georgetown in a given period.

Table 2.1 Demographics of All 277 Georgetown Students in the 1790s

FATHER'S OCCUPATION	(82 KNOWN)	%
Planter/merchant	24	29.2
Merchant	22	26.8
Artisan	8	9.7
Planter	7	8.5
Doctor	6	7.3
Lawyer	5	6.1
Politician	4	4.8
Merchant/politician	3	3.6
Lawyer/politician	2	2.4
Educator	1	1.2

NATION OR AREA OF ORIGIN	(253 KNOWN)	%
U.S.A.	206	81.4
Central America	40	15.8
Europe	6	2.4
Louisiana Territory	1	0.4

U.S. GEOGRAPHIC REGION	(204 KNOWN)	%
Local	163	79.9
Northeast	24	11.7
South	17	8.3

NATIVE STATE	(203 KNOWN)	%
Maryland	84	41.3
D.C.	78	38.4
Pennsylvania	15	7.4
Virginia	15	7.4
New York	7	3.4
Massachusetts	2	0.9
North Carolina	2	0.9

URBAN/RURAL LOCALE	(206 KNOWN)	%
Town	103	50.0
Country	59	28.7
City	44	21.3

ETHNIC GROUP	(276 KNOWN)	%
English	141	51.1
French	60	21.7
Irish	35	12.7
Scotch/Scotch-Irish	16	5.8
Hispanic	3	1.1
Italian	3	1.1
Scandinavian	3	1.1
Welsh	3	1.1
Dutch	2	0.7
French/Hispanic	2	0.7

ETHNIC GROUP, continued		
German/Swiss	2	0.7
Portuguese	2	0.7
English/German	1	0.4
English/Irish	1	0.4
English/Scotch-Irish	1	0.4
German	1	0.4

RELIGIOUS AFFILIATION	(227 KNOWN)	%
Catholic	219	79.1
Protestant	58	20.9

RELIGIOUS VOCATIONS	(8 KNOWN)	%
Society of Jesus	6	2.7
Diocesan clergy	2	0.9

FINANCIAL STATUS	(273 KNOWN)	%
Paid full tuition	196	71.7
Rec'd outside aid	27	9.9
Paid in cash & kind	25	8.4
Paid in kind	9	3.3
Paid with services	9	3.3
Paid reduced fees	3	1.1
Tuition waived	1	0.4

HOUSING STATUS	(277 KNOWN)	%
Campus boarders	146	52.7
Day students	110	39.7
Fenwick boarders	21	7.6

DISCIPLINARY STATUS		%
Expelled students	1	0.4

OCCUPATION OR CAREER*	(41 KNOWN)	%
Clergyman	9	20.9
Politician	9	20.9
Career military	4	9.3
Doctor	3	7.0
Lawyer	3	7.0
Lawyer/politician	3	7.0
Merchant	3	7.0
Planter	3	7.0
Artisan	1	2.3
Diplomat	1	2.3
Farmer	1	2.3
Gov't clerk	1	2.3

*Besides the students whose post-Georgetown occupations are tabulated here, it is known that two others (4.7%) died young, before going on to any adult career, work, or occupation.

Table 3.1   Demographics of All 256 Georgetown Students from 1812 to 1817

FATHER'S OCCUPATION	(38 KNOWN)	%
Government official/politician	10	26.3
Doctor	9	23.7
Merchant	8	21.0
Career military	3	7.9
Farmer	2	5.3
Planter	2	5.3
Architect	2	5.3
Clergyman	1	2.6
Editor	1	2.6

NATION OR AREA OF ORIGIN	(245 KNOWN)	%
U.S.A.	232	94.7
Central America	7	2.9
Europe	4	1.6
South America	2	0.8

U.S. GEOGRAPHIC REGION	(232 KNOWN)	%
Local	163	61.6
Northeast	24	23.3
South	17	13.8
Northcentral	3	1.3

NATIVE STATE	(232 KNOWN)	%
Maryland	84	36.2
D.C.	59	25.4
New York	35	15.1
Virginia	22	9.5
Pennsylvania	18	7.8
South Carolina	4	1.7
Kentucky	2	0.9
Louisiana	2	0.9
Ohio	2	0.9
Georgia	1	0.4
Illinois	1	0.4
New Jersey	1	0.4
North Carolina	1	0.4

URBAN/RURAL LOCALE	(224 KNOWN)	%
City	107	47.8
Country	61	27.2
Town	56	25.0

ETHNIC GROUP	(253 KNOWN)	%
English	158	62.5
Irish	41	16.2
French	24	9.5

ETHNIC GROUP, continued	(253 KNOWN)	%
German	11	4.3
Hispanic	4	1.6
Welsh	3	1.2
Italian	2	0.8
Scandinavian	2	0.8
Scotch-Irish	2	0.8
Dutch	1	0.4
English/German	1	0.4
English/Italian	1	0.4
English/Scotch	1	0.4
Portuguese	1	0.4
Scotch-Irish/English	1	0.4

RELIGIOUS AFFILIATION	(173 KNOWN)	%
Catholic	190	74.2
Protestant*	66	25.8

RELIGIOUS VOCATIONS	(26 KNOWN)	%
Society of Jesus	25	13.2
Diocesan clergy	1	0.5

FINANCIAL STATUS	(251 KNOWN)	%
Paid full tuition	193	76.9
Paid reduced fees	31	12.4
Rec'd outside aid	8	3.2
Tuition waived	6	2.4
Paid group rate	6	2.4
Paid in cash & kind	5	1.9
Paid in kind	2	1.2

HOUSING STATUS	(256 KNOWN)	%
Campus boarders	235	93.3
Day students	21	6.7

DISCPLINARY STATUS		%
Expelled students	10	3.9

OCCUPATION OR CAREER	(44 KNOWN)	%
Clergyman	22	50.0
Career military	5	11.3
Doctor	4	9.0
Editor/journalist	4	9.0
Businessman	3	6.8
Lawyer	3	6.8
Educator	1	2.3
Government employee	1	2.3
Lawyer/politician	1	2.3

*Of these Protestant students, it is known that nearly a tenth (6, or 9.0%) became Catholics during President Giovanni Grassi's tenure at Georgetown (1812–17).

Table 4.1 Demographics of All 175 Georgetown Students from 1820 to 1828

FATHER'S OCCUPATION	(25 KNOWN)	%
Merchant	11	44.0
Government official/diplomat	6	24.0
Planter	5	20.0
Artisan	1	4.0
Government clerk	1	4.0
Career military	1	4.0

NATION OR AREA OF ORIGIN	(157 KNOWN)	%
U.S.A.	148	94.3
Central America	4	2.5
South America	3	1.9
Europe	2	1.3

U.S. GEOGRAPHIC REGION	(148 KNOWN)	%
Local	111	75.0
South	31	20.9
Northeast	6	4.1

NATIVE STATE	(148 KNOWN)	%
D.C.	65	43.9
Maryland	46	31.1
Louisiana	16	10.8
Virginia	10	6.8
Pennsylvania	5	3.4
Georgia	2	1.4
Connecticut	1	0.7
Kentucky	1	0.7
Missouri	1	0.7
Tennessee	1	0.7

URBAN/RURAL LOCALE	(145 KNOWN)	%
City	79	54.5
Country	39	26.9
Town	27	18.6

ETHNIC GROUP	(173 KNOWN)	%
English	119	68.8
French	14	8.1
Irish	14	8.1
German	10	5.8
Hispanic	6	3.5
Scotch	4	2.3
Greek	3	1.7
Dutch	1	0.6
Portuguese	1	0.6
Welsh	1	0.6

RELIGIOUS AFFILIATION	(130 KNOWN)	%
Catholic	114	65.2
Protestant*	61	34.8

RELIGIOUS VOCATIONS	(5 KNOWN)	%
Society of Jesus	4	3.5
Diocesan clergy	1	0.8

FINANCIAL STATUS	(166 KNOWN)	%
Paid full tuition	111	66.9
Tuition waived	32	19.3
Paid reduced fees	11	6.6
Paid group rate	10	6.0
Rec'd outside aid	2	1.2

HOUSING STATUS	(175 KNOWN)	%
Campus boarders	116	66.6
Day students	59	33.4

DISCIPLINARY STATUS		%
Expelled students	12	6.9

DEGREES EARNED		%
A.B.	25	14.2

OCCUPATION OR CAREER	(24 KNOWN)	%
Doctor	5	20.8
Lawyer	5	20.8
Planter	4	16.6
Merchant/businessman	3	12.5
Writer/journalist	3	12.5
Clergyman	2	8.3
Career military	1	4.2
Educator	1	4.2

Of these Protestant students, it is known that 3 (4.8%) became Catholics in the 1820–28 period.

Table 5.1 Demographics of All 93 Georgetown Day Students from 1820 to 1829

FATHER'S OCCUPATION	(8 KNOWN)	%
Businessman/merchant	6	75.0
Doctor	1	12.5
Politician	1	12.5

ETHNIC GROUP	(93 KNOWN)	%
English	64	68.6
Irish	10	10.8
German	9	9.7
Scotch	6	6.5
French	3	3.3
Welsh	1	1

RELIGIOUS AFFILIATION	(75 KNOWN)	%
Catholic	26	28.0
Protestant*	67	72.0

FINANCIAL STATUS	(93 KNOWN)	%
Tuition waived	76	81.7
Paid full tuition	17	18.3

DISCIPLINARY STATUS		%
Expelled	7	7.5

DEGREES EARNED		%
A.B.	2	2.2

OCCUPATION OR CAREER	(3 KNOWN)	%
Doctor	1	33.3
Government employee	1	33.3
Lawyer	1	33.3

* Of these Protestant students, it is known certainly that only one (1.5%) became a Catholic in the 1820–29 period.

Table 6.1 Demographics of All 57 Georgetown Medical Students from 1851 to 1860

FATHER'S OCCUPATION	(1 KNOWN)	%
Government official	1	100.0

NATION OR AREA OF ORIGIN	(56 KNOWN)	%
U.S.A.	50	89.3
Europe	6	10.7

U.S. GEOGRAPHIC REGION	(50 KNOWN)	%
Local	26	52.0
South	10	20.0
Northeast	7	14.0
Northcentral	7	14.0

NATIVE STATE	(50 KNOWN)	%
D.C.	19	38.0
Maryland	7	14.0
Virginia	5	10.0
New York	3	6.0
Ohio	3	6.0
Indiana	2	4.0
Alabama	1	2.0
Arkansas	1	2.0
Connecticut	1	2.0
Iowa	1	2.0

NATIVE STATE, continued		%
Kentucky	1	2.0
Massachusetts	1	2.0
Michigan	1	2.0
Mississippi	1	2.0
Missouri	1	2.0
New Hampshire	1	2.0
Pennsylvania	1	2.0

URBAN/RURAL LOCALE	(26 KNOWN)	%
City	22	84.6
Country	3	11.5
Town	1	3.9

ETHNIC GROUP	(56 KNOWN)	%
English	36	64.3
Irish	9	16.1
French	6	10.7
Polish	2	3.6
German	1	1.8
Italian	1	1.8
Scandinavian	1	1.8

RELIGIOUS AFFILIATION	(24 KNOWN)	%
Catholic	16	66.6
Protestant	8	33.3

Table 7.1 Demographics of All 757 Georgetown College Students from 1830 to 1839*

FATHER'S OCCUPATION	(243 KNOWN)	%
Career military	49	20.2
Lawyer	40	16.5
Planter	35	14.4
Businessman	32	13.2
Doctor	26	10.7
Government employee	14	5.8
Politician	14	5.8
Lawyer/politician	12	4.9
Government official	9	3.7
Editor/journalist	4	1.6
Foreign diplomat	2	0.8
Artisan	1	0.4
Educator	1	0.4

NATION OR AREA OF ORIGIN	(736 KNOWN)	%
U.S.A.	700	95.0
Central America	15	2.0
Europe	10	1.4
Canada	8	1.1
South America	3	0.4

U.S. GEOGRAPHIC REGION	(700 KNOWN)	%
Local	321	45.8
South	282	40.2
Northeast	91	13.0
Northcentral	6	0.8

NATIVE STATE	(700 KNOWN)	%
D.C.	187	26.7
Virginia	146	20.9
Maryland	133	19.0
Louisiana	48	6.9
Pennsylvania	41	5.9
New York	39	5.6
Georgia	32	4.6
Alabama	11	1.6
Florida	10	1.4
Mississippi	9	1.3
North Carolina	7	1.0
South Carolina	7	1.0
Delaware	6	0.9
Missouri	4	0.6
Ohio	4	0.6
Tennessee	3	0.4
Illinois	2	0.3
Maine	2	0.3
New Jersey	2	0.3
New Hampshire	1	0.1
Kentucky	1	0.1

URBAN/RURAL LOCALE	(685 KNOWN)	%
City	323	47.1
Country	199	29.0
Town	163	23.9

ETHNIC GROUP	(749 KNOWN)	%
English	469	62.6
Irish	119	15.9
French	48	6.4
German	29	3.9
Hispanic	20	2.6
Scotch	20	2.7
Italian	11	1.4
English/Scotch	7	0.9
Welsh	7	0.9
English/Irish	3	0.4
Hungarian	3	0.4
Jews (European)	3	0.4
Dutch	2	0.2
Portuguese	2	0.2
Russian	2	0.2
Amerindian	1	0.1
English/French	1	0.1
English/Scotch-Irish	1	0.1
Slavic	1	0.1

RELIGIOUS AFFILIATION	(498 KNOWN)	%
Catholic	492	65.0
Protestant[†]	251	33.1
Jewish	2	0.2
Greek Orthodox	1	0.1

RELIGIOUS VOCATIONS	(25 KNOWN)	%
Society of Jesus	20	4.0
Diocesan clergy	5	1.0

FINANCIAL STATUS	(740 KNOWN)	%
Paid full tuition	629	85.0
Tuition waived	60	7.1
Paid reduced fees	31	4.2
Paid group rate	11	1.5
Paid in kind	5	0.6
Rec'd outside aid	4	0.5

HOUSING STATUS	(757 KNOWN)	%
Campus boarders	640	86.1
Half boarders	117	13.9

DISCIPLINARY STATUS		%
Expelled	51	6.7

Table 7.1, *continued*

DEGREES EARNED		%
A.B.	65	7.6

OCCUPATION OR CAREER[‡]	(160 KNOWN)	%
Lawyer	33	20.5
Doctor	27	16.7
Clergyman	22	13.6
Career military	21	13.0
Businessman	12	7.5
Lawyer/politician	7	4.4
Editor/writer	5	3.1
Farmer	5	3.1

OCCUPATION OR CAREER, *continued*		
Planter	5	3.1
Engineer	4	2.5
Clerk	3	1.9
Foreign diplomat	3	1.9
Government official	3	1.9
Politician	3	1.9
Sailor	3	1.9
Government clerk	2	1.2
Educator	1	0.6
Druggist	1	0.6

* For these students, the median entering age was 12 years and 11 months and the median departing age was 15 years and 3 months.

† Of these Protestant students, it is known that nearly a tenth (22, or 9%) became Catholics during this 1830–39 period.

‡ Besides the students whose post-Georgetown occupations are tabulated here, one other (0.6%) died young, before going on to any adult work, career, or profession.

Table 7.2 Demographics of All 640 Georgetown College Students from 1840 to 1849*

FATHER'S OCCUPATION	(223 KNOWN)	%
Lawyer	46	20.6
Career military	40	17.9
Doctor	30	13.4
Planter	29	13.0
Businessman	20	8.9
Politician	15	6.7
Government employee	12	5.4
Lawyer/politician	8	3.6
Artisan	4	1.7
Government official	4	1.7
Foreign diplomat	4	1.7
Clergyman	3	1.3
Dentist	3	1.3
Engineer	2	0.9
Architect	1	0.4
Editor	1	0.4
Farmer	1	0.4

NATION OR AREA OF ORIGIN	(634 KNOWN)	%
U.S.A.	586	92.4
Central America	20	3.2
Canada	15	2.4
South America	7	1.1
Europe	6	0.0

U.S. GEOGRAPHIC REGION	(586 KNOWN)	%
Local	266	45.3
South	263	44.8
Northeast	54	9.2
Northcentral	3	0.5

NATIVE STATE	(586 KNOWN)	%
D.C.	166	28.3
Louisiana	101	17.2
Maryland	98	16.7
Virginia	53	9.0
Georgia	38	6.5
Pennsylvania	29	4.9
New York	24	4.1
South Carolina	18	3.1
Alabama	14	2.4
Mississippi	9	1.5
North Carolina	9	1.5
Tennessee	7	1.2
Florida	7	1.2
Kentucky	5	0.8
Michigan	3	0.5
Arkansas	2	0.3
Delaware	1	0.2
Maine	1	0.2

Table 7.2 Demographics of All 640 Georgetown College Students from 1840 to 1849* (continued)

URBAN/RURAL LOCALE	(597 KNOWN)	%
City	251	42.0
Country	174	29.2
Town	172	28.7

ETHNIC GROUP	(639 KNOWN)	%
English	352	55.0
French	111	17.4
Irish	58	9.1
German	39	6.1
Hispanic	32	5.0
Scotch-Irish	12	1.8
Welsh	9	1.4
Italian	8	1.3
Jews (European)	3	0.5
English/German	2	0.3
English/Scotch-Irish	2	0.3
Polish	2	0.3
Portuguese	2	0.3
Dutch	1	0.2
English/French	1	0.2
English/Hispanic	1	0.2
English/Irish/French	1	0.2
French/Hispanic	1	0.2
French/Swiss	1	0.2
German/Irish	1	0.2
Russian	1	0.2

RELIGIOUS AFFILIATION	(491 KNOWN)	%
Catholic	460	71.8
Protestant†	177	27.8
Jewish	3	0.4

RELIGIOUS VOCATIONS		%
Society of Jesus	9	2.0

FINANCIAL STATUS	(628 KNOWN)	%
Paid full tuition	520	82.8
Paid reduced fees	44	7.0
Paid in cash & kind	25	4.0
Paid group rate	19	3.0
Tuition waived	18	2.9
Rec'd outside aid	1	0.2
Taught in exchange	1	0.2

HOUSING STATUS	(640 KNOWN)	%
Campus boarders	531	84.6
Day students	109	15.4

DEGREES EARNED		%
A.B.	66	10.3

DISCIPLINARY STATUS		%
Expelled students	18	2.8

OCCUPATION OR CAREER‡	(99 KNOWN)	%
Doctor	24	25.2
Lawyer	18	18.2
Career military	11	11.1
Lawyer/politician	9	9.1
Clergyman	7	7.0
Government clerk	6	6.1
Businessman	4	4.0
Editor/journalist	4	4.0
Educator	4	4.0
Farmer	3	3.0
Druggist	2	2.0
Government official	2	2.0
Politician	2	2.0
Engineer	1	1.0

* For these students, the median entering age was 14 years and 6 months and the median departing age was 16 years and 11 months.

† Of these Protestant students, it is known that 12 (6.8%) became Catholics in this 1840-49 period.

‡ Besides the students whose post-Georgetown occupations are tabulated here, two (2%) are known to have died young, before going on to any adult work, career, or profession.

Table 7.3 Demographics of All 1,174 Georgetown College Students from 1850 to 1859*

FATHER'S OCCUPATION	(251 KNOWN)	%
Doctor	66	26.3
Career military	51	20.3
Lawyer/politician	27	10.7
Lawyer	19	7.6
Businessman	17	6.7
Government clerk	14	5.5
Foreign diplomat	13	5.1
Politician	10	4.0
Planter	10	3.9
Government official	5	2.0
Educator	5	2.0
Farmer	4	1.6
Journalist/editor	4	1.6
Artist	2	0.8
Engineer	2	0.8
Artisan	1	0.4
Clergyman	1	0.4

NATION OR AREA OF ORIGIN	(1,172 KNOWN)	%
U.S.A.	1,097	93.6
Central America	35	3.0
South America	29	2.5
Europe	9	0.8
Canada	2	0.2

U.S. GEOGRAPHIC REGION	(1,097 KNOWN)	%
South	488	44.5
Local	468	42.6
Northeast	96	8.7
West	25	2.3
Northcentral	20	1.8

NATIVE STATE	(1,097 KNOWN)	%
D.C.	261	23.8
Maryland	205	18.7
Louisiana	166	15.1
Virginia	109	9.9
Georgia	47	4.3
Pennsylvania	47	4.3
South Carolina	39	3.6
Mississippi	38	3.5
New York	33	3.0
Alabama	29	2.6
California	20	1.8
North Carolina	16	1.5
Kentucky	12	1.1
Texas	12	1.1
Missouri	10	1.0

NATIVE STATE, continued		
Arkansas	8	0.7
Massachusetts	8	0.7
Indiana	4	0.4
Michigan	4	0.4
Tennessee	4	0.4
Maine	3	0.3
Minnesota	3	0.3
New Jersey	3	0.3
Ohio	3	0.3
Wisconsin	3	0.3
Illinois	2	0.2
Nebraska	2	0.2
Delaware	1	0.1
Florida	1	0.1
Iowa	1	0.1
Kansas	1	0.1
New Mexico	1	0.1
Vermont	1	0.1

URBAN/RURAL LOCALE	(1,131 KNOWN)	%
City	533	47.1
Country	331	29.3
Town	267	23.6

ETHNIC GROUP	(1,160 KNOWN)	%
English	627	54.0
Irish	183	15.7
French	119	10.2
German	74	6.2
Hispanic	59	5.0
Scotch-Irish/Scotch	29	2.5
Welsh	13	1.1
English/French	11	0.9
Italian	8	0.6
Portuguese	7	0.6
English/German	6	0.5
English/Scotch-Irish	6	0.5
English/Irish	4	0.3
Greek	3	0.2
Dutch	2	0.1
English/Dutch	2	0.1
Jews (European)	2	0.1
English/Italian	1	0.1
English/Welsh	1	0.1
German/Irish	1	0.1
Irish/Scotch/English	1	0.1
Polish	1	0.1
Scotch-Irish/French	1	0.1
Slavic	1	0.1

Table 7.3 Demographics of All 1,174 Georgetown College Students from 1850 to 1859* (continued)

RELIGIOUS AFFILIATION	(736 KNOWN)	%
Catholic	787	67.1
Protestant†	385	32.7
Jewish	2	0.2

RELIGIOUS VOCATIONS	(15 KNOWN)	%
Society of Jesus	12	1.5
Diocesan clergy	3	0.3

FINANCIAL STATUS	(1,161 KNOWN)	%
Paid full tuition	937	80.7
Paid reduced fees	133	11.4
Paid group rate	45	3.9
Tuition waived	29	2.5
Paid in cash & kind	13	1.2
Rec'd outside aid	4	0.2

HOUSING STATUS	(1,174 KNOWN)	%
Campus boarders	1,042	88.7
Half boarders	132	11.3

DISCIPLINARY STATUS		%
Expelled	10	0.8

DEGREES EARNED		%
A.B.	107	9.1

OCCUPATION OR CAREER‡	(191 KNOWN)	%
Lawyer	33	16.8
Doctor	27	13.8
Career military	17	8.7
Lawyer/politician	13	6.6
Businessman	11	5.6
Clergyman	11	5.6
Editor/journalist	11	5.6
Banker/industrial	9	4.6
Farmer	9	4.6
Government clerk	9	4.6
Government official	9	4.6
Politician	9	4.6
Clerk/manager	7	3.5
Planter	5	2.5
Educator	3	1.5
Public service emp.	3	1.5
Druggist	2	1.0
Actor	1	0.5
Dentist	1	0.5
Engineer	1	0.5

* For these students, the median entering age was 14 years and 2 months and the median departing age was 16 years and 1 month.

†Of these Protestant students, it is known that very few (10, or 2.9%) became Catholics during the 1850–59 period.

‡Besides the students whose post-Georgetown occupations are tabulated here, several died young (5, or 2.5%) before going on to any adult work, career, or profession.

Table 8.1 Demographics of All 64 Georgetown College Graduates in the 1830s

FATHER'S OCCUPATION	(23 KNOWN)	%
Businessman	6	26.1
Planter	5	21.7
Lawyer	4	17.4
Lawyer/politician	3	13.0
Career military	1	4.3
Doctor	1	4.3
Government clerk	1	4.3
Government official	1	4.3
Politician	1	4.3

NATION OR AREA OF ORIGIN	(64 KNOWN)	%
U.S.A.	62	96.9
Europe	2	3.1

U.S. GEOGRAPHIC REGION	(62 KNOWN)	%
South	25	40.3
Local	24	38.7
Northeast	13	20.9

NATIVE STATE	(62 KNOWN)	%
D.C.	12	19.4
Maryland	12	19.4
Louisiana	8	12.9
New York	8	12.9
Georgia	7	11.3
Virginia	7	11.3
Pennsylvania	4	6.5
Mississippi	2	3.2
Maine	1	1.6
Tennessee	1	1.6

URBAN/RURAL LOCALE	(61 KNOWN)	%
Country	23	37.7
City	22	36.1
Town	16	26.3

ETHNIC GROUP	(63 KNOWN)	%
English	35	55.6
Irish	15	23.8
French	5	7.9
English/Irish	2	3.2
German	2	3.2
Russian	2	3.2
Dutch	1	1.6
Slavic	1	1.6

RELIGIOUS AFFILIATION	(53 KNOWN)	%
Catholic	48	75.0
Protestant*	14	18.9
Orthodox	2	3.0

RELIGIOUS VOCATIONS		%
Society of Jesus	10	19.6

FINANCIAL STATUS	(61 KNOWN)	%
Paid full tuition	53	86.9
Paid reduced fees	5	8.2
Rec'd outside aid	2	3.2
Tuition waived	1	1.5

HOUSING STATUS	(64 KNOWN)	%
Campus boarders	56	87.5
Day students	8	12.5

OCCUPATION OR CAREER	(48 KNOWN)	%
Lawyer	16	33.3
Clergyman	9	18.7
Doctor	5	10.4
Lawyer/politician	4	8.3
Businessman	2	4.0
Engineer/surveyor	2	4.0
Government official	2	4.0
Banker	1	2.0
Career military	1	2.0
Editor	1	2.0
Educator	1	2.0
Lawyer/businessman	1	2.0
Lawyer/planter	1	2.0
Lawyer/publisher	1	2.0
Planter	1	2.0

Of these Protestant students, it is known that a little more than a fifth (3, or 21.4%) became Catholics in the 1830s.

Table 8.2 Demographics of All 66 Georgetown College Graduates in the 1840s

FATHER'S OCCUPATION	(28 KNOWN)	%
Lawyer	10	35.7
Doctor	5	22.2
Planter	4	17.8
Government clerk	3	10.7
Businessman	2	7.1
Clergyman	1	3.5
Dentist	1	3.5
Farmer	1	3.5
Lawyer/politician	1	3.5

NATION OR AREA OF ORIGIN	(66 KNOWN)	%
U.S.A.	64	97.0
Canada	2	3.0

U.S. GEOGRAPHIC REGION	(64 KNOWN)	%
Local	28	43.8
South	28	43.8
Northeast	8	12.5

NATIVE STATE	(64 KNOWN)	%
Maryland	15	23.4
D.C.	13	20.3
Louisiana	13	20.3
Virginia	6	9.4
New York	4	6.3
Pennsylvania	4	6.3
Alabama	2	3.1
Georgia	2	3.1
Tennessee	2	3.1
Mississippi	1	1.6
North Carolina	1	1.6
South Carolina	1	1.6

URBAN/RURAL LOCALE	(63 KNOWN)	%
City	29	46.0
Country	19	30.2
Town	15	23.8

ETHNIC GROUP	(65 KNOWN)	%
English	33	50.8
French	13	20.0
Irish	9	13.8
German	3	4.6

ETHNIC GROUP, continued		%
Scotch	2	3.1
English/Hispanic	1	1.5
German/Irish	1	1.5
Italian	1	1.5
Scotch-Irish/English	1	1.5
Swiss/French	1	1.5

RELIGIOUS AFFILIATION	(57 KNOWN)	%
Catholic	50	75.7
Protestant*	16	24.3

RELIGIOUS VOCATIONS		%
Society of Jesus	2	3.7

FINANCIAL STATUS	(64 KNOWN)	%
Paid full tuition	55	85.9
Paid group rate	3	4.7
Pad in cash and kind	2	3.1
Paid reduced fees	2	3.1
Paid by teaching	1	1.6
Tuition waived	1	1.6

HOUSING STATUS	(66 KNOWN)	%
Campus boarders	58	87.8
Day students	8	12.2

OCCUPATION OR CAREER	(32 KNOWN)	%
Lawyer	14	43.7
Doctor	3	9.3
Lawyer/politician	3	9.3
Farmer	2	6.2
Government clerk	2	6.2
Businessman	1	3.1
Career military	1	3.1
Clergyman	1	3.1
Doctor/politician	1	3.1
Editor	1	3.1
Lawyer/banker	1	3.1
Lawyer/journalist	1	3.1
Politician	1	3.1

Of these Protestant students, it is known that less than a fifth (3, or 18%) became Catholics in the 1840s.

Table 8.3 Demographics of All 107 Georgetown College Graduates in the 1850s

FATHER'S OCCUPATION	(26 KNOWN)	%
Lawyer	5	19.2
Businessman	3	11.5
Doctor	3	11.5
Lawyer/politician	2	7.7
Foreign diplomat	2	7.7
Planter	2	7.7
Writer	2	7.7
Career military	1	3.8
Clergyman	1	3.8
Clerk	1	3.8
Educator	1	3.8
Farmer	1	3.8
Lawyer/planter	1	3.8
Politician	1	3.8

NATION OR AREA OF ORIGIN	(107 KNOWN)	%
U.S.A.	96	89.7
South America	5	4.7
Central America	3	2.8
Europe	3	2.8

U.S. GEOGRAPHIC REGION	(96 KNOWN)	%
Local	38	39.5
South	38	39.5
Northeast	17	17.7
Northcentral	3	3.2

NATIVE STATE	(96 KNOWN)	%
Louisiana	20	20.8
D.C.	19	19.8
Maryland	19	19.8
Pennsylvania	9	9.4
Virginia	9	9.4
New York	6	6.3
South Carolina	3	3.1
Alabama	2	2.1
Georgia	1	1.0
Kentucky	1	1.0
Massachusetts	1	1.0
Ohio	1	1.0
Tennessee	1	1.0
Vermont	1	1.0
Wisconsin	1	1.0

URBAN/RURAL LOCALE	(104 KNOWN)	%
City	49	47.1
Country	28	27.0
Town	27	26.0

ETHNIC GROUP	(105 KNOWN)	%
English	48	45.6
Irish	24	22.8
French	13	12.4
Hispanic	8	7.5
German	3	2.8
Scotch	2	1.9
English/German	1	0.9
English/Irish	1	0.9
German/Irish	1	0.9
Jews (European)	1	0.9
Scotch-Irish/English	1	0.9
Scotch-Irish/French	1	0.9
Welsh	1	0.9

FINANCIAL STATUS	(107 KNOWN)	%
Paid full tuition	85	79.4
Paid reduced fees	15	14.0
Paid group rate	5	4.7
Tuition waived	2	1.9

RELIGIOUS AFFILIATION	(88 KNOWN)	%
Catholic	92	86.0
Protestant*	14	13.1
Jewish	1	0.9

RELIGIOUS VOCATIONS		%
Society of Jesus	4	4.3

HOUSING STATUS	(107 KNOWN)	%
Campus boarders	99	92.6
Day students	8	7.4

Table 8.3 Demographics of All 107 Georgetown College Graduates in the 1850s (continued)

OCCUPATION OR CAREER[†]	(60 KNOWN)	%
Lawyer	21	35.0
Lawyer/politician	5	8.3
Government official	4	6.6
Businessman	3	5.0
Doctor	3	5.0
Editor/journalist	3	5.0
Government clerk	3	5.0
Planter	3	5.0
Clergyman	2	3.3

OCCUPATION OR CAREER[†], continued		
Farmer	2	3.3
Farmer/politician	2	3.3
Lawyer/editor	2	3.3
Actor	1	1.6
Druggist	1	1.6
Engineer	1	1.6
Lawyer/banker	1	1.6
Librarian	1	1.6
Social worker	1	1.6

*Of these Protestant students, only one (0.9%) is known to have become a Catholic in the 1850s.
† Besides these students whose post-Georgetown occupations are tabulated here, one (1.6%) died young, before going into any adult work, career, or profession.

Table 9.1 The 1,085 Georgetown Alumni Who Served in the Civil War

COLLEGE OR PROFESSIONAL SCHOOL	UNION FORCES	CONFEDERATE FORCES	TOTAL ALUMNI IN UNIFORM
CAS (College of Arts & Sciences)	140	853	993
MED (Medical School)	71	13	84
CMD (College & Medical School)	6	1	7
LAW (Law School)	1	0	1
Total	**218**	**867**	**1,085**

Table 9.2 Demographics of the 867 Georgetown Alumni Who Served in the Confederate Military

SCHOOL OR COLLEGE	(867 KNOWN)	%
CAS	853	98.4
MED	13	1.5
CMD	1	0.1

FATHER'S OCCUPATION	(245 KNOWN)	%
Doctor	49	20.0
Career military	48	19.6
Lawyer/politician	33	13.4
Lawyer	30	12.2
Businessman	22	8.9
Planter	20	8.2
Editor/journalist	7	2.8
Government employee	7	2.8
Politician	7	2.8
Banker	4	1.6
Farmer	4	1.6
Architect/builder	3	1.2
Artisan/tradesman	3	1.2
Military/politician	3	1.2
Educator	2	0.8
Clerk	2	0.8
Clergyman	1	0.4

NATION OR AREA OF ORIGIN	(866 KNOWN)	%
U.S.A.	863	99.6
Europe	3	0.4

U.S. GEOGRAPHIC REGION	(863 KNOWN)	%
South	650	75.3
Local	211	24.4
Northcentral	1	0.1
West	1	0.1

NATIVE STATE	(863 KNOWN)	%
Louisiana*	208	24.1
Virginia*	167	19.3
Maryland	126	14.6
D.C.	85	9.8
Georgia*	74	8.5
Mississippi*	54	6.2
South Carolina*	42	4.8
Alabama*	40	4.6
North Carolina*	19	2.2

NATIVE STATE, *continued*		
Tennessee*	12	1.4
Arkansas*	9	1.0
Texas*	9	1.0
Florida*	7	0.8
Kentucky	6	0.7
Missouri	3	0.3
California	1	0.1
Michigan	1	0.1

URBAN/RURAL LOCALE	(834 KNOWN)	%
Country	333	39.9
City	283	33.9
Town	218	36.1

ETHNIC GROUP	(860 KNOWN)	%
English	501	58.2
French	139	16.1
Irish	90	10.5
German	28	3.2
Scotch-Irish/Scotch	23	2.6
Welsh	13	1.5
English/French	11	1.2
Hispanic	9	1.0
Italian	9	1.0
Scotch-Irish/English	7	0.8
English/German	5	0.5
English/Irish	4	0.4
Greek	4	0.4
Dutch	3	0.3
Jews (European)	3	0.3
Portuguese	3	0.3
German/Irish	2	0.2
Polish	2	0.2
English/Dutch	1	0.1
English/Italian	1	0.1
French/Hispanic	1	0.1
Scandinavian	1	0.1

RELIGIOUS AFFILIATION	(597 KNOWN)	%
Catholic	573	66.1
Protestant	291	33.5
Jewish	3	0.3

* The Confederate States. (The other states listed above remained in the Union, although some Georgetown alumni [222, or 25.6%] from them chose to serve in the Confederate armed forces.)

Table 9.2 Demographics of the 867 Georgetown Alumni Who Served in the Confederate Military (*continued*)

OCCUPATION OR CAREER	(196 KNOWN)	%	OCCUPATION OR CAREER, *continued*		
Doctor	51	26.0	Educator	4	2.0
Lawyer	36	18.3	Doctor/politician	3	1.5
Businessman	15	7.6	Druggist	2	1.0
Career military	15	7.6	Farmer/politician	2	1.0
Lawyer/politician	13	7.1	Lawyer/businessman	2	1.0
Farmer	10	5.1	Politician	2	1.0
Editor/journalist	8	4.0	Military/lawyer	2	1.0
Planter	8	4.0	Actor	1	0.5
Government employee	5	2.5	Banker	1	0.5
Clergyman	4	2.0	Banker/lawyer	1	0.5
Clerk	4	2.0	Librarian	1	0.5

Table 9.3 Demographics of the 218 Georgetown Alumni Who Served in the Union Military

SCHOOL OR COLLEGE	(218 KNOWN)	%	NATIVE STATE	(214 KNOWN)	%
CAS	140	64.3	D.C.*	61	28.5
MED	74	34.0	Pennsylvania*	38	17.7
CMD	3	1.3	New York*	30	14.0
LAW	1	0.4	Maryland*	27	12.6
			Massachusetts*	11	5.1
FATHER'S OCCUPATION	**(64 KNOWN)**	**%**	Virginia	7	3.2
Career military	21	32.8	Indiana*	5	2.3
Lawyer	8	12.5	Ohio*	5	2.3
Doctor	7	10.9	Connecticut*	4	1.8
Businessman	6	9.3	Maine*	4	1.8
Government employee	5	7.8	New Hampshire*	3	1.4
Lawyer/politician	5	7.8	Wisconsin*	3	1.4
Politician	4	6.2	Delaware*	2	0.9
Clergyman	3	4.6	Illinois*	2	0.9
Educator	1	1.5	Kansas*	2	0.9
Engineer	1	1.5	Kentucky*	2	0.9
Dentist	1	1.5	Arkansas	1	0.4
Government official	1	1.5	Georgia	1	0.4
Journalist/editor	1	1.5	Michigan*	1	0.4
			Missouri*	1	0.4
NATION OR AREA OF ORIGIN	**(218 KNOWN)**	**%**	New Jersey*	1	0.4
U.S.A.	214	98.1	North Carolina	1	0.4
Europe	3	1.3	Tennessee	1	0.4
Central America	1	0.4	Vermont*	1	0.4
U.S. GEOGRAPHIC REGION	**(214 KNOWN)**	**%**	**URBAN/RURAL LOCALE**	**(188 KNOWN)**	**%**
Northeast	93	43.4	City	114	60.6
Local	89	41.5	Town	40	21.2
Northcentral	17	7.9	Country	34	18.0
South	13	6.0			
West	2	0.9			

* These states remained in the Union. (The other states listed above joined South Carolina in secession and formed the Confederacy. However, some Georgetown alumni [11, or 4.8%] from them chose to remain loyal to the Union and served in the Union's armed forces.)

Table 9.3, *continued*

ETHNIC GROUP	(215 KNOWN)	%
English	137	63.7
Irish	32	14.8
German	15	7.0
Scotch-Irish/Scotch	12	5.6
French	6	2.7
English/German	3	1.4
English/French	2	0.9
Jews (European)	2	0.9
Dutch	1	0.4
English/Irish	1	0.4
German/Irish	1	0.4
Italian	1	0.4
Scotch-Irish/English	1	0.4
Welsh	1	0.4

RELIGIOUS AFFILIATION	(141 KNOWN)	%
Catholic	123	56.4
Protestant	92	42.2
Jewish	3	1.3

OCCUPATION OR CAREER	(142 KNOWN)	%
Doctor	65	45.7
Career military	36	25.3
Government clerk	7	4.9
Lawyer	7	4.9
Military/doctor	6	4.2
Businessman	5	3.5
Lawyer/politician	4	2.8
Druggist	2	1.4
Government official	2	1.4
Surveyor	2	1.4
Banker	1	0.7
Banker/lawyer	1	0.7
Clergyman	1	0.7
Doctor/businessman	1	0.7
Editor/journalist	1	0.7
Planter/businessman	1	0.7

Table 9.4 Demographics of All 138 Georgetown Medical Students from 1861 to 1865

FATHER'S OCCUPATION	(5 KNOWN)	%
Doctor	2	40.0
Clergyman	1	20.0
Lawyer	1	20.0
Military/doctor	1	20.0

NATION OR AREA OF ORIGIN	(136 KNOWN)	%
U.S.A.	133	97.9
Canada	1	0.7
Central America	1	0.7
Europe	1	0.7

U.S. GEOGRAPHIC REGION	(133 KNOWN)	%
Northeast	74	55.6
Local	34	25.5
Northcentral	18	13.5
South	5	3.7
West	2	1.5

NATIVE STATE	(133 KNOWN)	%
D.C.	26	19.5
New York	17	12.7
Pennsylvania	17	12.7
Massachusetts	12	9.0
Maryland	8	6.0
New Hampshire	8	6.0
New Jersey	7	5.2
Maine	6	4.5
Connecticut	5	3.7
Illinois	4	3.0
Minnesota	4	3.0
Virginia	4	3.0

NATIVE STATE, continued		
Indiana	2	1.5
Michigan	2	1.5
Missouri	2	1.5
Ohio	2	1.5
Vermont	2	1.5
Wisconsin	2	1.5
California	1	0.7
Oklahoma Territory	1	0.7
Tennessee	1	0.7

URBAN/RURAL LOCALE	(59 KNOWN)	%
City	39	66.1
Country	13	22.0
Town	7	11.8

ETHNIC GROUP	(134 KNOWN)	%
English	84	62.6
German	24	17.9
Irish	13	9.7
Dutch	3	2.2
Scotch-Irish/Scotch	3	2.2
Welsh	3	2.2
English/German	1	0.7
English/Irish	1	0.7
French	1	0.7
Scotch-Irish/English	1	0.7

RELIGIOUS AFFILIATION	(42 KNOWN)	%
Protestant	25	59.5
Catholic	16	38.1
Jewish	1	2.3

Table 10.1 Demographics of 340 of the 1870–79 Georgetown College Students*

FATHER'S OCCUPATION	(89 KNOWN)	%
Doctor	22	24.7
Businessman	16	17.9
Lawyer/politician	13	14.6
Lawyer	12	13.4
Career military	7	7.8
Politician	5	5.6
Editor/journalist	3	3.3
Foreign diplomat	2	2.2
Planter	2	2.2
Writer	2	2.2
Artist	1	1.1
Clergyman	1	1.1
Educator	1	1.1
Engineer	1	1.1
Government employee	1	1.1

NATION OR AREA OF ORIGIN	(340 KNOWN)	%
U.S.A.	312	91.8
Central America	18	5.3
Canada	4	1.1
South America	4	1.1
Europe	2	0.6

U.S. GEOGRAPHIC REGION	(312 KNOWN)	%
Local	102	32.6
South	99	31.7
Northeast	61	19.5
Northcentral	43	13.7
West	7	2.2

NATIVE STATE	(312 KNOWN)	%
D.C.	60	19.2
Maryland	42	13.4
New York	29	9.3
Louisiana	28	8.9
Missouri	21	6.7
Pennsylvania	19	6.0
Virginia	15	4.8
Georgia	13	4.1
West Virginia	10	3.2
Alabama	9	2.8
Illinois	8	2.5
Massachusetts	7	2.2
Ohio	7	2.2
South Carolina	6	1.9
Kentucky	5	1.6
Texas	5	1.6
Tennessee	4	1.2

NATIVE STATE, continued		
Michigan	3	0.9
Arkansas	2	0.6
California	2	0.6
Indiana	2	0.6
Maine	2	0.6
New Mexico	2	0.6
North Carolina	2	0.6
Wisconsin	2	0.6
Connecticut	1	0.3
Delaware	1	0.3
Florida	1	0.3
Mississippi	1	0.3
New Jersey	1	0.3
Rhode Island	1	0.3
Wyoming	1	0.3

URBAN/RURAL LOCALE	(315 KNOWN)	%
City	210	66.6
Town	55	17.4
Country	50	15.8

ETHNIC GROUP	(340 KNOWN)	%
English	121	35.6
Irish	107	31.5
French	31	9.1
German	26	7.6
Hispanic	25	7.3
English/Irish	5	1.2
Scotch-Irish/Scotch	5	1.2
Welsh	4	1.2
Slavic	3	0.9
English/Hispanic	2	0.6
French/Hispanic	2	0.6
Dutch	1	0.3
English/French	1	0.3
English/German	1	0.3
English/Scotch/German	1	0.3
English/Welsh	1	0.3
Scotch/English	1	0.3
Swiss/French	1	0.3

RELIGIOUS AFFILIATION	(336 KNOWN)	%
Catholic	263	77.3
Protestant[†]	75	22.0
Jewish	1	0.2
None (self-declared)	1	0.2

Table 10.1 Demographics of 340 of the 1870–79 Georgetown College Students* (*continued*)

RELIGIOUS VOCATIONS	(5 KNOWN)	%
Diocesan clergy	3	1.1
Society of Jesus	2	0.7

FINANCIAL STATUS	(331 KNOWN)	%
Paid full tuition	296	89.4
Paid reduced fees	15	4.5
Tuition waived	9	2.7
Paid group rate	7	2.1
Rec'd outside aid	3	0.9
Paid in cash & kind	1	0.3

HOUSING STATUS	(340 KNOWN)	%
Campus boarders	294	86.5
Day students	46	13.5

DEGREES EARNED	(54 KNOWN)	%
A.B.	46	13.5
LL.B.	4	1.2
M.D.	3	0.9
B.S.	1	0.3

DISCIPLINARY STATUS		%
Expelled students	12	3.5

OCCUPATION OR CAREER‡	(97 KNOWN)	%
Lawyer	30	30.3
Businessman	21	21.2
Doctor	14	14.1
Clergyman	5	5.0
Lawyer/politician	5	5.0
Editor/journalist	4	4.0
Career military	2	2.0
Engineering	2	2.0
Government official	2	2.0
Government worker	2	2.0
Politician	2	2.0
Tradesman	2	2.0
Actor	1	1.0
Dentist	1	1.0
Druggist	1	1.0
Educator	1	1.0
Planter	1	1.0
Scientist	1	1.0

* From 1870 to 1879, the median entering age of Georgetown students was 15 years and 1 month and the median departing age was 16 years and 10 months.

†Of these Protestant students, it is known that less than a twentieth (3, or 4.0%) became Catholics in the 1870–79 period.

‡Besides these students whose post-Georgetown occupations are tabulated here, two (2.0%) died young, before going into any adult work, career, or profession.

Table 10.2 Demographics of 50 of the 1870–79 Georgetown Law Students

FATHER'S OCCUPATION	(4 KNOWN)	%
Businessman	1	25.0
Doctor	1	25.0
Government clerk	1	25.0
Lawyer	1	25.0

NATION OR AREA OF ORIGIN	(40 KNOWN)	%
U.S.A.	39	97.5
Central America	1	2.5

U.S. GEOGRAPHIC REGION	(39 KNOWN)	%
Local	14	36.0
Northeast	13	33.3
Northcentral	8	20.5
South	4	10.2

NATIVE STATE	(39 KNOWN)	%
D.C.	13	33.3
Pennsylvania	6	15.4
Indiana	3	7.7
Maine	2	5.1
Massachusetts	2	5.1
Georgia	1	2.5
Illinois	1	2.5
Maryland	1	2.5
Michigan	1	2.5
Missouri	1	2.5
New Hampshire	1	2.5
New Jersey	1	2.5

NATIVE STATE, *continued*		
New York	1	2.5
North Carolina	1	2.5
Ohio	1	2.5
Virginia	1	2.5
West Virginia	1	2.5
Wisconsin	1	2.5

URBAN/RURAL LOCALE	(18 KNOWN)	%
City	15	83.3
Town	3	16.7

ETHNIC GROUP	(38 KNOWN)	%
English	24	63.1
German	4	10.5
Irish	3	7.9
Welsh	2	5.2
English/Irish	1	2.6
Hispanic	1	2.6
Irish/Hispanic	1	2.6
Scotch	1	2.6
Scotch/English	1	2.6

RELIGIOUS AFFILIATION	(16 KNOWN)	%
Catholic	11	68.7
Protestant	5	31.2

DEGREES EARNED		%
LL.B.	20	50.0

Table 10.3 Demographics of 83 of the 1870–79 Georgetown Medical Students

FATHER'S OCCUPATION	(8 KNOWN)	%
Businessman	2	25.0
Career military	2	25.0
Doctor	2	25.0
Clergyman	1	12.5
Lawyer	1	12.5

NATION OR AREA OF ORIGIN	(83 KNOWN)	%
U.S.A.	76	91.5
Europe	7	8.4

U.S. GEOGRAPHIC REGION	(76 KNOWN)	%
Local	26	34.2
Northeast	26	34.2
Northcentral	11	13.2
South	8	10.5
West	5	6.6

NATIVE STATE	(76 KNOWN)	%
D.C.	21	27.6
New York	14	18.4
Pennsylvania	9	11.8
Maryland	5	6.6
Ohio	5	6.6
Virginia	5	6.6
California	2	2.6
Illinois	2	2.6
Kansas	2	2.6
Kentucky	2	2.6
Massachusetts	1	1.3
Minnesota	1	1.3
Nebraska	1	1.3

NATIVE STATE, continued		
New Hampshire	1	1.3
Indiana	1	1.3
Iowa	1	1.3
Tennessee	1	1.3
Vermont	1	1.3
Wisconsin	1	1.3

URBAN/RURAL LOCALE	(48 KNOWN)	%
City	36	75.0
Country	6	12.5
Town	6	12.5

ETHNIC GROUP	(83 KNOWN)	%
English	45	54.2
German	15	18.0
Irish	14	16.8
Welsh	3	3.6
Jews (European)	2	2.4
Arab	1	1.2
English/French	1	1.2
French	1	1.2
Scotch	1	1.2

RELIGIOUS AFFILIATION	(42 KNOWN)	%
Protestant*	22	52.4
Catholic	18	42.8
Jewish	2	4.7

DEGREES EARNED		%
M.D.	49	59.0

* Of these Protestant students, only one (4.5%) is known to have become a Catholic in the 1870–79 period.

Table 11.1 Demographics of 223 of the 1880–89 Georgetown College Students

FATHER'S OCCUPATION	(65 KNOWN)	%
Businessman	12	18.5
Doctor	10	15.4
Career military	8	12.3
Lawyer	8	12.3
Lawyer/politician	8	12.3
Politician	4	6.2
Editor/journalist	3	4.6
Government employee	3	4.6
Educator	2	3.1
Foreign diplomat	2	3.1
Planter	2	3.1
Farmer	1	1.5
Librarian	1	1.5
Writer	1	1.5

NATION OR AREA OF ORIGIN	(221 KNOWN)	%
U.S.A.	214	96.5
Central America	4	1.8
Europe	2	0.9
Canada	1	0.4

U.S. GEOGRAPHIC REGION	(214 KNOWN)	%
Local	94	43.9
Northeast	54	25.2
South	34	15.9
Northcentral	22	10.2
West	10	4.7

NATIVE STATE	(214 KNOWN)	%
D.C.	68	31.7
Pennsylvania	25	11.6
Maryland	24	11.2
New York	23	10.7
Missouri	8	3.7
Louisiana	7	3.2
Georgia	6	2.8
Massachusetts	6	2.8
Virginia	6	2.8
Illinois	5	2.3
Ohio	5	2.3
Tennessee	4	1.8
Arkansas	3	1.4
Kansas	2	0.9
Kentucky	2	0.9
Minnesota	2	0.9
North Dakota	2	0.9

NATIVE STATE	(214 KNOWN)	%
Texas	2	0.9
Alabama	1	0.4
Colorado	1	0.4
Florida	1	0.4
Indiana	1	0.4
Iowa	1	0.4
Michigan	1	0.4
Montana	1	0.4
Nebraska	1	0.4
New Jersey	1	0.4
New Mexico	1	0.4
North Carolina	1	0.4
Rhode Island	1	0.4
Washington	1	0.4
West Virginia	1	0.4

URBAN/RURAL LOCALE	(217 KNOWN)	%
City	152	70.1
Town	40	18.4
Country	25	11.5

ETHNIC GROUP	(223 KNOWN)	%
English	97	43.5
Irish	68	30.5
German	13	5.8
French	11	4.9
Hispanic	9	4.0
Scotch	7	3.1
Italian	4	1.8
Dutch	3	1.3
English/German	3	1.3
English/Irish	3	1.3
German/Irish	2	0.9
English/French	1	0.4
Slavic	1	0.4
Welsh	1	0.4

RELIGIOUS AFFILIATION	(204 KNOWN)	%
Catholic	179	80.3
Protestant*	43	19.2
Jewish	1	0.4

RELIGIOUS VOCATIONS	(2 KNOWN)	%
Society of Jesus	1	0.5
Other clergy	1	0.5

Of these Protestant students, it is known that a few (3, or 6.9%) became Catholics in the 1880–89 period.

Table 11.1 Demographics of 223 of the 1880–89 Georgetown College Students (continued)

FINANCIAL STATUS	(212 KNOWN)	%		OCCUPATION OR CAREER†	(76 KNOWN)	%
Paid full tuition	185	85.3		Lawyer	33	42.8
Paid reduced fees	12	5.5		Businessman	14	18.1
Paid group rate	7	3.2		Doctor	8	10.4
Tuition waived	5	2.3		Lawyer/politician	4	5.2
Paid by teaching	2	0.9		Clerk/manager	3	3.9
Rec'd scholarship	1	0.4		Engineer	3	3.9
				Clergyman	2	2.6
HOUSING STATUS		%		Journalist/editor	2	2.6
Campus boarder	166	74.4		Politician	2	2.6
				Architect	1	1.3
DEGREES EARNED	(42 KNOWN)	%		Farmer	1	1.3
A.B.	36	16.1		Government official	1	1.3
B.S.	5	2.2		Librarian	1	1.3
Ph.B.	1	0.4		Marine pilot	1	1.3

DISCIPLINARY STATUS		%
Expelled students	7	3.1

†Besides these students whose post-Georgetown occupations are tabulated here, one (1.3%) died young, before going into any adult work, career, or profession.

Table 11.2 Demographics of 45 of the 1880–89 Georgetown Medical Students

FATHER'S OCCUPATION	(5 KNOWN)	%
Doctor	4	80.0
Businessman	1	20.0

NATION OR AREA OF ORIGIN	(45 KNOWN)	%
U.S.A.	39	86.7
Europe	6	13.3

U.S. GEOGRAPHIC REGION	(39 KNOWN)	%
Northeast	13	33.3
Local	12	30.7
Northcentral	9	23.1
South	4	10.3
West	1	2.5

NATIVE STATE	(39 KNOWN)	%
D.C.	9	23.0
New York	6	15.4
Illinois	3	7.7
Maryland	3	7.7
Massachusetts	3	7.7
Ohio	3	7.7
Pennsylvania	3	7.7
Virginia	2	5.1
Arkansas	1	2.5
Indiana	1	2.5
Kentucky	1	2.5
Minnesota	1	2.5
New Jersey	1	2.5
Washington	1	2.5
Wisconsin	1	2.5

URBAN/RURAL LOCALE	(22 KNOWN)	%
City	15	68.2
Country	4	18.2
Town	3	13.6

ETHNIC GROUP	(45 KNOWN)	%
English	27	60.0
German	6	13.3
Irish	5	11.1
French	3	6.7
English/German	1	2.2
English/Welsh	1	2.2
Scotch	1	2.2
Slavic	1	2.2

RELIGIOUS AFFILIATION	(20 KNOWN)	%
Protestant	11	55.0
Catholic	9	45.0

DEGREES EARNED		%
M.D.	33	73.3

OCCUPATION OR CAREER	(33 KNOWN)	%
Doctor	19	57.6
Doctor/teacher	7	21.2
Government doctor	7	21.2

Table 11.3 Demographics of 66 of the 1880–89 Georgetown Law Students

FATHER'S OCCUPATION	(9 KNOWN)	%
Doctor	2	22.2
Lawyer	2	22.2
Businessman	1	11.1
Farmer	1	11.1
Government clerk	1	11.1
Lawyer/politician	1	11.1
Librarian	1	11.1

NATION OR AREA OF ORIGIN	(66 KNOWN)	%
U.S.A.	66	100.0

U.S. GEOGRAPHIC REGION	(66 KNOWN)	%
Local	30	45.4
South	13	19.7
Northeast	12	18.2
Northcentral	8	12.1
West	3	4.6

NATIVE STATE	(66 KNOWN)	%
D.C.	26	39.4
Illinois	4	6.1
Pennsylvania	4	6.1
Virginia	4	6.1
Indiana	3	4.5
Maryland	3	4.5
New York	3	4.5
Maine	2	3.0
Tennessee	2	3.0
West Virginia	2	3.0
Arkansas	1	1.5
California	1	1.5
Colorado	1	1.5
Delaware	1	1.5
Georgia	1	1.5
Kentucky	1	1.5
Massachusetts	1	1.5
Minnesota	1	1.5
North Carolina	1	1.5

NATIVE STATE, continued		
Ohio	1	1.5
South Carolina	1	1.5
Vermont	1	1.5
Wyoming	1	1.5

URBAN/RURAL LOCALE	(59 KNOWN)	%
City	38	64.4
Town	14	23.7
Country	7	11.9

ETHNIC GROUP	(65 KNOWN)	%
English	40	61.5
Irish	17	26.1
Scotch	2	3.1
English/French	1	1.5
English/Scotch/German	1	1.5
French	1	1.5
German	1	1.5
Slavic	1	1.5
Welsh	1	1.5

RELIGIOUS AFFILIATION	(32 KNOWN)	%
Catholic	25	78.1
Protestant*	7	21.9

DEGREES EARNED		%
LL.B.	49	74.2

OCCUPATION OR CAREER	(53 KNOWN)	%
Lawyer	31	58.5
Lawyer/politician	6	11.3
Government employee	5	9.4
Lawyer/teacher	4	7.5
Clerk	2	3.7
Lawyer/editor	2	3.7
Businessman	1	1.9
Journalist	1	1.9
Lawyer/banker	1	1.9

Of these Protestant students, it is known that one (14.3%) became a Catholic in the 1880–89 period.

Notes

CHAPTER 1

1. Archives of the Sacred Congregation for Propagation of the Faith [hereafter APF], *Scritture riferite nei Congressi, America Centrale, I,* fols. 557r-v and 558r, September 1773; Thomas Hughes, SJ, *History of the Society of Jesus in North America: Colonial and Federal.* Text, 2 (London, 1917), 554–56.
2. James Hennesey, SJ, "Several Youth Sent from Here: Native-Born Priests and Religious of English America, 1634–1776," in Nelson H. Minnich et al., *Studies in Catholic History in Honor of John Tracy Ellis* (Wilmington, Del., 1985), 24.
3. Hennesey, 24; Herman Mattingly, *The Mattingly Family in Early America* (privately printed, 1975), 236–41.
4. Geoffrey Holt, SJ, *St. Omers and Bruges Colleges, 1593–1773: A Biographical Dictionary* (London, 1979). I am indebted to James McLachlan and Paul Mattingly for the comparative information.
5. James Hennesey, SJ, *American Catholics: A History of the Roman Catholic Community in the United States* (New York, 1981), 56.
6. Charles Carroll of Annapolis to Charles Carroll of Carrollton, July 14, 1760, in Kate Mason Rowland, *The Life of Charles Carroll of Carrollton, 1737–1832 with His Correspondence and Public Papers* (New York, 1898) I, 43.
7. Although 1769 has been commonly cited by Carroll's biographers as the year of his ordination, Thomas W. Spalding has recently established 1761 as the true date ("John Carroll: Corrigenda and Addenda," *The Catholic Historical Review* 71 [October 1985], 510).
8. Carroll to Thomas Ellerker [Rome, January 23, 1772 (1773), in Thomas O'Brien Hanley, SJ, The John Carroll Papers [hereafter CP] (Notre Dame, 1976), I, 27.
9. Carroll to Daniel Carroll, Bruges, September 11, 1773, CP, I, 32.
10. Carroll to Daniel Carroll, [Bruges, September 11, 1773], CP, I, 32; Annabelle M. Melville, *John Carroll of Baltimore: Founder of the American Catholic Hierarchy* (New York, 1955), 36–37.
11. John Carroll to Charles Plowden, Maryland, February 28, 1779, CP, I, 53. Charles Plowden (1743–1821) had studied at St. Omers before entering the Society in 1759. He was with Carroll at the English College at Brugge (Bruges) when the Society was suppressed. Plowden subsequently joined the faculty of the English Academy at Liège, which survived as a diocesan school under the local prince bishop. In 1784 he became both chaplain and tutor at Lulworth Castle, the home of Thomas Weld, who had been a student at the Brugge college in 1773. When the Liège school was forced to relocate to Stonyhurst in 1794, Plowden once again joined the faculty. Later he became the first novice master of the revived English Province of the Society, and in 1817 was appointed provincial. Henry Foley, *Records of the English Province of the Society of Jesus* (London, 1882) VII, 1, 601–03.

12. Charles Lee to John Hancock, February 27, 1776, *Researches*, 24 (July 1907), 225, in Melville, 44.

13. Draft of Memorandum of Carroll [1776], CP, I, 46–47.

14. February 28, 1779, CP, I, 53.

15. September 26, 1783, CP, I, 78.

16. "The Main Sheet Anchor: John Carroll and Catholic Higher Education," *Review of Politics* 38 (October 1976), 611.

17. Carroll to Plowden, Maryland, February 20, 1782, CP, I, 66.

18. "Report for His Eminence Cardinal Antonelli on the condition of religion in the sections of the United States of America," March 1, 1785, CP, I, 179.

19. Report of C. Hunter, SJ, July 23, 1765, in Thomas Hughes, SJ, *History of the Society of Jesus in North America. Documents*, I, Part 1, 335–38. There were also two small farms in southeastern Pennsylvania.

20. Hughes, *History, Documents*, I, Part 2, 609–14, 644–45; Francis Edwards, SJ, *The Jesuits in England: From 1580 to the Present Day* (London, 1985), 148.

21. The ex-Jesuits, in fact, were making what was in their day an unprecedented claim of autonomy for their "ecclesiastical" property. Carroll made a distinction between the temporal and spiritual realms of religion. In his enlightened thinking, just as church and state were separated, so were the material and spiritual orders. He was particularly concerned that no foreign power should control property. "A foreign temporal jurisdiction will never be tolerated here," he informed Plowden, "& even the Spiritual supremacy of the Pope is the only reason why in some of the United States, the full participation of all civil rights is not granted to the R.C. They [Propaganda] may therefore send their Agents, when they please; they will certainly return empty handed . . ." (September 26, 1783, CP, I, 78).

22. GUSC, Maryland Province Archives [hereafter MPA], 2 N 8d, [Carroll] to the Reverend Gentlemen of the Southern District, Maryland [1787] (draft).

23. Carroll to Jacques André Emery, SS [London, September 3, 1790], CP, I, 457.

24. Peter Guilday, *The Life and Times of John Carroll: Archbishop of Baltimore, 1735–1815* (New York, 1922), 1, 170.

25. Guilday, 203–4. Carroll was upset that Rome had acted on its own without even consulting the American clergy. He suspected that Propaganda Fide had feared that the Americans might choose one of their own as bishop and then get the blessing of the United States government for a *fait accompli*. "The propgda hope, by appointing a Bp now," he observed to Plowden, "to establish the precedent of appointing one hereafter . . ." (September 18, 1784, CP, I, 151).

26. Archives of the Archdiocese of Baltimore [hereafter AAB], 8 A 1, Strickland to Carroll, Liège, July 7, 1784. Strickland (1731–1819) remained as president at Liège until 1790. He subsequently played a key role in the restoration of the English Jesuit Province (Foley, *Records* VII, 2, 745–47).

27. Carroll to Ferdinand Farmer [December 1784], CP, I, 158.

28. Harvard (1636), William and Mary (1693), and Yale (1701) were the three oldest colleges. The College of New Jersey [Princeton] (1746), King's College [Columbia] (1754), the College of Philadelphia [Pennsylvania] (1755), the College of Rhode Island [Brown] (1765), Queen's College [Rutgers] (1766), and Dartmouth (1769) were the six founded during the Awakening era. The complete list is in Jurgen Herbst, *From Crisis to Crisis: American College Government, 1636–1819* (Cambridge, 1982), 244–53.

29. James McLachlan, *American Boarding Schools: A Historical Study* (New York, 1970), 35.

30. Herbst, 189; Howard Miller, *The Revolutionary College: American Presbyterian Higher Education 1707–1837* (New York, 1976), 133–49.

31. John F. Roche, *The Colonial Colleges in the War for American Independence* (Millwood, N.J., 1986), 150.

32. David W. Robson, *Educating Republicans: The College in the Era of the American Revolution, 1750–1800* (Westport, Conn., 1985), 32–33; Herbst, "The American Revolution and the American University," *Perspectives in American History* 10 (1976), 301–3.

33. Robson, 32.

34. CP, 1, 167.
35. Carroll to Farmer [December 1784], CP, I, 158; Carroll to John Thorpe, February 17, 1785, CP, I, 164.
36. Carroll to Leonardo Antonelli, March 1, 1785; Carroll to Joseph Edenshink, [April-June 1785]; Carroll to Francis Neale, June 17, 1785, in CP, I, 181, 186, 190. Hanley misidentifies the recipient of the letter as Francis's brother, Leonard.
37. Carroll to Plowden, December 15, 1785, CP, I, 198.
38. "I see at present," John Carroll observed in a letter to Charles Plowden, "no other advantage to us Catholics in the Annapolis College, than this, that it may be a place for our young lads, who have finished their Grammar education at Georgetown to pursue their higher studies of law, medicine &c. In other respects, it will be hurtful to our Institution" (February 24, 1790, CP, I, 431).
39. *An Address to the Roman Catholics of the United States of America by a Catholic Clergyman* (Annapolis, 1784). The title of Wharton's pamphlet was *Letter to the Roman Catholics of the City of Worcester* (Philadelphia, 1784). Wharton had his malicious "explanation" printed and published in Pennsylvania, not in the city where he distributed it.
40. Carroll to Farmer [December 1784], CP, I, 158.
41. This was equivalent roughly to a laborer's annual wage ($107 in Maryland dollars of that time).
42. Strickland estimated the expenses at £25 a year. Carroll may also have been calculating travel and other costs (AAB, 8 A 2, Strickland to Carroll, London, February 25, 1786; AAB, 7 V 8, Strickland to Carroll, London, January 21, 1789; Carroll to Beeston, Baltimore, March 22, 1788, CP, I, 292).
43. AAB, 6 J 1, Plowden to Carroll, London, April 4, 1784; AAB, 6 J 6, same to same, Lulworth Castle, February 28, 1785.
44. Carroll to Plowden, Baltimore, October 23, 1789, CP, I, 390.
45. Carroll to Beeston, Baltimore, March 22, 1788, CP, I, 292.
46. Carroll to Antonelli, March 13, 1786, CP, I, 209.
47. MPA, 2 N, Circular Letter of the general chapter on a diocesan bishop, November 24, 1786; "our great view," Carroll explained to Plowden, "is to form subjects capable of becoming useful members of the ministry; and to these a Bishop for Ordination, will be indispensably necessary (January 22, 1787; February 28, 1787, CP, I, 241).
48. MPA, 2 N 7, Proceeds of the Genl. Chapter in the year 1786 [November 16].
49. When a meeting was called in April 1788 to discuss ways to achieve the restoration of the Society in America, six of the thirteen Jesuits to attend were from those counties and had already sent the protest about the resolutions of the chapter (Hughes, *History*, Documents, I, Part 2, 683–84).
50. Carroll was more blunt in discussing it with Plowden. Any revival of the Society, a "very uncertain prospect[,] . . . ought not to hinder so essential a service to Religion: that the Society was instituted to save souls: & that souls were not made subservient to the temporal benefits of the Society" (February 28, 1787, CP, I, 246).
51. Carroll to unidentified Southern District member, February 7, 1787, CP, I, 249.
52. MPA, 2 N 8d, [Carroll] to the Reverend Gentlemen of the Southern District, Maryland [1787] (draft).
53. CP, 1, 249.
54. Carroll to Plowden, March 29, 1787, CP, I, 251–52.
55. APF, *Atti* (1789), ff. 369–78, quoted in Guilday, *John Carroll, I,* 352; Carroll to Plowden, Baltimore, March 20, 1789, CP, I, 351.
56. Carroll to Plowden, Baltimore, May 8, 1789, CP, I, 362.
57. APF, *Atti* (1789), fol. 378, in Guilday, *John Carroll,* I, 353.
58. Lib. J.G., No. 1. fol. 634 seq. in Hughes, *History*, Documents, I, Part 2, 723–26. The clergy subsequently chose "The Corporation of the Roman Catholic Clergymen" as the legal name of the body.
59. Carroll to Plowden, Rock Creek, January 22, 1787, Baltimore February 28, 1787, CP, I, 243–44.

60. There were twenty-eight agents in all, including Carroll, Charles Blake, John Blake, Chandler Brent, Baker Brooke, John Darnall, Robert Darnall, George Digges, Francis Hall, John Lancaster, William Matthews, Joseph Millard, Joseph Mosley, Bernard O'Neill, Edmund Plowden, Henry Rozer, John Tuitte, Marsham Waring, Ignatius Wheeler, and Notley Young—all of Maryland; Fitzsimmons and George Mead of Pennsylvania; George Brent and John Fitzgerald of Virginia; and Dominic Lynch of New York.

61. Phyllis Vine, "The Social Function of Eighteenth-Century Higher Education," *HEQ* 16 (Winter 1976), 409–13.

62. In New England the Phillips family gave over $100,000 in the late eighteenth century to establish Phillips Andover (MA) and Phillips Exeter (NH) (James McLachlan, *American Boarding Schools: A Historical Study* [New York, 1970], 42).

63. Quoted in James Alfred Haw, "Politics in Revolutionary Maryland, 1753–1788" (unpublished Ph.D. diss., University of Virginia, 1972), 390, cited in Herbst, "The American Revolution," 340.

64. Herbst, "The American Revolution and the American University," 303.

65. When Princeton was considering a European fund-raising mission, John Jay wrote its president that he did not "think it consistent with the dignity of a free and independent people, to solicit donations for that or any other purpose, from the subjects of any prince or state, whatever" (Roche, *Colonial Colleges,* 173–77).

66. AAB, 6 K 2, Plowden to Carroll, Lulworth Castle, 3 June 1787. "The English Catholic community at this time has been estimated to number between 80,000 and 90,000 persons" (John Bossey, *The English Catholic Community, 1570–1850* [New York, 1976], 422).

67. AAB, 8 A 5, Strickland to Carroll, London, October 11, 1788.

68. Carroll to James Frambach, Baltimore, October 1, 1787, CP, I, 264; Carroll to Smyth, April 8. 1788, CP, I, 295; Carroll to Betagh, July 9, 1788, CP, I, 314.

69. Patrick Smyth, *Present State of the Catholic Mission Conducted by the Ex-Jesuits in North-America* (Dublin, 1788), 26–27.

70. Reply to Smyth, [1789] (draft), CP, I, 337–46. Ironically, Strickland had written Carroll in June 1788: "I am told . . . that there is now in America a Gentleman of the name of Smith [sic], who is employd to examine the Ground & to raise an opposition to any measures you may adopt for the better Government of the country in Spirituals, unless they be such as agree with the wishes of his Employers. Mr. Halsey is said to be the Director of this Plan in London (AAB, 7 V 7, Strickland to Carroll, Liège, June 28, 1788). Smyth had arrived in Maryland earlier, during the discussion between Rome and the American clergy over the form of ecclesiastical government that was to be established.

71. Carroll to Matthew Carey, Baltimore, May 21, 1789, CP, I, 364.

72. AAB, 8 B G 7, Strickland to Carroll, London, April 18, 1788, cited in Guilday, John Carroll, I, 321.

73. AAB, 8 K 8, Thorpe to Carroll, Rome, August 8, 1790, cited in Guilday, John Carroll, I, 321.

74. Carroll to Antonelli, London, September 27, 1790, CP, I, 468.

75. Carroll to Antonelli, Baltimore, April 14, 1789, CP, I, 357; Carroll to Antonelli, February 6, 1790, CP, I, 428; APF, *Lettere Della S. Congregatione, dell' anno 1792,* vol. 262, fols. 558v to 568r, Propaganda Fide to Carroll, Rome, September 29, 1792; ibid., vol. 266, fols. 677r to 679r, P.F. to Carroll, Rome, December 20, 1794.

76. The largest gift, that from the ex-Jesuit, Peter Jenkins, for £200, was restricted through annuity payments of £10 each (Hughes, *History,* Documents, I, Part 2, 809).

77. MPA, 2 N 9, Proceedings of the General Chapter met at the White Marsh, May 11, 1789.

78. Carroll to Thomas Sim Lee, Georgetown, January 25, 1787, CP, I, 247–48.

79. Miller, 178.

80. Federal Census of 1790; Carville Earle and Ronald Hoffman, "Staple Crops and Urban Development in the Eighteenth-Century South," *Perspectives in American History* 10 (1976), 10.

81. Louis Philippe, *Diary of My Travels in America,* tr. Stephen E. Becker (New York, 1977), 21.
82. Harold W. Hurst, "The Maryland Gentry in Old Georgetown, 1783–1861," *Maryland Historical Magazine* 73 (Spring 1978), 1–2.
83. Earle and Hoffman, 49.
84. Earle and Hoffman, 50.
85. Terry D. Bilhartz, *Urban Religion and the Second Great Awakening: Church and Society in Early National Baltimore* (Rutherford, N.J., 1986), 12; Richard M. Bernard, "A Portrait of Baltimore in 1800: Economic and Occupational Patterns in an Early American City," *Maryland Historical Magazine* 69 (Winter 1974), 342.
86. Carroll himself earlier had thought that Philadelphia, then the largest city in the country, would be chosen (Carroll to Philadelphia laity, Baltimore, July 21, 1788, CP, I, 321); APF, *Atti* (1789), fol. 378, cited in Guilday, I, 353.
87. Guilday, *John Carroll,* I, 449.
88. Bilhartz, 22.
89. Paul Venable Turner, *Campus: An American Planning Tradition* (Cambridge, 1984), 106.
90. Lee W. Formwalt, "A Conversation between Two Rivers: A Debate on the Location of the U.S. Capital in Maryland," *Maryland Historical Magazine* 71 (Fall 1976), 310–21; Constance McLaughlin Green, *Washington: Village and Capital, 1800–1878* (Princeton, N.J., 1962), 7–13.
91. White Marsh, February 3, 1791, CP, I, 490. An oral tradition maintained that Carroll had intended to locate his academy on Jenkins Hill, the present Capitol Hill. The land belonged to Daniel Carroll of Duddington, the bishop's cousin. But, as Edward Devitt, who first reported the tradition, remarked, in 1786 "the place was 'too far away in the woods' for a boy's boarding school" (Edward I. Devitt, "Georgetown College in the Early Days," *Records of the Columbia Historical Society* 12 [1909], 21–37).
92. Carroll to Plowden, [London] September 2, 1790, CP, I, 454.
93. Green, 12.
94. March 1, 1788, CP, 1, 275.
95. MPA, 56 P 4a, "An Estimate of Roman Colliage in George Town by H. Carlisle," MPA 56 P 3. The contractors' suspicions about Carlisle's estimate seem to be confirmed by later bidding between Carlisle and another carpenter, William Eaton. The latter offered to do the carpentry in the building for £272, a figure substantially lower than the £328 estimated by Carlisle for the same work (MPA 56 P 4, "Estimate for Colliage by Henry Carlisle"; MPA 56 P 6, "An Estimate of Carpenters work to be done at the Colledge Geo.town").
96. Plowden had finally sent Carroll £50 for the school but to that point there is no record that anyone else in England had contributed (Carroll to Plowden, Baltimore, November 12, 1788, CP, I, 332).
97. GUA, 1.1, Deed to Parcel #1. The choice of 1789 as the founding date of the college stems not from this event but from a mistake made many years later, in the 1840s, in dating the construction of the first building. For more than two decades the founding of Georgetown was implicitly equated with the date of that first building, supposedly in 1789. The 1873 catalogue was the first to make it explicit: "Founded as a college 1789." On the scale of appropriate events, 1789 had the least claim among several years (including 1786, 1788, 1791, and 1792) as a founding date.
98. GUSC, John S. Sumner, SJ, Papers, Catholic Historical Manuscripts Collection [hereafter CHMC], "The Early History of Georgetown College."
99. American academies in general at this time were not boarding schools. Non-local students lived with private families in homes near the institution (McLachlan, *American Boarding Schools,* 45–46).
100. Miller, 177.
101. AAB, 9A-N3.
102. The "Constitution" alluded to is evidently that of Maryland, which in 1776 disestablished the Anglican Church and accorded religious freedom to all Christians

(Jews did not secure this right until 1826 in "The Free State"). (Richard Walsh and William Lloyd Fox, eds., *Maryland: A History, 1632–1974* [Baltimore, 1974], 98, 103).

103. Carroll to Plowden, Rock Creek, February 24, 1790, CP, I, 431.

104. Carroll to Plowden, Rock Creek, January 22, 1787; Baltimore, February 28, 1787, CP, I, 242.

105. AAB, 8 AS, Strickland to Carroll, London, October 11, 1788; AAB, 8 A 6, same to same, Liège, May 1789; AAB, 7 V 7, same to same, Liège, June 28, 1788.

106. AAB, 9A-N3.

107. As Philip Gleason has pointed out, Carroll's allusion to "the mere English teacher" and his perplexity about how to include geography in the curriculum in his plan for the academy casts some doubt on his desire to give equal prominence to the classics and the more utilitarian subjects. Curiously, he gave little thought to the teaching of religion—perhaps assuming that its role was understood. The section on "religious instruction" was left blank in his plan.

108. McLachlan, *American Boarding Schools,* 45.

109. Carroll undoubtedly had in mind St. John's in Annapolis, William and Mary, and Pennsylvania (MPA, 56 RI, "Proposals for establishing an Academy, at George-Town, Patowmack-River, Maryland" [17871; AAB, 9A-N3, Plan for Georgetown Academy, 1788].

110. Hubert Chadwick, SJ, *St. Omers to Stonyhurst: A History of two Centuries* (London, 1962), 40, 70–71, 270–71.

111. The institutions: Washington College, Liberty Hall Academy (1782); Hampden-Sydney College, Transylvania Seminary, Dickinson College (1783); St. John's College [Maryland] (1784); University of Georgia, Mt. Sion College [S.C.], College of Charleston, College of Cambridge [S.C.] (1785); Franklin College (1787); University of North Carolina (1789); University of Vermont (1791); Williams College (1793); Bowdoin College, Greeneville College [Tenn.], Blount College (1794). The list is given in Herbst, *From Crisis to Crisis,* 246–48.

112. *Journal of the Second Session of the Council of Censors,* August 27, 1784, cited in Herbst, "American Revolution," 335–36. Five years later the legislature compromised by restoring the rights of the old trustees, while preserving those of the new board. The consequence was two institutions, which merged two years later, with the governor of Pennsylvania named as president.

113. Herbst, *Crisis,* 195.

114. Herbst, *Crisis,* 192.

115. Herbst, *Crisis,* 201–2.

116. MPA, 56 R 4, "Georgetown College, District of Columbia" [Prospectus], 1814.

117. Carroll to Plowden, Baltimore, October 12, 1791, CP, I, 523–24.

CHAPTER 2

1. Carroll to Plowden, Rock Creek, January 22, 1787; Baltimore, February 28, 1787, CP, I, 242.

2. Rock Creek, February 24, 1790, CP, I, 431.

3. Baltimore, October 12, 1791, CP, I, 523–24.

4. Henry Foley, *Records of the English Province of the Society of Jesus* (London, 1882), VII, Part I, 608; Hughes, *History,* Documents, I, Part 2, 660, n. 51.

5. APF, *Scritte Riferiti nei Congressi Amer. Central* II, vol. 2 535r–536v.

6. David W. Robson, *Educating Republicans: The College in the Era of the American Revolution, 1750–1800* (Westport, 1985), 125, 144.

7. Carroll to Thomas Betagh, Baltimore, October 22, 1805, CP, II, 494.

8. Carroll to Plowden, September 7, 1790, CP, I, 460.

9. Carroll to Plowden, London, September 25, 1790, CP, I, 465–66.

10. Joseph William Ruane, SS, *The Beginnings of the Society of St. Sulpice in the United States (1791–1829)* (Washington, D.C., 1935), 32–34.

11. GUSC, John S. Sumner SJ, Papers, CHMC, 10:2.

12. *Souvenirs D'Edouard De Mondésir, 1789–1811* (Baltimore, 1942), 32.

13. CP, I, 243. The Maryland pound, during this period, was equivalent to 2.68 Maryland dollars.

14. University of North Carolina, Southern Historical Collection, Gaston Papers (hereafter GP), Gaston to [Mary Gaston], George Town, November 5, 1791.

15. Fleming had come to Philadelphia from Ireland a few years earlier, at the invitation of Catholic laity in that city. Carroll had originally put off the requests from the Catholic Philadelphians, but eventually he did agree to accept Fleming and quickly came to appreciate his abilities. By 1789 he had made the Dominican friar his vicar-general for the northern part of his diocese, a position Fleming held until he died ministering to the victims of the yellow fever epidemic in 1793. Presumably it was Carroll who made the arrangements to have Gaston study with Fleming while the academy construction was being completed (Carroll to [Philadelphia laity], Baltimore, July 21, 1788, CP, I, 321; Memorandum for John Heilbron, [Nov. 1789], CP, I, 392).

16. GP, Fleming to Mary Gaston, Baltimore, November 7, 1791.

17. Carroll to Plowden, Baltimore, March 1, 1792, CP, II, 21; GP, Gaston to [Mary Gaston], George Town, December 29, 1791.

18. GP, Gaston to Mary Gaston, George Town, June 17, 1792; ibid., same to same, Baltimore, September 24, 1792.

19. GP, Plunkett to Gaston, George Town, June 23, 1792.

20. GP, Gaston to Mary Gaston, George Town, November 5, 1791.

21. GP, Plunkett to Gaston, George Town, April 24, 1793.

22. "Master Billy," he wrote her in January 1793, "is as lively & as free of hypochon-driacal complaints & symptoms of a consumption as any student in the College. His cough & sore breast which I mentioned . . . , & which to my great regret has proved the occasion of such uneasiness to his worthy & affectionate parent have long since disappeared. In common with nine tenths of the Inhabitants of this town, he has lately taken a cold in consequence of damp weather & wet shoes, but neither his spirits, nor breast are impaired by it. . . ." (GP, Plunkett to [Mary Gaston], Geo Town, January 21, 1793).

23. *Pious Guide to Prayer and Devotion, Containing Various Practices of Piety Calculated to Answer the Various Demands of the Different Devout Members of the Roman Church* (Georgetown, 1792). Largely a compilation of Jesuit devotions, the *Guide* was published anonymously. Francis Neale seems its most likely compiler, and its publisher was James Doyle, one of Neale's parishioners at Holy Trinity in Georgetown.

24. GP, Neale to Gaston, George Town, July 14, 1794. In place of his customary "My Dear William," Neale addressed him in this letter: "My dear Sir."

25. A note on these statistics. A computerized study was made of the student body from 1791 to 1960. All known students from 1791 to 1870 are included, as well as the entering classes of every fifth year thereafter. For these students (10,621), data are accumulated for fifty-two variables, including place of origin (geographic regions or native state), family background, religious affiliation, ethnic group, age, academic concentration, history of education financing, reason for leaving Georgetown, career, military service, and family connections with the institution. A similar study with scaled-down variables was done for all the faculty from 1791 to 1960.

26. In an agricultural society that looked upon schooling as a seasonal complement to family work responsibilities, a broad range of ages was common in virtually all academies. At Exeter Academy in 1812, for instance, the age of students ranged from ten to twenty-eight. The age range at colleges was from the middle teens to the middle twenties. (See Joseph Kett, *Rites of Passage: Adolescence in America, 1790 to the Present* [New York, 1977]). Georgetown, with its base in the planter and merchant communities, had a more stable student population and with its European structure of education, a younger one than the typical college. Carroll in his plan for Georgetown originally set down eight as a minimum age. In practice there were a few younger children admitted. In general, however, the age of

Georgetown students seems not to have been as wide-ranging as at other schools, particularly the newer ones.

27. In this study urban areas with a population in excess of 10,000 are defined as cities.

28. Cohn Burke, *American Collegiate Populations: A Test of the Traditional View* (New York and London, 1982), 63.

29. CP, II, 45.

30. Yale, in 1795, charged $16 for tuition; Phillips Andover approximately $10 (Brooks Mather Kelley, *Yale: A History* [New Haven and London, 1974], 144; James McLachlan, *American Boarding Schools: A Historical Study* [New York, 1970], 44).

31. I am using the term Chesapeake Catholics to include Catholics from Maryland as well as those from the District of Columbia.

32. It is likely that the three Sim brothers were not Catholics. Their mother, Mary Carroll Sim, was Bishop John Carroll's niece. But her husband, Patrick, was not a Catholic. It was the custom in Maryland for the children of mixed marriages to be raised according to the religion of the parent of the same gender. In the case of the Sim family, however, both parents had died by the time the boys entered George-town in 1792. After the mother's death, their father had married Ariana Henderson, a Protestant. But, after his (Patrick's) death, the bishop's brother, Daniel Carroll, became their guardian and paid their bills at Georgetown. At any rate such religious practices among the Maryland gentry might have been another reason why Carroll planned to have Georgetown open to Catholics and non-Catholics alike.

33. Edward C. Papenfuse et al., *A Biographical Dictionary of the Maryland Legislature, 1635–1789*, I (Baltimore, 1979), 382.

34. Papenfuse, 652.

35. GUA, Financial Records Series, Ledger 1.A.1.b, 61.

36. John and Thomas Casey, for instance, had their tuitions paid, at least in part, by Adam King, a local merchant, and Felix Kirk, a member of the faculty. The mother of Joseph Maguire, another student, worked for the college in effect, since she made shirts and nightcaps for the students in exchange for her son's tuition. She also allowed the college to use some of her adjoining property.

37. Terry D. Bilhartz, *Urban Religion and the Second Great Awakening: Church and Society in Early National Baltimore* (Rutherford, 1986), 20–22.

38. Rock Creek, January 22, 1787; Baltimore, February 28, 1787, CP, I, 241.

39. Francis Neale apparently was prone to misread promise for commitment to the religious life in the young men who caught his eye. In 1803 he paid Joseph Stone's board, on the assumption that Stone, who had been at Georgetown since 1799, was prepared to enter the seminary upon completing his education. When Stone subsequently returned to his home in St. Mary's County a year later, Neale felt betrayed, but the youth later claimed that he had never given any indication that he was contemplating the priesthood (MPA, 203 R 7, Stone to Francis Neale, Head of St. Clements Bay, September 25, 1807).

40. GUA, Minutes of the Directors, Georgetown College, 1797–1815; St. Thomas Manor, November 28, 1797.

41. Burke, *Collegiate Populations,* 62.

42. Philip Gleason, "The Main Sheet Anchor: John Carroll and Catholic Higher Education," *The Review of Politics* 38 (October 1976), 580.

43. Carroll to Ferdinand Farmer [December 1784], CP, I, 158.

44. Ord had immigrated to the District of Columbia from Spain in 1790 or 1791, coming as a child with his supposed mother and uncle, Mary and James Ord. In 1800 he entered the college. His "uncle" later confessed that he knew little of the boy's origin except that he was the child of one of the sons of George III. A web of circumstantial evidence suggested that young James was indeed the offspring of a morganatic marriage in the 1780s between the future King George IV and a Catholic, Maria Anne (Smythe) Fitzherbert. In 1775 this same Maria Fitzherbert had married Edward Weld, of Lulworth Castle, Dorsetshire, who died the same year. Edward's younger brother, Thomas, succeeded him as owner of the estate. Thomas Weld, who had studied under John Carroll at Bruges in the early 1770s,

hosted Carroll's consecration as bishop in 1790 at Lulworth, shortly before the Ords brought the child to the United States. These newly arrived Ords were English Catholics who had gone to live in Spain in 1787 when James, a former seaman, apparently through high British connections, had received a commission as a shipbuilder for the King of Spain. Four years later they suddenly left with a child for the United States, where the older James Ord was employed as a shipbuilder by John Brent, one of Carroll's nephews. Ord worked first in Norfolk and then in Charles County, Maryland, but the young James Ord went to live with the Brents until his entrance into Georgetown under the care of another Carroll nephew, Notley Young (*The Dictionary of National Biography* [London: Oxford, 1937–38], 7:170–71; Shane Leslie, *Mrs Fitzherbert: A Life Chiefly from Unpublished Sources* [New York: Benziger Brothers, 1939], 8–9; GUA, Richards Letterbook 9:113–14, to Father Eyre, March 6, 1894; GUA, Memoranda Concerning James Ord, Who Died January 25th, 1873, by His Granddaughter Mary Ord Preston, 1896; GUA, Memoranda Concerning James Ord, I [the "older" James Ord], Who Died at the United States Navy Yard, Washington, D.C., October 12, 1810, by Mary Ord Preston, April 1896).

45. Scott was a man of considerable wealth and influence. When George Washington appealed to the Maryland legislature for a loan to construct the federal buildings, Scott and two associates secured the loan of $100,000 by personally guaranteeing it. Grace Dunlop Ecker, *Portrait of Old Georgetown* (Richmond, 1933), 19; Wilhelmus Bogart Bryan, *A History of the National Capital: 1815–1878* (New York, 1916) 11, 237–40, 287, 413; Stella Pickett Hardy, *Colonial Families of the Southern States of America* (Baltimore, 1981), 454; Papenfuse, 717–18.

46. CP, II, 409.

47. GUA, *College of George-Town, (Potomack) in the State of Maryland, United States of America* [Prospectus, 1798]. Besides the minimum age of eight the only other requirement that Carroll set for admission was literacy. This too was in the Jesuit tradition (Gleason, "The Main Sheet Anchor," 595–96; John W. Donohue, SJ, *Jesuit Education: An Essay on the Foundations of Its Idea* [New York, 1963], 35–38; Hubert Chadwick, SJ, *St. Omers to Stonyhurst: A History of Two Centuries* [London, 1962], 69–72).

48. GUA, *College of George-Town (Potomack) in the State of Maryland, United States of America* [Prospectus, 1798].

49. Gleason, "Main Sheet Anchor," 594.

50. The directions for the positioning of the arms, legs, head, etc., during discourse left no room for spontaneity or the imagination ("When the pupil has pronounced one sentence in the position thus described, the hand, as if lifeless, must drop down to the side, the very moment the last accented word is pronounced; and the body, without altering the place of the feet, poize [*sic*] itself on the left leg, while the left hand raises itself, into exactly the same position as the right was before, and continues . . ."). The advice for communicating emotions was less rigid. "Perhaps," Scott admitted, "the only instruction which can be given with advantage on this head, is this general one: Observe in what manner the several emotions or passions are expressed in real life, or by those who have with great labour and taste acquired a power of imitating nature; and accustom yourself either to follow the great original itself or the best copies you meet with . . ." William Scott, *Lessons in Elocution or a Selection of Pieces in Prose and Verse, For the Improvement of Youth in Reading and Speaking* (Philadelphia, 1791).

51. GP, F. Neale to Gaston, George Town, July 14, 1794.

52. Columbia as King's College (so chartered in 1754, then as Columbia College in 1784, and as Columbia University in the City of New York in 1896) was the first college to introduce French as a formal subject, in 1779, a year after the establishment of the American-French alliance (Frederick Rudolph, *Curriculum: A History of the American Undergraduate Course of Study since 1636* [San Francisco, 1977], 51–52).

53. Robert Walsh, Jr., to Robert Walsh, Georgetown, September 19, 1798, cited in Sr. M. Frederick Lochemes, *Robert Walsh: His Story* (New York, 1941), 17–18.

54. McLachlan, *American Boarding Schools*, 44.

55. A typical problem in the "Imports and Exports" section: "1. Suppose I import from Rotterdam 5 bales of paper, each at 10 rheams which with the charges there amounted to 29£. I pay duty here 6 P per rheam, for freight 19S porterage, 1S. What doth it stand me in per rheam, and how must I sell it per rheam, to gain 10 per cent?" John Gough, *Treatise of Arithmetic in Theory and Practice, Containing Everything Important in the Study of Abstract and Applicate Numbers. Adapted to the Commerce of Great Britain and Ireland to which are added many valuable additions and amendments; more particularly fitting the work for the improvement of the American Youth* by Benjamin Workman, A.M. (Philadelphia, 1792).

56. Robert Gibson, *A Treatise of Practical Surveying; Which is Demonstrated From Its First Principles Wherein Every Thing That is Useful and Curious in That Art, Is Fully considered and Explained*, 6th edition (Philadelphia, 1792).

57. By 1788, all eight colonial colleges had professorships of mathematics and natural philosophy (see Rudolph, *Curriculum*, 33–36).

58. [Georgetown] *Centinel of Liberty*, July 22, 1796.

59. GP, Gaston to Mrs. Gaston, Georgetown, December 26, 1792.

60. Carroll to Plowden, Baltimore, February 24, 1793, CP, II, 83–84. Eventually, in 1798, two members of the Liège faculty, Notley Young and Philip Laurenson, did join the Georgetown faculty, but neither was the president that Carroll wanted. Young, as the stepson of Carroll's sister, Mary, and the son of the elder Notley Young, had the perfect background for the position. Plowden found him "a very good tempered man, pious, & able . . ." who had returned to America only at his father's insistence. This younger Notley Young served on the faculty for five years but proved to be an alcoholic who plagued Carroll until the latter's death (AAB, 6 P 12, Plowden to Carroll [1798]; Carroll to Leonard Neale, Baltimore, October 18, 1813, CP, III, 236; Carroll to Francis Neale, Baltimore, October 3, 1815, CP, III, 361; Spalding, "John Carroll," *Catholic Historical Review* 71 [October 1985], 517).

61. MPA, 18 H 2, Plunkett to Ignatius Fenwick, Carrollsburg, August 20, 1795.

62. Carroll to Plowden, Baltimore, May 8, 1789, CP, I, 363.

63. GP, George Town, May 21, 1794.

64. Carroll to Antonelli, June 17, 1793, CP, II, 94.

65. MPA, 2 N 10, Proceedings of the General Chapter Met at the White Marsh on the 7th Day of November 1792.

66. John Gilmary Shea, *Memorial of the First Centenary of Georgetown College, D.C., Comprising a History of Georgetown University* (Washington, 1891), 20.

67. William W. Warner, *At Peace with Their Neighbours: Catholics and Catholicism in the National Capital, 1787–1860* (Washington, 1994), 238, n 26. Annual Report of the Treasury Historical Association (1991), 21.

68. Carroll to Plowden, Baltimore, November 13, 1795, CP, II, 158.

69. Louis Philippe, *Diary of My Travels in America*, tr. Stephen Becker (New York, 1977), 27.

70. APF, *Letteri Della S. Congregatione dell' anno 1792, 1794*, Propaganda Fide to Carroll, Rome, September 29, 1792, vol. 262, fols. 558v to 568r; same to same, Rome, December 20, 1794, vol. 266, fols. 677r to 679r. In November 1795 Carroll was still trying to locate "the last 300 Crowns" which the Propaganda had given to an agent in Rome to convey to the bishop for the college (Carroll to Charles Plowden, Baltimore, November 13, 1795, CP, II, 158).

71. It is very difficult to calculate the exact costs. The Corporation authorized $6,000 between 1794 and 1796 for the construction but in 1800 the college was seeking additional funding to complete the building (Hughes, *History*, Documents I, Part 2, 702–3, 747).

72. Plunkett gave them $2,000 from which he was to receive an annuity of $180 (9%) (MPA, 91.1, Proceedings of the Corporation of the Roman Catholic Clergy, February 25, 1794).

73. Phyllis Vine, "Another Look at Eighteenth-Century Colleges," *HEQ* 18 (Spring 1978), 61–69.

74. "Your good friend Robert," he wrote Plowden, "found the employment of president of this institution, too bustling & requiring too much energy for his good-natured,

& somewhat torpid disposition . . ." (Carroll to Plowden, Baltimore, September 24, 1796, CP, II, 189).

75. Five became bishops: Maréchal, Flaget, DuBourg, Jean Lefevre de Cheverus, John Dubois; others, preeminently the Sulpicians, dominated seminary education; still others, such as Philippine Duchesne, established religious communities (of women and of men) that became major shapers of Catholic society in America.

76. Jean-Edouard de Mondésir, "Mémoires," translated by W. S. Reilly, *The Voice*, 9 (November 1931), 24, in *Annabelle M. Melville, Louis William DuBourg: Bishop of Louisiana and the Floridas, Bishop of Montauban, and Archbishop of Besançon, 1766–1833* (Chicago, 1986), I, 54.

77. Melville, *DuBourg*, I, 50.

78. Boarman had entered the Society in 1770, after studying at Bruges for six years. He was a scholastic when the suppression occurred (Hennesey, "Several Youth," 22; Geoffrey Holt, SJ, *St. Omers and Bruges Colleges, 1593–1773: A Biographical Dictionary* [London, 1979], 41).

79. Carroll in his plan for the academy had directed that the students "be distinguished by some peculiar badge in their dress, without which they are never to appear in publick," but had suspended this requirement for the time being (AAB, 9A-N3). Uniforms had been traditional at St. Omers and the other recusant schools on the continent.

80. Constance McLaughlin Green, *Washington: Village and Capital, 1800–1878* (Princeton, 1962), 19.

81. Margaret B. Downing, "James and Joanna Gould Barry," *Historical Records and Studies* 15 (March 1921), 45–54; Melville, *DuBourg*, I, 63–64.

82. AAB, 8A H5, DuBourg to Carroll, Georgetown, May 22, 1797.

83. George M. Barringer, "They Came to GU: The French Sulpicians," *Georgetown Today* (July 1977), 7; Melville, *DuBourg*, I, 64.

84. Downing, 46.

85. MPA, 91.1, Proceedings of the Corporation of the Roman Catholic Clergy met at St. Thomas's Manor, June 2, 1796.

86. The Representatives, two from each of the three districts in Maryland into which the Select Body of the Clergy had been divided, were elected every third year. Their chief duty was to elect the five trustees of the corporation, which had been created in 1792 to preserve the property of the Society of Jesus in Maryland (MPA, 91–3, Proceedings of the Representatives of Roman Catholic Clergy, convened at St. Thomas Manor, June 3, 1795).

87. MPA, 91–3, Proceedings of the Representatives of the Roman Catholic Clergy met at St. Thomas's Manor, October 5, 1796; October 14, 1796.

88. MPA, 90 M 0, March 29, 1797.

89. The representatives had been claiming the power to regulate expenses on the basis of a resolution passed by representatives of the Select Body at the first meeting held after the incorporation of the property. The committee somewhat disingenuously found that the key phrase "Representative Body" referred not to the current representatives but to an earlier body (MPA 91.3, Proceedings of the Committee of the Select Body of the Roman Catholic Clergy, [St. Thomas Manor], September 1, 1797; MPA 91.1, Proceedings of the Roman Catholic Clergy convened at St. Thomas's Manor on the 4th day of October, 1793).

90. GUA, Minutes of the Directors, Georgetown College, 1797–1815, October 3, 1797.

91. GUA, Minutes of the Directors, Georgetown College, December 20, 1797.

92. Melville, *DuBourg*, I, 73.

93. GUA, Minutes of the Directors, Georgetown College, September 25–26, 1798.

94. "An Act to enable the corporation of the Roman catholic clergymen to receive a conveyance, and hold certain lands, and for other purposes therein mentioned," Lib. JG. No. 2. fol. 628, in William Kilty, *The Laws of Maryland*, vol. 2 (Annapolis, 1800), 78 A30.

95. MPA, 90 M 0, Proceedings of the Roman Catholic Clergy met at Newtown, December 3, 1798. What plan the trustees imagined the Sulpicians to be pursuing is

impossible to tell. The Select Body had agreed, apparently at Carroll's urging, that in the admission of future members, they would give preference to those trained at Georgetown and at the Sulpician Seminary in Baltimore. Perhaps some saw a Sulpician plot to take over the Select Body in this fashion (Carroll to Robert Plowden, George Town, July 7, 1797, CP, II, 218).

96. *The Centinel of Liberty and Georgetown and Washington Advertiser,* January 8, 1799, cited in Melville, DuBourg, I, 76.

97. Carroll to Plowden, Baltimore, December 11, 1798, CP, II, 248. Actually, only six of DuBourg's sixteen faculty appointments were French. Flaget was already there as vice-president when DuBourg arrived.

98. He wrote to Plowden: "Allow me to say to yourself alone that amongst our few remaining Brethren here [who have the charge of the administration of the property], there are some, whose violence will listen to no lessons of moderation; & others, whose knowledge & observations are too confined to comprehend that any thing useful can be learned, beyond what they know; or that any change of circumstances should suggest improvements suitable to time & situations, or cause the smallest deviation from the track, in which they once walked themselves." (Washington, September 3, 1800, CP, II, 318).

99. The four were George Fenwick, James Simpson, and the King brothers, Adam and George (AAB, 5 0 2, Francis Neale to John Carroll, Georgetown, April 26, 1797; AAB, 11 A 1, Trustees of Trinity Church to Bishop Carroll, Georgetown, 20 May 1797), cited in William Warner, *At Peace with All Their Neighbours,* 26.

100. Gleason, "Main Sheet Anchor," 608.

101. M. B. Brislen, OSF, "The Episcopacy of Leonard Neale, Second Archbishop of Baltimore," *Historical Records and Studies* 34 (1945), 20–111.

102. GUA, Minutes of Directors, October 3, 1797; *Centinel of Liberty and Georgetown Advertiser,* November 21, 1797.

103. The bishop noted: "Theory & experience are constantly at variance in this case: for tho' the principles of religion & morality command, or seem to command the Instructors of youth to restrain their pupils from almost every communication with the men and things of the world, yet that very restraint operates against the effects intended by it, and it is too often found, that on being delivered from it, young men, as when the pin that confined a spring, is loosened, burst out of confinement into licentiousness, & give way to errors & vices, which with more acquaintance with the manners & language of the world, they would have avoided" (Carroll to Plowden, Baltimore, March 12, 1802, CP, II, 383).

104. GUA, Minutes of the Directors, April 24, 1799.

105. AAB, 5 Q 1, Neale to Carroll, Georgetown, July 21, 1800.

106. Carroll thought that the term for prefecting should be limited to three years since it was "less honorable & more fatiguing" and would, unlike teaching, retard intellectual development (MPA, 56 Z 11/2, [Carroll], Observations on the College Oath).

107. GUA, Minutes of the Directors, White Marsh, 1–2 July 1800.

108. Undeniably there was much bad feeling between the ex-Jesuits and the Sulpicians during this period. For instance, the Bohemia estate in Cecil County, Maryland, which the Corporation, at Carroll's suggestion, had put under the management of the Sulpicians in 1793 to provide some income for them, was peremptorily reclaimed by the Corporation in April 1799 (Christopher J. Kauffman, *Tradition and Transformation in Catholic Culture: The Priests of Saint Sulpice in the United States from 1791 to the Present* [New York and London, 1988], 46).

109. AAB, 5 Q 1, Neale to Carroll, Georgetown, July 21, 1800. Also Carroll to Emery, [np], January 6, 1801, CP, II, 343.

110. Sulpician Archives, Baltimore, *Régistre du Resultat des Assemblées* (1791–1886), 6, cited in Vincent M. Eaton, S.S., "Sulpician Involvement in Educational Projects in the See and Province of Baltimore," *U.S. Catholic Historian* 2 (1982), 3–5.

111. Ruane, 106, citing Francis Nagot to Carroll, August 26, 1800; ibid., Carroll to Nagot, October 16, 1800.

112. *Régistre du Résultat des Assemblées (1791–1886)*, St. Mary's Seminary Archives, cited in Ruane, 87.

113. The trustees still felt it necessary to impress their clerical brethren with the importance of supporting Georgetown as a unique source of clergy for the rapidly growing needs of the church in America. Congregations in Maryland and Pennsylvania were without priests, to say nothing of those in Kentucky, Ohio, and the new territories in the West into which Catholics, along with so many other Americans, were pouring. Nor could they hope to receive further assistance from French emigres. "These; & many other obvious considerations," they concluded, "strongly inforce the necessity of encouraging the College, so that it may be productive of the principal advantage, contemplated at its Institution" (MPA, 91.3, Letter Addressed to the members of the Select Body of the R.C. Clergy residing in the different Districts, by the Trustees of Sd. Clergy, Newtown, October 15, 1802).

114. MPA, 91.3 [Meeting of the Select Body of the R. C. Clergy, Northern District], Conewago, November 17, 1802.

115. MPA, 91–1, Minutes of the Representatives of the Select Body of the Middle District, George Town College, November 16, 1802. This may have been in response to the information given them by the trustees that the Sulpician proposal contained certain conditions, "some of which will probably be thought inadmissible, [and] some requiring modifications . . ." (MPA, 91.3, Bolton to Select Body, October 15, 1802). Members of the district included Francis Neale, Robert Plunkett, Joseph Eden, John Dubois, Notley Young, and William Matthews.

116. Melville, *DuBourg*, I, 96.

117. Kauffman, 75; Ruane, 130–31.

118. Carroll to Plowden, Baltimore, 2 June 1809, CP, III, 86.

119. "Students of St. Mary's College," *Memorial Volume of the Centenary of St. Mary's Seminary of St. Sulpice* (Baltimore, 1891), 79–89.

120. Green, 29–30.

121. Michael B. Katz, "The Role of American Colleges in the Nineteenth Century," *HEQ* 23 (Summer 1983), 216.

122. Stonyhurst, the successor in England to St. Omers, ironically had approximately the same number of students at this time as St. Mary's (MPA, 203 Z 2, Nicholas Sewall to Charles Sewall, Portico, July 15, 1800).

CHAPTER 3

1. John Adams to Thomas Jefferson, Quincy, May 6, 1816, in Charles Francis Adams, ed., *The Works of John Adams* 10 (Boston, 1856), 219. Thomas Jefferson, who likewise regarded Jesuits as the embodiment of the worst of the old priest- and king-ridden order in Europe, readily agreed that it marked "a retrograde step from light towards darkness," but was more optimistic about republicanism's strength:

   > We shall have our follies without doubt . . . but ours will be the follies of enthusiasm, not of bigotry, not of Jesuitism. Bigotry is the disease of ignorance, of morbid minds; enthusiasm of the free and buoyant. Education and free discussion are the antidotes of both (Jefferson to John Adams, Monticello, August 1, 1816, in Adams, *Works*, X, 223).

   Had Jefferson known John Carroll, he would have realized soon enough how deeply the latter appreciated, if he did not fully share, Jefferson's convictions about education and free discussion in a republic. (Carroll was too much the Christian realist to endorse the romantic impulse that "enthusiasm" implied.) Carroll's academy had been founded partly on similar convictions about the role of an informed and free citizenry.

2. *American Catholic Historical Researches* [hereafter ACHR], viii, 25, Newtown, August 30, 1802, in Hughes, *History*, Documents, I, Part II, 815.

3. Although Carroll regarded the survival of the Russian Province as a providential sign of the eventual resurrection of the Society, still he had little hope that he and

his brethren would see it soon; in the meantime, to concentrate dreams and energies upon such a remnant in such a politically volatile place as Byelorussia was to distract them from the challenges facing the American church. Moreover, he felt that certain reforms needed to be introduced into both the Constitutions and the administrative structure of the Society in order to "suit it better to the great revolution in political establishments & principles since Ignatius's time." He believed, for instance, that any revived Society would need to be more republican and decentralized in its organization. "[D]o you think," he wrote Plowden in 1785, "that our Governments here or almost any one in Europe would allow of the dependence such as formerly existed, on a general residing at Rome?" In 1802 he was still dubious about the prospect of reviving a religious order on the strength of an assurance from a congregation official at the Holy See that ex-Jesuits around the world were free to unite themselves to their surviving brethren in Byelorussia. As he wrote to his friend Plowden, "This is going too fast for one who subscribed his submission to the destructive Brief" (Carroll to Charles Plowden, Maryland, September 26, 1783, CP, I, 79; same to same, Rock Creek, January 22, 1787; Baltimore, February 28, 1787, CP, I, 246; Carroll to Representatives of the Southern District, July 15, 1788, CP, I, 316–17; John M. Daley, SJ, *Georgetown University: Origin and Early Years* [Washington, 1957], 126; Rock Creek, December 15, 1785, CP, I, 197; EPA, Carroll to Plowden, December 15, 1800, in Hughes, *History,* Documents, I, Part 2, 815).

4. ACHR, viii, 25–26, St. Mary's and Charles Counties, April 25, 1803, in Hughes, *History,* Documents, I, Part 2, 816. The ex-Jesuits were Charles Sewall, Robert Molyneux, Sylvester Boarman, John Bolton, Charles Neale, and Ignatius Brooke. The other priests were Francis Neale, John Dubois, Francis Beeston, and William Matthews; the seminarians were Benedict and Enoch Fenwick, Benedict Eden, Thomas Poole, and Joseph Mobberly.

5. Those who had attended Georgetown were Charles Bowling (**C** 1802–6), Leonard Edelen (**C** 1799–1804), Benedict Fenwick (**C** 1793–1800), Enoch Fenwick (**C** 1793–97), James Ord (**C** 1800–6), William Queen (**C** 1800–6), James Spink (**C** 1797–1804), and Michael White (**C** 1804–6).

6. GUA, Minutes of the Directors, George Town, September 10, 1806.

7. MPA, 4 5 1, Leonard Neale to Marmaduke Stone, Geo. Town, March 15, 1805.

8. Members of the Society of Jesus, before they take final vows, are permitted to retain assets but they may not use them independently (MPA, folder 39, item 4S2, Stonyhurst transcripts, Anthony Kohlmann to William Strickland, Georgetown, February 23, 1807; MPA, 12 A 5, Recollections of John McElroy [1863]; GUA, Minutes of Directors, 28 February, 1–2 March 1809).

9. MPA, 4 5 2, Kohlmann to Strickland, Georgetown, February 23, 1807; MPA, 12 A 5, McElroy Recollections.

10. MPA, 4 5 1, Neale to Stone, Geo. Town, February 16, 1808.

11. Carroll to Thomas Betagh, Baltimore, October 22, 1805, CP, II, 494.

12. Baltimore, December 19, 1806, CP, II, 540.

13. Carroll to Molyneux, Baltimore, February 3, 1807, CP, III, 8.

14. Carroll to Molyneux, Baltimore, May 22, 1807, CP, III, 20.

15. MPA, Carroll to Strickland, December 8, 1808, CP, III, 75; Richard K. MacMaster, SJ, "Benedict Fenwick, Bishop of Boston, American Apprenticeship (1782–1817)," *Historical Records and Studies* 47 (1959), 100–101.

16. MPA, 4S2, Kohlmann to Strickland, New York, November 7, 1808, copy.

17. McMaster, "Benedict Fenwick," 109–10.

18. MPA, Fenwick to George Fenwick Sr., December 4, 1810, cited in MacMaster, 113.

19. MPA, 4 5 2, Stonyhurst transcripts, Kohlmann to Strickland, New York, September 14, 1810.

20. MPA, 4S2, Kohlmann to Strickland, New York, November 7, 1808.

21. MPA, 203 P 3, Carroll to Molyneux, Baltimore, July 1, 1808.

22. Francis X. Curran, SJ, "The Jesuit Colony in New York, 1808–1817," *HRS* 42 (1954), 69.

23. GUA, Minutes of Directors' Meeting, February 28, March 2, 1809.

24. MPA, 203 N 4, Kohlmann to [Grassi], New York, July 26, 1809.

25. MPA, 203 K 14, Benedict Fenwick to Francis Neale, New York, 10 June 1811.

26. Joseph Durkin, *William Matthews: Priest and Citizen* (New York, 1963), 9–16.

27. Giovanni [John] Grassi, who could only have received the information from the Neales, later wrote: "by weak indulgence to the boys and neglecting to control their prefects [he] brought the whole establishment into the most horrible confusion and disorder" (MPA, Stonyhurst Transcripts, Grassi to William Strickland, October 8, 1811, cited in Durkin, *Matthews,* 16).

28. Daley, 162–64.

29. In the 1820s one of Kavanaugh's college essays was used anonymously in the Maine constitutional convention to defeat a proposed clause barring Catholics from holding office.

30. James A. Henretta and Gregory H. Nobles, *Evolution and Revolution: American Society, 1600–1820* (Lexington, 1987), 223–225; Green, *Washington,* 27–28, 33–34, 36.

31. GUA, Minutes of Directors, September 9–12, 1809.

32. Joseph Hanson Clarke, "Reminiscences," *College Journal* [hereafter CJ] 8:26–27. Clarke had been sent by his father, a Hagerstown merchant, to Georgetown in 1804 to become a priest. He did not, but he did stay to teach classics at the college from 1810 to 1813. Later, as a layman he opened an English and classical school in Richmond, where Edgar Allan Poe was among his pupils.

33. Carroll to Plowden, [January 27, 1812], CP, III, 175.

34. *Archivum Romanum Societatis Iesu* [hereafter ARSI], *Marylandia* [hereafter MD], 1 IV 4, *Memoria sulla Compagnia di Gesu ristablilita negli Stati Uniti dell' America Settentrionale del 1810 al 1817.*

35. MPA, 4S3, Grassi to Strickland, October 8, 1811, Stonyhurst translation from the Italian.

36. English Province Archives [hereafter EPA], fol. 79, Foreign Correspondence, 1776–1859, Grassi to Korsak, Georgetown, November 27, 1812.

37. "Voyage of the Very Rev. Father John Anthony Grassi, SJ from Russia to America, January 1805-October 1810," *Woodstock Letters* [hereafter WL], 4 (1875), 115–36; Paul Horgan, "The Father President," *A Certain Climate: Essays in History, Arts, and Letters* (Middletown, 1988), 95–97.

38. Carroll to Grassi, Baltimore, July 9, 1812, CP, III, 185.

39. Carroll to Brzozowski, January 28, 1814, in CP, III, 252–53.

40. GUA, Minutes of the Board of Directors, Georgetown, August 11, 1812.

41. ARSI, MD, 1 IV 4; ARSI, Chartophylacium Desperamus to Grassi, St. Petersburg, May 10, 1812, in Hughes, *History,* Documents, I, Part 2, 833–34.

42. The other directors were Leonard and Francis Neale, William Matthews, and Enoch Fenwick (MPA, 91.1, Proceedings of the Corporation of Roman Catholic Clergymen, vol. I, September 22, 1812).

43. MPA, 203 C 15, Matthews to [Grassi], September 14, 1812; MPA, 203 C 11, Leonard Neale to Grassi, Georgetown, September 12, 1812.

44. MPA, 203 B 8 C, Charles Neale to [Grassi] December 1, 1812. Bishop Neale, his brother, took obvious offense at Grassi's attempt to claim authority over the college as superior general of the Mission. "I find myself summoned," he responded to Grassi's objection to having the finances of the college put outside the president's control, "to answer for my past proceedings whilst a Director of G. T. College at the bar of Your & Your Consultors tribunal—Without going into an enquiery whether you or your Board of Consultors have right to take cognicence of my proceedings whilst a Director . . ." (MPA, 203 C 11, Georgetown, September 12, 1812).

45. ARSI, Chartophylacium P. Desperamus, Epistolae VV.GG. in Russia, 1809–1814, Desperamus to Grassi, St. Petersburg, May 10, 1812, extract given in Hughes, *History,* Documents, I, Part 2, 833–34; Carroll to Brzozowski, January 28, 1814, CP, 111, 252–53.

46. EPA, f. 80, Grassi to William Strickland, Georgetown, November 28, 1812.

47. GUSC, Catholic Historical Manuscript Collection, Grassi Diary, May 8, 1811; ARSI, MD, 1 IV 4, *Memoria sulla Compagnia di Gesu.*

48. ARSI, MD, 1 IV 4.

49. GUA, Minutes of Directors, August 11, 1812.

50. D. B. Warden, *A Statistical, Political, and Historical Account of the United States of North America; from the period of Their First Colonization to the Present Day* (Edinburgh, 1819), 2: 157.

51. GUA, Minutes of the Board of Directors, May 24, 1813.

52. New York sent thirty-five students, a three and a half–fold increase from the previous twelve years; Pennsylvania more than quadrupled its figures from the same period, from four to eighteen. Virginia's twenty-two students accounted for nearly a tenth (9.5%) of the school's population; the state sent more students to Georgetown during Grassi's five years there than it had in the entire previous history of the institution.

53. GUSC, McElroy Diary, January 1, 1814.

54. Six of one hundred and ninety-eight students had been given reduced rates during the Neale years, thirty-one of two hundred and fifty-eight during Grassi's term.

55. With a much larger student body (approximately one hundred and thirty in 1817), St. Mary's sent thirty-one students to the seminary between the years 1803 and 1829; Mount St. Mary's, with about the same enrollment as Georgetown, sent four to the Baltimore seminary between 1807 and 1829, as well as a small number to its own seminary (Joseph William Ruane, *The Beginnings of the Society of St. Sulpice in the United States (1791–1829)* [Washington, 1935], 189).

56. Fewer than a fifth (17.9%) of the students in general had tuition waivers or reductions (Burke, 99).

57. For an excellent study of this development see David Allmendinger, Jr., *Paupers and Scholars: The Transformation of Student Life in Nineteenth-Century New England* (New York, 1975).

58. Hu Maxwell and H. L. Swisher, *History of Hampshire County, West Virginia* (Morgantown, 1897), 297–98.

59. Ironically the 1814 Prospectus was the first to make any public mention of the Catholic character of the school ("the institution is principally for students of the Catholic religion").

60. GUA, Georgetown College, District of Columbia [Prospectus], 1814; GUA, Georgetown College, D.C. [Prospectus], 1816; D. B. Warden, *Description statistique, historique et politique de l'amérique septentrionale, depuis l'époque des premiers établissements jusquà nos jours* (Paris, 1820), 5: 49.

61. Carroll to Plowden, Baltimore, October 13, 1815, CP, III, 368.

62. EPA, fol. 79, Foreign Correspondence, 1776–1859, Grassi to Korsak, Georgetown, November 27, 1812.

63. ARSI, MD, 1 IV 4.

64. In 1803 the directors of the college had recommended to Leonard Neale that "scholastic Exhibitions" involving "some original Production" be held at least four times a year, "to which the Friends of Literature shall be invited." There is no indication that Neale acted on this advice (GUA, Minutes of Directors, September 14–15, 1803).

65. MPA, 204 W 18, Grassi to Kohlmann, George Town, August 13, 1813; MacMaster, "Fenwick," 117.

66. MPA, 203 D 4, Strickland to Grassi, London, April 6, 1812.

67. MPA, 203 B 2, Carroll to Grassi, Baltimore, November 11, 1812.

68. MPA, Kohlmann to Grassi, May 18, 1813, cited in MacMaster, "Fenwick," 115.

69. MPA, 204 W 11, Grassi to B. Fenwick, [August 1813], copy.

70. MPA, 204 T 18, Kohlmann to Grassi, New York, October 25, 1813.

71. As he wrote in a final plea in 1815, a year after the Literary Institution had closed,

> . . . I promise you, you will have 2, or 300 children of the most respectable families not only of the union but of all the quarters of the World, from which

more vessels arrive at that port than at all others together: numbers of those children trained up in piety will enter the Society, . . . [in New York] you will have to deal not with that beggarly and low set of men, that would bargain with you like jews and almost pretend that you should take their children gratis, and afterwards not even pay the promised pension. . . . There . . . in about 20 years you will have as much as all yr plantations are worth, . . . there you would give edification to 110000 souls, put down heresy and make the Catholic religion a triumph in the Em[p]orium of America (MPA, 204 H 3, Kohlmann to Grassi, White Marsh, April 24, 1815).

Five years later Kohlmann was still pleading for a reestablishment of the school (ARSI, MD 2129, Kohlmann to Kenney, Washington, October 1, 1820).

72. MPA, 204 H 10, Kohlmann to Grassi, Wh[ite] M[arsh], May 23, 1815.
73. MPA, Brzozowski to Grassi, September 20, 1813.
74. MPA, 204 5 17, George Fenwick to [?], Georgetown, January 11, 1856.
75. MPA, 204 K 5, B. Fenwick to Grassi, New York, February 20, 1815.
76. *National Intelligencer,* September 6, 1813, cited in Daley, 184–85.
77. GUSC, Grassi Diary, September 9, 1813.
78. If there were any Georgetown alumni among the defenders of the capital in 1814, history has discreetly hidden their names. Of the Georgetown students, past or future, who fought in the War of 1812, sixteen are known. George Peter, son of the mayor, who as a fifteen-year-old had run away from the college in 1794 to join the state troops sent to quell the Whiskey Rebellion, had eventually joined the army, retired, then returned to command a squadron of flying artillery in 1813. William Queen, one of the first novices in the restored Society, had left the order to support his mother, became a doctor, and served as a surgeon in the Marine Corps. Another former Jesuit, James Ord, the reputed son of George IV, had entered the navy as a midshipman, then transferred to the army as a first lieutenant in the Thirty-Sixth Infantry. Richard Watts, Ignatius Young, and William Merrick also were officers in the Thirty-Sixth. Merrick had completed Rhetoric year at Georgetown in 1811, the highest course then offered. He subsequently became a prominent attorney in Maryland and represented that state in the United States Senate from 1838 to 1845. Richard McSherry, brother of Father William McSherry, SJ, and a classmate of Merrick, had gone from Georgetown in 1811 to the University of Pennsylvania to study medicine. In 1813 he joined the Virginia militia as a surgeon. William Weaver had also left Georgetown in 1811 at the age of nineteen to become a midshipman. Both ships on which he served were captured by the British; in the second engagement, in June 1813 on board the *Chesapeake,* Weaver was severely wounded but survived to become a commander after the war. Alexander Loughborough of Washington was less fortunate. Loughborough had entered the American navy in 1812 at the age of sixteen and become an ensign on the USS *Constitution*. He was killed in Florida while ashore looking for fresh water for the crew.

Charles Wederstrandt, the second student to enter the college, had joined the navy in 1797 but resigned in 1810. He subsequently settled in Baltimore, where he took part in the successful defense of that city in September 1814. Among his co-defenders at the "ramparts" was Joseph Judik, an immigrant from the Netherlands, who marched to Baltimore from Pennsylvania. Seven years later Judik entered the college as a twenty-five-year-old member of the Rudiments class and remained for five years. The other known participants in the war were Thomas Blackstone (**C** 1792–94), Charles Boarman (**C** 1803–8), William Ford (**C** 1799), Thomas Robinson (**C** 1792–93), John Rogers (**C** 1804–9), and Clement Sewall (**C** 1804).

79. Green, *Washington,* 61.
80. MPA, 12 A 5, Recollections of John McElroy.
81. GUSC, McElroy Diary, August 24–25, 1814.
82. GUSC, Grassi Diary, August 26, 1814.
83. Carroll to Grassi, Baltimore, September 30, 1814, CP, III, 297–98.

84. *National Intelligencer,* October 5, 1814.
85. GUSC, Grassi Diary, December 9, 1814.
86. "A new order of things is born." Given Kohlmann's less than complete command of English, it is doubtful he intended the pun here.
87. MPA, 204 M 18, Kohlmann to Grassi, New York, December 19, 1814.
88. "We praise thee oh God, we acknowledge thee oh Lord."
89. MPA 204 M 20, B. Fenwick to Grassi, New York, December 23, 1814.
90. GUA, Petition of Grassi to the Directors of Georgetown College, May 24, 1813; Grassi to Plowden, November 23, 1815, in Hughes, *History,* Documents, I, Part 2, 866.
91. Herbst, *From Crisis to Crisis,* 232–33.
92. Miller, *Revolutionary College,* 245.
93. Cf. John S. Whitehead, *The Separation of College and State: Columbia, Dartmouth, Harvard, and Yale, 1776–1876* (New Haven and London, 1973), 53–88.
94. Grassi apparently had in mind the Napoleonic university system, which put all institutions of higher education under a central university.
95. Irving Brant, *James Madison: The Virginia Revolutionist* (Indianapolis and New York, 1941), 1: 268–69; Brant, *James Madison: Father of the Constitution, 1787–1800* (Indianapolis and New York, 1950) vol. 3: 18, 420–21.
96. ARSI, MD, I IV 4.
97. Annals, Thirteenth Cong., third sess., p. 1106, cited in J. Herman Schauinger, *William Gaston, Carolinian* (Milwaukee, 1949), 78.
98. Daley, 190.
99. GUA, copy of Charter of Georgetown College, March 1, 1815.
100. Carroll to Plowden, Baltimore, October 13, 1815, CP, III: 368.
101. Last Will and Testament of Archbishop John Carroll [November 22, 1815], CP, III: 371–72; MPA, 204 F 12, Grassi to Enoch Fenwick, Georgetown, December 28, 1815.

CHAPTER 4

1. MPA, 208 G 6, R. McSherry to William McSherry, Martinsburg, November 27, 1828.
2. ARSI, MD, 2 I16, Neil to Grassi, New York, February 10, 1820.
3. James A. Henretta and Gregory H. Nobles, *Evolution and Revolution: American Society, 1600–1820* (Lexington, 1987), 225; Constance McLaughlin Green, *Washington: Village and Capital, 1800–1878* (Princeton, 1962), 82–86.
4. MPA, 206 R 9, John Walsh to Enoch Fenwick, Baltimore, August 15, 1823.
5. MPA, 205 G 6, Marshall to Enoch Fenwick, Georgetown, August 14, 1820.
6. David W. Robson, "College Founding in the New Republic, 1776–1800," *HEQ* 23 (Fall 1983), 323–41.
7. MPA, 206 R 22, Beschter to Dzierozynski, Baltimore, December 17, 1823.
8. Grassi, *Notizie vane sullo stato presente della repubblica degli Stati Uniti dell' America settentrionale scritte al principio del 1818* [Milano, 1819].
9. MPA, 204 R 19, Kohlmann to Grassi, New York, March 21, 1814.
10. *The Alexandria Controversy: Or a Series of Letters between M. B. & Quaero, on the Tenets of Catholicity* (Georgetown, 1817).
11. ARSI, MD, 4 VI, [Dubuisson] *Coup-D'Oeil Sur L'Histoire Intime De La Province du Maryland.*
12. Howard Miller, *The Revolutionary College: American Presbyterian Higher Education 1707–1837* (New York, 1976), 182; Thomas Bender, "Science and the Culture of American Communities: The Nineteenth Century," *HEQ* 16 (Spring 1976), 66–68; Hyman Kuritz, "The Popularization of Science in Nineteenth-Century America," *HEQ* 21 (Fall 1981), 260–61.
13. GUSC, Grassi Diary, July 31, 1816.
14. CUAA, Edward J[ames] Wallace Papers, Wallace to John Geddy (draft).
15. CUAA, Wallace to Geddy (draft).

16. ARSI, MD, 1 VIII 1, Maréchal to Grassi, Baltimore, April 21, 1817; ARSI, MD, 1 VIII 5, Grassi to Brzozowski, Rome, September 27, 1817; ARSI, MD, 1 IV 4.

17. Fenwick was supposed to go with him but the death of Leonard Neale a few days before their June departure kept Fenwick at Georgetown (EPA, Foreign Correspondence, 1776–1859, ff. 174, Grassi to Charles Plowden, January 20, 1820).

18. APF, American. Centrale IV, 621rv-622r, Grassi to Maréchal, Lyon, August 18, 1817.

19. ARSI, MD, 2 I14, Kohlmann to Grassi, Georgetown, 7 December 1819; MPA, 205 C 13, Grassi to Adam Marshall, Proieto, May 12, 1821.

20. MPA, 205 M 1, Grassi to Enoch Fenwick, Genoa, July 14, 1819.

21. EPA, Foreign Correspondence 1776–1854 ff. 141–2, Grassi to C. Plowden, Rome, November 21, 1818.

22. ARSI, MD, 1 VI 1, Kohlmann to [Grassi], W[hite] M[arsh], December 16, 1816.

23. ARSI, MD, 4 VI, Stephen Dubuisson, *L'Histoire Intime.*

24. Francis Eppes to Thomas Jefferson, Washington, December 28, 1817, in Edwin Morris Betts and James Adam Bear, Jr., eds., *The Family Letters of Thomas Jefferson* (Charlottesville, 1986), 420–21; Jefferson wrote to his grandson: "I do not wonder that you find the place where you are disagreeable, it's character, while I lived in Washington was that of being a seminary of mere sectarism" (Thomas Jefferson to Francis Eppes, Monticello, February 6, 1818, in *Family Letters,* 421). Eppes left the college the following spring. Ironically his mother, Martha Jefferson, had manifested a strong interest in Catholicism when she was with her father in Paris in the 1780s (John P. Boyd, ed. *The Papers of Thomas Jefferson,* vol. 14 [Princeton, 1958], 356).

25. ARSI, MD, 3 VIII 1, Dubuisson to Fortis, Georgetown, April 22, 1826.

26. Steven J. Novak, *The Rights of Youth: American Colleges and Student Revolt, 1798–1815* (Cambridge, 1977), 110–11, 126–28, 167–69.

27. Frederick Rudolph, *Curriculum: A History of the American Undergraduate Course of Study since 1636* (San Francisco, Washington, and London, 1977), 55–86.

28. CUAA, Wallace Papers, Wallace to Peter Kenney, April 29, 1820 (draft).

29. Wallace, iii–iv.

30. Talbot Hamlin, *Benjamin Henry Latrobe* (New York, 1955), 458.

31. How old John Swartout was at that time is unclear, but he was listed as a midshipman in the U.S. Navy when he entered the college in 1816.

32. ARSI, MD, 4 VI, Dubuisson, *L'Histoire Intime.*

33. MPA, 206 T 2, Neale to Marshall, Mount Carmel, July 8, 1822.

34. MPA, 206 P 0, Statement of money received and Expended by the General Fund from August 22, 1820, to January 1, 1824.

35. GUSC, McElroy Diary, 1816.

36. ARSI, MD, 2 15, Charles Neale to Brzozowski, [Port Tobacco] June 20, 1818.

37. CUAA, Wallace Papers, Wallace to Kenney, April 29, 1820 (draft). By 1822 McElroy was reporting that in the previous year the college had spent $2,000 more than it had taken in; total indebtedness was $10,434.14. Two years later the total debt had risen slightly to $11,000 (MPA, 206 P 0).

38. ARSI, Angl. 1011 V 2, Plowden to Grassi, January 11, 1819.

39. ARSI, Praep. Gen. In Russia, vi, Brzozowski to Kenney, April 23, 1819.

40. MPA, 205 M 6a, Kenney to Revd. Chas Aylmer, Georgetown, October 5, 1819.

41. MPA, Kenney to Grassi, Frederick, May 12, 1820.

42. ARSI, MD, 2 III 5, Kenny to Brzozowski, Georgetown, March 4, 1820.

43. "I have repeatedly written to the Genl on the necessity of having proper men to govern & to fill the chairs of higher studies," he noted to Francis Neale, "but I cannot entertain sanguine expectation when I know, that the whole interest of the King of Spain could only obtain nine men from Russia for South America" (MPA, 205 H 2, Kenney to Francis Neale, April 24, 1820).

44. GUSC, Charles Constantine Pise Papers, Journal, June 6, 1820.

45. AAB, 17 R 2, Kenney to Maréchal, Georgetown, October 6, 1819.

46. AAB, 17 R 3, Kenney to Maréchal, Georgetown, June 11, 1820.

47. Through Grassi's influence, Wallace had been asked by the Vicar General of the Society to take charge of the observatory at the Roman College, but the invitation

went unheeded (CUAA, Wallace Papers, Grassi to Wallace, Genoa, July 22, 1819; MPA, 205 H 2, Kenney to Francis Neale, April 24, 1820; ARSI, MD, 2 I 29, Kohlmann to Kenney, Washington, October 1, 1820; ARSI, MD, 2 I 31, Kohlmann to Fortis, Washington, February 4, 1821; ARSI, MD, 2 I 34, Kohlmann to Grassi, Washington, May 2, 1821).

48. M. LaBorde, M.D., *History of the Southern Carolina College* (Columbia, 1859), 187.

49. "Patriarcha amerykanskich Jezuitow, O Franciszek Dzierozynski SJ," in *Sacrum Poloniae Millenium* 7 (Rome: *Typis Pontificiae Universitatis Gregorianae*, 1960), 475–80, cited in Anthony J. Kuzniewski, SJ, "Francis Dzierozynski and the Jesuit Restoration in the United States," *Catholic Historical Review* LXXVIII (January 1992), 52.

50. Kuzniewski, 56.

51. MPA, 206 W 9a, Kenney to McElroy, Tullabey, Tullamere, June 20, 1822.

52. Calhoun to James Madison, Pendleton, May 13, 1827, in Robert L. Meriwether et al., eds., *Papers of John C. Calhoun* (Columbia, 1959/86–), 10:288–89.

53. J. Fairfax McLaughlin, *College Days at Georgetown: And Other Papers* (Philadelphia, 1899), 72–73.

54. ARSI, MD, 2 I 53a, Maximilian Rantzau to Fortis, Georgetown, May 10, 1822.

55. MPA, 205 G 4, E. Fenwick to Kohlmann, Baltimore, August 10, 1820.

56. MPA, 205 G 8, Enoch Fenwick to Francis Neale, Geo: Town College, September 6, 1820.

57. Both Daley and Durkin list Benedict Fenwick as succeeding his brother from 1822 to 1825. This appears to stem from a letter Benedict Fenwick wrote in 1822 in which he speaks of being appointed "to look after its [the college's] concerns . . ." (AAB, 16 P 34, B. Fenwick to Maréchal, November 30, 1822), but the younger Fenwick was actually procurator of the college then, not its president.

58. ARSI, MD, 2 I 51, Dzierozynski to Fortis, Georgetown, April 12, 1822.

59. Baxter, a very popular preacher, claimed facetiously that a bottle of wine was the best preparation. "He is too true to this method," one Belgian Jesuit remarked (ARSI, MD, 2 IV 3, McElroy to Grassi, Georgetown, May 6, 1821; ARSI, MD, 2 IV 11, De Theux to Fortis, Georgetown, June 18, 1823).

60. ARSI, MD, 2 161, Neale to Fortis, June 22, 1823.

61. John Clagett Proctor, "Early Days at George Washington University," Washington Sunday Star, April 9, 1933; Elmer Louis Kayser, *Bricks without Straw: The Evolution of George Washington University* (New York, 1970), 72.

62. Kayser, *Bricks without Straw,* 38.

63. McMaster, "Fenwick," 134–35.

64. ARSI, MD, 2 I 31, Kohlmann to Fortis, Washington, February 4, 1821.

65. ARSI, MD, 2 VII 7, Kohlmann to "Magisters," Washington, September 3, 1821.

66. ARSI, MD, 3 I 23, Ironside to Fortis, Washington, June 12, 1825.

67. ARSI, MD, 3 I 23, Ironside to Fortis, Washington, 12 June 1825.

68. The Jesuit president of the Washington Seminary, Jeremiah Keily, refused to carry out the suppression and attempted to continue classes in the Old Capitol building. Confirming Ironside's evaluation, many of the parents initially preferred to pay tuition to Keily rather than receive a free education at Georgetown, until they discovered that the seminary was now a private enterprise and no longer an official Jesuit institution (ARSI, MD, 3 V 4, Dzierozynski to Fortis, Georgetown, October 22, 1827).

69. ARSI, MD, 3 I 23, Ironside to Fortis, Washington, June 12, 1825.

70. Kohlmann to Lewis Wilcocks, White Marsh, March 16, 1824, extracted in *An Examination of a Protestant's Objections to the Popish Miracle Lately Wrought in America* (London 1824), 2–3. The Continental emigrès were particularly sensitive to the tide of conversions that seemed to be rising in the eastern cities. Kohlmann had experienced it firsthand in New York a decade before; then found the same phenomenon in Washington and Georgetown in the early 1820s. As one Marylander observed in the middle 1820s, "there is . . . a general fermentation as to Catholicism" (AAB, W[illiam Joseph] Williams to Samuel Eccleston, Baltimore, September 12, 1826).

71. *National Intelligencer,* April 1, 1824.
72. GUSC, Mobberly Diary, IV, November 5, 1824, quoting *National journal,* October 25, 1824.
73. Baxter, having left the Society while he was in England, returned to New York in 1826 where he attempted to join the clergy of that diocese. The next year he surfaced in Philadelphia as the vicar-general of the hapless Bishop Henry Conwell; and in May of 1827 he died of malaria (MPA, 206 5 15, Richard Hardy to George Fenwick, Georgetown, June 22, 1823; ARSI, MD, 3 I 25, Dzierozynski to Fortis, Washington, July 20, 1825; ARSI, MD, 3 I 27, Excerpts of letter from English Provincial, August 11, 1825; MPA, 209 F 6, Beschter to Dzierozynski, Baltimore, December 15, 1826; MPA, 208 W 1, Keily to Dzierozynski, Washington, April 6, 1827; MPA, 208 W 10, Henry Conwell to Dzierozynski, Philadelphia, May 24, 1827; MPA, 208 S 0, Kohlmann to George Fenwick, Rome, October 1, 1827).

    Levins was promptly invited to join the New York diocese. There he became involved with Catholic newspapers, the *Truth Teller* and the *New York Weekly Register and Catholic Diary.* In December 1824, Levins wrote John Calhoun, the secretary of war, about the possibility of securing a professorship in natural philosophy or mathematics in the University of Virginia. Even after he was well established in New York, he pursued this possibility. Calhoun in 1827 recommended him as "among the best mathematicians and scholars in our country" in proposing his name for the chair of mathematics at Virginia (W. Edwin Hemphill ed., *The Papers of John C. Calhoun,* IX [Columbia, 1976], Thomas C. Levins to Calhoun, December 10, 1824, 439–40; ibid. X [1977], Calhoun to James Madison, Pendleton, May 13, 1827, 288).

    In 1834 Levins found himself at odds with another emigré Frenchman, John Dubois, his bishop, who suspended him for disobedience. While he was suspended from the ministry, Levins helped design and construct the Croton aqueduct, still considered one of the engineering marvels of New York City's remarkable water system. He was restored to his priestly functions by Archbishop John Hughes and died in 1843. At his death he left his library to Georgetown, as well as his art collection, in exchange for scholarships for his nephews (GUA, House Diary, June 4, 1843).
74. ARSI, MD, 3 IV 5a, Dzierozynski to Fortis, Georgetown, February 12, 1825.
75. ARSI, MD, 3 I 28, Dzierozynski to Fortis, Georgetown, September 24, 1825.
76. ARSI, MD, 3 VIII 1, Dubuisson to Fortis, Georgetown, April 22, 1826.
77. ARSI, MD, 3 VIII 1, Dubuisson to Fortis, Georgetown, April 22, 1826.
78. ARSI, MD, 3 VIII 1; ARSI MD 3 IV 4, Dubuisson to Fortis, Georgetown, January 26, 1825.
79. ARSI, MD, 3 IV 12, Michael Dougherty to Fortis, Georgetown, February 5, 1827.
80. ARSI, MD, 3 I 38, Dzierozynski to Fortis, Georgetown, April 30, 1826.
81. ARSI, MD, 3 I 42, Beschter to Fortis, Baltimore, July 10, 1826.
82. MPA, 206 W 9a, Kenney to McElroy, Tullaby, Tullamere, June 20, 1822.
83. Adam Marshall, who had succeeded Kohlmann as president of the Washington Seminary and was the only feasible American candidate, had left the province about the same time as Baxter and Levins. Marshall had secured permission from his Jesuit superiors to accept an appointment as a naval chaplain aboard the *North Carolina* for the sake of his health. He died at sea from dysentery a year later (ARSI, MD, 3 I 15, Fortis to Dzierozynski, Georgetown, September 5, 1824; MPA, 207 N 9, Beschter to Dzierozynski, Baltimore, November 25, 1825).

    In the spring of 1826 John Dubois, the president-owner of Mount St. Mary's College in Emmitsburg who was then the bishop-elect of New York, offered his college to the Society of Jesus. (The Sulpicians had dismissed him from their society that January when he had refused to reduce his school from a major to a minor seminary.) Dzierozynski had no one to send to take over the institution, but for Dubois' sake, he offered to seek direction from the general in Rome. However, Dubois decided he could not wait that long and gave it to three priests of the Archdiocese of Baltimore (MPA, 207 H 4, Dubois to [McElroy?], Mount St. Mary's,

July 5, 1826; Kauffman, 83; ARSI, MD, 3 I 44, Dzierozynski to Fortis, Georgetown, September 28, 1826).

84. ARSI, MD, 3 IV 10, Feiner to Fortis, Georgetown, January 18, 1827.

85. GUA, Michael J. Rust, "The Georgetown Walks" (June 1, 1963), cited in Elizabeth Prelinger, "Architecture on the Hilltop," unpublished paper, 13–14.

86. ARSI, MD, 3 IV 16, Mulledy to [?], Georgetown, March 27, 1829.

87. When the Jesuits refused to recognize Maréchal's claims, he took the matter to Rome, where in 1822, with his good connections at Propaganda, the archbishop secured a brief from Pope Pius VII that ordered the Jesuits in Maryland to surrender White Marsh with all its slaves and other personal property to the archbishop. The Jesuits, both foreign and native, resisted, arguing that the prelate had no just claim. Through the efforts of William Matthews as well as two sympathetic allies at the State Department (George Ironside and Daniel Brent), then Secretary of State John Quincy Adams let it be known that the United States government would not tolerate such an invasion of American sovereignty. This opposition, coupled with the hostile reaction of both Catholics and Protestants to the publication of the brief, forced Archbishop Maréchal to drop his demand for the property.

88. MPA, 208 Z 12a, Dubuisson to Young, Rome, March 3, 1827.

89. ARSI, MD, 3 IV 16, Mulledy to [?], Georgetown, March 27, 1829.

90. MPA, 208 G 6, R. McSherry to William McSherry, Martinsburg, November 27, 1828.

91. MPA, 206 K 14, N. Sewall to Enoch Fenwick, Stonyhurst, September 28, 1824; MPA, 207 R 19, Grassi to McElroy, Turin, May 1825; MPA, 207 F 2, Kohlmann to McElroy, Roman College, December 1, 1826.

92. MPA, 208 H 4b, Kohlmann to McSherry, Rome, September 13, 1828.

CHAPTER 5

1. The father, an immigrant in the 1790s, managed to own four slaves by 1810 but was evidently never able to manage well enough to become self-supporting. As late as 1847 his daughter, Mary Mulledy, wrote to her brother Thomas that their father was talking "of raising cattle and making a fortune[,] yet he is doing worse than nothing on the farm[.] [S]everal hogs died from poverty[.] [H]e did not even try to get corn . . ." (MPA, 215 C, Mary Mulledy to Thomas Mulledy, Millcreek [Va.], January 31, 1847).

2. H. Maxwell and H. L. Swisher, *History of Hampshire County, West Virginia* (Morgantown, 1897), 297–98.

3. ARSI, MD, 2 VII 5, Kohlmann to Grassi, June 2, 1820.

4. GUSC, Charles Constantine Pise Papers, Journal, October 28, 1820.

5. GUSC, Thomas Mulledy Papers.

6. ARSI, MD, 3 I 53, Mulledy to Fortis, Genoa, September 8, 1828; ARSI, MD, 3 IV 17, Mulledy to [name not legible], Georgetown, March 27, 1829.

7. John J. Ryan, SJ, "Our Scholasticate-An Account of Its Growth and History to the Opening of Woodstock, 1805–1869," WL 33 (1904), 14–16; John T. Reily, *Collections and Recollections, In the Life and Times of Cardinal Gibbons,* II (Martinsburg, 1892–93), 384–85; Census of 1810, Jefferson Co., Va. The census return is for a "William McSherry" but the information on slaves and children (seven born by 1810) matches Richard McSherry exactly.

8. Barnard, who married a Catholic Michigander of French descent, became a distinguished educator, reforming the common school systems of Connecticut and Rhode Island and eventually serving as the first United States Commissioner of Education (Bernard C. Steiner, ed., "The South Atlantic States in 1833, as Seen by a New Englander," *Maryland Historical Magazine* 13 [1918], 289–90).

9. ARSI, MD, 3 IV 24, Ryder to Roothaan, Georgetown, February 18, 1830.

10. ARSI, MD, 3 I 74, Dubuisson to Roothaan, Georgetown, December 27, 1830.

11. ARSI, MD, 3 II 5, Dubuisson to Roothaan, Newtown, April 11, 1830.

12. ARSI, MD, 4 I 11, Dzierozynski to Roothaan, Georgetown, April 10, 1831.
13. Fidèle de Grivel reckoned there were 3,000 Catholics among the 7,500 inhabitants of Georgetown (ARSI, MD, 4 I 18, de Grivel to Alois Landes, Georgetown, February 14, 1831).
14. ARSI, MD, 3 IV 16, Mulledy to Roothaan [?], Georgetown, March 27, 1829.
15. ARSI, MD, 3 IV 20, Mulledy to Roothaan, Georgetown, January 7, 1830.
16. ARSI, MD, 4 III 5, McSherry to Roothaan, Georgetown, January 31, 1831.
17. Interestingly, of the total enrollment in 1830 only three day students were expelled or, compared to the boarders, less than half (eight boarders were dismissed, including the adopted son of the president of the United States) although the probable number of day students was virtually equal to that of the boarders. Indeed, over the previous five years more boarders (eight) had been expelled than day students (six), and Catholics equaled Protestants among those expelled.
18. Anna Maria Huarte de Iturbide had emigrated from Mexico to the United States in 1824 after the execution of her husband, Agustin de Iturbide, Emperor of Mexico from 1822 to 1823. She eventually settled in Georgetown with her seven children (Eleanore C. Sullivan, *Georgetown Visitation since 1799* [Baltimore, 1975], 78).

    Of the ninety-seven day students listed in 1830, the occupations of eleven of their fathers are known. There were three government workers, two lawyers, two military officers, two merchants, a planter, and a doctor. Most of the other fathers of the day students were artisans, craftsmen, and unskilled workers (ARSI, MD, 4 III 3, Mulledy to Roothaan, Georgetown, January 28, 1831).
19. ARSI, MD, 3 IV 27, Beschter to Roothaan, Georgetown, August 4, 1830; ARSI, MD, 3 IV 25, Dzierozynski to Roothaan, Georgetown, March 23, 1830.
20. ARSI, MD, 3 IV 25. Jackson's seventeen-year-old ward and grandnephew, Andrew Jackson Hutchings, was also a student at the college during the 1829–30 school year. He withdrew at the end of that year at the request of the faculty—a polite form of expulsion. Thirteen-year-old Smith Van Buren was enrolled in Second Humanities in 1830.
21. ARSI, MD, 3 IV 26, Dzierozynski to Roothaan, Georgetown, July 28, 1830.
22. ARSI, Register of the Generals' Responses for the American Mission (1830–1833) and Maryland Province (1833–1853) I, October 2, 1830, 17.
23. ARSI, MD, 4 III 13, Ryder to Roothaan, Georgetown, February 3, 1832.
24. ARSI, MD, 3 IV 20, Mulledy to Roothaan, Georgetown, January 7, 1830. In 1826 a group of citizens, including two prominent Washington physicians, Thomas Sim, president of the Medical Society of the District of Columbia, and Henry Huntt, an officer of the society and the first public health officer for the city, had together petitioned Congress to charter a medical school. A countermemorial from the faculty of the Columbian Medical Department had blocked this effort. In a letter to Father General Roothaan in August 1830 Mulledy speaks of "two principals" behind the move to secure Georgetown's sponsorship of a school, one a practicing Catholic, the other married to a Catholic. This duo could well have been Sim and Huntt (Elmer Louis Kayser, *A Medical Center: The Institutional Development of Medical Education in George Washington University* [Washington, 1973], 31–37; ARSI, MD, 3 IV 28, August 7, 1830).
25. ARSI, MD, 3 IV 28, Mulledy to Roothaan, August 7, 1830; ARSI, MD, 4 III 7, Charles Constantine Pise to Charles Maria Pedicine, Prefect of the Congregation of the Propagation of the Faith, Baltimore, June 6, 1831; ARSI, MD, 4 III 9, Mulledy to Roothaan, Georgetown, August 26, 1831.
26. ARSI, MD, 5 III 4, Mulledy to Roothaan, Georgetown, October 28, 1833.
27. ARSI, MD, 3 IV 20, Mulledy to Roothaan, Georgetown, January 7, 1830; ARSI, MD, 2 IV 12, Report of Anthony Kohlmann on the internal affairs of the American Mission [1823]. There were never more than a few slaves at Georgetown College, although more would occasionally be sent there temporarily. The Census of 1830 listed three males and one female.
28. ARSI, MD, 4 I 5, Dzierozynski to Roothaan, Georgetown, January 28, 1831.
29. MPA, 500: 61, Roothaan to Kenney, Rome, July 3, 1830.

30. According to the Constitutions of the Society of Jesus, the superior general appoints four members to serve as consultors to the provincial or regional superior. The consultors have advisory, not deliberative, power, but the superior is bound to seek their advice regularly on significant matters. They also draw up, together with the provincial superior, lists of three candidates (*terna*) for positions of leadership within the province. These lists go to Rome for final selection by the general.

31. ARSI, Register I, Roothaan to Dzierozynski, May 1, 1830. The superior general was particularly disturbed to learn that "our American fathers who have been in Italy . . . sometimes and perhaps more than sometimes amuse themselves by ridiculing Italy and what they have seen there; one would think that they found nothing good there; only things to blame" (ARSI, Register I, Roothaan to Dubuisson, May 1, 1830, 1–2).

32. MPA, 209 K2, Kenney to McElroy, Liverpool, September 15, 1830.

33. ARSI, MD, 4 I 3 Kenney to Roothaan, Frederick, January 10, 1831.

34. ARSI, MD, 4 III 9, Mulledy to Roothaan, Georgetown, August 26, 1831.

35. ARSI, MD, 4 I 12, Dzierozynski to Roothaan, Georgetown, August 10, 1831.

36. ARSI, MD, 4 III 11, George Fenwick to Roothaan, Georgetown, January 30, 1832.

37. During the 1830s non-Catholics accounted for more than a third (34.7%) of all students. By 1845 the proportion of non-Catholics was down (28.4%). Only in the 1850s were non-Catholics again a third (33.9%) of the student body. By contrast, St. Mary's in Baltimore, whose enrollment of both boarders and day students was also rising rapidly during this period, remained heavily Protestant. That pattern, together with the consequent few vocations to the ministry, was a major factor in the suppression of the college in 1852 (Kauffman, *Tradition and Transformation*, 124, 136–137).

38. ARSI, Register I, Roothaan to Dzierozynski, May 29, 1830.

39. MPA, 210 H9, Kenney to McElroy, Philadelphia, April 14, 1833.

40. ARSI, MD, 3 IV 28, Mulledy to Roothaan, Georgetown, August 7, 1830.

41. ARSI, MD, 4 III 7, Charles Constantine Pise to Charles Maria Pedicine, Prefect of the Congregation for the Propagation of the Faith, Baltimore, June 6, 1831.

42. GUSC, Kenney Papers, Kenney to McSherry, New York, July 24, 1833.

43. ARSI, Register I, Roothaan to Mulledy, October 3, 1830, 20.

44. ARSI, Register I, Roothaan to Mulledy, May 1, 1830, 5.

45. ARSI, Register I, Roothaan to Dubuisson [October 1830], 18; ARSI, MD, 4 I 5, Dzierozynski to Roothaan, January 28, 1831; ARSI, Register I, Roothaan to Kenney, April 19, 1831, 27–28; ARSI, Register I, Roothaan to Kenney, June 2, 1831, 35–36.

46. ARSI, Register I, *Decretum erectionis Provinciae Marylandiae Societatis Jesu in Statibus Unitis Americae*, 70.

47. ARSI, MD, 4 I 12, Dzierozynski to Roothaan, Georgetown, August 10, 1831; ARSI, MD, 4 I 18, same to same, Georgetown, February 17, 1832.

48. GUA, Rector's Consultation Book, February 8, 1832; ARSI, MD, 4 III 4, Ryder to Roothaan, Georgetown, January 29, 1831; ARSI, MD, 4 I 20, McSherry to Roothaan, St. Louis, April 23, 1832; GUA, Financial Accounts, January 28, 1832. In 1848 the width of the building was doubled, which added another set of rooms on each floor.

49. ARSI, MD, 4 I 18, Dzierozynski to Roothaan, Georgetown, February 17, 1832.

50. GUA, Rector's Consultation Book, March 31, 1832; ibid., April 10, 1832.

51. MPA, 210 S 1b, Benedict Fenwick to George Fenwick, Boston, November 4, 1831; MPA, 210 S 4, same to same, Boston, December 21, 1831.

52. MPA, 210 R 11, Kenney to McSherry, Georgetown, June 18, 1832.

53. MPA, 210 R 11, Kenney to McSherry, Georgetown, June 18, 1832; MPA, 210 R 13, Kenney to McElroy, Georgetown, June 19, 1832; MPA, 210 F 8, Kenney to McSherry, New York, July 24, 1833; MPA, 210 F 11, Kenney to McSherry [New York], August 9, 1833; ARSI, Register I, Roothaan to McSherry, February 14, 1834.

54. MPA, 211 Z 4, de Grivel to McSherry, White Marsh, January 21, 1834.

55. Ibid.

56. "There is no nobility as such in the United States," Dubuisson noted, "nonetheless, he would be at a disadvantage, even among youth," a judgment that McElroy himself echoed a few years later (ARSI, MD, 5 I 27, Dubuisson [notes for Roothaan] [1836?]; MPA, 215 W 5, McElroy to Peter Verhaegen, Frederick, July 29, 1845).

57. ARSI, Register I, Roothaan to McSherry, August 23, 1833, 102; ARSI, MD, 5 I 24, McSherry to Roothaan, Georgetown, August 30, 1835.

58. ARSI, MD, 5 I 46, Peter Havermans to Roothaan, Georgetown, December 13, 1837.

59. MPA, 211 W 2, James Ward et al. to Samuel Barber, Georgetown, April 15, 1834. "Almost every bank is broken, or failed in some manner or other," another Jesuit reported to Barber and another American Jesuit in Rome. "[B]usiness is dull . . . because nothing but hard money [gold and silver in specie] passes" (MPA, 211 W 3, George Fenwick to Barber and Samuel Mulledy, Georgetown, April 16, 1834).

60. By 1837 the college was still paying an annual interest of $535.20 (6%); then in June $9,018.12 was paid to Neill, with the apparent agreement that the previous interest payments would be counted as part of the capital (GUA, Financial Records Series, Ledger I.A.3.i).

61. GUA, Financial Records Series, Ledger I.A.3.g. The contract for the student center (Mulledy building) called for the complete payment of the entire $11,000 cost by the time the building was occupied (GUA, "Buildings," Box 1 of 6).

62. ARSI, MD, 4 III 13, Ryder to Roothaan, Georgetown, February 3, 1832.

63. ARSI, MD, 5 III 6, Mulledy to Roothaan, Georgetown, March 8, 1835.

64. 22nd Congress, Session II, Ch. 86, 1833. Statute II, March 2, 1833; in *Journal of the Senate of the United States of America*, Dec. 3, 1832–March 2, 1833 (Washington, 1832), 228, 248. Mulledy did attempt to persuade the Congress to give the college the value of the land in cash, but predictably, to no avail (ARSI, MD, 5 III 4, Mulledy to Roothaan, Georgetown, October 28, 1833; ARSI, MD, 5 I 14, Vespré to Roothaan, Georgetown, April 5, 1834; GUA, House Diary, March 1, 1833).

65. Mrs. Decatur had long been seeking to obtain the prize money that the government had owed to her husband (as a bounty) for the destruction of a pirated American frigate in Tripoli harbor in 1804. In 1837 the United States awarded her a widow's pension of approximately $10,000 (MPA 212 T 7, McSherry to McElroy, November 23, 1837; GUSC, Dennis C. Terez, "The Long and Involved Claim of Susan Decatur and the Men Who Burned the Philadelphia").

66. ARSI, MD, 5 I 45, McSherry to Roothaan, Frederick, November 12, 1837.

67. ARSI, MD, 7 III 3, McSherry to Roothaan, Georgetown, January 16, 1838; ARSI, MD, 5 III 14, Mulledy to Roothaan, Georgetown, December 7, 1837; MPA, 56 W 3, Procurator's Report, January 1, 1838.

68. ARSI, MD, 7 III 3, McSherry to Roothaan, Georgetown College, January 16, 1838.

69. MPA, *Acta Primae Congregationis, Provinciae Marylandiae Societatis Jesu*, 1835.

70. See Robert Emmett Curran, "'Splendid Poverty': Jesuit Slaveholding in Maryland, 1805–1838," in Jon Wakelyn and Randall Miller, eds., *Catholics in the Old South* (Macon, 1983), 125–46.

71. ARSI, MD, 5 I 21, Fidèle de Grivel, *Mémoire sur la Congregation Prov. du Maryland commences . . . le 8 Juillet 1835.*

72. These are figures computed from the 1860 census in Barbara Jeanne Fields, *Slavery and Freedom on the Middle Ground: Maryland during the Nineteenth Century* (New Haven, 1985), 24–25.

73. Fields has calculated that fewer than a fifth (16%) of the slaves sold in Maryland between 1830 and 1840 left the state (*Slavery and Freedom*, 24).

74. The European Jesuits tended to regard the slaves simply as American serfs, whose living conditions were better than those of most of the peasants they had known in France and Poland, or even the day laborers in urban America. As late as 1855 Father Bernard Wiget, a German, found the slaves in Charles County "a happy lot of people compared to the poor Irish in Boston. These [Irish] are equal to slaves in ignorance & hundred other ways, have no master to take care of them in sickness & old age, no kind mistress to teach their children their prayers & to keep them in the Church" (MPA, 224 W 9, Wiget to Charles Stonestreet, August 28, 1855).

75. MPA, 500.76.d, Roothaan to McSherry, October 27, 1836; ARSI, Register I, Roothaan to McSherry, December 27, 1836, 131–32.

76. ARSI, MD, 5 II 1, de Grivel to Alois Landes, St. Ignatius, October 24, 1834.

77. ARSI, MD, 7 I 5, Mulledy to Roothaan, Fredericktown, August 9, 1838; GUA 531–1, Rector's Consultations, July 9, 1840. In time, the college authorities began to claim that the loan had been an outright gift, but thirty years later a provincial superior ordered the college to return the money to the province (MPA, 56 N 1).

78. ARSI, MD, 7 II 7, Thomas Lilly to Roothaan, St. Thomas, July 2, 1838.

79. ARSI, MD, 7 I 9, Havermans to Roothaan, Newtown, October 20, 1838. Havermans left the Society four years later. The sale of the slaves seems to have been a major source of his alienation from the American Jesuits. He afterward served as a priest in the New York diocese.

80. GUA, Devitt Papers, Thomas Hughes to Edward Devitt, Rome, January 29, 1907; MPA, 212 G 9, de Grivel to Charles C. Lancaster, Georgetown, May 4, 1839; MPA, 112 W O, Newtown Account Book; MPA, 212 M 5a, de Grivel to C. C. Lancaster, Georgetown, November 11, 1838.

81. ARSI, Register I, Roothaan to Mulledy, August 25, 1838, 152.

82. In an accompanying letter the archbishop urged the general's "paternal indulgence in [Mulledy's] behalf . . . whose many excellent & distinguished qualities are known to me, as well as the weaknesses which have pained both you & myself. The services which he has rendered & is still calculated to render to religion, his sound principles of piety and goodness of heart have endeared him to me, notwithstanding his occasional failings . . ." (ARSI, MD, 7 I, Eccleston to Roothaan, Georgetown, June 27, 1839).

83. MPA, 500: 84b, Roothaan to McSherry, Rome, August 3, 1839.

84. ARSI, Register I, Roothaan to Vespré, December 31, 1839, 169.

85. MPA, 212 D 8, de Grivel to Charles Lancaster, Georgetown, December 14, 1839.

86. MPA, 213 T 4a, de Grivel to Lancaster, Georgetown, October 31, 1840.

87. ARSI, MD, 7 I 52, Dzierozynski to Roothaan, Georgetown, October 29, 1842.

88. MPA, 214 N 4, Ryder to McElroy, Georgetown, March 7, 1844.

89. ARSI, MD, 8 I 15, Rey to Roothaan, Georgetown, January 14, 1846; ARSI, MD, 9 XIV [Verhaegen], Georgetown, September 25, 1847; GUA, Directors' Minutes, August 7, 1848.

90. David B. Potts, "American Colleges in the Nineteenth Century: From Localism to Denominationalism," *HEQ* 11 (Winter 1971), 368; James Edward Scanlon, *Randolph-Macon College: A Southern History 1825–1867* (Charlottesville, 1983), 215.

91. GUA, House Diary, February 12, 1841; March 4, 1841.

92. Robert Seager II, *And Tyler Too: A Biography of John and Julia Gardiner Tyler* (New York, 1963), 436.

93. ARSI, MD, 7 III 9, Ryder to Roothaan, Georgetown, November 12, 1840; ARSI, MD, 7 I 46, Dzierozynski to Roothaan, Georgetown, March 29, 1842.

94. The delegates to the second provincial congregation sought permission from the superior general to have the province assume the debts. They apparently felt they had no choice. In 1839 the procurator reported that the builders were still owed "many thousand dollars" and feared that they would soon sue (ARSI, MD, 7 II 9, Vespré to Roothaan, Georgetown, September 21, 1841; MPA, 212 D 7 Vespré to Dzierozynski, Georgetown, December 22, 1839).

95. New York Province Archives, John Larkin to F. W. Gockeln, Fordham, November 15, 1852.

96. MPA, 213 Z 6b, de Grivel to Lancaster, Georgetown, February 29, 1840.

97. As early as 1839, Thomas Mulledy was reporting to the superior general that the Bishop of Philadelphia possessed "love letters," apparently from the woman to Ryder (ARSI, MD, 7 I 12, Mulledy to Roothaan, Georgetown, April 17, 1839).

98. ARSI, Register I, Roothaan to Ryder, April 10, 1846.

99. *Imminent Dangers to the Free Institutions of the United States through Foreign Immigrations* (New York, 1835), 25. To be sure, there were public defenders of the Society. When ex-President John Quincy Adams was reported to have attacked the Jesuits as

persecutors of Galileo, he did not hesitate to refute that malicious charge in writing and instead pronounced the Jesuits "intimate friends, the disciples, the protectors of Galileo," as well as successful rivals in the development of astronomy and physics. Adams also reminded his readers that when the great Copernican (and Lutheran) astronomer Johann Kepler was forced to leave Tubingen because of the complaints that Lutheran theologians had made against his work, he found "asylum among— God save the mark! the Jesuits at Gratz!" (Quoted in *Baltimore Catholic Herald,* December 10, 1843).

100. MPA, 211 N 12, Ward et al. to Samuel Barber [1835].
101. MPA, 211 H 10, Dubuisson to McSherry, Rome, October 8, 1836.
102. Thomas S. Harding, *College Literary Societies: Their Contribution to Higher Education in the United States, 1815–1876* (New York, 1971), 395.
103. E. Merton Coulter, *College Life in the Old South* (New York, 1928), 150–51.
104. ARSI, MD, 7 V 13, Vespré to Roothaan, Frederick, June 5, 1844.
105. See Warner, *At Peace with All Their Neighbours.*
106. MPA, 214 M 4, Ryder to McElroy, Georgetown, May 12, 1844.
107. ARSI, MD, 7 I 49, extract of a letter of Anthony Rey, May 21, 1842; GUA, Minister's Diary, May 9–11, 1842.
108. ARSI, MD, 7 I 49, quoted in a letter from Stephen Dubuisson to Jan Roothaan, Aix-ci, Marseilles, June 30, 1842.
109. ARSI, MD, 8 I 17, Peter Verhaegen to Roothaan, Worcester, June 5, 1846.
110. ARSI, MD, 8 I 28, Verhaegen to Roothaan, Georgetown, October 7, 1847; John McElroy, "Chaplains for the Mexican War—1846" WL, 16 (1887), 226.
111. Donald G. Tewksbury in his study of *The Founding of American Colleges and Universities before the Civil War* (New York, 1932) found 133 permanent institutions tracing their roots to the three decades before the Civil War (16), but Natalie Naylor has shown that Tewksbury overlooked some 159 institutions that at least eventually became colleges ("The Ante-Bellum College Movement: A Reappraisal of Tewksbury's *Founding of American Colleges and Universities,*" HEQ 13 [Fall 1973], 263).
112. Colin B. Burke, "The Quiet Influence: The American Colleges and Their Students" (Ph.D. diss. Washington University, 1974), cited in James McLachlan, "The American College in the Nineteenth Century: Toward a Reappraisal," *Teachers College Record* 80 (December 1978), 295; Burke, *American Collegiate Populations: A Test of the Traditional View* (New York, 1982), 54–56.
113. Absalom Peters, *Discourse before the Society for the Promotion of Collegiate and Theological Education at the West* (1851), 13, quoted in Tewksbury, *Founding,* 1.
114. The figures are based on Edward J. Power, *A History of Catholic Higher Education in the United States* (Milwaukee, 1958), Appendix A.
115. David B. Potts has argued, from the evidence of Baptist institutions in this period, that the so-called denominational colleges were primarily local colleges, "closely tied with the local, cultural, and economic ambitions of citizens, parents, and students." ("American Colleges in the Nineteenth Century: From Localism to Denominational-ism," HEQ 11 [Winter 1971], 363–80; Potts, "'College Enthusiasm!' As Public Response, 1800–1860," *Harvard Educational Review* 47 [February 1977], 28–42.
116. Colin Burke, *American Collegiate Populations,* 39, 52.
117. "Changing and Remaining the Same: A Look at the Record," *Current Issues in Catholic Higher Education* 10 (Summer 1989), 4–5.
118. Gerald McKevitt, SJ, *The University of Santa Clara: A History, 1851–1977* (Stanford, 1979), 40.
119. Kauffman, *Tradition and Transformation,* 123.
120. ARSI, MD, 5 I 47, McSherry to Roothaan, George Town, October 12, 1837; ARSI, MD, 5 III 14, Mulledy to Roothaan, Georgetown, December 7, 1837.
121. ARSI, Register I, Roothaan to Mulledy, March 10, 1838, 144.
122. MPA, 214 Z 5, Benedict Fenwick to Dzierozynski, Boston, February 4, 1843; in 1838 he had written to his brother, George: "I shall erect a College into which no Protestant shall ever set foot" (November 29, 1838, quoted in James W. Sander, "19th Century Boston Catholics and the School Question," Working Papers Series:

Center for the Study of American Catholicism [Fall 1977], 3–4). Sanders cites the letter as being in the Fordham Archives but it cannot be located there, nor is it with the George Fenwick papers within the Maryland Province Archives.

123. Walter J. Meagher, SJ, and William J. Grattan, *The Spires of Fenwick: A History of the College of Holy Cross, 1843–1963* (New York, 1966), 36–42; ARSI, MD, 7 VIII 1, Dzierozynski to Roothaan, Georgetown, September 6, 1842; ARSI, MD, 7 VIII 2, same to same, March 14, 1843; ARSI, MD, 7 I 55, same to same, Georgetown, April 30, 1843.

124. ARSI, MD, 8 II 8, Brocard to Roothaan, Georgetown, August 16, 1848; ARSI, MD, 8 II 9, same to same, November 8, 1849; *Boston Pilot*, October 6, 1849; ARSI, MD, 8 II 36, Brocard to Roothaan, March 16, 1851.

125. Nicholas Varga, *Baltimore's Loyola, Loyola's Baltimore 1851–1986* (Baltimore, 1990), 27–29, 142–45.

126. Nearly one hundred students enrolled at St. Joseph's during its initial year (1851–52); fewer than fifty did so during Boston College's first academic year (1864–65) (Francis X. Talbot, SJ, *Jesuit Education in Philadelphia: Saint Joseph's College, 1851–1926* [Philadelphia, 1927], 39–41; David R. Dunigan, SJ, *A History of Boston College* [Milwaukee, 1947], 85).

CHAPTER 6

1. MPA, 216 P 2, Grassi to John McElroy, Rome, June 8, 1848.

2. "Autobiography of Father Burchard Villiger," WL 32 (1903), 51–81.

3. ARSI, MD, 8 II 5, Brocard to Roothaan, Georgetown, April 16, 1848.

4. GUSC, Catholic Historical MSS. Collection 8:11, James Ryder Papers, 23–27, Joseph C. Shaw to Ryder, Boston, October 5, 1848.

5. Pietro Galetti, *Memorie Storiche intorno al P. Ugo Molza e alla Compagnia di Gesu in Rome durante il secolo XIX* (Rome, 1912), 32–33; English Province Archives, Foreign Correspondence, 1776–1859, fol. 411, Torquatus Armillini to Charles Brooke, Georgetown, December 8, 1848; Carlos Sommervogel, SJ, *Bibliotheque de la Compagnie de Jésus*, tome VIII (Brussels and Paris, 1898), 642–43.

6. Quoted in the *Boston Pilot*, November 25, 1848, 3.

7. Twenty-five of the Germans remained at the college, including all twenty-one of the scholastics. The rest went on to Missouri.

8. *Catalogus Provinciae Marylandiae Societatis Jesu Ineunte Anno* MDCC–CLI (Georgetown, 1851).

9. ARSI, MD, 8 II 4, Combs to Roothaan, Georgetown, February 15, 1848.

10. Burke suggests that the Mexican American war may have contributed to the decline, but that seems at most to have had a marginal impact at Georgetown (Burke, *American Collegiate Populations*, 56–57, 272n11).

11. GUSC, Thomas Lilly Diary, October 28, 1849.

12. The German, Joseph Duverney, who was charged with the spiritual direction of the scholastics, both native and foreign, advised the refugees to keep complaining to their superiors in Europe until they would be recalled (ARSI, MD, 8 II 39, Joseph Ashwanden to Roothaan, Georgetown, April 25, 1851). When Duverney was giving lectures to the scholastics in January of 1849, the Americans rebelled against his rigoristic interpretation of the Society's Constitutions and manner of living. Duverney's response was to discontinue the talks and deal directly only with the Germans and some Italians (ARSI, MD, 8 II 17, Brocard to Roothaan, Georgetown, October 6, 1849).

13. ARSI, MD, 7 III 4, Philip Sacchi to Roothaan, Georgetown, January 23, 1839.

14. ARSI, MD, 5 111 7, Stephen Gabaria to Roothaan, Georgetown, August 7, 1835.

15. ARSI, MD, 8 II 11, Brocard to Roothaan, Georgetown, February 27, 1849.

16. ARSI, MD, 8 II 43, Brocard to Roothaan, Georgetown, December 23, 1851.

17. ARSI, MD, 8 III 6, Stonestreet to Beckx, Georgetown, January 30, 1854; GUA, Minister's Diary, July 8–11, 1853, January 16, 1854.

18. ARSI, MD, 9 XXII 3, Bapst to Beckx, Bangor, January 10, 1855; William Leo Lucey, SJ, *The Catholic Church in Maine* (Francestown, N.H., 1957), 118–35. Bapst's experience affected him more deeply than he realized at the time. He ended his life in an asylum, haunted by nightmares of attackers storming his room (WL, 16 [1887], 324–25, cited in Hennesey, *American Catholics,* 125).

19. The New York Observer, cited in Thomas W. Spalding, *The Premier See: A History of the Archdiocese of Baltimore, 1789–1989* (Baltimore and London, 1989), 155.

20. MPA, 219 T 9, Alexius Jamison to Samuel Barber, Georgetown, April 25, 1851.

21. Jean H. Baker, *Ambivalent Americans: The Know-Nothing Party in Maryland* (Baltimore and London, 1977), 23.

22. GUSC, Lilly Diary 2, September 12, 1851.

23. National Archives, Thirty-First Congress, 1st Session. Memorial of the President & Directors of the George Town College praying that certain Real estate held by said College may be excepted from the corporate limits of Geo. Town, June 28, 1850.

24. Ibid., H. Addison, Robt. Ould, P. F. Berry, A. H. Dody, and Wm. S. Nicholls, F. W. Risque, to the Hon. John Mason, Chairman of the Senate Committee on the District of Columbia, Georgetown, September 20, 1850. The bill was subsequently recommitted. Ould and Risque had children at the college in later years. Nicholls apparently had had two sons attend for a few months in 1845.

25. WL 31 (1902), 221–22.

26. ARSI, MD, 8 III 9, James Ward to Beckx, Baltimore, November 17, 1854.

27. ARSI, MD, 8 III 17, Stonestreet to Beckx, Boston, March 11, 1856. Two years earlier Stonestreet had already begun to consider opening houses in the Deep South, where he thought there was less opposition to Catholics and less danger of persecution (ARSI, MD 8 III 8, Stonestreet to Beckx, Georgetown, November 4, 1854).

28. ARSI, MD, 8 II 24, Brocard to Roothaan, Georgetown, April 12, 1850; ARSI, MD, 8 II 41, Brocard to Roothaan, Georgetown, October 31, 1851; ARSI, MD, 8 II 43, same to same, Georgetown, December 23, 1851.

29. Burke, 49.

30. MPA, 225 N, Maguire to Stonestreet, George Town College, October 2, 1857.

31. Ronald Story, *The Forging of an Aristocracy: Harvard and the Boston Upper Class, 1800–1870* (Middletown, Conn., 1980), 83.

32. David F. Musto, "A Survey of the American Observatory Movement, 1800–1850," Vistas in Astronomy 8 (1968), 89–90.

33. GUSC, Curley Papers, Box 1, folder 4; "Fr. James Curley," WL 18 (1889), 381–82.

34. GUSC, Curley Papers, Box 1, folder 4; ARSI, MD, 7155, Dzierozynski to Roothaan, Georgetown, April 30, 1843.

35. "The college," he wrote Roothaan, "could easily pay its debt provided they do not build that observatory; . . . but everyone, especially Father Rector, is so fixed on this point . . ."(ARSI, MD, 7 I 54, Vespré to Roothaan, Georgetown, January 12, 1843).

36. Francis J. Heyden, SJ, *The Beginning and End of a Jesuit Observatory* (1841–1972) (Manila, n.d.), 3; MPA, 56 W 4; Guralnick, 89.

37. ARSI, MD, 711114, Curley to Roothaan, Georgetown, December 24, 1843.

38. Musto, 90.

39. ARSI, Register I, Roothaan to Curley, February 15, 1844, 217–18.

40. GUA, Directors' Minutes, July 24, 1844; GUA, House Diary, April 4, 1844.

41. GUA, Financial Records Series, Ledger I.A.3.k; Heyden, *Beginning and End,* 3. A year earlier Harvard had appropriated approximately the same amount, some $25,000, to construct and outfit an observatory (Bessie Zaban Jones and Lyle Gifford Boyd, *The Harvard College Observatory: The First Four Directorships, 1839–1919* [Cambridge, 1971], 50–51).

42. ARSI, MD, 8 II, Brocard to Roothaan, Georgetown, August 24, 1848.

43. ARSI, MD, 9 XIV 6, Sestini to Roothaan, Georgetown, December 30, 1848; ARSI, MD, 9 XIV 7, same to same, Georgetown, March 2, 1849; ARSI, MD, 9 XIV 12, same to same, Georgetown, September 17, 1849.

44. *Astronomical Observations for 1847,* vol. 3 (Washington, 1853).

45. "Sestini, Benedict," in Clark Elliott, ed., *Biographic Dictionary of American Science* (Westport, Conn., 1979), 233.

46. McLaughlin, College Days, 96; Shea, Memorial, 159.

47. William F. Rigge, SJ, *Jesuit Astronomy Part II, The Restored Society, 1814–1904* (Northfield, Minn., 1904), 36–37; Giorgio Abetti, "(Pietro) Angelo Secchi," *Dictionary of Scientific Biography* 12, 266–70.

48. [James Curley, SJ] *Annals of the Astronomical Observatory of Georgetown, D.C.* (New York, 1852), 157–87.

49. In 1837 the college, through Vespré, had acquired a printing press in France but the publication of these books was done by commercial firms.

50. Marc Rothenberg, "The Educational and Intellectual Background of American Astronomers, 1825–1875," Bryn Mawr College dissertation, 1974, 153–157.

51. Magali Sarfatti Larson, *The Rise of Professionalism: A Sociological Analysis* (Berkeley, 1979), 128–33.

52. Joseph Kett, *The Formation of the American Medical Profession: The Role of Institutions, 1780–1860* (New Haven, 1968), 164–67; William G. Rothstein, *American Medical Schools and the Practice of Medicine: A History* (New York, 1987), 31–32, 49.

53. Pamela Ginsbach, "A History of the Georgetown University Medical School," unpublished ms., II, 1.

54. Kett, *Formation of the American Medical Profession,* 45. The specific catalyst in Washington for the formation of a second medical school was a dispute in the Washington Medical Society in 1849 over the selection of delegates to a meeting of the American Medical Association. Noble Young, a local physician unconnected with the Columbian Medical Department, proposed that the delegates be chosen from among those members of the profession who were not professors in colleges. The motion lost. Ten months later Young led the group that formed the Georgetown Medical Department (*History of the Medical Society of the District of Columbia, 1817–1909* [Washington, 19091, 15–16).

 Such medical rivalry seems to have been at the root of the initial proposal to form a medical department at Georgetown in the 1820s. In 1826, the year that Columbian College established a medical department, a memorial was presented to Congress by a group of local citizens, including eight physicians, asking that Congress charter a medical college. A counter-memorial from faculty members of the new medical department at Columbian contended that there was no need for one. At any rate, Congress issued no charter, and a few years later a group of doctors attempted to begin a school under Georgetown's charter, as we have seen (Elmer Louis Kayser, *A Medical Center: The Institutional Development of Medical Education in George Washington University* [Washington, 1973], 31–34).

55. Ginsbach, II, 2.

56. GUA, Rector's Consultations, November 28, 1849.

57. GUA, Minutes of the Directors of the Georgetown University Medical School, Noble Young et al. to President and Faculty of Georgetown College, District of Columbia, October 12, 1849, cited in Milton Corn, "Medical Education at Georgetown: A Historical Overview," in William McFadden, SJ, ed., *Georgetown at Two Hundred: Faculty Reflections on the University's Future* (Washington, 1990), 295–96.

58. Ginsbach, II, 5–7.

59. Ginsbach, II, 4.

60. Ginsbach, II, 5.

61. *History of the Medical Society,* 232.

62. GUA, Dr. Llewellin Elliot, "The History of the Foundation of the Medical Department of Georgetown University," (1907); GUA 19.1, W. W. Johnston, "History of the Medical Society of the District of Columbia," delivered February 16, 1894, at Seventy-Fifth Anniversary of the Society; Samuel H. Holland, "Charles H. Liebermann, M.D. An Early Russian-born Physician of Washington, D.C.," *Medical Annals of the District of Columbia,* 38 (Sept. 1969), 499–504.

63. Eliot, "History"; Corn, "Medical Education at Georgetown," 297–98.

64. Rothstein, 6.

65. GUA, Medical Faculty Minutes, April 12, 1850.

66. GUA, Medical Faculty Minutes, March 18, 1850.

67. GUA, Medical Faculty Minutes, April 12, 1850. Some of the members apparently had been having second thoughts about their ability to finance the school. In March 1850 a committee reported to the faculty that "it is fair to have a full understanding prior to commencing as to probable & actual expenses in order that every gentleman may decide whether he will incur expense and how far he can afford to provide with what seems to him more or less of an experiment." It was already obvious that more money than they had initially calculated would be necessary even to renovate the building for their needs. The prospects of a new building meant a radical increase in their anticipated expenditures (GUA, Medical Faculty Minutes, March 18, 1850).

68. GUA, Medical Faculty Minutes, October 25, 1852.

69. GUA, Medical Faculty Minutes, June 11, 1852.

70. National Archives, Thirty-First Congress, First Session, June 1850; discharged February 1851; GUA, Medical Faculty Minutes, October 7, 1850.

71. GUA, Medical Faculty Minutes, September 24, 1850.

72. MPA, 219 T 14, Aloysius Jordan to Samuel Barber, Georgetown, May 13, 1851.

73. GUA, Joshua Ritchie to Daniel Lynch, July 1852; GUA, Faculty Minutes, August 5, 1850; February 25, 1851; March 3, 1851; March 25, 1851.

74. GUA, Ritchie to Lynch, July 1852.

75. GUA, Medical Faculty Minutes, December 12, 1853.

76. Green, *Washington: Village and Capital,* 213.

77. GUA, Catalogue, 1853.

78. Colin Burke points out that there were more physicians in the United States in 1860 than there were lawyers or ministers, indeed more per capita than at any other time in American history (*Collegiate Populations,* 186).

79. Kayser, *A Medical Center,* 50.

80. Information on Georgetown medical students for the first decade, with the exception of the few alumni of the college, is limited to graduates. Medical schools in general graduated only a third or so of their students. The University of Pennsylvania had one of the highest rates of graduation from 1830 to 1859—37 percent. Harvard graduated fewer than a quarter of its medical students. By 1866–75 Georgetown was graduating 61 percent of those who enrolled, close to the national norm for the period (Rothstein, 50, 93).

81. *The National Cyclopedia of American Biography,* 7:46–47.

82. Between 1851 and 1870 only seventeen medical students out of a total of 422 were alumni of Georgetown College.

83. GUA, Catalogue of 1855.

84. William K. Beatty, "Daniel Roberts Brower—Neurologist, Psychiatrist, and Medico-Legal Expert," *Proceedings of the Institute of Medicine in Chicago,* 41 (1988), 96.

85. Daniel Lamb, *Hoya* 7 (1925), 8.

86. GUA, Medical Faculty Minutes, May 23, 1860.

87. Johns, for instance, was so remembered. See Lamb reminiscences.

88. GUA, Medical Faculty Minutes, January 16, 1859. The faculty and student body of National Medical College [Columbian] immediately issued a formal denial that it had anything to do with the deed (GUA, Medical Faculty Minutes, February 7, 1859).

89. GUA, Medical Faculty Minutes, March 7, 1853.

90. GUA, Medical Faculty Minutes, October 17, 1853.

91. GUA, Medical Faculty Minutes, November 13, 1858; ibid., July 9, 1859.

92. GUA, Medical Faculty Minutes, March 23, 1858.

93. Noble Young, *Valedictory Address to the Graduating Class of the Medical Department,* March 12, 1857, 6–7, cited in GUA, Joseph T. Durkin, SJ, "The History of the Medical School of Georgetown University" (unpublished), 6.

94. Thomas Antisell, *Valedictory Address to the Graduating Class of the Medical Department of Georgetown College, Delivered at the Smithsonian Institution, March 10, 1859* (Washington, 1859), 12.

95. GUA, Medical Faculty Minutes, John Morgan Evans to Dean, Handegley, England, June 24, 1859; Medical Faculty Minutes, September 15, 1859.
96. GUA, Early Papers, John C. Goulstone to John Early, Radnorshire, England, April 29, 1860.
97. GUA, Medical Faculty Minutes, February 28, 1861. Subsequently Evans requested that the degree be backdated to 1858, but there is no evidence that the faculty honored this last variation on his attempt to buy a degree (GUA, Medical Faculty Minutes, July 15, 1861).
98. GUA, Medical Faculty Minutes, November 18, 1857.
99. GUA, Medical Faculty Minutes, September 7–11, 1860.
100. GUA, Medical Faculty Minutes, December 8, 1860; December 29, 1861.
101. *History of the Medical Society*, II, 41.
102. ARSI, MD, 8 II 52, Aschwanden to Roothaan, Georgetown, June 2, 1852; "Father Charles Stonestreet," WL, 14 (1885) 400–403.
103. In March 1852, Brocard had cut his finger while exercising. He soon experienced dizziness and a severe fever. The doctors diagnosed erysipelas but it proved to be typhoid fever. He was dead within a week, perhaps the worst loss the province had suffered in its brief history.
104. "Fr. Bernard A. Maguire," WL, 15 (1886), 232.
105. MPA, 219 B 1, Joseph Hegan to Samuel Barber, Georgetown, April 1, [1851?].
106. Maguire, who had a fine singing voice as well, was not above serenading the students on special occasions. James Ryder Randall recalled that he "had one song, only one, a rollicking ditty, commencing *A Frog, He Would A-Wooing Go*. He intoned it with tremendous effect at our banquets, but . . . on one feast day, when importuned to sing, he said: 'I know only one song and you have all heard it too often. I suspect some mischief.' Still he consented to sing it once more" ("Reminiscences of Father Maguire," CJ, 35 [October 1906], 24–26).
107. GUA, Rector's Consultations, [1851].
108. GUA, Rector's Consultations, September 1, 1856.
109. MPA, 216 S 5, Ryder to Brocard, Worcester, April 3, 1848.
110. A decade later an agreement was reached with the Potomac Water Works to provide water for the campus (GUA, Directors' Minutes, September 10, 1850; January 23, 1860).
111. ARSI, MD, 8 III 7, Stonestreet to Beckx, Georgetown, August 9, 1854; GUA, Directors' Minutes, July 8, 1855, 15.

CHAPTER 7

1. Burke, *American Collegiate Populations: A Test of the Traditional View* (New York, 1982), 126. By the 1850s the South was sending twice as many students per thousand white males to colleges as any other region of the country (E. Merton Coulter, *College Life in the Old South* [New York, 1928], 241).
2. Burke points out that average college costs rose from one-third of a skilled manual laborer's income in 1800 to approximately two-thirds in 1860, with the inevitable consequence of growing economic elitism in the colleges (Burke, *American Collegiate Populations*, 50–51).
3. No doubt, the reluctance of the Chesapeake middle class to invest in education reinforced this cost freeze. When Benedict Fenwick was preparing to open a college in New England in the early 1830s, he warned his brother that "my price will be so much cheaper than yours (only $130 pr. an.) that I should not be surprised, if the half of your College should be running to this Yankee land for education. You ought to know by this time what a wonderful liking Marylanders have for things that are both cheap & good" (MPA 210 F 10, Benedict Fenwick to George Fenwick, Boston, August 1, 1833). There was a chronic struggle to collect fees from parents and guardians. By the 1850s college treasurers were employing alumni in Maryland and elsewhere as collectors.

4. ARSI, MD, 7 I 36, Report to Rome, [1840–1841].

5. Leonard D. White, *The Jacksonians: A Study in Administrative History 1829–1861* (New York and London, 1954), 438.

6. Constance McLaughlin Green, *Washington: Village and Capital, 1800–1878* (Princeton, 1962), 198.

7. Green, Washington, 147, 157, 196–98.

8. *Sixth Census of the United States, 1830; Seventh Census of the United States, 1850; Eighth Census of the United States, 1860.*

9. Benedict Joseph Semmes to Jorantha Semmes, Washington, October 9, 1857; same to same, Washington, October 23, 1857, in Anderson Humphreys and Curt Guenther, *Semmes America* (Memphis, Tenn., 1989), 336.

10. These sons of Raphael Semmes were Benedict Joseph (**C** 1835–1840), Thomas Jenkins (**C** 1838–42, A.B.); Alexander Jenkins (**C** 1837–46), Raphael (**C** 1848–51), and Peregrine Warfield (**C** 1851–60, A.B.). The Semmes family traced its roots back six generations to the first doorkeeper of the Maryland assembly. By the late seventeenth century the second generation were major landholders in Charles County and were sending sons and daughters abroad to St. Omers and to French convents. In the second quarter of the nineteenth century there were Semmeses in Maryland, Georgia, and the District of Columbia, and all branches of the family sent sons to the college (Harry Wright Newman, *The Maryland Semmes and other Families*, [Baltimore, 1956], 1).

11. The number of Georgetown students in both the preparatory department and the college increased from 35 in the 1830s to 86 in the 1850s. Significantly, the occupations of only 17 of the 86 student fathers of the students in the latter decade are known, compared to 18 known of the 35 total in the former years. In the 1830s all were merchants, lawyers, doctors, or military officers; in the 1850s, there were an artisan and farmer besides one merchant and fourteen professionals. Nearly a fifth of all students received financial aid in the 1850s, nearly double the figure for the previous decade.

12. Barbara Jeanne Fields, *Slavery and Freedom on the Middle Ground: Maryland during the Nineteenth Century* (New Haven and London, 1985), 6–7.

13. Census of 1830, Charles County, Maryland, Roll 56.

14. Burke, *American Collegiate Populations*, 80.

15. Burke, 80–81.

16. Thomas Jefferson Wertenbaker, *Princeton, 1746–1896* (Princeton, 1946), 265–66.

17. MPA, 225 F 9, H[enry] B. Thompson to Stonestreet, Perote, Pike Co., August 24, 1856.

18. Of the occupations of the 1850–59 Southern fathers (271 known for 1,103 total Southern students), 102 (32.6%) were lawyer/politicians, 66 (31.5%) military, 53 (16.9%) doctors, and 50 planters (16.2%).

19. Census of 1830, Virginia, Fauquier Co., M-19 Roll 194, p. 435; Census of 1840, Virginia, Fauquier Co., M 704 Roll 558, p. 184.

20. Census of 1840, Georgia, Hancock Co., M 704, Roll 43, p. 212.

21. John Rozier, ed., *The Granite Farm Letters: The Civil War Correspondence of Edgeworth & Sallie Bird* (Athens and London, 1988), xxi–xxiv.

22. Joseph Kett, *Rites of Passage: Adolescence in America, 1790 to the Present* (New York, 1977), 43.

23. ARSI, Register of Father General Roothaan's Letters, I, Roothaan to McSherry, April 26, 1834, 99; ARSI, MD, 8 VI 3, *Puncta quaedam, de quibus in Consultae ARPN cum PP Assistentibus et P. Felice Sopranis . . . actum est et stat utum, ut ea introducantur in Ordinatione toti Americae Septentrionali communi* [1860].

24. David F. Allmendinger, Jr., *Paupers and Scholars: The Transformation of Student Life in Nineteenth Century New England* (New York, 1975), chapter 7.

25. Allmendinger, *Paupers and Scholars*, 97–105.

26. Isidorio Errázuriz, *Diario de don Isidorio Errázuriz. 1851–1856* (Santiago, 1947), September 18, 1851, 1–2.

27. Robin Ruff [James Doonan, SJ], "College Days Fifty Years Ago," CJ, 35 (October 1906), 16; Randall, "Letters from Famous Old Boys," CJ, 35 (December 1906), 109.

28. Edward Devitt, "Georgetown College in the Early Days," *Records of the Columbia Historical Society 12* (1909), 34.

29. CJ, 35 (December 1906), 109.

30. GUA, Refectory Diary, 1825; Richard X. Evans, "Alexander Dimitry, Georgetown Student," CJ, 59 (January 1931), 171–72.

31. Ruff, "College Days" CJ, 35 (February 1907), 219.

32. GUA, Rector's Consultations, February 25, 1846.

33. ARSI, MD, 10 I 8, Angelo Paresce to Beckx, Baltimore, December 13, 1864.

34. His mother was Rachel Mordecai. His cousin, Jacob Mordecai, the son of a North Carolina circuit judge, had entered Georgetown a year before Lazarus. Jacob's mother was a gentile and a Christian.

35. GUA, Minister's Diary, November 25, 1831.

36. *Diario,* October 4, 1851, 13–14.

37. *Diario,* October 5, 1851, 14–15.

38. Augustus J. Thébaud, *Forty Years in the United States of America* (1839–1885) (New York, 1904), 359–60.

39. MPA 216 uncoded, W. S. Gibson to Fenwick [n.d.].

40. ARSI, MD, 5 I 16, McSherry to Roothaan, St. Thomas Manor, June 27, 1834.

41. GUA, Fleming Gardner Papers, Fleming Gardner to Charles Miller, Georgetown, April 2, 1836.

42. GUA, Gardner to Miller, August 27, 1836.

43. GUA, Bernard Maguire notes, 9–10.

44. GUA, Reminiscences of Robert Ray.

45. GUA, House Diary, April 7, 1837; CJ, 16 (February 1888), 58.

46. MPA, 205 C 10, Jerome Mudd to Thomas Mulledy and William McSherry, Georgetown, May 2, 1821.

47. Stephen Mallory, "Letters from Famous Old Boys," CJ, 35 (December 1906), 115.

48. John Carroll Brent to Emily C. Brent, October 7, 1830, printed in *Library Associates Newsletter,* November 1994.

49. GUA, Stonestreet Diary, September 25, 1840.

50. GUA, Directors' Minutes, July 11, 1853.

51. GUA, Joseph O'Callaghan Diary, April 1, 1856.

52. SHC, Randall Diary, September 18, 1855; GUA, O'Callaghan Diary, October 9, 1856.

53. GUA, O'Callaghan Diary, November 4, 1856.

54. *Diario,* May 24–25, 1852, 170–74.

55. To reach Louisiana in the 1830s entailed a trip of nearly a month. Henry Strawbridge of Covington, Louisiana, came home through Virginia by rail, then switched to stagecoach on turnpikes that reminded him of rockpiles. On one such trip " . . . we were jolted about and battered to mummies," he reported. Then at Cincinnati he boarded a steamer that ran aground in Mississippi River waters five times before finally reaching New Orleans in early September (GUA, H. H. Strawbridge to "Ritchie," Covington, La., September 6, 1837).

56. MPA, 205 C 10, Mudd to Mulledy and McSherry, Georgetown College, May 2, 1821.

57. Ibid.

58. MPA, 218 R 6, Sanders to Ignatius Brocard, White Marsh, July 18, 1850; MPA, 218 R 15, Edward Thomas McNerhany to Samuel Barber, Georgetown, July 29, 1850.

59. GUA, Directors' Minutes, Vol. II, May 4, 1871.

60. Charles E. Rosenberg, *The Cholera Years: The United States in 1832, 1849, and 1866* (Chicago and London, 1987), 25, 57.

61. ARSI, MD, 4 I 21, Wharton to Kohlmann, Washington, August 25, 1832.

62. MPA, 210 N 2, James Whitfield to John McElroy, Baltimore, September 12, 1832.

63. MPA, 4 S 6, Fidèle de Grivel to Nicholas Sewall, Georgetown, July 9, 1833.

64. GUA, Minister's Diary, September 28, 1832; ibid., October 7, 1832; ARSI, MD, 4 I 25, extract of letter Peter Kenney to William McSherry [Georgetown], September 27, 1832.

65. GUA, Minister's Diary, December 1, 1832.

66. MPA, 217 K 9, Edward Thomas McNerhany to Samuel Barber, Georgetown, September 13, 1849.

67. GUA, Stonestreet Diary, October 2–3, 1843; GUA, Minister's Diary, October 1–3, 1843; *Washington Intelligencer,* October 2, 1843.

68. Grassi, 26–27. An Episcopal priest from New England who resigned as the headmaster of an academy in Raleigh, North Carolina, in 1834, was even more emphatic about the deleterious consequences of slavery for education: "Little or nothing can be done in the most important part of education, the formation of character and the fixing of good moral principles and habits, while such a portion of the community is in so degraded and wretched a condition" (Joseph Green Cogswell to Mrs. Prescott, September 14, 1834, in Anna Ticknor, *Cogswell,* 192–193, as cited in McLachlan, *American Boarding Schools,* 101).

69. "Father James A. Ward: A Sketch," WL, 25 (1896), 420.

70. Bertram Wyatt-Brown, *Southern Honor: Ethics and Behavior in the Old South* (New York, 1982), 118–74.

71. *Diario,* October 15, 1851, 22–23.

72. MPA 213 Uncoded, William Burke to George Fenwick, Red Sulphur, January 8, 1840.

73. Robert V. Remini, *Andrew Jackson and the Course of American Freedom, 1822–1832* (New York, 1981), 3.

74. MPA, 215 C, John Pendleton to Mulledy, Culpeper County, September 22, 1847.

75. W. J. Rorabaugh, *The Alcoholic Republic: An American Tradition* (New York, 1979), 10.

76. GUA, House Diary, June 4, 1827.

77. GUA, House Diary, December 10, 1836.

78. GUA, Rector's Consultations, January 20, 1841.

79. MPA, 213 uncoded, Hugh Caperton to Fenwick, Union, Monroe Cty., August 15, 1840.

80. GUA, Rector's Consultations, May 19, 1845.

81. Although the rule was certainly in force, in practice students were often readmitted for one reason or another. After Aristides L. Aubert, a student from Louisiana, was dismissed in 1852 because a whiskey bottle fell out of his pocket on the campus, President Stonestreet readmitted him when all the members of the upper three classes solemnly promised to abstain from all liquor for a year if Aubert received a second chance (GUA, Rector's Consultations, February 4, 1852).

82. MPA, 213 Uncoded, Ryder to G. Fenwick, Georgetown, September 15, 1841.

83. One student recalled that the only faculty member known to smoke was Father Fenwick, and he in his room (GUSC, Dundas Papers, William Dundas to Joseph Himmel, SJ, April 18, 1909). The Jesuit farms, of course, continued to raise tobacco. In 1860 a Cuban student, apparently by request or as a gift from his family, brought back to school an enormous bag of Cuban tobacco seed; enough, one Jesuit thought, "to put the whole state of Maryland in tobacco!" The seed was sent on to Baltimore to be distributed to the farms in southern Maryland (MPA, 56 M 2, L. Nota to Calvert, Georgetown, December 1, 1860).

84. GUA, Stonestreet Diary.

85. GUA, "Regulations for the Students of Georgetown College."

86. "Ward," 421.

87. GUA, Rector's Consultations, October 17, 1838.

88. GUA, House Diary, November 2–3, 1833; MPA, 211 W 2, James Ward et al. to Samuel Barber, Georgetown College, April 15, 1834.

89. MPA, 211 W 6, Barbelin to Samuel Mulledy and Samuel Barber, Georgetown, January 22, 1834; ARSI, MD, 5 I 10, McSherry to Roothaan, St. Thomas, December 31, 1833; ARSI, MD, 5 I 12, Francis Dzierozynski to Roothaan, Georgetown, February 20, 1834.

90. Jennings L. Wagoner Jr., "Honor and Dishonor at Mr. Jefferson's University: The Antebellum Years," *HEQ* 26 (Summer 1986), 177.

91. At Franklin College [University of Georgia], for instance, a school smaller than Georgetown, 176 students were expelled between 1830 and 1873 for everything from profanity to having firearms in the classroom (Coulter, *College Life,* 115).

92. This draconian enforcement of authority ultimately proved to be Mulledy's undoing as a president. Later, while he was rector of St. John's College in Frederick (1850–1854), Mulledy precipitated a mass walk-out of the older students, most of whom he expelled. St. John's never recovered from Mulledy's purge.

93. ARSI, MD, 5 III 8, Mulledy to Roothaan, Georgetown, August 13, 1835.

94. GUA, Morris to President and Faculty of Georgetown College, June 5, 1850.

95. Kett, *Rites of Passage,* 59.

96. GUA, Lilly Diary 2, January 16, 1850; GUA, House Diary, January 14–16, 1850.

97. GUA, Robert Ray Reminiscences.

98. GUA, House Diary, January 16, 1850.

99. *Republic,* January 21, 1850.

100. GUA, Minister's Diary, January 17–19, 1850; ARSI, MD, 8 II 33, Brocard to Roothaan, Georgetown, December 21, 1850.

101. GUA, Ray Reminiscences.

102. GUA, Lilly Diary 2, January 19–22, 1850; ARSI, MD, 8 II 22, Brocard to Roothaan, Georgetown, January 23, 1850; ARSI, MD, 8 II 24, same to same, April 12, 1850; Durkin, *Middle Years* (Washington, 1963), 30–31; GUA, Maguire notes.

103. MPA, 220 M 16, J. O'Callaghan to George Fenwick, Georgetown, October 31, 1852.

CHAPTER 8

1. GUA, Address of John C. C. Hamilton to Philodemic Society, July 3, 1862.

2. Ibid.

3. In the famous "Yale Report of 1828," the foundation of education was identified as "intellectual culture . . . the discipline and . . . furniture of the mind; expanding its powers, and storing it with knowledge." The Report called for the study of language, philosophy, mathematics, and science, those subjects best suited to cultivate *"all* the important mental faculties. . . ." Barely a nod was given to the imagination (Richard Hofstadter and Wilson Smith, eds. *American Higher Education: A Documentary History,* I [Chicago and London, 1961], 275–291).

4. Robert R. Newton, *Reflections on the Educational Principles of the Spiritual Exercises* (Washington, 1977), 10.

5. In practice the students were assigned to mathematics and French classes according to their level of proficiency in the subjects, regardless of what "class" (Rhetoric, First Humanities, etc.) they were assigned within the course of studies.

6. Mark Jenkins left Georgetown shortly afterwards and later graduated from the University of Virginia (MPA, 206 K 24, Thomas Jenkins to Enoch Fenwick, Baltimore, September 26, 1824).

7. Frederick Rudolph, *Curriculum: A History of the American Undergraduate Course of Study since 1636* (San Francisco, Washington, and London, 1977), 64.

8. GUA, Rector's consultations, March 14, 1859.

9. *Notizie vane sullo stato presente della repubblica degli Stati Uniti dell' America settentrionale scritte al principio del 1818* [Milano, 1819], 29.

10. Donald C. Stewart, "The Nineteenth Century," in Winifred Byran Homer, ed., *The Present State of Scholarship in Historical and Contemporary Rhetoric,* 2nd ed., rev. (Columbia and London, 1990), 154–55.

11. ARSI, MD, 4 III 2, George Fenwick to Roothaan, Georgetown, January 28, 1831.

12. Davies, *Elements of Geometry and Trigonometry* (1834 et sequi); Davies, *Elements of Algebra* (1835 et sequi); Davies, *Elements of Analytical Geometry* (1836); Stanley Guralnick, *Science and the Ante-Bellum American College* (Philadelphia, 1975), 51–59.

13. ARSI, [Samuel Barber], *Litterae Annua Prov. Maryl. SJ a 11a Januarii 1845 ad 1am Jan. 1846.*

14. Southern Historical Collection, Diary of James Ryder Randall, September 15–17, 1855.

15. GUSC, Evans Papers Collection 1, Box 2, Folder 8, Alexander Dimitry to Alfred Lewis, Georgetown College, May 25, 1825.

16. GUA, *Theses from Natural Theology,* LXXXV, 1853–54.

17. GUA, Joseph O'Callaghan SJ, Diary, November 10, 1853.

18. See Herbert Hovenkamp, *Science and Religion in America, 1800–1860* (Philadelphia, 1978), 19–56.

19. ARSI, [Samuel Barber], *Litterae Annua Prov. Maryl. SJ a 11a Januarii 1845 ad 1ay em Jan. 1846.*

20. William C. McFadden, SJ, "'Catechism at 4 for All the Schools': Religious Instruction at Georgetown," in McFadden, ed., *Georgetown at Two Hundred: Faculty Reflections on the University's Future* (Washington, 1990), 144–45.

21. Inevitably they found ways to avoid the drudgery. One non-Catholic during the Civil War took to raising challenges to the doctrine being recited as a way of distracting the teacher from his own lack of preparation. Eventually, the young scholastic caught onto the game and demanded that the challenger recite his lines, which he invariably failed to do, thus landing in detention hall, or "jug," where he seemed to be a permanent resident, accumulating more and more memorized lines of Latin (GUSC, James Longyear Reminiscences).

22. ARSI, MD, 7 III 11, Thomas Meredith Jenkins to Roothaan, Georgetown, December 18, 1841.

23. SHC, Randall Diary, September 18–21, 1855.

24. MPA, 216 uncoded, J. Doyle, J. R. Pearson, H. H. Strawbridge to Thomas Mulledy, n.d.

25. The text used was Mrs. Lincoln's Botany (Guralnick, 110–18).

26. GUA, House Diary, July 23, 1844.

27. GUA, House Diary, November 26, 1844.

28. GUA, House Diary, May 28, 1844.

29. "Georgetown College," *Catholic Almanac* (1833), 62–63.

30. GUSC, Aylmer Papers, Henry Aylmer to Robert Aylmer, Petersburg, March 6, 1837.

31. GUA, Minister's Diary, March 16, 1829.

32. GUA, G. T. Beauregard to Early, New Orleans, November 22, 1859.

33. ARSI, MD, 8 VI, Ordinations of Felix Sopranis, 1860.

34. Once enrollments began to rise again at Loyola, the commercial course was quietly dropped (Nicholas Varga, *Baltimore's Loyola, Loyola's Baltimore, 1851–1986* [Baltimore, 1990], 65; David H. Burton and Frank Gerrity, *St. Joseph's College: A Family Portrait, 1851–1976* [Philadelphia, 1977], 8–9).

35. Walter J. Meagher, SJ, and William J. Grattan, *The Spires of Fenwick: A History of the College of the Holy Cross, 1843–1963* (New York, 1966), 58–60.

36. General Joseph Hernandez of St. Augustine (Florida) asked that one of the two sons he was sending to the college be given an education that would fit him for "mercantile pursuits." Both boys, whom Hernandez admitted were "rather deficient," were placed in the lowest class of Rudiments and stayed only a year (MPA, 212 misc., Joseph Hernandez to William McSherry, St. Augustine, December 15, 1839).

37. This section draws extensively from [George Barringer], "The Georgetown University Library: A Historical Sketch," unpublished paper in GUSC.

38. Lawrence Carleton Chamberlain, "Georgetown University Library: 1789–1937," M.S. thesis (Catholic University of America, 1962), 42.

39. GUA, House Diary, June 4, 1843.

40. GUSC, George Barringer, "History of the Library," 63. In 1848 the heirs of Thomas C. Levins in a legal transaction gave the college his collections, estimated at $4,000, in return for scholarships for persons nominated "from time to time" by Levins's two brothers or their heirs "so long as the . . . College shall continue." One nephew attended Georgetown for three years shortly thereafter. Forty years later, Peter Levins, Thomas's surviving brother, requested that his son be given the scholarship. However, for some years in the early twentieth century it was not given because the agreement could not be found. Finally, in the 1920s it was located and subsequently

other Levins heirs received the scholarship. As late as 1952 Georgetown granted the scholarship to Peter Thomas Levins, Jr., although by that time the treasurer was under the mistaken impression that the original gift had been "a collection of minerals which . . . have long since disappeared" and thought a work-study scholarship appropriate, a suggestion that Georgetown's president mistakenly agreed to make a condition of the 1952 award (GUA, 439–7, Box 30, Folder 542). In fact, the "disappeared" mineral collection had been included in an 1847 sale of precious stones for which the college received $4,000 (GUA, Rector's Consultations, October 7, 1846; January 24, 1847).

41. Kenneth J. Brough, *Scholar's Workshop: Evolving Conceptions of Library Service* (Urbana, 1953), 14–15, cited in Arthur T. Hamlin, *The University Library in the United States: Its Origins and Development* (Philadelphia, 1981), 230.

42. Brough, *Scholar's Workshop,* 12, cited in Hamlin, *The University Library,* 43–44.

43. In 1847 Joseph M. Finotti, one of the Italian scholastics brought to Georgetown by Ryder, tabulated part of the holdings of the library, counting some 13,437 volumes (GUA, 444.3 "Manual to the Library of Georgetown College, March 30, 1847").

44. ARSI, MD, 9 XIV 18, Stonestreet to Roothaan, Georgetown, August 28, 1852.

45. GUA, Longyear reminiscences.

46. *Diario de don Isidorio Errázuriz. 1851–1856* (Santiago, 1947), November 18, 1851.

47. GUA, Prefect's Report, Ash Wednesday 1842.

48. GUA, Prefect's Report, Ash Wednesday, 1843.

49. GUA, Prefect of Schools, Middle Examination Report, February 1858.

50. Some other theses: "Human authority in matters of fact, even when not full and complete, is to be considered as a safe rule, which we may follow in judging and acting"; "Since good consists in some perfection; evil, which is the absence of good, is properly termed the privation of some perfection due to the subject"; " . . . the soul is not matter, nor a modification, nor a quality of matter, but a substance entirely simple" (MPA, 56 K 17–22, *Theses from Rational Philosophy,* 1853–54).

51. Diario, June 28, 1852, 200; July 12, 1852, 210.

52. SHC, Randall Diary, September 23, 1855.

53. GUA, "History of the Philodemic Society, Georgetown College, First Year 1830–1831"; Eric M. George, "The Cultivation of Eloquence at Georgetown College: A History of the Philodemic Society from 1830–1890," in Joseph Durkin, SJ, ed., *Swift Potomac's Lovely Daughter: Two Centuries at Georgetown through Students' Eyes* (Washington, 1990), 103–4.

54. GUA, House Diary, February 22, 1831.

55. GUA, Philodemic Society Papers, Box 1, Folder 6, "Constitution of the Philodemic Society of Georgetown College."

56. Shea, *History of Georgetown College,* 92.

57. When James Randall was urged to join as a Philosopher, his initial response was to found a countersociety, the "Philomessheim, . . . having for its object the procuration and consumption of edibles." But he accepted membership, all the same (SHC, Randall Diary, September 23, 1855).

58. MPA, 213 uncoded, John M. Hearde, John L. Kirkpatrick, and John C. Thompson to Samuel Barber.

59. GUA, Philodemic Society Papers, Box 1, Folder 5.

60. GUA, Philodemic Society Papers, Box 2, Folder 5, Minutes of meeting on June 28, 1848.

61. Thomas S. Harding, *College Literary Societies: Their Contribution to Higher Education in the United States, 1815–1876* (New York, 1971), 179–95. Harding notes a critical shift, in line with public opinion, toward pro-slavery advocacy after 1840. Georgetown seems to have lagged behind this trend.

62. GUA, Bird Papers, Edgeworth Bird to Frances Casey Bird, Georgetown College, March 21, 1844; ibid., Frances Bird to Edgeworth Bird, Sparta, April 2, 1844.

63. GUA, Philodemic Society Papers, Box 4, Folder 5, Minutes of Meeting on May 17, 1857.

64. GUA, Rector's Consultations, October 28, 1859.
65. GUA, Robert Aylmer to parents, George Town College, November 4, 1836.
66. E. Merton Coulter, *College Life in the Old South* (New York, 1928), 60–61.
67. John Lombard and Justin Davis, "The Georgetown College Cadets," in Durkin, *Swift Potomac's Lovely Daughter,* 249–59.
68. Clement S. Lancaster, SJ, CJ 35 (1907), 340.
69. William H. McCabe, *An Introduction to Jesuit Theatre: A Posthumous Work,* Louis J. Oldani, SJ, ed. (St. Louis, 1983), 11–60.
70. GUA, Diary of Thomas Lilly, April 1, 1850.
71. Like the Philodemic, the Association elected its members as well as its president (Thomas Steinthal and Daniel Hood, "Dramatics at Georgetown: The Mask and Bauble Society," in Durkin, *Swift Potomac's Lovely Daughter,* 160).
72. GUA, O'Callaghan Diary, April 2, 1857.
73. MPA, 215 W 4, William Clarke to Samuel Barber, Georgetown College, June 18, 1845.
74. GUA, Fleming Gardner to Charles Miller, Christiansburg, August 27, 1836.
75. CJ, 1 (November 1873).
76. William Faux, "Memorable Days in America, 1819–1820," cited in CJ, 59 (April 1931).
77. GUA, Minister's Diary, July 26, 1832.
78. Two died in college.
79. Ronald Story, *The Forging of an Aristocracy: Harvard and the Boston Upper Class* (Middletown, Conn., 1980), 95; Colin Burke, *American Collegiate Populations: A Test of the Traditional View, 1800–1870* (New York, 1982), 184–85.
80. This is 18.7% of all the 2,701 students who entered the college between 1830 and 1860.
81. Burke, *Collegiate Populations,* 187.
82. Bertram Wallace Korn, "Jews and Negro Slavery in the Old South, 1789–1865," in Leonard Dinnerstein and Mary Dale Palsson, eds., *Jews in the South* (Baton Rouge, La., 1973), 130–31.
83. Burke, *Collegiate Populations,* 188.
84. Burke, *Collegiate Populations,* 185–86.
85. Burke, *Collegiate Populations,* 141.

CHAPTER 9

1. J. Fairfax McLaughlin, *College Days,* 97–98; GUA, Philodemic Society Papers, Box 4, Folder 6, Minutes, December 11–18, 1859.
2. Nicholas Varga, *Baltimore's Loyola, Loyola's Baltimore, 1851–1986* (Baltimore, 1990), 14–16; McLaughlin, *College Days,* 186.
3. GUA, Philodemic Papers, Box 4, Folder 7.
4. GUSC, Evans Papers Collection I, Box 2, Folder 11, Alexander Dimitry to Mary Powell Dimitry, Leon, January 26, 1861.
5. Benson J. Lossing, *Pictorial History of the Civil War* (Hartford, Conn., and Philadelphia, n.d.), I, 313, cited in David T. Maul, "A Man and His Book," *The Register of the Kentucky Historical Society* 65 (July 1967), 233.
6. C. Vann Woodward and Elisabeth Muhlenfeld, eds., *The Private Mary Chestnut: The Unpublished Civil War Diaries* (New York and Oxford, 1984), 56.
7. ARSI, MD, 8 IV 24, Villiger to Beckx, Baltimore, December 13, 1860.
8. ARSI, MD, 8 IV 26, Villiger to Beckx, Baltimore, February 27, 1861.
9. GUA, Minister's Diary, January 4, 1861.
10. GUA, John Shelton to Early, Raymond, Miss., January 3, 1861.
11. GUA, Rector's Consultations, February 18, 1861.
12. GUA, Gabriel A. Fournet et al. to Early, April 10, 1861.
13. GUA, Early Papers, Col. William Byran to Early, Cleveland, April 21, 1861.
14. GUA, Early Papers, E. A. Porter to Early, Richmond, May 6, 1861.

15. Verses 1 and 9. Randall wrote two other songs for the Confederacy: "There's Life in the Old Land Yet" and "The Battle Cry of the South."

16. Library of Congress website, "I Hear America Singing."

17. It has been estimated that about three-quarters (between 70% and 80%) of all Southern white men of military age served in the Civil War (McPherson, *Battle Cry of Freedom*, 615, n. 46).

18. Negro slavery, he had written, was only one aspect of "the manifold cruelties that labor elsewhere suffers at the hands of capital . . ." (Bertram Korn, "Jews and Negro Slavery in the Old South, 1789–1865," in Leonard Dinnerstein and Mary Dale Palsson, eds., *Jews in the South* [Baton Rouge, 1973], 130).

19. National Archives, Record Group No. 109, John Prevust Marshall to Hon. G. W. Randolph, Camp Winder, April 17, 1862.

20. Only a few families connected with Georgetown were divided by the war. Edmund P. Hickey (**C** 1855–58) of Washington, the son of General William Hickey, secretary of the United States Senate, joined the First Maryland Cavalry of the Confederacy. Lawrence Abert Williams (**C** 1844–47), the son of a U.S. Army officer, was assistant adjutant general to the Union's General George B. McClellan; his brother, Orton, joined the Confederacy and was hanged as a spy in Tennessee. The Sheckell brothers, Abraham and Marinus (**C** 1848–52), of the District, fought for the Blue and Gray, respectively. Charles Throckmorton (**C** 1855–57) of Virginia was commissioned a first lieutenant in the Fourth United States Artillery; his father volunteered as a private in the Sixth Virginia Cavalry. At First Manassas the son found his battery engaging his father's regiment. Both survived that battle, but afterwards Charles secured a transfer to the western theatre of operations.

21. In all, ninety-one Georgetown medical alumni participated in the war, seventy-seven of them (85.5%) in the service of the Union. But nearly half the medical alumni to serve in the war entered as students *after* Appomattox.

22. ARSI, MD, 9 XIV 21, Early to Peter Beckx, Georgetown, May 12, 1861.

23. "I have rigidly enjoined all superiors," he added, "that they diligently read all letters of Ours; and mail none in which even the least allusion is made to political affairs" (ARSI, MD, 8 V 7, Paresce to Beckx, Baltimore, November 26, 1861).

24. Diary of Martin Whelan, SJ, cited in James S. Ruby, ed., *Blue and Gray: Georgetown University and the Civil War* (Washington, 1961), 6–7.

25. CJ, 7 (December 1878), "A Remembrance of the War," [George Gibson Huntt], 20–21; when the fourteen-year-old John Longyear entered Georgetown in January 1864, he found the college still a Confederate stronghold within the nation's capital. Most of his classmates in the preparatory department were from below the Mason-Dixon line. Several students from Louisiana had not heard from their families for three years. Those from the Deep South, Longyear recalled vividly in later years, were especially "of the fire-eating Secession type, and were fierce in their denunciation of the Yankees." Longyear, the son of a Michigan congressman, made no attempt to disguise his feelings about the Confederacy and its leaders, and quickly caught the attention of the Southerners and their sympathizers. In the fall of 1864 the younger boys conducted a mock presidential election in their play yard; unsurprisingly Jefferson Davis overwhelmingly defeated Abraham Lincoln. But victory was not enough for the fire-eaters. Someone shouted: "Let's ride some damn Yankee on a rail." "Skinny," someone else suggested, pointing toward the five-foot ten-inch, ninety-eight-pound Longyear. A mob instantly had him on their shoulders, but some prefects, overhearing the tumult, rescued him from his Confederate captors (GUA, Longyear Reminiscences).

26. GUA, Early Papers, Box 1, Folder 1.

27. GUSC, Sumner Papers, B[ernard] C. McMahon to Sumner, Georgetown College, May 10, 1861.

28. GUA, Philodemic Society Papers.

29. GUA, House Diary, 1861. One relative of a recent graduate of the college, an Alabama woman, wrote a friend: "Since the commencement of our national

troubles, few things have occured to grieve me so much as the melancholy fact of that venerable and hitherto venerated Sanctuary of learning and religon, George-town College, being used as Barracks for old Abe's cutthroats. Oh! how the mighty has fallen, and the holy places been profaned by those modern barbarians" (Archives of the Sisters of Charity, Nazareth, Ky., Ann Martin Baxter to a Sister of Charity, Tuscumbia, June 17, 1861). Courtesy of Brother Jordan Baxter, ST, of Trinity Missions, Silver Spring, Md. The relative was James Owen Martin (**C** 1856–59) of New Orleans.

30. Christopher Charles Callan to wife, July 14, 1861, cited in James S. Ruby, "Callans Forever: The Texas Ranger, the FBI and Georgetown," *Georgetown University Alumni Magazine* (May 1956), 6.

31. Louis Otto Hem, *Memories of Long Ago* (New York and London, 1925), 27.

32. McLaughlin, *College Days,* 187.

33. Hem, 28.

34. William C. Davis, *Battle at Bull Run: A History of the First Major Campaign of the Civil War* (New York, 1977), 218–19.

35. GUA, Early Papers, Box 1, Folder 1, Garesché to Early, July 22, 1861.

36. GUA, Minister's Diary, 550–11, July 22, 1861.

37. "Father Joseph B. O'Hagan," WL, 8 (1879), 178–79; ARSI, *Litterae Annual. Prov. Maryland VI* (1860–62), 21–29.

38. At the Episcopal College of St. James in Hagerstown, with three-quarters of its students from the South and, like Georgetown, exclusively dependent on tuition for revenue, enrollment dropped below fifty by 1862. The school finally closed its doors in 1864, after its buildings were occupied and its faculty arrested during Jubal Early's summer raid (Richard R. Duncan, "The Impact of the Civil War on Education in Maryland," *MHM* [March 1966], 37–52; Duncan, "The College of St. James and the Civil War: A Casualty of War," *Historical Magazine of the Protestant Episcopal Church* 39 [September 1970], 286).

39. Even if the country survived the war, McElroy observed, there were now four other Jesuit colleges in the South and six in the North. Nevertheless, as a central location for a Jesuit house of higher studies, Georgetown was still ideal (MPA, 226 G 6, McElroy to Angelo Paresce, Boston, February 6, 1862).

40. MPA, 226 E 3, James Clark to Paresce, Worcester, September 4, 1862.

41. Mary Mitchell, *Divided Town* (Barre, Massachusetts, 1868), 89.

42. GUA, Soper to Coleman Nevils, Glendale, Calif., January 18, 1929.

43. GUA, Rector's Consultations, May 1, 1862.

44. GUA, *Address to the Philodemic Society* (Washington, 1862), 13–14.

45. James McPherson, *Battle Cry of Freedom: The Civil War Era* (New York, 1988), 414.

46. GUA, E[dward] S. Reily to Mary Reily et al., Georgetown, April 6, 1862.

47. "O'Hagan," 179–80.

48. Edgeworth Bird to Sallie Bird, his wife, and Sallie (Saida), his daughter, Richmond, July 29, 1862, in John Rozier, ed., *The Granite Farm Letters: The Civil War Correspondence of Edgeworth & Sallie Bird* (Athens and London, Georgia, 1988), 94.

49. Joseph T. Durkin, SJ, ed., *John Dooley, Confederate Soldier: His War Journal* (Notre Dame, Ind., 1963), 21–23.

50. *History of the Medical Society of the District of Columbia, 1817–1909* (Washington, D.C., 1909), 233–34.

51. Margaret Leech, *Reveille in Washington, 1860–1865* (New York, 1941), 239–41.

52. *Dooley,* 30, 38–39.

53. "I felt a little hurt," Dooley admitted, "but endeavoured to shew myself as cordial towards him as he seemed to feel towards me . . . He wanted to do so many things for me, and even tried to induce me to accept some of his clothing. Good-hearted Jack!" (Dooley, 26–29). Davis subsequently joined the Third Maryland Cavalry of the U.S. Army before receiving an appointment to the United States Military Academy at West Point in the fall of 1863.

54. Dooley, 47.

55. He wrote to ask his mother to let him know when he would turn nineteen (Alexander Dimitry to Mary Powell Dimitry, September 28, 1862, in CJ, 59 [1930–31], 179).

56. Mary D. Gouverneur to J. F. McLaughlin, Knoxville, Md., November 26, 1889, in McLaughlin, *College Days,* 171–73.

57. O'Hagan to Wiget, near Falmouth, November 30, 1862, in WL, 15 (1886), 111–12.

58. *Dooley, 80.*

59. O'Hagan to Wiget, Falmouth, December 18, 1862, in WL, 15 (1886), 112–13.

60. GUA, Early Papers, Box 1, Folder 1; David Fulghum,"The War That Gave the School Its Colors," *Georgetown Magazine* (May–June *1983*), 4.

61. GUA, Minister's Diary, September 1, 1862.

62. GUA, Minister's Diary, September 14, 1862.

63. Edward I. Devitt, SJ,"Trinity Church, Georgetown: An Historical Discourse," WL, 33 (1904), 321–22.

64. Peter Cozzens, *No Better Place to Die: The Battle of Stones River* (Urbana and Chicago, *1990*), 166.

65. GUA, Minister's Diary, May 10, 1863.

66. Diary, February 19, 1863, in William L. Lucey, SJ, ed., "The Diary of Joseph B. O'Hagan, SJ, Chaplain of the Excelsior Brigade," *Civil War History* 6 (1960), 409.

67. B. J. Semmes to Iorantha Semmes, Fayetteville, May 1863, in *Semmes America,* 345.

68. Dooley, 97.

69. James Dougherty (1852–57; AB), a Harrisburg banker, was taken prisoner by J. E. B. Stuart's cavalry during the invasion but was released when he discovered several of his former classmates among Stuart's troopers (GUSC, Augustine Neale Reminiscences).

70. Edwin B. Coddington, *The Gettysburg Campaign: A Study in Command* (New York, 1968), 263–74.

71. Dooley, 101.

72. Dooley, 103–6.

73. Coddington, 517–18; James Longstreet,"Lee's Right Wing at Gettysburg," *Battles and Leaders of the Civil War,* vol. 3 (New York, 1884), 347.

74. Gerald F. Linderman, *Embattled Courage: The Experience of Combat in the American Civil War* (New York and London, 1987), 160–61.

75. Bird to Sallie Bird, July 7, 1863, in *Granite Farm Letters,* 114–19.

76. Edgeworth Bird to Sallie Bird, Williamsport, Md., July 12, 1863; same to same, near Bunker Hill, Va., July 19, 1863, in *Granite Farm Letters,* 123, 125.

77. GUSC, John Barrister, SJ, to John Cattani, SJ, Alexandria, July 17, 1863.

78. Elmer Louis Kayser, *A Medical Center: The Institutional Development of Medical Education in George Washington University* (Washington, D.C., 1973), 68–69.

79. GUA, Minutes of the Medical Department, February 2, 1863.

80. This two-session schedule survived for several years after the war (GUA, Medical Department, Minutes, February 10, 1864; February 25, 1864; GUA, Daniel S. Lamb, "'Reminiscences of the Old Medical School," *Hoya* 7 [1925], 8).

81. GUA, Medical Department, Minutes, September 6, 1864. The Sisters of Mercy had opened Providence Hospital in June 1861 for the medical care of the poor. Several Georgetown Medical Department faculty members, including Noble Young and Johnson Eliot, had been instrumental in procuring a $6,000 grant from the Congress to fund it (John Clagett Proctor, "Hospital Progress," [Washington] *Sunday Star,* September 29, 1946).

82. William A. Tidwell et al., *Come Retribution: The Confederate Secret Service and the Assassination of Lincoln* (Jackson, Miss. and London, 1988), 242–47.

83. GUSC, Reminiscences of John M. Longyear.

84. "I believe myself," he added, "that when Lincoln issued his Proclamation calling on the negroes to rise upon their masters, if we had then declared that we would neither give nor take quarter, that the enemy never could have raised such large armies to invade the South" (B. J. Semmes to his sons, Dalton, Georgia, March 8, 1864, in *Semmes America,* 350).

85. Bird to Sallie Bird, near Richmond, June 1, 1864, in *Granite Farm Letters,* 169–70.
86. W. W. Goldsborough, *The Maryland Line in the Confederate Army, 1861–1865* (Baltimore, 1900), 268–71; Augustine Neale, "Georgetown Men in the Confederate Army," CJ, 29 (March 1901), 253.
87. GUSC, Longyear Reminiscences.
88. ARSI, MD, 10 XXIII 1, Wiget to Beckx, Washington, July 22, 1864.
89. Atlanta, August 21, 1864, in *Semmes America,* 355.
90. B. J. Semmes to Iorantha Semmes, Barnesville, September 4, 1864, in *Semmes America,* 356.
91. Edgeworth Bird to Sallie Bird, near Richmond, August 4, 1864, in *Granite Farm Letters,* 179.
92. Edgeworth Bird to Wilson Bird, Richmond, November 26, 1864, in *Granite Farm Letters,* 212.
93. B. J. Semmes to Iorantha Semmes, Barnesville, September 4, 1864; September 7, 1864, in *Semmes America,* 356–57.
94. B. J. Semmes to Iorantha Semmes, near Aberdeen, January 12, 1865, in *Semmes America,* 360–61.
95. Edgeworth Bird to Sallie Bird, Petersburg, July 17, 1864, in *Granite Farm Letters,* 176.
96. John J. Ryan, "Our Scholasticate—An Account of Its Growth and History to the Opening of Woodstock, 1805–1869," WL, 33 (1904), 150.
97. Edgeworth Bird to Sallie Bird, Richmond, January 7, 1865, in *Granite Farm Letters,* 231.
98. ARSI, MD, Paresce to Beckx, Baltimore, February 23, 1865.
99. GUA, Minister's Diary, February 22, 1865.
100. CJ, 32 (July 1904), 486.
101. In late February, Confederate officials had indeed begun to shift stores to this region (the Virginia Piedmont), and Lee was making preparations to shift his forces west before Grant could attack. Rumors abounded to this effect in Richmond (*Come Retribution,* 369–74).
102. Dooley, 181.
103. Dooley, 187–200.
104. GUSC, Longyear Reminiscences.
105. Ward, *Chicago Tribune,* April 14, 1932.
106. GUA, Minister's Diary, April 15–16, 1865.
107. "Rev. John B. Guida," WL, 49 (1920), 124.
108. Tidwell, *Come Retribution,* 334–38.
109. Both served only three years of their sentences. In 1867, there was an outbreak of yellow fever at Fort Jefferson in Florida, where they were both imprisoned. The medical officer at the fort, a Georgetown medical graduate (Joseph S. Smith [**M** 1855–57; MD]), died during the epidemic and Mudd heroically replaced him. For his efforts he was pardoned by President Andrew Johnson.
110. Queen (**C** 1800–06) had been one of the first to join the restored Society of Jesus in 1806, but he had to leave to support his mother in 1810.
111. In *Come Retribution* the authors make a provocative case that the conspiracy to kidnap Lincoln, if not to assassinate him, was not "one mad act" of an individual, but a well-organized plan that originated with the officials of the Confederate government, partially in retaliation for Dahlgren's raid. In this planning, many Confederate agents and sympathizers seem to have been involved, including Thomas H. Harbin, the father of George F. Harbin (**C** 1890–02, A.B.). Mudd had introduced Harbin to Booth, who sought his assistance in the capture of Lincoln. Harbin agreed, presumably with the approval of his superiors in Richmond, and provided both contacts and material help in forwarding Booth's plans. When Booth and Herold arrived in Virginia, Harbin furnished horses and food. He shortly thereafter left for Cuba (*Come Retribution,* 337–42).
112. Thomas Reed Turner in his study of the popular reaction to the assassination points out how many Protestant clergy in Washington and elsewhere stoked the fires of revenge, but they confined their targets to Confederate leaders and their

sympathizers (Turner, *Beware the People Weeping: Public Opinion and the Assassination of Abraham Lincoln* [Baton Rouge, 1982], 25–52; 77–89).

113. Ruby, ed., *Blue and Gray.*

114. "Letters from Famous Old Boys," CJ, 35 (December 1906), 114.

CHAPTER 10

1. Constance McLaughlin Green, *Washington: Village and Capital, 1800–1878* (Princeton, 1962), 303.

2. MPA, 56 M 12, E. J. Young, SJ, to C. C. Lancaster, Georgetown, January 22, 1866 [1867].

3. "Universal Suffrage," CJ, 3 (May 1875), 76.

4. "Retrocession," CJ, 3 (March 1875), 54.

5. "Thrift," CJ, 2 (October 1874), 114.

6. GUA, Dooley Papers, "Lines Addressed to the Bronze Statue of the Goddess of Liberty Which Crowns the Capitol's Dome, Washington, D.C.," October 1, 1870.

7. GUA, Francis Barnum, SJ, Collection of Chronological Notes for a History of Georgetown College, Box 1, 43.

8. Mary Mitchell, *Chronicles of Georgetown Life, 1865–1900* (Washington, 1986), 47.

9. GUA, John Early Diary, July 25, 1871.

10. GUA, Directors' Minutes, May 16, 1866.

11. Green, 288, 340–58.

12. GUA, Rector's Consultations, November 7, 1872. The college had already been remunerated $800 for repairs that had been necessitated by the federal occupation of the buildings (GUA, Directors' Minutes, December 22, 1863).

13. GUA, Rector's Consultations, April 5, 1873; NARA, Quartermaster General's Office, Claims Branch, 1861–1889, Document File, Quartermaster Stores (Act of July 4, 1864), Rent Services and Miscellaneous Claims, Book F 1873 1182–1246, Box No. 86, 4136 of 1873, Cl. F 1208/1873.

14. GUA, Early Diary, February 15, 1871; GUA, Rector's Consultations, November 7, 1872.

15. GUA, Early Diary, June 18–21, 1872; GUA, James Curley Diary, July 5, 1872.

16. GUA, Minister's Diary, February 11, 1866; GUA, Curley Diary, March 15, 1869; GUA, Early Diary, December 11, 1871; GUA, House Diary, October 22, 1872.

17. "Election Day," CJ, 1 (December 1872), 6.

18. "Inauguration of President Grant," CJ, 1 (April 1873), 43.

19. GUA, House Diary, September 17, 1874; January 8, 1875; March 22, 1875; March 6, 1876; March 30, 1876.

20. GUA, House Diary, November 7, 1876; CJ, 6 (December 1876), 26.

21. GUA, House Diary, November 24, 1876.

22. GUA, House Diary, March 5, 1877.

23. ARSI, MD, 10 I 36, *Navigatio Funestra Patrum Procuratorum qui ex America Romam venerant, anno 1866;* GUA, Curley Diary, February 11–19, 1869.

24. Albert Foley, SJ, *Dream of an Outcaste* (Tuscaloosa, 1976), 1–43.

25. MPA, 218 N 3, Early to Ignatius Brocard, College of the Holy Cross, September 9, 1850.

26. *Archivum Provinciae Belgicae Septemtrionalis Soc. Jesu,* Inv. B 23/15: *Liber continens Theses ex Universa Philosophia et Theologia, Pro Examine ad Gradum Prov. Belg.*

27. "Letters from Famous Old Boys," CJ, 35 (December 1906), 117.

28. GUA, John Early Diary, May 1, 1872.

29. ARSI, MD, 10 II 4, Keller to Beckx, Baltimore, September 21, 1869.

30. GUA, Prefect's Report, 1870.

31. MPARP, *Acta Consultationum Prov. Maryl.,* January 8, 1845 [to] December 17, 1883 (hereafter Province Consultors' Minutes), September 9, 1845.

32. ARSI, MD, 8 111 15, Stonestreet to Beckx, December 5, 1855.

33. ARSI, MD, 8 IV 5, Villiger to Beckx, Frederick, February 2, 1859.

34. MPARP, Province Consultors' Minutes, January 24, 1861.

35. The expenses for the year 1861 were $17,440.02. That same year the farms produced only $14,961 (ARSI, MD, 8 V 9, Paresce to Beckx [1862]). By 1862 the Boston operation represented over half the expenses of the province (ARSI, MD, 8 V 14, Paresce to Beckx, Baltimore, February 16, 1863).

36. MPARP, Province Consultors' Minutes, December 12, 1861.

37. ARSI, MD 10 I 3, Paresce to Beckx, Georgetown, April 19, 1864; Patrick J. Dooley, "Woodstock and Its Makers," WL, 56 (1927), 5.

38. GUA, Maguire Notes.

39. Whereas, for instance, military officers had accounted for a little more than two-fifths (41%) of the fathers with known occupations of day students who had entered during the war years, they made up only a little more than a fifth (22%) of those whose sons entered during the five years following the war.

40. GUA, House Diary, October 13, 1869.

41. GUA, Rector's Consultations, October 25, 1870.

42. GUA, Maguire notes.

43. GUA, Payne, *Some Reminiscences in My Life for My Children and Grandchildren* [nd.], 6–7.

44. GUA, James H. French to [Bernard Maguire], Pearisburg, Giles County, Va., November 26, 1867.

45. GUA, Payne, *Reminiscences,* 9.

46. GUA, Payne, *Reminiscences,* 9.

47. ARSI, MD, 10 XXII 1, McAtee to Beckx, St. Thomas Manor, January 25, 1871.

48. GUA, B[arton] B[ennett] Simmes to Maguire, Whitehall, [La.], June 8, 1867.

49. GUA, Minister's Diary, May 27, 1869; GUA, Barnum, Notes, 39.

50. See R. Emmett Curran, ed., *American Jesuit Spirituality: The Maryland Tradition, 1634–1900* (New York and Mahwah, N.J., 1988), 34–37.

51. Southern Maryland Room, Charles County Community College, LaPlata, Md., Hamilton Family Papers, George Hamilton to John Hamilton, Georgetown, November 10, 1870.

52. GUA, John Early Diary, November 24, 1870.

53. GUA, Address of professors and students to "Our Holy Father Pius IX," June 16, 1871.

54. ARSI, MD, 10 II 17, Keller to Beckx, Baltimore, May 21, 1871.

55. GUA, John Sumner to Silas M. Chatard, Georgetown, July 2, 1871 (copy).

56. "Georgetown College and the Pilgrimage," CJ, 2 (June 1874), 74.

57. GUSC, Ives Papers, Box 1, Folder 4, Cora Semmes Ives to Patrick Healy, Feldkirch, Austria, July 23, 1874.

58. CJ, 2 (October 1874), 109–10.

59. GUA, House Diary, May 8, 1873.

60. Thomas Steinthal and Daniel Hood, "Dramatics at Georgetown: The Mask and Bauble Society," in Durkin, *Swift Potomac's Lovely Daughter,* 162.

61. GUA, Barnum Notes, 37.

62. Gerald F. Linderman, *Embattled Courage: The Experience of Combat in the American Civil War* (London and New York, 1987), 271–72.

63. GUA, Rector's Consultations, March 8 and May 4, 1871.

64. GUA, Rector's Consultations, Minutes, January 12, 1872; GUA, Early Diary, January 12, 1872; CJ, 1 (February 1873), 22.

65. CJ, 1 (December 1872), 6; Christopher Donesa, "History of the Georgetown College Journal," in Durkin, *Swift Potomac's Lovely Daughter,* 3–17.

66. "Our History," CJ, 1 (February 1873), 22.

67. GUA, Minister's Diary, April 15, 1869.

68. GUA, Barnum Notes, 28.

69. Harold Seymour, *Baseball: The Early Years* (New York, 1960), 40–41.

70. Ronald A. Smith, *Sports and Freedom: The Rise of Big-Time College Athletics* (New York and Oxford, 1988), 56–58.

71. GUA, Barnum Notes.

72. GUA, House Diary, October 14, 1869.

73. GUA, House Diary, September 30, 1872.

74. GUA, Curley Diary, May 6, 1870.

75. Payne, "Letters from Famous Old Boys," CJ, 35 (December 1906), 120.

76. "Baseball," CJ, 1 (December 1872), 3.

77. GUA, John Early Diary, June 11–24, 1872.

78. GUA, Directors' Minutes, December 22, 1863, [m.d.] April 1865; September 5, 1865; October 3, 1865; June 4, 1866; June 16, 1866; September 24, 1867.

79. In 1867 Mary Browne left her entire estate to Georgetown College. When her brother contested the will, a settlement was reached in which the college received $15,000 (MPA 103.5 S 1 fols.); also in 1867 Elizabeth H. Hughes left her estate in Charles County to the college, which it sold for $5,600 (MPA, 107 K 2). The most controversial gift was that of an alumnus, Raphael Boarman, who in his will in 1859 bequeathed $18,672 to the college. That represented the total amounts he had previously loaned to Gonzaga and Loyola colleges. When he died in 1861, the officials at the two latter places claimed that the gift was meant as a cancellation of the loans already made and not an "instruction" to Gonzaga and Loyola to pay back their loans to Georgetown, and that Boarman had simply equated Georgetown with the regional Jesuits in general. The superior general, to whom the matter was finally appealed, ruled in 1865 that the money should be split among the three colleges and Boarman's heirs. Georgetown received $4,474 from the Loyola and Gonzaga communities (ARSI, MD, 9 XIV 20, Will of Rapl. H. Boarman, August 24, 1859 [copy]; MPA, 95 B 2, Statement of Thomas Carbery, Executor of R. H. Boarman, November 1, 1862; ARSI, MD, 10 XV 1, Paresce to Beckx, Baltimore, April 11, 1864; ARSI, MD, 10 I 3, Paresce to Beckx, Georgetown, April 19, 1864; ARSI MD, 10 XV 3, Stonestreet to Beckx, Georgetown, August 8, 1864; ARSI, MD, 10 I 7, Paresce to Beckx, Baltimore, September 23, 1864; ARSI, MD, 10 I 8, Paresce to Beckx, Baltimore, December 13, 1864; ARSI, MD, 10 XV 6, Paresce to Beckx, Baltimore, December 29, 1865; ARSI, MD, 10 XV 7, Wiget to Beckx, Washington, January 2, 1866).

80. ARSI, MD, 8 IV 2, Villiger to Beckx, Georgetown, December 1, 1858; ARSI, MD, 8 IV 6, Villiger to Beckx, Georgetown, March 1, 1859.

81. ARSI, MD, 10 XV 8, Paresce to Beckx, Baltimore, February 19, 1867.

82. Robert Stevens, *Law School: Legal Education in America from the 1850s to the 1980s* (Chapel Hill and London, 1983), 3–8, 24.

83. Stevens, 23.

84. Stevens, 24.

85. GUA, 379–1, Law 1870–1899, William Merrick to Early, Washington, June 9, 1859.

86. GUA, House Diary, September 15, 1869.

87. GUA, Martin F. Morris, "Address to the Students," [n.d.] October 1891, cited in "A Partial History of G.U. Law Center," 3.

88. GUA, Directors' Minutes, March 21, 1870.

89. GUA, Directors' Minutes, March 21, 1870; June 4, 1870; September 16, 1870.

90. *The Daily News* (Frederick), December 28, 1896.

91. GUA, "Statement of Yearly Expenses, 1870–1871," in "Partial History," 12.

92. "Thomas Ewing," *The National Cyclopedia of American Biography*, 1516.

93. GUA, Charles P. James, "Address," June 4, 1872, 6–7.

94. GUA, Catalogue of Georgetown College, 1871–72.

95. Stevens, 26–27.

96. GUA, "Address," 16–18.

97. GUA, "Statement of Yearly Expenses, 1871–1872," cited in "Partial History," 17.

98. GUA, Law Ledger B III A.1.A., Financial Statement of the Law Department of Georgetown University for the year ending June 30, 1876.

99. GUA, Medical Department Minutes, March 9, 1867.

100. GUA, Medical School Minutes, March 28, 1874.

101. Elmer Kayser, *A Medical Center* (Washington, 1973), 78.

102. GUA, Medical Department Minutes, April 6, 1867.

103. GUA, Minutes of Medical Department, May 20, 1867.

104. By 1874 there was a special card for students that listed the textbooks for the various courses (GUA, Medical Department Minutes, September 2, 1874).

105. GUA, Medical Faculty Minutes, August 27, 1869.

106. GUA, Medical Faculty Minutes, August 27, 1869.

107. GUA, Medical Faculty Minutes, March 14–21, 1868.

108. "Benjamin Sherwood Hedrick," *National Cyclopedia of American Biography,* 127–28.

109. GUA, Medical Faculty Minutes, September 9–16, 1867; March 21, 1868.

110. GUA, Catalogue, 1874.

111. GUA, Medical Faculty Minutes, March 28, 1868.

112. GUA, Medical Faculty Minutes, September 1, 1870.

113. ARSI, MD, 10 II 6, Keller to Beckx, Baltimore, December 13, 1869.

114. MPARP, Province Consultors' Minutes, April 21, 1870; ARSI, MD, 10 II 8, Keller to Beckx, Frederick, March 2, 1870.

115. MPARP, Province Consultors' Minutes, March 19, 1870; April 21, 1870; GUA, Directors' Minutes, July 14, 1870.

116. John Gilmary Shea, *Memorial of the First Centenary of Georgetown College, D.C.* (Washington, 1891), 247.

117. GUA, House Diary, May 23–24, 1873; GUA, Directors' Minutes, May 24, 1873. Superior General Beckx was less than pleased with the initiative of the Georgetown directors. He indicated to Keller in September 1873 that he "was not opposed to" making Healy vice-rector or acting rector of the college. In fact, that was Healy's official status for his first year in office (ARSI, Generals' Register II, Beckx to Keller, Rome, September 10, 1873, 219).

CHAPTER 11

1. M[aurice] F[rancis] E[gan], *Philadelphia Catholic Standard,* quoted in CJ, 4 (February 1876), 56.

2. GUA, *Acta in Consultatione ext raordinaria de ampliando Collegio Georgiopolitano,* February 12, 1874.

3. GUA, Patrick Healy Papers, Beckx to Healy, Fiesole, December 6, 1875.

4. Frederick Rudolph, *The American College and University: A History* (New York, 1962), 330.

5. Rudolph, *College,* 333.

6. Frederick Rudolph, *Curriculum: A History of the American Undergraduate Course of Study since 1636* (San Francisco, Washington, and London, 1977), 116–19.

7. Rudolph, *Curriculum,* 136. "When the American university appears," Eliot insisted, "it will not be a copy of foreign institutions . . . but the slow and natural outgrowth of American social and political habits, and an expression of the average aims and ambitions of the better educated classes. The American college is an institution without parallel; the American university will be equally original" ("The New Education," in *Atlantic Monthly* [February 1869], 210, quoted in Peter Dobkin Hall, *The Organization of American Culture, 1700–1900: Private Institutions, Elites, and the Origins of American Nationality* [New York, 1982], 261).

8. Hall, 256.

9. James M. Garnett to Gilman, February 27, 1884, Gilman Papers, quoted in Hugh Hawkins, "Charles W. Eliot, Daniel C. Gilman and the Nurture of American Scholarship," *The New England Quarterly* 39 (September 1966), 307.

10. Edward Shils, "The Order of Learning in the United States: The Ascendancy of the University," in Alexandra Oleson and John Voss, eds., *The Organization of Knowledge in Modern America, 1860–1920* (Baltimore and London, 1979), 28.

11. *Concilii Plenarii Baltimorensis II, in Ecciesia Metropolitana Baltimorensi . . . Decreta* (Baltimore, 1868), 228; C. Joseph Nuesse, *The Catholic University of America: A Centennial History* (Washington, 1990), 10–11.

12. "Shall We Have a Catholic Congress?" *Catholic World* 8 (November 1868), 224–28; CW 12 (1872), 122, cited in Nuesse, 23.

13. *Tablet*, August 28, 1875. The editor was James S. Mullaly (1873, A. B.).

14. "Ought We Not to Have a Catholic University?" CJ, 4 (October 1875), 6–7.

15. *"De Quibusdam Rebus,"* CJ, 4 (February 1876), 49.

16. CJ, 4 (October 1875), 6–7.

17. GUA, Rector's Consultations, February 12, 1874.

18. GUA, Rector's Consultations, April 23, 1873; October 27, 1873.

19. Elizabeth Prelinger, "'From Her Spires and Steeples Beaming': Mission and Image in Bricks and Stone," in William McFadden, ed., *Georgetown at Two Hundred* (Washington, D.C., 1990), 340.

20. GUA, House Diary, March 27, 1876; March 29, 1876; May 16, 1876.

21. GUA, Beckx to Healy, Fiesole, August 8, 1876; February 22, 1877.

22. An alumnus and future Jesuit, Francis Barnum, was an associate of the bank and had persuaded John Early and other college officials to invest the bulk of the college's money there (ARSI, MD, 10 II 27, Keller to Beckx, Woodstock, April 13, 1875; ARSI, MD, 10 II 29, Keller to Beckx [Baltimore], May 9, 1876).

23. GUA, Beckx to Healy, Fiesole, August 8, 1876.

24. GUA, House Diary, October 6, 1877; October 7, 1877; October 15, 1877; January 6, 1878; January 16, 1878; July 1, 1878.

25. GUA, House Diary, May 27–29, 1878; July 18, 1878.

26. "Tax on Georgetown College," CJ, 6 (March 1878), 69; "Brief Mention," CJ, 7 (March 1879), 57.

27. GUA, Beckx to Healy, Fiesole, August 8, 1876.

28. GUA, Healy to Corcoran [December 3, 1877], draft; GUA, House Diary, December 3, 1877.

29. From the early 1870s until his death in 1888, Corcoran contributed nearly $200,000 in real estate and money to Columbian (Elmer Louis Kayser, *Bricks without Straw: The Evolution of George Washington University* [New York, 19701, 146, 160, 169); CJ, 1 (January 1873), 12.

30. Shea, *Memorial of the First Centenary of Georgetown College, D.C.* (New York, 1891), 265; Albert Foley, SJ, *Dream of an Outcaste,* 187.

31. "The Alumni Meeting," CJ, 9 (July 1881), 111.

32. GUA, House Diary, June 26, 1883; Shea, 292; G. E. Hamilton et al. to James A. Doonan, Washington, December 18, 1883, quoted in CJ, 12 (December 1883), 39.

33. "It had often been in my mind," he wrote in his diary, "to ask leave to go in the hope that I might do something to further the financial interests of the College. I thought, as did others, that it was worth the trial" (Holy Cross Archives, Patrick Healy Diary no. 3, November 30, 1878; GUA, House Diary, November 28, 1878).

34. CJ, 9 (February 1881), 54.

35. Hall, *Organization of American Culture,* 262.

36. Howard Hawkins, *Between Harvard and America: The Educational Leadership of Charles W. Eliot* (New York, 1972), 186.

37. Hardy George, "Georgetown University's Healy Building," *Journal of the Society of Architectural Historians* XXI (1972), 210; GUA, House Diary, December 12–13, 1877.

38. GUA, House Diary, July 4, 1878.

39. GUA, Patrick Healy Papers, John Mullaly to Patrick Healy, Georgetown, December 22, 1878.

40. GUA, Patrick Healy Papers, Mullaly to Healy, Georgetown, January 30, 1879.

41. GUA, Patrick Healy Papers, Mullaly to Healy, Georgetown, April 9, 1879.

42. GUA, Patrick Healy Papers, Mullaly to Healy, Georgetown, April 28, 1879.

43. GUA, House Diary, November 15, 1879.

44. GUA, Directors' Minutes, April 15, 1880.

45. Foley, *Dream,* 200.

46. Foley, 211.

47. GUA, House Diary, October 1, 1881.

48. GUA, House Diary, February 19, 1873.

49. CJ, 2 (October 1874), 117.

50. GUA, Patrick Healy Papers, John Mullaly to Healy, Georgetown, July 16, 1879.

51. Shea, *Memorial,* 287.

52. GUA, Directors' Minutes, Vol. II, October 16, 1876.

53. GUA, House Diary, February 23, 1878; September 12, 1878.

54. "The Fathers at Georgetown were lenient to us," he recalled, "so long as we observed the proprieties and went into good society" (Egan, Recollections, 61–82).

55. There was growing restiveness, among the collegians, about the dominance of prep schoolers on campus. "It *does* seem as if this system, our legacy from the past, might be dispensed with about this time. Circumstances have probably changed since the College, in order to maintain itself, had to open its doors to students of all grades" (CJ, 4 [March 1876], 67). In fact, the major circumstance, the lack of Catholic secondary schooling, had not significantly changed. And Georgetown obviously depended on the preparatory students for the bulk of its annual revenue.

56. In 1872, when he was still prefect (dean of students) and responsible for admissions, Healy wrote to an old classmate in Belgium about the wisdom of having non-Catholic students in a Catholic school. His classmate suggested that exclusion was the best policy, inasmuch as the piety of Catholic students tended to suffer from the presence of non-Catholics (GUA, J. A. Dequesne to Healy, Namur, March 16, 1872).

57. GUA, Directors' Minutes, December 1, 1880.

58. "The Commencement," CJ, 2 (August and September 1874), 104.

59. This revised requirement presumably would not have excluded the three Japanese applicants who had sought admission to the college in 1872. But they were three years too early. On hearing that they were not interested in studying Latin and Greek, President Early informed them that they should choose some other institution "more in harmony with their plan of study" (Shea, *Memorial,* 243). This non-classical course was first announced in the 1876–77 catalogue, but the *College Journal* had already reported in the summer of 1875 that "Arrangements have been recently made . . . by which students may pursue a course in English alone" ("Georgetown College," CJ, 3 [August and September 1875], 111).

60. "College Jottings: A Scientific Course," CJ, 1 (1872), 9.

61. Hawkins, *Between Harvard and America,* 83.

62. Nevertheless, by the 1880s there were a few internal dissenters surfacing over the matter of the curriculum. One student in 1884, in his senior essay, attacked the *sine qua non* status of the classics by denying that there was a necessary relationship between them and mental discipline or *eloquentia perfecta* or classical culture (GUA, 186.5, Henry Latshaw, "Is It a College Fetish?" 1884, cited in Sally A. DeSando, "Student Thought at Georgetown Expressed in Their Writings," M.A. thesis, Georgetown, 1963, 78–81).

63. CJ, 9 (January 1881), 41; CJ, 9 (February 1881), 52.

64. "Book Notices," CJ, 10 (April 1882), 89.

65. Frank W. Clark, SJ, A *Report on the Teaching of Chemistry and Physics in the United States* (Washington, 1880), cited in Liam S. Donohue, "The History of Chemistry at Georgetown University (1789–1900)," in Durkin, ed., *Swift Potomac's Lovely Daughter,* 432.

66. "Scientific Studies at Georgetown II," CJ, 7 (June 1879), 90.

67. "Astronomy Class," CJ, 14 (April 1886), 77.

68. "Laboratory Practice," CJ, 12 (October 1883), 5.

69. CJ, 10 (May 1882), 109.

70. "Specimen in Physics," CJ, 4 (February 1876), 54; "Specimen in Natural Philosophy," CJ, 4 (May 1876), 93.

71. "Specimen in Natural Science," CJ, 6 (June 1878), 94, citing Charles S. Schoolfield, "The Navigation of the Air."

72. "Specimen in Natural Science," CJ, 6 (June 1878), 94.

73. Archbishop Connolly of Halifax, "Darwinism," CJ, 2 (February 1874), 33.

74. CJ, 13 (December 1884), 28.

75. "Science Lectures," CJ, 9 (February 1881), 52; "The Toner Scientific Circle," CJ, 10 (November 1881), 22.

76. CJ, 10 (June 1882), 120; Shea, *Memorial,* 283.

77. "College Jottings," CJ, 11 (May 1874), 65.

78. "On Universal Suffrage," CJ, 4 (June 1876), 103.

79. CJ, 1 (October 1873), 94; "Middle Examination," CJ, 4 (March 1876), 66.

80. "School Matters," CJ, 4 (November 1875), 17.

81. David F. Allmendinger Jr., *Paupers and Scholars: The Transformation of Student Life in Nineteenth-Century New England* (New York, 1975), 121–24.

82. "Our Commencement," CJ, 3 (August and September 1875), 114.

83. "Entertainment by the Reading Club," CJ, 3 (April 1875), 68.

84. "Libraries in the College," CJ, 4 (February 1876), 56.

85. "Society Libraries," CJ, 3 (November 1874), 9.

86. "Our Society Libraries," CJ, 4 (February 1876), 54; CJ, 8 (April 1880), 64; "General News," CJ, 16 (March 1888), 73.

87. "The Rebellion of the Civil Power," CJ, 3 (May 1875), 78.

88. CJ, 3 (May 1875), 78. If the *Journal* and student opinion at Georgetown were decidedly anti-black in their opposition to Reconstruction, they were consistently pro-Indian and always supportive of native Americans in the West. A constant was their opposition to the intrusion of the federal government. In the West, the Indians were seen as the victims of such intervention; while in the South, the Afro-Americans were its perceived beneficiaries ("Indian Policies Contrasted," CJ, 2 [April 1874], 51; "Final Notes," CJ, 1 [October 1873], 93).

89. "The Principles of Civil Liberty," CJ, 2 (February 1874), 30. The legacy of Civil War statecraft, the student editors quoted the *New York Sun* with approval, was "the establishment of a well-nigh countless horde of agents and officers of the central government, under one or another name, and with vast and almost inconceivable ramifications of corruption, fraud, and political immorality" ("What Congress Ought to Do," CJ, 6 [February 1878], 56).

90. "Excess in Legislation," CJ, 2 (May 1874), 66.

91. "Excess in Legislation, II," CJ, 2 (June 1874), 78.

92. "Communism," CJ, 3 (April 1875), 65.

93. CJ, 6 (June 1878), 94.

94. Hawkins, *Between Harvard and America,* 110–11.

95. William Henry Dennis, "Rev. Patrick F. Healy, SJ at an Appreciation," CJ, 41 (January 1913), 226.

96. "Mass-meeting," CJ, 3 (December 1874), 22.

97. "Meetings," CJ, 9 (November 1880), 16–17.

98. GUA, House Diary, November 11, 1879.

99. Ronald A. Smith, *Sports and Freedom: The Rise of Big-Time College Athletics* (New York, 1988), 33–34.

100. Smith, 42–51.

101. GUA, House Diary, May 5, 1876; CJ, 4 (April 1876), 80; CJ, 4 (May 1876), 89; CJ, 4 (July 1876), 115.

102. GUA, House Diary, June 1, 1876.

103. Sports under Patrick Healy were entirely self-supporting, or rather student-supported. When the Boat Club approached the president in the spring of 1877 for a loan of $100 to buy a boat, he turned them down. The boat house alone cost $1,100 (GUA, House Diary, May 5, 1876; May 9, 1876; May 23, 1876; September 19, 1876; December 19, 1876; February 16, 1877; March 4, 1877; April 24, 1877; May 29, 1877; CJ, 4 [May 1876], 89; Lawrence H. Cooke, "The History of the Georgetown Crew: Guardian of the Blue and Gray," in Durkin, *Lovely Daughter,* 327–28.

104. "Here and There," CJ, 9 (March 1881), 69; Cooke, "Georgetown Crew," 331.

105. GUA, Stonestreet Diary, September 25, 1840.

106. "Mass-Meeting," CJ, 3 (December 1874), 22.

107. "The College Societies," CJ, 12 (December 1883), 41; Hugh J. Golden, "Georgetown Football: A Complete History (1874–1987)," unpublished paper [1989].

108. GUA, House Diary, October 30, 1888.

109. Rory F. Quirk, *Hoya Saxa: Georgetown Football, 1874–1978* (Washington, 1979).

110. "Preparations for the Carnival," CJ, 4 (March 1876), 65; "The Carnival at Georgetown," CJ, 4 (April 1876), 82; "Mardi Gras," CJ, 5 (February 1877), 57; "Masquerade," CJ, 6 (March 1878); "Mardi Gras," CJ, 9 (February 1881), 57.

111. Hawkins, *Between Harvard and America*, 58.

112. Rothstein, *American Medical Schools*, 99–113.

113. "Opening of the Medical School," CJ, 3 (February 1875), 8.

114. GUA, House Diary, March 22–25, 1876; April 20, 1876; GUA, 531–1, Rector's Consultations, April 20, 1876; GUA, Directors' Minutes, October 1, 1876. Healy, like most Jesuit presidents of the era, tended to use the consultors (by Jesuit law appointed to advise a rector or religious superior) in making decisions regarding policy and governance in the university. Again, like other Jesuit presidents, he used the board of directors mainly for legal purposes, such as the sale of property and the awarding of degrees. Usually the two bodies had the same members.

115. *History of the Medical Society of the District of Columbia, 1817–1909* (Washington, D.C., 1909), 286; *Washington Post*, May 21, 1905.

116. "Swan Moses Burnett," *National Cyclopedia of American Biography* [hereafter NCAB], 439.

117. "John Brown Hamilton," NCAB, 245–246.

118. In the academic year in which Baker was appointed, a demonstrator of anatomy resigned because of the students' lack of interest and their failure even to purchase materials needed for dissection. Under Baker, dissection became a rigorous portion of each student's training (GUA, L. Eliot to Faculty, Washington, February 18; GUA, F. B. Bailey et al. to Faculty, 1886).

119. "Frank Baker," DAB 1, 519; Francis A. Tondorf, comp. and ed., *Frank Baker, M.D., AM., Ph.D., LL.D.* (1841–1918). *Professor of Anatomy Georgetown University Medical School from 1883–1918* (Washington, 1923), 5–10.

120. C. H. A. Kleinschmidt to the editor of the *Journal of the American Medical Association*, Washington, July 20, 1890, quoted in CJ (October 1890), 11.

121. As Georgetown was implementing the three-year course, the recently formed American Medical College Association, to which Georgetown belonged, convened in special session to consider ways to adopt a standard system of formation that was "more in harmony with the requirements of the age," including a three-year program (GUA, "Call for a convention of All American medical Colleges to be Held in the City of Atlanta, Ga., beginning at 10 A.M., Friday, May 2, 1879" [printed circular]). Only seven of the more than one hundred medical schools in the country had a similar program (GUA, Lovejoy, "History of the Medical College Prepared and Read by the Dean at the Opening of the Session, Oct. 4th, 1886" [typescript]). Approximately half the medical schools still had terms of fewer than six months (Rothstein, 104).

122. GUA, C. Eliot to [Patrick Healy], Boston, April 22, 1878.

123. Louis Kolipinski, CJ, 36 (October 1907), 40–41.

124. GUA, John C. Riley to Johnson Eliot, Washington, October 22, 1875.

125. George Rosen, M.D., Ph.D., "From Frontier Surgeon to Industrial Hygienist: The Strange Career of George M. Kober," *American Journal of Public Health* 65 (June 1975), 638–41.

126. Robert Stevens asserts that Georgetown, by the 1890s, was operating "one of the largest and most lucrative part-time programs in the nation," with nearly a thousand students on its rolls (*Law School: Legal Education in America from the 1850s to the 1980s* [Chapel Hill, N.C., and London, 1983], 75). In truth, the school's nineteenth-century population peaked at three hundred and eight in 1897 and did not approach the thousand mark until 1912.

127. GUA, "Annual Statement, 1878–79," cited in an untitled history of Georgetown University Law Center [hereafter GULC History] (ca. 1970), chapter II, 4.

128. GUA, Faculty Minutes, May 1, 1883.

129. Elmer Kayser, *Bricks without Straw*, 130, 156.

130. GUA, Faculty Minutes, May 1, 1883.

131. James S. Easby-Smith, *Georgetown University in the District of Columbia,* Vol. I (New York, 1907), 432.

132. GUA, Financial Statement of Law School, 1883–84.

133. Durkin, *Middle Years,* 126–27.

134. GULC History, chapter II, 18.

135. The province officials had intended that Healy retire in 1880 when they recommended three other persons to Rome as the next rector of Georgetown. Officials in the Jesuit curia in Rome obviously decided otherwise (MPARP, *Acta Consultationum Prov. Maryl.,* July 24, 1880).

136. GUA, House Diary, February 9, 1882; February 12, 1882.

137. GUA, House Diary, February 17, 1882.

138. "Our Ex-President," CJ, 10 (March 1882), 71–72.

CHAPTER 12

1. A testament to Georgetown's original link to the Society of Jesus through the remnant that had been helped to survive in Byelorussia (GUSC, Richards Papers, Letterbook 3, to Daniel Donovan, March 8, 1889.)

2. GUA, 505–14, House Diary, February 22, 1889.

3. Cited in John Gilmary Shea, *Memorial of the First Century of Georgetown College, D.C.* (New York, 1891), 339.

4. The first evidence of this mid-1840s dating error is in a paper written by an immigrant Jesuit, Anthony Rey, for a European audience. Rey was in residence at the college at the time (MPA 3 B 2, *"Notice historique de l'établissement et des progrès de la Religione catholique dans les Etats Unis"*). In 1851 the first catalogue of the University stated that "in 1789 the first house was built." This information was repeated in every catalogue for the next twenty years until the 1873 catalogue declared on the inside cover "Founded as a college 1789," thereby implicitly equating the completion of construction of the first academic building and the academy's founding.

   A recent graduate, in the course of reading Shea's history of the university, discovered the mistake—possibly in the spring of 1892. But when, à propos of this discovery, President Richards sought advice about changing the foundation date, former President Healy replied, "I can see no possible advantage in going backwards. . . . A change of date against the dictum of tradition can hardly fail to provoke undesirable comment" (GUA, Richards Papers, Letterbook 6, to James A. Doonan, June 14, 1892; ibid., to Patrick F. Healy, Providence, 1892).

5. In 1887 the Hickory Hill farm and the Tenleytown villa were sold for $60,000 each. In that same year Brother Thomas Dougherty, a tailor at the college, inherited $51,000 from his brother's estate (GUA, 550–14, House Diary, June 4, 1887; June 6, 1887; July 1, 1887; GUA, Directors' Minutes, February 27, 1887; May 15, 1887).

6. ARSI, MD, 11 I 7, Thomas Campbell to Anton Anderledy, New York, July 7, 1888.

7. GUA, Box 2, Folder 7, Campbell to Richards, New York, August 23, 1888; ARSI, *Annuaria Historiae, Collegium Georgiopolitanum, 1886–1889.*

8. Cited in Shea, *History of Georgetown College,* 304–5.

9. Shea, *History of Georgetown College,* 321.

10. J. Havens Richards, *A Loyal Life: A Biography of Henry Livingston Richards* (New York, 1913).

11. "Richards," WL 53 (1924), 251.

12. GUA, Rector's Consultations, October 2, 1888; October 12, 1888.

13. ARSI, MD, 11, I, 12, Campbell to Anderledy, Boston, January 23, 1889.

14. GUA 550–14, House Diary, 1884 to 1892, 173.

15. "Father John Hagen, SJ," WL 60 (1931), 282–85.

16. Ibid., 370–371.

17. Ibid., 350–51.

18. Ibid., 382.

19. Ibid., 400.
20. ARSI, *Litterae Annuae, Collegii Georgiopolitani,* 1886–1889.
21. Father Joseph Carberry and his brother, Thomas Carberry, had, sixty years earlier, removed seven cannons from St. Mary's river at the sites of two former forts. They were subsequently distributed to various locations around the state, including one to the lawn of the statehouse in Annapolis, and the last two to Georgetown (Donald G. Shomette, "The Guns of St. Mary's," *Maryland Historical Magazine* (Winter 1998), 477–98.
22. *Georgetown College Journal,* 62 (1933–34), 462.
23. Daniel J. Geary, "American Catholics and Higher Education," in Shea, *Memorial,* 418.
24. Ibid., 353.
25. Remarks of George E. Hamilton, Esq. in response to the toast: "The Law Department," ibid., 395.
26. As early as 1882, the Georgetown administrators were complaining that the provincial superior, on his official visit to the campus from his headquarters in New York City, "was lamentably ignorant of the standard to which Geo'town had risen under Fr. Healy's administration" (GUA, House Diary, June 30, 1882).
27. Ibid., 385–86.
28. The Jesuit provincial superior, Thomas Campbell, warned the superior general not to consent to supply any faculty to the new university. He reminded him "who are the Biships [sic] who are directing this future university. Since all are disciples of Cardinal Manning, they have a low opinion of religious, especially us. They are not exactly supporters of Henry George, but minimally are in accord with the Archbishop of New York who has condemned him (The Archbishop himself is only nominally in favor of this university scheme). They are all doctrinaire about total abstinence, and go on *ad nauseam* with their absurd notions about American Catholicity . . ." (ARSI, MD, 11 I 10, Campbell to Anderledy, New York, December 15, 1888).
29. E. J. Burrus, SJ, "Historical Notes: Father Joseph Havens Richards' Notes on Georgetown and the Catholic University," WL 83 (1954), 83.
30. Burrus, 86.

Bibliography

PRIMARY SOURCES

Archives

Archives of the Archdiocese of Baltimore
Archives of the Sacred Congregation for Propagation of the Faith
    Scritture riferte nei congressi, America Centrale
Archives of the Sisters of Charity, Nazareth, KY
Archivum Provinciae Belgicae Septemtrionalis Societatis Jesu
Archivum Romanum Societatis Jesu
    Litterae Annuales Provinciae Marylandiae
    Marylandia
    Navigatio Funestra Patrum Procuratorum qui ex America Romam venerant, anno 1866
    Register of the Generals' Responses for the American Mission (1830–33) and
        Maryland Province (1833–53)
Catholic University of America Archives
    Edward J. Wallace Papers
Charles County Community College, LaPlata, MD, Southern Maryland Room
    Hamilton Family Papers
English Province Archives
    Foreign Correspondence, 1776–1859
Georgetown University Special Collections
    Augustine Neale Reminiscences
    Bird Papers
    Catholic Historical Manuscript Collection
      Giovanni Grassi Diary
    Charles Constantine Pise Papers
    Dennis C. Terez. "The Long and Involved Claim of Susan Decatur and the Men Who
        Burned the *Philadelphia*."
    Evans Papers Collection
    George Barringer. "The Georgetown University Library: A Historical Sketch."
        Unpublished paper, n.d.
    Georgetown University Archives
      Acta in Consultatione extraordinaria de ampliando Collegio Georgiopolitano
      Address to the Philodemic Society. Washington, DC: Published by the Society, 1862.
      Aylmar Family Papers
      Bernard Maguire, SJ, Notes
      Catalogues
      Charles Henry Stonestreet, SJ, Diary

Diary of the Administrator of the Jesuit Community (House Diary)
Edward Devitt, SJ, Papers
Financial Records Series
Fleming Gardner Papers
Francis Barnum, SJ. Collection of Chronological Notes for a History of Georgetown
    College
"History of the Philodemic Society, Georgetown College, First Year 1830–1831"
John Dooley, SJ, Papers
John Early, SJ, Papers
    John Early Diary
Joseph Havens Richards, SJ, Letterbooks, 14 vols., 1888–98
Joseph O'Callaghan, SJ, Diary
Law School
    Financial Ledgers
    James Therry. "A Partial History of the Georgetown University Law School."
        Unpublished typescript, n.d.
Medical Department Minutes
Medical School
    Daniel S. Lamb. "Reminiscences of the Old Medical School." Hoya, 1925, 8.
    James W. Lovejoy. "History of the Medical College Prepared and Read by the
        Dean at the Opening of the Session, Oct. 4th, 1886."
    Joseph T. Durkin, SJ. "The History of the Medical School of Georgetown
        University." Unpublished manuscript.
    Llewellin Elliot. "The History of the Foundation of the Medical Department of
        Georgetown University." 1907.
    Medical Faculty Minutes
    Medical School Minutes
    Pamela Ginsbach. "A History of the Georgetown University Medical School."
        Unpublished manuscript.
    W. W. Johnston. "History of the Medical Society of the District of Columbia."
        Delivered February 16, 1894, at the Seventy-Fifth Anniversary of the
        Medical Society.
Minister's Diary
Minutes of the Directors, 1797–1889
Patrick Healy, SJ, Papers
Philodemic Society Papers
Prefect's Reports
Rector's Consultations
Refectory Diary
Reminiscences of Robert Ray
    Ives Family Papers
James Curley, SJ, Papers
    James Curley Diary
James Longyear Reminiscences
John McElroy, SJ, Diary
John S. Sumner, SJ, Papers
Joseph Mobberly, SJ, Diary
Peter Kenney, SJ, Papers
Thomas Lilly, SJ, Diary
Thomas Mulledy, SJ, Papers
William Dundas Papers
Holy Cross Archives
Patrick Healy, SJ, Diary
Maryland Province Archives
Acta Primae Congregationis, Provinciae Marylandiae Societatis Jesu
Fidèle de Grivel. *Mémoire sur la Congregation Prov. du Maryland commences . . .
    le 8 Juillet 1835.*

Proceedings of the General Chapter
Proceedings of the Roman Catholic Clergy
Procurator's Report
Recollections of John McElroy, SJ
Stonyhurst Transcripts

National Archives
Censuses of 1790, 1810, 1830, 1840, 1850, 1860
Quartermaster General's Office, Claims Branch, 1861–89
Record Group 109
Thirty-first Congress, 1st session

New York Province Archives of the Society of Jesus

University of North Carolina, Southern Historical Collection
James Ryder Randall Diary
William Gaston Papers

Newspapers

Baltimore Catholic Herald
Boston Pilot
(Frederick) *Daily News*
[Georgetown] *Sentinel of Liberty*
Georgetown University *Hoya*
National Intelligencer
Washington Evening Star
Washington Intelligencer
Washington Post
[Washington] *Sunday Star*

Magazines and Bulletins

Catholic Historical Review
Georgetown College Journal
Georgetown University Alumni Magazine
Historical Records and Studies
History of Education Quarterly
Maryland Historical Magazine
Review of Politics
Washington History
Woodstock Letters

Books

Antisell, Thomas. *Valedictory Address to the Graduating Class of the Medical Department of Georgetown College, Delivered at the Smithsonian Institution, March 10, 1859.* Washington, DC: H. Polkinhorn, 1859.
"Autobiography of Father Burchard Villiger." *Woodstock Letters* 32 (1903): 51–81.
Egan, Maurice Francis. *Recollections of a Happy Life.* New York: George H. Doran Co., 1924.
Galletti, Pietro. *Memorie Storiche intorno a P. Ugo Molza e alla Compagnia di Gsu in Rome durante il secolo XIX.* Prato: Giashetti, 1914.
Grassi, Giovanni, SJ. *Notzie varie sulo stato presente della republica degli Stati Uniti dell' America settentrionale scritte al principio del 1818.* Milano: Per Giovanni Silvestri, 1819.
Mondésir, Édouard de. *Souvenirs D'Édouard De Mondésir, 1789–1811.* Baltimore: Johns Hopkins University Press, 1942.
Morse, Samuel F. B. *Imminent Dangers to the Free Institutions of the United States through Foreign Immigrations.* New York: E. B. Clayton, 1835.
Richards, J. Havens. *A Loyal Life: A Biography of Henry Livingston Richards.* New York: B. Herder, 1913.
Rozier, John, ed. *The Granite Farm Letters: The Civil War Correspondence of Edgeworth and Sallie Bird.* Athens: University of Georgia Press, 1988.

Thébaud, Augustus J. *Forty Years in the United States of America (1839–1885)*. New York: United States Catholic Historical Society, 1904.

Articles

McElroy, John, SJ. "Chaplains for the Mexican War, 1846." *Woodstock Letters* 16 (1887): 225ff.

Payne, John Carroll. *Some Reminiscences in My Life for My Children and Grandchildren*. [n.d.]

Steiner, Bernard C., ed. "The South Atlantic States in 1833, As Seen by a New England-er." *Maryland Historical Magazine* (1918).

SECONDARY SOURCES

Books and Articles

GENERAL

Abetti, Giorgio. "(Pietro) Angelo Secchi." *Dictionary of Scientific Biography*. Vol. 12. New York: Charles Scribner's Sons, 1970–80.

Adams, Charles Francis, ed. *The Works of John Adams*. Vol. 10. Boston: Little, Brown and Co., 1856.

Allmendinger, David F., Jr. *Paupers and Scholars: The Transformation of Student Life in Nineteenth Century New England*. New York: St. Martin's Press, 1975.

Astronomical Observations for 1847. Vol. 3. Washington, DC: Georgetown University, 1853.

Baker, Jean H. *Ambivalent Americans: The Know-Nothing Party in Maryland*. Baltimore: Johns Hopkins University Press, 1977.

Bender, Thomas. "Science and the Culture of American Communities: The Nineteenth Century." *History of Education Quarterly* 16 (Spring 1976): 63–77.

Betts, Edwin Morris, and James Adam Bear Jr., eds. *The Family Letters of Thomas Jefferson*. Charlottesville: Published for the Thomas Jefferson Memorial Foundation by the University Press of Virginia, 1986.

Bilhartz, Terry D. *Urban Religion and the Second Great Awakening: Church and Society in Early National Baltimore*. Rutherford, NJ: Fairleigh Dickinson University Press, 1986.

Boyd, John P., ed. *The Papers of Thomas Jefferson*. Vol. 14. Princeton, NJ: Princeton University Press, 1958.

Brant, Irving. *James Madison: Father of the Constitution, 1787–1800*. Vol. 3. Indianapolis: Bobbs-Merrill, 1950.

———. *James Madison: The Virginia Revolutionist*. Vol. 1. Indianapolis: Bobbs-Merrill, 1941.

Burke, Colin B. *American Collegiate Populations: A Test of the Traditional View*. New York: New York University Press, 1982.

Coddington, Edwin B. *The Gettysburg Campaign: A Study in Command*. New York: Scribner's, 1968.

Coulter, E. Merton. *College Life in the Old South*. New York: Macmillan, 1928.

Cozzens, Peter. *No Better Place to Die: The Battle of Stones River*. Urbana: University of Illinois Press, 1990.

Davis, William C. *Battle at Bull Run: A History of the First Major Campaign of the Civil War*. Garden City, NY: Doubleday, 1977.

The Dictionary of National Biography. London: Oxford University Press, 1937–38.

Dooley, Patrick J. "Woodstock and Its Makers." *Woodstock Letters* 56 (1927): 5.

Downing, Margaret B. "James and Joanna Gould Barry." *Historical Records and Studies* 15 (March 1921): 45–54.

Duncan, Richard R. "The College of St. James and the Civil War: A Casualty of War." *Historical Magazine of the Protestant Episcopal Church*, September 1970, 265–86.

———. "The Impact of the Civil War on Education in Maryland." *Maryland Historical Magazine*, March 1966, 37–52.

Dunigan, David R., SJ. *A History of Boston College*. Milwaukee, WI: Bruce, 1947.

Durkin, Joseph T., SJ, ed. *John Dooley, Confederate Soldier: His War Journal*. Notre Dame, IN: University of Notre Dame Press, 1963.

Earle, Carville, and Ronald Hoffman. "Staple Crops and Urban Development in the Eighteenth-Century South." *Perspectives in American History* 10 (1976): 7–78.

Elliott, Clark, ed. *Biographic Dictionary of American Science.* Westport, CT: Greenwood Press, 1979.

Fields, Barbara Jeanne. *Slavery and Freedom on the Middle Ground: Maryland during the Nineteenth Century.* New Haven, CT: Yale University Press, 1985.

Gibson, Robert. *A Treatise of Practical Surveying; Which Is Demonstrated from Its First Principles Wherein Every Thing That Is Useful and Curious in That Art, Is Fully Considered and Explained.* 6th ed. Philadelphia, 1792.

Goldsborough, W. W. *The Maryland Line in the Confederate Army, 1861–1865.* Baltimore: Press of Guggenheim, Weil & Co., 1900.

Gough, John. *Treatise of Arithmetic in Theory and Practice, Containing Everything Important in the Study of Abstract and Applicate Numbers. Adapted to the Commerce of Great Britain and Ireland to which are added many valuable additions and amendments; more particularly fitting the work for the improvement of the American Youth* by Benjamin Workman, AM. Philadelphia, 1792.

Green, Constance McLaughlin. *Washington: Village and Capital, 1800–1878.* Princeton, NJ: Princeton University Press, 1962.

Guralnick, Stanley M. *Science and the Ante-Bellum American College.* Philadelphia: American Philosophical Society, 1975.

Hall, Peter Dobkin. *The Organization of American Culture, 1700–1900: Private Institutions, Elites, and the Origins of American Nationality.* New York: New York University Press, 1982.

Hamlin, Arthur T. *The University Library in the United States: Its Origins and Development.* Philadelphia: University of Pennsylvania Press, 1981.

Hamlin, Talbot. *Benjamin Henry Latrobe.* New York: Oxford University Press, 1955.

Harding, Thomas S. *College Literary Societies: Their Contribution to Higher Education in the United States, 1815–1876.* New York: Pageant Press, 1971.

Hardy, Stella Pickett. *Colonial Families of the Southern States of America.* Baltimore: Genealogical, 1981.

Hawkins, Hugh. *Between Harvard and America: The Educational Leadership of Charles W. Eliot.* New York: Oxford University Press, 1972.

———. "Charles W. Eliot, Daniel C. Gilman and the Nurture of American Scholarship." *New England Quarterly* 39 (September 1966): 291–308.

Hein, Louis Otto. *Memories of Long Ago.* New York: G. P. Putnam's Sons, 1925.

Hemphill, W. Edwin, ed. *The Papers of John C. Calhoun.* Vol. 9. Columbia: University of South Carolina Press for the South Caroliniana Society, 1976.

Henretta, James A., and Gregory H. Nobles. *Evolution and Revolution: American Society, 1600–1820.* Lexington, MA: Heath, 1987.

Herbst, Jurgen. "The American Revolution and the American University." *Perspectives in American History* 10 (1976): 301–3.

———. *From Crisis to Crisis: American College Government, 1636–1819.* Cambridge, MA: Harvard University Press, 1982.

Hofstadter, Richard, and Wilson Smith, eds. *American Higher Education: A Documentary History.* Vol. 1. Chicago: University of Chicago Press, 1961.

Hovenkamp, Herbert. *Science and Religion in America, 1800–1860.* Philadelphia: University of Pennsylvania Press, 1978.

Jones, Bessie Zaban, and Lyle Gifford Boyd. *The Harvard College Observatory: The First Four Directorships, 1839–1919.* Cambridge, MA: Belknap Press of Harvard University Press, 1971.

Katz, Michael B. "The Role of American Colleges in the Nineteenth Century." *History of Education Quarterly* 23 (Summer 1983): 215–23.

Kayser, Elmer Louis. *Bricks without Straw: The Evolution of George Washington University.* New York: Appleton-Century-Crofts, 1970.

———. *A Medical Center: The Institutional Development of Medical Education in George Washington University.* Washington, DC: George Washington University Press, 1973.

Kelley, Brooks Mather. *Yale: A History.* New Haven, CT: Yale University Press, 1974.

Kett, Joseph. *The Formation of the American Medical Profession: The Role of Institutions, 1780–1860.* New Haven, CT: Yale University Press, 1968.

———. *Rites of Passage: Adolescence in America, 1790 to the Present.* New York: Basic, 1977.

Korn, Bertram Wallace. "Jews and Negro Slavery in the Old South, 1789–1865." In *Jews in the South,* ed. Leonard Dinnerstein and Mary Dale Palsson, 89–134. Baton Rouge: Louisiana State University Press, 1973.

Kuritz, Hyman. "The Popularization of Science in Nineteenth-Century America." *History of Education Quarterly* 21 (Fall 1981): 259–74.

LaBorde, M. *History of the Southern Carolina College.* Columbia, SC: P. B. Glass, 1859.

Lamb, D. S., et al. *History of the Medical Society of the District of Columbia, 1817–1909.* Washington, DC: The Society, 1909.

Larson, Magali Sarfatti. *The Rise of Professionalism: A Sociological Analysis.* Berkeley: University of California Press, 1979.

Leech, Margaret. *Reveille in Washington, 1860–1865.* Garden City, NY: Garden City Publishing, 1941.

Leslie, Shane. *Mrs Fitzherbert: A Life Chiefly from Unpublished Sources.* New York: Benziger Brothers, 1939.

Linderman, Gerald F. *Embattled Courage: The Experience of Combat in the American Civil War.* New York: Free Press, 1987.

Lochemes, M. Frederick. *Robert Walsh: His Story.* New York: American Irish Historical Society, 1941.

Longstreet, James. "Lee's Right Wing at Gettysburg." In *Battles and Leaders of the Civil War,* vol. 3, 339–54. New York: Century Co., 1884.

Lucey, William L., SJ, ed. "The Diary of Joseph B. O'Hagen, S.J., Chaplain of the Excelsior Brigade." *Civil War History* 6 (1960).

Mattingly, Herman. *The Mattingly Family in Early America.* Privately printed, 1975.

Maul, David T. "A Man and His Book." *Register of the Kentucky Historical Society* 65 (July 1967): 212–29.

Maxwell, Hu, and H. L. Swisher. *History of Hampshire County, West Virginia.* Morgantown, WV: A. Brown Boughner, 1897.

McLachlan, James. *American Boarding Schools: A Historical Study.* New York: Scribner, 1970.

———. "The American College in the Nineteenth Century: Toward a Reappraisal." *Teachers College Record* 80 (December 1978).

McPherson, James. *Battle Cry of Freedom: The Civil War Era.* New York: Oxford University Press, 1988.

Meriwether, Robert L., ed. *Papers of John C. Calhoun.* Columbia: University of South Carolina Press for the South Caroliniana Society, 1959–86.

Miller, Howard. *The Revolutionary College: American Presbyterian Higher Education, 1707–1837.* New York: New York University Press, 1976.

Mitchell, Mary. *Divided Town.* Barre, MA: Barre Publishers, 1968.

Musto, David F. "A Survey of the American Observatory Movement, 1800–1850." *Vistas in Astronomy* 8 (1968): 87–92.

The National Cyclopedia of American Biography. Vol. 7. New York: J. T. White.

Naylor, Natalie. "The Ante-Bellum College Movement: A Reappraisal of Tewksbury's *Founding of American Colleges and Universities.*" *History of Education Quarterly* 13 (Fall 1973): 261–74.

Novak, Steven J. *The Rights of Youth: American Colleges and Student Revolution, 1798–1815.* Cambridge, MA: Harvard University Press, 1977.

Nuesse, C. Joseph. *The Catholic University of America: A Centennial History.* Washington, DC: Catholic University of America Press, 1990.

Philippe, Louis. *Diary of My Travels in America,* trans. Stephen E. Becker. New York: Delacorte Press, 1977.

Potts, David B. "American Colleges in the Nineteenth Century: From Localism to Denominationalism." *History of Education Quarterly* 11 (Winter 1971): 363–80.

———. "'College Enthusiasm!' As Public Response, 1800–1860." *Harvard Educational Review* 47 (February 1977): 28–42.

Proctor, John Clagett. "Early Days at George Washington University," [Washington] *Sunday Star,* April 9, 1933.

Remini, Robert. *Andrew Jackson and the Course of American Freedom, 1822–1832.* New York: Harper & Row, 1981.

Robson, David W. "College Founding in the New Republic, 1776–1800." *History of Education Quarterly* 23 (Fall 1983): 323–41.

———. *Educating Republicans: The College in the Era of the American Revolution, 1750–1800.* Westport, CT: Greenwood Press, 1985.

Roche, John F. *The Colonial Colleges in the War for American Independence.* Millwood, NY: Associated Faculty Press, 1986.

Rorabaugh, W. J. *The Alcoholic Republic: An American Tradition.* New York: Oxford University Press, 1979.

Rosenberg, Charles E. *The Cholera Years: The United States in 1832, 1849, and 1866.* Chicago: University of Chicago Press, 1987.

Rothenberg, Marc. "The Educational and Intellectual Background of American Astronomers, 1825–1875." Dissertation, Bryn Mawr College, 1974.

Rothstein, William G. *American Medical Schools and the Practice of Medicine: A History.* New York: Oxford University Press, 1987.

Rudolph, Frederick. *The American College and University: A History.* New York: Knopf, 1962.

———. *Curriculum: A History of the American Undergraduate Course of Study since 1636.* San Francisco: Jossey-Bass, 1977.

Ruffner, Kevin Conley. "Civil War Letters of a Washington Rebel." *Washington History* (Fall–Winter 1992–93): 57–71.

Scanlon, James Edward. *Randolph-Macon College: A Southern History, 1825–1967.* Charlottesville: University Press of Virginia, 1983.

Scott, William. *Lessons in Elocution or a Selection of Pieces in Prose and Verse, For the Improvement of Youth in Reading and Speaking.* Philadelphia, 1791.

Seager, Robert, II. *And Tyler Too: A Biography of John and Julia Gardiner Tyler.* New York: McGraw-Hill, 1963.

Seymour, Harold. *Baseball: The Early Years.* New York: Oxford University Press, 1960.

Shils, Edward. "The Order of Learning in the United States: The Ascendancy of the University." In *The Organization of Knowledge in Modern America, 1860–1920,* ed. Alexandra Oleson and John Voss, 19–50. Baltimore: Johns Hopkins University Press, 1979.

Shomette, Donald G. "The Guns of St. Mary's." *Maryland Historical Magazine,* Winter 1998, 477–98.

Smith, Ronald A. *Sports and Freedom: The Rise of Big-Time College Athletics.* New York: Oxford University Press, 1988.

Stevens, Robert. *Law School: Legal Education in America from the 1850s to the 1980s.* Chapel Hill: University of North Carolina Press, 1983.

Stewart, Donald C. "The Nineteenth Century." In *The Present State of Scholarship in Historical and Contemporary Rhetoric,* ed. Winifred Byran Homer, 2nd rev. ed. Columbia: University of Missouri Press, 1990.

Stone, Lawrence. "Prosopography." *Daedalus* 100 (Winter 1971): 46–49.

Story, Ronald. *The Forging of an Aristocracy: Harvard and the Boston Upper Class, 1800–1870.* Middletown, CT: Wesleyan University Press, 1980.

Tewksbury, Donald. *The Founding of American Colleges and Universities before the Civil War.* New York: Teachers College, Columbia University, 1932.

Tidwell, William A., et al. *Come Retribution: The Confederate Secret Service and the Assassination of Lincoln.* Jackson: University Press of Mississippi, 1988.

Turner, Paul Venable. *Campus: An American Planning Tradition.* Cambridge, MA: MIT Press, 1984.

Turner, Thomas Reed. *Beware the People Weeping: Public Opinion and the Assassination of Abraham Lincoln.* Baton Rouge: Louisiana State University Press, 1982.

U.S. Congress. *Senate Journal.* 22nd Cong., 2nd sess., March 2, 1833.

Vine, Phyllis. "Another Look at Eighteenth-Century Colleges." *History of Education Quarterly* 18 (Spring 1978): 61–69.

———."The Social Function of Eighteenth-Century Higher Education." *History of Education Quarterly* 16 (Winter 1976): 409–13.

Wagoner, Jennings L., Jr. "Honor and Dishonor at Mr. Jefferson's University: The Antebellum Years." *History of Education Quarterly* 26 (Summer 1986): 155–79.

Warden, D. B. *Description statistique, historique et politique des Etats-Unis de l'amérique septentrionale, depuis l'époque des premiers établissements jusquà nos jours.* Paris: Chez Rey et Gravier, 1820.

———. *A Statistical, Political, and Historical Account of the United States of North America; From the Period of Their First Colonization to the Present Day.* Edinburgh: Printed for A. Constable and Co., 1819.

Wertenbaker, Thomas Jefferson. *Princeton, 1746–1896.* Princeton, NJ: Princeton University Press, 1946.

White, Leonard D. *The Jacksonians: A Study in Administrative History, 1829–1861.* New York: Macmillan, 1954.

Whitehead, John S. *The Separation of College and State: Columbia, Dartmouth, Harvard, and Yale, 1776–1876.* New Haven, CT: Yale University Press, 1973.

Woodward, C. Vann, and Elisabeth Muhlenfeld, eds. *The Private Mary Chesnut: The Unpublished Civil War Diaries.* New York: Oxford University Press, 1984.

Wyatt-Brown, Bertram. *Southern Honor: Ethics and Behavior in the Old South.* New York: Oxford University Press, 1982.

GEORGETOWN UNIVERSITY HISTORY AND RELATED DOCUMENTS

Barringer, George M. "They Came to GU: The French Sulpicians." *Georgetown Today,* July 1977.

Beatty, William K. "Daniel Roberts Brower: Neurologist, Psychiatrist, and Medico-Legal Expert." *Proceedings of the Institute of Medicine in Chicago* 41 (1988).

Bernard, Richard M. "A Portrait of Baltimore in 1800: Economic and Occupational Patterns in an Early American City." *Maryland Historical Magazine,* Winter 1974, 341–60.

Brislen, M. B., OSF. "The Episcopacy of Leonard Neale, Second Archbishop of Baltimore." *Historical Records and Studies* 34 (1945): 20–111.

Bryan, Wilhelmus Bogart. *A History of the National Capital: 1815–1878.* New York: Macmillan, 1916.

Burrus, E. J., SJ. "Historical Notes: Father Joseph Havens Richards' Notes on Georgetown and the Catholic University." *Woodstock Letters* 83 (1954).

Chamberlain, Lawrence Carleton. "Georgetown University Library, 1789–1937." MSLS thesis, Catholic University of America, 1962.

Clarke, Joseph Hanson. "Reminiscences." *Georgetown College Journal* 8 (November 1879): 26–27.

Cooke, Lawrence H. "The History of the Georgetown Crew: Guardian of the Blue and Gray." In *Swift Potomac's Lovely Daughter: Two Centuries at Georgetown through Students' Eyes,* ed. Joseph Durkin, SJ, 321–39. Washington, DC: Georgetown University Press, 1990.

Corn, Milton. "Medical Education at Georgetown: A Historical Overview." In *Georgetown at Two Hundred: Faculty Reflections on the University's Future,* ed. William McFadden, SJ, 293–319. Washington, DC: Georgetown University Press, 1990.

Curley, James, SJ. *Annals of the Astronomical Observatory of Georgetown, D.C.* New York: Edward Dunigan & Brother, 1852.

Curran, Robert Emmett. "'Splendid Poverty': Jesuit Slaveholding in Maryland, 1805–1838." In *Catholics in the Old South,* ed. Jon Wakelyn and Randall Miller, 125–46. Macon, GA: Mercer University Press, 1983.

Daley, John M., SJ. *Georgetown University: Origin and Early Years.* Washington, DC: Georgetown University Press, 1957.

Dennis, William Henry. "Rev. Patrick F. Healy, SJ, at an Appreciation." *Georgetown College Journal,* January 1913, 226.

DeSando, Sally A. "Student Thought at Georgetown Expressed in Their Writings." Master's thesis, Georgetown University, 1963.

Devitt, Edward I. "Georgetown College in the Early Days." *Records of the Columbia Historical Society* 12 (1909): 21–37.

Devitt, Edward I., SJ. "Trinity Church, Georgetown: An Historical Discourse." *Woodstock Letters* 33 (1904).

Donesa, Christopher. "History of the *Georgetown College Journal.*" In *Swift Potomac's Lovely Daughter: Two Centuries at Georgetown through Students' Eyes,* ed. Joseph Durkin, SJ, 3–29. Washington, DC: Georgetown University Press, 1990.

Donohue, Liam S. "The History of Chemistry at Georgetown University (1798–1900)." In *Swift Potomac's Lovely Daughter: Two Centuries at Georgetown through Students' Eyes,* ed. Joseph Durkin, SJ, 421–39. Washington, DC: Georgetown University Press, 1990.

Durkin, Joseph T., SJ. *Georgetown University: The Middle Years (1840–1900).* Washington, DC: Georgetown University Press, 1963.

———. *William Matthews: Priest and Citizen.* New York: Benziger Brothers, 1963.

Easby-Smith, James S. *Georgetown University in the District of Columbia.* 2 vols. New York: Lewis, 1907.

Ecker, Grace Dunlop. *Portrait of Old Georgetown.* Richmond, VA: Dietz Press, 1933.

Errazuriz, Isidoro. *Diario de don Isidorro Errazuriz, 1851–1856.* Santiago de Chile, 1947.

Evans, Richard X. "Alexander Dimitry, Georgetown Student." *Georgetown College Journal,* January 1931, 171–72.

Foley, Albert Sidney, SJ. *Dream of an Outcaste.* Tuscaloosa, AL: Portals Press, 1976.

Formwalt, Lee W. "A Conversation between Two Rivers: A Debate on the Location of the U.S. Capital in Maryland." *Maryland Historical Magazine,* Fall 1976.

Fulghum, David. "The War That Gave the School Its Colors." *Georgetown Magazine,* May–June 1983.

Geary, Daniel J. "American Catholics and Higher Education." In *Memorial of the First Centenary of Georgetown College, D.C. Comprising a History of Georgetown University,* ed. John Gilmary Shea, 411–18. Washington, DC: Published for the College by P. F. Collier, 1891.

George, Eric M. "The Cultivation of Eloquence at Georgetown College: A History of the Philodemic Society from 1830–1890." In *Swift Potomac's Lovely Daughter: Two Centuries at Georgetown through Students' Eyes,* ed. Joseph Durkin, SJ, 103–19. Washington, DC: Georgetown University Press, 1990.

Gleason, Philip. "The Main Sheet Anchor: John Carroll and Catholic Higher Education." *Review of Politics* 38 (October 1976): 576–613.

Golden, Hugh J. "Georgetown Football: A Complete History (1874–1987)." Unpublished Paper, 1989.

Guilday, Peter. *The Life and Times of John Carroll: Archbishop of Baltimore, 1735–1815.* 2 vols. New York: Encyclopedia Press, 1922.

Hanley, Thomas O'Brien, SJ, ed. *The John Carroll Papers.* 3 vols. Notre Dame, IN: University of Notre Dame Press, 1976.

Hardy, George. "Georgetown University's Healy Building." *Journal of the Society of Architectural Historians* 21 (1972).

Heyden, Francis J., SJ. *The Beginning and End of a Jesuit Observatory (1841–1972).* Quezon City, Philippines, n.d.

Holland, Samuel H. "Charles H. Liebermann, M.D.: An Early Russian-born Physician of Washington, D.C." *Medical Annals of the District of Columbia* 38 (September 1969): 499–504.

Horgan, Paul. "The Father President." In *A Certain Climate: Essays in History, Arts, and Letters.* Middletown, CT: Wesleyan University Press, 1988.

Humphreys, Anderson, and Curt Guenther. *Semmes America.* Memphis, TN: Humphreys, Ink., 1989.

Hurst, Harold W. "The Maryland Gentry in Old Georgetown, 1783–1861." *Maryland Historical Magazine,* Spring 1978, 1–2.

Kilty, William. *The Laws of Maryland.* Vol. 2. Annapolis, MD: Printed by Frederick Green, printer to the state, 1800.

Kuzniewski, Anthony J., SJ. "Francis Dzierozynski and the Jesuit Restoration in the United States." *Catholic Historical Review* 78 (January 1992): 51–73.

Lombard, John, and Justin Davis. "The Georgetown College Cadets." In *Swift Potomac's Lovely Daughter: Two Centuries at Georgetown through Students' Eyes,* ed. Joseph Durkin, SJ, 249–59. Washington, DC: Georgetown University Press, 1990.

Mallory, Stephen. "Letters from Famous Old Boys." *Georgetown College Journal,* December 1906, 115.

McFadden, William C., SJ, ed. *Georgetown at Two Hundred: Faculty Reflections on the University's Future.* Washington, DC: Georgetown University Press, 1990.

McLaughlin, J. Fairfax. *College Days at Georgetown, and Other Papers.* Philadelphia, 1899.

Melville, Annabelle M. *John Carroll of Baltimore: Founder of the American Catholic Hierarchy.* New York: Scribner, 1955.

———. Louis *William DuBourg: Bishop of Louisiana and the Floridas, Bishop of Montauban and Archbishop of Besançon, 1766–1833.* 2 vols. Chicago: Loyola University Press, 1986.

Mitchell, Mary. *Chronicles of Georgetown Life, 1865–1900.* Cabin John, MD: Seven Locks Press, 1986.

Neale, Augustine. "Georgetown Men in the Confederate Army." *Georgetown College Journal,* March 1901, 253.

Newman, Harry Wright. *The Maryland Semmes and Other Families.* Baltimore: Heritage Books, 1956.

Papenfuse, Edward C., et al. *A Biographical Dictionary of the Maryland Legislature, 1635–1789.* Vol. 1. Baltimore: Johns Hopkins University Press, 1979.

Payne, John Carroll. "Letters from Famous Old Boys." *Georgetown College Journal,* December 1906, 115.

Prelinger, Elizabeth. "Architecture on the Hilltop." Unpublished paper, [1988].

———. "'From Her Spires and Steeples Beaming': Mission and Image in Bricks and Stone." In *Georgetown at Two Hundred: Faculty Reflections on the University's Future,* ed. William McFadden, SJ, 335–53. Washington, DC: Georgetown University Press, 1990.

Proctor, John Clagett. "Hospital Progress." [Washington] *Sunday Star,* September 29, 1946.

Quirk, Rory F. *Hoya Saxa: Georgetown Football, 1874–1978.* Washington, DC: Privately printed, 1979.

Randall, James Ryder. "Letters from Famous Old Boys." *Georgetown College Journal,* December 1906, 109.

Rigge, William F., SJ. *Jesuit Astronomy.* Part 2, *The Restored Society, 1814–1904.* Northfield, MN: n.p., 1904.

Rosen, George. "From Frontier Surgeon to Industrial Hygienist: The Strange Career of George M. Kober." *American Journal of Public Health* 65 (June 1975): 638–43.

Rowland, Kate Mason. *The Life of Charles Carroll of Carrollton, 1737–1832, with His Correspondence and Public Papers.* New York: G. P. Putnam's Sons, 1898.

Ruby, James, ed. *Blue and Gray: Georgetown University and the Civil War.* Washington, DC: Georgetown University Alumni Association, 1961.

———. "Callans Forever: The Texas Ranger, the FBI and Georgetown." *Georgetown University Alumni Magazine,* May 1956.

Ruff, Robin [James Doonan, SJ]. "College Days Fifty Years Ago." *Georgetown College Journal,* October 1906, 16.

Schauinger, J. Herman. *William Gaston, Carolinian.* Milwaukee, WI: Bruce, 1949.

Shea, John Gilmary. *Memorial of the First Centenary of Georgetown College, D.C. Comprising a History of Georgetown University.* Washington, DC: Published for the College by P. F. Collier, 1891.

Spalding. "John Carroll." *Catholic Historical Review* 71 (October 1985): 505–18.

Steinthal, Thomas, and Daniel Hood. "Dramatics at Georgetown: The Mask and Bauble Society." In *Swift Potomac's Lovely Daughter: Two Centuries at Georgetown through Students' Eyes,* ed. Joseph Durkin, SJ, 159–78. Washington, DC: Georgetown University Press, 1990.

Tondorf, Francis A., comp. and ed. *Frank Baker, M.D., A.J., Ph.D., LL.D. (1841–1918): Professor of Anatomy Georgetown University Medical School from 1883–1918.* Washington, DC: n.p., 1923.

Walsh, Richard, and William Lloyd Fox, eds. *Maryland: A History, 1632–1974.* Baltimore: Maryland Historical Society, 1974.

Warner, William W. *At Peace with All Their Neighbors: Catholics and Catholicism in the National Capital, 1787–1860.* Washington, DC: Georgetown University Press, 1994.

JESUIT AND CATHOLIC EDUCATIONAL HISTORY

An Address to the Roman Catholics of the United States of America by a Catholic Clergyman. Annapolis, MD: 1784.

The Alexandria Controversy: Or a Series of Letters between M. B. & Quaero, on the Tenets of Catholicity. Georgetown, DC, 1817.

Archbishop Connolly of Halifax. "Darwinism." *Georgetown College Journal,* February 1874, 33.

Bossy, John. *The English Catholic Community, 1570–1850.* New York: Oxford University Press, 1976.

Burton, David H., and Frank Gerrity. *St. Joseph's College: A Family Portrait, 1851–1976.* Philadelphia: St. Joseph's College Press, 1977.

Catalogus Provinciae Marylandiae Societatis Jesu Ineunte Anno MDCC–CLI. Georgetown, DC, 1851.

Chadwick, Hubert, SJ. *St. Omers to Stonyhurst: A History of Two Centuries.* London: Burns & Oates, 1962.

Concilii Plenarii Baltimorensis II, in Ecciesia Metropolitana Baltimorensi . . . Decreta. Baltimore: Excudebat Joannes Murphy, 1868.

Curran, Francis X., SJ. "The Jesuit Colony in New York, 1808–1817." HRS 42 (1954).

Curran, R. Emmett, ed. *American Jesuit Spirituality: The Maryland Tradition, 1634–1900.* New York: Paulist Press, 1988.

Donohue, John W., SJ. *Jesuit Education: An Essay on the Foundations of Its Idea.* New York: Fordham University Press, 1963.

Dunigan, David R., SJ. *A History of Boston College.* Milwaukee, WI: Bruce, 1947.

Eaton, Vincent M., SS. "Sulpician Involvement in Educational Projects in the See and Province of Baltimore." *U.S. Catholic Historian* 2 (1982): 3–5.

An Examination of a Protestant's Objections to the Popish Miracle Lately Wrought in America. London, 1824.

Edwards, Francis, SJ. *The Jesuits in England: From 1580 to the Present Day.* Tunbridge Wells, Kent: Burns & Oates, 1985.

Foley, Henry, SJ. *Records of the English Province of the Society of Jesus.* Vol. 7. London: Burns & Oates, 1882.

Hennesey, James, SJ. *American Catholics: A History of the Roman Catholic Community in the United States.* New York: Oxford University Press, 1981.

———. "Several Youth Sent from Here: Native-Born Priests and Religious of English America, 1634–1776." In *Studies in Catholic History in Honor of John Tracy Ellis,* ed. Nelson H. Minnich, Robert B. Eno, SS, and Robert Trisco, 1–26. Wilmington, DE: M. Glazier, 1985.

Holt, Geoffrey, SJ. *St. Omers and Bruges Colleges, 1593–1773: A Biographical Dictionary.* London: Catholic Record Society, 1979.

Hughes, Thomas, SJ. *History of the Society of Jesus in North America: Colonial and Federal.* 2 vols. London: Longmans, Green, and Co., 1917.

Kauffman, Christopher J. *Tradition and Transformation in Catholic Culture: The Priests of Saint Sulpice in the United States from 1791 to the Present.* New York: Macmillan, 1988.

Lucey, William Leo, SJ. *The Catholic Church in Maine.* Francestown, NH: M. Jones Co., 1957.

McCabe, William H., SJ. *An Introduction to the Jesuit Theatre: A Posthumous Work.* Ed. Louis J. Oldani, SJ. St. Louis, MO: Institute of Jesuit Sources, 1983.

McKevitt, Gerald, SJ. *The University of Santa Clara: A History, 1851–1977.* Stanford, CA: Stanford University Press, 1979.

McMaster, Richard. "Benedict Fenwick, Bishop of Boston, American Apprenticeship (1782–1817)." *Historical Records and Studies* 47 (1959).

Meagher, Walter J., SJ, and William J. Grattan. *The Spires of Fenwick: The History of the College of the Holy Cross, 1843–1963.* New York: Vantage Press, 1966.

Newton, Robert R. *Reflections on the Educational Principles of the Spiritual Exercises.* Washington, DC: Jesuit Secondary Education Association, 1977.

Pious Guide to Prayer and Devotion, Containing Various Practices of Piety Calculated to Answer the Various Demands of the Different Devout Members of the Roman Church. Georgetown, MD, 1792.

Power, Edward J. *A History of Catholic Higher Education in the United States.* Milwaukee, WI: Bruce, 1958.

Reily, John T. *Collections and Recollections, In the Life and Times of Cardinal Gibbons.* Vol. 2. Martinsburg, WV: Herald Print., 1892–93.

Ruane, Joseph William, SS. *The Beginnings of the Society of St. Sulpice in the United States (1791–1829).* Washington, DC: Catholic University of America, 1935.

Ryan, John J., SJ. "Our Scholasticate: An Account of Its Growth and History to the Opening of Woodstock, 1805–1869." *Woodstock Letters* 33 (1904): 14–16.

Sanders, James W. "Nineteenth-Century Boston Catholics and the School Question." Working Papers Series, Center for the Study of American Catholicism, Fall 1977.

Smyth, Patrick. *Present State of the Catholic Mission Conducted by the Ex-Jesuits in North-America.* Dublin, 1788.

Sommervogel, Carlos, SJ. *Bibliotheque de la Compagnie de Jésus.* Tome 8. Brussels: O. Schepens, 1898.

Spalding, Thomas W. *The Premier See: A History of the Archdiocese of Baltimore, 1789–1989.* Baltimore: Johns Hopkins University Press, 1989.

"Students of St. Mary's College." *Memorial Volume of the Centenary of St. Mary's Seminary of St. Sulpice, 79–89.* Baltimore: John Murphy, 1891.

Sullivan, Eleanore C. *Georgetown Visitation since 1799.* Baltimore: French-Bray, 1975.

Talbot, Francis X., SJ. *Jesuit Education in Philadelphia: Saint Joseph's College, 1851–1926.* Philadelphia: St. Joseph's College, 1927.

Varga, Nicholas. *Baltimore's Loyola, Loyola's Baltimore, 1851–1986.* Baltimore: Maryland Historical Society, 1990.

"Voyage of the Very Rev. Father John Anthony Grassi, SJ, from Russia to America, January 1805–October 1810." *Woodstock Letters* 4 (1875): 115–36.

Wharton, Charles H. *Letter to the Roman Catholics of the City of Worcester.* Philadelphia, 1784.

About the Author

Robert Emmett Curran is professor emeritus of history at Georgetown University. He was born in Baltimore, Maryland, and attended the College of Holy Cross, where he received a BA with honors in history. He later received an MA in history from Fordham University before earning a PhD in history from Yale University. In addition to writing numerous journal articles and chapters and reviews, Curran has published three books: *Michael Augustine Corrigan and the Shaping of Conservative Catholicism in America, 1878–1902*; *American Jesuit Spirituality: The Maryland Tradition, 1634–1900*; and *The Bicentennial History of Georgetown University, 1789–1889*. After teaching at Georgetown for more than thirty years, he now lives with his wife, Eileen, in Richmond, Kentucky, where his nonacademic interests include running, playing the banjo, and choral singing.

Index